Happy Birthday J J !

I hope you enjoy this Devotional Book. The author, Kay Powell lives in Cookeville.

love, Gloria Bell

Moon Over My Shoulder

Kathryn Powell

MOON
over my
shoulder

Shining words of encouragement upon your path

A 365 day devotional

DEDICATION

This book is dedicated to my mother and grandmother, who with differing perspectives on life, influenced me with a unique view on life. Each, in her own way, nurtured independence, strength, and nudged me toward my relationship with Jesus.

It is also dedicated to my family, who by the grace of God, found their foundation in Jesus. To my children, Whitney, Blair, and Trevor; you have been a bright spot in my world since the moment you were born and continue to bring joy and love into my life. To my grandchildren, Addison, Benjamin, Asher, Ian, Elizabeth, Bryn, and Anna; I never could have foreseen the blessings of knowing each of you. To my in-laws, you have been an unspeakable blessing to have in my family; I could not have chosen more wisely than God had ordained. Thank you all for your support in making this book possible.

To my local body of Believers, our pastors, support staff, and my "forever family", thank you from the depth of my soul! You have spared me great hardship, stood with me in the trenches of spiritual warfare, lifted me up in my sorrow, and prayed steadfastly for this book. May the Lord bless you abundantly!

This book is dedicated to every heart that needs a home; you will find in Jesus more than you can possibly imagine. I pray you find your place of peace and acceptance in His presence daily.

"When the call of Christ sears a hole through your self-protectiveness, you go wherever He leads whether or not you feel like you fit."
Beth Moore

Moon Over My Shoulder Introduction

Revisiting my stash of dusty journals, I opened the cover of the one labeled "Journal #1", rather shocked at the inscription greeting me: "I think I need to write a book." It was inscribed thirty years ago. The world is full of authors, and Gutenberg himself would be speechless at the number of books published since the advent of his printing press. The world did not need another book, to be certain, and it did not need mine, not even knowing what "mine" be! I thought I had no story, nothing of value to fill the pages; God said otherwise. I was wrong, so terribly wrong, but His timing was perfectly right.

Returning home on one of the first evenings of spring, I rejoiced in the warmth of the clear, dark, night with stars sparkling against a crisp, sharply black sky. Suspended just above the treetops, the crescent moon appeared as a silver bowl, hung perfectly upside down. And the words, "Moon over my shoulder" softly dropped into my spirit. I had no idea what that meant, but it was comforting and pleasant. I knew if it was important, I would not be able to put those words aside. And I could not.

Days passed and the notion that a book was in my future seemed to be linked to those words, and that I had been given a title for it. Never have I considered myself a "writer"—I am more of a "journal-er", an observer of life, and an encourager. My Bible study group had read a few of the pages I had written, so I gingerly tossed the absurd concept out to them. I was stunned, as they enthusiastically endorsed the idea.

That night, it was confirmed, despite my reservations, that a book was in my future. I am totally and completely inadequate, broken and flawed; but as Cindy, Amy and Abbey have taught me, so are all people God has called to step into His plan; so will be every person He ever calls for His purpose. And now a completed book rests in your hands.

He has shaped and formed me to quietly share encouragement with other broken vessels and turn their hope to Jesus. Through my experience and adventures with Him, I can extend you an invitation to know Him, love Him, and receive His amazing love in return. I pray that He will become the "Moon Over My Shoulder" for you, as well.

January

Another Year!

On any given holiday, my neighbor's teenage boys gleefully send fireworks over my rooftop, the later in the night the better. So last night, New Year's Eve, I snuggled down under the blankets at eleven o'clock, fully expecting to be awakened by bursts of gunpowder and barking dogs. Whether I slept blissfully through the entire event, or they saved their money this year, I am extremely grateful.

Last night, as I considered the year behind me and the bright shiny new one that begins today, I couldn't see much difference. The year past counted 365 new days of work, family, relationships, chores, ordinary life; some were sad, others mundane, a few, absolutely blissful. There were periods of upheaval in the world, days of peaceful lulls; some days fell short of dollars while others were days of plenty. And I had food to eat every day this year, not something all the world's population can boast. Because I am learning day by day to trust in God, they were all days of contentment.

Every year can be our best year, even if it was the worst year of our lives. Even though I have had whole years I would rather forget, I would not wish them away or change them. With each hardship endured, pain suffered, brokenness experienced, each twist and turn led me home to Jesus, to a fuller understanding of who I am, and leaning harder on Him. Through them, I learned to be more like Him, increasingly resembling the One who has lifted me when I could not stand on my own.

I have found Him to be extraordinarily trustworthy, loving, generous, merciful, and kind. If each day draws me into more dependence on Him, if my struggles encourage trust in Him instead of reliance upon myself, then each day brings me closer to my heavenly Father. I can trust Him with the day before me, too, recognizing that today is all I have; on New Year's Day, we are not promised another 364.

Greeting someone yesterday with the words, "I hope you have your best year ever!" I reconsidered my year, wondering what I would say in retrospect on my next New Year's Day. Looking back at the past year, the evidence is blatant—everything was under God's control. I see His hand in each of the 365 days that passed, each unfolding like an origami paper crane, revealing His interactions with me; tiny folds revealing His plan for me. Because I can trust Him, I believe I will be able to state that this was my best year ever, too.

"You will keep in perfect peace him whose mind is steadfast, because he trusts in you."

Isaiah 26:3

The Right Rita   January 2

A lady in our Bible study group described her attempt to connect with a mutual friend by phone for the first time. The contact's photo came up, she glanced at it, and proceeded to call; but the call did not reach her friend. It had connected to a Rita, just not the one she thought it was. During the conversation, trying to determine who she had reached, she found that the woman had recently lost her son, was grieving, and lonely.

Debbie could easily have been too busy to listen, had more important things to do, or been agitated at the delay in her day. She could have had a list drawing her to check off the "to-do's" and been fatigued and irritated with the interruption. She could have brushed off the call, easily relegating it to the wrong number bin. But she listened. The "wrong Rita" ended the conversation by asking Debbie if she would be her friend. Jesus knew that Debbie had called the "right Rita", the one who needed His comforting touch through the gentle voice of my friend.

Many times, I have witnessed what our pastor calls "God-cidences". They are times when our paths are altered, and our inconvenience becomes a chance to express His compassion and care for hurting people. Those moments most often become a choice to be the hands and heart of Jesus to a weary and broken world; or keeping to ourselves the grace, love, and forgiveness we have received.

We are easily consumed with our own priorities, lists, and control of our day. When our plans are disrupted; our paths redirected; our day in disarray; and our hopes dashed, is it time to look deeper and find the "right Rita", the reason God is turning our eyes in a different direction?

With God, there are no accidents, only opportunities to grow in His grace through loving Him and loving the people He loves. Those same opportunities provide reminders daily of what God's priorities are and how His plan often differ from ours. But I also find that God always rewards obedience, sometimes with replacement of the losses and sacrifices we made, but always with the satisfaction of knowing our Father is pleased.

Administer His love to the "Rita" who may be right in front of your eyes. She may show up on your caller ID like Rita, or in the grocery check-out line, in the break room at work, or on the shut-in list at church. The "Rita's" are all around us, with abundant opportunities to be the hands and feet of Jesus.

"But a Samaritan, as he traveled, came where the man was; and when he saw him, he took pity on him. He went to him and bandaged his wounds, pouring on oil and wine. Then he put the man on his own donkey, took him to an inn, and took care of him. The next day he took out two silver coins and gave them to the innkeeper. 'Look after him,' he said, 'and when I return, I will reimburse you for any extra expense you may have.' Which of these three do you think was a neighbor to the man who fell into the hands of the robbers? The expert in the law replied, 'The one who had mercy on him.' Jesus told him, 'Go and do likewise.'" Luke 10:33-37

An Orca, the largest member of the porpoise family, was to be my first encounter with a whale. I was surprised to find that it was not a whale at all, but impressive, nonetheless. At Sea World, the Orca, slightly smaller in size than a school bus, flew from the water as though propelled by a cannon, picking the dangling fish from the trainer's hand high above. Water, on cue, rained down on elated show-goers as the Orca re-entered its liquid domain.

Whales have captured my fascination ever since, with curiosity and great respect for the largest mammals ever to grace the earth. These creatures breathe air yet live in water. They cannot sleep deeply lest they drown. They swim slowly or station themselves upright to sleep, half of their brains sleeping for as long as they can hold their breaths. They make countless journeys to the surface to breathe over a lifetime of decades.

I find my life in Christ to be similarly dependent. The Bible calls it "abiding", and it becomes like breathing. I have found that the times I am not abiding in Jesus are characterized by fear, distant and mechanical communications with Him, loneliness, a vague feeling of separation, and emptiness. The world is full of distractions, diversions, deceit, and darkness; but when I enter His Presence again, perspective returns. When I whisper, "Jesus", it is as though I am breathing a fresh breath of air, enabling me to function again.

When we live deeply in a suffocating world, we can rise to the surface and capture a new vital breath of fresh air, a little bit of heaven, enough to suffice for the moment. Deprived of His life-giving air, we will die, as surely as a whale without the ability to surface. Jesus is the air we breathe, the life-sustaining Spirit of God we cannot live without. Daily I feel the urgency to breathe Him in. And though I sometimes ignore it, God's Spirit continually draws me back to Him, whispering, "Just breathe!"

"We know that we live in him and he in us because he has given us of his Spirit."

I John 4:13

"Remain in me and I will remain in you…I am the vine; you are the branches. If a man remains in me and I in him, he will bear much fruit; apart from me you can do nothing." John 15:4a-5

Visiting my friend on her mini-farm, I was introduced to sheep for the first time. Let me just say, I wasn't very impressed. I love toasty, wool sweaters, but that was about the only connection I could find to them. They were not the soft, fluffy, bright-white huggable creatures I imagined them to be. And on top of that disappointment, they were not smart but very stubborn. A donkey was their companion to protect them from predators, and I found him more to my liking than sheep.

Nearly all references in the Bible, aside from the sacrifice of lambs, had to do with people being compared to sheep. I was a bit offended by that after being introduced to actual sheep. However, it didn't take long to see the resemblance, after giving it some consideration. Sheep don't like to follow and must be led, stray easily, won't drink from fast-flowing water, and can actually drown themselves by looking up in heavy rain. They are a predator's favorite meal, following chicken, of course. They need a protector, provider, and physician constantly.

Some phrases from the Old Testament reveal the characteristics of sheep: We all went astray like sheep; the sheep will be scattered; like sheep without a shepherd; like lost sheep. In contrast, the New Testament phrases are: Go to the lost sheep; I am the Good Shepherd; calls His sheep by name; lay down my life for the sheep; my sheep hear my voice; I know them.

The 23rd Psalm famously speaks about sheep and a Shepherd, but until you understand the qualities of the sheep, you will never understand the passage. Until one grasps the tendencies of sheep, one cannot understand why God would compare one of His less-appealing creatures to those made in His very own image. You will not appreciate the depth of its meaning, nor why I am now happy to be called His sheep.

Please allow me to offer my translation of these verses: "The all-powerful, all-knowing One is my leader and protector, I shall not need anything He cannot provide. He makes me rest, not strive, in fields that are not parched, but lush and comforting. He leads me without anger or impatience, beside, not across, waters I cannot swim in; not raging waters but still water where I can comfortingly drink in His Presence. He quiets my soul. He does not push, but counsels me, in paths according to His wisdom for order and good, for His name's sake, for His glory and my good."

"I am the good shepherd; I know my sheep and my sheep know me---just as the Father knows me and I know the Father---and I lay down my life for the sheep." John 10:14

Computers the size of rooms, not desktops, nor handheld, required operating systems that were set up using key-punch cards. My husband, studying business in college, was required to complete a computer class in "DOS", carting around stacks of those key-punch cards. I could not have imagined the impact those beasts in the university computer center would have on my future. The "apps" we use today were then just a figment of someone's imagination.

The handheld computers, alias smartphones, we tote everywhere on God's earth, are laden with hundreds of apps that function as telephone books, maps, compasses, photo albums, recipe books, nightly news, and even cable channels. I have an app for my favorite word game, a carpenter's level, and shopping at my fingertips any given time of day. I can record or listen to music, measure the ambient room temperature, locate someone to repair my car, or find the latest weather forecast. The information highway on-ramp is seconds away, with the latest and greatest.

As the saying goes, "There's an app for that!" Wouldn't it be wonderful if there was a "Jesus App"?! One on which I could find immediate answers to all my deepest questions? One where I could contact Him at any time of day? Where I could request Him to show up when I wished, like a hologram? It could send me notifications of His voice-mail answers, or His wanting to contact me.

Many apps do these things already! The Bible app on my phone gives me answers to my deepest questions, found in God's Word. Other apps can send notifications for devotional passages. Others display reminders to set aside time to talk personally with Jesus. And though He won't show up in a hologram, He is constantly with me. Through the Spirit, there is a world more expansive than any computer app can generate. It is more powerful than the latest and greatest model, and one which no computer scientist can conjure; the spiritual world where Jesus walks by your side.

The Holy Spirit speaks to us and guides us through every single day. I don't require notification of His wanting to contact me; it's a given--He wants to talk with me any time I will be still long enough to listen. No app is needed for that, just ears to hear!

"And my God will meet all your needs according to his glorious riches in Christ Jesus."

Philippians 4:19

"But when he, the Spirit of truth, comes, he will guide you into all truth."   John 16:13

Forgetful Like a Child

Having observed children living in families that love them, the characteristics that define their childhoods are that they tend to be healthy, secure, and protected. They understand they are not in charge, but when they need anything, they promptly ask, and keep asking. They look at everything with surface observations, simply trusting their parents for what they need; and they are always needy, asking unashamedly for more. A child fails many times a day while learning something new but doesn't give up. They never feel like a failure, and just try again.

A child sees wonder in everything around him yet lives simply in the present. (Hence you never mention an event a week beforehand, lest you suffer the unrelenting queries of the said child). The world is colored by his imagination, where nothing is impossible, and safety is taken for granted. A child who is secure in a loving, protective family sees an unhindered future and unlimited possibilities.

There is wonder, too, at the forgetfulness of a child. Children have been corrected thousands of times as they grow up, learning not to touch hot stoves, staying out of the street, not touching matches, and not wandering away in a crowd. They do not feel guilt for their failures; they get up and try again, and again, and again. Often, I wondered as I raised my children, how many more times they would prompt my correction by the same behavior, but eventually, by the grace of God, they remembered and survived.

It would be helpful if I could routinely forget my failures, as a child of God, focusing on laying my guilt down, trying again with trust and determination to do what pleases Him. Exhibiting the characteristics of a child would be a simple and natural process, but sin gets in the way, and guilt warps our understanding of God's corrections. We view His discipline as punishment instead of the life-giving process it is intended to be. Trusting His good intentions toward us, accepting His corrections in simple faith, and living in the present, we are not trapped in a past of failures and defeat.

A child's security within a family builds a firm foundation for their future belief in a heavenly Father, who offers them love, protection, forgiveness, and trust. We find that security a hundred times over, as a child of God. God's intentions toward you are wonderfully loving, more so than you can imagine, and His discipline is wise and life-giving. As a child prized and treasured by the King, you can trust His best for you, too; but only through forgetfulness like a child can we grow up to be mature in Christ.

"Endure hardship as discipline; God is treating you as his children. For what children are not disciplined by their father?" Hebrews 12:7

Endless Highway

The early years of my youth were spent in northern Illinois, just outside Chicago, in a flat, uninteresting landscape of mostly trees. It seems that the trees hid the small hills and ripples of earth; there were state parks with cliffs and valleys witnessing to that fact, which we frequented on the weekends with picnic lunches. But the roads were what I considered straight, flat, and monotonous, until a trip through Nebraska.

A song my children sang, "This Is the Song that Never Ends", would have come to mind, had I known it at that time. I had never experienced a road running headlong into the horizon, with pavement as far as I could see, for hours, and hours, and hours. I marveled at the expanses of "farmland", appearing nothing like the fertile farm soil of my great uncle's dairy farm in southern Illinois.

On the positive side, rain was rare, the driver had an endless view of the road, including the occasional wayward cow or goat; and there was ample room for native Nebraskan drivers to pass. Eventually, we reached our destination of the western border of Nebraska, and on the new horizon was my first glimpse of the purple-hazed Rocky Mountain ridge.

Like that endless highway, I have most often viewed life as similarly unending, as though I will always have that horizon before me, aiming for a destination which never really manifests. Human beings rarely believe their own lives are truly limited upon this earth; but at some point, a person loved will be a person gone. Until death is truly imminent in our own lives, we see no end.

On that unending road, I have planned my stops, for convenience and out of necessity. I have experienced breakdowns and been slowed because of obstacles. Gazing in the rearview mirror, I can see that what I planned was never as good as what God had prepared along the way. At the unexpected stops, He always had a reason. Delays were for His purpose. But He has always been present, always provided, and always protected.

Wherever your highway leads, a day will come when the horizon is reached, and your eventual destination arrived. If Jesus has traveled your "endless highway" with you, your destination will be sweeter than anyplace you have traveled or can imagine. The real endless highway will have just begun, as you experience a majestic eternity with the King of Kings.

"Oh, the depth of the riches of the wisdom and knowledge of God! How unsearchable his judgments, and his paths beyond tracing out! Who has known the mind of the Lord? Or who has been his counselor? For from him and through him and to him are all things."

Romans 11:33-36a

Moving southward, after growing up in the Midwestern United States, the cultural discrepancies became glaringly obvious, at first shockingly so. A childhood game, peek-a-boo, became one of my first introductions to the new culture I had begun to assimilate. Having borne my first child in the state of North Carolina, I was fascinated by the transformation of peek-a-boo into "peep eye". My baby could not care less about the name of the game; she enjoyed every second of it, giggling and cooing.

The fascinating thing about a young child playing "peep-eye" is that when they hide behind their own hands, they believe you cannot see them. And the one playing the game with them is not real until they reveal their face. How funny we are, as adults, playing this same game with God! We believe that when we hide our face from Him, we become protected from His gaze, becoming invisible to Him.

Can you imagine how amusing this is to God? Your Creator, the God of the universe, counts the number of hairs on your head, and sees you from conception to your last breath. He knows what you think before you think it. However, there was a time when God covered His face, and we could not see Him because of our sin. We could see that God existed, but we could not see His face. Now, though, through Jesus, we can know Him; now His face is uncovered, and we have no reason to hide.

Jesus sought us and brought us to the Father, revealing His loving face to us through His Spirit. When we sin, we feel God hides from us, but it is not true; we only need to repent and turn from our sin. Then, like the child believing she is invisible when hiding behind her hands, we only need to uncover our eyes and gaze into His. There we find His forgiveness and love. Hopefully, we will understand that He never disappeared, we just thought we did.

"And without faith it is impossible to please God, because anyone who comes to him must believe that he exists and that he rewards those who earnestly seek him." Hebrews 11:6

"Where can I go from your Spirit? Where can I flee from your presence? If I go up to the heavens, you are there; if I make my bed in the depths, you are there. If I rise on the wings of the dawn, if I settle on the far side of the sea, even there your hand will guide me, your right hand will hold me fast." Psalm 139:7-10

Even though I no longer enter my dogs in dog shows, I have learned a great deal about dogs and have owned only one breed for many years. As small and cute as they are, my little Maltese dogs are still canines. They are, by deepest nature, animals who survive, and thrive, in packs. Solitary life is threatening to them, and when one howls, they all howl. My three Maltese dogs are no different; when one howls, the other two chime right in. They know they are not alone, as they listen to each other.

When they begin howling for no apparent reason, I assume it is because they can hear something not within my range of hearing. However, I am certain that occasionally they do it just to hear themselves. One day, they all began howling and it brought to mind a comment my friend Amy made during our Bible study. She said, "Unhappy people are simply groaning for the world to be made right, just as the earth is groaning for restoration." We are not alone in our pain on this earth, not alone in our suffering. It is common to human beings, and all creation is subject to it.

Though we live in a fallen world, subject to its challenges and frustrations, we, who know Christ Jesus, are not alone, either. Jesus died to send us the Holy Spirit, our Helper and Comforter. He is the one we can trust and in whom we find our hope and peace. From the cross, Jesus heard all our groans, something akin to the howling of my little dogs, in our spirits. Rising from the dead, He delivered us into freedom from sin and death.

While we may encounter people who are groaning under the weight of this life, we can offer them the hope we have in Jesus. Ours is the lasting hope, not in a little god, but hope in the living God, King of Glory, who holds us in His hands. We are not alone.

"I consider that our present sufferings are not worth comparing with the glory that will be revealed in us. The creation waits in eager expectation for the sons of God to be revealed…We know that the whole creation has been groaning as in the pains of childbirth right up to the present time. No only so, but we ourselves, who have the firstfruits of the Spirit, groan inwardly as we wait eagerly for our adoption as sons, the redemption of our bodies. For in this hope we were saved…In the same way, the Spirit helps us in our weakness. We do not know what we ought to pray for, but the Spirit himself intercedes for us with groans that words cannot express. And he who searches our hearts knows the mind of the Spirit, because the Spirit intercedes for the saints in accordance with God's will." Romans 8:18-19, 22-24, 26-27

It appeared dead from my kitchen view, and the next day, it hadn't appeared to have moved. Surprisingly, later that afternoon, the "dead" cat had vanished, only to find this stray on the cushy deck chair instead, from which she didn't move for hours at a time. Ever after, she has been "Dead Cat" to me. One day she brought a spouse home and that is when the trouble began. Dead Cat and partner began scouting out dinner via my birdhouse, home to a newly hatched batch of wrens.

I woke too early one morning to the sound of my beautiful birdhouse and its contents crashing to the floor of the porch. I dashed to the door, interrupting the culprits who had one paw stretched inside the front door of the little house. Chasing them off in fury, I righted the house, peered inside, and spotted one of the tiny birds thrashing about, on top of what I assumed to be the other three babies buried in nest materials. There was nothing apparent I could do to save them; the damage had been done. So, I barricaded the house on the table, surrounding it with potted plants and an old steel watering can.

Later that afternoon, the sound of everything crashing down rang the alarm. I arrived on the scene, once again finding the invaders with a paw reaching where it shouldn't. Those poor little birds are probably flying in dizzy circles today. They survived the pounding once again and lived long enough to leave home, once I moved the birdhouse, one last time, far out of the reach of Dead Cat and friend. Since that last encounter, Dead Cat moved to a new home and her friend never frequented our porch again.

What's the moral of this story? Temptation is just, well...tempting. If, like Dead Cat, you cannot resist the temptation confronting you, remove yourself from its proximity. Though your temptation is not unique, your enemy, the devil, knows your weaknesses. He is as patient as Dead Cat, and just as stealthy.

However, you have Someone on your side who can stand beside you in your weakness, strengthening and enabling you to stand without being overcome; His name is Jesus. He has the answer you need, just ask! Don't wait until your world collapses.

"No temptation has seized you except what is common to man. And God is faithful; he will not let you be tempted beyond what you can bear. But when you are tempted, he will also provide a way out so that you can stand up under it." 1 Corinthians 10:12-13

"When tempted, no one should say, 'God is tempting me.' For God cannot be tempted by evil, nor does he tempt anyone; but each one is tempted when, by his own evil desire, he is dragged away and enticed. Then, after desire has conceived, it gives birth to sin; and sin, when it is full-grown, gives birth to death." James 1:13-15

Cracked January 11

Wood, once vibrantly alive in a forest, came to live at my house. All three of my brothers learned woodworking skills, and two of the three have gifted me a hand-turned wooden bowl. Ron also crafted a duplicate of my grandmother's measuring scoop, always found in her flour bin, sculpting the replica by hand. A beautiful walnut rice bowl, with jade inlays and chopsticks that mounted to the bowl, became a treasured gift another year.

Because it was once living, there is just something special about the connection to wood, different from plastic and metal. Once beautiful in the forest, it is now beautiful in my hands and on my table. As wood is subject to do, one of my oak bowls developed a crack as it aged, rendering it unusable for kitchen purposes. The bowl was too valuable to me to discard, so I repurposed it to hold colorful rolled dishcloths, which brightened a corner of my countertop.

Many of us feel that because we are flawed, we must be disqualified from service to God. There is no one who "qualifies", not one perfect; "flawed" is all that God has to work with! No one has credentials substantial enough to impress God, or a resume' which is acceptable. There is only one qualifier, one letter of recommendation which will gain entrance to His throne, and that stipulation requires trusting His only and beloved son Jesus. Unless we "qualify" by way of His Son, there is no one acceptable in God's eyes.

Sometimes, my flaws become my excuse to avoid God, my guilt an obstacle to approaching Him. My "cracks", I believe, disqualify me from entering His presence and fulfilling my calling. God can use even the most unlikely and humble, if we will but trust Him. Like my beloved bowl, carved especially for me, God's loving hands formed me for His purpose. And His purpose may turn out to be entirely different than what I expected; I just need be willing to go where He sends me, cracks and all.

"But we have this treasure in jars of clay to show that this all-surpassing power is from God, not from us." 2 Corinthians 4:7

"This is love for God: to obey his commands. And his commands are not burdensome, for everyone born of God overcomes the world. This is the victory that has overcome the world, even our faith. Who is it who overcomes the world? Only he who believes that Jesus is the Son of God." I John 5:3-5

The lights are out, and the power has shut down for millions of people. This is not happening in a third-world country, but in California, the United States of America, and no one can say how long they will be in darkness. Gradually, they will adapt, if necessary. Stumbling in the dark at first, they will learn to function as much as possible during daylight hours. Many will wish they had been better prepared to prepare meals without power. Some will wish they had on hand ways to source light at night. Others will regret not having ordered extra medications, stored extra water, or bought a little extra food for their pets. Without light, life changes dramatically.

We cannot anticipate all of life's events, and we are to trust God's provision, not storing up treasures on earth. However, we are called to be wise stewards of what He gives us. Being wise means being as prepared as we can be to meet emergencies, obsession defining the dividing line. Being prepared for the dark is also being prepared to help your neighbor when the lights go out.

The ultimate darkness results not from a power failure, though, but from a Power failure. I have experienced many brief power outages over the years, and they are unnerving, but the darkness in which I lived spiritually far outweighed the physical darkness. Fear inhabited every shadowed corner of my soul, paralyzing my life in many ways. When Jesus stepped in, His light shone in one dark spot after another, illuminating and exposing sin, brokenness, and despair, filling them instead with His powerful light of love.

We can live in darkness, stumbling along, gradually adapting, and barely noticing the depth of it. Or we can trust in Jesus, connecting to the true Power source, the one who provides for and protects those who love Him. When we begin to allow Jesus to shine His light of life into our hearts, the tool most needed is trust; it serves as an emergency beacon in times of stress. He is the Source who never fails. As He walks us from darkness into His Light of love, we will be well prepared for any emergency, and able to share His Light with those around us.

"When Jesus spoke again to the people, he said, 'I am the light of the world. Whoever follows me will never walk in darkness but will have the light of life.'" John 8:12

"For with you is the fountain of life; in your light we see light." Psalm 36:9

"You are my lamp, O Lord; the Lord turns my darkness into light." 2 Samuel 22:29

In this world, we live amid many dangers, most of which we become so accustomed to that we rarely consider them threatening at all. An F4 tornado, one of the deadliest on record in the United States, awakened our populous to the threat of severe storms. A pandemic lurks on the horizon and most people remain oblivious to the implications until it storms their doors. Car accidents are the number one killer in the nation, but we blissfully believe we will arrive at our destinations until proven otherwise. We are oblivious to many dangers until the threat becomes a personal reality.

Fear is a form of distrust, looking to the world for solutions or escape, forgetting that it is God who is our provider and protector. I have been keenly familiar with fear most of my life; lingering in the background of my mind is an awareness of the threats most people never consider. Some causes were real, while others remained vague. My bent toward being fearful lends very well to searching my Bible for answers, and I found something very interesting early in my walk with Jesus—He discourages fear, strongly!

There are actions He strongly encourages, too. The first is His command to "**Be** still" (Psalm 46:10), not to fret, but to quietly look to God. He promises to "**Be** our guide" (Psalm 48:14) and trusting Him, we are to "**Be** not shaken" (Psalm 16:8). We are to "**Be** strong and courageous" (1 Chronicles 22:13), "**Be** joyful" (Romans 12:12), and "**Be** transformed by the renewing of your mind. Then you will **be** able to test and approve what God's will is—His good, pleasing and perfect will" (Romans 12:2).

As a result of the "**Be's**", those acts of trusting God, other "**Be's**" become part of our character. "**Be** *self-controlled*" (1 Thessalonians 5:8), "**Be** *completely humble and gentle*; **be** *patient, bearing with one another in love.*" (Ephesians 4:2), "**Be** *encouraged*" (Colossians 2:2), "**Be** *of one mind and one spirit*" (2 Corinthians 13:11).

Fear has consumed me in the past, but I refuse to succumb to it now. When we become well acquainted with who God is, how can we not trust Him? He is always faithful to remind me through His word, and learning of His attributes. Fear will flee as I obediently trust the Almighty, all-powerful, Sovereign God. I have no need which He is insufficient to secure on my behalf. My greatest need is only to remember the "**Be's**".

"Jesus answered, 'The work of God is this: to believe in the one he has sent.'"   John 6:29

"For I am the Lord, your God, who takes hold of your right hand and says to you, 'Do not fear; I will help you.'" Isaiah 41:13

As fascinating as they are to my grandson, spiders have caused me great anxiety since I was about eight years old. A very large, black spider crawled out of the overflow drain as I was taking a bath. You can barely imagine my horror and panic, I'm sure! I screamed, and can't remember many times even as a child, that I screamed. My howling prompted great alarm from my mother, who with her own horrified expression, removed it. She was not fond of the arachnid, either, so I am pretty certain her disdain was only a notch below the panic I felt.

Fear is promoted in movies and media, as if we couldn't manufacture enough of it in our daily lives! Some threats are very real and others very imagined. We can become so accustomed to it that we barely notice fear until its stranglehold is choking off life itself. Fear can creep in like a spider, quietly closing in on its prey, or it can confront and paralyze you, in a matter of seconds. It can insidiously linger in the background of our lives, affecting our emotions and behavior, disguised and undetected for years uncountable. It is the basis of unhealthy relationships, the food of predators, and fuel for abuse.

And for those who read this and think I am exaggerating, examine your own life and I believe you will quickly identify your own subtle, hidden sources of fear. No one is immune to it. It is a residual element from our rebellious origins, universal to the human condition. It is a condition that can only be overcome through the power and the love of the God we rebel against. It is, next to pride, the tool Satan most loves to use against us, undermining our trust in God.

Mistrust is at the root of fear, which is why God firmly commands, "Do not fear". Fear belies our lack of confidence in the character and power of God, implying that He is too weak, too distant, or incapable of protecting or providing for us; and even worse, that He doesn't truly love us. I am guilty of it daily---I forget so easily who my God is. In *Isaiah 41:10*, His command is to "**Be not** dismayed!" In *Deuteronomy 31:6* He says, "Be strong and courageous. **Do not be afraid** or terrified because of them, for the Lord your God goes with you. He will never leave you nor forsake you."

It has been said there is a "fear not" in the Bible for every day of the year, 365 of them. Though I haven't personally counted them, I have a hunch there are just as many "**trust Me's**". We have His assurance that He will hear and guide us, quiet our spirits, and strengthen our hearts to rebuff the fear. I am still learning to trust Him daily, "not to be" afraid, "not to be" fearful, "not to be" weak; but "**to be**" strong in the Lord, trusting in His love for me.

"Peace I leave with you; my peace I give you. I do not give to you as the world gives. Do not let your hearts be troubled and *do not be afraid*." John 14:27

In a dream strange enough to remember upon waking, I had been searching my Bible for a word from the Lord and was directed to the book of Hebrews. But when I looked in the book of Hebrews, I found some of its pages missing. The beginning and very end were there, but the part I needed was gone, as though a section of the book had fallen out. I looked everywhere for the missing pages but woke up before finding them.

In my morning quiet time with the Lord, I remembered my dream and went to the section of Hebrews which had been missing. It was Hebrews 12, concerning enduring hardship as discipline from the Lord. Verses 12 and 13 were of particular interest. Though I have read this chapter many times, I never understood verse 12. I was about to skip over it but was drawn back and could not let it go. It says, *"Therefore strengthen (restore or make strong) your feeble arms and weak knees. Make level paths for your feet, so that the lame may not be disabled, but rather healed (to be healed or made free)."* AMP

In the preceding verses, discipline is defined as such that sons receive. A father does not discipline to destroy the sons he loves; God, even more so, intends not to destroy those who love Him, but to restore and heal. When we accept His discipline, we will look for the elements in it which will strengthen us, not searching for escape, but seeking His face. We will, in the end, find freedom through God's discipline. In August 2001, I read *"Secrets of the Vine"* by Bruce Wilkenson, which expressed this same principle; God disciplines those He loves, not for destruction, but restoration; and He does it as tenderly, wisely, and gently as is possible.

Many of the traumatic experiences we have in life are for our infinite good in God's eyes, weaning us from dependencies upon the world, with its fleeting pleasures and diversions. From the magnetic attraction of self, His discipline teaches us humility and service. From the powerful tug of wealth and power, He leads us to far greater rewards in an eternal realm instead. Our Father is infinitely good and full of grace. The "missing pages" are always available to us when we refocus our gaze on the One who loves us beyond all we can imagine.

"Moreover, we have all had human fathers who disciplined us and we respected them for it. How much more should we submit to the Father of our spirits and live! Our fathers disciplined us for a little while as they thought best; but God disciplines us for our good, that we may share in his holiness. No discipline seems pleasant at the time, but painful. Later on, however, it produces a harvest of righteousness and peace for those who have been trained by it." Hebrews 12:9-11

Precious Treasure   January 16

My daughter had spent the night with her friends at a slumber party. Upon her return home, she noticed her treasured necklace was missing, and the search was on. We combed through her belongings, her bag, and bedding. We called her friend's family to put them on alert, prompting them to scour their house as well, all to no avail. It was simply gone. Before she went to bed that night, she prayed that God would bring her precious treasure back, trusting that He would.

When she awoke in the morning, her necklace was lying beside her, perfectly formed, as if around someone's neck. God showed up that morning in a most unlikely way! If you are saying to yourself, "That can't happen, someone put it there," I assure you it is a minor thing for God to retrieve a necklace. My family has witnessed God working in much greater ways over the years. Jesus did not offer an empty promise when He encouraged us to "seek and you will find", He loves, when we trust Him, to surprise and amaze us, as any good Father does.

Because fear has been a stronghold in my life, I have sought God quite often, needing His protection, provision, and deliverance. Psalm 34 has become my "life" chapter, a model of relationship with God, to which He continuously draws me. It begins with praise and acknowledgment, settles into seeking God, and ends with salvation and deliverance. Step by step, diving into God's Word, asking for His help multitudes of times, I am finally learning to trust Him for every conceivable need. I am finally able to proclaim deliverance from the chokehold of fear.

We go to God searching for comfort and answers, some as simple as restoring what was lost, others more complex and just as seemingly impossible. It is fear which most often drives us away from God, fear from lack of knowledge of who God is, or fear that we will not have what we ask. But God's love is greater than any fear we have. Running to Him with every variety of fear, holding it up to His scrutiny, I find I can trust His promises; and I can trust in His power to overcome whatever obstacle I face. Seeking His face, I have come to realize God's great and precious treasure is found in His Son, Jesus, and our answers are always discovered in Him.

"My soul will boast in the Lord; let the afflicted hear and rejoice. Glorify the Lord with me: let us exalt his name together." Psalm 34:2

"The righteous cry out, and the Lord hears them; he delivers them from all their troubles." Psalm 34:17-18

In the months following my husband's passing into heaven, I knew God had placed me into a rather forced season of resting. He knew the condition of my body, mind, and spirit following years of exhaustion caring for family members. He also knew that I would pursue busyness as a distraction from the pain of my loss. I am not the "resting" type, always able to find something to occupy my time.

Suddenly, everything in my life stalled. My finances took a hit; I didn't fit into social groups comfortably; my family was busy with their own lives, and I was home. That time alone was, when I considered the healing taking place, exactly what I had needed but did not realize. That realization did not come easily—I fought it at the beginning, struggling with loneliness and pain. Gradually I turned my focus more to Jesus, becoming thankful for the time with Him. I was able to re-group, deeply rest, recover relationships that had been strained, and regain my bearings with the Lord.

Out of the un-rest of activity and distractions, in His wisdom, He placed me in a profound time of rest. In comfort and healing, I found "me", and God's presence. He was never missing, always present in the trials, but my focus became clearer. My joy was restored, and I was able to step into the next phase of life as a widow, with the confidence that God is an ever-present help in time of need. He set my feet on new paths and continued growth. He has endowed me with new freedom and expanded my boundaries.

When God created mankind, He ordained times of rest. He created us with a need for it and a directive to observe it. The seventh day of the week is made for rest; the night was created for rest; feasts and festivals marked the mandates for rest. And seasons of life force rest. God knew we would need it, and daily He directs us in paths that reinforce it, enabling us to shed the busyness of un-rest for the rest only to be found in a close relationship with Him. This is expressed beautifully in the Complete Jewish Bible's translation of **Psalm 23**:

"Adonai is my shepherd; I lack nothing. He has me lie down in grassy pastures, he leads me by quiet water, he restores my inner person. He guides me in right paths for the sake of his own name. Even if I pass through death-dark ravines, I will fear no disaster, for you are with me; your rod and staff reassure me. You prepare a table for me, even as my enemies watch; you anoint my head with oil from an overflowing cup. Goodness and mercy will pursue me every day of my life; and I will live in the house of Adonai for years and years to come."

I stood behind her, observing my precious charge, the ninety-two-year-old lady whom I had become quite fond of over the nearly two years of assisting her. Meticulously well-kept hair swept back in perfection, make-up fastidiously accurate— she sat fretting over the little scar on her forehead. She peered into her 10X magnification mirror, the same kind I use every morning. Though mine is a tool for failing eyesight, hers is a tool for perfecting her dignified image with still-amazingly good visual acuity.

One morning, I gently insisted that no one else can see what she sees in her mirror; they don't have the advantage of the magnification. It was mostly to no avail, but I had to smile; in my mirror that very morning I had gone through a similar process. Every day we both utilize our mirrors to concentrate on our "imperfections". It is easy to be consumed with the details while gazing into the magnifying mirror, believing that the tiny distractions are of major importance.

While details may affect a proofreader or scientist, in our daily lives, many details are not only irrelevant, they are a distraction from what God has for us. Details consume our time and focus, distracting us from God's purpose and relationship with Him. We become less observant of His interaction in our lives and miss the elephant while focusing on the fly. Details are also a diversion from gratitude, focusing on the annoying minutia instead of being grateful for God's greater blessings.

10X vision can be a blessing, or a curse, depending upon our focus. When our primary focus is Jesus, imperfections fall away from view, and our sight is aligned with His, no matter our ages or details of our lives. He allows us to see a bigger picture as we trust in Him; instead of our focus on an ice crystal, He may show us the glacier!

"Find rest, O my soul, in God alone; my hope comes from him." Psalm 62:5

"Cease striving and know that I am God." Psalm 46:10a

"Jesus replied, 'Love the Lord your God with all your heart and with all your soul and with all your mind.'" Matthew 22:37

Waking to a fully charged phone, there was only one problem—it wouldn't turn on, rendering my phone as helpful as a brick. It was an unexpected and unwanted delay on a busy morning; I borrowed a phone and called technical support, everything on hold while I spent an hour in a queue, then talking with the service representative to define the problem. He graciously walked me through the restoration process, and I finally emerged from the technical abyss with a fully functioning device.

When life strands us with nary an answer in sight, Jesus is our source for all the "technical help" we can ever need. After all, He wrote the original owner's manual! God's Word is our source of truth, strength, guidance, direction, and healing. When we flounder in the details or are overwhelmed by the big picture, He reveals the solutions. He understands how we were made, and He lived as we live. He alone knows how to restore function to our disfunction, and healing to our pain. Only He can reconnect our broken connections with God and man. Every answer to any problem can be found in Jesus; His promises are certain, and His help reliable.

If I had chosen to forego calling the technical support line, my life would have been negatively impacted, not even able to call 911 in an emergency. My calendar, contact numbers, and many other functions would have been lost. Likewise, choosing to forego calling on Jesus for help will also yield a negative impact. Jesus said to seek God and His Kingdom first; He should never be our last resort, but rather, our first choice. It is up to the "user" to seek help from the ultimate "Technical Support".

"I will instruct and teach you in this way that you are to go; I will give you counsel; my eyes will be watching you." Psalm 32:8

"For the eyes of the Lord range throughout the earth to strengthen those whose hearts are fully committed to him." 2 Chronicles 16:9

"Ask and it will be given to you; seek and you will find; knock and the door will be opened to you. For everyone who asks receives; he who seeks finds; and to him who knocks, the door will be opened." Matthew 7:7-8

On the shelf in my living room, handcrafted pottery items I have collected over the years reside. A perfectly symmetrical mug was thrown on the wheel and meticulously glazed with soft colors, of lovely greens and browns. Another was purchased in Alaska; it is an oversized mug of ice blue and white to remind me of my visit there. Three matching oil lamps, squatty and round, are reminiscent of my three children; they were purchased as an example of Biblical truths.

Raku pottery, in varied forms, is displayed, courtesy of my son's interest in that method of finishing. Another piece is a slab-form plate made by my first grandson, simple and clean. The last is a relic of my early experimentation with coil construction, nothing more special than a fond memory.

Though very different, the pottery pieces on my shelf have several things in common: They were all made by human beings, not a machined piece among them. They are all constructed from clay. They have all been fired in a kiln. They are all glazed or finished uniquely.

Like the pottery on my shelf, God's children may appear very different from culture to culture, by physical appearance, personality traits, status, or position; but they are all made by the same Creator. Every single one is constructed in His image and crafted with a body, soul, and spirit. They are all fired in the kiln of life, experiencing brokenness, trial, heartache, and trouble. And all are uniquely finished, though similar, with specific qualities and gifts that suit God's purpose for them on this earth.

For those of us who sit on God's shelf, it is impossible to gain the perspective God has. We see our fellow shelf-sitters, as a mystery to us; we see their "glaze", "construction", or use as different than ours. We find it difficult to accept those differences, or we compare ourselves to them. Yet God sees each as an individual on the shelf, fitting exactly where it needs to be properly displayed, precisely filling the position of His gifting and purpose. What God sees is vastly different than what we see.

Instead of comparing myself to the rest of the pots, I am beginning to look at the unique ways we have been formed and "glazed". Looking to the Potter, I can trust that all things work together for good. I can rest on His shelf, knowing that He has a unique plan, into which I somehow perfectly fit. Though I'm not a perfect pot, I fit perfectly into His perfect plan, and so do you.

"Yet, O Lord, you are our Father. We are the clay, you are the potter; we are all the work of your hand." Isaiah 64:8

"We know that all things work together for the good of those who love God: those who are called according to His purpose." Romans 8:28

Do You See What I See? January 21

My friend, seated to the right of me, began to talk about the light coming on outside the window. As I gazed through the glass panes, I had to wonder what in the world she was seeing. The more she insisted, the more I questioned. Finally, rising out of my chair and walking behind hers, I bent down behind her and peered in the direction of her line of sight. And there was the light I could not see; my field of vision had been obscured by a post. Until I viewed the world from her perspective, I could not understand the world she saw.

As I considered that situation, God revealed that I can apply that metaphor in many ways to my life, especially in relationships. It is particularly applicable to understanding people who differ in opinion, values, or life experience. When their opinions differ from mine, it is because they have life experiences that alter their perspectives; if I could step behind them and view life from their angle, I am certain that the things they see would be clearer to me.

We don't meet by mistake, interact by happenstance, or escape God's created order of life; it is all training our eyes to His perspective. Through life's interactions with God's people, we come to recognize, love, and follow Him in greater dependence. We learn to trust Him as we grow up in Him. And only God sees all the angles, every perspective, and the most obscure views of each soul. Only He understands all our life-shaping events, the sharp-edged painful ones, as well as the tender precious moments. He knows intimately the tears shed in secret, and the hopes lost in fear; He alone can skillfully restore hope and trust, even in seeming impossibility. Jesus peers into our hidden places without condemnation, beckoning us to step toward Him, where He can show us a better view.

In Christ, there is not a perspective that cannot be changed, despair that cannot find hope, problem lacking a solution; no lost trust which cannot be restored, and no path to Him which can be blocked. Miniscule faith He still honors. Our vision can be narrow, but He can enlarge our view. With God, all things are possible... So, step behind me and let me ask you this question: "Do you see what I see?"

"'But if you can do anything, take pity on us and help us.' 'If you can?' said Jesus. 'Everything is possible for him who believes." Mark 9:22b-23

"For the Lord gives wisdom and from his mouth come knowledge and understanding. He holds victory in store for the upright, he is a shield to those whose walk is blameless, for he guards the course of the just and protects the way of his faithful ones. Then you will understand what is right and just and fair---every good path." Proverbs 2:6-9

Moon Over My Shoulder

Failure to Future January 22

Like every human inhabiting the earth, I wondered why God had placed me on the planet and what great plan He had for my life. I saw nothing special about my presence here. My failures far outnumbered my successes, at least in my own eyes, and I suspect the eyes of the world, as well. Some people realize their dreams and understand their purpose early in life; for me, it has been a long and arduous journey on a twisting mountainous path, with many trials and obstacles along the way.

Moses and Joseph became my Biblical mentors, examples of later-in-life "success" stories, exemplars of enduring faith in God, perseverance, and trust in His promises. Both were nothing in the world's eyes during their youth, and both could lay claim to some major mistakes. Both also had a calling from God, including trials to endure along the path to fulfillment of that calling. Joseph endured decades of dishonor before his eventual position of honor. And Moses was no youngster when he confronted Pharaoh and led the Israelites out of Egypt to their Promised Land. Their examples gave me hope.

Even though I knew not what I was preparing for, God knew. As he strengthened me ahead of each new challenge, I began to consider it a training ground. What I found during these seasons surprised me! Every training season became an opportunity to stretch, grow in faith and trust, and prepare for that which I did not know was coming. I began to discern God's method of discipline, training, and tempering. I found Him to be my oasis, my trust growing even in the wastelands, as He drew me near and watered my soul.

Because God is sovereign, loving, and intentional, we can trust that our valleys and "wastelands" are simply challenges to trust God more. God does not prepare us for what can be seen on earth alone; we are being refined and prepared for heaven also. My place on this earth is not about me; it is about fulfilling His purpose in and through me. It is only through His wise plans that we are taken from failure to future, hope to fulfillment, and glory to glory; all to His Glory.

"For the word of the Lord is right and true; he is faithful in all he does…From heaven the Lord looks down and sees all mankind; from his dwelling place he watches all who live on earth---he who forms the hearts of all, who considers everything they do…We wait in hope for the Lord; he is our help and our shield. In him our hearts rejoice, for we trust in his holy name." Psalm 33:4, 13-15, 20-21

A Vertical Life   January 23

Once thought to be vicious killers, the enormous sperm whale could demolish a boat with a flick of its tail. Normally docile, it is a staunch adversary when preyed upon. Since 1988, the sperm whale has been studied instead of hunted and found to have remarkably gentle ways. One of the most fascinating comments I heard during a recent documentary was that the sperm whale "leads a very vertical life".

Known to dive as deep as 3,200 feet in search of squid and fish, a ton a day, they plummet into the dark depths, rising straight to the surface again to breathe. They even appear to nap in a vertical position near the surface. Except for brief times breathing, resting, and playing, life is occupied with deep diving for food.

As I watched the footage of the whales in this process of disappearing into the depths of darkness, I considered the difficult times in my life recently. And it occurred to me that in those depths, I found the choicest foods. It was where I have drawn so much on the Lord's strength, and where my character was refined. It had been dark and solitary; I could not see or understand where I was going. It was those darker places that necessitated relying on Jesus, the food He provided in His Word and by His Spirit. I learned better to rely on His direction.

God made the whales able to instinctively find their food in the depths of darkness. He created human beings with a similar "knowing" of our need for Him, leading us to the source of our nourishment, Jesus. Rising to the surface, I could breathe deeply, drawing in His Presence. Floating there, in the light, was to revel in His love and care, recognizing His provision, and expressing my gratitude. Those were periods of rest and restoration to prepare me for the next dive.

In the depths, God feeds our souls, when we feast on Him. The darkness is our training, the Light is our life. Whether in the light above or the darkness below, God is never absent, and the journey between the two is a vertical life.

"The God who made the world and everything in it is the Lord of heaven and earth and does not live in temples built by hand. And he is not served by human hands, as if he needed anything, because he himself gives all men life and breath and everything else. From one man he made every nation of men, that they should inhabit the whole earth; and he determined the times set for them and the exact places where they should live. God did this so that men would seek him and perhaps reach out for him and find him, though he is not far from each one of us. 'For in him we live and move and have our being.'"   Acts 17:24-28a

My vision began to gradually change from a perfect 20/20 to perfectly awful, with cataracts compounding the problem at a too early age. At first, reading glasses were adequate; I didn't even realize that trees were gradually transforming into green blobs, and road signs had become guessing games. Once I transitioned from readers to multi-focus lenses, my world changed. The freedom I hadn't known I had lost caused me to realize what I couldn't see, until wearing the correct lenses. Vision is a priceless gift we all take so much for granted until we begin to lose it.

The same thing happened when I realized I had lost sight of who God is. It happens periodically in my life when my schedule intrudes, and the world encroaches upon my quiet reflections with Him. The signs, as clearly as green-blob-trees, mark my days. One sign says "Insecure", another says "No Awe", one fairly screams in bold print "No Praise"; and the last is most indicative, "No Gratitude". It is then I realize I have turned my line of sight to the circumstances, becoming confused, and isolated from God; He does not seem real, as though I can only see Him from a very far distance.

When I recognize the symptoms of my nearsightedness, I realize my lenses need to change. God has not changed, nor has He moved farther away. His promises have not changed, either. So, it is up to me to be proactive in changing my perspective, to actively pursue and trust Him again. There is no condemnation from Him, just gentle admonishment that it is up to me. If I want to have a relationship with Him, I must be determined to spend time with Him. If I want to see life more clearly, it is up to me to pick up His Word and read it. If my lenses are to change, it is up to me to pick them up and put them on each day.

Spiritual nearsightedness is not unique to anyone, and it happens throughout life. I am so very thankful we have a Savior who understands how we are made and the struggles we have. He is always willing to accept us as we are, gently nudging us to peer through the corrective lens of Truth. With correct vision, we will see Him as He is, not distant and vague, but as the loving, forgiving Father who can be fully trusted and relied upon.

"If you love me, you will obey what I command. And I will ask the Father, and he will give you another Counselor to be with you forever---the Spirit of truth. The world cannot accept him because it neither sees him nor knows him. But you know him, for he lives with you and will be in you."   John 14:15-17

"You are my God, and I will give you thanks; you are my God, and I will exalt you. Give thanks to the Lord, for he is good; his love endures forever."   Psalm 118:28-29

The Butter Bell

My butter sat at room temperature, comfortably convenient in a handmade, pottery butter-bell. Finished with a lovely soft blue glaze, it had graced my table for years. As if a simple butter dish would never do, it had been an item I felt I couldn't live without. Entering the kitchen one morning, the pieces of my butter-bell laid on the countertop neatly stacked. The butter dish now seemed like a perfectly fine container for my butter, and though disappointed at the loss of my lovely butter-bell, I wasn't heartbroken over it.

I hadn't witnessed its demise, but my son confessed that it had slipped from his hand, stating that he would administer the necessary repairs. He was true to his word and meticulously glued the misshapen pieces, restoring it to a resemblance of its former glory. How he managed to reassemble it so well I don't know, but even with the fracture lines visible, it otherwise housed the butter perfectly, continuing its functionality, if not beauty, for many more years. Now I don't even notice the fracture lines.

We, too, were perfectly made, formed by God's own hand in the very beginning. Similarly, we too were formed out of clay, and into God's image. Sin entered the world and shattered the work of God's hands, leaving us broken, as shards in the hands of the Restorer. There is no hope in this world, no perfection through worldly means, and try as I may, I cannot restore myself to perfection. The only glue that will adhere, the only bond with sufficient strength, and the only one who knows how to fit it all together again, is Jesus.

Cracks are still apparent, but the butter-bell I thought was beyond repair has been restored. The cracks are a reminder of its former brokenness, but even more of the loving restoration it received. Through Jesus, God no longer sees the cracks but sees us as already fully restored. His grace alone makes us fully functional and sets us in a place of honor in His kingdom.

God leaves some cracks visible in His restoration process, too, not because He cannot heal them; the cracks remain throughout a lifetime, serving to remind us to look to Him, and to remind us of our need for His love. The cracks are a reminder that this is not our home, and our full restoration and final destinations are not of this world, but the one to come.

"And the God of all grace, who called you to his eternal glory in Christ, after you have suffered a little while, will himself restore you and make you strong, firm and steadfast. To him be the power, forever and ever. Amen." 1 Peter 5:10-11

Emptying the box of its contents, the table filled with one thousand pieces of an intricate puzzle, its picture unfolding only on the lid of its container. Confusion reigned, until piece by piece my friend Mary Lu distributed them onto separate mats by color and pattern. Corner pieces and outside edges began to frame the graphic design of cupcakes, aligned on a striped background. As the exacting process proceeded, puzzle pieces were matched to their perfect partners, forming clusters of assembled sections, then joined to complete the picture.

The puzzles Mary Lu enjoys the most are unique, by virtue of their manufacturing. Every piece in the puzzle die is an individually shaped cut, thicker than average, and no two pieces cut exactly alike. This process makes the puzzle, with unique high-quality graphic images, more challenging and more satisfying to assemble. I have observed the completion of several of Mary Lou's beautiful puzzles, and marvel at her patient tenacity in finding the perfect match for every piece.

It leads me to ponder the miracle of patience displayed in God's creation. Even though He spoke the world into existence, so many processes of nature are wrought over long periods of time. A snowflake doesn't simply fall to Earth, it is caught up in the turbulence of the clouds and modified many times before making its graceful descent. Water drips for years on end before cutting through a rock. Trees grow to maturity over decades. The moon takes weeks to circle the earth. And babies grow to adulthood through many tears and trials.

All the while, God is putting the puzzle together, matching the pieces, fitting His plan to His purpose. How incomprehensible is His wisdom and strategy! He lovingly completes each section of this Divine perplexity, aligns and matches each combination, then sets them exactly where they need to be positioned. It is through Jesus that we find our place in His intricate puzzle, discovering that the perfect match to our weakness is God's strength, and to our need is His provision.

"For you created my inmost being; you knit me together in my mother's womb. I praise you because I am fearfully and wonderfully made; your works are wonderful, I know that full well...All the days ordained for me were written in your book before one of them came to be." Isaiah 139:13-14, 16b

"The God who made the world and everything in it is the Lord of heaven and earth and does not live in temples built by hands. And he is not served by human hands, as if he needed anything, because he himself gives all men life and breath and everything else." Acts 17:24-25

They are attached to everything, the words in fine print, the "legal-eze", the terms of agreement which place conditions upon our use of every service and device. Most of us read none of the fine print. We pray that we never need to acknowledge such irrelevant nonsense, while recognizing that it could return one day, like a rabid dog to bite us. We tend to believe it never will, until it does.

God was into contractual agreements from man's beginning and gave a pretty lengthy list of consequences to the Israelites in the book of Deuteronomy, chapters 28-30. I read His list of penalties for breaking the agreement, or covenant, and they weren't pretty: defeat, sickness, confusion, captivity and slavery, no rest, an anxious mind, despair, wasting diseases, and worse. The list was long and the outlook bleak.

At one point in my life, God was convicting me to repent of a specific sin, and I would not. I could identify with most of the listed penalties, one especially; being filled with dread day and night. Persisting in my headstrong ways, dread robbed me of all peace, as well as many a night's sleep. I remember thinking He surely would protect, me regardless of my rebellion, but when His Word states that He will not be mocked, that is an understatement. God is not a deceiver; He means what He says.

There are always severe consequences for rebellion; especially for us who He calls His children. The world may not know better, but we are expected to. The progression of penalties I accrued lasted for eighteen months; but once I humbly repented, God in His infinite mercy forgave me, restored me, and infused my life with peace.

God doesn't command us to do what we are incapable of doing, either. He is simply outlining what the terms of agreement are: **"Carefully follow the terms of the covenant so that you may prosper in all that you do."** He said in chapter 30, verse 11, **"Now what I am commanding you today is not too difficult for you or beyond your reach."** God's rules empower us with His promises and protect us from our enemy.

Repenting of our broken trust with the Father brings healing and restoration of His promises. **"...When you and your children return to the Lord your God and obey him with all your heart according to everything I command you today, then the Lord your God will restore your fortunes and have compassion on you..."** (v.2) Lesson learned! God restored me, healed me, and set me on a fresh path. He was teaching me that obedience has its rewards, and His terms of agreement are always for our loving protection.

Pondering what I would most wish to convey to my grandchildren about living well on this earth, I stumbled upon a short, but powerful, list that the apostle Paul wrote. In *1 Thessalonians 5:1-22,* he sums it up far better than I can. In an abbreviated form, the list is as follows:

- Be on your guard (as children of the light), alert and clear-headed, not asleep like the others (children of the darkness).
- Encourage and build each other up.
- Honor your spiritual leaders, showing them great respect and wholehearted love.
- Live peaceably with each other.
- Warn those who are lazy, encourage the timid, take tender care of the weak. Be patient with everyone.
- Do not pay back evil for evil, but try to do good to each other, and all people.
- Always be joyful. Be thankful in all circumstances.
- Never stop praying.
- Do not stifle the Holy Spirit.
- Hold on to what is good and stay away from every kind of evil.

My grandchildren, and we, are living in a world filled to overflowing with bright, shiny objects, digital splendors, mind-bending technology, and pleasures beyond anything the world has previously conceived. The promises of the world will be appealing and enticing. They will find themselves caught up in infinite possibilities and unlimited dreams. It is the allure of the same world that was offered to Jesus in the wilderness—your dreams-beyond-limits *if* you will submit your will to, and worship, the prince of darkness instead of God.

They will, as we humans tend to do, avert their eyes from the suffering of the lost in this world until Jesus disrupts their comfort and distraction. They will satisfy themselves until the suffering of others skims the hem of their own garment, or rudely splashes mud unexpectedly upon them.

If they will only open their eyes to it, there is a flip side to the world's allure. There is a world of pain and darkness, the consequences of injustice, poverty, sin, and its destruction. When the sorrows of their exposure to life overtake them, I pray they will turn to Jesus, the only one who can enable them to live out "the list" in love. I pray that they will then share God's message of peace and reconciliation with all whose lives they touch. I pray that they will intimately become acquainted with the Man of Sorrows and the Prince of Peace, who enables us all to accomplish His will on earth. His shortlist on life is summed up by loving God and loving our neighbor.

"May God himself, the God of peace, sanctify you through and through. May your whole spirit, soul, and body be kept blameless at the coming of our Lord Jesus Christ. The one who calls you is faithful and he will do it." 1 Thessalonians 5:23

Every weekday afternoon at precisely 3:45, a blue Ford Galaxy pulled onto the concrete driveway. We knew what to expect next. The car door closed, and the back door opened. Grandpa walked directly downstairs to the shower, peeling off his shirt (full of burn holes from welding sparks at the factory), on his way. Climbing the stairs, he walked to the refrigerator and pulled out, not a drink for himself but a carrot for Penny, the family's Manchester terrier. He slowly cut slivers of the carrot, while Penny sat hopeful and expectant before him.

As Gram cooked supper, Penny waited patiently in the doorway, carefully staying out of the kitchen fray, only her eyes following Gram's steps. She had every reason to be hopeful since Gram cooked two dinners, one for us and another for Penny. Penny was blessed with freshly cooked chicken nearly every night, turning her nose up at store-bought dog food, which is probably why she lived to the amazing age of 18. She then slept on Grandpa's lap every evening, never lacking in loving attention.

As excited as Penny was when Grandpa arrived home, there was never a speck of anxiety in it. She knew what to expect from experience, trusting because she knew Grandpa loved her and was kind. I learned something from that little dog as I observed her interactions with him; there is hope for what is yet to come, and there is trust in the character of the provider.

God's goodness and character tell us that we can trust Him. He is faithful, consistent, and true...all the time, never varying. He keeps His promises, never wavers in His commitment, and is generous, steadfast, loving, and kind. And we can have hope. He does not change like shifting shadows, promises never to leave nor forsake us and to provide for our future.

While sliced carrots didn't seem like much to me, to Penny, they were a bit of heaven from Grandpa's hand. God is my Provider, meeting me where I am, feeding me what I need, caring for my peace, and loving me while knowing well my imperfections--all because of Christ's sacrifice on the cross. Like Penny, we can confidently hope in The One we trust, steadfastly waiting, for our God is wonderful beyond imagining!

"Because of the Lord's great love, we are not consumed, for his compassions never fail. They are new every morning; great is your faithfulness. I say to myself, 'The Lord is my portion: therefore, I will wait for him.' The Lord is good to those whose hope is in him, to the one who seeks him; it is good to wait quietly for the salvation of the Lord."

Lamentations 3:22-26

"Don't be deceived, my dear brothers. Every good and perfect gift is from above, coming down from the Father of the Heavenly lights, who does not change like shifting shadows."

James 1:16-17

Tied in Knots

A fair number of years passed without the need of tying a square knot, and if I had tied one, it was purely accidental. The only knots I had needed to execute were the French knot of embroidery and a simple knot to end my thread. When my son enrolled in a Boy Scout troop, the world of knots expanded far and wide, as he earned his badges. And I will admit that since then, that square knot has come in pretty handily.

Perfectionist that I have been most of my life, I can peer into the chasm of time-past and admit that I spent a fair portion of it tied up in those proverbial knots. Drawing a horse for an art contest in seventh grade became a lesson in creative paralysis. Grades in school were a fixation. A card game loss became a compulsion to win. And I discovered that camping was an exercise in controlling fear, leaving my stomach tied in knots (my greatest pleasure is the sound of the words, "It's time to load up!").

I don't believe I am alone in my quest for control. I meet many people who struggle to have the perfect family, perfect life, perfect possessions, and perfect relationships. This may come as a surprise to you, as it did me, but nothing in life is perfect. In life, almost everything tends to tilt toward chaos and being riddled with flaws. Those of us who haven't figured this out yet lean toward looking down a bit on the rest of humanity, from the height of pride in our "perfect" accomplishments. For those people, I feel a bit sorry, and regretful that I ever saw anyone else that way.

Every stage of life presents its own unique set of challenges, to say nothing of the raw cataclysmic world each of us encounters daily. The upheavals in life are perfectly suited to cure the worst perfectionist, bringing our inaccurate sense of control under God's control, our pride down one step for each rung on life's ladder. The knots tied in my soul by my perfectionism He has been able to unravel. He has smoothed out the wrinkles with His peace; and as He has done so, the tension and strain have eased as well.

Tension is in opposition to trust, something I wish I could remember more often. Tension tugs the knots tighter and makes life harder. Fear opposes trust, whispering that we don't need God, that independence is the way. And what if "it" doesn't turn out as we wished? What if??? Jesus came to release the knots; and to teach us to trust His nimble and wise hands, wherever in life He takes us. The only knot that matters is the blood-soaked cords that bind my heart to His.

"In you, our fathers put their trust; they trusted and you delivered them. They cried to you and were saved; in you they trusted and were not disappointed." Psalm 22:4-5

"Do not let your hearts be troubled. Trust in God; trust also in me." John 14:1

This Is My Story, and I'm Sticking to It! January 31

My first journals were no more than spiral notebooks in the beginning, the genesis of my writing thirty years ago. The journals progressed to hard-cover and eventually settled into leather-bound. The physical changes in bindings mirrored the physical changes of life, the leather becoming more comfortable in my "maturing" hands than the rest. All along the way, I never viewed myself as a writer, just someone filling a need to think slowly, process words at my own pace, and reassemble them in my mind.

Those journals became an accounting of mundane life, deeper thoughts, but most of all, the changes God worked in me as He carried out His intentional transformations, bit by bit. Some of the entries were painful to read, bringing to the surface my losses and failures. Others reminded me of the blissfully good times, especially with our children as they grew up, and the experiences we shared as a family. Each page became a marker on my timeline. Each was evidence of God's workings, and His interactions with me.

We all have a story to tell. We are created in God's image, and each one of us has a purpose on this earth. We discount our importance to God, yet He sent His only Son, Jesus, to a sinner's cruel death on a cross; He destroyed sin and death on our behalf and raised Him to life with the promise of eternity. Why??? Because He loves us. And because of His amazing love, we have a story to tell the world, His story through our testimony of faith in Jesus.

I found my story, and my mission, in His timing and through His leading—the book you are holding is proof of it. And my hope is that it leads each person reading it back to the Author of Life. However, the only book that ultimately matters is the one God Himself inscribes with our names. It is the Book of Life, the recording of each Believer who has placed his or her faith in God's precious Son. I pray your name is written there with mine, and that you will share your story with the world as the Holy Spirit leads you, too. This is my story, and I'm sticking with it!

"Nothing impure will ever enter it (the new heaven), nor will anyone who does what is shameful or deceitful, but only those whose names are written in the Lamb's book of life." Revelation 21:27

"Jesus did many other things as well. If every one of them were written down, I suppose that even the whole world would not have room for the books that would be written." John 21:25

February

No to Cherubs

Their cute little chubby cheeks, sweet smiles, and roly-poly baby bodies adorn greeting cards, shoot love arrows for Valentine's Day, and swing from hooks on Christmas trees, except at my house. I have said "no" to cherubs. I don't have anything against angels, only the common concept that cherubs are an accurate representation of angelic beings. Something tells me we have the concept of cherubs all wrong.

Cherubim are referenced in the Bible as guardians, first of the Garden of Eden, then perched atop the Ark of the Covenant, and on both sides of the throne of God, pretty serious business. Angels wield great power, often portrayed as bearing swords. They are "mighty creatures who do God's bidding", whether acting as messengers who bear God's own words, protectors, envoys through dreams, or ministers of comfort. And God's angels will always direct our attention to him, the Lord of Hosts.

There are hierarchies of angels, in various forms. Archangels to seraphim, each perform specific duties, all worshiping God and obeying His commands. Those who rebelled under Satan, another angelic being, were cast out of heaven. Angels are not passive and baby-like.

At Christmas, Gabriel, an archangel, brought the message of God's calling on Mary's life and spoke to Joseph in dreams. Angels appeared to shepherds, spoke to the Magi in a dream, and burst through the barriers of heave, casting streams of glory into the night at Christ's birth, as they displayed the majesty of heaven. Angels tended to Jesus' needs after the trial of fasting forty days in the desert. The angels awaited the bidding of Jesus at His crucifixion, and I cannot imagine the willpower it required to resist summoning them in His agony.

Angels pour out the wrath of God upon the earth at the ending of days, in judgment for mankind's rejection of His authority and sovereignty. The praises abounding in heaven are the voices of the angels combined with the voices of the children of God, in unrestrained, jubilant praise and adoration for the King of Glory!

They can be found in miracles and amid crowds, a traveler among us, or a barrier for us. Man's version of chunky angels with rosy cheeks is fine for people who do not need protection and provision. But I will admit to being needy and am thankful for strong, mighty angels capable of doing God's will, and of helping me in a dark and difficult world. So, I will say "no to cherubs" and "yes" to the mighty angels who do God's bidding.

"If you make the Most High your dwelling---even the Lord, who is my refuge---then no harm will befall you, no disaster will come near your tent. For he will command his angels concerning you to guard you in all your ways; they will lift you up in their hands, so that you will not strike your foot against a stone." Psalm 91:9-12

Listening to a technology expert enlightening his audience about the advances in current science, his message didn't startle me, since I have kept a close eye on it for decades and recognize the trends. The friend whom I later spoke with had no clue. And she was happy to have no clue about the trans-human projects, the robotic mosquito-sized weapons of warfare, or the climate generating machines already in operation. Robotics and AI (artificial intelligence) alone are staggering in their future impacts on the world as we know it.

As technology booms, human beings tend to increasingly cede control of their lives to it, becoming more dependent upon the little gods of this world. Thinking themselves secure, they are content to silently wrest control from God's hand, "independent" of needing Him. I see it in my own life: the cellphone submerging me in the technologically inclined universe, the fascination and "shiny ball syndrome" of it. The tendency is to nudge the Big God over a bit, to make way for the little god who seems more easily accessed.

The words flashing before my eyes warn of descent into such folly: **"You shall have no other gods beside me."** (Deuteronomy 5:7) There is little to no struggle in following the path to worldly pleasures and fulfillment of needs; but that path will, without fail, lead to destruction. I have experienced this rebuke and command many times in my life, and with every yielding to the desires of my flesh, devastation has followed. It is our human tendency not only to be distracted but to cheerfully follow the little gods of self and worldly glitter.

In Christ is life and abundance, that which the world will always be incapable of giving. Only God can repair our hearts, fulfill our deepest needs, and refresh our spirits. Jesus knows the world well and told us that He came into it to give us peace. AI and technology may enhance our lives, but only Jesus saves us. The little gods of this realm are no match whatsoever for the Lord Almighty. In Him, I will trust and not be afraid.

"To the Lord your God belong the heavens, even the highest heavens, the earth and everything in it…For the Lord your God is God of gods and Lord of lords, the great God, mighty and awesome, who shows no partiality and accepts no bribes.…Fear the Lord your God and serve him. Hold fast to him and take your oaths in his name. He is your praise; he is your God…" Exodus 10:14, 17, 20, 21a

One friend was in the excruciating grip of a family conflict, another requested prayer for a dire financial crisis. Another was experiencing critical medical issues which may render her a widow far sooner than she had hoped. I am also praying for a precious friend whose son has divorced unpleasantly (I don't believe there is any other kind of divorce) and is sorting through the shards of relationships strewn in its wake. Amid car accidents, abuse, critical illnesses, addictions, losses, and trials of all kinds, I have many friends going through upheaval.

After talking with one of those friends this morning, I leafed through my journal looking for a verse of encouragement for her. In a Psalm, I stumbled upon a very simple verse where I had drawn a box around two of the words. I paused, contemplating their weight; their meaning was profound if I considered all the possibilities.

"EVEN THERE, **your hand will guide me, your right hand will hold me fast." Psalm 139:10** The first two words stunned me. I realized that no matter where we are in life, whatever the situation; when there seems to be no solution to my problems, no water in my desert, no sun in my sky, God is there. When I am oppressed, depressed, weighed down, or pushed into a corner, *even there* His hand will guide me. When I am isolated, or in a crowd, pressed from all sides, or have no one on my side, His hand will hold me fast. When I cannot see the way, am blindsided, or the darkness is closing in, and there seems no way out, His hand will guide me.

EVEN THERE, wherever your "there" is, whether you are confined to a hospital bed, a relationship, a circumstance, or a season of life, God is there. He is not absent. He is not distant. He is not detached. He is there with you, whether you feel His presence or not. It is His promise; Jesus stated that He will NEVER leave or forsake you. You are His child and He does not abandon His children—EVER. So be encouraged, precious one! You can expect help is on the way and that He will provide what you need, exactly when you need it. Trust that *EVEN THERE,* where you reside this moment, He sees you, understands, and He will supply all your needs in His timing, and according to His perfect plan.

"And my God will meet all your needs according to his glorious riches in Christ Jesus."

Philippians 4:19

"Cast all your anxiety upon him because he cares for you." I Peter 5:7

"My times are in your hands." Psalm 31:15

Welcome Home! February 4

Flying into LAX airport in Los Angeles for the first time, a stark contrast greeted me. An expansive view of the terrain appeared as an unending river of concrete, glass, and metal flowing into the horizon. There was little vegetation and lots of asphalt. Walking from my hotel to the venue for my event, concrete planters, and an occasional palm tree, dotted the route. It was indeed quite the contrast from the lushness surrounding the Nashville airport from which I had departed such a short time before. The phrase from the Wizard of Oz repeated in my mind, "There's no place like home."

If you have ever experienced being stranded away from home, you can most likely relate to my insecurity. Even when traveling across town, we so much take for granted our access to food, water, money, a place to rest, transportation, and security. There are moments when I feel that life on this planet is similarly unfamiliar and dangerous, that I am living rather precariously in the uncertainties of survival. Bills need to be paid in months short of cash, and accidents happen when least expected. Relationships flounder in flash floods of tears. Upheavals around the world rock my security, and decisions by leaders, with whom I do not agree, and whose agendas I oppose. Cataclysmic events rupture the physical world surrounding me. And the threat of illnesses lurk, some having pounced already.

How thankful I am that Jesus holds my times in His hands, that He extends hope and a future, not only in heaven but also today. Amidst all the turmoil of this world, He walked, too; He understands and knows full well the threats we face, the evil we battle, the crushing forces at hand. Yet, He came to give us life, not in meager measure, but life to its fullest, life abundantly. He came to offer us hope and a future extending like an ocean to the horizon. It is life we cannot, in our limited abilities, even imagine.

Jesus is standing at the door of your heart and extending His arms, inviting you to trust Him alone. Then watch what He can do with the smidgeon of resources you think you have. He can do more than we can ask or imagine if we will but trust Him. He stands at the door of peace and abundance, welcoming you home, home to your place in His Kingdom and His Presence, the only place of security on this earth.

"Taste and see that the Lord is good; blessed is the man who takes refuge in him. Fear the Lord, you his saints, for those who fear him lack nothing. The lions may grow weak and hungry, but those who seek the Lord lack no good thing." Psalm 34:8-10

No, it's not the word you think it is, though that word you are thinking has become pervasive in our media and our culture. The "F" word to which I refer is FEAR. In the world we inhabit, fear abounds and is magnified by the media. Advertisers promote the fear of lack and fear of unacceptance. The latest news parades a never-ending litany of current dangers and fears of the day, the latest catastrophe de jour. Where news was once factual, it has now become "may be true". Sources are secret or non-existent, reality blurred, and fear promoted.

If pride is our enemy's first weapon of choice, fear is the tool of second choice in our enemy's arsenal. There is plenty to fear in the mere living of life, whether from disease, loss of loved ones, inability to earn what we need, accidents, conflicts large and small, natural disasters, and more. Relationships dissolve and brokenness abounds. Sounds dismal, doesn't it? Living in a world overflowing with fear drowns our hope and leaves us dogpaddling for our very lives.

This all comes as no surprise to God. When He created mankind in His image, one unique quality set us on the path to determining how much fear would rule in our lives. He gifted us with the ability of choice. At the crossroad of choice is the alternative of fear or faith, the other "F" word. Follow God, trusting Him no matter what the circumstances appear to be, or take the road of fear. Listen to His instructions, stepping closer to Him in faith; or take the worldly route, which leads to increasing panic. Draw courage and strength through fellowship with Him or cower in the corner of fear.

Fear will be thrust upon us by the world in which we live, but the choice is ours whether we will bow to fear or bow to the Throne, subject to the enemy or a subject of the King. God has given us the weapons required to fight whatever battles we face, and He never leaves us alone; but it is a choice as to whether we will take up the armor. Jesus used the Word of God as His primary weapon; prayer and solitude with His Father gave Him strength; His mission to save us gave Him purpose; the Spirit of God gave Him the power to do His Father's will. We have the same weapons available to us. Today, which "F" word will you choose, fear or faith?

"Jesus answered, 'It is written: "Man does not live by bread alone, but on every word that comes from the mouth of God."'" Matthew 4:4

"Put on the full armor of God so that you can take your stand against the devil's schemes…Stand firm then, with the belt of truth buckled around your waist, with the breastplate of righteousness in place, and with your feet fitted with the readiness that comes from the gospel of peace. In addition to all this, take up the shield of faith, with which you can extinguish all the flaming arrows of the evil one. Take the helmet of salvation and the sword of the Spirit, which is the word of God." Ephesians 6:10-11, 14-17

Blind Encounter

Upon waking each morning, I routinely count heads, fully expecting to find three little Maltese dogs greeting me. This morning, the oldest was missing! I carefully peeked under furniture and in all her favorite spots, but she was nowhere to be found. Searching even the places she could not access in the house, still, there was no Tiffy. Alarmed by that, I began to well up with tears, realizing something truly was amiss.

I had gazed down the stairwell and had seen nothing at the bottom, but as I descended the stairs, Tiffy happily trotted out of the bedroom to greet me. The muffled sound I had ignored as I was waking was Tiffy tumbling down the stairs. My aging dog, with limited vision, had misjudged the top step and promptly arrived at the bottom, thankfully unharmed. The door to the stairs is now kept closed.

Jesus also does a headcount of all the children He created, loves, and for whom He sacrificed Himself. Jesus came to set us free from the sin and bondage which ensnares us, trapping us at the "bottom of the stairs". Jesus left the ninety-nine sheep and went in search of the missing blind one. He protects us in our waywardness, even before we are found. He comforts us in our shortsightedness and blunders.

He did not give up, become distracted, or demand a reward for finding it. He loves His sheep. When one is wayward or has strayed from the flock, He is determined to find it. That is His heart, His purpose for stepping out of heaven and into flesh; to seek and save that which is lost. I am so grateful that He found me! Like Tiffy, I would have remained isolated and in danger if He had not sought me.

When I carried Tiffy back up the stairs and set her down, she was immediately greeted and welcomed back by the rest of my little white dogs. I cannot express my relief and the outpouring of love I felt at that time, thankful to God that she was rescued and had not been hurt. The Bible says that when one sinner claims their salvation in Christ, there is great rejoicing in heaven. I'm pretty sure Jesus, too, is elated when we who are blind are found, and placed in the safety and security of His protective care.

"When he saw the crowds, he had compassion on them, because they were harassed and helpless, like sheep without a shepherd." Matthew 9:36

"And if he finds it, I tell you the truth, he is happier about that one sheep than about the ninety-nine that did not wander off. In the same way your Father in heaven is not willing that any of these little ones should be lost." Matthew 18:13-14

My close friend was experiencing the heartbreak of watching one of her children go through the devastation of divorce. It was what she had suffered as a mother, and now was witnessing in her son. Now it was affecting relationships she had built for many years. She could only look on helplessly as her grandchildren withdrew in confusion and debilitating pain. Her own heart crumbled in numbness and bewilderment, as she prayed for the family, gathered the fragmented hearts, and pressed on in ministry to each one.

A son wanders into drugs, a daughter refuses a relationship, a move to distant lands divides hearts, illness changes personalities, and conflicts divide families. Economic pressures, eroding familial connections, and changing cultural norms can all gnaw at our family relationships; many are the reasons for family distress and brokenness. Where is Jesus in the relational storms we all experience? How can He possibly understand our pain when He had no family of His own?

Jesus' family, I realized, was dysfunctional, too, though not for the same reasons as most of us experience. His brothers did not support His ministry, nor believe that He was the Son of God, until after His crucifixion. They resented Him for stirring up what they perceived as trouble, bringing the whole family under the scrutiny of the ruling religious class.

Jesus could do few miracles in Nazareth due to the unbelief of His friends and neighbors. He spent nearly all His time with His disciples, even His mother having to track him down, asking to be seen. He was opposed at every turn, despised by many. He wept at the brokenness of those surrounding Him.

I had forgotten about those earthly relationships, believing that Jesus could not understand the pain of my failures. He understands them well, but He also points me to the perfect relationship, the one with His Heavenly Father. Jesus talked with His Dad constantly, knew His Father loved him, and fully relied on His protection and provision perfectly. The sinless Son knew His magnificent Father intimately.

There was only one moment where fellowship between Father and Son was broken. On the cross, the Father turned away from the sin Jesus carried there in my place. The whole point of His walking the earth was to bring us into the same fellowship with His Father that He enjoyed, a Father who eagerly scoops us into His arms, loving us as He loves His only Son. Reflecting on Jesus' ability to empathize with my broken relationships, I can only whisper, "He understands," and trust Him with the ones I love.

"He was despised and rejected by men, a man of sorrows and familiar with suffering. Like one from whom men hide their faces he was despised and we esteemed him not." Isaiah 53:3

"For even his own brothers did not believe in him." John 7:5

Hide and Seek   February 8

There was an odd closet in the house in which I grew up, and it was in my bedroom. To maximize space in the second-floor room, the closet ran narrow and deep. With the rod hanging across the front, the back of the closet was difficult to access, so when playing hide and seek, it was my favorite nook. There was an additional aspect to that closet; it had a "shelf" where I fit snuggly, curled up. When sad or lonely, it was my hiding place, and I hid a lot.

Whatever our pain is, we have a tendency, as Adam and Eve did in the garden, and I did in my closet, to attempt to hide from God. Hiding is a symptom of brokenness due to sin, shame, fear, or guilt. Just as I hid in my special closet for comfort, we can find comfort in hiding, isolating ourselves from God and others. But the funny thing is that everyone knew where to find me. It was, after all, my favorite hiding place. And God knows just where to find you in your special hiding place.

Our heavenly Father knows our pain and seeks us in our weakness. He understands our brokenness, the area we believe no one knows. Before we can find His comfort, though, we must acknowledge the wound and that He can heal us. As believers in Jesus, we accept that He went to the cross, suffered, and died in our place to bring healing, as well as salvation. Countless times, I have witnessed His healing power in His children as they have submitted themselves to His grace and love, and I am one of them.

Isolation is a natural inclination when injured, proven in medicine of the millennia. It is part of the healing process, a time of quiet for our bodies to recover their strength and recuperate. Spiritual wounds are no different, but continued isolation has the detrimental effect of festering them. By bringing them into the light of Christ Jesus, and trusting His ways as outlined in His Word, any wound can be healed, and any believer made whole in body and spirit. He died to set us free. He seeks us out, beckoning us to leave the dark and enter into His wonderful light of love and restoration. In Him, there is no condemnation for those who believe and trust Him. And He always wins in the game of hide-and-seek.

"Where can I go from your Spirit? Where can I flee from your presence? If I go up to the heavens, you are there; if I make my bed in the depths, you are there. If I rise on the wings of the dawn, if I settle on the far side of the sea, even there your hand will guide me, your right hand will hold me fast."   Psalm 139:7-10

"Now the Lord is the Spirit, and where the Spirit of the Lord is, there is freedom."
2 Corinthians 3:17

Throughout my early years, my mother volunteered with various drama clubs, working on the sets, wardrobe, and make-up teams. My brothers and I were the baggage she toted on location. Later, when I entered high school, my stepfather was a drama instructor. I was also cast as a character in productions and worked on sets. All my background in drama gives me a good understanding of memorizing lines, staying "on script", and not deviating from the conversation which the play-write intended.

Going "off script" means that the actor has taken the liberty to make an impromptu deviation, which could alter the whole storyline of the play. Changing one line could affect the tone of the current scene or the outcome of the ending. Only the director can make that judgment, taking responsibility for the ultimate success or failure of the production.

We all have a part to play in this drama called life and have been cast in the perfect role. It is the role of a lifetime, as an individual created by God to fit His plan and purpose. Honestly, there have been many difficult times when I have been dissatisfied with my role, wishing I had someone else's part to play instead of my own. But the more I examine the roles of other players, the more I understand that we all have difficult parts to play. Life is universally painful, especially when we go "off script", making choices that are contrary to God's clearly laid out script.

The director is the key to the success of the play, determining the staging and taking responsibility for the outcome. Largely, his success is dependent upon the trust the actors and support team have in his judgment calls. Actors, who are self-centered and will not take direction, may hinder everyone else involved. Disasters happen on sets, as well as in real life. It is the director's judgment calls that save the play.

It is no different for us; our trust must be in Jesus, the Director, for our character development and His production plan. Our Director is ever-present and can intervene in the play, bringing about success in the end. He sees the whole play from beginning to end; and holds the power to change the elements of the play at any time, even when we seem to go "off-script". Nothing surprises Him, nothing hinders Him. He is always on-script.

"The Lord Almighty has sworn, 'Surely, as I have planned, so it will be, and as I have purposed, so it will stand.'" Isaiah 14:24

A divorced woman with four children ages 6 and under, limited education, no child support, and no government assistance constituted a dire situation. She had been advised to give up the children for adoption but refused. Now her headstrong tenacity, which had precipitated the current circumstances, became her strength. With my grandmother's hard work and support supplying the basic family needs, she went on to raise me and my brothers.

During one of those difficult days, I went to the cabinet and found that there was only a partial jar of peanut butter and a box of saltine crackers for supper. I can't say that we ever starved, as my mother continued her education over those five years. However, it did reinforce the fear of not having enough and contributed to my tendency to find comfort in a full pantry.

Many years later, I found myself a Christian with a perplexing problem. How could I be so fearful of not having enough when there was ample evidence all around me that God had provided well? I have never been without food, clothing, shelter, or transportation. My bills have always been paid, and I have generously given to others in need. Not only have I had enough, but I have also had more than enough. One would think the answer to be obvious, but it took me years to figure it out.

The answer may have been obvious, but it was not easy to change the fear hidden in my heart as a young child. Fear is often subtly embedded in the soil of our hearts; and because we are vulnerable at young ages, it is left there to grow in the darkness. Inquiring of my heavenly Father, I asked Him to reveal the truth to me.

As God began to bring this fear into His healing light, I have been able to recognize it more readily. Trusting Jesus has released me from fear and set my feet on His promises instead. Daily, I realize new areas of my life where fear attempts to crawl in through a crack. But, also daily, as I trust my heavenly Father, I walk in profound freedom. When fear bubbles to the surface, I now recognize the truth hidden within my heart—Jesus is sufficient. He is my "enough".

"Therefore, I tell you, do not worry about your life, what you will eat or drink; or about your body, what you will wear. Is not life more important than food, and the body more important than clothes? Look at the birds of the air; they do not sow or reap or store away in barns, and yet your heavenly Father feeds them. Are you not much more valuable than they? Who of you by worrying can add a single hour to his life?" Matthew 6:25-27

An article published in World Magazine featured an elderly woman who had been writing letters to her family, sharing the truths she had learned, as well as her experiences. She had written an incredible 777 letters to various family members over the years, imparting her life, wisdom, and love. Each precious page spilled drops of her life into theirs, touching and connecting their hearts in ways, I am certain, that she could never imagine.

Our heavenly Father expresses Himself too, in a remarkably similar way, through letters found in the Bible. They were written to share truths with us through the experiences of His children's past, as well as through His instructions. The letters begin in the Old Testament, many chapters long, including genealogies, chronologies, historic events, and prophecies; some are poetry and one is even a love letter.

With the love of a father, He includes letters of encouragement, rebuke, and discipline in the New Testament. He explains His family lineage, recounts the life of His son, Jesus, and His journey walking the earth in human flesh. He explains what happened on the cross of death, gives us hope and courage to trust His plan, then offers us a continued presence through His Spirit. Finally, He explains what we will encounter on earth and offers us heaven's citizenship.

As if that were not enough, God sends us memos daily, sticky notes of sorts. Through "coincidences" each day, holy "accidents" are randomly placed in our paths, some subtle and others glaringly obvious. We are not often paying attention, distracted by our busy lives. At times, God has to allow major disruption to our agenda, dislodging our attention, and directing it back to Himself. I have been known to stumble through a day, never noticing one; other days my eyes are open to the awe of His presence and love, like a mailbag being dumped over my head!

God's intention has always been to communicate with His children, to have a close-knit family relationship. 777 letters never opened by the woman's family would have been a crime; they would have missed out on the love and wisdom she shared with them. It is equally tragic when we, the children of the Most High God, leave His letters untouched, His heart and wisdom neglected. May we open our eyes to His Word and His Spirit speaking to us today, missing not one of His letters, the expressions of His love.

"The Spirit himself testifies with our spirit that we are God's children."   **Romans 8:16**

"The Lord confides in those who fear him; he makes his covenant known to them."

Psalm 25:14

My precious friend called me, and I could tell by her voice that she was struggling. Her husband, a wonderful man, had been ill. His health declined over the past several years, and he now seemed to be resigning himself to it, giving up hope of healing. Having walked through that experience myself, she has turned to me for comfort, which I feel ill-prepared to give. Her situation brought a startling picture into view, as I contemplated how to encourage her.

Picture the amazing perfection of the Garden of Eden, home to God's premium model of human beings, created in His very own likeness. They were the pinnacle of Creation, radiant with beauty, and sparkling with the energy of perpetual youth. They were glowing with the Divine presence, with the very fingerprint of God upon them, the perfect couple, and the blueprint for mankind. God walked with them in perfect harmony daily, until they thought themselves wiser than their Maker, resulting in cataclysmic brokenness of unimaginable proportion.

The first sin initiated catastrophic events, which they could never have imagined, and a nightmare they could never have foreseen. The first signs of their vulnerability in a fallen world would have been injuries like broken bones, cuts, bruises, and the searing reality of pain! Just imagine experiencing pain for the first time in the history of the world.

Immediately, another element of shattered perfection began to prey on the first couple, as they experienced aging. They were the first to grow old, to experience loss of divine energy, and to witness sagging muscles and wrinkling skin. As they sank into sickness, they faced the eventual loss of their partner, who was made by God's perfect plan just for them. How wrenching the unfathomable loss must have been for the perfect couple, to be finally separated by death! This was never meant to be.

The comfort in this scenario is that it was no surprise to God that man would choose sin. All along, He planned for our rescue. And the comfort for us today, amid the suffering and pain, the agonies of aging, and the brokenness of the world is that God cares so much. We may not understand why we must suffer, but we are not the first to suffer. He is present in our every moment of weakness, holds our tears in His hands, and hears our cries. Life turned to death for the perfect couple, but we turn from death to life through Christ Jesus, with perfection still to come.

"Three times I pleaded with the Lord to take it away from me. But he said to me, 'My grace is sufficient for you, for my power is made perfect in weakness.'" 2 Corinthians 12:8,9

"For God so loved the world that he gave his one and only Son, that whoever believes in him shall not perish, but have eternal life." John 3:16

The opinions surrounding the tiny candy hearts, of Valentine's Day notoriety, are nearly as intense as political opinions. The parties are of two sects, one cheering on the original Conversation Hearts, the other, Sweet Tart hearts. The opponents of Conversation Hearts critique it as too chalky, or too sweet, which is beyond my understanding. The opposition to Sweet Tart hearts is that they are too hard or too sour.

Conversation Hearts, tiny treats with sweet messages, harken back to my childhood and a century more. They were inexpensive, portable, their messages fun but not particularly meaningful, and could be selectively distributed by relevant messages. One little box met many relational needs: Cute! Kiss Me! Love You! Hug! Or Be Mine. No one took their messages very seriously, which made them even more appealing.

All these years later, I can look back on dating, marriage, and relationships of all kinds, thankful for the love shown to me, and the many different expressions of love that I didn't even realize at the time. Some were as simple as a smile or an unexpected hug, praise for a job well done, an act of kindness, or a compliment extended. The one making the strongest impression, though, was the unconditional love my husband showed to his flawed and broken spouse, eventually leading me to seek the very same type of love from my Savior, Jesus.

We can search the world over for the mate our hearts long for, seek love in every corner of the globe, but we will never find anyone who can satisfy the emptiness within us. I know it full well, having experienced that hunger myself. Even my husband could never fill that role; it is impossible to substitute anything on earth for the love that only Christ can give.

As God expressed His love for me over the years, I began to understand. He is faithful to send "tiny heart messages" through any means possible to impress us, whether it is in a sunset, a painting, music, the chirp of a tree frog, or a loving touch. He expresses His love through His provision of daily necessities, smiles, problems solved, the warm gaze of a pet, or unexpected help to solve a problem. If we fail to respond to His messages, we will miss the Love of our lives.

Whether Conversation Heart or Sweet Tart, all of God's messages can be summarized on one tiny heart candy, "Be Mine!" His desire on Valentine's Day, and every day, is to have our surrendered hearts. He asks that we love Him first and foremost, not because He is selfish or controlling, but because He loves us so much that He would sacrifice all He had to capture our hearts.

"I will give you a new heart and put a new spirit in you; I will remove from you your heart of stone and give you a heart of flesh. And I will put my Spirit in you and move you to follow my decrees and be careful to keep my laws." Ezekiel 36:26

Hearted   February 14

Much to my disappointment, my husband's business trip took him to Fort Wayne and kept him there through Valentine's Day. I had little time to think about it, though, as my day pressed forward, packed with the family demands. The children finally were tucked into bed, pets cared for, and the house locked up. I finished a salad at 11:15, cleaned up the kitchen, made notes about all that needed attention the next day, and was happy to be dropping into bed.

As I wearily tossed pillows from my side of the bed to Gary's, the red foil "hearted" (as my daughter, Blair, used to say) Valentine box, shining in the lamplight, caught my eye. Gary had tucked it under my pillow before leaving on his trip. My heart crumbled with gratitude and awe, amazed at this man God had given me. I have heard people say that they didn't deserve someone; I am one of those people. I have been so blessed, and admittedly, at times ungrateful for the mate God had given me.

That night, I thanked God for the gift of Gary, His most generous and thoughtful gift, given to one very undeserving woman. That night, I thanked God for the miraculous gift of Jesus, as well, the one who had redeemed our marriage, saving it from certain ruination years earlier.

I also pondered, that night, what a generous and wonderful God I serve, considering that I, being so blessed, am often just as ungrateful for what my Savior has done for me. His heart is ever bent toward me, granting me His favor, protection, and bounty. His love is unfathomable. His gifts are beyond generous, His forgiveness abounding, and His grace unlimited.

God's love is the red "hearted" box that I didn't expect or deserve, the once-in-a-lifetime relationship that is once in an eternity. I don't deserve it, but just as I opened the "hearted" box and tasted the candy I didn't merit, Jesus bids me keep my heart open to His love, and to taste and see that He, too, is good.

"You see, at just the right time, when we were still powerless, Christ died for the ungodly. Very rarely will anyone die for a righteous man, though for a good man someone might possibly dare to die. But God demonstrates his own love for us in this: While we were still sinners, Christ died for us."   Romans 5:6-8

"O God, you are my God, earnestly I seek you; my soul thirsts for you, my body longs for you, in a dry and weary land where there is no water. I have seen you in the sanctuary and beheld your power and your glory. Because your love is better than life, my lips will glorify you. I will praise you as long as I live, and in your name I will lift up my hands. My soul will be satisfied as with the richest of foods; with singing lips my mouth will praise you." Psalm 63:1-5

Black ice, the invisible villain spreading itself thinly over my driveway, catapulted me into the air and landed me flat on my back, leaving me staring in disbelief at a frigid sky with no help to be found. Obedience paid off when I had earlier listened to the still, small voice whispering to tuck my phone into my pocket before heading out the door. I called my neighbor, who is usually not home at that time of day, and he came, along with his adult son, who normally doesn't visit at that time, either. My neighbor and son picked me up, not too gracefully, from the ice and assisted my hobbling self into the warm house.

Being a paramedic for years, he looked at my ankle, fairly certain of a sprain. Through the night, my ankle complained loudly enough that I headed to the urgent care clinic for an X-ray the following morning. I did have a severe sprain, but the X-ray revealed a fracture as well. The first fracture of my life was confirmed by the doctor, a cast applied, and six miserable weeks of navigating my home on one leg ensued.

It was the X-ray that revealed what the eye could not see, the bone buried deep within my flesh. When the film was read and the diagnosis given, it would have done no good if treatment had not been administered. God's law is like that X-ray, revealing our brokenness, our sin. Jesus is the physician who prescribes the treatment through His grace. We can refuse treatment, go home, and live with our pain, or we can accept His forgiveness, trust Him, and be healed.

The choice is ultimately ours, not only for salvation, but to also trust God daily, taking our sorrows, brokenness, and pain to Him. He knows us more thoroughly than an X-ray machine. Though physicians care, Jesus loves; He alone can tend our wounds, heal our pain, touch our sorrows, and love us through rehabilitation. He never tires of us and never complains. He's never frustrated, always lovingly patient, correct in His assessment and treatment. The Great Physician is the Healer of our souls, mender of our wounds, and our ultimate prescription for our wholeness.

"On hearing this, Jesus said, 'It is not the healthy who need a doctor, but the sick. But go and learn what this means: "I desire mercy, not sacrifice." For I have not come to call the righteous, but sinners.'" Matthew 9:12-13

"And when the men of that place recognized Jesus, they sent word to all the surrounding region. People brought all the sick to Him and begged Him just to let them touch the fringe of His cloak. And all who touched Him were healed." Matthew 14:35-36

Many winter evenings, after supper dishes had been washed and darkness descended on the old farmhouse, my seven cousins and aunt pulled chairs up to the quilting frame. They learned from young ages French knots, leaf stitches, and such. Once the quilt top was embroidered, it was layered with batting and backing. Painstakingly quilted with its delicate pattern, the quilting bound it all together. The quilts they produced were rare treasures, mine received at my wedding.

Believing I was protecting my priceless quilt, I tucked it away in a trunk in the attic. Years later, as we prepared to move, I opened the trunk to find my quilt had a large water spot on it, a dark stain about 12 inches in diameter. I was stunned and baffled, learning later that I had committed the cardinal sin; attic condensation had taken its toll. The quilt, ugly scar and all, remains a treasure to me because of the care and love which produced it.

I, like my precious quilt, have been exquisitely created by my Heavenly Father. I was wonderfully made in His very image, crafted in my mother's womb, and endowed with talents and a specific personality. I was created by Him to fit perfectly into His pattern, positioned in this time to do that for which He designed me. As my quilt was made by loving hands for beauty and warmth, so God has suited me for sharing His beauty and love with all who wish to know Him.

Marred by trauma and stained by sin, I felt for a long time that my existence and purpose had been invalidated. I felt unwanted and impossibly broken, beyond repair, seeking validation by the world, and totally unworthy of God's love. Jesus went to the cross to prove me wrong. He removed my stain by pouring His priceless blood over it. We are each stained, and yet, through Jesus, God sees us as restored.

My quilt, in expert hands, can also be repaired, restored to its original beauty by removing the damaged area and meticulously piecing in new cloth. But I think I will leave it just as it is, a reminder that God sees a perfect quilt, one suited to His purpose and plan. When I insist on pointing out the stain, He asks, "What stain?" as though it never existed, a pristine quilt of exquisite value, beloved and treasured.

"In him we have redemption through his blood, the forgiveness of sins, in accordance with the riches of God's grace that he lavished on us with all wisdom and understanding."

Ephesians 1:7

Approaching the mountains of Alaska by air, the timing could not have been more perfect. All the passengers on the much-too-long flight had succumbed to sleep, save me and my friend. As we chatted the night away, sudden splendor caught our rapt attention as the sun broke the darkness in morning glory that happens once in a lifetime.

A vast expanse of cumulus clouds stretched before us, the big fluffy variety, turning golden tints, and reaching high into the sky. Beneath them were "stepping-stone" clouds, fire-red on the bottom and charcoal gray, flat on the tops with cracks, appearing as molten lava flowing into the horizon. Rays of sun burst through it all as if to herald a special welcome. And below, the snow-capped mountains came into view, with large lakes tucked in between; the mirror-like water reflected perfectly the brilliant scene above them.

I have witnessed many wonders of God's creation, but never anything so breathtaking as this. I could not drink in the view enough, wishing it to continue indefinitely. I remain in awe of the beauty and wonder of a God so immense, so creative, and so generous that He would share this fingerprint of His glory with me.

His wonders are created to open my eyes to see Him as He is, to know and understand His majesty, to taste His goodness, and to realize His power. His glory is simply a demonstration of His beauty in its many facets, which He displays for us all to see. It is meant to lead us to Him, awaken our desire for Him, and invite us to know Him. We, the people created in His image, are His greatest desire, to fellowship with and to have a relationship with us. Imagine, the God of the universe desiring a personal relationship with me, and you! Therein lays the true glory of the morning.

"His glory covered the heavens and his praise filled the earth. His splendor was like the sunrise; rays flashed from his hand, where his power was hidden." Habakkuk 3:3-4

"The heavens declare the glory of God; the skies proclaim the work of his hands. Day after day they pour forth speech; night after night they display knowledge." Psalm 19:1-2

"The Word became flesh and made his dwelling among us. We have seen his glory, the glory of the One and Only, who came from the Father, full of grace and truth." John 1:14

Deep Fire February 18

The hardwood, mostly oak and maple, was cut to 18-inch lengths and stacked neatly in a long row. The frost had descended the night prior, the thermometer not rising above 40 degrees even late in the morning. The days that had waned into early darkness, had begun to lengthen, with spring but a wink away. Our woodstove stood, another chilly night, at the ready.

We began using wood as supplemental heat the year Gary was laid off his job, with money sparse in the five months of winter with no work. One evening when he was away, the coals had completely died, leaving me to begin from a small heap of bark and kindling. As I lighted it, tiny sparks grew to lapping flames skirting the wood. It was a rather lengthy process, requiring patient tending; for the fire to last, it had to burn deeply into the wood, producing the red-hot coals which would sustain our warmth throughout the night.

Though there are wonderfully warm and bright days in my life, I have learned to also expect there will come winter. Each of us experiences challenges, whether they are from illness, job loss, financial problems, relational stress, war, and strife, or just plain evil touching our lives. They are things no one predicted or could have foreseen. Jesus guaranteed we would live in a world of trials, a world that is broken with sin. Yet we tend to desire a surface relationship with the only One who can give us comfort, protection, and provision.

It is no accident that God was revealed in a burning bush for Moses, or that God gave the Israelites a pillar of fire to guide them at night. Holy sacrifices were consumed in flames, flaming chariots appeared on a hillside, and a mountain top was burnt, the very rocks melting in the Presence of God. Tongues of flame descended upon the Disciples at Pentecost. And at Jesus' return, Revelation describes His eyes as blazing with fire.

Jesus patiently waits for us to seek Him in His fullness, to burn not on the surface of our souls, but with deep fire in our hearts, a fire that lasts through the trials. His fire consumes the trivial and the distractions, lighting our paths, and warming our spirits. His fire takes patient tending on our part, pushing steadfastly against the drafts of the world. But only through seeking Jesus daily can we truly access His deep fire in our souls and spirits.

"Do not put out the Spirit's fire; do not treat prophecies with contempt. Test everything. Hold on to the good. Avoid every kind of evil. May God himself, the God of peace, sanctify you through and through. May your whole spirit, soul, and body be kept blameless at the coming of our Lord Jesus Christ. The one who calls you is faithful, and he will do it."
1 Thessalonians 5:19-24

Snow White   February 19

Snowfall in the Chicago area, where I lived as a child, was exciting, but not particularly beautiful. We were routinely cautioned about not eating the snow, fearing nuclear fallout in it. And though white, after forcing its way through the smog, it always seemed a bit "off-white". We built snow forts, snowmen, and dug tunnels through the 32 inches which descended one day. The gray smog of the city would settle onto the surface of it all. Coal cinders were used to coat the snow-laden sidewalks and streets, and plows would churn pavement dust into the mix.

Halfway into high school, we moved to Colorado, where I experienced my first "real" snow. Walking with my new friends through a mountain forest, the moonlight glinted in unimaginable brilliance off the pristine blanket of snow. The stars on a black, velvet night twinkled like gems on a jeweler's cloth, winking back at the snow with a million eyes. My friends explained that skiers, and I would soon become one, called this "deep powder". But that night, I had never seen snow so white, or heard a quiet so deep, nor experienced moonlight so pure and bright as that, and haven't since.

It would have been difficult, quite impossible, for me to imagine the brilliance and peace of that Colorado snowfall. My only point of reference was the soiled snow of my childhood, a stark and wonderful difference. In many ways, my life has taken on new brilliance and wonder, like that perfect snow, since I have come to know Jesus. Looking back to the sin-stained, dark, and broken life I lived without Him is very much like that. I had lived thinking I was all right and not so bad. But when He brought me into His magnificent light, I discovered cleansing, healing, and purifying light. My life is so much different than I ever could have imagined.

God's desire, the passion of His heart, is to restore us, like that mountain snow, to bright white brilliance through Jesus. He is the one who forgives and purifies, restoring us to fellowship with our heavenly Father. Becoming His child, we are ushered into His Presence in stunningly white robes, radiant snow-white, washed and cleansed, healed and restored to the ultimate beauty He had in mind from the beginning. Though difficult to remember while walking this earth, it is worthwhile to reflect on His powerful transformation, reminding ourselves of what Jesus did on our behalf, not a magical memory, but fact for eternity. In Christ, by His grace, we are forever radiant, snow-white.

"Though your sins are like scarlet, they shall be as white as snow; though they are red as crimson, they shall be like wool." Isaiah 1:18

The screen saver on my television randomly displays photographs, some taken by photographers, some from NASA or Google Earth, so I never know when I glance up what picture will be on the screen. At first, I thought, "Oh, what pretty fabric!" It looked as though it was woven of fine threads in blues and whites. I found the title and credits in the corner of the frame and it stunned me! What I was seeing was a glacier from the satellite view.

To stand at the foot of a glacier versus gazing at it from satellite view invokes a much different response. I've seen a glacier up close and could understand the colors of the ice chasms, with sharp edges broken into deep blues, turquoise, and ice blue layers, blanketed on top with pristine white snow. Where the glacier breaks off and crashes into the sea, it leaves ice cliffs hundreds of feet high, displaying the compressed blue coldness within the ice. The difference between the view of the glaciers from the satellite and ground level is profound, not even fathomable.

This provoked a question, "Who do you say I am?" Yes, it sounds random, but stay with me for a moment. Jesus asked it of Peter (in Mark 8:29) and His disciples, but I never thought to ask it of anyone. Surprisingly though, a close friend of mine was completing a form and asked me that very question, worded a bit differently; basically, she was asking me how I see her. I told my friend that she was "oozing mercy"! She is compassionate and merciful, caring, and makes a wonderful nurse for all those reasons.

So, I ventured to ask God, "Who do you say I am?" His answer, a perspective as radically different from mine as the view from the satellite, is from the foot of the glacier, and His eternal perspective is far superior to my limited view. His answer goes something like this, according to what He said in the Bible: *You are chosen. You are a child of the King, the only God, Ruler of the Universe. You have been adopted, and the adoption can never be undone. You are powerful through the blood of Jesus and you have been cleansed by that same blood. You have been given priestly garments, pure and white. A crown awaits you in heaven. You have a royal seal, that of His Holy Spirit. You are precious, treasured, restored, and healed. He delights in you, loves you, and treasures you. You are the object of His delight, for when He sees you, He sees His only Son.* And when you ask that question, you will receive the same answer.

"But, whenever anyone turns to the Lord, the veil is taken away. Now the Lord is the Spirit, and where the Spirit of the Lord is, there is freedom. And we, who with unveiled faces all reflect the Lord's glory, are being transformed into his likeness, with ever-increasing glory, which comes from the Lord, who is the Spirit." 2 Corinthians 3:16-18

The brilliant flakes of snow sparkled in the porch light against a velvety, black sky. I ran for my camera. To catch the wonder of it would be so cool! It never occurred to me that it was too dark, and the flakes were falling too fast to capture the image of the tiny crystals. Aiming at the darkness, I clicked away and was stunned when I loaded the images on the computer to view. No, there weren't any perfect snowflakes gracing my lens, but what I did see amounted to a spectacular miniature universe.

I had never considered a universe of snowflakes, but they had reflected the light in a show of "planets" and "stars" on my lens; it was just like looking into a cloudless, night sky. Some appeared small and separate, but the most impressive flakes were those joined to others, forming a cluster. Those reflected the most brilliant light.

No two snowflakes are identical, each unique, with all sorts of scientific explanations about how that process works. I don't believe it is accidental that we humans have that in common with the white fluffy stuff. Can your mind imagine how many snowflakes are in the drift outside your door, or the branches of one tree, or the crystal field shimmering in the moonlight? Can you imagine how many human beings have lived upon the earth since the very first, or even in the past century? Yet all are without duplicates. We are each like those snowflakes, floating in the vastness of humanity yet created to be unique, and all part of one universe.

So it is with those of us who choose to follow Jesus. We are set against a dark sky, reflecting the Light of Christ. And we shine most strongly when we are bound together with our brothers and sisters, each unique and gifted differently. That is when we shine most brilliantly and reflect Jesus the most, as we walk in love and unity.

I want to keep that snowflake universe before me, remembering each of you and how special you are. I want to value you, as God values you and holds you dear. You are created to have much to offer. You have a purpose in God's kingdom. He has a plan for you, which is incomplete, or you wouldn't still be here. I am looking forward to what the Lord has in store, as we link together and form our "clusters" of beautiful snowflakes in His kingdom.

"Do everything without complaining or arguing, so that you may become blameless and pure, children of God without fault in a crooked and depraved generation, in which you shine like stars in the universe as you hold out the word of life…" Philippians 2:14-15

Where the Sun Shines

It had been very cold during the night, dropping well below freezing. Gazing out my kitchen window, the low temperature was very apparent. As morning birthed golden rays, they glinted off an even coating of crystalline frost cloaking the landscape. I noticed the sunshine peeking around the corner of my house as it rose to greet the day, and every hint of frost had vaporized at its touch, leaving the shaded area perfectly frozen. It was the literal difference between night and day.

The message did not escape my notice, nor did it take more than a few seconds for me to realize what was encrypted in the scene: Wherever the sun shines, darkness and coldness dissipate. The immediate leap of faith was the realization that "Wherever the Son shines, darkness and coldness dissipate." Where the Son is allowed to shine in my heart, to warm and change it, the coldness of darkness and deception diffuse, and doubt is dispelled.

Where the sunbeams touched the grass, the line was distinct and easily discernible. There was no guessing whether the sun had risen; it was very apparent. When Jesus arrives, the changed heart begins to melt, thaw, soften, and warm, too. The changes may be sudden and dramatic for some, a bit more gradual for others; but transitioning, just the same, into Son-light, reflecting His very image in our hearts. The development of our character, the essence of who we are shifts to reflect "Whose" we are, Christians, Christ-like, "little Christs", as the early believers were named.

The early morning sun inches across the yard as it yawns deeply from its slumber. It does not overtake the shadows all at once. But it never fails to rise, and refuses to retreat, always advancing against the dark places, filtering into every hollow and ravine. God shines His light into our dark places, too, advancing steadily and faithfully into the hidden and protected places, bidding us release those to Him, as well. In the darkness and cold is death and denial; where the Son shines, His warmth illuminates what has been placed firmly into His hand. Wholeness is regenerated, and hope restored.

"I keep asking that the God of our Lord Jesus Christ, the glorious Father, may give you the Spirit of wisdom and revelation, so that you may know him better. I pray also that the eyes of your heart may be enlightened in order that you may know the hope to which he has called you, the riches of his glorious inheritance in the saints, and his incomparably great power for us who believe."   Ephesians 2:17-19a

The Right Key   February 23

The itch to rid my home of accumulating clutter arrived right on time, along with the daffodils, forsythia, and record flooding rains, forcing early spring cleaning. Treasures were rediscovered in the process of sorting, one being a colorful woven rattan box, coins from years past tucked secretly away. Another item was a set of mystery keys. I attempted to unlock several locks with the newly found keys. Finally, I relegated them to joining their cousins on the lost keys hook, hoping one day to unlock another treasure, long hidden.

There is a lock on our hearts as well, and we wander through life looking for the right key, the one that will unlock happiness, fulfillment, and love. It's a tough lock, which even the best earthly locksmith has no power to overcome. There is only one key that fits, only one which turns the tumblers in the correct sequence. Though we wander the earth searching through the stash of keys, there are none but His with the power to overcome our resistance and pain. God has fitted our hearts with His lock, and only He holds the key to it.

There is a cover over the lock on our hearts and it is moved by our will to choose to accept the key, or to deny its entrance. We have the power to keep God out or allow Him the freedom to enter; He will honor our choices. When we close ourselves off from His entrance, we get to keep what is inside; inside is pain, sin, darkness, and damage. What He unlocks when He enters is healing, forgiveness, peace, light, and restoration. We are finally able to see with the spiritual eyes He intended, eyes to see and a heart to love Him. The unlocking of our hearts results in transformation, becoming more like Him day to day, and year by year.

It was a late winter day when my neighbor ran breathlessly to my door, exclaiming when I opened it, "Jesus told me to tell you that He loves you!" She immediately turned and went back to her house, leaving me with the decision to accept that key or deny His insertion into my life. As spring melted the cold, God melted my heart. I allowed the Lord of Life entry into mine, the right key, at last, the perfect and life-changing Key. He has resided here ever since, quietly and persistently cleaning the house of my heart, forever unlocked to His presence there.

"Ask and it will be given to you; seek and you will find; knock and the door will be opened to you. For everyone who asks receives; he who seeks finds; and to him who knocks, the door will be opened." Matthew 7:7

Clothed in Green   February 24

Naked brown and grey branches dominated the early spring day as I drove home in the lengthening daylight, and in them was a stunning form. It was a tree clothed in green, the flush of new growth vibrant on the backdrop of receding winter, starkly standing out. Its branches extended hope of new life and the strength of regeneration. I sighed in relief that spring had so boldly announced itself and winter was officially gone, not by virtue of a calendar date, but of actual evidence.

We, as Christians, followers of Christ Jesus, are like that tree, displaying the garment of salvation and regeneration of our spirits through Jesus. We stand out against the backdrop of the brown and broken world, lively in green life, in contrast to death and defeat. We display vivid life lived in truth and honor, in comparison to the deceit and lies of the world around us. God has called us to be different, to be imitators of Christ, walking humbly, but in strength and power.

As I looked through the Scriptures with this idea of being "clothed" in mind, I noted that there were three that specifically mentioned clothing ourselves: The first instructs us in Romans 13:14, to **"Rather, clothe yourselves with the Lord Jesus Christ, and do not think about how to gratify the desires of the sinful nature."** This is our first and most important way of clothing ourselves; donning the mind of Christ instructs all the rest of our thinking.

The second is found in Colossians 3:12: **"Therefore, as God's chosen people, holy and dearly loved, clothe yourselves with compassion, kindness, humility, gentleness, and patience. Bear with each other and forgive whatever grievances you may have against one another. Forgive as the Lord forgave you. And over all these virtues put on love, which binds them all together in perfect unity."**

The third is 1 Peter 5:5b-6. **"All of you, clothe yourselves with humility toward one another, because, 'God opposes the proud but gives grace to the humble.' Humble yourselves, therefore, under God's mighty hand, that he may lift you up in due time."**

As I considered the clothing outlined in these Scriptures, and these are not the only references by far, it occurred to me that it is this clothing that sets us apart. In a dark and spiritually dead world waiting to be awakened through God's Spirit of life, we are the trees clothed in green. Set against that dreary backdrop of sin and hopelessness, we are offering hope of spring to the hearts of those around us.

The morning flew into high gear right away, as was normal in our growing household, with cereal bowls hurriedly carried into the kitchen and everyone rushing in separate directions. I was the only one who had not been in the kitchen yet to witness the explosion of millions of microscopic lives spread across my countertop. They were the product of my sourdough starter which had decided, in the middle of the night, to exponentially multiply. The sight was a disgusting mess!

All over the countertop, in a puddle surrounding the Mason jar, the mass had spread out to encompass about two square feet. Clumps of glue-like masses had dried onto the exterior of the jar, and everything it had touched had transformed into a formidable cleaning task, contaminating and bringing to ruin anything crossing its path. The bread resulting from the remains inside the jar was the only benefit of the experience.

It was a stark reminder of what Jesus taught in the Bible about sin resembling yeast. Just as that yeast spilled over the sides, down the jar, and spread over the countertop, touching everything around it, so does sin. It silently poisons all those around us, our friendships, businesses, even our culture, as it insidiously penetrates all it touches.

Our propensity for rebellion is well documented. Robbie Zacharias summed up sin's demands best, "Sin will take you farther than you want to go, keep you longer than you want to stay, and cost you more than you want to pay." It can result in broken homes, broken dreams, severed relationships, damaged reputations, and unimaginable loss. Sin's most consequential effects are on our families, resulting in bitterness, resentment, lies, unbridled tongues, and making demands on people which only God can fulfill.

My kitchen countertop took a vast effort to clean up, and sin often does also, costing more than we ever imagined. I have experienced many examples first-hand; but I also know that through a repentant heart, God's forgiveness can heal, losses can be restored, and relationships mended. With and through the Lord, there is always hope, and redemption through Christ Jesus.

Mary Magdalene had sinned about as much as anyone could, yet she shines throughout the historical record as the perfect example of the flip side of sin. Forgiven and whole, she was the one who had loved Jesus most because she had been forgiven much. That is the experience of all, who with a humble heart, fall at Jesus' feet. There, beauty blooms, peace finds its home, and hope is born in the gaze of Him who loves us unconditionally and fully. Through Jesus, we can also become the perfect example of His forgiveness and hope.

"Do not be deceived: God cannot be mocked. A man reaps what he sows. The one who sows to please his sinful nature, from that nature will reap destruction; the one who sows to please the Spirit, from the Spirit will receive eternal life. Let us not grow weary in doing good, for at the proper time we will reap a harvest if we do not give up. Therefore, as we have opportunity, let us do good to all people, especially to those who belong to the family of believers." Galatians 6:7-10

The words pierced my heart as soon as they were spoken, "I don't like this! I should have been content with what I had. I hate it!" The gift of curls, for the thirteen-year-old with perfectly straight hair, resulted in an unruly and unmanageable mess instantaneously. It was the very gift she had desired for three years, a gift I had saved sacrificially to obtain for her, and it was her only birthday present from me that year. Now, watching her at her wit's end with how to handle her newfound bounty, I ached for her loss but decided to allow the unruly locks to bide their time. Life doesn't always turn out as we hope, and there are consequences to every decision.

I anticipated the needs and desires of my children, planned and saved, spending great time and effort to give them the gift which would satisfy them, while balancing their developmental stages and interests. I cannot number the hours spent choosing the right gifts for their birthdays, Christmases, Easters, and graduations. My love was expressed through every gift, at every age.

Our Father, too, planned for eternity and made an inconceivably great effort throughout creation to give me the ultimate gift, just what I needed, Jesus. He additionally provides good gifts daily, intended just for me, desiring that I will be content and delighted with them. He created me, knows me, loves me, and desires His best for me. His gifts may not always appear to be exactly what I was wishing for and are sometimes wrapped in a paper I may not recognize as "gift wrap"; but He is a thoughtful Father, always having my eternal best interests at heart.

Have you ever given a gift that was despised? God did, too, I realized as I coped with my sadness over my daughter's gift gone awry. I cannot fathom God's disappointment and longing when we reject the gift of His only Son, the ultimate gift of staggering expense, and the gift that cannot be undone or taken back. Have I ever given a gift that was despised? Just one. So has God, just One.

"Blessed is the man who makes the Lord his trust, who does not look to the proud, to those who turn aside to false gods. Many, O Lord my God, are the wonders you have done. The things you planned for us no one can recount to you; were I to speak and tell of them, they would be too many to declare."   Psalm 40:4-5

"For the wages of sin is death, but the gift of God is eternal life in Christ Jesus our Lord."
Romans 6:23

A strange voice chattered away as I picked up the weighty receiver from its even heavier base, the white numbers tucked inside the finger holes of the dial. At my grandparent's house, making a telephone call was akin to trying to jump rope in tandem; making your move at precisely the right time was tricky, not bumping the other jumper out before they were ready to depart.

It was considered rude to interrupt and great patience was often required, the other party not always ready to relinquish the coveted line. And it wasn't only one "party" vying for the line; there were five families on each one. They were strangers all, but I would wager that they got to "know" one another, eavesdropping being too great a temptation, I think. The party line eventually gave way to private lines for everyone, beneficial for all concerned, but they may have also missed one another.

Even those of us who don't particularly enjoy talking on the phone are reluctant to end a call to someone dearly loved and missed. There are times when it is a gift to hear a loved one's voice more than the words spoken, a connection hearing a breath in place of a phrase. And I think prayer must be similar, connecting us to God in an intimate way. Even though we cannot hear His audible words, we can feel His presence, and even in a sense, His breathe.

The beauty of that "phone call" to God is that there is no party line, just a direct call on a secure line. He hears every word we utter to Him. He is never too busy to answer or listen. We are His only focus on that call, not competing with five other families or nine billion other people. It is just a Father waiting for the call from His precious child, a dad anticipating an exchange with His child who stays too busy to call, and too distracted to realize how much he is missed. How often I am that child!

I have a direct line to my heavenly Father through His Son, Jesus, yet I take it very much for granted most often. What a privilege I forfeit when I neglect to call on Him! The God of the Universe is at the other end of that call, Immanuel, God "with us", as close as our next breath. He is the One with all the answers to life's dilemmas, and comfort for all our sorrows. How about the "phone" in your hand---when will you call your Father?

"In the same way, the Spirit helps us in our weakness. We do not know what we ought to pray for, but the Spirit himself intercedes for us with groans that words cannot express. And he who searches our hearts knows the mind of the Spirit, because the Spirit intercedes for the saints in accordance with God's will." Romans 8:26-27

Saving the Best for Last February 28

There is a reason my mother always made us finish our meal before being served dessert, and a reason there are bedtime stories at the end of the day. There is a reason that repose follows hard work, and spring blooms after winter. There is a reason rewards fall on the heels of honorable acts, and blessings are unfurled in the rainbow's delicate tints, gracing the clouds after the storm. There is a reason childhood is crowned with eventual adulthood, following decades of training and discipline.

It is savoring the caught fish after the toil of catching, the prize at the end of the competition, and the satisfaction of finding the solution to a perplexingly difficult puzzle. It is in the paycheck at the end of the work cycle. It is overcoming impossibilities and being crowned with the courage to face the next obstacle. All this is part of the pattern God established in His creation of human beings; we require the structure and discipline of each of those cycles to become more like Him.

To learn His patience, we are patiently taught by the Master to wait. To learn His love, we are lovingly guided to unlovable people and taught to sacrifice self, first. To learn His humble heart, we are gently brought low so that our pride sets itself above no one, for God is no respecter of persons. To learn diligence, He leads us to tasks not easily mastered. To learn wisdom, He trains us to search for its riches in Him rather than the world. And to learn generosity, He sometimes requires sacrifice. God's order to life produces rewards following labor, security following trust, and maturity following growth. It is all intended to point us to our heavenly Father.

I have had friends over the years who ate dessert before their meal, some who played before they worked, and others who have grown up later than they should have, by the world's standards. We are uniquely made, and God can use even our mistakes and untimely behavior for His purposes. There are individual exceptions, but the overall pattern of saving the best for last is an eternal principle written in the handbook of life. They are principles for our good and God's honor.

Life may be difficult, disheartening, and painful while we labor on this earth. But earth will give way one day, and we will step into the glory He has reserved for us. In the presence of Jesus, we will find that God has saved His best for last.

"As the heavens are higher than the earth, so are my ways higher than your ways and my thoughts than your thoughts." Isaiah 59:9

March

Chance of Showers   March 1

Donning my gardening attire, I glanced upward, noting the few gray clouds skirting the sun. As I turned the pot over in my hand and it released its holdings, I realized some time had passed and the one percent chance of rain was upon me. I heard the drops bouncing off the trees, then the car and pavement. It approached ever so gently, then quietly retreated; within minutes, the one percent chance of showers had come and gone, the sun returning from its catnap under its blanket of clouds.

Most days, my expectations are one hundred percent sunny, and a chance of showers never clouds my thoughts. I fully expect a perfect day, with no delays, distractions, and nothing to deter me from my plans; notice I said, "my" plans. I may briefly consult God, but generally, not until something goes awry, and the one percent chance of "rain" shows up to rearrange my day. Whether it is a fleeting shower or a full-blown storm, life has a way of making certain I do not become overly confident in my forecasts.

The beauty of walking with Jesus is that He fully understands my propensity for self-absorption and naïve optimism, or complete oblivion. I trust that He has spared me more unpleasantness than I will know until eternity reveals it. But even Jesus said that in this world we will have troubles and trials, crucibles, and storms along the way. The very things I would send away, He sends my way to disrupt my dependence on and fascination with the world.

The chance of disruption of life through innumerable painful disruptions and upheavals is nearly one hundred percent on any given day. Only by His protection do we get reprieves, and through His grace do we receive rest. Not one of us is immune to the trials; but because of God's loving-kindness, He carries us through them, bringing us out again into the sun to rest. We are not to linger for long slumbers, but to cat nap for a time, rest and recover, and then offer encouragement and comfort to others.

In a way, it is a wonderful characteristic our Father alone fathoms—that we do not know our own frailty. On the other hand, we would do well to look to our Creator with a bit more respect and a lot of gratitude. His generosity is vastly overlooked in every day's forecast, and it is His hand that determines every day's chance of showers, whether I acknowledge it or not.

"And he passed in front of Moses, proclaiming, 'The Lord, the Lord, the compassionate and gracious God, slow to anger, abounding in love and faithfulness, maintaining love to thousands, and forgiving wickedness, rebellion and sin." Exodus 34:6,7

Beautiful Legs

The photo captivated me as if time had suddenly paused. It was a stop-action photo of horses running through water, while the rain fell all around them, in a blizzard of raindrops. In the middle of the dynamic scene was a stunning set of legs, fully extended, and veritably flying over the water. Those legs were attached to a very young colt amid the fully-grown herd. I wondered at his ability to peacefully fly in perfect synchronization with the adults. What beautiful legs, carrying the small body, long and disproportionate, able to run as effortlessly as the breeze which carried the rain!

I marveled at our Creator's imagining such a creature and forming its magnificent structure, such that even a very young horse could keep pace with the adults. Those beautiful, straight, long legs enabled that baby to wrap itself in the protection of the herd, and with such grace and beauty, as to be nearly angelic.

Our Creator also imagined beautiful legs for the creation He patterned after Himself, man, made in His image. Our legs are made to walk with Him, to run after Him, and to follow Him. At first, we stumble along, unsure of our footing, falling at times like that newborn colt. As we grow in faith, our legs become stronger; and we can follow through the rain, storms, and unsure footing. Each step strengthens our next. Soon, we are doing what we are created to do, to run on beautiful legs!

Just as that colt was not meant to run alone, so are we created to run together as believers, to protect and encourage the young among us, and to keep pace with the Holy Spirit. Running with Him means that even when we feel vulnerable, we can trust He is with us. In sadness, He is present. In His presence, there is peace. As that colt followed the lead stallion, so we can follow our Savior confidently, on beautiful legs.

"You made him a little lower than the heavenly beings and crowned him with glory and honor." Psalm 8:5

"But those who hope in the Lord will renew their strength. They will soar on wings like eagles; they will run and not grow weary, they will walk and not be faint." Isaiah 40:31

Place at The Table   March 3

Before their passing into God's presence, Liebert, Winnie, and Geraldine had been seated at the same table every day, and now each place at the table had a different, unfamiliar face. The words of Psalm 103:15 came flooding into my spirit at that moment: **"As for man, his days are like grass, he flourishes like a flower of the field; the wind blows over it and it is gone, and its place remembers it no more."** I was saddened at the truth of it. Many people bustled through that dining room that day, and I am fairly certain not one of them thought of the faces who so long frequented that table. Life and busyness continue unabated.

As I contemplated my own losses, they are not felt any less keenly today as they were when first experienced, but there is truth in the fact that the acute pain subsides over time. I realized that time is a blessing as it dulls, just a bit, the pain of the loss. Our loved ones don't lose importance and the pain doesn't disappear, but the remembrances are spaced farther apart, as life's demands fill in the holes of our hearts. It is a normal and natural process, not betrayal.

Years ago, I drove down a road in South Carolina where vines were growing boldly across the pavement, as if in a rush to overtake it before the next car broke through their expanding barrier. Much of nature will adapt to and fill in the spaces from fires, floods, volcanoes, and earthquakes. Flowers bloom within days of lava flows cooling, and trees spring up from the ashes following a forest fire. The earth was created, in God's wisdom, to heal itself in a relatively short time. As the transformations occur, their places are remembered no more.

Perhaps God, in His infinite mercy, created us as He did the rest of his creation, equipping us with the ability to heal, over time, while functioning in the face of loss. Notice that the two verses below bookend verse 15, as I quoted above; our Father's love and compassion envelope us in our loss. He is faithful to remind us of His unfailing goodness amid our grieving. For those who love Him, we will all one day find our place at His table, together with those who have gone before us.

"As a father has compassion on his children, so the Lord has compassion on those who fear him; for he knows how we are formed, he remembers that we are dust." Psalm 103:13

"But from everlasting to everlasting the Lord's love is with those who fear him, and his righteousness with their children's children—with those who keep his covenant and remember to obey his precepts." Psalm 103:16

A family in our community was the envy of many around them, married, three children, decent income, supportive friends; a "normal" family. As their story unraveled, the details stunned everyone; the husband and wife revealed that one of the children belonged to a different father, the marriage of the father and mother was on shaky ground, and the children wrestled with problems of their own. Hurt feelings, emotional distancing, and lashing out because of their pain—that was the real "normal" family.

Growing up in a highly dysfunctional family myself, I naturally envied the "normal" families. Through years of observation, and raising my own, I came to realize "normal" to be largely a fantasy. Families experience trials, testing, friction, fear, distress, and the normal pains of life on this planet. We all struggle with relationships on some level; and because of our close bonds within families, those conflicts can be more intense.

Even Jesus' family was not perfect. His brothers did not believe in Him. There was friction within their family over expectations and jealousy. The community never believed the story of Jesus's claim to be the Son of God, and Jesus was accused as a criminal. Do you really believe Jesus' family had no fragile relationships? And if His earthly family wasn't stress-free, do you believe yours will be? No family is, after all, perfect. It can be a wonderful family, but it will never be a perfect one.

My expectations for perfection and "normal" only hindered me in resolving conflicts within my family. Then I began to realize that even those of us who know Jesus as our Lord and Savior cannot achieve any resemblance of perfection on our own. However, through trusting Him, we are given the insights and tools we need within our family relationships. God has given us freedom from fear, the ability to forgive, and access to His Spirit for peace and revelation. He has given us His word to instruct us and His directions on how to live godly lives.

Instead of demanding perfection from the frail human beings in our families, we fix our gaze on Him, understanding that Christ alone is truly our provider. We, as well as our families, benefit as we to look to Jesus to fulfill our needs and desires. He is our hope, our only hope, of fulfillment on this earth. God's desire for each of us is for us to draw our strength, guidance, and direction ultimately from Him. He asks for our love, trust, and devotion in return so that we can be reflections of His presence; as we mirror His Son, God draws people to Himself, even our families. Only through Christ can we experience a "new normal" in our relationships.

"Look to the Lord and his strength; seek his face always." Psalm 105:4

"For in him we live and move and have our being." Acts 17:28

Clear Vision

The age of thirty-nine was an eye-opening year. It was the year aging became reality, with the advent of visual acuity decline. My first pair of reading glasses progressed eventually to other types of lenses, then contact lenses, and back to multi-focal lenses. As my vision declined, cataracts advanced, and I mourned my 20/20 days bygone. Recent surgical removal of my cataracts, and the implant of new lenses, permanently adjusted my vision closer to the 20/20 of the past.

As I have lost my physical vision, I have gained spiritual vision. My spiritual eyes have become increasingly opened, deciphering the heavenly truths of God's Word with greater depth and understanding. God makes clear in His Word who I am, but I had squinted and stared, not comprehending it, until recently. Though I often struggle to see with my spiritual eyes, I am beginning to see a glimmer of truth: I am like my Father, made in His very image, and a miraculous creature.

My faith in Christ Jesus transforms me by the power of His blood into "clean" and "beautiful", even "delightful" in His eyes. My soiled clothing has been exchanged for exquisite robes, my diseases healed, and my body restored. I am now ageless with no hint of time, and I can look forward to an eternity of gazing into His face in awe, and with praise. In this world, that perfection is not yet visible, but I am still like Him. I was created to fulfill the role meant for me in this world, and in the age to come.

I am like my Father, though I have not yet arrived in heaven. Like His Son, I am being perfected in this life. I continue to require my Father's love, discipline, and forgiveness. I will place my trust in Him, knowing that He will give me the eyes I need, to increasingly recognize the paths He desires me to walk.

How clear our vision will be one day when He parts the clouds, returning in brilliance and power! We will see Him as He truly is; with unmatched acuity, we will see the Truth Himself. In the meantime, He is Immanuel, God with Us, and God with me. I recognize that I am His delightful child, whether I feel it or not, whether I see it or not, and whether I acknowledge it or not. How wonderful it is to embrace that truth, crediting Him for my salvation and transformation through Jesus! Jesus is squarely in the center of my vision now!

"To them, God has chosen to make known among the Gentiles the glorious riches of this mystery, which is Christ in you, the hope of glory." Colossians 3:15

When I began my independent weight loss journey, it necessitated the elimination of fast foods, which simply means I either cook nearly all my food or go hungry. Hunger not being a pleasant option, I learned to cook new foods, and began adapting to the extra hours required of me in the kitchen. One of those evenings of "extra hours", the kitchen was growing darker by the minute as I scrambled to finish.

Realizing the absurdity of working in the encroaching shadows, I thought, "Isn't this silly to work in the dark when all I need to do is flip the switch and have light?!" What a privilege that we take so much for granted; light at our fingertips! The power of electricity is all around us, yet most of us are oblivious to this extraordinary blessing, never giving it a moment's notice during our hectic schedules.

Suddenly, I realized that Power, far beyond that of electricity, envelopes me at all times. In my days and nights, in all the places I roam, whether power lines are present or not, God's power is available to me. The simple realization is that it is up to me to flip the switch; to access the power of God, I need only ask. He is ever-present and all-powerful, my help in every need; the switch is in the asking, the access in the trusting. Like working in the darkness, living without awareness of God is counterproductive. Living without His Presence and power leaves us wandering without Light, stumbling through our days.

Many days I have strained to see in the evening light, forgetting my need of Him. I want today to be different. This Power source is reliable and trustworthy, with never a power shortage or brownout; the lines are never down, and access is never denied. Today, I will run to my heavenly Father when I am in need. When I grow aware of darkness edging into my day, I will ask for His assistance. When confusion creeps in like twilight, I will flip the switch on, whispering the name of Jesus. His light will surge into my day when I simply remember to ask for His power and Presence. He is the "switch" that changes everything.

"You, O Lord, keep my lamp burning; my God turns my darkness into light." Psalm 28:13

"Blessed are those who have learned to acclaim you, who walk in the light of your presence, O Lord. They rejoice in your name all day long; they exult in your righteousness."
Psalm 89:15-16

"The sun will no more be your light by day, nor will the brightness of the moon shine on you, for the Lord will be your everlasting light, and your God will be your glory."
Isaiah 60:19

Butter Is Better

The activity in the milking barn on my great uncle's farm, escalated in the early dawn as the sun's rays barely filtered through the pasture's boundary line of trees. The faithful farm dog had already guided the herd to the barn. In a stall, each cow stood with hay at her head to keep her occupied, and her attention off the milking machine being attached to the other end of her. (My uncle had once been the object of his cow's sudden kicks, resulting in a serious injury.) Water puddled on the concrete floor, and the humidity mingled the scent of fresh milk with hay, pleasant and comforting.

My great aunt carried her share of the milk to the old farmhouse, separated the cream, and put it into the butter churn. Two things were always on the table at meals, a fresh pitcher of milk and a bowl of butter. Being a city kid, raised on pasteurized milk and margarine, I found whole milk a bit too strong for my liking, but my first taste of fresh butter was the beginning of a lifelong love affair. In opposition to the synthetic, man-made, yellow food-colored margarine, there was no flavor as pleasing as that of wholesome, organic butter melting into a hot fresh biscuit. I never could go back to margarine.

That first taste of fresh, homemade butter became a life-changing event, though a small and rather insignificant one in most people's view. I, however, am very grateful for it. That introduction to butter flavored the following decades of many meals. Like my affection for butter, though incomparably more significant, Jesus affected my life when I tasted His love, wonderful beyond all measure. One small taste of His goodness leaves us craving more of Him. One mouthful of His forgiveness brings us back to the table of His mercy and grace. There is no flavor on earth as uniquely satisfying as the love of God through Jesus.

God sets your table daily with the choice of margarine, the artificial and flavorless substitute of what the world offers, or the real and satisfying alternative of His promises. We have the freedom to choose between the power of this world and the power of Heaven. The option we choose determines how our lives are flavored from that point on---as I could never return to margarine, so I can never return to a life barren of Jesus. He has flavored every day of my life as only He can. Butter is better, and so is Jesus!

"Taste and see that the Lord is good; blessed is the man who takes refuge in him."

Psalm 34:8

"Like newborn babies, crave pure spiritual milk, so that by it you may grow up in your salvation, now that you have tasted that the Lord is good." 1 Peter 2:2-3

Each of my children, at the approximate age of four, experienced night terrors. My son once "woke up" in the middle of the night screaming, eyes wide open, that his bed was on fire, seeing leaping flames all around him. It took a minute to understand that he was not awake and was having a nightmare, a very vivid one at that. Those night terrors never seemed to spill over into fear during the day, and many children who experience this at a young age outgrow it within a year.

It was exactly the opposite for another child I know. He became increasingly fearful as he approached his teen years. With an incredibly gifted imagination, his thoughts had begun running wild, causing fear to increase. The torment of fear was causing him to dread the night, and sleep. Wanting to encourage him and give him hope, I developed this simple "Bible study" for him, which I have also found useful.

My emotions are not truth—God's Word is the truth. **"Sanctify them by the truth; your word is truth." John 17:17**
Because our thoughts steer our emotions, I must train my thoughts to be in line with what God says. My emotions will follow like a caboose following the engine. Once I give my wrong thoughts to Jesus, He destroys them. It is my decision to give them to Him or keep them. **"We demolish arguments and every pretention that raises itself up against the knowledge of God; we take every thought captive to make it obedient to Christ."** 2 Corinthians 10:5

This feeling will pass, this time will pass, this circumstance will pass. The beauty of time is that it causes change eventually, and God is in control of my times. **"My times are in your hands." Psalm 31:15**

Jesus is not everyone's Savior, but he is MY Savior. He loves me, made me exactly who He wants me to be, is here for me now, and will never leave or forsake me. **"The Lord delights in those who fear him, who put their hope in his unfailing love." Psalm 147:11 "And I will ask the Father, and he will give you another Counselor to be with you forever—the Spirit of truth." John 14:16**

I am loved deeply by God, and He will help me. **"For God so loved the world (me) that he gave his one and only Son, that whoever believes in him shall not perish but have eternal life." John 3:16 "So do not fear, for I am with you; do not be afraid, for I am your God. I will strengthen you and help you; I will uphold you with my righteous right hand." Isaiah 41:1**

We each encounter fear almost daily. We can allow it to intimidate us into surrender, or we can surrender it to the only one who can subdue it, Jesus. Fear is used by our enemy to separate us from the only One who can help us. Fear is a weapon wielded against us, but God's weapons of love and truth are eternal and powerful, for the children of the King of Kings who will trust in Him, and fear not.

Piggy Back

Whether it is actually a custom in South Korea or totally fictional, nearly every Korean production I have viewed has someone carrying another person on his back. These aren't babies in carriers or slings; they are adults who were sick, injured, or incapacitated. I found it rather interesting because, in my culture, this is rarely done, except with small children, who often fall asleep in the process.

One day I read a passage in the Bible that surprised me, never noticing it the multiple times I had previously read the book of Deuteronomy:

About Benjamin, he said: "Let the beloved of the Lord rest secure in him, for he shields him all day long, and the one the Lord loves rests between his shoulders." Deuteronomy 33:12

What a beautiful passage! And it is a personal one. Because Jesus is my security in the relationship with my heavenly Father, I can replace Benjamin's name with my own. So, it is I who am beloved, I who rest secure in him, I who am shielded all day long, and I, whom the Lord loves, resting between his shoulders. Wow! My heavenly Father is carrying **me** piggyback through this day!

Even for a small child, trust and peacefulness result from being carried on someone's back. Being carried piggyback surrenders all control to the carrier, not determining the steps or direction. It is admitting that I do not have the ability or strength to go where I need to go. As I begin this day, I pray, Lord, that I, too, will trust you enough to relinquish control and rest between your shoulders. Allow Him to carry you, too, Child.

What's for Dinner? March 10

I recall hearing that question nearly every day my children were growing up, and sometimes my oldest would ask days in advance for the anticipated menu. It was one of my greatest challenges, to produce a varied menu while maintaining my unvarying budget, for a husband and three children. It seems I am not unique in this respect, as nearly every woman I talk with has experienced the same daily dilemma.

Thinking it unfair, I considered that Eve didn't have to cook! Really, think about it! All that was required was that she wander through the garden, picking what she wanted from a tree. She didn't even need to bend over! Adam likely followed her around and ate whatever Eve picked for dinner, and I don't think men or children have changed much since then. No brick ovens were required—the original fast food was really fast. Grain hadn't entered the picture yet, so there was no milling, kneading, or baking. Animals were off-limits until God himself instituted sacrifices, so no hunting, processing, smoking, or drying, either.

From the day Eve chomped down on the forbidden fruit, and God leveled the death sentence on mankind, producing dinner became one of life's most challenging tasks. We don't think much of the consequences of sin—they have become our daily routine, as routine as cooking a meal, plowing a field, or going to work. Only when the routine becomes burdensome, or bothersome, do we notice and understand that something is amiss. There is a vague prompting in our spirits, that this life is not what God intended for the children made in His image. The original plan was His best plan.

Something tells me that God thinks meals shared are pretty important, too. I wonder if Martha knew she was preparing a meal for God? Or the disciples comprehended, on that beach, that the Son of God was preparing a meal of fish for them? Or that the 5000 men, and their families, grasped that the Son of Man had provided the banquet of fish and loaves out of thin air?

Eve's dinner choice in the garden initiated God's restoration plan, to bring us all back to garden-like fellowship with Him through Jesus. When the pinnacle of time and eternity meet, what do you imagine will be on the table at the wedding banquet of the Bride of Christ and the Lamb of God? Whatever it is, it will have been divinely planned and perfectly prepared. My mouth is watering as I ask, "Lord, what's for dinner!?!"

"Then God said, 'I give you every seed-bearing plant on the face of the whole earth and every tree that has fruit with see in it. They will be yours for food.'" Genesis 1:29

"Then the angel said to me, 'Write: "Blessed are those who are invited to the wedding supper of the Lamb!"'" Revelation19:9

A livestock farmer stated that shepherding sheep requires more hands-on work than any other livestock farming, with little recognition accompanying it. Curious about his statement, I did a little digging online, finding that one of my presumptions was entirely wrong—sheep are not stupid. They are usually very quiet and gentle, and highly social. Sheep have excellent hearing; loud noises and abrupt movements startle them, making them nervous and difficult to handle, but they are not stupid.

Sheep are best known for their strong flocking and following instincts, becoming highly agitated when separated from the rest of the flock. And when one sheep moves, the rest will follow, even if it is detrimental to them. They are also reluctant to go where they cannot see. The shepherd trains them to his voice, giving them good things to eat to encourage following him.

This is probably more than you care to know about sheep, but I find it fascinating since Jesus spoke at length, comparing people to them., People, similar to sheep, are not stupid; but we are definitely "flock prone" and "followers", highly social, and do poorly when separated from the flock. We are easily distracted, easily startled, quick to become lost, and quick to become prey as we wander away from our Shepherd. We are reluctant to walk where we cannot see, and mistrust of our Savior becomes evident as faith eludes us.

We are followers to a fault, following any diversion along the path, prone to easily wander off and into danger. We tend to follow the Good Shepherd only when He is feeding us good things, what we consider tasty, then avoiding His hand when it is guiding us other than where we want to go. Life's hardships startle, frighten, and cause us to withdraw from the Shepherd, though He is our lifeline and sustenance. When His calm and wise voice should be our comfort and strength, we avoid Him.

The shepherd I read about, Craig Rogers, has a motto concerning his sheep, "Tending to the flock but caring for the individual". Jesus also came for the whole human race but died for individuals. While loving all, He singularly cares for each of us. You and I are the flock of His pasture, the lambs He loves. In following such a Shepherd, there is simple bliss through trusting Him, and residing in His pasture of peace.

"He tends his flock like a shepherd: He gathers the lambs in his arms and carries them close to his heart; he gently leads those that have young." Psalm 40:11

Just Humbled

Working as a part-time caregiver, I sat on the patio with my charge, whom I affectionately called "Ladybug". An elderly woman approached, greeted us, and sat down to begin a conversation. She opened with the question, "Have you ever worked more than a part-time job in your life?" Considering my age, I found that question demeaning at first, then I laughed gently at the absurdity of it. Continuing to smile, I assured her I had.

Though her question was clearly prideful, insinuating that she was of superior status, my answer could have also been equally prideful. I flipped back through the mental resume' of my life: I have dined at a governor's mansion, traveled, lived many places, owned businesses, worked as a professional, learned multiple new skills, and gone back to college late in life. I have designed a house, raised and shown dogs, and raised a pretty remarkable family. I could have given a worldly and prideful response, but I did not.

Considering my life, it should have been quite different, given the extremely humble beginnings from which I rose. As a child, I had no hope and meager dreams. Yet few people would recognize me today, set free from the poverty of mind and emotions, confident, and humbled by the ways God has intervened in my life. I cannot be prideful about anything at all. Only due to His repeated interventions has good transpired.

Because of His layers of forgiveness and outpourings of love, abundant guidance, and heaps of mercy am I here today. Through overwhelming numbers of protections and deliverances have I arrived here, wholly dependent upon Jesus, claiming no worldly status but Christ-follower. Like Paul, I can boast in nothing but Jesus. Rather than prideful, I am humbled, undeserving, and grateful to a loving and merciful God. Just humbled.

"Be sensitive to each other's needs — don't think yourselves better than others; but make humble people your friends. Don't be conceited." Romans 12:16

"Likewise, you who are less experienced, submit to leaders. Further, all of you should clothe yourselves in humility toward one another, because God opposes the arrogant, but to the humble he gives grace." 1 Peter 5:5

"Therefore, humble yourselves under the mighty hand of God, so that at the right time he may lift you up." 1 Peter 5:6

There is a dividing line drawn horizontally across one of the last pages of journal number six. Above the line, these words are written boldly: "I am drawing the line on my life." It was a defining moment when I made the conscious, and purposeful, decision to change the trajectory of my life. I would finally allow God to take the controls that my fingernails were dug into so deeply. "I am laying down guilt, shame, and wondering if I am good enough. I am laying down comparisons of myself to others, feelings of abandonment, and wondering if I can hear God," was the final sentence on the page.

What followed on the next page was a page-high cross dividing it into two lists. One heading was titled "Surviving" and the other "Abiding". On the surviving side, the words penned were "whining"; "trying"; "struggling"; "unworthiness"; "doubt"; and "wallowing". There was no redeeming that list, not with self-help, not with the right sermon, and not with the help of others. I had already tried it all but was left bereft in a sea of guilt, bobbing on a raft of self-pity and failure.

The words listed under the "Abiding" title were familiar, yet alien because I had not soaked them into my spirit. It was like a lighthouse beam far away, with no sense of how to draw closer to it. The words under the "Abiding" header became life for me, as I learned to trust God with everything, emphasis on **everything**.; "Promises", "peace", "love", "cleansing", "rest", "worthy", "power", and "healing" graced the list; and as trust grew, they permeated my life in growing measure.

"Freedom" is the last word on that list, though I think not accidentally. It is the result of living, and deeply knowing, the other words on the list as reality. It is confidence in the work of Jesus in my life, knowing that all my failures past, all my sin, and all of my doubts are washed away by the blood He shed on my behalf. There is no longer any condemnation; none. No man, angelic being, nor any power in heaven or earth can change that statement of fact. I am bought and paid for by the blood of the Lamb of God. But until I believe it, I will live as though the "surviving" list is true.

The "Surviving" list is one of lies, and the "Abiding" list is the truth. We always have a choice as to which we will believe. The results will always be the same; lies leading to destruction, or truth leading to life and peace. Belief leads to action, and actions change our lives. So, my question for you today is, "Whom will *you* believe?" Your life depends on the line you draw, too.

"Now the Lord is Spirit, and where the Spirit of the Lord is, there is freedom. And we, who with unveiled faces all reflect the Lord's glory, are being transformed into his likeness with ever-increasing glory, which comes from the Lord, who is the Spirit."

2 Corinthians 3:17-18

Spotlight March 14

The chairs were plump and comfortable as I waited in the lobby, walled by two-story windows. Off to the right of the receptionist's desk, an anteroom sat in the afternoon shadows, with a bookcase, chairs, and a table lamp illuminating the space. Beneath the table, a shaft of the afternoon's sun spotlighted a spider web, marring the otherwise perfect setting. Immediately, I was impressed by the Spirit, affirming that it is He who shines His light into the darkness, revealing sin, and exposing evil.

God brings to light not only the deeds of individuals but also shines His spotlight into the halls of organizations and governments, exposing corruption and decay long-festering beneath the surface. It is much like the spider webs, hidden in the dark corners, the spiders meticulously building their lairs for many years, some for generations. I wondered at that moment why people would perpetrate evil and willingly welcome darkness. The answer is not pleasant.

There is a spiritual battle for men's souls which rages in the realms we cannot see. It spills over into our physical realm, manifesting itself in human lives as strife, addictions, wars, the breakdown of cultures, violence, and destruction. As I consider the enemy of our souls, I am coming to realize that it is not random destruction he desires; his ire is directed upon each human being. He will utilize every method at his disposal to destroy each one, especially delighting in using us to harm one another.

One of our enemy's most effective weapons is the lure to power, with implied protection for those who side with him. It is one of his best lies. It is one we all succumb to at some point; we desire to control and manipulate life instead of yielding control to God; it is anything we seek to "own". Pride was Satan's sin, and often ours, believing we know better than God. We believe life is ours to dictate, and it is his ultimate deception.

Like the sunlight revealing the cobweb, if we could only see the contrast of God's love and Satan's hatred, why would any of us choose darkness? Because we are children of darkness. Until we choose the Light, sin blinds us to God's love and the light of truth. We have a choice, ultimately, embracing the father of lies or the Father's spotlight of truth, the path of darkness and destruction, or the Way, the Truth and the Life, Jesus.

"This is the verdict: Light has come into the world, but men loved darkness instead of light because their deeds were evil. Everyone who does evil hates the light, and will not come into the light for fear that his deeds will be exposed. But whoever lives by the truth comes into the light, so that it may be seen plainly that what he has done has been done through God." John 3:19-21

The tidy home to two hatchings through the summer, its snippets of leaves and twigs occupied the inner corner of the porch roof. We had counted four tiny bobbing heads in each hatching, now turned fledglings, and gone. Their watchful mama and daddy would return, finding their way home as they had the summer prior, to raise the next generation of Tree Swallows this spring.

Bird watching has long been a favored pastime, but I never gave much thought to the fact that nests are for nesting. Nesting is raising young; adult birds do not occupy nests as permanent abodes. I always pictured birds retreating to their nests during storms, or at night, but no, most really don't. They are building and occupying nests only while raising babies.

Reading Matthew 8:20, Jesus replied to a teacher of the law who volunteered to follow him wherever he went, **"Foxes have dens and birds of the air have nests, but the Son of Man has no place to lay his head."** I was puzzled by His response since the teacher appeared to be a willing follower. Jesus seemed to be deterring him. Considering the birds, I realized, perhaps in part, what Jesus was communicating.

Jesus did not come to live a conventional life, including children and a stable home. The birds of the air were a picture of that lifestyle. Jesus was indicating that His followers may be disappointed if they were looking for a traditional leader with a home, family, and the trappings of power. He would have no permanent home on earth. Born in a stable, the home of His childhood would be the only earthbound home He would ever know. His family was His followers, and His home was wherever His Father directed Him to rest His head.

Jesus said those words to indicate that His real home was in the presence of His heavenly Father, in the glistening halls of heaven, seated upon the throne, ruling in power and might; quite the contrast from His earthly nomadic ministry. We, followers of Jesus, need also to recognize that this is not our permanent residence, but a temporary stopping point in our journey. Our true home is reserved and promise-sealed, by the blood of the Lamb. There is a season for nesting, a season for flying, and a season for going home, to our real and permanent home, in His presence and glory. The way to our real home is always, and will ever be through Jesus, the Son of God.

"Jesus replied, 'If anyone loves me, he will obey my teaching. My Father will love him, and we will come to him and make our home with him." John 14:23

Little Miracles March 16

The toasted almonds were still hot as they sank into the deep brown, velvety chocolate. The nuts quickly became coated with semi-sweet goodness and were poured onto waxed paper to cool. I set the bowl in the sink, heading for my favorite chair while they cooled. I relaxed right into a long Sunday nap, totally forgetting the chocolate on the kitchen counter.

Finally, back in the kitchen, I washed the bowl I had used and tucked a few dishes back into their cupboard. Leaving the cabinet door open, I turned away for a second, reached for another dish, and in my peripheral vision saw an object falling. With a thud, it landed on the cooled almond bark, which I had forgotten to move, instead of the stone countertop. That object was a heavy glass that would have surely injured me if it had shattered within inches of my hand. I voiced my gratitude to God immediately.

I could have dismissed the whole incident as coincidence but would have overlooked one of the "little miracles" God intended me to witness as a testament to His loving presence in my life. There are many such instances every day, but I, in my self-importance and busyness, overlook them or reject them as insignificant. A near miss on the highway, a wrong step righted on a stairway, rain that stops when I get to my parking space, a compliment on a day I don't feel deserving, an unexpected check arriving in a financial crunch. They are all part of God showering me with His love, as any father would, through protection, provision, understanding, and grace.

Jesus showed us expressions of God's love while He was among us. He heaped up the nets of the fishermen quite unexpectedly; they could have thought it coincidence and dismissed the incident, but instead recognized who caused it and praised Him. Peter finding the coin in the fish's mouth was some coincidence, right?! When Jesus told Jairus, "Don't be afraid; just believe, and she will be healed," Jairus could have passed it off as a coincidence, refusing to believe that God intervened to spare his precious daughter from her brush with death.

No matter how big the miracle is, we humans tend to dismiss it as if God is incapable. Or perhaps, we cannot believe because our understanding is so limited. Every day, God is working on our behalf, whether the "miracle" is small or large in our eyes. He is able, and lovingly willing, to work miracles in the world He created, the world He alone sustains for our benefit. I pray He will open my eyes today to the many "little miracles" around me, some big ones, too, and that I will be excited to give Him the praise, thanking Him for each one.

"You are the God who performs miracles; you display your power among the peoples."

Psalm 77:14

"Jesus did many other things as well. If every one of them were written down, I suppose that even the whole world would not have room for the books that would be written."

John 21:25

Sunbeams bounced cheerfully off the new spring foliage. Braced against the sky in vivid green, trees brightly bloomed in brilliant pinks, and perky yellow tulips encouraged even the faint of heart. Spring was apparent everywhere my gaze landed, and it was a welcome sight the day before Easter. Easter Day's outlook was dismal, to say the least, with a forecast of very heavy rain and possible flooding, which, regrettably, came to pass exactly as predicted.

I awoke Easter morning to the sounds of wind in the treetops and rain pounding on the roof. It was relentless for the entire day with barely room for a sigh between the gusts tugging at the treetops. Normally, I could have shrugged off the rainy day, but this season of historic quarantine had already confined me to the inside of my home for nearly a month. In addition to not being able to attend Easter worship, the rain now dampened my mood as thoroughly as it drenched the grass in my yard.

"Attending" an online service, singing along happily, I was rudely interrupted by water from another unwelcome source, an unexplainable leak in a twenty-gallon aquarium. Three hours later, searching for another online service, I felt a bit beleaguered and a lot disheartened as the rain ran in rivers across our street, still no sign of ceasing. As I sat to listen to the sermon and Bible teaching, my heart found its home again, the place of peace, where rain was insignificant, the unexpected events of the day were irrelevant, and my dreary attitude flexed into a quiet smile.

Ironically, the word for the day in a devotional book I had read that very morning focused on gratitude, the same day that I had grumbled away half of it. I had overlooked the one element I needed most, Jesus; I had heartily complained to Him, but I had not expressed gratitude for the rain, or that I noticed the aquarium emptying before it had expelled all twenty gallons, or that I had a heater and fan to help dry it. I had not thanked Him with all my heart for the food on my plate, or that my house was dry, excepting the aquarium.

Most of all, I was finally noticing that God had it all under control. I did not have the day I wanted to have in the forecast, but it was a blessed day when I finally aligned my attitude with God's instruction. We have not the ability to forecast today's events, but we do have the ability to walk through the day with gratitude. And we can acknowledge that a Sovereign and loving God has absolute control, even when we don't.

"Let the peace of Christ rule in your hearts, since as members of one body you were called to peace. And be thankful." Colossians 3:15

Incalculable Gifts March 18

My granddaughter, Elizabeth, is very gifted with music, playing the violin with ever-increasing skill. I could easily see her love of music from the time she was very young, singing like a happy fledgling discovering it had wings. It was no surprise to anyone that she would excel in music; but she will not master it, nor see its rewards, without hard work and many hours of practice.

Attempting to learn a new language, I realize how amazing the gifts of reading and writing are. They open the world to me for exploration, pleasure, communication, and earning a living. Without the ability to read and write, my life would not just be less enjoyable, it would not remotely resemble my life with them. How immeasurably different, and more difficult, my life would have been without words!

Another gift I have received, happily, is the gift of a morning song. My joy every morning is the wonder of God's sense of humor (I seem to be tone-deaf!) and the pleasure of His gifting me with a song when I awaken. Each morning, before my eyes fully open, God's Spirit drops the words of a song into my heart, and it becomes the "song of the day". It may be a part of a hymn, or a phrase of praise, but it stays with me until my head hits the pillow again. And I can count on God showing me, at some point during that day, how the words of that song apply to my relationship with Him.

However, retaining the song requires a focus on my Father during the day. It is obvious that reading, writing, and music take lengthy practice and great commitment; but we often brush aside the value of coming to know and understand God. All relationships, to flourish, require the work necessary to develop understanding.

It must grieve His heart to see me place such a high priority on developing temporary skills, for use in the world He created, and to ignore its very Creator. Still, He meets me where I am, at the level of my willingness, and invites me to accept the incalculable gift of His very Presence. He never turns a seeking heart away. For this gift, I am the most grateful.

"Because you are my help, I sing in the shadow of your wings. My soul clings to you; your right hand upholds me." Psalm 63:7-8

"And without faith, it is impossible to please God because anyone who comes to him must believe that he exists and that he rewards those who earnestly seek him." Hebrews 11:6

Full Bloom

The advent of spring brought great anticipation of my garden erupting in a bounty of vegetation and flowers as the planting was nearly finished. As I surveyed my work and asked God's blessings on it, I spotted something ominous making its way onto my newly cleaned porch—a poisonous vine of undetermined variety. I only know it is not poison ivy, but it had all the characteristics of a noxious invasive weed with a staggering rate of growth. And it was heading directly toward my pot of Alstromeria, which had been carefully wintered over in my greenhouse, now in full bloom.

Just as my life appeared to be leveling out, and I had overcome several major obstacles through faith, hope bloomed, growing lavishly where bare soil had been raked raw. At just the time when I felt God's hand guiding me most strongly, just when I was most involved in what I believe He called me to do, a seed was planted in my most vulnerable soil, fear of rejection. Though I recognized it for what it was, I did not thoroughly eradicate it and allowed it ever so little room to grow. It wrapped its insidious tendrils around the blossoms of my faith, almost overnight. Doubt and fear began to multiply faster than the blossoms.

Fear assails us with a constant barrage of possibilities, from the moment we are born to the day of our passage from this earth into the halls of heaven. The world is currently in upheaval as I write this, and fear embraces each country's populace as lockdowns sweep our citizens and economies. Livelihoods and lives are at risk, our freedoms taken; but there are always reasons to fear, even without seismic global events.

Fear, in any of its destructive forms, can be given a foothold in our spirits. It assures us that we cannot trust God, that His written Word is not true, and that His promises are only credible for someone else, but not for us. It is a strangling vine creeping out of the darkness, attempting to subdue the light of God. Fear does not come from our heavenly Father. Fear is our default setting, and faith is what overcomes it.

When God instructs us to not be afraid, which He does hundreds of times in the Bible, He means it. *Stop being afraid*. Stop. Do the opposite—*trust God*. Trusting God is the only antidote to fear, the only means of tearing the roots apart, and utterly destroying them. Confess your fear, then stand firmly trusting God's goodness toward you. Taking God at His word and truly trusting Him is the only way we can each live in full bloom.

"I cry out to God Most High, to God, who fulfills his purpose for me. He sends from heaven and saves me, rebuking those who hotly pursue me; God sends his love and his faithfulness." Psalm 57:2,3

This Is Your Captain Speaking March 20

The calm, friendly, capable voice streamed throughout the airliner cabin, "Good afternoon, everyone! This is your captain speaking." The seasoned flyers, belying their experience with a touch of arrogance, settled into their seats with little attention diverted to the formalities. They, and I, had heard them many times prior; and it was, admittedly, purely out of respect that I restrained my activities, making a minor effort at being attentive. The bustle of the passengers largely continued unabated.

A marked difference in response became evident as the plane bounced over rough turbulence, much like one of the bucking horses I had witnessed at a rodeo. Looks of concern electrified the cabin, all activities abandoned, as we pitched and rolled over the billowing clouds. All eyes were focused on the cockpit as if to summon the captain for an explanation. Every ear was finely attuned to the calm and capable voicing of his assessment over the same speaker system, previously disregarded. Immediate respect is commanded for the pilot in an emergency.

When life is flowing smoothly, with little turbulence and no headwind, we humans tend to ignore the Captain's instructions, too, believing we have everything under control. "I know the drill. I've been here before; the Pilot will take care of His part and leave me to do as I wish. Sure, His instructions are important; I know them by heart. I don't need to listen to the announcement," until I am shocked into full attentiveness in the emergency.

That would be the moment I rush to the cockpit door, persistently knocking, demanding an answer to my dilemma, and wondering why there is not an urgent response. My heavenly Father, though, is not panicked; He had the answer all along and would have communicated it willingly if I had listened to His instruction at the beginning of the trip. His plan is laid out in the Bible, and the calm, steady, capable voice of His Holy Spirit was speaking to me when I would listen; when I didn't, He poured out His grace and mercy instead.

God has filed life's flight plan well in advance, anticipates the storms, knows where turbulence will be encountered, and has established life-saving rules of conduct for us. He not only knows how to fly the plane, He intimately knows each passenger and how to lead each one to safety. He has much to communicate with His passengers on this flight of life, if we will simply shift our attention when He whispers the words to our spirits, "This is your Captain speaking!"

"Then a cloud appeared and enveloped them, and a voice came from the cloud: 'This is my Son, whom I love. Listen to him!'" Mark 9:7

"Now choose life, so that you and your children may live and that you may love the Lord your God, listen to his voice, and hold fast to him." Deuteronomy 30:19b-20a

For eleven years, the cottage, a five hundred square foot "tiny house", resided in our backyard. The first years were a comfort, knowing I could look after my father-in-law's needs. The remainder of its occupation witnessed many trials, as life with dementia became increasingly challenging. My husband's health worsened. My mother moved nearby following her tangle with an 18-wheel big rig. My mother-in-law's health worsened in a nursing home, and one of my daughters experienced two premature births. By the time my father-in-law moved out of the cottage, the cottage itself had become an obstacle to maintain.

Deciding to sell the cottage, my son and I concentrated our energy and resources on renovation, doing all the work ourselves. One year later, its new owners and I waited on various moving companies, who promised week by week to appear, weeks yawning into months. Now, it sat in my yard perched on two huge steel beams high above its foundation. It was awaiting loading onto the trailer, paid in full, ready for its service to new owners in another town.

As the trailer sailed down the road at a snail's pace, I shed not one tear, praising and thanking my God for His deliverance and provision. I stood in my yard waving goodbye to broken pipes, Carpenter bees, broken appliances, slow drains, and a few demons! Through those eleven years, I recognized God's hand. He has drawn me closer to Himself, kept His promises, and taught me to be more dependent upon Him.

How did I know this was all God's timing? I was completely out of money to pay my house payment on the very day they loaded the cottage on the beams. The day the cottage sale was notarized, and payment in hand, was only **hours** before my house payment was due!

Our trials are not a surprise to God. They do not catch him off guard, nor does He have limited time or resources. His promises are true, and He is capable of fulfilling them. No matter how dire my situation seems, He is asking me to come to Him for the help I need, and to trust His goodness. He is never early, teaching me patience and trust; but He is never late, though at times His ways seem to run at a snail's pace, compared to mine.

"So do not fear, for I am with you; do not be dismayed, for I am your God. I will strengthen and help you; I will uphold you with my righteous right hand." Isaiah 41:10

"And my God will meet all your needs according to his glorious riches in Christ Jesus." Philippians 4:19

Hands-On

Her hands were folded, palms up, as Jeannette gently held the soft pink Begonia blossom in her fingertips. The contrast between her aged grasp and the delicate new petals was stunning. That photograph is one of my all-time favorites, unveiling one of the mysteries of aging; the wrinkles and changes we abhor are testimonies of storms weathered, hardships endured, and service rendered. The hands betraying age are also telling a story, if we will open our hearts to it.

From her history, I know that the hands in the photograph sewed clothing, cooked countless meals, tended the flowers she loved and shared, and set thoughtful place settings for guests. They taught and nurtured not only her children but the community's as well. She raised a family, tended to chores, and was a wife of great worth to her husband as she nursed him through a prolonged illness. Her hands dried the tears of others, as well as her own when life served up loss. They folded in prayer and turned the pages of praise, reaching out to God and extending a hand to others.

I have been guilty of believing that the "little" things I did were of no value, but have learned by observing those older than myself, that each of those acts done in love can be life-changing to those around me, whether family, a friend, or a stranger. The hands lifted to God in praise are of untold value, and the hand offering a cup of water, Jesus sees. The hands that work quietly in the background, hands that labor, hands that sew and sow, the hands that nurture the young and tend to the old, hands mending the sick and broken, that take the hand of the weak and saddened, are all of great worth.

God bestows His grace every day through hands serving Him while serving His people. Each day presents fresh opportunities to love as He loves, to go where He leads, and to serve with willing hands; we are called to be "hands-on" people, resembling the Savior we love. Jesus Himself aged only thirty-three earthly years, and each day of that allotted time, He placed His hands onto people, serving and blessing them, often to the point of exhaustion.

My own hands are changing, no longer smooth and youthful, aching now and then, foretelling transitions to come. What a privilege to witness it! Each sign of age is also a testimony of a life lived, love extended, and abilities spent. We, as Christ-followers are called to be imitators, caring for people as He did, "hands-on", as we trust Him for strength and direction to carry out His plan.

"God is not unjust; he will not forget your work and the love you have shown him as you have helped his people and continue to help them." Hebrews 6:10

Do You Know Who You're Dealing With? March 23

"Do you know who you're dealing with???" It's the classic question, incredulously asked of anyone considered a minion. Most often we hear such a tone from the all mighty and powerful banker, lawmaker, Mafioso, gang leader, etc. This is the point of no return, acknowledging the power of the station or confronting it, most likely with utter destruction ensuing. Power is more sought after than gold, possessions, or position, all of which are simply tools to obtain it. However, seeking power is not allocated to the rich only; it is part of the human condition, raising its ugly head wherever human beings reside.

We eventually realize that power struggles surround us. But they are also within us. Originating before creation, the ultimate power grab was attempted by Satan as he sought to dethrone the Almighty. Wielding absolute power will ultimately destroy everything of importance in its path, and those who believe they have evaded its influence are generally proven wrong in the end. There is only one exception, only One, who acts in perfect power.

The ascent to power undergirds the sinful heart of every man, as we seek to wrest control from the hand of God. So, the question I must ask when confronted by my attempts at control is, "Who are you dealing with?" and the answer is a resounding, but quiet, "Oh." Contemplating the sovereignty and holiness of God, His power and might, all-consuming fire, the majesty and awe of Him, and His omniscience and omnipotence, how can I presume to question Him? Like Job, I must unequivocally concede that I have no business doing so.

More than His power, I dare not question His intentions toward me. That would be the appropriate time to ask, "Do you know who you are dealing with?" He is the Holy One, acting from the deepest and purest love, who birthed Himself in human form. Bathed in Light, He stepped into a dark world and voluntarily climbed Golgotha, to the cross of ultimate suffering. All because of His incomprehensible love for people who thirst for power and are steeped in sin.

Though fear would be wholly appropriate, His power I do not need to fear. God's wrath is no longer directed toward me, because of Jesus. Through Him, the Father looks upon me in mercy, forgiveness, love, and compassion. The only power I need to concern myself with is the usurping of His—it is best to leave control in His capable hands, focusing on submitting rather than controlling. I can trust His power to raise up and bring down, to exalt and destroy, in His time and according to His will. Yes, I know Who I am dealing with.

"Let the name of the Lord be praised, both now and forevermore. From the rising of the sun to the place where it sets, the name of the Lord is to be praised. The Lord is exalted over all the nations, his glory above the heavens. Who is like the Lord our God, the One who sits enthroned on high, who stoops down to look on the heavens and the earth?" Psalm 113:2-6

The Greatest Asset March 24

Entering my freshman year of college, my proud, but thrifty, grandmother treated me to a shopping trip at her local department store. I don't recall anything from that trip except the deep brown, velvety suede jacket, its leather buttons skipping down the front, and streaming long, narrow fringe dancing up one sleeve, across the yoke, and down the other.

That short jacket cost my grandmother a week's pay, hard-earned by standing on her feet, dressing ladies' hair all day. The sacrifice was well worth it in my mind, if not hers; though she may be gone now, I have retained it to this day, thankful for the love she expressed through it, remembering her fondly each time I touch the soft textured leather. My jacket may not be worth five dollars today, but it is one of my most valuable assets, steeped in sweet memories of a sacrificial gift given by irreplaceable love. And little did she know that some of her great-grandchildren would also wear it.

Taking it down from the clothes rod one day, I noticed tiny holes in the front panel—something had made a feast of my precious cowhide at some point, leaving my treasure damaged for life. All these years later, worn with time, dust adorning its now sagging shoulders, God found a new purpose for it, reminding me of another life lesson. The words of Jesus rang in my heart, **"Do not store up for yourselves treasures on earth, where moth and rust destroy, and where thieves break in and steal. But store up for yourselves treasures in heaven, where moth and rust do not destroy, and where thieves do not break in and steal. For where your treasure is, there your heart will be also."** (Matthew 6:19-21)

I am admittedly a bit of a worrier, a habit which lends well to storing up things I might "need" in the future. The world's wisdom dictates storing up wealth, in ways that may sound quite reasonable, such as "rainy day" emergency funds, retirement, investments, and hard assets for wealth stability. Weathering life's storms taught me not to anticipate events so far in advance, but rather to trust God's leading. I look back at the times I had saved for a rainy day, a deluge overcoming me instead, but God had prepared me in advance. Other times, I had nothing when a storm descended upon me and God provided in most miraculous ways.

Overall, the balance comes from trusting Him moment by moment, with gratitude for what He has already generously given, and preparing ahead when He nudges me to do so. There is no magic formula to life, not for anyone; there is only trust in God or trust in self, which God seems to delight in upending, so that we can, in the end, trust Him more. Jesus' desire, above all, is that the love He expressed in His birth, death and resurrection, be returned. As we love Him, trusting Him to be and provide all we need, He becomes our greatest asset.

"And my God will meet all your needs according to his glorious riches in Christ Jesus."

Philippians 4:9

An interesting perspective on patience was revealed by author Tony Campolo in his book, *"Everything They Told You Is Wrong"*. "Patience, he said, was something we had with people whom we consider to be better than, or beneficial to us. We have patience with those whom we do not want to risk losing. We have extraordinary patience when dating, or with those who influence our careers. We find exceptional perseverance, as we interact with those who wield power."

In contrast, we are impatient with people we consider to be of lesser status than ourselves, or those we feel we are not in danger of losing. People in this category may be food servers, clerks, the poor, handicapped, and even worse, our families, spouses, and children.

I knew immediately that his assessment was correct. I remembered the times I was short-tempered when my children were slow to respond, my husband disappointed me, or my expectations were quashed. I had to search the depths of my soul for it when plans were ruined, or appointments were turned upside down. There was another element to my impatience, which suddenly became very apparent as well—pride. Pride seems to be very closely associated with patience, or the lack of it.

Pride deceives us into imagining that we are elevated in some way over others. It invades our souls so subtly, so insidiously, disguising itself as necessity or concern; it is, in reality, an effort to control our environment and those around us, believing we know better than they. All at once, I could see as clearly as if the clouds had parted and rays of sun burst through, that this was the reason God hates pride so much. It is the deception of entitlement and control which makes us feel elevated above others.

I am learning to recognize my need for humility when extending patience to others. It is one of God's lessons I wish I had learned much sooner and applied more freely. Patience and humility are by-products of love. Can this be why God calls us to love others, as much as we love ourselves? Out of God's inexplicable love, flows extraordinary patience, not control. Only because of His love and patience do we have the opportunity for salvation, and closeness with Him. When we lay down "self", pride and prejudice usually sleep with it.

"The end of a matter is better than its beginning, and patience is better than pride. Do not be quickly provoked in your spirit, for anger resides in the lap of fools." Ecclesiastes 7:8-9

"A man's wisdom gives him patience; it is to his glory to overlook an offense."
Proverbs 19:11

Road Trip

Far from home, my speaking engagement had taken me to a venue high above the city, overlooking the wide river. As I gazed over the downtown hugging its shores, doubts chased my confidence in circles. I had made changes to my speech that was to be delivered the next morning. And as much as I dreaded the speech, the very long drive home, through unfamiliar territory, would follow; I did not relish, nor could I escape either one.

I could not trust in past successes to see me through this speech, but I remembered Whom I could trust. I softly whispered a plea for help, and just as He had never let me down before, He was faithful to answer yet again. The speech I was so uncertain in presenting, God poured His grace upon; to His credit, many compliments followed.

Then there was the long drive home. Once again, I whispered my prayer, shifted into drive, and pulled onto the road. Many hours later, as I turned into my driveway, I realized that the unfamiliar roads had not been unfamiliar to God, and I was never out of His reach. The peaceful drive, and beautiful landscape draping the roads, elicited praise and thanksgiving all the way home; the trip I dreaded was, throughout the miles, one of the most wonderful I had ever driven.

The problems we anticipate in the road trip of life may happen, but most of our imaginings will never materialize. I know this well, having quite an active imagination myself. What God has taught me, and continues to instruct, is that even if the worst comes about, He is still there and has been all along. He is quite capable, often in amazingly creative ways, of meeting our needs. And He delights in surprising us with His abilities, with solutions far beyond anything we can ask or imagine.

I find myself underestimating God far more than overestimating Him, if that were even possible. In place of fear, He is teaching me to lean upon Him fully, beyond my understanding, experience, and competence. Life will continue to present challenges, providing ample opportunities to trust Him more, and myself less. On this road trip of life, He is correcting my error of underestimation and tutoring me daily in trust.

"I pray that out of his glorious riches he may strengthen you with power through his Spirit in your inner being, so that Christ may dwell in your hearts through faith. And I pray that you, being rooted and established in love, may have power, together with all the saints, to grasp how wide and long and high and deep is the love of Christ, and to know this love that surpasses knowledge---that you may be filled to the measure of all the fullness of God. Now to him who is able to do immeasurably more than all we can ask or imagine, according to his power that is at work within us." Ephesians 3:14-20

Speechless

The closer I came to my home, the fewer words I could assemble into complete thoughts or sentences, alarming my adult son who was listening over the car's Bluetooth device. As I pulled into my driveway, nary a sentence could be formed, my thoughts suddenly as incoherent as my spoken words. Never had a migraine headache caused such upheaval in my thoughts or speech, and an ambulance was my next mode of transportation. A hospital, I later found, without a guardian, is no place to be speechless!

Words are our link to sanity, I discovered, during that experience. They are also the link to our identities, the very core of who we are, what life is about, and the value we hold in this world. It is truly frightening to be silenced, whether through health, social pressure, family dynamics, or the physical world's limitations. Silence may be momentarily golden, but to have my voice silenced, with no way to accurately communicate, was a revelation.

That day, unable to hear the voice of Jesus, seemed quite empty and hopeless. Had I been able to think clearly, I would have immediately remembered Him who never leaves me and is always able to hear my cry for help. The thought, nay the lie, of believing that we can exist in this world without Jesus, without the love of God, or His gracious guidance and care, is so deeply ingrained into human beings that it shocks me to my core, repeatedly. It is unfathomable, yet exactly what I do.

My fragile memory forgets so easily every past rescue, each grace applied, each key to the unlocking of a solution, and every password of escape issued on my behalf. But whether I am near or far, blessed or broken, walking near or stranded in the desert, He understands my weakness, protecting me because I am, simply weak.

Because God keeps every one of His promises, I know I can count on His promise to protect and keep me, whether I feel it or not, expect it or not, remember or not. So, I remind myself again. I may find myself speechless, but my God is not helpless. He sees me, knows my need, loves me still, and will ever provide exactly what I need, simply because of Jesus. And because He loves me, and you, even when we are speechless.

"But the eyes of the Lord are on those who fear him, on those whose hope is in his unfailing love, to deliver them from death and keep them alive in famine. We wait in hope for the Lord; he is our help and our shield. In him our hearts rejoice, for we trust in his holy name. May your unfailing love rest upon us, O Lord, even as we put our hope in you."
Psalm 33:18-22

It is no small wonder that the Creator, and Lord of the vast universe, loves me, me in whom so many faults are to be found. Why would the human race, in general, be worthy of His attention, let alone a compassionate and consuming love? Why would He invest so much for such a meager return, so little love and respect from His creation? Why does He endure the rebellion, the insurrection seething in the hearts of men, and the unjustified blame we lay at His feet for all the sin, in which He had no part? I think it is that He is a father, that He has the original and perfect father's heart.

Adoption is a concept that is God-inspired and patterned after His own unselfish, and self-sacrificial, fatherly love. A young child, who has known only abandonment and pain, filth, rebellion, hurt to his core being, who is then shown unconditional loving acceptance and nurture, transforms over time. Subtle changes become increasingly obvious, then blatant, eventually overwhelming, as the transformation is fixed into adulthood. That child finally becomes an adult, able to give and receive love like that which he has received.

Similarly, this must be God's reason for loving us unconditionally, to the point of ultimate personal sacrifice. He alone can see the beginning, and ahead to the end, the transformation of His children. When adopted in Christ, we transform from hopelessness to radiant confidence, from filth to a brilliantly clean reflection of His Son. He witnesses the captives freed, their hunger and thirst satisfied, their wounds healed, and their final transformation into His very likeness. He sees what He meant for us to be, ever since we were just an idea in His mind.

We are being transformed, from children of darkness and desperation, into children of the Light, fully capable of receiving His love and returning love unceasingly to Him. And I am so thankful for my Father's infinite mercy and forgiveness, His compassion, and grace, which are extended to me through Christ Jesus. His love has transformed my life from that of a very needy orphan to the title, Child of the Most High God. I am a slave bought at a great price, set free, then adopted into the family of the King. No, it is not a small wonder at all; it is a very great wonder indeed!

"Praise be to the God and Father of our Lord Jesus Christ, who has blessed us in the heavenly realms with every spiritual blessing in Christ. For he chose us in him before the creation of the world to be holy and blameless in his sight. In love, he predestined us to be adopted as his sons through Jesus Christ, in accordance with his pleasure and will---to the praise of his glorious grace, which he has freely given us in the One he loves. In him we have redemption through his blood, the forgiveness of sins, in accordance with the riches of God's grace that he lavished on us with all wisdom and understanding." Ephesians 1:3-8

Waterfalls and Whales March 29

An amusing picture formed in my mind as I parked my car. A waterfall with a whale awkwardly pitching headlong over the edge of the falls and plopping unceremoniously into the pool below made me smile until I realized...I was the whale!

You see, I have always, and I do mean always, questioned why I was placed on this planet. I questioned God's plan, figuring He must have left an important piece to my puzzle in the box. I haven't been able to put any of the pieces together, to assemble a picture that made any sense. And as I have aged, that idea was reinforced, believing my insignificance in "God's plan". I have been the whale without an ocean.

From my limited view, I could not see where or how the Lord has used me, nor the gifts and talents He endowed. I have made the grave mistake of comparing my gifts with others, to my detriment. And in doing so, I undermined God's glory and credit for what He gave me. Some examples of this, now that I reconsider, are as follow:
He gave me three children to raise, and I threw in all the imagination, determination, creativity, and sweat equity I could muster, loving everything about the gift of motherhood. They grew up, and I gave in to the thoughts that what I did couldn't have been enough, though the evidence is to the contrary.

He gave me many hats to wear, figuratively speaking. I became a speaker, cake decorator, florist, designer, entrepreneur, business owner, instructor, artist, writer, and student. And in none of them did I feel successful. Interestingly, someone recently walked up to me and stated that the cake decorating I had taught her had been such a blessing to her family and that she often remembered me for it.

He gave me many friends over the years, most of whom I did not deserve. Yet they have stuck with me for the greater part of my life and through the worst of trials. I may have underestimated those relationships a bit.

After considering these points, I realized, yes, I am the whale, but just thought I should be swimming in the river when I was really swimming in the ocean! I always felt out of place because I didn't see God's greater plan. My perspective wasn't big enough. My job isn't to choose where to swim, it's simply to trust Him and swim! I have so much more liberty, not looking to the world's standards of achievements, but swimming freely in the vastness of God's possibilities. I'm a WHALE! And I'm finally free to swim where He leads, swimming in the vast ocean of freedom through Christ Jesus!

"If the Son sets you free, you will be free indeed!" John 8:36

Many of my friends are campers and lovers of the great outdoors, feeling very much at home in the wooded camping areas. I was, on the other hand, raised a city girl, and knew nothing more about camping than what I learned in Girl Scouts and from our very scant yard. My husband joked that my idea of camping was occupying a hotel room with a mint on the pillow. The first question I always asked when camping or hiking the wooded trails was, "Can we go home now?"

Understanding fully the attraction to nature (I really do), I am content to observe it from my porch or window, at this point in life, and am blessed to live where wildlife wanders through our yard regularly. It never ceases to amaze me how God's creation testifies of His vast imagination, the many varieties of species He created, and the intricate designs they display. I marvel at the ability to hibernate, sleeping through cold unpleasant months to awaken in spring. The habits and colorations of the many species of birds, living in my yard alone, are quite amazing.

God has taught me much through observing nature, even from my porch. They have been lessons about provision, protection, and trusting Him. Reading the book of Job one day, I came across this passage: **"But *ask* the animals—*they will teach you*— and the birds in the air—*they will tell you*; or speak to the earth—*it will teach you*—and the fish in the sea *will inform you*: every one of them knows that the hand of God has done this! In his hand is the life of every living thing and the spirit of every human being." Job 12:7-10**

God's creation is meant to teach and inform us about His character and power, His ultimate control, His care for His creatures, and His people. In short, God is telling us He loves us. The keyword in that passage from Job is "ask", ask the animals, the birds, the earth, the fish; from God's creation, we will receive the resounding answer— God did all this for you because of His love!

He is speaking through His creation directly to you and me. If we inquire of Him, God will answer. Whether it is a result of observing His creation, speaking through His servants, or His words in the Holy Bible, God desires to reveal His character to us. If only we ask, He is faithful to show us who He is and how much He cares for us. He encourages us to find Him, for in finding Him, we find life, health, and peace. So, today, Lord, I come, just asking for eyes to see you in your creation, ears to hear your Spirit's leading, and a heart to know and love You.

Many Robins

Against the dreary, damp, brown grass, a sudden movement revealed the robin's flash of a rosy breast. I noticed another nearby as they plucked tasty treats from the rain-soaked mat of grass, then another, and another. None were immediately visible in the low morning light, dimmed by misting rain, but in total, nine robins were counted. Eventually, they became visible only as they moved about the dull patch of yard, hidden in plain sight.

I similarly approached my Bible, with its massive page count and hidden meanings obscuring the "robins". Countless people have read the Bible over millennia of generations, and many complained of its elusive content, or that it contradicted itself. Readers are simply put off by the sheer volume of 66 books, its complex history, and meticulous lineage listings. I had complained of it all while reading my Bible and not grasping its passages. Feeling it dry and empty, especially as a new Christian, I was often frustrated by my lack of understanding.

My eyes began to open to more than the dry grass, the robins appearing one at a time. I would find a bright spot through learning a verse, digging a little deeper, and prayerfully seeking what God could be communicating to me. As I have grown, read my Bible through and through, end to end many times, I searched for answers and asked for more understanding. God has opened my eyes to more fullness, revealing many "robins", more than I ever could have imagined.

The beauty of God's word is in layer upon layer of wisdom, His outpouring of love, and even His careful discipline. The mystery of His plan gently unfolds, and our hope in Christ grows. The Word is the display of His power, the glory of His Being, and the promise of His eternal care. But what I love most about His word is the revelation of God's character. I am in awe that He laid aside the splendor of His holiness as He was birthed as one of His very own creations. Living in plain sight, few recognized the King of Glory.

So, is the Bible worth studying? I would shout a resounding "YES!" It is God's very words spoken to those who have ears to hear and eyes to see. It is light for the lost, love for the lonely, and food for every hungry heart. It is our unbreakable chain, the link to our eternal and almighty God, the foundation of our trust and faith. And through it, He will reveal many "robins" of revelation as we seek Him.

"How sweet are your words to my taste, sweeter than honey to my mouth! I gain understanding from your precepts…your word is a lamp to my feet and a light for my path…The unfolding of your words gives light; it gives understanding to the simple….All your words are true; all your righteous laws are eternal." Psalm 119:103, 105, 130, 160

"For the word of God is living and active. Sharper than any double-edged sword, it penetrates even to dividing soul and spirit, joints and marrow; it judges the thoughts and attitudes of the heart." Hebrews 4:12

April

Moon Over My Shoulder

This Moment

Nothing is as brilliantly beautiful as spring's newness. The vibrant daffodils brave the last snowfall, poking their sunny faces above its chill. The spring storms scrub newly born leaves into riotous greens. New lives appear in the fields, and the days are bathed in new light. Spring bears an expectation of new beginnings, and hope hung on rainbows. Its lengthening days give rise to increased opportunity. It is a season of birthing and wonder, the silence of death exploding to re-energized life.

Last spring, I noticed that its colors are very much like the colors of autumn, more subdued, but similar. The trees on the hillsides hinted at reds, greens, and yellows, not shouting their presence, but gently coloring the mosaic of the forest. Autumn, with no reservation, shouts umber, crimson, and gold. Both seasons share tints the same, just differing intensities.

Reflecting on life again, I realized why I had always focused on spring—it is a beginning. It is a clean slate, a fresh perspective, daring and audacious, pregnant with possibility. Summer fuels our days with expectation. Autumn counts down to the launch of winter, death, stillness, and the quietness of hibernation. That is how most of us process the seasonal changes. Today, however, I am changing my mind. Today I will not focus on what is ahead, reminding myself instead to focus upon this moment.

How spectacular life can be when all my focus is on today, this moment, this season. How much more exciting life is, in every season, when I do not wish away the days at hand! It is the same with the seasons of life; I can long for my spring, chase after my summer-gone, but must acknowledge my autumn has come, and winter will follow.

Today is the day for me to shout in brilliant colors, and to softly serve in the shortening daylight. It is my time to revel in all God has done in the length of my days, and to testify of His mercies never failing, in every season. Today is the opportunity to live life to its fullest, to drink in the colors along the path the Lord has laid out for me. In Him, there is hope never failing, and the adventure of spring in every path, as I am following the Creator of Seasons. His intentions toward me are good, with a sound hope for the future, whatever my season.

"There is a time for everything, and a season for every activity under heaven: A time to be born and a time to die, a time to plant and a time to uproot…"   Ecclesiastes 3:1-2

"But I trust in you, O Lord; I say, 'You are my God.' My times are in your hands…" Psalm 31:14-15a

Tornado!   April 2

The emergency siren for our town simultaneously blared with the alert on my phone. Still deep in dreams, it startled me awake. Launching from my bed, which is not characteristic of my morning routine, I ran to the back door. The sky seemed normal, just rain and fast-moving low clouds from the south. Walking to the front of the house and gazing over the eastern sky, I again saw only rain and light wind. Three young men stood on the neighbor's porch calmly observing, too. "Typical guys, they're not going inside," I thought. That's when I prayed!

By the time I whispered my request for protection, the wind was quite gusty. The young men next door, now nowhere to be seen—spoke volumes! Suddenly, the trees bent to nearly 90 degrees under the blast of wind, and the rain became a deafening downpour. In an instant, a wall of water began swirling horizontally around our house in a circle; and I knew it was too late to run. It was over as quickly as it began. The storm left three trees down, thankfully not on top of our house. And mysteriously, everything on our porch was saturated in places never before touched, yet nothing out of place.

It was obvious to me that God had answered my breathless prayer, and placed His hand over our house, as well as the young men on the porch next door. Many thanks flowed from my heart and through my mouth that day. We have a God who hears us and watches over us. I wondered, though, if things had turned out differently, could I still have thanked my Father? Gazing in retrospect over my life, I would have to say yes, I could. There have been many hardships, tragedies, and trials along the way. I have learned to trust Him in the darkness, to thank Him for His goodness, and look for His protection and provision in them.

God does not leave us in difficult or tragic times. I believe that if we search for Him, He is always willing to be found. He does not hide; He does not run away. When the disciples were on a boat in a dangerous storm, Jesus slept. He was present; they just didn't call on Him until they couldn't do anything on their own. And when they did call on Him, He did not delay their rescue.

When I have the most difficulty finding Jesus, I discover it is most often I who have hidden or run away. The reasons for running from Him are many. For me, they tend to be guilt, or not feeling worthy of His love and care. He simply asks me to trust Him in the storm, even if it turns into a tornado. And whether I can see Him, or He seems invisible, I am exceedingly thankful that He holds me, even when I let go of Him. Storms don't last forever, and every storm in life will eventually pass, but His love and care never will.

"The disciples went and woke him, saying, 'Master, Master, we're going to drown!' He got up and rebuked the wind and the raging waters; the storm subsided, and all was calm. 'Where is your faith?' he asked his disciples." Luke 8:24

Too Many Mockingbirds April 3

On the porch railing outside my window, a fledgling mockingbird puffed out her new downy plumage and settled in, awaiting the next tasty morsel from her mama. Suddenly her brother lighted on the railing beside her and hopped along until he found a cozy spot to scan the horizon for his mama's return. It was a treat for me to witness this family adventure, to see up close that which is normally hidden.

Six weeks later, I noticed several full-grown Mockingbirds playing in my backyard. I have never been a fan of these imposters. They perch in the tree outside my window at night, making a racket without ceasing. They mimic the other songbirds, trying to lure them away from their nests, invading and robbing them, eating their eggs. The Mockingbirds were cute and fun to watch as young ones, but completely annoying and destructive as adults.

I don't believe it is an accident that God placed Mockingbirds in our lives. To me, they are a constant reminder of another common enemy, Satan. We tend to see him as not very threatening, and sometimes even cute and somewhat lovable, like a cartoon character. We embrace his deceptions with welcome arms when they please us. His distractions are entertaining, and his diversions are welcomed when God's way seems too difficult. But his deceit is alluring, captivating, and then dangerous; it is eventually fatal for us, as surely as the eggs in the songbird's nest.

It often takes a trained ear, hearing the real thing, to distinguish which song is the actual songbird's and which is the Mockingbird's imitation. It has taken years to figure it out. So it is, also, separating the voice and tactics of the enemy of humankind, from the voice of its Savior. One seeks to destroy; the other offers life.

The only way I have learned to tell the difference is by training my heart to the sound of Jesus's voice alone, then comparing it with what I am hearing in the world. Jesus's voice comes alive through His words. His words speak truth and life; He never lies, never deceives, never kills, steals, or destroys. He is faithful, self-sacrificing, and loving. He brings hope, healing, forgiveness, grace, and clarifies the difference between the Mockingbird liar and the Spirit of Truth. And in this case, one Mockingbird is too many.

"My sheep hear my voice, and I know them, and they follow Me; and I give eternal life to them, and they will never perish; and no one will snatch them out of my hand." John 10:27

"The thief comes only to steal, and kill, and destroy. I have come that they may have life and have it abundantly." John 10:10

A planner by nature and usually punctual, I will admit to being a tad more relaxed about perfect timing lately. On a day where I could not afford to be one minute late, of course, the unexpected event would intrude on my schedule, completely throwing off the timing. I prayed continually to my destination, sighing with relief as I pulled into the parking space. I had arrived right on time, exactly where God wanted me to be, even though it seemed there was no chance of it an hour prior.

I am thoroughly convinced, through many such incidents, that God is ultimately in control of time. He can remove obstacles and expand and stretch time as necessary to achieve His purposes. He steps in and intervenes when the impossible is, well, impossible. God made the sun stand still to ensure victory for His people and held back the roaring waters of the split sea until Israel's pursuers were positioned for defeat. At the very moment the Hebrew children were thrown into the fire, God deemed them fireproof, and as Daniel was tossed into the lion's den, hungry as they were, God instantly sealed their mouths until dawn.

God showed up right on time when Jesus happened to be walking the road where Zaccheus was hanging out in a tree. And in the crush of a crowd, the woman in need of healing was able to skim the hem of His robe, instantly healed. Jesus appeared at just the right time to heal Peter's mother-in-law. Raising Lazarus from the dead after four days, though everyone strenuously protested, solidified the identity of Jesus as the Son of God.

Every instance in the Bible and every moment of our lives, God is ever-present but seems to delight in showing up when we least expect, always in perfect timing, if not ours, always His. My husband, as a new Christian, began to quote, "God is never early, but He is never late." And I have found it to be quite true, as evidenced not only in my life but throughout the Bible.

The flip side is, of course, the tragedies where we wonder where God was in its timing. He is there, too, and though we cannot, in our finite minds, comprehend the "why", we trust the "Who". His timing in all things is perfect; He works His plan in heavenly wisdom and ultimate love. We can trust that He holds each of us in the palm of His hand, not allowing anything which will not work for our eternal good and His infinite Glory. He is never early, nor ever late, but always right on time.

"Find rest, O my soul, in God alone; my hope comes from him…Trust in him at all times, O people; pour out your heart to him, for God is our refuge." Psalm 62:5, 8

"Peace I leave with you; my peace I give you. I do not give to your as the world gives. Do not let your hearts be troubled and do not be afraid." John 14:27

Building Plans   April 5

From the age of six, I began drawing floor plans. Houses, particularly, fascinated me. They seemed like puzzles to be assembled, finding the right order of it, the necessary flow that would make it beneficial. Since then, I have observed many houses being built, and am ever curious about the process and logic of it. I remain fascinated by architecture and building today, many years removed from six.

Curiosity pricked at me concerning the cornerstones mentioned in the Bible. They are not used as much in today's construction methods. Looking up the definition, I understood it to be the first stone laid at the foundation of a new building, but oh, it is so much more! I watched a YouTube video by a stonemason who defined it well. He said that the cornerstone is the best stone, having no fissures or flaws so it can support the weight of the building without cracking. It is also the quality of stone by which the rest of the stones will be matched, the representation of the rest of the stones to be used. Equally important, it is the key to the orientation of the building; it is the plumb line and level which measures true in all directions. If the cornerstone is off, the building will tilt and eventually succumb to gravity. Cornerstones are also sometimes used at the top corner of a building in its completion.

Now the full weight of the meaning began to settle in my heart. Our Creator laid the foundations of our world and named Jesus as its cornerstone. Jesus is the one beyond compare, the quality stone that the entire foundation of God's kingdom would be built upon, a stone rare and pure, of unequaled strength and beauty. He is the stone to which the other stones are compared, the key to the direction and strength of the building, the Body of Christ. He is our beginning foundation, and He is also our cornerstone capping off the building of our faith. Jesus is my foundation and my direction, the Chief Cornerstone of His Father's amazing building plans.

"As you come to him, the living Stone, rejected by men but chosen by God and precious to him---you also, like living stones are being built into a spiritual house to be a holy priesthood...." I Peter 2:4

"For He rescued us from the domain of darkness and transferred us to the kingdom of His beloved Son, in whom we have redemption, the forgiveness of sins. He is the image of the invisible God, the firstborn of all creation. For by Him all things were created, both in the heavens and on earth, visible and invisible, whether thrones or dominions or ruler or authorities---all things have been created through Him and for Him. He is before all things, and in Him all things hold together. He is also the head of the body, the church; and He is the beginning, the firstborn from the dead, so that He Himself will come to have first place in everything..." Colossians 1:13-19

Three excruciating trials circled my head like vultures, awaiting the last breath of their prey. One of the trials dragged on and on, a seemingly never-ending saga of painful dealings with a giant company, not at all interested in resolving the problem at hand. The second "hover-er" was related to taxes and the IRS, and it seemed the waiting would never end. The third vulture, was completely out of my hands, requiring prayer for protection and resolution. The only way forward was to trust God with each of them, day by day.

Each day, I prayed, and every day I trusted that God would take care of the problems, but the problems greeted each day unresolved for months. Every day, two of the three grew worse instead of better. The horizon appeared murky and unclear, quite dark at times, but in the middle of my trifecta storm, there was peace. I had no idea how God would resolve any of the problems, but I have walked with Jesus long enough to know that no problem is beyond His power.

Burdens can abound, troubles can agitate, conflicts can irritate, but only Jesus can initiate peace in the middle of them. Jesus slept on a fishing boat being swamped by waves, tossed at their tops, and pitched into their bottoms; the threat of sinking real enough to alarm seasoned captains. Yet when His fishermen-disciples awakened Him, he was dismayed by their fear. His words were unsettlingly calm, His command to the sea firm, "Be still!" As if calming a naughty child, He spoke, yet the wind and waves immediately obeyed the Master of the Universe.

Jesus understands our difficulties, but He is not upset by them. He is upset, rather, by the tendency we have, as His children, to underestimate His ability to help us and His power to save us. There is not a problem that exists in this world that He cannot resolve, but we must trust that when He appears to be sleeping, not attentive to our needs, He is still in control.

I do not understand why it was necessary to walk through the three problems and may never. One problem was finally resolved, by the grace of God, with adequate closure. The second turned out overwhelmingly in my favor, and the third is ongoing; no intervention but prayer will suffice. I was able to thank God profusely for all of them, trusting that each, in some way, was for my ultimate good. In His hand only is the power to change everything that confounds, exasperates, and binds me. Like the waves on the sea and the gale winds driving my boat, Jesus is with me; and when the time is right, He will command, and they will obey. The darkness will eventually depart, but even if not, my hope will remain in Him alone, day by day.

"The Lord is gracious and righteous; our God is full of compassion. The Lord protects the simple-hearted; when I was in great need, he saved me. Be at rest once more, O my soul, for the Lord has been good to you." Psalm 116:5-7

Extreme Opposites

Listening expectantly, I hear the gentle pings of water drops on the roof of my drought-parched house, gliding over the shingles and trickling through the gutters. It has been a witheringly hot season, scorching my grass and wilting my basil. Though I welcomed the rain, across our country many have experienced massive flooding, which devastated crops and washed through whole communities. Elsewhere in the world, catastrophic rivers flowed where none previously existed, bobbing cars and houses on their currents. Rain can be desired and welcomed or dreaded.

Bonfires and fire pits evoke thoughts of hot dogs and S'mores, warmth, and sparks fleeting innocuously into the air on a fall evening. At the same time this year, volcanoes in Hawaii and Guatemala are erupting, spewing ash skyward, emitting deadly gasses, and forcing red-hot lava flows through entire neighborhoods on their trek to the ocean. Like water, fire can be desirable or lethal.

Just as rain and fire can be welcoming or dreadful, so is there a day coming for every human being on earth. It is the day of death. Death will place us at the feet of the Living God and will be recognized as judgment day. There is no escaping it—it is a certainty, as much so as the floodwaters rushing toward us, or the lava flowing with certainty on its inevitable path.

Our choice must be made on this side of the divide, a choice to embrace Jesus or reject the Son of God. If having lived life rejecting Him, then I will stand on my own merits. I know instinctively that regardless of my good intentions, I have failed to live perfectly in the eyes of our Holy and Righteous God, who can accept nothing less than perfection. Thankfully, I have chosen wisely to follow Jesus, who has forgiven and cleansed me. When I stand in welcome reunion with Him after passing from this life, there will be no condemnation, never-ending flames, nor the absence of His Presence. I will pass into the brilliant light of His love, into Paradise unimaginable, and unending peace for eternity. Until then, I will trust that no matter what life brings, He can overcome any "extreme" I face.

"But you have come to Mount Zion, to the heavenly Jerusalem, the city of the living God. You have come to thousands upon thousands of angels in joyful assembly, to the church of the firstborn, whose names are written in heaven. You have come to God, the judge of all men, to the spirits of righteous men made perfect, to Jesus the mediator of a new covenant, and to the sprinkled blood that speaks a better word than the blood of Abel. See to it that you do not refuse him who speaks…Therefore since we are receiving a kingdom that cannot be shaken, let us be thankful and so worship God acceptably with reverence and awe, for our God is a consuming fire." Hebrews 12:22-25a, 28, 29

A Face I Will Never Forget   April 8

It couldn't have been more than a month or two old, standing on the shoulder of Interstate 40 in the summer's sweltering heat. The young fawn still displayed its baby spots as it wobbled on weary, long legs. It was trembling visibly as it tried to breathe, exhausted in the heat. The fawn's mouth was open, parched tongue hanging, head drooped as it wearily gazed across the lanes of traffic moving at 80 miles per hour. Its mother had made it across the highway, but it had not.

It was only visible for about 3 seconds as I passed but was eternally etched upon my mind. To this day, it brings tears to my eyes knowing that its fate was evident; without its mother to guide it, death was the only outcome possible. That moment, God brought words to my mind, so vividly that I will never forget them, either. "That is you without Me."

I realized that my need for Him is so great, primal, and complete that I will die without Him. Without Him, I can do nothing. I cannot breathe, cannot heal, cannot function. Without Him, I cannot be forgiven. I am not capable of standing in His holy Presence. Without Him, I am merely dust. Without Him, I am that fawn on the edge of the highway destined to die.

Our "divide", the highway of certain death needing to be crossed, is the temptation to sin, that every human being instinctively understands. We intuitively understand that we can never overcome it on our own. We recognize good and evil, and intuitively know there is a righteous and holy God we will have to stand before one day.

Unless there is a guide to deliver me safely to the other side, I will languish in my self-will, in this stubborn, rebellious flesh that I contend with every day. Within my heart is resistance to doing anything God's way; insisting on my control is one of the deadly vehicles that will mow me down. And the world itself, the powers that rule it, and the one who seeks to destroy God's children, will happily try, as well.

As that doe was most certainly distraught by the absence of her fawn, Jesus expressed something similar in His parable of the lost sheep. He is not content to leave us abandoned. He seeks us out, then rejoices when we are "found" and brought back to our rightful place by His side. As we abide there, we find comfort for our souls that we can find nowhere else.

It has been five years since I witnessed that fawn hopelessly clinging to his place within a mere thirty-six inches of traffic, and I can still see it as if it was an hour ago. Whenever I need to find my place at Jesus' side again, I need to remember; He is the rescuer of the weak, lost, and weary. He is the One I need to follow, without hesitation wherever He leads, and the face I need never forget.

"My sheep listen to my voice; I know them, and they follow me." John 10:27

Car Quest April 9

With three teens in the house and the first approaching licensing status, I can recount the frenzy of thoughts swirling like a tornado in my mind: Which car will she be able to safely drive? Can I afford another car? What options do I need? What about servicing? Where do I look? How much should I pay? Do I trade my old one in or sell it outright? How long will mine last until I can afford another? How will we afford so many drivers in the family???

It is so easy to work myself into a panic as I face any challenge life brings and consider all the possibilities. (Feel free to replace "car" with anything in your life you are worried about—just saying!) Looking back at that car quest years later, I recognize that all my worry was fruitless. All three children ended up with vehicles to drive, we did not go broke, and thankfully they all had a minor fender-bender (instilling the better part of caution in them).

Thankfully, most things in life are like that car quest. Problems may loom as obstacles in our paths, but how we face them, the trust we place in ourselves or God, determine the stress level we encounter. The less trust I place in my heavenly Father to provide for and protect me, the more burden I place on my own back, and the heavier the load to carry.

How easy it is to forget that my Father understands my needs and provides for me! There is peace in trusting Him to provide what He knows I need. He knows before I know, and He honors my trust in Him. I have learned much about not being anxious, as He has proved himself many times over the years. You can trust Him, too, whatever quest you encounter; I promise.

"Jesus said, 'For this reason I say to you, do not be worried about your life, as to what you will eat or what you will drink; nor for your body, what you will put on.'" Matthew 6:25 (And I would add, "Or what you will drive!")

"Your heavenly Father knows that you need these things." Matthew 6:32

Free to Be Loved   April 10

Though treasured dearly, my Bible study groups were not easy to stick with. At one point, my "reason" was that my husband was ill with a chronic disease. Later, after he passed, it was that I was single and didn't fit with couples, or that I was older, or... Even after finding the group I currently attend, I struggled to "fit".

I have learned much about myself over the recent years and have a better understanding of the "problem", which is *me*. Thinking of myself as an extrovert all these years, it was shocking to me to realize I am quite an introvert. But I found something even more fundamentally broken, and that is my understanding of how God sees me. If I don't understand and accept that God not only loves me, but likes and delights in me as His child through Christ, how can I feel secure in myself, and my relationships with others? The bottom line is that I cannot.

I realized much of this as I read one of my journal entries from twenty years ago. It startled me to see that I had not changed much in my understanding of what Jesus had done for me. I remained in guilt and fear, largely because I believed I had to FEEL loved and accepted. Emotions are not reliable, even when they involve God. Whether I feel loved and saved by His grace, or not, doesn't change the FACT that I AM LOVED, and SAVED. Once I began to grasp that, my relationship with my Father changed, because it was no longer based on emotion.

The beauty of this realization was that it freed me to be who my Father, in His wisdom, created me to be. It has freed me to be more authentic with people, and more real within my relationships. It has freed me from fear and doubt because I know, even as a young child trusts her daddy to protect and provide for her, that I can trust my heavenly Father. I may not LIKE things I have to go through, but I have His peace and know His love while walking through them.

I am not alone in being raised without a father here on earth. There are many, many individuals in our culture and worldwide who have never known a father's love and care, who have no example to compare to God. I can tell you, though, that it matters not with God the Father. Regardless of your circumstances, He desires to show Himself to you and to keep His promises. He knows no restrictions, and no boundaries in His love toward you. In a relationship with Jesus, you are free to be loved.

"We have come to know and have believed the love which God has for us. God is love and the one who abides in love abides in God, and God abides in him...We love because he first loved us." I John 4:16, 19

Dropping Anchor

The old anchor stood stalwartly on guard at the entrance to the bay, an ancient reminder of mariners sailing in and out to sea. This beast of an anchor was painted white, I presume to inhibit rust, and propped in an upright position of honor; the full weight of its authority against the tides and currents on display. It is difficult to imagine this mammoth chunk of iron being hoisted and lowered by anything short of a miracle in a frothing ocean.

The decision to drop anchor was the captain's decision, which was relayed to the ship's crew, who executed the order. The anchor would then sink to the full extension of its chain, digging into the water's bottom. Holding down the end of the chain, it essentially tethered the ship. Without an anchor, the ship would continually drift, carried by the currents into hazardous rocks and reefs.

Each day, we choose the type of anchor we will drop into the ocean of our lives. There is a choice to be made about the type of anchor we decide to use. We can choose to drop an anchor of fear, one that holds us back, preventing us from reaching what God has for us. That anchor keeps us from making headway in our journey with God, paralyzing us in the water. Or we can choose an anchor of trust, one which plants us firmly into the ocean bed of faith in God, an anchor which protects us from destruction in the storms.

Having weathered many tempests, I confess that my faith during some of the storms has, at times, wavered and my anchor dropped on the side of fear rather than faith. But God is always faithful, always gentle, and always secure. He teaches me, through the experience of each storm, that the only anchor I can depend on is weighted in Him. And His cross stands stalwartly in the bay of my life; I can rely on no other anchor to prevent my inclination to drift. Dropping the dependable anchor of trust in what Jesus has done on my behalf brings me life each day.

"We have this hope as an anchor for the soul, firm and secure. It enters the inner sanctuary behind the curtain, where Jesus, who went before us, has entered on our behalf." Hebrews 6:19

"This is what the Lord says: 'Cursed is the one who trusts in man, who depends on flesh for his strength and whose heart turns away from the Lord…But blessed is the man who trusts in the Lord, whose confidence is in him. He will be like a tree planted by the water that sends out its roots by the stream. It does not fear when heat comes; its leaves are always green. It has no worries in a year of drought and never fails to bear fruit.'" Jeremiah 17:5, 7-8

The Sink Hole April 12

Considering all the rocks in my part of the world, I was alarmed and amazed that this area is at such great risk for sinkholes, one of the highest in the country. A sinkhole is, essentially, the underlying rock eroding and the topsoil collapsing into a large, previously underground, cavern. They can be any size, but many are a hundred feet in diameter and can be that many feet deep. And I found that I live near a whole string of them!

The ground can drop at any moment, accompanied by houses, cars, trees, cows, or whatever is sitting on that idyllic land, with no prior notice. One of the largest in the United States is the "Golly Hole" and located in Shelby County in central Alabama. That sinkhole is the size of a football field and 120 feet deep.

That is pretty scary, but not nearly as scary as an interview I heard with a popular actor a long time ago. When asked if he was at peace with himself, he answered, "There's one thing that's still inside, and that's kind of a yearning. What that yearning is I'm not totally sure. But whatever it is, it can't quite get quenched. I think it's a need, a seeking of completeness. I think that's one quality of life that's common to all of us."

When I finished reading his comments, my heart sank; I understood what he was expressing, because my heart, also, had once experienced the same emptiness, a heart without Jesus. The heart without Jesus is similar to that sinkhole, with nothing supporting it, and nothing in it. There is no purpose to life, no real meaning, just empty holes needing something to fill them.

And those holes are dangerous to the people around them because the people we love cannot fill that hole, either. We forever search for someone, or something, to fill it. We look to bucket-list experiences, emotional rushes, adrenaline kicks, anything to fill the nagging gap in our souls. Cars, houses, material things of all sorts, cannot fill it. Sports, money, games, clothes, animals, nothing works for long, leaving a lonely, bottomless pit beneath our feet.

Because of Jesus, the hole in my heart has been filled to overflowing and the pit of despair filled to the brim with Living Water. His limitless mercy has flooded my soul, and His forgiveness vanquished the depth of the darkness awaiting me. God's love plumbed the cave of despair and broke its bonds, freeing this captive by His grace, and setting my feet once again on solid rock. The fear is overcome and peace rests in its place. The sinkhole in every heart, whether it can be realized by them or not, is the essential need of Jesus.

"Salvation is found in no one else, for there is no other name under heaven given to men by which we must be saved." Acts 4:12

Lying awake in the middle of the night, fear slashed at my heart, carving out any courage remaining. Bills had come due that I had no practical way of paying, and I could find no path of escape. I knew that I could expect the calls for collection to come, as surely as the approaching dawn. Though it was many years ago, I remember that grip of fear, of the feeling of desperation with no rescuer in sight, and I was at wit's end.

Many prayers had ascended on my behalf, but the path before me had not dissolved, and a resolution still lingered in the fog. As I hovered in my tenuous position, my Father heard my prayers but did not send the expected answer. Instead of sending the proverbial cavalry, He sent an insight as to why I had to embrace the pain. It was time to deal with the fear.

Fear was the insidious dark root choking me to death financially, fearing that I wouldn't have what I wanted or needed, and fearing people's expectations. I was also fearful of what I might lose. And pride worked as a potent fertilizer. I had to reexamine the level of trust I had with my heavenly Father, and when it came to my finances, my trust was like a vapor gone with the morning sun. I knew what the answer was; it all boiled down to training myself to trust God with all my wants *and* needs.

Slowly, I worked my way out of debt, learned to save more, and trained myself to be less focused on possessions. Being content with what God had given me meant holding everything with an open hand, not a clenched fist. In the beginning, I came into this world with nothing, and I will leave it the same way. Possessions are meaningless in the grand scheme of eternity.

That was the point Jesus was making in **Hebrews 13:5: "Keep your lives free from the love of money _and_ be content with what you have, _because_ God has said, 'Never will I leave you; never will I forsake you.'"** I did not need to worry or fear, but trust in the One who will never leave me; WHO I need far outweighs WHAT I need.

I weathered the crisis, and God set my feet on solid ground. I learned to trust His principles of money, and I have lived on less. Though there is always more to learn, trust in my Father has grown and the lessons are less painful, as well as less frequent. His purpose is never to deprive us, but always to bless us. Trusting Him, the stress is removed, and peace prevails. My Father is faithful, sleep is peaceful, and I find myself rarely at wit's end.

"So we say with confidence, 'The Lord is my helper, I will not be afraid. What can man do to me?'" Hebrews 13:6

"But godliness with contentment is great gain. For we brought nothing into the world, and we can take nothing out of it. But if we have food and clothing, we will be content with that." 1 Timothy 6:6-8

Two pair of round black eyes, set in fluffy white coats, peered expectantly at me, as persuasively as possible for two little Maltese dogs. I had placed their food bowls in the normal spot and walked away. My dogs have been so spoiled, so entitled, that even a bag rustling in the kitchen draws their sassy demands. Now, with those coaxing gazes, they were clearly conveying their message to me, "Where's the rest???" They were disappointed at the contents, pleading for the "good stuff" that I had so callously denied them, and they felt strongly entitled to more.

To make matters worse, I laughed. It was so funny to me because I suddenly saw a mental picture of myself with God, asking for "more" when I clearly had enough, or for something different than what He had given me. I ask for situations to change, and they don't. I ask for more money, I end up having less income. I ask for increased wisdom, and my foolishness surfaces. Sometimes, I simply neglect to ask altogether. You get the idea; we have all been on the asking end of prayers that seem to never find the answers or timing we desire, no matter how noble.

When the requests don't appear to match the answers, I am learning to do two things. The first is to examine my request; if it doesn't line up with what God outlines in Scripture, it will likely not be answered. God often protects us from ourselves through His non-response to these requests; sometimes, we don't see how our request will affect us, or others, in the future. Sometimes, no matter what Sunday-best in which we dress them, our requests are purely selfish or self-serving. Our motives often disqualify our requests.

The second thing I am learning is that God is Sovereign and powerful, enough so to take care of anything in life that comes my way. He knows me and created me for His purpose on this earth. He designed me to be part of His plan of revealing Jesus to the world. He also intimately knows what I need. He formed me, shaping my personality and inner being to fulfill that role, plus much more. He created me to fellowship and walk closely with Him, to follow the sound of His voice, and hear the whisper of His heart.

We can turn our "entitlement" into trust. God, our Father, is pleased with our expectant prayers and the boldness of our requests. And I believe, even our demands for His attention He finds delightful. We are His children, children He dearly loves, children of the King. When we come to Him, even with our skewed expectations, because of Jesus we are entitled to our Father's favor and blessing, not because we deserve it, but because Jesus does.

"Be joyful always; pray continually; give thanks in all circumstances, for this is god's will for you in Christ Jesus." 1 Thessalonians 5:16-18

"But seek first his kingdom and his righteousness, and all these things will be given to you as well." Matthew 6:33

Monkey's Transformation

Pocketbook draped around her neck and "Monkey" tucked under her arm, our daughter Blair found the two accessories indispensable. Monkey was a second-hand sock monkey when she adopted him, and he never left her side thereafter. Many stitches and emergency surgeries ensued in that monkey's lifetime, and after a while, not even stitches would keep him together.

One day, when the stitches I lovingly placed wouldn't hold, Blair took Monkey to her daddy to fix. What is the one "fix" most dads have on hand? Duct tape, of course! Over time, Monkey's duct tape "Band-Aid" was expanded and layered, until he was finally dubbed "Space Monkey". It was a transformation that enabled him to follow Blair on her adventures, much longer than he would otherwise have lasted.

Thinking back on that transformation, I realized I am a lot like that sock monkey. When I was younger, I had little need for "repairs". I felt I had much of my life under control. However, life saw to it that receiving my share of disappointments, hurts, and wounds, I was not overlooked. I was finally willing to admit that virtually nothing, except my personal decisions, was under my control.

Upon becoming a Christian, I, like Monkey, have undergone a similar transformation. With each wound, I ran to my Father God, and He lovingly dressed it in Band-Aids when they were small, and battle dressings when they were overwhelming. He administered His special "duct tape" to hold me together when the wounds were deep. So, in a sense, I guess you could say I have completed the transformation to "space suit".

The "suit" I wear on this earth will not last indefinitely. And when I arrive at my final destination, I will be issued attire suitable for heaven, one which will never require mending. It will last through every adventure and journey I encounter in eternity, and I will have undergone the best, and final, transformation. For now, I have begun running to Him, not just for mending, but because I love Him.

Like Monkey, I am ready for every adventure, not in my limited capabilities, but through those of my Savior. His covering of grace is all the transformation, and spacesuit, I need.

"For our citizenship is in heaven, from which also we eagerly wait for a Savior, the Lord Jesus Christ; who will transform the body of our humble state into conformity with the body of His glory, by the exertion of the power that He has even to subject all things to Himself."
Philippians 3:20, 21

A Perfect World

If I could change everything I *wanted* to change, could ask God to change everything I *couldn't* change, and could be happy with everything that *wouldn't* change, I would be content, right? Somehow, it just doesn't work that way. The days I have strategically laid out morph uncontrollably into changes I neither planned nor welcomed. An unexpected trip to the hospital—change! Family and friends absent during a pandemic—change! The washer and dryer needing to be urgently replaced—change! A traffic accident—change!

Life is always changing, schedules are disrupted with the unexpected, and rarely have I been happy with the changes such as friends who have moved far away, family members who have passed to the next life, the transitions of life stages, children who make choices where the painful consequences are apparent to me, but not to them. Changing residences, finding new friends, employment issues, medical and/or financial stress, all force modifications in life.

The quip, "The only thing you can count on in life is death and taxes" would be more accurate if it included "death, taxes, and change". I have become less daunted by the daily changes as I have recognized that change is inevitable and often wonderful. The change of jobs can be refreshing and exciting. A new baby brings a new depth of love, delight, and wonder, as well as the increased task load and lack of sleep. A new season often brings growth opportunities, if I am willing to embrace them.

It is a wonderful thing that God does not task me with approving all the changes in my life. Many exquisite gifts would have been overlooked and many precious times never realized, if my wisdom had prevailed over His. I am learning, albeit slowly, to roll with the changes, trusting God's superior wisdom for my life, and appreciating the wonders of His provision and protection throughout them all.

How many things in my life would I change? Honestly, not many. Each change has instructed me, taught me patience, understanding, trust, and even love. I have learned, and am learning, to appreciate what I have at this moment, to be content with little or much, to trust my Father for all I need, and to be thankful in everything. No, this is not a perfect world, and it will never be—until Jesus returns to rule it. And that one will be nothing short of heaven, and the most welcome change of all.

"I know what it is to be in need, and I know what it is to have plenty. I have learned the secret of being content in any and every situation, whether well fed or hungry, whether living in plenty or in want. I can do everything through him who gives me strength."
Philippians 4:12-13

The Interstate highway was, as usual, nearly bumper to bumper with big-rig trucks, cars, and every type of vehicle. We had embarked on our family's first trip into the city. Together with our teenage children, for the first time in quite a while, we were all looking forward to our time together on this rain-soaked Saturday. After my husband passed one of the eighteen-wheelers, he eased his way back into the right lane and onto water-filled grooves in the pavement, propelling us into a free-wheeling hydroplane.

The sudden impact with the guard rail sent our fifteen-year-old son flying out of the car, onto the pavement. Thankfully, the very eighteen-wheelers we had passed, slowed traffic behind them and prevented our son from being run over. In the 30 minutes it took the ambulance to deliver him to the hospital, I could only repeat, "Thank you, Jesus!" Quite miraculously, he sustained no internal injuries, no head injury, and no broken bones.

The night before we embarked on that trip, we talked about the day we would have, what time we would leave, where we would go, and our return. We anticipated wonderful memories. We assumed our day. Yet nothing turned out as we had planned. A totaled car was not in the plan; a hospital visit was not in the schedule; the resultant memories and nightmares were not anticipated; the reality of being far from home for such an event had been unthinkable. Our plan had been disrupted and our confidence was shaken.

After analyzing the event and speaking with a state highway patrolman, we learned that many people had hydroplaned in that section each time it rained. Many had died on that stretch of highway, including one woman who had died that very day, following our incident. As we considered each detail of that accident, we could also see the details of God's provision. A bystander had offered an umbrella; the motorcycle trying to avoid us slid within inches of my husband as he exited the car; the ambulance hydroplaned three times on the way to the hospital, yet arrived safely; the truckers aligned to protect us by blocking traffic.

Many times, since that incident, it has come to mind that though we make plans, it is God who orders our day. It is God who commands the outcome of every event. Our pride has us believe that we control everything. In reality, we control nothing but our will to trust Him, or not. Whether the day delivers good news or unwanted revelations, we can trust our Father who loves us in our todays and holds us in our tomorrows.

"Now listen, you who say, 'Today or tomorrow we will go to this or that city, spend a year there, carry on business and make money.' Why, you do not even know what will happen tomorrow. What is your life: You are a mist that appears for a little while and then vanishes. Instead, you ought to say, 'If it is the Lord's will, we will live and do this or that.'"
James 4:13-15

A Chipper Morning April 18

Very early on a Saturday morning, too early, in my opinion, my phone rang, and I was informed that the tree removal crew had arrived. A very large pine tree had fallen from our neighbor's yard and hung itself in the top of our River Birch during a storm. At seven A.M. on a Saturday morning, I repeat, they descended on my yard with chain saws and chipper roaring.

I was fascinated by one very nimble man, with a blazing chainsaw in hand, who walked the inclined trunk like a cat balancing on the back of a living room couch. He sawed off each limb as he made his way rather quickly up the thick trunk, jumping up and down gingerly to test its stability near the top. Men scrambled about under him dragging each branch to the monster chipper, which greedily devoured each one.

The last step in the process was cutting the huge trunk, surprisingly beginning from the bottom instead of the top. Step by step, they sized up the lengths to be cut, drew their blades through the wood, and the tree that was so tall slowly shrank, as though melting in the early morning sun. Another machine picked up the pieces and loaded them into the massive chipper, as my mouth dropped in awe; that chipper swallowed even the massive trunk sections, making them disappear almost immediately. The early morning rise was worth every minute, just to watch the chipper in action.

I gazed in fascination as it occurred to me that God disposes of all our sins just like that massive chipper, as thoroughly and dramatically. When He says He casts our sins as far as the east is from the west, it is as though they are thrown into that giant woodchipper; and God's ability to remove sin makes that chipper look pretty lame. Jesus paid a hefty price, one that is inconceivable to our understanding, making us free of our sins once and for all.

If you tend to keep remembering your sins, just picture the giant woodchipper. Toss those sins into God's gracious hands! He has already disposed of your guilt through the blood of Jesus, and your sins were shredded and hauled away, never to be remembered again. Make it a "chipper morning" as you begin your day, fresh and whole in the love of Jesus.

"The Lord is compassionate and gracious, slow to anger, abounding in love. He will not always accuse, nor will he harbor his anger forever; he does not treat us as our sins deserve or repay us according to our iniquities. For as high as the heavens are above the earth, so great is his love for those who fear him; as far as the east is from the west, so far has he removed our transgressions from us." Psalm 103:8-12

Shifting Light April 19

The morning light slid between the slats of the blinds, settling softly on the bedspread and carpet. As I rested my gaze upon the faint glow, I noticed something I had never seen in my entire life, startling me into intense concentration upon that scene. The entirety of the light faded and returned in such rapid succession that it reminded me of a strobe light effect. It changed from dark to light an estimated 25 times in the span of that minute.

Sunlight shone, was gone, then appeared again! Finally realizing that the sun was being filtered by fast-paced clouds, I was still surprised that I had never noticed this rapid-fire exchange anywhere before that day. It was as if I had witnessed time being accelerated.

Living on earth, we see time in slow motion, as we wish it away, or in fast forward as we wish it to come speedily. God created time for mankind; and in His infinite wisdom, He marked our existence with days and nights, for working and resting. We have come to mark our days in hours and minutes, then fractions of minutes, and now in nanoseconds.

Isn't it ironic that the more we fractionalize our time, the less time we seem to have? The more we fill our time with busy-ness, the more time slips through our fingers. Time marches on, and on, and on in a monotonous beat which intensifies with each unrelenting year, and then life is suddenly over, always sooner than it should be.

God's plan to mark our time has always been to do so for our benefit, but also His glory, pointing us to the One who supplies all our needs. I believe He is also pointing us to His character, which never shifts and changes, like the light on the bed covering. He, who is the Author and Finisher of our faith, is also Faithful and True from the beginning of time to the end. He is the constant Presence in the shifting light of change.

"But I trust in you, O Lord; I say, 'You are my God.' My times are in your hands; deliver me from my enemies and from those who pursue me. Let your face shine on your servant; save me in your unfailing love." Psalm 31:14-16

A fatherless child, the unclaimed daughter of a man having long ago moved on to another family and distant place, she was the progeny of a nameless face for the rest of her life. She was the girl who grew to womanhood carrying the ravages of abandonment. Deep ran the scars, searching for acceptance in every face, longing for a safe place and unfailing love, only to find conflict, rejection, and abandonment. She was the product of the failure of human beings—doing what flawed human beings do.

Sounds depressing, doesn't it? Or tragic? Or exaggerated? But it is none of those. It is the reality of every woman I have known who was abandoned by a father or mother, and I believe the consequences, as most social studies will prove, are even more devastating for boys. I was one of those children growing up with no idea what a father's love was. I had no mental or emotional framework to build relationships upon, feeling my way through the process, and not doing a very admirable job of it. Until I became my Father's child.

Submitting my life to God through Jesus, I found that I had access to my heavenly Father. That newly found relationship inspired my journey of discovering the relationship with my heavenly Father that had eluded me in a relationship here on earth. He gently and methodically expressed His love for me, lovingly guided, and yes, disciplined me. He showed me His character and what fathers should look like.

I found the most beautiful examples of a father's love in the fellowship of other Believers. In the protection of their children, they displayed my Father's care for me. In their fairness and firmness, I saw the likeness of my Father's discipline. In their provision, I witnessed my Father's generosity. And in the tenderness and adoration they displayed, I saw the love expressed toward me in my Father's eyes. My heavenly Father is very expressive of His love for me, and since He is even better than some fathers I know, I would even describe Him as a "doting" Father.

I am finally beginning to understand that the Father adores His children, loving them even to the point of sacrificing Himself to death. He did that for me, and you. He loves and adores me, and you. No earth-bound father can match our Father's love. I am my Father's child. Are you? He desires nothing more than for you to come home to Him and be your Father's child.

"Though my father and mother forsake me, the Lord will receive me." Psalm 27:10

"A father to the fatherless, a defender of widows, is God in his holy dwelling. God sets the lonely in families, he leads forth the prisoners with singing…" Psalm 68:5,6a

Mary in the Morning

My friend, Cindy, was voicing a complaint that echoed in my soul and has reverberated throughout Christendom, ever since Jesus gently chastised Martha for the complaint she voiced. It was Martha, after all, who first opened her home to Jesus, but it was Mary who sat listening eagerly and attentively. It was Martha who worked hard to assure His comfort, but Mary knew the timeless and priceless presence of the Son of God. Martha worked hard and strived to please all in attendance; Mary listened while Jesus' words were fresh, first-hand, and fed her heart.

Ironically, Cindy, like Martha, is a cook, quite famous in her own right, preparing mega meals for hundreds of mouths at a time. She is a Martha through and through in the labor of meal-making, but she was voicing her desire to be more of a Mary, eagerly awaiting every word of His lips, in the early morning hours. Also, ironically, I can think of no one who sits at Jesus' feet, no one more open to His leading or teaching, no one who loves Him more than Cindy.

Formerly believing most people to be "Marys" more than "Marthas", I am beginning to realize that I had it completely backward. I can see that He was speaking to most of us, not the exception. It's a pretty safe bet that there are far fewer ears attuned to Jesus' communication, on any given morning, than those who have skipped the conversation altogether.

Jesus was correct, as He always is, to re-focus Martha's, and my, order of priorities. I can barely restrain my thoughts from drifting to the demands of the crowd, keeping my schedule intact, and yielding to the squeakiest wheel. Bumping Jesus to a tenuous position on my daily to-do list, I am missing communication and fellowship with the One who sacrificed Holy blood on my behalf. The irony is that Jesus, who is all-wise and all-powerful, holds time and the order of the universe in His hands, so I know He can handle my day.

Like Martha, when I am focused on the demands of the day, I miss the day's greatest Treasure. Jesus understands our weakness but never condones it; and cannot because of His vast love for us. We are exchanging the glory of His presence for the hollowness of "busy", the Bread of Life for a dry, hard, molded crust. I would not feed that to my children, and neither would He to His. He desires His best for us, and the best is found only at His feet, as a "Mary in the morning".

"As Jesus and his disciples were on their way, he came to a village where a woman named Martha opened her home to him. She had a sister called Mary, who sat at the Lord's feet listening to what he said. But Martha was distracted by all the preparations that had to be made. She came to him and asked, 'Lord, don't you care that my sister has left me to do the work by myself? Tell her to help me!' 'Martha, Martha,' the Lord answered, 'you are worried and upset about many things, but only one thing is needed. Mary has chosen what is better, and it will not be taken away from her.'" Luke 10:38-41

Forever and a Day

When stringing beads, each bead is strung with a definite beginning, ending, and a carefully calculated pattern between the two. Following someone's pattern requires far less calculation, and headache, I found. Laying out the beads in said pattern, I strung them one by one; lifting the end of the string to tie it off, the beads rolled and bounced my beautiful pattern across the table and floor. I had neglected to knot the other end.

Though today may seem to stretch far into the distance, it is a string of pearls with a loose end. We know not the number of our pearls, our days. Life is laid out in advance, by our heavenly Father, with a specified beginning and an ending. If we can inspect ourselves with honest eyes, we will see the willful detours from His will, and the choices that upended the beautiful design He had originally set out for us. But for those who know Jesus as Lord and Savior, grace produces a re-threading of our pattern, re-configuring it into a string of pearls befitting a King. He alone can make my failures, pain, and trials into a pattern of Holy origin, beautiful in His eyes and fit for His use.

When the string of this life will come to an end, we do not know. Life's thread can be very short or exceedingly long, with no hint of its termination. Make your peace with God and man today while you are able, then live, understanding that you know not the length of your days. Hold tightly your precious relationships, give your care generously to others, and speak carefully.

Your string of pearls may appear to be strung far into the future, forever and a day, but only God knows. Our time is always spilled into eternity long before we feel it should be finished here on earth, no matter how many days we were allotted.

"I know that everything God does will endure forever; nothing can be added to it and nothing taken from it. God does it so that men will revere him." Ecclesiastes 3:14

"Sow for yourselves righteousness, reap the fruit of unfailing love, and break up your unplowed ground; for it is time to seek the Lord, until he comes and showers righteousness on you." Hosea 10:12

"For he says, 'In the time of my favor I heard you, and in the day of salvation I helped you.' I tell you, now is the time of God's favor, now is the day of salvation." 2 Corinthians 2:2

Not everyone loves vegetables, and I will admit that many of them have taken time, and repeated trials, before being added to my "love" classification. Corn, beans, peas, carrots, and tomatoes were at the top of my list as a child, but as my tastes matured, I later added Brussel sprouts, lima beans, cauliflower, cabbage, and squash. Spinach and asparagus never made the list at all but cooked properly, I can abide them occasionally. Vegetables, whether we love them or not, contain life-giving nutrients that sustain our bodies.

Following Jesus, I have discovered, requires a similar discipline as eating your vegetables. There are parts of following Him that I love and can't consume in excess; praising Him through worship songs is one of my favorites. I love spending quiet moments with Him, and I especially love the mini revelations He lavishes on me when I least expect them. I love admiring Him through His creation and in His word. I love His nudging, and the quiet ways He makes Himself known to me.

Slowly God has added to my list of "vegetables", as He drew me into diligent prayer, quiet times, Bible study, giving, and service. But these, like the vegetables I could tolerate, were not my first choice, requiring more persistence, diligence, and discipline. It wasn't that I didn't desire to do any of those things, but they were not as easy for me, and not quite as natural as the rest. I was created with different gifts, and those naturally are easier.

Yet these are all vital nutrients to a Christian. Through them, God works in us to build the Body of Christ. We do not live in isolation as Christ-followers; we live within the body of believers. And God uses the gift of discipline to train us, molding us into the image of Jesus, for the good of the whole body; like individual cells are nourished by the nutrients in our vegetables, we are strengthened as we become more like Christ, unified into His body.

If you are struggling in your understanding of Jesus or walking through times of discipline and training, you may find yourself pushing against God instead of accepting your "vegetables". It may be time to ask Him to clarify what He is requiring of you, or simply accepting that this "vegetable" may also be an acquired taste. Our Father will not force your will, but I have found that if I keep refusing what He is teaching, the lesson, or "vegetable", will show up time after time. When God is placing the same "vegetable" on my plate, I am learning to recognize the pattern and trust that whatever vital nutrient I am missing is to be found there.

"Do not be wise in your own eyes; fear the Lord and shun evil. This will bring health to your body and nourishment to your bones…My son, do not despise the Lord's discipline and do not resent his rebuke, because the Lord disciplines those he loves, as a father the son he delights in." Proverbs 3:7-8, 11-12

"'My food,' said Jesus, 'is to do the will of him who sent me and to finish his work.'" John 4:34

The Power of One   April 24

An eight-year-old boy died of a brain tumor, and his photo, such a handsome young face, has circulated on the internet, his life touching hearts of netizens around the world. The death of a forty-seven-year-old diplomat sparked an international investigation of espionage. A young woman handed roses to each policeman on duty and thanked them for their service. A reporter balked at the demand that he sacrifice his integrity, then ventured out on his own, becoming well renowned for his honest reporting.

There is power in numbers, but the most often underestimated number is the number one. One stone sets a hundred ripples into motion. One voice can be silenced, but it can also spark a flame roaring in the darkness of oppression and evil. One act of kindness can be the catalyst for many, "paying it forward". The kind word of one stranger can alter the course of the day. The undervalued power of one, whether used for good or evil, depending on the choices we make, is what we individually overlook in our daily lives.

The Bible is replete with examples of the power of one, plus God: Mary, a young virgin, consented to the will of God and became a vessel yielded to carrying the Son of God in her womb, and into the world. Joseph, sold into slavery at a tender age, believed God's promises and became the deliverer of his family, and a nation. Moses stood singularly against the culture of his day and led God's people through the Red Sea. Daniel prayed when prayer was prohibited and did so where everyone could witness his faith. David, Ester, Rahab, Stephen, Paul—the list is vast.

When you feel isolated, insignificant, or powerless, just remember the power of one, plus God. He sees you, knows your circumstances, and understands your heart. He has also prepared you for the moment you face right now. Your experiences, your life, the gifts and talents He has bestowed on you, your temperament and personality, are not accidental. When one individual partners with God to stand for what is right, to dream big dreams, or to be a force for good in a dark world, the world changes, even if you cannot see it; only eternity will reveal it in many cases.

The key to understanding God's plan is to wait for His timing, go where He leads, be obedient to His calling on your life, and surrender your will to His. It is to work on your character and to strive, no matter what happens, to be more like Jesus, conforming not to this world, but the image of Christ. Do not underestimate the power of God to work on your behalf and in your heart; His intentions toward you are good. The power of one, plus God, is far greater than you can imagine.

"I will remember the deeds of the Lord; yes, I will remember your miracles of long ago. I will meditate on all your works and consider all your mighty deeds. Your ways, O God, are holy. What god is so great as our God? You are the God who performs miracles; you display your power among the peoples." Psalm 77:11-14

Small Fish, Big Ocean April 25

The early morning light found me relaxing on a dock, the tide gently but surely surging in, while I observed the life sustained by it. On this morning, I longed to know more of God, asking how I could remember how awesome He is. Immediately, a school of Finger Mullet, darting beneath the dock, came into view. Thousands occupied the space between the two piers, darting and turning as though one unit, graceful and quick. Each one was an individual, breaking away for a moment, but quickly resuming its position in the body of flashing quicksilver.

My attention turned to the water that was their world. They did not see beyond the piers, not knowing the water that sustained them gave life itself. In the water, they lived, breathed, moved, and had their being. Yet the water stretched far beyond the piers; into the bay; beyond that into the Gulf; the Gulf into the ocean; and beyond the ocean into the great depths.

And my God has not asked a tiny Finger Mullet to dwell in the power of the sea's pounding waves, or the presence of the great creatures of the deep, in the crushing pressures of the depths, nor the rushing currents of the surf. He placed it in community, in the shallow waters between two piers, exactly where it was made to be, in all the vastness of waters. He has similarly placed me exactly where I need to be, though I often question His wisdom. I fail to understand that I am a tiny fish swimming in His ocean.

I swim about in my surge of activity, darting here and there, unaware of the One to whom I owe my very life. If I could see beyond my school of tiny fish; beyond my world between the piers; if only I could know, His very Presence is the water around me! How limited is my knowledge of God and His unbridled, unlimited power displayed throughout the universe and eternity!

Finally, my eyes are opened, and I can see the Water around me, sustaining me. I can see that He extends beyond my piers and beyond the bay. I may never see the fullness of who He is; but as long as I am hungry to know Him, He will always reveal more. I am learning to become content, as a small fish in the vast ocean of my God.

"For in him we live and move and have our being." Acts 17:28

"Who has measured the waters in the hollow of his hand, or with the breadth of his hand marked off the heavens? …or weighed the mountains on the scales and the hills in a balance? Who has understood the mind of the Lord, or instructed him as his counselor? He sits enthroned above the circle of the earth, and its people are like grasshoppers. He stretches out the heavens like a canopy, and spreads them out like a tent to live in." Isaiah 40:12-13, 22

Left Behind

From the exterior of the white brick house, it was natural to assume that the interior was decked out in similar fashion, neatly and stylishly. Its owner, a white-haired, slender, elderly woman apparently lived solitarily with her antique aqua-blue Chevy, perfectly parked in its double garage. Though I never met her, I could see that she enjoyed being in her yard, planting Iris beds along the side of her driveway.

Driving by her house several months ago, I noticed that she had apparently moved. The beautiful house she had built had been left behind. Her lovely home had been leased to a family sporting a big-rig truck in the driveway. Driving by again today, my heart sank as I noticed the tell-tale signs of her absence. The yard had been neglected, the garage was piled high with junk where the pristine antique car once lived, and the shades in the windows were perched askew.

I wondered if that possibility had crossed the mind of the lady who had built that house in her later years. It has certainly occurred to me, that whatever is currently in my possession is only temporarily mine, and ultimately not mine at all. I consider it often; what I hold in my hand today will be someone else's tomorrow. Will they treasure or care for it the way I do? Not likely. Even if they do, it won't be theirs very long, either.

Jesus assured His disciples, repeatedly, that their heavenly Father could supply their needs, even when it appeared impossible to them. He understood this temporal world, teaching His disciples to hold everything loosely in their hands. He knew they would soon leave behind everything they could see and touch for what was far better, for what was lasting and eternal.

It is not easy to focus on the unseen when the visible is so tantalizingly "real" and alluring. I am learning to trust God for every need and ask His guidance, holding with open hands my treasures in this world. God prizes my heart and my trust far more than any "thing" I can offer Him. Everything else, whatever "it" is, you can be dead sure it will be left behind, sooner or later.

"And do not set your heart on what you will eat or drink; do not worry about it. For the pagan world runs after all such things, and your Father knows that you need them. But seek his kingdom, and these things will be given to you as well…Sell your possessions and give to the poor. Provide purses for yourselves that will not wear out, a treasure in heaven that will not be exhausted, where no thief comes near and no moth destroys. For where your treasure is, there your heart will be also." Luke 12:29-30, 33-34

Six Cylinders April 27

Buying my current vehicle included the normal dilemmas of such a purchase. As I attempted to sort through the options, it necessitated choosing between what could be considered essential, and what options I could afford, while staying within my tight budget. Of the major options, a choice had to be made whether to buy a four-cylinder or higher-powered six-cylinder vehicle. I considered the miles I had traveled on my previous four-cylinder, and the narrowly margined brushes with other vehicles where a bit more power would have made a difference.

Purchasing the six-cylinder, I received a bit of criticism for not being economical, that I could have "gotten along" on four cylinders. Those comments still surface in my memory each time I encounter an on-ramp with 80 MPH rocket-like big rigs barreling down on me. I put my foot on that gas pedal and promptly scoot beyond the impending disaster, thanking God I decided on the not-so-economical engine. It has paid for itself many times over by extending my life, if not repair costs.

My relationship with God through Christ Jesus is like the choice between a just-to-get-by car and a higher-powered vehicle. Sounds ridiculous, doesn't it? But I find it to be true in my life. I have experienced both kinds of relationships with my God, one a type of surface relationship, only understanding that God is there when I need him; the other, a deeper "knowing" Him, and experiencing a deep abiding love for Him.

The time I spend getting to know Him and the relationship I build with Him can be just enough to get by. Or it can be a relationship where I count on Him, know His character, and experience His power in my life. When busyness dominates and my day seems to be flowing smoothly, I tend to allow my relationship to slide a bit, sometimes more than a bit. I forget that my sufficiency doesn't include the word "self" and comes only through Christ, that my dependency on Him is not only for "spiritual" things but for *everything*.

As human beings, we find ourselves unwittingly prideful and arrogant—it is part of the fallen nature of man, as sin obscures our need for God. We are reminded of our need through difficulty, hardship, and pain; at least I am. I am not ashamed to say that I need Jesus' saving power, grace, forgiveness, and mercy daily. I could "get along" living on four-cylinder power, but I want to live in a six-cylinder relationship, through His power in all circumstances, every day I am graced to live.

"Love the Lord your God with all your heart and with all your soul and with all your strength." Exodus 6:5

The children were largely unaware of the challenges their father had been confronting at work for the prior 18 months, but they did know he was looking for another job. My husband had recently received a serious diagnosis of a debilitating disease, and we had no idea how long he would be able to work, his prospects narrowing further. New management had been installed at his current company; to say that their ethical standard was subpar is a vast understatement. They made it abundantly clear that they wanted the last Christian on staff to go away. With a family depending upon him, he did not consider the option of resigning, as he continued to search for a new position.

In his search, my husband had been using professional recruiters and had been on several interviews, with no offer in hand. It began to take its toll on him as he slid into depression. We had few options available, as I continued to pray for God's direction. Agonizing months passed.

As I prayed one morning, I felt the Lord was speaking very clearly to my heart. "Do not go to the secular world any longer. Go to my people." Gary had resisted inquiring of our friends at church, but those words were so strong that I finally convinced him to take his resume to three men, and simply ask if they knew of a job, would they please prayerfully consider him. One of those men was a QC Manager of a large local company, an upstanding Christian who lived his convictions. I know he prayed much over what to do with Gary's resume since he was well aware of our situation.

When the news came late one evening that he had been accepted at that company, there was tremendous rejoicing at our house. And there was no doubt in any of our minds where this job originated, and Whom to credit. Many people had sent up a barrage of prayers on our behalf. We had much to be thankful for—we didn't incur the expense or upheaval of moving, the children were able to keep their friends and schools, and we could keep our home.

There are many details I could fill in to underscore what a miracle from God this was, but the bottom line is that when God opens a door, no one can close it; when He closes the door, no one can open it, and anyone who wants God's best will not try to force it open but wait for Him to unlock it! He will always answer, in due time.

"But I trust in your grace, my heart rejoices as you bring me to safety. I will sing to the Lord because he gives me even more than I need." Psalm 13:6

"For our light and momentary troubles are achieving for us an eternal glory that far outweighs them all." 2 Corinthians 4:17

Ian was chasing bugs since the time he could crawl. As a two-year-old, I vividly remember the Cicada he adamantly refused to release from his tightly clutched fist, and no strategy of persuasion changed the release of his prize. Though Ian is not yet grown, the trajectory of his gifting has been launched. The question in my mind is, what will he be when he grows up? Ian, like every child created in God's image, is custom-made for God's plan.

Most of us, as children, dream of what we will be when we grow up. We are perplexed as we explore our purpose as young adults, and tortured as adults, who feel they may have missed "it". Why are we so confused as we search for our purpose in life, the fulfillment of our gifting? Perhaps it is because we mistake our "gifting" for our "calling". I have found there to be a difference between the two.

Our gifting is what we are given at birth; it is a talent or interest with a multitude of paths to choose from. A calling is using that gift where we have been specifically directed, according to God's plan, not just our own. This is the biggest secret of life that I can share with you—lots of people have gifts, many have talents, a few follow their calling.

For many years I trudged through this process of learning what my gift from God was and would have found it much earlier if I had been willing to embrace it. Words were my gift, but my calling was uncovered through sharing encouragement, words beckoning people to come to the only Source who can supply every need.

I thought I was too late to begin, but God said otherwise. Whether we follow His leading early or late in life, God's timing is always right. It is not dependent on circumstances, your past, or your status. Moses began at age 80, and Abraham at 100. Joseph's calling began following slavery and imprisonment; Ruth found her calling after losing her husband, and Paul, after killing Christians. Peter found his calling after denying Jesus. In every instance, it is plain to see that each was gifted to fit precisely into God's plan at just the right time for His kingdom.

The bottom line is that you have a gift, and you have a calling in God's kingdom. You were custom-made for exactly this time. The only question remaining is, "Will you follow where He leads?"

"But each man has his own gift from God; one has this gift, another has that."

2 Corinthians 7:7

Predictably Unpredictable April 30

Each visit I made with my grandfather was predictable, until it wasn't. Grandpa's car predictably found its way to his mother's house every Saturday. The roads were curvy and a bit hilly, and the trip took nearly an hour before pulling onto the dirt driveway between the old barn and the tidy but ancient, small white house. Inside, the floors were wavy hardwood, with unpredictable footings, like walking in a carnival house of mirrors. And I could never recall the location of the next wave.

The black and white spotted pony grazing beyond her back fence would come to be petted, only until he found there was no food in my hand, then nipped my negligent, offending fingers. The flowers intertwining the rusting fence were pretty until finding how attractive they were to the bees, too. There was an equally ancient outhouse, which I would avoid if possible, finding that spiders didn't seem to mind the smell at all. And the only drinking water came from a well, equipped with a tin ladle to dip the water out of the bucket, which everyone used; I avoided it, too, if possible.

My life has been very much like Grandma Becker's farmhouse. I have strived to maintain its tidy appearance, despite its shortcomings. I have neatly tucked my china plates into the wooden cabinets, memories stacked on the shelves with them. My gate is getting a bit rusty, and the weeds are persistent despite my efforts to tame them. My water Source, though, is an ancient one that I can trust; everyone who is thirsty can drink from the same Cup without hesitation.

The sweet fragrance of the flowers attracts the bees, but I am no longer fearful of what may happen; the sting of death has been rendered powerless. The floors are wavy, and though I don't always have my precise footing, I understand that Someone will guide me and pick me up if I fall. The dust has been swept out, including dust bunnies hidden in places I wasn't even aware of; but He was.

I learned not to offer my gifts with fingers exposed but with an open palm, because ponies are ordinarily ornery, as are some humans. Life's necessities will take me to places where spiders naturally linger, but I cannot fear; they will be exposed as the Light shines ahead of me. And the road may have seemed long at the beginning of the journey, but it will be only an instant in the rear-view mirror of eternity.

Life has been predictably unpredictable, exactly as our Creator intended, or my faith would have remained small. As Moses will attest, and Joseph, and Abraham, and all the rest, that God never did the expected, but nudged them, as He will every one of us, into situations that require our trust and faith to rest in Him. Our unpredictable God has an unwavering plan that always leading us predictably into a deeper relationship with our loving Father through Jesus, His son.

"By faith, Abraham..." Hebrews 11:11b   "By faith, Joseph..." Hebrews 11:22a

"By faith, Moses..." Hebrews 11:24a

May

Many Umbrellas

The mall had decorated its multi-storied atrium by suspending umbrellas, of all sizes and colors, from the ceiling. From the top floor looking down, it was quite a beautiful sight. Some were very fancy umbrellas, with lovely patterns of geometrics and plaids, while others sported photographic scenes. Golf umbrellas looked like circus tents, sporting their bold stripes of color. Some umbrellas stretched fine, printed fabrics across their frames, while others appeared as giant flowers fully opened.

There are umbrellas not worthy of display, those that are shabby, worn, and unlovely with broken ribs and sprained handles. They are the ones most often used every day. Some could be repaired if we could just get around to it. The most damaged umbrellas are destined soon for the trash heap if we could only part with them. As I considered the umbrellas, I thought that even the black, plain ones look very lovely when they are serving their purpose.

Umbrellas, I thought, are very much like people. People, too, are a very diverse creation, actually with no two alike. Some are quite beautiful, grabbing our attention immediately. Some are quite creative, admirable for their stunning contributions. The less common ones are larger than life, and everyone seeks to run to them. Others are sporting the geometric print or plaid, a bit more ordinary. Then there are a lot of common, black umbrellas, looking very plain.

There are many perfect umbrellas, but there are no perfect people. We, to the man, woman, and child, have wounds and scars, broken ribs and handles, whether they are readily visible by others, or not. We are faded from sin, torn from scraping against the hard things of life, and battered by the winds of strife. Honestly, a lot of us are ready to collapse from the strain of the storm.

So, what do we do? We cling for all we're worth to the only One who can fix our damaged frame, the only One who can renew the fabric of our souls, the One who can anchor us in the winds, Jesus. Call on Him. He will never refuse to hear you, even in the mightiest storm. Jesus, in His compassion, looks at us from the top floor of the atrium. From His vantage point, He sees what we can become, "many umbrellas" of all colors and sizes, designs and uses, an intricately patterned creation, perfectly suiting His plan.

"I have told you these things so that in me you may have peace. In this world, you will have trouble. But take heart! I have overcome the world." John 16:33

"For I am the Lord, your God, who takes hold of your right hand and says to you,' Do not fear; I will help you.'" Isaiah 41:13

Ripples and Storms

At two o'clock in the morning, life changed for many people in our community as a devastating tornado ravaged homes and businesses. Many died that night, and the search continued, house by house, for scores still missing. Many were sound asleep in the safety of their beds when the disaster struck with little warning. It is no surprise that the tally of the dead rises as the search continues, adding to the twenty-two lost as of this morning. Sorrow and pain have pierced the hearts of so many, as a realization of the losses ripple across our landscape, as over a deep lake.

My optician was touched by the tragedy, losing a long-time friend. My banker was well-acquainted with another victim. Another friend of mine recounted the lives wrecked along the highway, big rigs and cars tossed like toys, as she battled to get home in the aftermath. Each loss touches many other lives, the ripples intersecting and crossing, weaving a tapestry of connection; each story connecting in a multitude of unexpected ways.

The thread which ties us all together is the realization of our vulnerability to death, loss, and suffering in this world. It is set before us so blatantly that we are unable to overlook or deny its existence. We question with broken hearts, swollen eyes, and torn souls, "God, why???" Yet, in the storm, His quiet voice resounds, "Trust me!"

There is no comfort or real peace without Him, inside or outside the storms. We have no future nor hope but by His hand. Jesus was intensely familiar with each victim. His nail-pierced, scarred hand wore our pain and sorrows. He is not distant, and He has not abandoned us in our trauma and troubles. Over history, He has acted on behalf of those who love Him, who trusted that God is good above all else.

In times when our strength is little and our resolve is weakened, He is there. When our pain is heightened and souls wrecked, He has not abandoned us. He alone can bring beauty from the ashes of destruction, and our trust in Him is never misplaced.

In heart-wrenching tragedy, we can help one another by being the hands and feet of Jesus. Sending hope through our ripples of connection to a lost world, we can direct them to the One who never fails us, even in the storms.

"One day Jesus said to his disciples, 'Let's go over to the other side of the lake.' So they got into a boat and set out. As they sailed, he fell asleep. A squall came down on the lake so that the boat was being swamped, and they were in great danger. The disciples went and woke him, saying, 'Master, Master, we're going to drown!' He got up and rebuked the wind and the raging waters; the storm subsided, and all was calm. 'Where is your faith?' he asked his disciples. In fear and amazement, they asked one another, 'Who is this? He commands even the winds and the water, and they obey him.'" Luke 8:22,25

A Long-Distance Relationship   May 3

Both my daughters and my son married their long-distance courtship partners, as I did mine. It is a challenging way to go about the process, but over many miles, long-distance phone calls, letters, and digital communications, their relationships deepened. Marriages resulted, and the commitments have run deep in their hearts and families. It requires a focused effort to communicate, to stay true to the one you love, and to have hope for the future.

In so many ways, my relationship with Jesus is a long-distance one. He seems so far away at times, and this earthly journey, though very brief, seems a very protracted one. Some days feel lonely and distant; I long to see Him, touch Him, hear His voice, and simply sit in His presence.

Then I remember that the One I love is not absent at all. Because He loves me so much, He gave me His Holy Spirit to connect me directly to Him, to communicate with me, and to speak His love to me. He gave me a wonderful, and long, love letter, the Bible, a powerful statement of His love, with specific encouragement and directions for my life. You don't believe me? In just two chapters, Psalm 31 and 32, He communicates all this to me:

I can trust him. ("But I, I trust you, O Lord; I say, 'You are my God.' My times are in your hands." Chapter 31:15, 16)

He wants good things for me. ("But oh, how great is your goodness, which you have stored up for those who fear you, which you do for those who take refuge in you, before people's very eyes!" Chapter 31:20)

He forgives me completely. ("How blessed are those whose offense is forgiven, those whose sin is covered! How blessed those to whom the Lord imputes no guilt, in whose spirit is no deceit!" Chapter 32:1,2

He protects me. ("You are a hiding place for me, you will keep me from distress; you will surround me with songs of deliverance." Chapter 32:7)

He instructs me. ("I will instruct and teach you in this way you are to go; I will give you counsel; my eyes will be watching you." Chapter32:8)

He gives me grace. ("Many are the torments of the wicked, but grace surrounds those who trust in the Lord." Chapter 32:10)

He hears me. ("Nevertheless, you heard my pleas when I cried out to you." Chapter 31:23b)

He gives me hope. ("Be strong, and fill your hearts with courage, all of you who hope in the Lord." Chapter 31:25

He accepts my repentance and gives me freedom. ("When I acknowledged my sin to you, when I stopped concealing my guilt, and said, 'I will confess my offenses to the Lord'; then you forgave the guilt of my sin." Chapter 32:5

God is not as distant as we feel or imagine. As with earthly relationships, it requires a focused effort to communicate, to stay true to the one you love, and to have hope for the future. It's a relationship well worth the effort and really not as long distance as you may think.

Watching the stick horse, Pokey, "throw" its rider was pretty amusing. Trevor was four years old, completely decked out in a plaid western shirt, jeans, cowboy boots, and too-big-for-his-head cowboy hat, which rested more on his ears than his head. Forget outer space, dinosaurs, and firemen—Trevor's world was fully focused on western adventure and keeping Pokey in line. Years passed, Pokey stood faithfully in the corner, and Trevor's hat eventually became too small.

Childhood passes much too quickly, most of us can agree. As a child, time stretches endlessly ahead of us; but in reality, all our years are brief, like a vapor in the noon sun. Only when we gaze backward can we see them for the blink of an eye they are. That is one of the ironic benefits of age; the less time you have left, the more you can see just how limited days on this earth are. Between the beginnings of youth and the endings of aging, there is, though, the opportunity for growing and learning.

Isn't growth a wonderful component of God's creation? It is thoroughly incredible that children grow, explore, and learn. Even as adults, we are created to continue to explore, create, wonder, and tinker with new ideas. We are created in God's image to imitate HIM! He is never stagnant, boring, fragile, nor decaying. He is vibrant, exciting, and continually calling us to follow, learn from, and imitate Him. He invites us to unceasingly grow in knowledge and grace.

God draws us to Himself, calling us as His little children, to be humble and recognize who our heavenly Father is. We are invited to love Him and continue growing in resemblance to Him. I want to find myself fully engaged with this amazing Father, to understand the fullness of His love, and enter into the family business, on this earth, and in the world to come. Like Trevor, I want to go on adventures with God, to follow Him, know Him, and grow up to the full adult, in Christ, He desires me to be. I want my hat to become too small and my toys too dull, as today I adventure with my Father, the King!

"For we are God's handiwork, created in Christ Jesus to do good works, which God prepared in advance for us to do." Ephesians 2:10

The breeze was gentle and the air heavy, as I sat on the porch gazing at the clouds amassing. A summer storm was edging nearer, as evidenced by the sudden burst of wind, which suddenly changed directions, heaving the tree branches from side to side. The rain was coming; there was no doubt. A deep growl of thunder in the distance, amid many flashes of light, confirmed it was heading in my direction. Then there was sudden quiet, and I listened carefully. I could hear it before seeing it; the light rain sweeping over the landscape, from my left to my right, changed to pressure-washing status as it flew over my car parked in the driveway.

It made me think of this passage in the book of **Job 37:3-5: "He unleashes his lightning beneath the whole heaven and sends it to the ends of the earth. After that comes the sound of his roar; he thunders with his majestic voice. When his voice resounds, he holds nothing back. God's voice thunders in marvelous ways; he does great things beyond our understanding."**

In the darkness of my storms, I question where God is. I feel abandoned, cowering in fear; but I am learning, instead, to quietly watch the storm and look for Him in it. At times, His voice can be clearly heard, loudly as the thunder, as He crashes through my resistance. Other times, the wind of His direction will nudge me along a path I am hesitant to travel. And then there are the times when I need to be very still and listen for the sound of the rain approaching before I can even see it, watching patiently for His presence to be known.

When in the middle of the storms of life, it is very normal to fear the storm itself, looking upon it as beyond our control and all-consuming. But in that storm, He reveals truths I could not have seen without it. And when the storm has swept through, even the destruction I believed was beyond my control, was always under His dominion. I am finding that when I become quiet in the storm, trusting my God, His voice becomes the whisper in the storm, and He never left me, no matter how intense the storm was.

"Stop *striving* and know that I am God; I will be exalted among the nations; I will be exalted

on the earth." Psalm 46:10

Movement caught my attention as I washed dishes, drawing my eyes to the window in front of me. At first, I thought it was on the interior, but looking more closely, realized it was caught between the screen and glass. A tiny fruit fly had entered through the screen and furtively darted back and forth, attempting to find its way of escape. Ironically, if it had just stopped in place, the vast squares of screen forming an ocean of opportunity would have allowed it to easily pass through.

As I attempted to sleep last night, I found myself doing what the fruit fly was doing. I had a problem and instead of stopping the cycle of worry, I tangled myself in a knot of anxiety, with no solution, only loss of sleep. My mind darted back and forth and back to the beginning again. My efforts accomplished negative results, a day running on far too little sleep. I know better; I know where to find the answer I was seeking. I have a Savior who listens, a God I can trust, the Spirit who gives not only peace but solutions—if only I would be still and wait.

The beauty of that fruit fly is in the lesson it taught me this morning. What a wonderful Father I have, who will use an insect to reveal His object lesson to me, one who is made in His image, and infinitely higher than a fruit fly! As I frantically darted, about attempting to find my own way, I revealed my weakness; it was a lack of belief in Who He is and a faith too weak to believe that He can provide a way out.

As I rebuked myself for my obvious lack, He gently reminded me that He understands how I am made. He forgives me and invites me to be still, wait for His Spirit's presence, and walk in the ways that He will open for my "escape". Just wait in peace. How precious is God's patience!

"We wait in hope for the Lord; he is our help and our shield. In him our hearts rejoice, for we trust in his holy name. May your unfailing love rest upon us, O Lord, even as we put our hope in you." Psalm 33:20-22

"I sought the Lord, and he answered me; he delivered me from all my fears. Those who look to him are radiant; their faces are never covered with shame." Psalm 34:4-5

"What is man that you are mindful of him, the son of man that you care for him? You made him a little lower than the angels; you crowned him with glory and honor and put everything under his feet." Hebrews 2:6-8

Stranger in the Mirror

There is a stranger in my mirror! Her nose is bigger, and her ears, too. Her hair is thinning, creases parenthesize her smile, and strange brown spots have dotted her skin. She has confided to me that she also has aches and pains in places she never knew could act so, and not as much energy as she once had. Her clothing does not fit as well as her earlier days, buttons pulled a bit snugger, zippers a thing of the past; Lycra and Spandex have become much more familiar companions. Makeup takes less time, though, because there is no longer much point in exerting the effort.

The aging countenance of the person in the mirror is me, but not really. The outside may change to decay, but the inside is changing to life. The inside reveals the identity of an eternal being, of transformation not unto death, but to radiant glowing life in Christ. The moment I was born again through faith in Jesus, I became ageless, growing in grace but not in age; age became irrelevant from that point on.

We understand deep within our spirits that aging is not "normal". It may seem normal in the world in which we live, but our spirits testify to the opposite. We were created to stay forever young, an eternal age of companionship with an eternal God. From birth, we know not the number of our days; believing we do, we act as though eternity is at our disposal. Children and young adults are notorious for their perspective of invulnerability, dangerously so at times; only the tempering of trials and loss convince them otherwise.

The stranger in the mirror will continue to show signs of aging, and they will not be pretty. They will be agonizingly difficult at times, as they gradually lead to the countdown of her transition from this world, into the ageless and perfect body awaiting her. While she is here, though, she will find there is no age limit on growth, and it is never too late to yield to God's conforming hand, to heal, change, and be transformed. Living God's purpose for her here on earth will require trust, listening to His voice, and acting obediently. And beginning today is preferable to tomorrow—too many tomorrows have become yesterdays already.

"But our citizenship is in heaven. And we eagerly await a Savior from there, the Lord Jesus Christ, who, by the power that enables him to bring everything under his control, will transform our lowly bodies so that they will be like his glorious body." Philippians 3:20-21

"And we, who with unveiled faces all reflect the Lord's glory, are being transformed into his likeness with ever-increasing glory, which comes from the Lord, who is the Spirit."
2 Corinthians 3:18

We, as humans, consider ourselves so wise and intelligent. And in God's image, we were certainly created to be so, though, in our fallen state, we exhibit undeniable flaws and limited insight. That was the error in my thinking as I considered the similarity of personality traits, in relationship to birth order; I have witnessed this commonality consistently bob to the surface in most families I have known. Could it be possible there is a retro-engineering we are not considering? That, perhaps, there is perfect order to the birth order?

My immediate question was, "If God foreknew each of us, how is it that our personalities are shaped by such a common thing as the order in which we arrive in life?" I never once, before today, considered that perhaps because God foreknew us, He *planned* what family we were to be born to, and in what order we would arrive; utilizing that family and order, He shaped and molded us for *His purpose.*

In most families, there do appear to be traits common to first, second, third, and single children. Each person is uniquely an individual, yet shares common traits, even as they walk quite different lives. And the beauty of God's plan is that He fits us all together perfectly to accomplish His will on earth, as perfectly as He assembled all the universe, to its most minute workings.

That thought came as a great encouragement to me—our God is not the God of random accidents. He is purposeful, meticulous, thoughtful, omniscient, and intentional. Because He is loving, long-suffering, full of mercy, and overflowing in grace, He has carefully considered each of our paths. He is not a god of generality; He is the God of intentionality.

You are not an accident on this earth, and neither am I. We were created for a relationship with this very God, to walk with Him daily, moment by moment, touching lives with His love, wherever He leads. He is available through His Holy Spirit, given through faith in Christ Jesus, who is the very evidence of the vastness of God's love for us. He tempers, molds, and refits our personalities through our encounters with the hardships of life. He is refining and refitting us for heaven, intentionally, lovingly, and in His perfect order.

"You are worthy, our Lord and God, to receive glory and honor and power, for you created all things, and by your will they were created and have their being." Revelation 4:11

"For it is God who works in you to will and to act according to his good purpose."
Philippians 2:13

My mother's words, "This, too, shall pass," ring in my ears often as life presents the difficulties of each day. The difficulties that necessitated reciting them in the past seemed to come in longer intervals, but now, mere months flee before they ring out again. And they are always associated with hard times, which are difficult to understand and even more difficult to walk; a broken heart, an illness, a sick bank account, a wounded relationship, and worse. Eventually, an end to the problem will step forward and the pain of that event, even if not forgotten, will slowly lessen.

I find myself reciting my mother's words even more often lately, given the tumultuous times in which we live. But the Lord has revealed an additional application for them, too: While waiting for the difficult times to pass, do not let the good times slip away without notice or gratitude. It is best to remember that even the good times pass much too quickly.

I have a tendency, along with the rest of humankind, to take very much for granted the many blessings which come mixed thoroughly into the hardships. A glimpse of red as a cardinal perches on the tip of a branch, swaying in the breeze. The smile of a stranger pushing a grocery cart, passing mine. A random word of encouragement by a friend. The food on my plate at the end of the day. And often, we brush away the understanding that as bad as things may seem, they can always be worse.

God breathes blessings into our lives, no matter how dire the circumstance may be. Whether you can hear Him or not, sense His presence or not, He has not run away. He knows your every tear, every thought, weakness, and failing. And still, He stays. Jesus promises never to leave or forsake His children.

I recently heard a statement made by President Donald J. Trump: "Often, bumpy roads lead to beautiful places." It startled me. I had never heard those words, but they were worth remembering. God may lead us over some rugged terrain as we walk with Him, but we can always trust that He knows the way and that there is a reward in the end for those who love Him. The joy in the journey can be found only in Jesus, and remembering that whatever you are experiencing, bad or good, this too shall pass.

"And the peace of God, which transcends all understanding, will guard your hearts and your minds in Christ Jesus." Philippians 4:7

"The LORD himself goes before you and will be with you; he will never leave you nor forsake you. Do not be afraid; do not be discouraged." Deuteronomy 31:8

The Expiration Date   **May 10**

My seed packets from the prior year had an expiration date, which I ignored, happily tucking the seeds into their cozy dark soil, watering, and waiting. A few days passed before their tiny green faces appeared, to my delight! Not all of the seeds germinated, but most did; that was the risk of planting seeds past their "use by" date. Nothing appeared wrong with the ones that didn't turn into plants; they had simply aged out of their life span. But the plants which grew from the viable seeds produced tomatoes galore throughout the hot summer days.

We carry another type of seed with us daily, unseen, waiting to be planted, one born inside us. It is the seed of God, a deep knowing that He exists, drawing us to connection with Himself. He will not plant the seed in our hearts for us; He leaves that decision to each individual. Nor will He force the timing of our planting. He waits patiently, day by day, year by year, but eventually, there will be an expiration date.

Like the viability of the seed, the longer we wait, the less likely the seed is to be planted, and when finally planted, less time to yield a harvest. Denial of relationship with Him sends us into the pursuit of self and the world, causing disenchantment, hardening of our hearts, and yielding a harvest of pain.

Once that seed is planted, though, it yields ever-increasing fulfillment, life, and abundance. God is the patient farmer, bringing the perfect amounts of sun, rain, and tilling when most needed. The fruits pleasing to Him, peace, patience, kindness, self-control, and love, were quite unfamiliar to me until I began patiently enduring the growth process. And like my garden plants, I continue to mature. The fruit of the Spirit of God, whether in early fruition, or spanning a lifetime before fully maturing, becomes irrepressible, abundant, and blesses the world it touches.

People have an "expiration date", an unknown time when the seed of life will no longer be viable. One day, we will be planted in darkness and emerge in another realm. We know not when the end date is, nor the hour; today is not a promise, but an opportunity. I pray that you will plant the seed of faith in Christ Jesus firmly in your heart today if you have not yet done so. It is a planting you will never regret. As you grow closer to Jesus, have confidence that He only plants viable seeds, watering them with the promise of His Presence now, and throughout eternity to come.

"Jesus said to her, 'I am the resurrection and the life. He who believes in me will live, even though he dies." John 11:25

Be the Weed

Gardening in Tennessee is one of the most frustrating activities of my life, bar none. I have never encountered weeds so invasive, so pervasive, or tenacious as these. It's not that they have wonderful soil in which to flourish. The "soil" here is clay and rocks, with a spattering of something resembling soil. It is why we are known for producing livestock and trees, not bountiful garden crops.

There is abundant evidence across the landscape of the dominance common weeds of the region hold. Thistles and painfully thorny things abound here, as if to serve a warning to anyone even thinking about breaking ground for a garden. Vines and ivies are prolific. Poke plants pop up out of nowhere and proliferate themselves, as if by magic. After a decade of attempting to grow vegetables, I have concluded that raised beds and constant diligence are the only alternatives.

Knowing what I know about the weeds in my yard, I have decided to imitate their annoying qualities, and to become like the worst weed, even of nightmares. Have you ever attempted to pull a weed out of the dry ground? That is how I want to be planted. I want to be rooted and grounded in God's love, unmovable. I want my roots to sink deeply, with a strong thistle-like tap root, firmly clinging to the soil of faith in Christ. No matter how hard the world tugs, I will not yield or be uprooted.

I want to grow into cracks and crevices, finding every tiny space of encouragement the Lord speaks into my day. Like Kudzu, I will grow a foot a day, growing even at night. I will search out His daily revelations of Himself in the world around me. I will soak up every drop of moisture from His Word, taking nourishment from it and holding resolutely to it. I want to be the weed the Son shines on.

I want faith as small as a mustard seed, or even the seed of the dandelion. I want a faith that God honors and fertilizes. I will be prolific in sharing Jesus, multiplying, and distributing the seed He planted in me. I want to thrive in adversity, profusely, like the grasses of the fields, depending solely on my God and King. Tender greens and beautiful flowers will not survive the storms of life here, but weeds will always prosper. Lesson learned; I will be the weed.

"I pray that out of his glorious riches he may strengthen you with power through his Spirit in your inner being, so that Christ may dwell in your hearts through faith. And I pray that you, being rooted and established in love, may have power, together with all the saints, to grasp how wide and long and high and deep is the love of Christ, and to know this love that surpasses knowledge---that you may be filled to the measure of all the fullness of God."
Ephesians 3:16-19

Evening Light May 12

In the cloudy evening light, my hand rested on the steering wheel as I made my way home. I have never given much thought to my hands (most of us take them very much for granted), but tonight I happened to glance down at them. I was surprised to find myself thinking they appeared rather young and pretty. Then a cloud drifted away, exposing just a tad more light, revealing the true age and status of the hands on the steering wheel, not quite so pretty and very much older than first perceived.

As a child, I woke at dawn without fail, to the chagrin of a night-owl mother. I loved the early light, the excitement of a breaking day. I awoke in early morning most of my life, resenting the fading glow of evening. And I have never enjoyed night much at all! God truly has a sense of humor in pairing me with a husband who, like my mother, thrived in the night. But whether I approved or not, daytime has passed, and evening descended, without fail.

Life is much the same. It has passed without my permission, defiantly and unceasingly. Whether its days please or torment us, the daylight comes then fades away. Life is like one long day, youth breaking forth as an early explosion of yellow rays, midday arriving in a rush, carrying trials upon its shoulders. Late afternoon yields to a slowing pace and somber knowing that the day has slipped by, before we were prepared for it. Night will silently nudge the light from the sky, as surely as aging will march to the precipice of eternity with Jesus.

I am content now to see fewer flaws, feel less rushed, have more refined priorities, more grace, and greater love. I am thankful for the experiences I've been gifted, and the people encountered. I am grateful for a wider perspective and deeper knowledge. In the evening light, life appears like a deep lake with sun-saturated ripples, sun setting with memories of yesterdays, and tempered hopes of tomorrows yet to dawn.

"Jesus Christ is the same yesterday and today and forever." Hebrews 13:8

"And those who know Your name will put their trust in You, For You, O Lord, have not forsaken those who seek You." Psalm 9:10

"As for man, his days are like grass; as a flower of the field, so he flourishes. When the wind has passed over it, it is no longer. But the lovingkindness of the Lord is from everlasting to everlasting on those who fear Him." Psalm 103:14-17

No matter the setting, my washing machine simply would not spin, or even complete a cycle. And it decided to take its rest while digesting a particularly unsavory load! This would not have been a problem at a time when my bank account was bloated with excess cash, but instead, it was looking quite lean, close to starving. I could live without my dryer, but the washing machine—no way!

Without alternative options, my last resort, of course, was to pray. Then I checked appliance prices online to see what a replacement would cost. The cheapest model would clean out every cent I could scrape together. I knew, too, that for someone to just step into my house for an estimate, would be beyond the value of the very aged machine. I decided to wait for God to answer my request for a solution, and trust that He had one. He did—I just had to be patient.

The answer came in the form of my son, Trevor, who looked up the problem online. He found the solution to the error code, dragged the hulk of a washing machine to its knees, and tightened A BOLT! Seriously, it was as "simple" (subduing a washing machine to get to its underbelly is never simple) as one bolt needing a wrench. Cost of repair—FREE! Value of my son—PRICELESS!

The Lord answered my prayer in time to save my wash load from mildew, and to show me that He is, indeed, trustworthy in every detail of my life. This was just laundry. But God's answer to my problem spoke volumes to my heart, which spilled over into other areas of my life. The Lord Jesus is present, hears, and answers when I ask and am patient enough to wait. If I had not been patient, and not trusted Him, my accounts would have been cleaned out, resulting in a more stressful situation later.

Don't many of our problems stem from impatience? And doesn't impatience stem from not trusting God to bring resolutions to our requests? I don't understand why I do not ask God for help *first* when problems arise, nor why I am so resistant to waiting for His answers. I can only chalk it up to the deep rebellion buried in this sinful flesh. through His Spirit, He gives us words of encouragement, reminders of His presence, forgiveness, and faithfulness. He is constantly in the process of taming the beast that lies within each of us.

"This is what the Sovereign Lord, the Holy One of Israel, says: 'In repentance and rest is your salvation, in quietness and trust is your strength, *but you would have none of it.*" Isaiah 30:15

"But as for me, I watch in hope for the Lord, I wait for God my Savior; my God will hear me." Micah7:7

A Perfect Day

The window framed a perfectly beautiful day—an ultra-blue cloudless sky, summer foliage, gentle breeze whispering in the leaves, a bird soaring into view, then gone again. This is also my expectation of life, what I believe it should be, and I doubt I am alone. I have a deep yearning within my spirit for that perfect day—every day, but sensing something is broken. Ultimately, isn't that why I am constantly surprised and disappointed at the twists, turns, and up-endings in my life?

Perhaps our spirits recognize what our minds do not. This world was perfectly designed, perfectly created, perfectly ordered; then shattered irreparably by the ugliness of sin and rebellion. A world that was designed by a perfect, holy, and loving God became a dysfunctional, dangerous, and degrading planet by way of sin, disobedience, and rebellion against Him. It was disoriented from its Creator, separated from its King, and vanquished from Perfection.

Thankfully, God didn't leave us. He didn't throw His hands in the air and walk away. He didn't give up as people often do. He didn't wipe out the planet and make a new one. He knew it would happen, though, and already had an emergency plan in place; He sent a rescuer, Jesus, who would set the repair procedure into place. And one day, Jesus will restore even this devastation to its original perfection. He will bring us into a perfect relationship with our Father, in a perfect place, heaven; and in a perfect time, eternity.

Until that day, He has left us with the Mediator, His Holy Spirit, who can still work His perfecting power in our world, and in our lives, as we trust in Jesus. My life may not appear perfect to me, but with faith in His goodness, it can become better. With trust in His provision and protection and understanding of His unfailing love for me, I can view life through His window and see a perfect day, knowing He holds it all in His hand.

"Therefore, do not worry about tomorrow, for tomorrow will worry about itself. Each day has enough trouble of its own." Matthew 6:34

"For we walk by faith, not by sight." 2 Corinthians 5:7

"Do not conform any longer to the pattern of this world but be transformed by the renewing of your mind. Then you will be able to test and approve what God's will is---his good, pleasing and perfect will." Romans 12:2

Not a great risk-taker, my life "on the edge" can be defined most days as using a garden hoe, driving my car, or bagging my groceries. A real adventure for me could be a drive through the countryside, an airline flight, or a visit to family or friends. Not much of a risk, you might say, but I would differ with you; life itself is a risk, and we rarely acknowledge it until a random event pries our fingers loose from the controls.

Every day, we believe we have the whole course of time ahead, options and choices all along the way, until something goes wrong. Until a family member has an accident, someone becomes critically ill, a job loss blindsides us, or a conflict arises with a friend. The evening walk after supper, the high school graduation, the trip to the grocery store can all be interrupted, or disrupted, by life.

We do not get to choose what happens to us, or to those we love. Other people make bad choices, nature careens out of control, wars escalate beyond our scope of understanding—life is in constant flux. The possibilities are nearly endless, yet we treat each day as though it is ordinary, with no cause for concern. While each day is special, each breath and every thought precious, life is truly lived on the edge of eternity, and the precipice of change. Even time works against us and transforms our lives sooner than we can estimate possible.

Largely, we view life as we want it to be, as we know it was intended to be, eternal. We view God as a distant star in a far-off galaxy during many of our days, until we see life in the precarious position it is. When life suddenly careens out of control, can I know that wherever I am walking, God is with me, whether I feel that way or not? The answer is a resounding "YES!"

Many days, I cannot tell you that I "feel" God, but God never made that a requirement for His presence or His promises. Whether I feel it or not, whether pain has fractured my heart or broken my body, God promised to hold me. Whether the earth gives way or the sky falls, whether the mountains crash into the sea or the wind roars, He will never let go. While the storm rages and the waves of life threaten to swallow me, He will be steadfast. Whether I live life on the edge or in relative safety, I can trust that "there" He is lovingly present.

"O Lord, you have searched me and you know me. You know when I sit and when I rise; you perceive my thoughts from afar. You discern my going out and my lying down; you are familiar with all my ways. Before a word is on my tongue you know it completely, O Lord. You hem me in---behind and before; you have laid your hand upon me. Such knowledge is too wonderful for me, too lofty for me to attain. Where can I go from your Spirit? Where can I flee from your presence? If I go up to the heavens, you are there; if I make my bed in the depths, you are there…All the days ordained for me were written in your book before one of them came to be." Psalm 139:1-8, 16b

Perfect Connection

My phone rang and the caller ID sent me into full alert. My brother was calling, and as much as I love and pray for him, it is a call I am rarely anticipating with joy. My brother does not share my faith, values, or politics; what we have in common are many unpleasant memories of growing up together in a highly dysfunctional and broken family. Communication had broken down, and he had become angry; the reason, I am still attempting to decipher. This call, like others, did not end well, and as I hung up, my spirit was grieved. It upset me greatly.

Guilt would have been my normal reaction, followed by a need to apologize, though I had done nothing wrong. Many other conflicts in the past dictated that I would mull it over a thousand times, trying to decode my mistake that had triggered his anger. However, later that evening I was listening to a Christian brother's podcast and had to smile. He admonished not to be upset by other people's opinions of you, nor by those who don't like or approve of you. He charged his listeners to not allow those people to become an obstacle to communicating with God. God knows me so well and had sent this message at just the moment I needed it!

Writing an entry in my journal, I marveled at some of my notes from years prior, concerning how God speaks to me. That was followed by these words in my "Jesus Calling" daily devotional reading: "I speak to you continually. My nature is to communicate, though not always in words...I speak softly in the depths of your spirit, where I have taken up residence...gradually you will find me in more and more of your moments." I am so thankful for the ability to communicate with my heavenly Father freely.

God does not want our communication with Him to be stifled by guilt, emotions, or even by sin. His desire is that we will run to Him constantly, with happy and thankful hearts; souls filled with sadness, and hearts spilling over with repentance, when it is truly appropriate. The bottom line is that God wishes to communicate with each of us--His greatest desire is to connect with us one on one. This is my greatest joy and most profound mystery: Jesus made it possible to have an open line with the God of the Universe, always connected, access guaranteed 24/7. And in His still, small voice, as I listen carefully in the wake of years of training, He speaks in return, through the perfect connection, His Holy Spirit.

"And your ears shall hear a word behind thee, saying, 'This is the way, walk in it, when you turn to the right and when you turn to the left.'" Isaiah 30:21

"I will instruct you and teach you in the way you should go; I will counsel you with my eye upon you." Psalm 32:8

I waited eagerly, but patiently, as the attendant circled the machine, safety-checking each passenger and engaging the lock on every section. As he wearily strolled back to the control panel, he finally barked out final instructions about keeping feet and hands inside the vehicle. As the slow growl of the machinery ramped up, my long-anticipated ride at last started.

The wheels of the roller coaster clacked loudly on the rails as the red-painted beast labored up the incline, suddenly topping the rise and plummeting us into riotous twists and breathtaking dips. In less than three minutes, we were returned to our starting point, the end of the beginning. Though breathless, I was ready for more right away, but there would be plenty of time to recover as I stood in the very long line again.

Having children is pretty much the same feeling of anticipation, exhilaration, and intense emotion. You are on the ride for what you expect to be a prolonged thrill, but before even acclimating to each stage, the ride is over at what feels like the beginning. Suddenly a new generation is standing in your place in line, eager to sit in the seat you just vacated, believing as you did, that this ride would last a very long time. And you smile a knowing smile.

Each phase of life is another ride in the park, different in appearance, varying in speed, launching you in different directions, but over before it begins, in the grand scheme of life. Careers begin, and retirement knocks at the door sooner than you could imagine; marriages with expectations of fifty-year anniversaries fall far short of the celebration, and all anticipated beginnings end much too soon. Everything but God has a beginning and an ending, a season, a reason to exist, and a destiny of closure.

The stars orbit the galaxies and the galaxies traverse the universe, all suspended in passages of time, all with an origin and a trajectory of eventual death. Not one physical thing in this world will carry over to the next; nothing existing in eternity, not even time, nothing will break that unseen barrier. But the miracle of it all is a God who gives a new beginning each day we awake, each time we ask His forgiveness, and every time we trust Him more deeply. At His feet, starting even now, is the real and never-ending beginning.

"In the beginning you laid the foundations of the earth, and the heavens are the work of your hands. They will perish, but you remain; they will all wear out like a garment. Like clothing you will change them and they will be discarded. But you remain the same and your years will never end. The children of your servants will live in your presence; their descendants will be established before you." Psalm 102:25-28

It is worse than I ever thought! Yes, the stories I discovered buried deep in the dust bins of history were more depraved, and more evil than I ever imagined—and I imagined some pretty bad things! It seems that human depravity, rooted in sin, coupled with evil forces, is a fine pairing for death and destruction the world over. They are equally present in our current times, riding just beneath the surface of our culture like a stealth submarine.

Sounds dark and dire, doesn't it? It is, and I will not diminish the dangers and threats to human existence on this planet. I have lived in one realm of purposeful oblivion to them, and in another with acute awareness and fear. My early life was steeped in fear, and I carried it like a hundred-pound stone most of the days I have breathed on this earth. I did my very best to ignore and shut out the daily gnawing of the "what ifs" and "might happens", as my remedy. Fear is the greatest tool our enemy has universally employed against humankind, and I was as vulnerable to it as any human has ever been.

Until one day in 1981. That was the day I accepted Jesus Christ as my Savior, and the day the enemy began to loosen his grip on me, and increasingly since then. Every day since, the enemy has lost more control, and Christ has gained it. It has not been an easy process. It has been one of the most difficult aspects of my relationship with God. Sometimes fear is comfortable because it is all you know. Often, it gives you a sense of control, in a twisted sort of way.

As I have given up my idea of control and safety, I have gained unmatched freedom. As I, day by day, moment by moment, trust Jesus, I find increased peace. Faith is a peaceful trust that acknowledges God's plan and Sovereignty, but also His protection. So, what do I do when scary things happen? I reach out to Jesus, trusting His ability to use every situation to produce growth in me, encourage others going through similar trials, or, if He chooses, to completely change the situation. The key takeaway is that I can trust Him every single time, with any "news".

God proves to me every day that He holds my life in His hand. Evil may seem to prevail, but it cannot hold me down, discourage me, or cause me to give up. And I have even become dangerous! I have become courageous enough to stand up and fight against the kingdom of destruction, against the enemy of our families, and our faith. Jesus won at the cross, not just for the time He lived in the flesh, but for eternity. I am on the winning team, and we already know the end of the story. That's the news you never hear—the enemy of your soul will keep it from you at all costs. God's news, Christ in me, is truly GOOD NEWS!

"So do not fear, for I am with you; do not be dismayed, for I am your God. I will strengthen you and help you; I will uphold you with my righteous right hand." Isaiah 41:10

"They will have no fear of bad news; their hearts are steadfast, trusting in the LORD." Psalm 112:7

Most Beautiful Baby May 19

The county fair boasts a "fairest of the fair" beauty contest each year, pageants of princess-like prodigies vying for the coveted crown. The classifications begin at the earliest of ages, typically named "Most Beautiful Baby", infants and toddlers decked out in plumage and puffery befitting royalty and putting most peacocks to shame. I would argue that most parents and grandparents believe, without the grandeur, that their babies are the most beautiful and worthy of any grand prize; I certainly did!

There is an innate attachment and wonder for our babies, a hallmark of parenthood. Were it not for that God-given affection, few of us would survive; it is built into us, understanding the wonder of producing offspring, marveling at the miracle of life. There is a certain amount of "baby blindness" in each parent, a recognition of the special qualities endowed by God to this unique individual held in our arms; as they grow, we are on high alert to identify their strengths and gifts. But it does not take long to see that each has its flaws, inherited through the human race.

Selfishness, temper flare-ups, tantrums, lies, and defiance show up alarmingly early. I noticed the demanding nature of my babies early on, each subsequent sibling confirming what God had clearly shown me---this is a picture of me! It was not difficult to connect the dots; I could see my defiance, selfishness, and temper tantrums, my unwillingness to be guided and taught by God, my resistance to His will and ways. The stubbornness of my heart, though, was no match for His grace.

When I accepted Jesus as my Savior, my heart began to change, at first in subtle ways, as I came to know Him, yielding my stubborn will to His sovereign will. I began to grow up from a willful toddler into a child willing to learn and to follow. Maturing into a full-grown adult in Christ has been a process, a lifetime of trusting Him instead of hanging onto my baby-like will, one day at a time, over time.

I believe our heavenly Father sees us each as His "beautiful babies", uniquely and wonderfully made by His hands. He, however, does not have "baby blindness" and sees us exactly as we are, immersed in sin at birth and in need of a Savior. Once we come to Christ, though, we are restored to our original beauty as the Father views us through the sacrificial blood of his Son, each becoming the most beautiful baby in the world, worthy of wearing the crown of heaven.

"Yet to all who received him, to those who believed in his name, he gave the right to become children of God---children born not of natural descent, nor of human decision or a husband's will, but born of God." John 1:12

"How great is the love the Father has lavished on us, that we should be called children of God! And that is what we are! The reason the world does not know us is that it did not know him." I John 3:1

Don't Weary

My charge sat quietly, aligning strands of fringe on her shawl perfectly, and steadfastly refusing interruption or assistance. It is only one small instance in a day's activities, consumed with compulsively ordering everything around her. Old disciplines bubbled to the surface, and a form of OCD (Obsessive Compulsive Disorder) due to aging, kicked into high gear. It is an unrelenting taskmaster, driving her to exhaustion, and I recognize the same tendencies in myself.

There have been countless situations in which I am certain that I wore myself, and others, out with my leanings toward perfectionism, as I attempted to control the world around me and maintain an ordered life. But I have learned to separate the motive from the action; perfectionism is born of fear. It is a desperate attempt to control my environment, making it predictable and safe. Instead, it produces anxiety and worry.

A precious friend shared with me a profound truth, something her son had said when he was very young. Believing he was telling her not to worry, he said, "Don't weary!" Worry wears us out, drains our emotional resources, and keeps our attention focused on the problem, as surely as the elderly OCD lady was focused on her fringe. Worry limits our view, preventing us from seeing beyond our problems. It prevents us from obtaining the peace God has for us, and sometimes, even missing miracles.

Like every season, there is a time to pursue details and a time to walk away from them, a time to strive for more, and a time to open our hands and let go. In every season, control of our lives must rest in the hands of the Almighty God, acknowledging His sovereignty over every looming detail. One of the questions I ask myself when driven into perfectionism by worry is, "What is my focus accomplishing that is of eternal value?"

The antidote to worry is trusting God with not only the big picture but also the details. Worry makes us weary, but trust brings life, peace, and rest. We can accomplish all God has for us when we rest in His timing, provision, and plan; there is a time for attention to detail, but it must be synchronized to God's timing and direction. When we are open to His leading, even in the details, we will not grow weary but grow in trust. Faith in God is never wasted, always producing a harvest of peace. Child of God, don't weary!

"He who trusts in himself is a fool, but he who walks in wisdom is kept safe."

Proverbs 28:26

"Find rest, O my soul, in God alone; my hope comes from him. He alone is my rock and my salvation; he is my fortress, I will not be shaken. My salvation and my honor depend on God; he is my mighty rock, my refuge. Trust in him at all times, O people; pour out your hearts to him, for God is our refuge." Psalm 62:5-8

Field of View

My photography education began in a Nikon class many years ago, and more recently in a series of photography classes for graphic designers. Other than light, one of the most important elements of a good photo is its framing, fitting the subject of the photo into the "field of view" of the camera. How the subject is positioned determines the photo's balance, making it appealing.

We often see individuals in "snapshots", glimpses of who they are. What we do not see is the rest of their story, their experiences outside the framed picture, and beyond our field of view. Learning more about them, we understand better who they truly are, but only God knows the full picture.

It is our tendency, by God's design, to categorize people, to sort everything mentally, and assign names, placements, and numbers to each encounter. Adam, immediately following his creation by God's hand, was assigned the task of naming all the animals inhabiting the garden with him. Our minds similarly analyze nearly everything we encounter, flowing so naturally that we are unaware of it. Recognizing differences is natural and beneficial; it is only when we level judgment upon people, without knowing what is outside their "field of view" that we encroach upon God's territory and into dangerous dealings.

"The bigger picture" is another way of saying "outside the field of view", and it is the bigger picture that shows us the context of someone else's life. God would have us consider everyone's bigger picture, nearly impossible for us with our limited view, and to trust Him when we cannot see it. I will admit that this is one of my most difficult tasks, the assignment from my Father to love and forgive, to understand those whose field of view is mostly shielded from my view.

However, when I cannot understand someone else, I know I can trust God instead. Conversely, when I cannot understand criticisms from others and their misunderstandings of me, I must also remember that they have a limited "field of view". He knows my whole story, outside the framing of my pictures, and He knows yours. Jesus knows. He orders our lives, whispers our names, and bids us come into the panorama of His field of view. Through Him, we are known, loved, and can share His love without judgment, to love as He loves us.

"And this is his command: to believe in the name of his Son, Jesus Christ, and to love one another as he commanded us. Those who obey his commands live in him, and he in them. And this is how we know that he lives in us: We know it by the Spirit he gave us."

1 John 3:23-24

The Beautiful Desert May 22

The Colorado Rocky Mountains descend to meet the desert on their western slope. It is quite the contrast to the eastern slope, which snags the rainfall off the mountain tops. It was my first encounter with a desert, and I was not impressed; it felt barren, dry, and bereft of life. The colors appeared monotone tan, but as my perspective changed, the desert manifested muted gray-greens, rusts, and browns of all variations. With spring, vivid reds, yellows, and bright pinks dotted the cacti. The desert became beautiful in its own way.

A desert ecology class revealed much more life than I had previously deciphered, too. Jack rabbits, hawks, and barn owls resided there, though I never saw the owls. I did see some of the more unpleasant, in my humble opinion, residents like desert rats, lizards, scorpions, varieties of rattlesnakes, and to my horror, really big, hairy spiders. I heard there were bobcats, mountain lions, and coyotes, too; but never ran across any of them on our weekly field studies, thankfully. And I found there was more water in the desert than met the eye, if only you knew where to find it.

In everyone's lives, there are times when we feel as though we have been vanquished to the desert. I walked through one of those deserts for years, feeling very alone, in a monochromatic world of brown and gray. As I began to understand that God had not abandoned me, and trusted His promises, I became increasingly grateful for small, invisible blessings, such as sunlight streaming through the window on a bitter cold day; my pillow and blankets; my Bible; each meal; and every family member. And though I felt alone, I knew that I was not. Little by little, my desert became more beautiful as I discovered nuanced shades of color.

Gratitude is the brush which paints my deserts, lifting me up to new life and out of my sorrows. It is the discovery every day that God's grace and provision never fail. And the desert is a revelatory training ground, which God can use to refine our focus, disciple His children, and reveal beauty we were never able to see without it. There is always water in my spiritual deserts, too, streams of Living Water, just as Jesus promised. Generous gratitude leads us to drink in His Spirit, which will revive even the most parched wanderer. Our God is good, and our desert is temporary, even beautiful.

"If anyone is thirsty, let him come to me and drink. Whoever believes in me, as the Scripture has said, streams of living water will flow from within him." John 7:37b-38

A Choice Family

We are not afforded the option to choose the family into which we are born, but my children were blessed with one that loves them very much, all the way into adulthood, and for the rest of their lives. If I could have chosen my children, I would have chosen exactly the ones I received from God.

While we cannot choose our physical family, we are given a choice about which spiritual family we will join. The choice is simple, just two options---Satan's or God's. The choice is not complicated, not nearly as complex as we humans tend to make it. When all the noise is filtered out, two voices beckon us to follow: One is the voice of deception and lies, that whispers to elevate "self"; the other is the voice of truth and light, asking us to lay down "self". One calls us to a family of destruction and death while dressing it in worldly glamour; the other beckons us to a family of humble love and sacrificial life.

I have to question, "Why would anyone choose a family of evil, one that hated him, hurt, and attempted to destroy him? Why would he choose lies and deceit, deception and destruction, over love and truth?" The reality is, we all choose that dark family until God somehow breaks through to us with His love. We are comfortable in our dark family, for a season, tolerant of the destruction the enemy wreaks in our lives, until God's light dawns in the darkness. At that point, we realize there is a heavenly Father who desires good for us instead of evil, love instead of destruction and death.

When we choose God's family by accepting Jesus, God has a very special gift in mind for us. We receive the indwelling of the Holy Spirit when we receive Jesus as our Savior, deposited in us as evidence of our place in His family; we are sealed with His love for all time. We are forever transplanted from the kingdom and family of darkness, adopted into God's kingdom and family, living in the light of our Savior. He, who paid the price in full, gives us all the benefits of living in the Family of God, my "choice family" forever, and I hope yours, also.

"Jesus answered: 'Don't you know me, Philip, even after I have been among you such a long time? Anyone who has seen me has seen the Father...And I will ask the Father, and he will give you another Counselor to be with you forever---the Spirit of truth. The world cannot accept him, because it neither sees him nor knows him. But you know him, for he lives with you and will be in you." John 14:9, 16-17

"For you were once darkness, but now you are light in the Lord. Live as children of light (for the fruit of the light consists in all goodness, righteousness and truth) and find out what pleases the Lord. Have nothing to do with the fruitless deeds of darkness, but rather expose them. For it is shameful even to mention what the disobedient do in secret." Ephesians 5:8-12

Whitney was eight years old when she entered the kitchen with the statement, "Mom, I want to learn to play the piano." I, with uncharacteristic wisdom, replied, "Ok, but you have to commit to practicing every day for two years. Come back with your answer when you are ready." She retreated to her bedroom and I figured I had squashed that idea soundly; we didn't even own a piano for her to practice. Later that evening, she stood in front of me and said she would do it. And she did. When her commitment time had expired, she continued with music lessons far beyond those two years.

Her piano, a very vintage, ornate, upright model, stayed at our home far longer than Whitney did. When she married, her husband bought her a new digital piano; moving the very ancient, very heavy one became less likely. It sat un-tuned and un-played for years, needing a major overhaul and restoration.

We all looked at that old piano fondly, with many fond memories. But until Whitney contacted the original manufacturer, we had no idea of its worth. Finding the piano to be 123 years old and unique, it was only in the context of full restoration value that we could see more than emotional attachment. Its restoration was the key; its value nearly tripled with renewal by a master craftsman. Recently moved to its new home, it now shares the room with her digital piano. Who can know what beautiful music is yet to come?

By way of His son, Jesus, the master craftsman begins His delicate work of restringing broken hearts and tuning the discord of our pain. As He does so, He is bringing us into the restoration of our relationship with Him. Frequently, I look at the unfinished restoration of my heart and life, doubting His plan. It seems a process too slow, too difficult, and too painful. I forget that it is a process of submission to His will, timing, and wise plan.

This restoration will be ongoing, throughout my remaining time on earth. But through His unmatched knowledge and skill, working over a lifetime, He is producing a priceless instrument, like Whitney's piano, worthy of beautiful music.

"And we know that in all things God works for the good of those who love him, who have been called according to his purpose." Romans 8:28

"I will instruct you and teach you in the way you should go; I will counsel you and watch over you." Psalm 32:8

A Happy Ending   May 25

A drama series with a fascinating storyline captured my imagination recently, featuring a cartoonist whose cartoon world became a parallel second dimension. In the cartoon dimension, the lead character began making self-determining decisions, bypassing the creator. As he attempted to alter the ending, the storyline became a tangled mess, which he was helpless to remedy. The definitive factor, in the end, was the character's resolution to take responsibility for his actions and accept the outcome; flowing out of that decision, a happy ending resulted.

It struck me halfway through the series that the characters, fighting through their difficulties on their own, relying only on themselves, and attempting to bypass the creator, were a pretty hopeless bunch. And I believe that is an accurate portrayal of what most of us do, as we fight through life on our own, without God's input, and resist His assistance. Things get jumbled and tossed upside-down while we refuse to acknowledge Him or ask for His help.

We seem to be blind to the Creator, who, living in the ultimate alternative dimension, knows, sees, and controls ALL. We push, to our detriment, the agenda we believe will deliver our happiest ending, never realizing that we ultimately have little control. Assuming the mantle of "self-determination", the rebellion of mankind against his Creator seemingly knows no bounds.

God, the Creator, made the rules of this dimension and guides our storyline, not for His amusement or gain, but out of the purest and deepest love. Attempting to navigate this world without Him delivers confusion, pain, and isolation from Him. But when we come to Him, asking for His will, guidance, and help, we open up a new dimension that is impossible for the world to see. It is a dimension of love and power that is super-natural, flowing from the realms of Heaven itself, through His Spirit.

God does not restrict our free will, and we know that His story has a plan which cannot be thwarted. It is based on the sacrificial love of Jesus Christ, and His perfect plan to save all who will come to Him. Though every day may not contain the happy ending we desire, we can be certain that God the Father holds every one of our days in His hand. And in the ultimate storyline playing out in our universe, the happiest of all possible endings awaits; God wins!

"The mind of sinful man is death, but the mind controlled by the Spirit is life and peace."

Romans 8:6

Pig I Will

Read by their dad with great "character development", Richard Scarry's "Pig Will and Pig Won't", was one of my children's favorite books. When Gary read Pig Will's part, he used a sweet smile and kind voice, Pig Will being the polite pig he was; but when he read the Pig Won't part, a scowl and petulant voice prevailed. The giggles from the children added to his motivation for acting the parts, which in turn, added to their delight.

Many times in my life I have assumed the role of Pig Won't when called by God to make changes, especially those requiring painful partings with a "little god" in my heart. Each little god, like Pig I Won't, stubbornly digs in and holds on with both hands, refusing to obey. One of the most tenacious little gods for me is "security", with tentacles of fear sinking to unfathomable depths within my soul. It shows up in nearly every sector of my life.

At the root of insecurity is a lack of trust in God, and I can vouch for its insidiousness. It is at the heart of every relationship; though I cannot change other people, can I trust God whether they change or not? Can I trust God to provide the next meal and the ones a month from now? I can add layers of protection to my life, but at what point do I trust God to protect me? Can I trust God for the money I need? Or to use me in every place He plants me for His glory?

God tells us to trust Him with *everything,* and I cannot find an exception to His instructions anywhere in the Bible. He gave us a multitude of examples: Daniel faced down hungry lions, David stared up at the likes of Goliath, Joseph was sold into slavery and languished in prison, Ruth was without a family, Matthew left his counting tables, and Stephen confronted death with a heavenly smile. The disciples counted thousands of mouths to be fed in the middle of nowhere, Ester stared down extermination, Saul became Paul, and John was exiled on an island.

God did not abandon one of them and was their help in time of trial, so He will be for us in whatever we face. That is His promise, and He never changes. It is my choice to act as "Pig I Will" or stubbornly resist as "Pig I Won't". I can choose to trust in the goodness of God in Christ Jesus, or continue in my stubborn, willful ways. No matter what I choose, Jesus remains the same, faithful to every promise.

"For thus said the Lord God, the Holy One of Israel: In returning [to Me] and resting [in Me] you shall be saved; in quietness and in [trusting] confidence shall be your strength. But you would not." Isaiah 30:15 AMP

"Jesus Christ is the same yesterday and today and forever." Hebrews 13:8

"Lean on, trust in, and be confident in the Lord with all your heart and mind and do not rely on your own insight or understanding." Proverbs 3:5 AMP

Battle Plans

My life's conflicts had me weary and ashamed, always apologetic for having struggles, and enduring what seemed to be never-ending battles. Why was life so difficult for me while everyone else seemed to be doing ok?! The answer is probably not such a big secret to anyone else, but it eluded me for decades.

Living this life free of battles is abnormal; if someone is not in a battle yet, he or she is about to be. That was confirmed as I read Psalm 27, which jolted me into reality—my life is completely normal! Life is a war zone with battles being fought on every front. This world is fraught with booby traps, land mines, and tripwires just along the next path. Satan's troops stalk and snipe at us one minute, and the next, they hold up the white flag, deceiving us into thinking they have surrendered and are no longer a threat.

In verse 5 of Psalm 27, this stood out to me: **"He will conceal me in His shelter, hide me in the folds of His tent, and set me high on a rock, lifting my head above my surrounding foes."** This tells me that for every battle, He is present with a plan of protection, provision, and victory. He has intelligent information I will never see, and a plan meticulously, flawlessly put together. My greatest responsibility is to praise Him while trusting and seeking Him in every battle. I lose the battle when I attempt to exert control over the situation, forgetting that my strength is in trusting the General in charge of the battle plan.

The important thing to remember is that battles are normal; they are components of war, and we live in a war zone on planet Earth. Our war is a fierce one being waged for the souls of men. For soldiers in the field, this is a normal way of life; they anticipate the next battle and continuously plan for winning the war. The battles will be many, no truce negotiations possible, a fight unto death. Perseverance is key.

I have exposed two of my enemy's weapons of choice in this battle—making me feel weary and ashamed. He has a huge arsenal from which to choose, using self-pity, shame, and defeat to his advantage. But now that his plan is exposed, I will stand guard, alert at my post, vigilant until the General appears, or I am taken off the field. In the end, God wins through Christ Jesus; and throughout the war against God's people, He is faithful to execute His perfect battle plans to secure the victory of the ages.

"For our struggle is not against flesh and blood, but against the rulers, against the authorities, against the powers of this dark world, and against the spiritual forces of evil in the heavenly realms. Therefore, put on the full armor of God, so that when the day of evil comes, you may be able to stand your ground, and after you have done everything, to stand."
Ephesians 6:10-13

Companion Planting

The deep brown soil flowed between my fingers as I pulled the peat moss up through the potting mix, tiny specks of white vermiculite dotting it like confetti. It was spring planting season, and tender young plants in their sectioned pots waited to be snugged into their respective containers in my porch garden. Pulling up each vegetable on my phone's screen, its companion plant was identified, the plant which grows best with it and is mutually beneficial.

Rosemary teamed up with Nasturtiums to repel tenacious cats and Cabbage Butterfly, marigolds adorned the pots of sturdy tomato plants, along with garlic to throw tomato worms off the scent of their favorite meal. Squashes bedded down with thyme, and sage nestled between beans. My dread enemy, aphids, find Nasturtiums and garlic appalling, while the hated slugs detest rosemary leaves sprinkled on the soil. And one more, of what seems to be many uses for Nasturtiums, is that White Fly find them highly distasteful, to my delight!

Couldn't we all benefit from "companion planting"? Imagine the perfect companion who fends off depression, or one who, at the perfect time, lifts our spirit. Perhaps there is one who defends us when no one else is willing, or steps between us and a potential disaster. Perhaps there is another who sits quietly by our sides just as we need to talk through a problem; a companion who just likes us for who we are, or knows our hearts, understands our weariness, or comforts us in our brokenness.

Our hearts are hungry for one Companion who satisfies our cravings, and His name is Jesus. He is the perfect companion who is everything we need when we need it. He alone can honor the promise "never to leave or forsake" us. He alone can fulfill our needs, and He alone is the deepest desire of our hearts. He is closer than the air we breathe, warmer than the sunshine, and more caring than we can imagine.

I tend to resist His best offers, making every type of excuse. I deny His power, refuse to yield to His control, and resist His promises—I am human. But still, He extends His hand and offers His heart. It is truly up to me; Jesus has done all He can do, more than anyone on earth could do, sacrificially offering Himself in my place. He has made peace and every blessing available to me through the blood He shed on the cross, grace upon grace poured out on my behalf. As I walk beside Him, I truly have found the perfect "companion planting".

"The Lord himself goes before you and will be with you; he will never leave you nor forsake you. Do not be afraid; do not be discouraged." Deuteronomy 31:8

Fancy and plain, small and large, some were shaped like flowers, others sparkling balls. Buttons by the hundreds filled my grandmother's button box. The "box" was a round tin, oddly stored in a drawer in the bedroom, rather than with her sewing machine. Every childhood visit found me lifting the tin lid, gazing at the variety and beauty of the buttons she had collected over the years. My fingers ran through them like sand, and the buttons felt somehow comforting and familiar.

When a button was found unattached, it made its way to the tin; and a button vacancy on a garment found a button to attach. Some of the buttons adorned the pretty flannel nightgowns Gram made for me, her only granddaughter. One tiny, white-pearled button restored my brother's dress shirt for Sunday school. Many years later, two round, black beady-looking buttons fit perfectly as eyes for the stuffed animal I made for my soon-to-be husband. The buttons were useful whether plain or beautiful; ultimately, they were buttons, after all.

God made each of us to serve a purpose in His kingdom, a role to play in His plan for this world. Some, like the buttons, seem plain and rather nondescript, quietly going about God's business in the background. Others are sparkly, noticeable immediately for their bright dominant roles in life; but both functions serve God's purpose. We are not created to be simple adornments in this world, but rather, we are to be useful, lending our hands and feet to God's plan.

God invites us to serve Him by serving others, with the talents and gifts He graciously bestowed on each of us. We are not to serve out of pride or self, but to show our love for Him by imitating His. He will always lead us, through His Holy Spirit, to the place of service He planned for us when our hearts seek Him most and are willing to bend to His will above our own.

I don't understand why God created man to act as God's earthly hands, feet, and lips. I don't understand why He would choose "buttons" of all sizes, shapes, colors, and temperaments to carry out His plan for humankind, entrusting us with conveying His love to those around us. I know that we were not created to just show off God's love only in words to the world, though. We were not made to simply be beautiful, we are made in His image to be His messengers and real helpers, after all.

"Serve wholeheartedly, as if you were serving the Lord, not men, because you know that the Lord will reward everyone for whatever good he does, whether he is slave or free."

Ephesians 6:7-8

Cow Birds

Rude, obnoxious birds, driving out the beautiful songbirds, leaving the air bristling with their abrasive chatter—that is a flock of Cow Birds. Our trees were once alive with Song Sparrows, Finches, Cardinals, and Bluebirds. Now they bustle with the antics of Cow Birds—plain, homely, brown-and-black Cow Birds. If I knew how to get rid of them, they would no longer crowd our lawn, nor stir such a din; but alas, there appears to be no remedy, and nothing to entice the songbirds to return.

Though there appears no cure for my Cow Bird dilemma, the Lord showed me a better perspective. I pictured the Cow Birds invading a tranquil scene with their noise and number, causing all peace to flee. And I knew that these troublesome Cow Birds were a picture of the worries disturbing the peace in my spirit. There is nothing I can do about the physical Cow Birds in my yard, but the spiritual Cow Birds may be vanquished, if I will just place my trust in Jesus. He promises peace, perfect peace, and order amid the chaos.

Despite the Cow Birds, I have learned to focus on one family of House Sparrows, one of Mockingbirds, and one of Blue Jays, none of which are my favorite birds, but are beautiful in their own way. In the same way, my focus needs to shift, not to the source of worry, but my Source of all peace and provision, Jesus. The clamor of the world will fade into the background, and I will begin to see my circumstances in a different perspective, as I fix my attention on Jesus. The "Cow Birds" of worry must scatter before His Presence and light in trees other than mine.

"Peace I leave with you; my peace I give to you. I do not give to you as the world gives. Do not let your hearts be troubled and do not be afraid." John 14:27

A Full Cup

The sun was setting, the heat subsided a bit, and it was the perfect time to inspect my garden for its daily yield. My bucket began to fill with tomatoes, cucumbers, and an overly grown zucchini. The last stop of the evening was strawberry picking, gently placing the cup full of fragile berries on top of the harvested vegetables. It was a satisfying feeling, bringing in produce from a garden planted solely on my porch and stairs, enough to feed myself through my labor and God's blessing.

Sorting it onto the countertop, the cup full of berries that appeared so perfect in the evening light looked less than perfect under the bright kitchen light. Notably, tiny worms were enjoying some of my berries too much. Not to be defeated by a few naughty worms, I promptly cut around them and, with sweet revenge, locked them into a plastic bag of death. The cup full of strawberries still yielded enough for the night's dessert.

Life recently had taken a similar turn, events springing up from nowhere to ruin otherwise pleasant summer days. They were the ordinary annoying events of a checking account not balancing, hours spent on a "help-line" which was much less than helpful, paired with a nerve-wracking encounter with the phone company. Like the little worms consuming my strawberries, these little nagging problems were robbing me of my joy.

The solution is as simple as the knife in my kitchen, which deftly sliced away the annoyance of tiny worms. Turning my attention back to Jesus required only a simple song, repeated as often as necessary, yielding sweet fruit, minus the worms of destruction. And though the solution is simple, it is never easy; it is much easier, at first, to continue cursing the "worms" than to sing that song of praise, but it is the song of praise that carves out the rotten spots. It is the praise that salvages the fruit, turning it from garbage into dessert.

Jesus is worthy of ALL praise, honor, and glory, regardless of our circumstances, attitude, or plight. It is praise which releases His power into our conditions, lifting us above them, carving away the decay, and revealing the real fruit. How wonderful is our God that He gives us this option, never forced but always blessed, to praise the One who is worthy of all we can give! Yielding even the smallest bit to Him will always increase our blessing, to an overflowing "full cup" in return.

"Sing to the Lord, all the earth; proclaim his salvation day after day. Declare his glory among the nations, his marvelous deeds among all peoples. For great is the Lord and most worthy of praise; he is to be feared above all gods. For all the gods of the nations are idols, but the Lord made the heavens. Splendor and majesty are before him; strength and joy in his dwelling place. Ascribe to the Lord, O families of nations, ascribe to the Lord glory and strength, ascribe to the Lord the glory due his name." 1 Chronicles 16:23-28

June

The Beach House

They weren't difficult to find, but they were very difficult to avoid. The seashells, of all sizes and many shapes, littered the beach. And what first appeared to be tiny brown pebbles, were minuscule shells and broken fragments of shells with sharp jagged edges. Seashells seemed to abound everywhere our gaze landed, and many were intact, a prize for everyone searching for an authentic beach souvenir!

The broken shells could be identified as parts of larger shells by their shapes, colors, and lines. There were fragments of homes to clams, oysters, conch, and whelks. Transverse Arcs, King's Crowns, and Olive shells abounded. And each home was perfectly suited to its inhabitant's salty lifestyle. No matter the home each creature of the sea occupied, it was inevitably temporary, eventually dashed in the surf, and washed clean of its inhabitant.

We all live in "beach homes" of varying styles, like each of those billion seashells, occupying very temporary bodies while on this earth. We care for, preen, pamper, and groom them. We feed them, sometimes excessively, and then starve them half to death. We spend mountains of money on them, exercise, use and abuse them, then attempt to repair them. We complain about them and link our self-esteem to them. We expend them and then try to rejuvenate them. But inevitably, they expire, leaving an empty shell on the sands, our beach houses vacated.

As inevitably as each sea critter surrendered its home to the ocean, we will surrender these bodies, which serve as the house for our spirits, back to the ocean of life from which they came. The beach house of all our intense focus will be as an empty shell, left behind on the shores of the vast ocean of life.

But one of the great promises of God is a new body, un-aging, unfailing, resurrection-new, just waiting to be claimed. Leaving this home, with Jesus as our Savior, a magnificent new home awaits, one perfectly suited for eternity, and the promise of a new life. In light of the new "beach house" awaiting me, in all its splendor, perhaps the comparative shabbiness of the one I have now shouldn't really be that important.

"So it will be with the resurrection of the dead. The body that is sown is perishable, it is raised imperishable; it is sown in dishonor, it is raised in glory; it is sown in weakness, it is raised in power, it is sown a natural body, it is raised a spiritual body."

1 Corinthians 15:42-44

Family Feud

The television game show, Family Feud, pits family against family, in hope of taking home a new vehicle. Each family is wonderfully cohesive, lobbing high fives, embracing, and chanting family cheers on-air. The younger members are energetic and out-going, the older generation setting decorum, and cheering them on. How wonderful it would be if all families acted as though they were on TV all the time! But it isn't the reality we live in day-to-day. The bottom line is that there are no perfect families.

Holidays tend to bring out the worst qualities of many family members. Stress, time crunches, high expectations, and past experiences contribute to the pressures built during that season. I will confess that some of my "worst moments ever" happened during a holiday season: Introvert + crowd + time constraints + logistics + past wounds = Disaster. Though I have often failed, and cannot redeem those days, with God every day is a new opportunity. There, grace and hope abound, and though I cannot change what is past, I can trust God with today.

Family relationships are incredibly difficult to place into God's hands because they are so close to our hearts. Yet, those are the ones we most need to entrust to Him. And in my family, during a relatively brief time, one I never could have imagined would experience bitterness and strife, Jesus became my only hope. The situation required my surrender of each loved one solely into His care and timing. The changes were not easy, the asking and giving of forgiveness was painful, and the waiting, excruciatingly long. However, God brought healing and restoration in His timing, and I found that experience prepared me for what was to come in future world events.

I have witnessed what God can do to restore relationships, renew fellowship, and heal my pain. Real family feuds are most often the ones only God's formula can heal. Jesus + Forgiveness + Prayer + Time = Healing. I came to realize that Jesus *can* change anything if hearts are willing and that even if my family doesn't change, I can. His is the only relationship I cannot live without. With Christ Jesus, real family feuds may just possibly begin to look more like the television version, in the end. With God, all things are possible.

"So watch yourselves. If your brother sins, rebuke him, and if he repents, forgive him. If he sins against you seven times in a day, and seven times comes back to you and says, 'I repent', forgive him." Luke 17:3

"When a man's ways are pleasing to the Lord, he makes even his enemies live at peace with him." Proverbs 16:7

166   **Moon Over My Shoulder**

A Breath Away June 3

Whitney approached me after church with a puzzled expression, followed by a question. Her twelve-year-old mind was wrestling with how the air was filled with things that couldn't be seen. It has water in it, but the only time we can see it is when it becomes dense, or "solid", as in rain, fog, snow, or clouds. Oxygen, carbon dioxide, helium, and a multitude of other elements ride, too, on the winds. There is an invisible realm of dust, pollen, and microscopic organisms finding passage on the air currents, truly a universe of its own. As that universe fills our lungs, life truly is always a breath away.

Another realm surrounds us as certainly as the air, a realm teeming with energy and life, one that affects us just as surely. It is the spirit realm, hidden from our natural sight, but no less real than the natural air enveloping our bodies. Because we cannot see the air, we do not deny its existence; because we cannot see the spiritual realm, it is not rendered nonexistent. We feel its influences and sense its movements, though we tend to dismiss them because we cannot understand them.

Within that realm, angels tread, ministering God's love to mankind. Demons plot and torment, and there the true battles are fought. Its events are glimpsed as their evidence spills into our realm at times, defying logic, and highlighting God's power in lightning-flash episodes. Momentarily, our eyes are opened to the wonders normally hidden from view. God's miracles surround us like the air.

Even now, through the blood of Christ, we have become conquerors, wielding the deadly sword of the Spirit and the Word of God. God's assurance is that even when it appears that we are losing, we have already won if Jesus is our King. Though our battles may be hard and the wounds extensive, everything we need can still be found in Him. Jesus is our victor in the invisible war, and eternal victory is only a breath away.

"Finally, be strong in the Lord and in his mighty power. Put on the full armor of God so that you can take your stand against the devil's schemes. For our struggle is not against flesh and blood, but against the rulers, against the powers of this dark world, and against the spiritual forces of evil in the heavenly realms. Therefore, put on the full armor of God, so that when the day of evil comes, you may be able to stand your ground, and after you have done everything, to stand. Stand firm then, with the belt of truth buckled around your waist, with the breastplate of righteousness in place, and with your feet fitted with the readiness that comes from the gospel of peace. In addition to all this, take up the shield of faith, with which you can extinguish all the flaming arrows of the evil one. Take the helmet of salvation and the sword of the Spirit, which is the word of God. And pray in the Spirit on all occasions with all kinds of prayers and requests. With this in mind, be alert and always keep on praying for all the saints." Ephesians 6:10-18

Strawberries Fields Forever   June 4

If the timing of my stay with my grandparents was just right, just after summer vacation began at the close of the school year, a trip to the strawberry fields was inevitable. It was one of my grandmother's favorite foods, as evidenced by my grandfather's comment upon every visit to the fields, "They need to weigh your grandmother before, and after, she picks." No one grasped that concept until they followed my grandmother down a row; one strawberry landed in her basket, while one flew to her mouth!

As I cut my ripe berries into a bowl, I remembered my grandmother, missing those hot sunny days spent with her in the field, then in her kitchen. There, we quickly plucked their green leafy tops, then sliced them into a pan, making strawberry jam. My berries, fresh from the grocery store, don't smell as sweet or seem as dark red as the berries of my memory. As I sorted them, a couple of strawberries were already molding, and more had difficult-to-see bruises. Some were still unripe on top or had brown spots forming on their bottoms.

The similarities to frail human beings were rather striking as I continued my strawberry processing. We humans, made in God's image, are innately beautiful to Him. It is sin that spoils us, rotting us from the inside and causing brown spots to appear, eventually, on the exterior. Some of us are bruised by rough handling during our lives on this earth, those bruises glaringly evident at times, other times not so obvious. And though we are reluctant to admit our frailty, we, too, have a short shelf-life.

As God our Father gazes down the long rows, He sees us and accepts us just as we are, and He still delights in His creation. He detests the sin and corruption of this world, all that is the cause of our damage and destruction. The wonder is that He sent His son, Jesus, into that very corrupt world to be our remedy and our Restorer. On that precious Son's shoulders, it was His Father's will to lay the cross, bruising Him in my place, and crushing Him under the weight of my sin.

The good news of the resurrection of Jesus is that when God raised Him from the dead, He raised me to new life, fresh and clean, reborn in His spotless image. When I stand before Him, He sees only Jesus, the perfection of His Son, and welcomes me without condemnation. Perfection is found in Christ alone and for me, and you, that is called grace. Like the strawberries in the field, we will not live forever on this sin-ridden earth. Eternity with Christ is the only strawberry field that is forever.

"But he was pierced for our transgressions, he was crushed for our iniquities; the punishment that brought us peace was upon him, and by his wounds we are healed. We all, like sheep, have gone astray, each of us has turned to his own way; and the Lord has laid on him the iniquity of us all." Isaiah 53:5-6

Over-comer

Chubby hands and tender feet struggled up the steep slope of the ladder, every rung a threat to the toddler's safety. Advancing ever so cautiously, he could hear the gentle words of encouragement from his daddy. Then he pulled himself, with all his toddler might, onto the next step.

At last, there was a platform to sit and contemplate for a moment what he had accomplished. But another word from his father prompted him on, another hurdle to overcome. He had gotten to the top—now how would he get down? He had never done this before and was hesitating. It was hot, so far up, and such a looong way down.

His eyes widened with fear as he reservedly gazed down the path he must travel. He couldn't go back down the ladder; that was unthinkable after all he had gone through to climb up. Again, the soft word of encouragement from below, and he pushed off! Picking up momentum, the fears fell away, and exhilaration slid into their place as the pace accelerated. Just as the speed transitioned into fear, strong and gentle arms enfolded him at the bottom of the slide.

Safely in his daddy's arms, looking over his comfortable shoulder, he gazed at the formidable challenge he had just overcome. For now, he'd enjoy being up high in his daddy's arms; there was no better, nor safer, place to be.

We are never so old or too wise that we no longer face daunting obstacles in our lives. The ladder is steep, the steps difficult, and the challenges overwhelming. Through it all, though, we can trust our Father's instructions, His guidance, and the safety of His presence. He is our provider, protector, strength, and mighty power. When we listen to His words of encouragement and follow His direction, we, over-comers through Jesus, can rest peacefully in His arms, knowing that whatever happens, He will still be in control.

"Have no fear of sudden disaster or of the ruin that overtakes the wicked, for the Lord will be your confidence and will keep your foot from being snared." Proverbs 3:25-26

"Trust in the Lord and do good; dwell in the land and enjoy safe pasture. Delight yourself in the Lord and he will give you the desires of your heart." Psalm 37:3-4

"Trust in the Lord with all your heart and lean not on your own understanding; in all your ways acknowledge him, and he will make your paths straight." Proverbs 3:5-6

Still Standing

Marsha had suffered greatly over the past year, as pain moved from one joint to another. Her back had improved, but now, as she sang the hymn in the early morning worship service, one knee gave way. And her face expressed the searing pain she experienced. As that knee buckled, I saw her husband, Ed, move closer to her side and hold her with his arm around her back, acting as a standing brace, perfectly aligned to her slight frame.

I was immediately impacted by the scene before me. We are all "Marshas". As frail beings living on a fallen earth, we are crippled in our sin and too weak to stand on our own. For those who will allow Him to interact in our lives, Jesus becomes our "Ed", standing alongside us. He is strong enough to meet every need, able to secure and protect us. He is watchful over us, ready to steady us with His close presence and calm influence. He knows our pain and anticipates our weaknesses. Yet we are hardly aware of Him until we give way and cannot stand on our own.

Many of us are too prideful and stubborn to ask for His help. I know I am. However, I am learning to depend on Jesus more each day, recognizing that I am fully inadequate, and not even able to control my heartbeat, or the next breath I take. Aren't we amazingly brilliant and wonderful creatures made in God's very image? And at the same time, aren't we the densest and most rebellious creatures, to our detriment?

Yet God does not leave us to ourselves but invites us to stand alongside Him. There He supports us in loving-kindness, forgiveness, and full acceptance in Christ. Only because of Him are we still standing.

"Jesus said to him, 'I am the way, and the truth, and the life; no one comes to the Father but through Me.'" John 14:6

"Peace I leave with you; My peace I give to you; not as the world gives do I give to you. Do not let your heart be troubled, nor let it be fearful." John 14:27

Learning piano at a late, very late, age is daunting for many reasons. It is a complicated instrument with a steep learning curve, requiring decades of instruction and practice. I prayed and thought long and hard about the value of it, before purchasing an instrument. After its arrival, my first few days yielded a simple song with one hand; a couple of weeks produced a slightly more complex melody played with two hands and even a bit of improvisation. It is hard work, but it brings joy to my soul.

Then it dawned on me, like a clearing of the clouds—my new journey with music is simply a matter of being available and willing. If I compare myself to others, I have little hope of being proficient, but if I say, "Here I am, Lord! Take me where you want on this journey," the possibilities are truly endless. He is the God of the impossible. Every journey and every gift have value, even if it is a single song that brings joy to one soul.

It is inherently human to compare, measuring the differences, and assessing the worth of pretty much everything in this world, including each other. When we are simply comparing and not criticizing our differences, that quality is innocuous. However, when our assessment of those differences is affected by pride, trouble ensues. When we belittle the gifts and talents of those around us because they appear insignificant to us, we diminish God's presence in this world; He is pleased with the smallest of offerings.

Criticism abounds in our world and encouragement is in short supply. Instead of evaluating someone's performance and questioning their worth, I am reminded to look at my obedience to God's calling. Diligence, patience, labor, failures, and intermittent successes are all part of God's personal improvement plan. He encourages us to trust Him with everything, as He leads us on the paths He desires us to walk. Every human being is gifted in some way to bring good into the world.

We are to be a blessing in our time on earth and prepared for heaven to come. For each of us, God only requires simple willingness to be available, allowing Him to guide us, even against the flow, if necessary. Trust him for His timing, and leading. His blessings and rewards are ours every day as we cry out, "Lord, here I am!" Then step out, even if in baby steps, to accomplish that to which He has called and equipped you, no matter how humble.

"O Lord Almighty, blessed is the man who trusts in you." Psalm 84:12

"Before his downfall a man's heart is proud, but humility comes before honor."

Proverbs 18:12

Car Polish

From his youth, Gary's fascination with automobiles became a life-long pursuit. It was an attraction stronger than any other in his life. Vintage models, particularly, caught his attention no matter where we went. Many are the times we stopped in front of a house to admire a vehicle. Saturdays were often spent at car shows, car lots, and even parking lots, identifying the models and customizations. Gary could pinpoint a vehicle's age within a year, tell what items were stock or custom, and if they had been wrecked or restored.

After many years of being apprenticed to Gary through marriage, I can finally distinguish a good paint job from a very fine paint job. Bad paint is obvious to almost anyone, but it takes a more experienced eye to separate the good from the exceptional. With paint, the quality shows in the reflection.

Being a Christian is somewhat comparable to the quality of the paint job on cars. The quality shows up in the reflection. Some of us still have pretty blatant imperfections, which have not been yielded to the sanding and buffing process. Some of us appear good, until the Light hits from a certain angle, and the rough areas are exposed. In a very few, there is a brilliance of refinement which reflects the Master painter in near perfection. That perfecting came in the form of many washings, sandings, buffings, and polishings—many "yieldings". It is that fine paint job that reflects the Image in it, sharply and clearly.

Will my "paint" clearly reflect Jesus, and am I willing to submit to His hand for further refinement? Will my "paint" reflect Him clearly, or will His likeness appear hazy, distorted, or not visible at all? What will the world around me see? Lord, help me be more willing to undergo the refining process you have for me, conforming me to the perfect image of your Son. Like the car polish, I want to reflect You.

"And we, who with unveiled faces all reflect the Lord's glory, are being transformed into his likeness with ever-increasing glory, which comes from the Lord, who is the Spirit."

2 Corinthians 3:18

Ride to Crazy

The power sizzled overhead, crackling across the metal ceiling, while the drivers pressed down on the pedal hoping to be the first to take off. One could tell who the real competitors were by their intense gaze of anticipation, waiting to pounce upon the nearest bumper car that would dare obstruct their mad circular dash. It was one place where aggression was permitted and strategy imperative, lest you be snagged in a stalled cluster of cars, the epitome of frustration. Still, it was one of my favorite rides in the amusement park, truly a ride to crazy.

My strategy, driving bumper cars, has improved with age and real driving experience. I now know to look ahead as much as possible, to stay to the outside of the pack, and to watch for openings. It pays to avoid the aggressive drivers and to be kind to the timid. Making headway depends upon shrewd strategy, and still, frustration abounds. When stopped dead in my tracks in the middle of chaos, for it is only a matter of time, it will all change in a few seconds anyway.

So goes my life! I have realized the wisdom to be forward-thinking, but not too tied to the future to be able to live in the present. There is wisdom in having plans, but I have also realized that waiting a bit, the situation will change anyway. We humans need each other, and that's all right, but I have also learned to be content walking alone with Jesus; listening to what God has to say, instead of people all the time, is simply wisdom. And when I am stopped dead in my tracks, frustrated and annoyed, it is generally time to wake up to a lesson God is trying to impress on me.

There have been a few times in my life when I wanted to get off this ride-to-crazy, to escape the frenzy and the pain. But I have also been fascinated by it as I have watched God intervene and guide events. I have learned more about Him from each round I am blessed to ride, and through interacting with the people God loves.

With the experiences my Father has given me, I have become so much better at driving this bumper car of life. God has used each event to better equip me for the next. As we witness God's hand at work in a chaotic and dark world, we are privileged to observe His displays of power and love. And each day is a new opportunity to know Him and bless others on this "ride to crazy".

"All the days ordained for me were written in your book before one of them came to be."
Psalm 139:16b

"In his heart a man plans his course, but the Lord determines his steps." Proverbs 16:9

"He will have no fear of bad news; his heart is steadfast, trusting in the Lord." Psalm 112:7

The Best Resort   June 10

Listening as the group of young women discussed which was their favorite beach destination, many of the best resorts of the Southeastern United States were mentioned. Of the popular beaches, I reminisced, I have been to most of them in years past. Many memories floated to the surface of my mind, bobbing momentarily, then I nudged them neatly into their place of mental storage. I miss those times of travel and exploration, of seeing new places, and the relational closeness that develops from tight quarters. I miss the sights and sounds, the cultures which are similar enough to be comforting and unique enough to be stimulating.

As the best memories come to mind, inevitably the worst memories surface in comparison. There were a few truly awful experiences in my travels such as bedbugs in a newly renovated hotel, a drug deal transpiring as I walked by two men outside a motel office, and an uncleaned bathroom and unchanged sheets in three separate rooms at the same motel, leading to a night in their Presidential Suite. A hotel in Orlando advertised a buffet breakfast and instead offered bagels and toast. Another in New Orleans boasted water-soaked carpets. Without these experiences, though, I may have very much taken for granted their wonderful counterparts, those who provided all they promised, with a smile included.

Oddly, when it comes to our relationship with God, most of us settle for the worst resort instead of the best. We will spend our precious time soaking up the sun at a worldly resort but avoid time with the One who made the universe. We don't hesitate to talk with a friend about our problems but try to hide them from the Solution. We thirst for acceptance, yet spiritually dehydrate, resisting Him who begs us to come to Him. We run to a doctor but refuse treatment from the Great Physician. We bury our pain when our relief is but a prayer away, and we cower in the darkness of shame when there is a Savior who longs to shine His forgiving light.

Oh, that I would learn to run to the Best Resort, Jesus, before using Him as my last resort! Oh, that I would pray before lingering in the worst places. Oh, that I would find His comfort and healing instead of seeking the weaker choices first. He may allow me to reside in those last resorts at times, to show me that they are not His best for me. He may give me the ability to see His goodness in stark contrast to the worst resorts. But He will always lead me, in the end, to the best Resort in the world, at the feet of Jesus, exactly where I should be.

"I say to myself, 'The Lord is my portion; therefore I will wait for him. The Lord is good to those whose hope is in him, to the one who seeks him; it is good to wait quietly for the salvation of the Lord.'" Lamentations 3:24-26

The Top of the Heap

My soon-to-be husband and I shared a common interest of "running the roads" for relaxation and entertainment. He loved to drive, and I loved the peaceful sightseeing. As I marveled at the landscape, my imagination flapped in the breeze stirred by the open windows. Passing a very old and very dilapidated house, with furniture stacked to the ceiling of the broad front porch, something caught my eye. I excitedly directed Gary to back up and pull into the driveway. Tall oak trees and an elderly lady greeted us as we approached.

On the top of the heap was a very old rocker, partially held together with screws. It sported a plywood seat which had long ago separated its layers, as it withstood many baths in rain. It had little finish left on its ancient wood, but it was solid, and the price was right—just five dollars! Making a bargain with Gary, I agreed to strip, sand, and refinish it if he would make a new seat for it.

It was our first official furniture for our new home together. Outfitted with its new cherry-wood slatted seat, that chair taken from the top of the heap became one of my prized possessions. Its wide flat arms and the low arc of its rockers became my favorite perch as I later rocked our babies. It sits in my living room today, a sweet and tender reminder of a family raised together.

If I could assign feelings to that old chair, it probably lost hope long before being lifted to the top of the heap; there is no guessing how many years it sat on that mountain of junk. Even after we purchased it, it endured much sanding, washing, more sanding, grinding, cutting, staining, and finishing before it was prepped for its mission.

Many of us, like that chair, are on the top of the heap of life, feeling discarded, lonely, and useless, with no purpose, but that would be a lie. God values each of His children, and I have learned, and perhaps am still learning, that if I am breathing that is a good sign that God has a plan not yet completed. There is a purpose for my being here, a "mission" of some kind, a value to Him which I cannot see or feel in a tangible way, yet important no less.

God's way is to carry us to a better place, though it may not feel that way at first. And I had imagined God was finished with me, too, after years of prepping, but He wasn't—He was actually just getting started. So, I would encourage you to embrace the prepping, and since you are still walking the planet, God has a purpose for you. He brought you off the top of the heap and into His loving arms for a reason. The best may still be yet to come.

"Yet, O Lord, you are our Father. We are the clay, you are the potter; we are all the work of your hand." Isaiah 64:8

"For I know the plans I have for you," declares the LORD, "plans to prosper you and not to harm you, plans to give you hope and a future." Jeremiah 29:11

The prediction model for the weather was simple in days before the advent of computer-generated forecast models. It was predictable and accurate. Farmers knew the forecast by observing the movement and forms of the clouds throughout the past millennia. For me, clouds indicate weather changes, but they are much more of a fascination as sky sculptures, another element of nature directing my attention to the hand of God in creation.

This summer I have witnessed two "sculptures" I have never seen in all my years of attention directed to the sky. One was a bank of thin clouds suspended above the trees; topped with curls, they appeared almost as if pin-curled. The curls all flowed in the same direction like waves in a child's drawing, symmetrical and evenly spaced. The other was a thin tube of cloud yawning across the sky with top and bottom wisps fanning out like a feather. Both formations were obviously clouds, not jet generated, and were so unique that I was compelled to record them on my camera.

Clouds capture our imaginations, intrigue us with their diversity, and even strike fear in our hearts. Some are indicators of sunny days ahead, some signal rain approaching. Others amass power and destruction, spinning a tornado across the landscape. Some toss lightning bolts like spears of fire. Clouds can hide the sun, obscure a mountain, and reflect God's glory in sunrise majesty. I will confess that there is another reason I intently watch the clouds.

One day clouds, which the earth has never beheld, will amass in such a way that they cannot be dismissed as "just another storm" or a pretty sunset over the ocean. I am looking for that particular gathering of clouds, anticipating the Son of Man returning on a cloud with great glory; it will be the same way He exited this world. I am looking forward to His coming, my spirit groaning with anticipation of freedom from the chains of sin and despair which bind the world in brokenness.

Cloud gazing gives my heart hope and a sense of wonder at God's creation. It reminds me to trust in His promise of return; that He will set everything right again; that under His Kingship peace will be restored. He is present with me now in Spirit; but when He comes again, we will see Him as He truly is. Until then, I will continue to peer into the sky. I will delight in the gathering wisps and strands, billows, and furls. I will unleash my imagination amid His amazing sky sculptures, anticipating my Savior's sure return.

"At that time they will see the Son of Man coming in a cloud with power and great glory. When these things begin to take place, stand up and lift up your heads, because your redemption is drawing near." Luke 21:27-28

Carried Away June 13

Laid out on the closed street near our home was the envelope of a hot-air balloon, perfectly flat as if painted on the pavement. Its suspension cables were attached to the envelope, running back to the basket, as a crowd of puzzled neighbors gathered to witness the event. I had enlisted the hot-air balloon tethered-ride for a non-profit organization; for a nominal extra fee, they had offered my husband and me an un-tethered excursion, with take-off from our neighborhood. We were about to be carried away, and fear began rising before the balloon did.

As the envelope filled, becoming a billow of colorful cloud, it began rising slowly, pushing against the sky as if defying its superiority. Finally positioned over the basket, we climbed in; and to the sound of the burner flaring, we began floating upward like the bob on a fishing line, faster as the hot air fed the envelope. Higher and higher above the treetops, above the sounds of barking dogs and laughing children, strung between heaven and earth, the quiet was broken only by the intermittent burner igniting.

I was excited at the prospect of the adventure, and terrified of the possibilities. Life is very much the same with challenges and hurdles, which in our own strength, we are not sure we can handle. Some of life's events are dangerous, some mundane; some are compounded with problems stacked atop one another. Some of them are of our own making, others are often simply by-products of living in a fallen world.

The perfect balance is found in trusting that Someone has my life in His hands, that God is ultimately in control and has the power to change whatever He deems necessary. The unchangeable events are the very ones producing His greatest transformation in me, altering my way of thinking, cleansing my impurities, stretching my "envelope", and nudging me in directions I would not otherwise go.

When it seems that life has carried you away and you have no control, look up, knowing that God the Father is looking down. Jesus has tethered Himself with unbreakable bonds, no matter the stress and tension the circumstances apply. The stress-testing has already been done by Jesus, and the world conquered through His death and resurrection. During every challenge and trial, His love has not lessened, care not diminished, and heart not changed toward us. And it is He who holds the burner cord, He who reads the map and guides the way. He is the anchor that holds fast, never permitting you to be carried away, or beyond His reach.

"Cast your cares on the Lord and he will sustain you; he will never let the righteous fall…When I am afraid, I will trust in you. In God, whose word I praise, in God I trust; I will not be afraid." Psalm 55:22, 56:3a

"We have this hope as an anchor for the soul, firm and secure." Hebrews 6:19a

There is something fundamentally reassuring about harvest time. I spent part of my summers on my great-uncle's farm watching him plow and till with his old John Deere tractor. I don't think most people, unless you are a serious gardener or farmer, consider that the rows have to be plowed in a straight line to be able to reap. How you go about plowing determines the abundance of your harvest. Like driving a car, tractor, or even oxen, if your focus is not straight ahead, you drift, naturally plowing a curvy line. Your crooked rows and lack of focus will be revealed at harvest, rendering it destructive and unprofitable.

In Luke 9:57-62, Jesus spoke most to farmers in the crowds (v.62), **"To him, Jesus said, 'No one who puts his hand to the plow and keeps looking back is fit to serve in the kingdom of God.'"** The significance of His statement spoke to the people. It resonated because they depended upon those harvests.

Today, we have difficulty understanding the parables Jesus told because they seem irrelevant in our culture. We rarely go without food, the supermarket isn't far away, and we depend on only two percent of our population in the United States to grow most of our food. But as Jesus walked outside the city gates and spoke to people in the countryside, the parables were impactful. It was their lives, and those of their families, on the line; if fortunate enough to own them, they relied on the power and strength of oxen to plow those lines straight.

An older, mature, trained ox would be yoked together with a younger ox, essentially "training" it to move with the older ox, instead of pulling against it. Training a young ox required patience and kindness, or they became afraid and unruly, but well-trained oxen were a very valuable asset in an agrarian culture. And young oxen, refusing to bend to the yoke of their masters, were useful only for food.

Jesus, knowing so well our weaknesses and immaturity, invites us to walk humbly next to Him. Matthew 11:29 says it so well: **"Take my yoke upon you and learn from me, for I am gentle and humble in heart, and you will find rest for your souls. For my yoke is easy and my burden is light."** Jesus is inviting us to plow with Him, becoming our guide and our trainer. He is patient and gently directs us on the rows of life best suited for our abilities and needs. And when we rebel against the yoke and refuse Him, we are headed for destruction.

By His grace, as many times as I plowed that wavy line, He has walked alongside me and straightened it. He has promised not to leave me when I don't plow willingly or correctly, continuing my "training". The cool thing about farming is that if you survive this season, there will come another season and the promise of a new harvest. Jesus also gives us second chances. He knows that our only hope of a good "crop" is in Him--anything else is looking back!

A Teacup Full

My family loved observing the running battle of the male hummingbirds, as they defended their territory of the solitary feeder, dangling from our porch ceiling. One day, while home alone and making a bed, something in the window caught my eye. The feeder I intended to clean and refill days before appeared odd; something was dangling from the bottom of it. Stepping up to the window, I could see that the "something" was a hummingbird hanging by its feet, clutched to the feeder perch!

I ran to the kitchen, grabbed a teacup, and flew out to the porch. Ever so gently, I pried the minuscule toes off the perch, sliding her delicate body into the cup. I had no idea what I was going to do with the bird in a cup. The only remedy I could concoct was to quickly dissolve some sugar in warm water. Finding an eyedropper, I sucked some of the sweet solution into it, and held it up to the needle-like beak. Nothing—not the slightest stir. Seeing no other recourse, I delicately lifted the tiny beak and inserted it into the dropper.

Suddenly, an even tinier tongue extended, flicking away at the sugary liquid. Only a few seconds passed, as I tenderly stroked her back. Suddenly, movement in her body, a wonderful thing for her, indicated a crisis for me. I quickly realized a hummingbird turned loose in my house posed a dangerous situation for her.

I headed to the door as fast as I could, with one hand carrying the cup, the other roofed over the top. As I set the teacup gently on the railing, I stepped back as she aroused to full life. Her mate was waiting for her in a nearby tree. Swooshing to the cup, he hovered for a moment, when suddenly, she sprang out from it, as if from a slingshot! They flew off into the sunset to live happily at someone else's feeder.

Our God is like this, rescuing us when we were yet dead to Him, raising us to new life through Christ. He will not drown us with His presence but invites us to taste and see that He is good; as we taste, we thirst for more of Him. As we drink from the Source of Life, Jesus, we gain the strength to fly. He waits patiently for us to come. We are worth so much more to Him than a teacup filled with a hummingbird, or a sparrow.

"Are not two sparrows sold for a penny? Yet not one of them will fall to the ground apart from the will of your Father. And even the very hairs of your head are all numbered. So don't be afraid; you are worth more than many sparrows." Matthew 10:29-31

The wooden bleacher seats were too hard, the sun too hot, and the game a little too slow to hold my attention, until my grandfather stepped up to the plate. He played in the adult baseball league, and Grandpa was really good. Despite a major accident where his knee was decimated, he was determined to play. He loved baseball so much that he could often be found listening to one game on the radio while watching another game simultaneously on the television.

When the pitcher saw my grandpa step up to the plate, the signals between the pitcher and the catcher indicated they were bringing everything they had to strike him out. The ball ripped through the air and blistered into the catcher's mitt, "Ball one!" ringing out from the umpire. Again, the released ball spun through the air and dropped its trajectory ever so slightly. With a crack of the bat as it impacted, the cry, "Foul ball!" decided the play. The next pitch landed squarely in the strike zone as Grandpa's bat connected dead-center with the ball, bouncing a double play into place.

Jesus may not have played baseball, but He played against the cagiest competitor ever, His mortal and spiritual foe, Satan. Satan was confident of his ability to defeat Jesus, stranded on His competitor's field of play, alone in the desert. Satan threw the first pitch, certain he could corrupt Jesus, famished following forty days of hunger, by tempting Him to distrust His Father's provision. **"But Jesus told him, 'It is written: "Man does not live by bread alone, but on every word that comes from the mouth of God."'"**

Satan lobbed his second pitch, offering Jesus all the kingdoms of the world if He would only worship him. Foul play! It all belonged to Jesus from the beginning anyway! Satan attempted to deceive Jesus, to have Him believe that His Father would withhold what He had promised. But Jesus answered, **"It is written: Worship the Lord your God and serve him only."**

The final fastball was, "Just throw yourself down from this height and the angels will save you!" Satan hoped Jesus would test His Father's will instead of yielding to it. This time, Jesus hit the ball out of the park with His answer, **"It says: Do not put the Lord your God to the test."** The devil admitted only temporary defeat as he slinked away, leaving Jesus "until another opportune time". (Quotes taken from Matthew 4 and Luke 4)

The bottom line is, Satan doesn't play fair, doesn't want you to win, and will use primarily three things to defeat you, the same things he used against Jesus: He will tempt you to shortcut God's provision, His plan, and His power in your life. He will manipulate the truth every single time, trying to get you to swing at anything. God's will for us is to trust Him in everything, really, *everything*! To do anything without trust in Him is to hit a foul ball, out of bounds, unproductive, and, eventually, in defeat. Trust in Jesus—that's the winning game!

Dead End

On my great aunt and uncle's farm, we were often cautioned to wear our shoes while playing in their spacious yard, surrounding the huge oak trees and wrap-around porch. It only required one time of disregarding the instructions from the adults to make believers out of us. Bees love clover flowers even more than I, a pertinent fact relevant to the wearing of shoes in said clover field.

Walking barefoot in the clover is such a lovely scene when on a movie screen, but in real life can yield some very unpleasant consequences. Once stung—never forgotten. The bee may live on for a short time, along with a memory that lasts a lifetime, but the bee soon dies. The only advantage to being stung by the bee is that once it has stung, it cannot ever sting again, a "dead end", I say with a smile.

Death can be viewed in much the same way. When Jesus walked in the desert, through heat and intense temptation, it was as though a menacing bee taunted Him for forty days. That bee pursued Him throughout His life on earth, attempting to kill Him, and not realizing that by doing so, he would be destroying his power over humankind. After Jesus was crucified, after the sting of death, the bee, like death, became stinger-less for us. Jesus has removed its stinger and death has no potency, no venom that can affect us.

The stinger which Jesus removed through His death and resurrection was the power of sin over us. The chasm of separation between us and the Father was forever bridged. Once the stinger was removed, forgiveness and reconciliation with God, through the blood of the Lamb, became possible again. Satan's power has been conquered, and he is no longer to be feared, any more than the stinger-less bee.

He may still buzz around our heads, distracting and annoying us, attempting to convince us of his power. Though attempting to bring us into submission to the law, he is powerless to overcome the work of Jesus on our behalf. Satan's "dead end" will have no hold on us; he will be as innocuous as the bee which has lost its stinger, I say with a smile. Where, oh death, is your sting?! Jesus has robbed the bee of its stinger, rendering the ultimate dead end.

"For the perishable must clothe itself with the imperishable, and the mortal with immortality. When the perishable has been clothed with the imperishable, and the mortal with immortality, then the saying that is written will come true: 'Death has been swallowed up in victory.' Where O death, is your victory? Where, O death, is your sting?' The sting of death is sin, and the power of sin is the law. But thanks be to God" He gives us the victory through our Lord Jesus Christ." 1 Corinthians 15:53-56

The boat dock laid claim to no boat, but it was the favorite gathering spot for my mother's, and her best friend's, children. We swam and frolicked there, along the wooded riverfront, twenty miles from the sweltering, summer heat of our paved streets. It was more dangerous than our neighborhood swimming pool, but an exhilarating swim, in the wake of speed boats on the river. But my favorite time was when everyone else wearily abandoned the boat dock and wandered to the house.

As I laid on that bobbing wooden platform, far from the sounds of the city, I found a place of peace. Floating upon the pulsing waves, closing my eyes and shutting out all but the sounds of gentle lapping water, I was comforted by the rising and falling cadence. Hours could pass without my knowing, like driving an endless highway, the countryside along the way a blur—the time just passed without notice. In that place, there was solace and rest.

Few places, other than home (and often too many distractions even there), have supplied that same comforting solitude, a quietness where I could hear the voice of God. The busyness of life strips us of our ability to sense His Presence, to explore the depth of who He is, and to listen to His gentle voice. So often, it takes a major event in our lives to stop us in our tracks, commanding silence and surrendering our "control", or illusion thereof. In His presence, there is peace, security, and a sense of His assurance that He is quite well equipped to meet any need.

A discordant and deafening world actively works against our hearts, vying for every thought. It is in Jesus we find what the world is incapable of bestowing, real and lasting peace. The name of Jesus becomes our bastion of peace when we gently speak it, focusing at that moment on Him alone. Like the waves lapping at the dock, His still small voice can be heard if we will but calm our minds and listen for it. In Him, we find the place of peace we seek.

"You will keep in perfect peace him whose mind is steadfast, because he trusts in you." Isaiah 26:3

"Now choose life, so that you and your children may live and that you may love the Lord your God, listen to his voice, and hold fast to him." Deuteronomy 30:19b

"But the Counselor, the Holy Spirit, whom the Father will send in my name, will teach you all things and will remind you of everything I have said to you. Peace I leave with you; my peace I give you. I do not give as the world gives. Do not let your hearts be troubled and do not be afraid." John 14:25-27

Three small things made big impressions on me when I spent time at my grandmother's business, a hair and nail salon simply named "Edna's Beauty Shop". A black lacquered, quite small, manicure table sat to one side, with nail polishes arranged in neat rows. How I loved sitting at that table watching Gram apply polish to her customer's nails, then as the table became vacant, applying it to my own.

The second was the large red aluminum Coca-Cola ice chest, yes, really, "ice chest", where the large block of ice was delivered weekly by the ice delivery man. The remains of the previous week's block were drained, and Gram signed for the new ice; my job was to place the bottles into the chest on the new ice block. I was rewarded with a bottle of Coke, made only in small 6.5 oz. green, glass bottles at that time.

The third impressive area of Gram's shop was the "mixing closet", hair coloring dyes neatly organized in rows on the shelves. Gram would go to the closet, precisely measuring each component; her client patiently waited, seated in the black swivel chair. I was fascinated by all the colors and formulas in the closet that seemed so vast, until I grew up and returned.

Now, gazing back in time, I see that my fascination with the manicure table, and hovering presence, may have been a hindrance to my grandmother's work. The "job" I did in filling the ice chest may have filled her with a bit of trepidation as I handled the glass bottles, and the mixing closet was, in reality, a very cramped space. Though these were all very happy memories for me, I remind myself that the unpleasant memories can be a bit warped by emotion, time, and perspective, also.

Our memories are colored by our emotions and can alter the way we see the world around us. I have found this truth an important thing to remember in life. Just as that mixing closet seemed so big, yet shrank in size when viewed from adulthood, so my view of things changes when I recognize my skewed memories, releasing the painful ones to the Lord.

If I could see my painful experiences from God's point of view, they may not seem quite as painful. He alone can bring beauty from ashes, good from evil, and His glory from what was intended to destroy. The "bad" memories have been used for my good and, eventually, God's glory; God was in control throughout them all. From Edna's Beauty Shop to God's hand, day by day, I am becoming more like Jesus, as I release my memories, as well as my future, into His hands.

"But I am like an olive tree flourishing in the house of God; I trust in God's unfailing love forever and ever. I will praise you forever for what you have done; in your name I will hope, for your name is good. I will praise you in the presence of your saints." Psalm 52:8-9

Staying a few weeks in the summer with my grandparents, far from home, landed me in a far different world, one I relished and would have chosen to live in permanently. At home with a very stressed single mother, anger flared, tempers and blame abounded, and brokenness cut at the hearts of all. Grandpa and Gram's house was much the opposite; peace abounded, unless my brothers were also there. The baseball park, amusement park and zoo, penny candy at Mr. Purdy's store, and trips with Grandpa to visit his even-more-elderly mom on the farm, all soothed my soul.

The local zoo had one popular attraction I found intriguing. It was a ship in the middle of a large pond that housed the monkeys during the warm, summer months. It was fascinating to watch them climbing through the portholes, throwing things at each other, and chasing one another up and down the masts. Occasionally they would screech shrilly, objecting to the food stolen or territory encroached upon. While the onlookers laughed from shore, the monkeys peered back at them in curiosity as to what could be that funny.

While the memory strikes me as humorous now, I remember thinking of the monkeys not as funny, but somehow rather sad. I felt I was looking at the home in which I lived versus the home I visited in the summers of my youth. The monkeys made a mess of everything, that being a monkey's nature; the nature of God is to bring order, peace, and trust. That was the difference between home and my grandparent's house, one a place of no trust in God and the strife which resulted, the other trusting in God and the peace emanating from those who followed Him.

I would later meet and marry my husband, beginning our life together in unbelief and strife, selfishness and destruction, patterned on our worldly views. Jesus was invited in and peace prevailed, more abundantly as we both grew in faith, learning how to trust God with our lives and family. The changes were not sudden, but as we ordered our lives, taking small steps of faith, our ship of unruly monkeys began to transform into a ship of peace.

Because of Jesus, my life did not resemble that of my mother's, though I learned much from her tenacity and determination to raise us. Instead of monkeys on a ship, by God's grace, my children experienced a home which more closely resembled the one I longed for, at my grandparent's house, only because of Jesus.

"Now the Lord is the Spirit, and where the Spirit of the Lord is, there is freedom. And we, who with unveiled faces all reflect the Lord's glory, are being transformed into his likeness with ever-increasing glory, which comes from the Lord, who is the Spirit."

2 Corinthians 3:17-18

The Sweet Illusion

It was a peaceful walk to Edna's Beauty Shop, my grandmother's place of business. And once I crossed the proverbial railroad tracks, a neighborhood conspicuously more prosperous than that of my grandparents opened before me. The houses were larger with neatly manicured, expansive yards, stately trees, and meticulous landscaping. When I approached the "boulevard", with what appeared to be a park in the center of the street, I knew I was only three blocks from my destination.

Every house on the boulevard appeared perfect, and I marveled at the varying styles of architecture lining both sides of the street. One was Tudor, another a ranch style, the next more of a modern design; all were in good repair and nothing seemed out of order. They were in direct contrast to my life, which seemed in a constant state of tension and out of control.

Passing the perfect houses on the journey from my grandparent's modest, but very neatly kept house, I can now understand that behind each door, like my own, there were problems. Each home housed its secrets, pains, and sorrows, no matter how proper they appeared. That is the nature of human beings living in a broken and fallen world. We are all ever so flawed, no matter the sweet illusion of careful appearance we display to the world.

We all succumb to carefully crafting our appearances and believing that we are safely hidden. If we can only maintain the exterior perfection while guarding our interior secrets, what can go wrong? "Pride comes before the fall" has not been written in God's word for naught, tripping up those who resist humility most.

I have realized that Jesus did not come for perfect people, nor can He find one on the face of the earth. He did not come for the prideful, accomplished, haughty, or arrogant. He asks instead that those who hide behind their perfect exteriors open their doors to Him, humbly, like children. In repentance and admission of our sins, He will bring healing to our souls and new life to our spirits.

He came, not seductively offering a sweet illusion, but with genuine restoration to relationship with Himself. He can supply every need and bind every wound, and His name is, thankfully, Immanuel, God with us. He came to save the lost, to heal the sick, to mend the brokenhearted, to restore the hope of the hopeless, as only He can, through His priceless blood shed on the cross and the power of His resurrection.

"Like newborn babies, crave pure spiritual milk, so that by it you may grow up in your salvation, now that you have tasted that the Lord is good." I Peter 2: 2-3

"On hearing this, Jesus said to them, 'It is not the healthy who need a doctor, but the sick. I have not come to call the righteous, but sinners.'" Mark 2:17

One of my assignments when visiting the family farm was to help set the table, mainly because this city kid was not much use in the bustling, expansive kitchen. I was always in awe of the enormity of the table, utilized in so many ways between meals, accommodating the canning of produce, sorting the massive mounds of laundry, laying out quilt patterns, etc. When the dinner bell rang, 14 or more people pulled their chairs up, bowing their heads to pray. My uncle, seated at the head of the table, was dressed in a clean white t-shirt with blue denim overalls, his arms and face well-tanned by the summer sun.

When everyone arrived and was seated, we spanned immediate family, farmhands, the extended family which included me and my grandparents, and anyone else who "happened by". Conversations were always lively, opinions varied, occasionally strong, but never disrespectful or angry. That was one of my favorite aspects of the table; its guests may have differed but were never disrespected. No one was agitated or aggressive, though tense moments hovered, at times, in the air like the scent of bacon freshly fried in Aunt Nora's iron skillet.

I hope heaven will be like that giant table. With Jesus seated at the head, He will gaze lovingly over His children, happily gathered over one awesome feast, sprinkled generously with lively conversation and laughter. I wish it could be like that here on earth, but with broken people seated at the table and an enemy who delights in deception and disruption, we are granted mere glimpses of it, and those only because of Jesus.

Heaven's table will offer a distinct advantage, affording us a heavenly perspective of absolute accuracy and inerrancy about who Jesus is, who we are, and what God's plan was all along. We will be fully understanding of our brothers and sisters in Christ when, given the opportunity to view from God's perspective, we see the paths of trial, learning, and hardships they endured. We will be able to clearly see the interferences and obstructions the enemy placed on their road to understanding God. And we will see them through the loving eyes of Jesus only.

God's children possess many common traits, but none are the same; we all see life a bit differently, each with his or her unique perspective. All are at different stages of understanding, but Jesus, nonetheless, calls us to love one another, agreeing to disagree without anger or offense. We are to be kind, patient, and gentle to each other while holding to the teachings of Jesus to the best of our understanding. Generous in our mercy and bountiful in grace, forgiving, and carefully guiding one another to the feet of Jesus, we are to imitate the Master at the head of the table.

"A new command I give you: Love one another. As I have loved you, so you must love one another. By this all men will know that you are my disciples, if you love one another."

John 15:4

There were too few days of summer with my grandparents. Eight days a week wouldn't have been enough! Whether I filled the hours with paint-by-number crafts, cruised the concrete driveway on my metal-wheeled skates, or ate ice-pops in their array of colors, the time melted in the summer rays. When Grandpa arrived home at 3:30, he watered Gram's flowers, tomato plants, and me, with the cold water from the garden hose. The thin towel, used too many times by the frugal family, dried me just in time to pick tomatoes before supper.

Weekends scooted by even faster. Gram worked until five o'clock; grocery shopping filled the early evening immediately after supper, then there was ice cream before bed on Fridays. Saturdays, Gram baked pies for the next day, Grandpa grilled hamburgers for supper; baths followed for everyone, and preparation of lessons for Sunday School topped off the night. Church, lunch, a brief nap, snapping beans or peeling potatoes on the front porch for supper, and the weekend quietly tip-toed into the night. The week evaporated as fast as the water on the hot sidewalk.

Whatever rhythms of life fill our days, they will all pass like steam rising off the lake in the morning sun. We will likely yearn for more of them. For me, there are more things I want to do, inquiries to make, puzzles to solve, and words to speak. I have ideas to explore, roads to ponder, too many to squeeze into the seven days a week allotted to my calendar. Time is the most valuable commodity in life and the one most taken for granted.

Jesus displayed His stunning power over nature and time by calming the storm at sea, with only three words, "Peace! Be still!" He was giving us a glimpse, an incredibly tiny exhibit of the extent of His power. He displayed His power over time by granting the request of Joshua for the sun and moon to stand still (Joshua 10:12). His is the power to expand and contract time, but in His wisdom, He has marked our days in weeks of seven.

A time will arrive, the Father's perfect time, when the cadence of these days will slow and cease. Our breaths will expire one final time, and we will awaken in Christ; the dawn of the eighth day, our day of new beginning, we will breathe our next breath in the hidden kingdom of heaven. Our hope of one more day, or one more hour, will never be remembered again, as our new week stretches forward to infinity in Jesus' presence.

"I will praise the Lord who counsels me; even at night my heart instructs me. I have set the Lord always before me. Because he is at my right hand, I will not be shaken. Therefore my heart is glad and my tongue rejoices; my body also will rest secure, because you will not abandon me to the grave, nor will you let your Holy One see decay. You have made known to me the path of life; you will fill me with joy in your presence, with eternal pleasures at your right hand." Psalm 16:7-11

Traveling back to the house where I spent most of my childhood happened only one time. The house was painted the same color but appeared much smaller than I remembered. The yard was not the vast expanse embedded in my memory, either, and the mature trees that cradled my frame in the summer breezes were gone. It seemed more foreign than familiar, positioned in a city neighborhood now far from home.

My city memories were fading with it. Memories of riding the bus to the movie theater for the Saturday matinee, shopping downtown, and walking to school counting down the city blocks were becoming more distant. Ice skating and swimming, playing card games, and Monopoly with friends entertained us, and we ate supper at home. Then I arrived on the streets of a tiny western town at age 16.

My first live rodeo shook this timid city kid down to the boots, attesting to the dramatically different culture I had been thrown into. Dust flew in billowing clouds, as real cowboys risked life and limb for a few-second thrill. Bulls charged and leaped into the air, twisting and thrusting unwanted cowboy baggage to the ground, something of a picture of how displaced I felt. But people were friendly, helped each other, and sat together quietly, closing the days in the diminishing sunlight of the Rocky Mountains.

Whether in the city or the country, I never truly felt I fit. It would be many states and much later than 16 years old, where I finally found my place on this earth. I arrived "home" in Tennessee, decades ago and staked my claim to the culture I love, a wonderful mix of city streets and cowboy boots. But even this is not my real home. There is only one place that is truly home.

With the eyes of an immortal body and a spirit regenerated by the blood of Christ, I will one day understand how fragile this "house", the body of my current dwelling, was. I will be able to see with fresh eyes that the size of my problems was not at all accurate and that I should have relied more on Jesus. The possessions were not important, the relationships priceless, and love invaluable. Not fitting into this "foreign" culture of life, I have been a city kid in cowboy boots all along, but in God's presence, at home in heaven, I will fit perfectly. In Christ, I already do.

"But because of his great love for us, God, who is rich in mercy, made us alive with Christ even when we were dead in transgressions---it is by grace you have been saved. And God raised us up with Christ and seated us with him in the heavenly realms in Christ Jesus, in order that in the coming ages he might show the incomparable riches of his grace, expressing in his kindness to us in Christ Jesus." Ephesians 2:4-7

Hundreds of feet above the canyon floor, the swaying of the rope bridge with each step was nearly unbearable. The Rocky Mountains were truly named appropriately, I acknowledged, as I timidly gazed through the wood slats under my feet at the stream far below. It flowed briskly, tumbling over nothing but rocks. My feet did not want to move, and I was paralyzed with fear one-third of the way across the bridge, unable to press forward, and unable to turn back. My fear of heights was forever solidified, but as you can guess, I finally made it across and am alive to tell about it.

Sharing my faith in Jesus was akin to walking the planks of that rope bridge as a new believer. I was paralyzed with fear of rejection, which was my "canyon" to cross. My fear of the loss of relationships, essentially abandonment, was so overwhelming that it took years to overcome. It would not be through thoughtful reasoning, being "talked down from the ledge" with soothing words, or the "right sharing methods" which would see me to the other side.

Step by baby-step, my security grew in simply knowing Jesus, trusting my heavenly Father, and holding the hand of the Holy Spirit as He guided me. And just as I found that relationship to be secure footing, I also began to desire to share Jesus, in a kind, gentle, and tender way, with those also paralyzed by fear, burdened under the weight of life, and in need of peace. That doesn't mean that everyone I shared with was accepting, and I lost some relationships anyway; relationships only work when both parties want it.

I have learned to listen more, wait on God's timing and leading, and be respectful of people's experiences, while sharing my own. I am comforted by the fact that the Bible says that God is no respecter of persons. He essentially treats us all the same when it comes to accepting Jesus—we either do, or we do not. The consequences and rewards for that decision are an equal opportunity for all; either accepting His grace, forgiveness, Lordship, and sovereignty or rebelling and consequently rejecting eternal life in God's presence.

This is the reason I am "alive to tell about it", alive in Christ and living on this earth. I am alive because Christ lives in me, therefore, alive to tell others about the great love of Jesus. He has rescued me countless times from my fear and set my feet on the solid ground of faith. For the duration of my journey in this alien land called Earth, I will share the hope I have in Christ, hopeful that others may draw close to Him as their bridges sway and they face their fears.

"Then Peter began to speak: 'I now realize how true it is that God does not show favoritism but accepts men from every nation who fear him and do what is right. You know the message God sent to the people of Israel, telling the good news of peace through Jesus Christ, who is Lord of all.'" Acts 10:34-36

The old maple tree, with a hefty trunk and sturdy, horizontal lower branches, made the perfect perch overlooking the street below. During the summer I could sit in the security of its screen-of-green, neatly tucked away from the fray, and watch my brothers playing catch below. Passers-by would rarely look up, leaving me quietly unnoticed and quite invisible. It was my summer sanctuary.

Free from distractions, I peered through the parting branches at the clouds floating above, forming white puffy images, parading through my ever-expanding imagination. I dreaded summer's end when my hideaway would be exposed. My sanctuary drifted to the ground to be raked into heaps, dry and blown by the wind, with a vague promise of newness in spring.

During my younger years of having no father, attending to three younger brothers, and a mother working while attempting to complete a college degree, I found few places of escape. Safety and security became synonymous with "alone"; and in my summer sanctuary tree, I was free to think, dream, and find comfort.

Each of us needs a place of sanctuary, a secure place of safety and rest. Sanctuary is by primary definition "the holiest room or area in a religious building"; but the secondary definitions are numerous, most notably a place of safety and security. Many dictionary entries reference a place called "home"; my home, growing up, was neither safe nor secure, but God had a better plan than a summer maple tree. Jesus became my every-season sanctuary, no building required.

It is no accident that the Bible describes God as our Hiding Place, Refuge, Strong Tower, and Deliverer. He provides peace in the storms of life, shelter from turbulence, and provision at all times. He is our safe place, the arms which never fail, the hand that never releases ours. He is our quiet confidant, our closest friend who never abandons us; and He is the security we seek. He is not a building or empty sanctuary, but He will become your only Sanctuary, your home, and refuge, now and always, if only you ask.

"The Lord is my rock, my fortress and my deliverer; my God is my rock, in whom I take refuge, my shield and the horn of my salvation. He is my stronghold, my refuge and my savior." Psalm 22:2-3a

"Taste and see that the Lord is good; blessed is the man who takes refuge in him." Psalm 34:8

Daybreak and Broken June 27

June in Alaska yields unending daylight, in varying degrees throughout the night, so I wasn't expecting to witness "sunrise" my first morning in Anchorage. The sun had never truly set, but suddenly, in radiant display, it spread golden rays before me. They peeked from under clouds, suspended a bit above the mountains. It seemed the sun had broken through a crevice between the heavens and earth, spilling its glory out for my viewing. What a wonderful introduction to Alaska it was!

That morning brought hope and wonder, as I considered the ruggedness of the terrain. The dangers were real, even in the city, even in the neighborhood we walked. The dangers I might encounter were outlined while listening to the "precautions" speech (a couple of which came to fruition concerning bears and moose). The realities of this new environment were settling into my awareness. And I had arrived in Alaska, already broken.

Appendicitis and bronchitis had traveled with me on the plane, but they were not the only passengers. I had disembarked with a broken and weary heart, struggling under the weight of caregiving, and recognizing the loss of my loved one was not far off. I probably never should have traveled at that time, but I knew I was, for whatever reason, supposed to be there.

Upon my return home, I recovered from bronchitis just in time to have an emergency appendectomy. I did not die in Alaska of either cause and lived to tell about my encounters with a bear in a trash can and a mother moose with her calf on a playground. Despite my fragile emotional and physical conditions, God met me in Alaska, turning my attention to Him as I witnessed His glory there. It was much like the sun spilling its gold from between the sandwich of mountains and clouds, spreading hope through my heart as I trusted Him with each step.

God taught me a lot about being broken, and that it is not accidental—it is purposeful and never wasted. Our broken hearts are the direct result of living in a horrifically broken world; but God's intention in allowing the brokenness is to turn our attention from ourselves, back to Him, our hearts' rightful focus. There is no "broken" He doesn't understand. When yielded to Him, "broken" always directs us to the Restorer, Healer, Redeemer, and infinite Lover of Our Souls. It is in "broken" that we begin to understand trust, and where God's glory spills out in our lives.

"The Lord is close to the brokenhearted and saves those who are crushed in spirit."

Psalm 34:18

Easily Distracted

A conversation with my adult son produced laughter, and subsequent revelation, as we reflected on a few of my driving experiences. While riding with me, he has more than once asked me where I was going, as I missed an exit or turn. It wasn't that I was forgetful, I was just talking, and my mind was not focused on the path I needed to follow. I became distracted by the conversation instead of focusing on the directions.

I was a good sport about the laughter but realized a greater revelation; it is a human tendency to become easily distracted. Multi-tasking, white noise, interactions with other people, and unexpected events keep our brains constantly juggling the intrusions, to say nothing of media bombardment. The distractions keep my brain, and my spirit, engaged in the wrong direction. It is those distractions that keep my focus on myself, or the world around me, instead of God.

I don't know when the world has ever seen a greater number, or intensity, of distractions, or more ways to divert our eyes from the God who loves us. They compete on an unprecedented plane, demanding that we look here, then immediately look there, from the time we wake until the time we fall asleep with their frequencies buzzing in our ears. We are uneasy with solitude and pressured to comply with the cacophony of the world.

When the distractions drain away my very soul, leaving me parched and weary, I have forgotten who I am, and who Jesus is. The longer I allow myself to be distracted, the more difficult life becomes, and the more my agitation spills onto the people I love. After prolonged resistance, God will eventually intervene with forced solitude, often through unpleasant circumstances, giving me time to refocus and to find my center in Him again.

Thanks be to God that He loves us so much that He will not allow us to stray too far in our distracted state, or to lose our direction permanently! In His grace, He lovingly draws our attention, through whatever means necessary, back to Himself, who is our very sustenance and life. He never loses sight of us, never takes a wrong turn, and is never overwhelmed by the commotion of the world. And I am eternally grateful that my God and Savior is not easily distracted.

"But Martha was distracted by all the preparations that had to be made. She came to him and asked, 'Lord, don't you care that my sister has left me to do the work by myself? Tell her to help me!' 'Martha, Martha, the Lord answered, 'you are worried and upset about many things, but only one thing is needed. Mary has chosen what is better, and it will not be taken away from her.'" Luke 10:40-41

One perfectly sunny and temperate day, my front porch became my parade review stand as I observed the procession. One by one, they passed in neat order across a vivid blue spring sky. First, a rowdy puppy skipped ahead. Next, a piglet dashed across the expanse before morphing into a seahorse, as it faded from view. A smoke-breathing dragon fleetingly flew by. And finally, a rhinoceros chased them all into oblivion. The clouds each dissipated quickly, giving way to the one behind it as they marched across the treetops.

What a beautiful gift from the Creator our imaginations are! My smile persisted during the whole procession of fluffy white fantasies taking shape before my very eyes, existing for mere seconds before forever changing. I take such delight in the ability to "see" through my imagination, the fun and wholesome, interesting images. It was not always so; fear had consumed my imagination for many years, the result of childhood trauma, and presented itself most painfully in nearly every area of my life.

Fear is not what God intends for us. Jesus came to save us from fear, freeing us of one of the most pervasive curses of sin. We were not created to be fearful; we were created to be focused. It requires effort on our part, upon the promises of God, for it does not come as naturally as the fear we are fighting. The self-discipline of placing those God's words before our eyes and tucking them away in our souls is elemental in conquering fear. It requires diligence, too. Our enemy insidiously injects it through any means possible, to place a wedge between God and His children.

After coming into God's family through Christ Jesus, I found Him to be wholly trustworthy. He proved His love through His sacrifice on the cross, but He also proves to be a daily supply of peace. We, through Christ, can take our fear, which usually resides in our natural thoughts, and hold it captive to Jesus, then command it to surrender to His sovereign rule.

We can tame our imaginations, bringing them into submission along with our thoughts. We are then freed from the bonds of slavery to fear through the power of Christ. His promises are real, His power is irresistible, and His love beyond anything we can imagine or measure. We can align with what God says is factual, for He does not lie. Only through holding my fearful thoughts captive to Christ have I found a transformation from fear to peace possible. The parade review can be riddled with fear and dread if left to my mind's playground or, by the power of Christ, it can transform into a sweet and pleasant imagining from my porch.

"The weapons we fight with are not the weapons of the world. On the contrary, they have divine power to demolish strongholds. We demolish arguments and every pretension that sets itself up against the knowledge of God, and we take captive every thought to make it obedient to Christ."   2 Corinthians 10:4-5

"I sought the Lord, and he answered me; he delivered me from all my fears." Psalm 34:4

Weather or Not

The breeze rolling across my porch was a welcome relief from the heat of the day, but not so for the small moth struggling against it. I observed its attempts to navigate the strong current for several seconds; I do not know if it eventually overcame the wind it fought against, took another route, or waited for a better day to find its way home. One thing did occur to me, though; I, like that moth, had been flying against the wind much of the past few years.

Everyone alive on this earth will find themselves, sooner or later, flying against the wind, some on sunny days, some in tornado-like winds. But every person will have struggles, obstacles, sorrows, pain, and regret. Some will come in the form of illness, some in loss of income, others will find their pain in the choices they have made. Some will struggle through the loss of loved ones, and others in friction and conflict; some against the mountains of bureaucracy. Many will encounter natural disasters, political upheaval, or unimaginable losses, and some will suffer persecution. This is the nature of the world in which we live, but only temporarily.

Like the moth, when flying against the winds, we must fix our attention, and focus our "radar", training our gazes on Jesus. Through struggling against the winds, we learn to attach our eyes to Him amid every challenge, every obstacle, and every loss. We will find that He is the source of peace amid craziness, our only hope in distress, and the only answer to every question. He is the calm in our storms, the light in every darkness, and the fulfillment of every need.

If we find ourselves overcome by the wind, too weak to fight on our own, Jesus is faithful to His promise, never leaving or forsaking His children. The testing and trials are proving grounds of faith and builders of character, as we, more and more, reflect His. In Jesus, there is always hope, always love, always growth. And even if we never realize the answers in this life, the answers to our "why's" can be entrusted to His wise plan. That is what faith is, trust in God though we cannot see the answer. It is trust in His goodness, "weather or not".

"For he spoke and stirred up a tempest that lifted high the waves. They mounted up to the heavens and went down to the depths; in their peril their courage melted away. They reeled and staggered like drunken men; they were at their wits' end. Then they cried out to the Lord in their trouble, and he brought them out of their distress. He stilled the storm to a whisper; the waves of the sea were hushed. They were glad when it grew calm, and he guided them to their desired haven. Let them give thanks to the Lord for his unfailing love and his wonderful deeds for men." Psalm 107:25-31

July

The massive and ornate carousel sat at the center of the amusement park, horses chomping at the bit to gallop endlessly beneath the circular canape. It was my favorite ride at the park, perhaps due to my love of horses, unfulfilled by the real thing. Choosing the right horse, in the seconds before someone else snagged it, was my greatest challenge. And no one wanted to be left riding in the stationary polar bear seat. Once the steed was selected, I would lift myself by way of the real stirrup onto the back of my magnificent equine.

Holding the reins, off we sailed, chasing the horse in front of us, as imagination took flight. The man at the controls, in the red stationary center of the carousel, watched with indifference as we whirred by, mirrors attached to all but his doorway, as though attempting to remain invisible. The horses slowed their up and down movement too soon. The platform gradually came to a stop, the obvious signal it was time to dismount. Reluctantly, I let the reins drop, gave my horse a final stroke, and dropped to the floor—until next year.

That exquisite carousel, imported from Germany, came back to mind lately as I contemplated my tendency to be caught up in the affairs of life. Running headlong, I chase activities that make me feel as though I am on that carousal, attempting to keep up with the horse ahead of me, but never able to catch it. Then I remembered the man in the center who operated the controls. When life seems out of control, I just need to remember that God is at the center. He operates the controls with love and wisdom.

Just as a dancer looks to a stationary object when spinning to avoid dizziness, I need to look to my "center", who is Jesus. He is untouched by my frantic life and bids me to focus on Him alone, to remove my gaze from the horse in front of me and fix my attention on Him. His love never fails to hold my life together when He is the sole object of my trust. The control which I cling to so rigidly, He bids me yield into His worthy hands, because just as the horse on the carousel was an illusion of control, so is life.

"It is through his Son that we have redemption---that is, our sins have been forgiven. He is the visible image of the invisible God. He is supreme over all creation because in connection with him were all things created---in heaven and on earth, visible and invisible, whether thrones, lordships, rulers, or authorities---they have all been created through him and for him. *He existed before all things, and he holds all things together.*" Colossians 1:14-17

"You will keep him in perfect peace, whose mind is stayed on you because he trusts in you." Isaiah 26:3

A Crumby Life

The fairytale of Hansel and Gretel wandering through the forest revealed the fatal flaw in the strategy of dropping breadcrumbs to find their way home. Their breadcrumbs were gobbled up by the birds, leaving that brilliant idea in the bellies of well-fed crows, while stranding the children in a dark and dangerous place.

One day, I thought, "I like the idea of leaving breadcrumbs everywhere I go!" Of course, I wasn't considering littering my path with actual bread, but littering my path with little words of encouragement to people I encounter each day. It is easy to see when I open my eyes and heart to the people around me, the hunger for God's goodness.

Human beings are all born hungry, not only physically, but spiritually, requiring both words of encouragement and words leading to the Bread of Life Himself. And we don't all search for bread in the same places, or at the same times in life. I have discovered, too, that most people don't need a "full meal", but are hungry for crumbs, little bites at a time.

Living a "crumby life" requires that judgments are not made, either. There was once a time I did not follow the trail of breadcrumbs myself, though that time has become more and more difficult to remember. My belly has become so full and satisfied that I forget what it was like to be hungry, empty, and searching for God's table of life-giving bread.

However, at some point on the path, all of us search the scrapheaps of the world, even scouring the garbage bins, instead of eating the choice foods of God's table. Without the Bread of Life, Jesus, we are like Hansel and Gretel, stranded in a dark and dangerous place, subject to eternal death and destruction.

So, I am learning to delightfully lead a "crumby life", leaving small bites of encouragement, leading to the Bread of Life Himself. I hope to leave such a trail of crumbs that the birds will flock to them, that they will find the hope of Jesus, crumbs leading them to His gentle hand, instead of the clumsiness of mine. I pray that they will delight in the meal He has prepared for them, preferring it over the crumbs I offered, that they will eat and be satisfied, as only He can do. And ultimately, I pray they will find their way home and dine with Him, in all the splendor of heaven, at the wedding feast of Jesus.

"For the bread of God is he who comes down from heaven and gives life to the world...Then Jesus declared, 'I am the bread of life. He who comes to me will never go hungry, and he who believes in me will never be thirsty...For my Father's will is that everyone who looks to the Son and believes in him shall have eternal life, and I will raise him up at the last day.'"

John 6:33, 35, 40

You Are

I hesitated to put poetry in this book, but I feel this is a good page to return to when you need a reminder of the character of the God we serve. Dog-ear this page and come back often:

You are the Number-er of grains of sand,
Your boundaries set, marking land.
Your power upending ocean waves,
The mighty waters you sustain.

You are true Master of the universe,
Clock-smith of the galaxy, you set its vast course.
The winds of time swept by your hand,
No man's imaginings can comprehend.

You are binder of wounds, encourager of hearts,
You are God of uncountable, unimaginable fresh starts,
Who whispers every dream and tries every soul,
God of new beginnings, God in full control.

You are healer of hurt, a friend to sheep,
Our Protector who never slumbers, our God who never sleeps.
You feed every mouth and hold every hand,
Guiding and providing, quietly revealing your plan.

You are present at each baby's birth, its breath,
The heartbeat of nations, every life, and death.
Present in a father's strength and mother's touch,
A friend's embrace, a loved one—loved much.

You are life that flows through miles of veins.
Light in the storm, dark times, and trying days.
You are the warmth of touch, and tender glance,
The dream of the lonely, and every romance.

You are accepting of repentant hearts,
God of our beginnings, endings, stops, and starts.
Humble, gentle, forgiving, and kind,
You are God of little children, of fragile, broken minds.

You are giver of purpose, and generous gifts,
Disciple-r and discipline-r, your plan always fits.
You treasure our tears, and shower with favor,
Lifting us up, drawing us closer to our Savior.

You are Redeemer, brother, friend to the low,
You are Lord of Life, Jesus, never too late or too slow.
You are rest, peace, shelter, and love.
You are Healer of bodies, perfect Gift from above.

Independence Day

Like a little child, my heart becomes anxious, my thoughts weary, and my body worn from the schedules, decisions, and circumstances of the day. Declaring my independence from my Father and going my own way, I often believe that the Lord is absent from my choices. I eventually reap the consequences of such folly. I am prone to running from my heavenly Father's input. Then, I imagine Him tensely sitting on the edge of His lofty throne, hands clasped together, eagerly watching to see what will transpire next. That thought is thoroughly laughable, if I would stop to consider the truth of that mental picture.

The God of the universe is not wringing His hands and wondering what to do, or how He will accomplish everything on His list for the day. Only I am. Up-ended plans wreak havoc in my world, but not so for God. I struggle for solutions and quest for answers; I claw for control even as life's events careen beyond my grasp. My natural tendency is to mentally replay difficulties over and over, seeking the key to unlocking the mystery of what just transpired, often to no avail. My flubs and errors confront me without end, though less than in the past.

I am the puzzled child obsessed with learning the trick to winning the game instead of quietly observing and learning from the Master. I am a student who will not sit long enough to listen. But one step at a time, and many Holy Spirit promptings later, God is teaching this hard-headed child to be still and with childlike faith, to consult Him first, then trust Him. He reminds me that He already knows all that concerns me and that nothing surprises Him or catches Him off guard.

There is no commanding an answer from the God who commands everything; He is perfectly peaceful, decidedly calm, and coolly in control. God will do His part, but I have an important role, as well. Mine is to remember that it is only He who can hold my life in perfect balance, to quiet my heart, discipline my thoughts, and look to Him for the answers He desires me to have. It is good to live "in-dependence" on God every day.

"You will keep in perfect peace those whose minds are steadfast, because they trust in you."
Isaiah 26:3

"There is no fear in love. But perfect love drives out fear, because fear has to do with punishment. The one who fears is not made perfect in love." 1 John 4:18

"Do not be anxious about anything, but in every situation, by prayer and petition, with thanksgiving, present your requests to God." Philippians 4:6

That None May Be Wasted

A major reorganization of my refrigerator shelf was going to be necessary. Emptying it, I spotted a plastic bag stuffed into the wastelands of refrigeration, the back of the shelf. A few blueberries were bunched in the corner of the bag; and from the outside, I could see the tell-tale signs of spoilage.

My first reaction was to toss the bag into the trashcan, but the words, "That none may be wasted," came so immediately and strongly that I stopped mid-action. Opening the bag, I poured the few blueberries into my hand. Upon examination, and to my surprise, less than half were bad. As I picked them from my hand, leaving the good berries, I understood the words.

The world is filled with good and evil. It's not always apparent which is which. We wonder why God allows us to inhabit the same planet, subjecting His people to interact with those who would inflict pain and suffering. It is also our tendency to judge the people who are doing the inflicting. Our hearts rebel against the command to forgive and to love.

I wouldn't pretend to know the mind of God, but I do know from His Word that we live to influence those around us, touching the "not so pleasant" for the Perfect One. He calls us to walk with the humility of Jesus, who forgave the worst people on earth. He was gentle in the face of hideous violence and vehement hatred directed toward Him. He was strong in His love for all men, and He forgave and loved even enemies, who would place second-to-none throughout history. His humility and submission to His Father bought my freedom.

It gave me great comfort as I examined those berries in my hand and removed the rotten ones. God is not unaware of the world He holds in His hand. His timing is perfect, His ways are perfect, and He looks lovingly on His creation, even as it looks a mess to us. Rinsing the good berries in my hand, I slowly savored each one and thought, "What a happy time it will be for our heavenly Father when all His children are in His presence forever". It will be the sweet harvest planned long ago, with His amazing love and grace, for the here and now.

We cannot know in this lifetime the ultimate destination of souls, the hearts of those who will yet come to Him. Some will appear beyond salvaging, but they are never beyond His reach. Some will appear hopeless, but they are never beyond His love. Some will appear damaged, but they are never beyond His touch. Yet, some will never accept His loving grace; it's simply not my place to say who that is. I believe His promise that for those who do, a humble and gentle Savior awaits them. And none will have been wasted.

"And this is the will of him who sent me, that I shall lose none of all that he has given me, but raise them up at the last day. For my Father's will is that everyone who looks to the Son and believes in him shall have eternal life and I will raise him up at the last day."

John 6:39, 40

Saturated

Within four months, four separate "water events" struck my domicile, thoroughly saturating flooring, carpet, ceilings, and everything in between. The first unhappy event involved record spring rains, which invaded our finished basement with sufficient volumes as to have a running current. The second incident did not, thankfully, overflow its boundaries, but a kitchen drain that does not drain is not much better; even the plumber was perplexed with its resistance to function as it was intended.

The third encounter, a twenty-nine-gallon aquarium on the second story, relentlessly seeped into my bedroom ceiling. And the finale', a cracked water supply line to a toilet, spewed its contents, against my wishes, across the room, seeping once again into the aforementioned basement. Did I mention these events all graced my home within four months? The plumber offered a frequent customer card with a taunting smile, which I handily refused with my daring frown.

Amid the trials by water, it was tempting to complain, and I cannot truthfully say that I complained not. But there was also much to be thankful for in the moment of mopping; I could call for help, I possessed tools to aid the cleanup, and in all but one incident, I had someone to assist in the repair and cleanup process. I still had a house to live in when it was all over, as well. God provided. Every event seemed quite overwhelming in the moment, but in the end resolution reigned.

No matter how many trials, annoyances, and perplexities arise in a day, no matter how complex the problems, I am so very grateful for the ability to talk to my Father in heaven. Without prayer, even the middle-of-emergency version, I could not breathe. Not knowing, without a doubt, that my heavenly Father had my best interest at heart, could I face the problems arising in any single day.

Thankfully, God has no long list of requirements or qualifications for our pleas. He knows us and sees every detail of our existence. He understands fully how we are made, our weaknesses and frailties, our tendencies to overly complicate life. He alone perceives our full propensity for blindness, our defenselessness in the face of our enemy. And there is only one remedy—saturation in Him, as fully as the water running through my house.

"For we are the temple of the living God. As God has said: 'I will live with them and walk among them, and I will be their God, and they will be my people...I will be a Father to you, and you will be my sons and daughters, says the Lord Almighty.'" 2 Corinthians 6:16b, 18

"He will have no fear of bad news; his heart is steadfast, trusting in the Lord." Psalm 112:7

"I love the Lord, for he heard my voice; he heard my cry for mercy. Because he turned his ear to me, I will call on him as long as I live." Psalm 116:1-2

The Evening Rainbow

I am technically considered "elderly", and in all my existence on earth, I have never witnessed a rainbow after sunset. It was quite an amazing picture! The sun was below the horizon, yet the gentle colors of the bow reached down, gently kissing the summer hilltop, a prism of light defying the dark.

What expresses God's glory more beautifully than the wonder of a rainbow, and the miracle of it at dusk with no rain clouds visible? God showed up for me in the shadow of twilight on a difficult day that hadn't made sense, reinforcing His presence through a rainbow in the dark.

Words of encouragement to the weary and broken are much the same as that gentle rainbow. They touch a heart darkened by grief, sorrow, or pain. Though they don't light the entire sky, they defy the darkness for a moment. They give relief and perhaps even a new perspective, but even more, they express care. We all need encouragement, and in some way, small or large, we can all administer encouragement.

I have received encouragement and encouraged others, but I have never considered the gift of encouragement to be an extravagant gift. It is the quiet gift dwelling mostly in the background, being whispered to the hurting or bewildered. It is usually personal and quiet, the gift of a note written, or the touch of a gentle hand on a weary shoulder. It is quietly listening to a heart filled with pain. It is an expression of caring from Jesus Himself, the gift of "a cup of water" to those who thirst, or a word of encouragement to those who cannot see their worth and value in the eyes of their Savior.

The most important use of the gift encouragers give is not just to cheer someone on, it is to lead him or her onto the path that takes them to the One who can supply all their needs, according to His riches, not mine. We are not what they need, only the vehicle to get them to the **One** they need. He will be their Provider and Savior because He alone understands their fragility and the depth of their pain.

He is our gentle rainbow in the bright light of day and in the twilight of evening. Since He was able to make a rainbow in the dark for me, He can make one in the darkness for you, too.

"You will show me the path of life; in Your presence is fullness of joy; at Your right hand are pleasures forevermore." Psalm 16:11

On the beach, our young daughter played happily in the water lapping the shore when she suddenly began screaming in pain. I scooped her up, trying to figure out what had happened. A jellyfish had wrapped its long tentacles around her small torso, leaving stinging stripes of welts. "It just so happened" that a woman was nearby who had the unlikely remedy for relief, alcohol and meat tenderizer!

Enjoying the meal with his family, the restaurant had only one other guest at a nearby table. The son-in-law, father, and husband to those at the family gathering, suddenly began choking on a piece of food, unable to breathe. Being a large man, no one at his table could get their arms into a suitable position to administer the Heimlich maneuver. It "just so happened" that the man dining nearby could, and he did. He sprung into position and the food dislodged, saving a life. Countless times I have heard similar stories of automobile collisions, accidents, and sudden illnesses where it "just so happened" that help showed up in an unlikely coincidence.

The flip side of this is that there are also times when it seems help is nowhere to be found. It "just so happened" that someone was at the wrong place, at the wrong time. A procedure ends up killing someone unexpectedly. No one shows up to help because of misdirection. A car entered the intersection at the wrong second, or someone's attention diverted at exactly the wrong time. The ending on this side of events is tragic and painful. So, I wondered which side God is on, and I must conclude it is both, the "good" and the "bad".

When everything falls into place and our days flow with ease, we believe we are in control and God is looking with favor upon us. When the raw events of life disrupt them, we are rattled to our core, often prone to blaming God. I have come to realize that Job was the most accurate in his assessment when he came to the end of his trials: **"Then Job replied to the Lord: 'I know that you can do all things; no plan of yours can be thwarted. You asked, 'Who is this that obscures my counsel without knowledge?' Surely I spoke of things I did not understand, things too wonderful for me to know." Job 42:13** Though I cannot understand why God allows the painful, unhappy incidents, along with the spectacular "saves", I can trust that He is good, wise, and just in all His ways.

The Lord blessed Job many times over following the tragedies He initially allowed in Job's life. But I noticed one verse never used in commentary on God's ultimate sway over events, also in the book of Job: **"Men at ease have contempt for misfortune as the fate of those whose feet are slipping." Job 11:5.** As we live in a fallen world, we are all subject to tragedy. We, as believers, can offer comfort with the same comfort we have been given, offering encouragement and hope, trusting the Sovereign Lord, with whatever "just so happens".

One of the greatest obstacles to the sale of an item is an obscure or missing price, as I confirmed personally on a recent visit to the grocery store. A price tag was displayed for every item on the shelf; but for my jar of olives, no price tag was visible. I grudgingly placed it back on the shelf and walked away, knowing I would have to go to another store to find it again. But at that moment, I did not have time to wander the aisles, only possibly stumbling upon an employee or scanner.

People do not buy anything unless they know the price, certainly not big-ticket items. If it is important to them, they may; but most often they will walk away. The truth is, everyone wants to understand the cost before making a deal, and it is no different with Jesus. When He asks us to follow Him, He also informs us of the price— we will be required to lay down our lives, perhaps literally, but certainly figuratively.

Coming to this realization, I was, frankly, scared to death! "What will He ask of me?" "Can I lay down my life for Him?" The weight of eternity anchored those questions to my soul. To better understand what, exactly, I was bargaining for and Who I was dealing with, I headed to my most reliable source, the Bible, and discovered the answers which sealed the deal.

I found that Jesus is the Son of God, and even the demons did not question that fact but acknowledged Him to be the Son of the Most High God. He bought salvation through His blood on the cross and rose again in triumph over death. He is everything He claimed to be, sent His Holy Spirit to testify, confirming all He said and did. He has proven Himself to me countless times, and in impactful ways, over decades of my relationship with Him, too.

So, is Jesus worth the cost of following Him when He requires total dependence upon Him? Is He worth the price when He does things in a way I don't expect or understand? When I am asked to go where I do not wish to go, or where I never have been, is following Him worth the cost? My answer is a resounding, "Yes!"

My commitment is a pittance compared to the life He laid down for me, the vast love He has shown me, and the grace He has showered upon me. He made the price of a relationship with Him clear, and I have accepted the exchange. Surrendering my heart in payment to the Son, I have truly received the better end of the deal.

"A man who has everything plus God is not a whit richer than the man who only has God." Dan Hively

"Then Jesus said to his disciples, 'If anyone would come after me, he must deny himself and take up his cross and follow me. For whoever wants to save his life will lose it, but whoever loses his life for me will find it.'" Matthew 16:24-25

Diligent Weeding July 10

Tennessee soil being the weed haven of the world, I could never keep up with my garden's proliferation of infiltrators. Pokeweed is popping up everywhere, and a mystery vine has decided to entwine itself at blistering speed along my porch rail. Even after relocating my "garden" to my porch, the weeds eventually, and irritatingly, found their way even into the pots of tomatoes, herbs, and flowers. My plants require diligent weeding, even on my porch.

The remedy for weeds is not weed killers, which can be even more dangerous to the user than the weeds, but diligence. Weeds in my yard have overtaken anything which is not diligently tended weekly. Weeds propagate insanely while plants we cultivate take more effort. Life seems to mirror my garden, porch, or otherwise; the weeds grow easily while everything else takes disproportionate effort.

The poor habits I have allowed, the 'little' sins, such as the neglect of time with my Creator and avoiding reconciliation in relationships, all become weeds growing at exponential rates in my life. Compared to the effort I must make in correcting them, they seem to grow freely, as if on a fertilization regimen. Our pride would lead us to believe our weeds are not so bad, certainly not as bad as someone else's; but God scrutinizes our motives and hearts. He sees where the roots are growing.

Spiritual weeds may have taken strong root, becoming thoroughly entwined in our hearts, but Jesus will free us from their hold. Warning: It will not be easy and will require diligence over time. It will take work and a keen eye to spot the infiltrators when they attempt resurgence; they will keep trying to reappear, just as stubbornly as the weeds in my garden.

Take heart and be encouraged, though. We have a Savior who conquered sin, and who is a present help in our struggles against it. God calls us, as His children, to be diligent in coming to Him with our "weeds", confessing our sins, and seeking His guidance in eradicating them. He does not condemn us for having weeds; He is our remedy for them.

"So then, just as you received Christ Jesus as Lord, continue to live in him, rooted and built up in him, strengthened in the faith as you were taught, and overflowing with thankfulness." Colossians 2:6-7

"We speak for Christ when we plead, 'Come back to God!' For God made Christ, who never sinned, to be the offering for our sin, so that we could be made right with God through Christ." 2 Corinthians 5:20b-21

Buried Treasure

Trevor had more than any child should have the right to possess, of Lego building blocks, that is. They migrated mysteriously to every part of the house, painfully underfoot at times, as evidenced by the sudden howl of family members. Castles sprang up, were conquered, and crumbled before bedtime. Mysterious cities rose and fell. The pirate ship, outfitted with a treasure chest, was filled with a bounty of even smaller "pieces of eight", which could be "hidden away" on a deserted island grid; it sailed for weeks, then morphed into a fortress in a far country. His imagination was limited only by the number of blocks available.

A time eventually came when the Lego structures were each dismantled, pieces rattling together in the storage box, and carefully tucked away. Years of young adulthood gave way to other interests. He was much too mature for Legos until the tide turned, and he discovered the storage box again. Fond memories flooded into the present day, and though they are not assembled into structures, the attachment is clear; the blocks would not be finding a new home, with the hope that one day he would build with his son.

Every Christ-follower has a treasure buried within, the "word of their testimony". I was puzzled by that phrase when I became a new Christian, but the meaning has become very apparent to me. Lazarus was a great example; he died and was buried in the tomb for four days when Jesus called his name and boldly told him to come forth. From that moment on, Lazarus gave the word of his testimony, as he recounted who Jesus is and what he had done for him to all who would listen.

Numerous examples fill the New Testament pages, of those who interacted with Jesus: a woman condemned to death, fishermen, a woman sick for 12 years, a tax collector, a doctor, a man lame his entire life, and a religious leader—they all shared their experiences freely, and to all who would listen. Why? Because only Jesus can give us true hope, eternal life, and change our hearts, souls, and bodies. They understood that He is the Son of God, and we, as children of the Father, are indebted to Him who sacrificed Himself for us.

The word of our testimony is simple. It is sharing with people what God has done for us. It is the excitement of being set free from our chains of bondage to sin, and the simple Gospel message. When I find myself reluctant to share, I have one of two problems; one, I am not remembering who He is and what He has done; or two, I am fearful of what the worldly reaction will be. Both have remedies. By sharing that Jesus is the treasure of the Father and the priceless Son of God, we reveal the buried treasure the world is seeking.

"After they had further proclaimed the word of the Lord and testified about Jesus, Peter and John returned to Jerusalem, preaching the gospel in many Samaritan villages." Acts 8:25

Flying High

Glancing upward at the billowy, summer clouds, a far distant object caught my attention. Flying high between them in a clear, blue sky, a large bird soared in lazy circles, becoming smaller and smaller until it disappeared from view. Whether it was an eagle, or a buzzard, was undiscernible and irrelevant. The bird was enjoying its ride on the thermal winds above me, and oblivious to the world beneath it.

Finding myself a bit envious, I reflected upon the times I have flown above the clouds. I love flying, being above the details of life, and having a bird's eye view of the earth. On various flights, a junkyard in the desert became a glittering scatter of jewels with the reflections of the sun bouncing off of windshields and bumpers in a junkyard; swimming pools in Houston became like inlaid jade; and circular irrigation in Texas like the geometric patterns of a dress I had long ago. Lakes have shown as mirrors, commuter's cars as Matchbox toys, and mountains as ripples in the carpet of earth.

Populated with black clouds in a night sky, spears of lightning shot between them. One flight highlighted gold-fringed clouds. On another, the clouds separated and broke out in the deepest reds of volcanic looking steppingstones to the next cloud beyond, reaching far into the distance. Yet another flight yielded an entire vista of popcorn-shaped, white fluffy clouds scattered across the sky as though it were spilled on the carpet of a movie theater. Flying is a source of amazement and wonder to me.

When I glimpse snippets of the character of God, the ways He demonstrates His love and presence in my life, I find that same sense of wonder and amazement. I wonder at the God of the universe, the Creator of galaxies and unimaginable power unleashed, the controller of orbits and destinies of stars, that He could love me. I marvel at love so great, so pure, Holy and just, that would sacrifice Himself to restore peace to my soul. I am humbled by the righteous God desiring a relationship with me, whom He could rightly reject, but by the blood of His only Son.

With the love of Jesus under my wings, I feel I can also soar above the clouds of this earth. But only when I keep my focus on Him, on the wings of trust, do I rise. Then, the problems I have encountered, conflicts and friction, shrink in size; some even beginning to appear like jewels in the desert, reflecting the Son. On those wings of trust, flying high, my perspective changes, and the details melt away, leaving only the beauty of His Presence in my view.

"You will keep him in perfect peace, whose mind is stayed on You, because he trusts in You."

Isaiah 26:3

Whether they do it intentionally or not, books, television, movies, games, and even the nightly news, tell stories. As I watched a powerful tale of integrity vs. blatant manipulation and intrigue, the ever-present tension between good and evil resurfaced. Since every captivating story is a reflection of our all-powerful, loving, and wise God, in the end, good prevailed, as it should.

Overcoming hardship, opposition, defeat, and evil are hidden deep within the human heart. We instinctively know that good should win and evil should lose. It is written in our spirits because we are all made in the image of God; without Him, we have no hope. Stories without a "happy ending" leave us, also, with no hope.

Every individual has a story. How can I emphasize it enough? Every human being has a story! Each has similarities in experiencing joys, sorrows, loves and love-lost, betrayal, friendships, family or lack of one, work, and a search for their value in the world. And God is the author of each storyline. He is the author and finisher of our faith, but every detail of life is also within His control—we make choices, but He ultimately guides the plot and storyline of each individual.

I have begun to see a glimmer of what God sees when He looks upon us. With our own unique stories, He alone has witnessed our conceptions, births, and childhoods (which I believe He treasures). He witnesses our struggles as teens to discover who He created us to be, and our arrogant tendencies in young adulthood. He is acutely aware of the elation of our love, our pain as we suffer the hardships of life, sorrows in losing those close to us, and the loneliness of aging. Each story may be similar, but no two are the same.

Jesus' story is similar, but, oh, so different. He was conceived, as God and man joined in the flesh. He grew up in a family with joys, sorrows, hardship, good memories, close ties, strained relationships, weddings, and funerals. He learned to work in His father's business while also tending to His heavenly Father's business. He led a company (of disciples), struggled against the powers of this world, kept His integrity to the end, and died the cruelest of deaths.

His happy ending is the best of happy endings, and one that gives us eternal hope--resurrection overcoming death! Hope triumphed forever over hopelessness, and because of Jesus' happy ending, in life and death, we all have hope. As we trust and love Him in this life, He is present in the story of our today, and writing our happy ending yet to come, an eternity in His presence.

"Let us fix our eyes on Jesus, the author and perfecter of our faith, who for the joy set before him endured the cross, scorning its shame, and sat down at the right hand of the throne of God." Hebrews 12:1-2

"You killed the author of life, but God raised him from the dead." Acts 3:15

Squeals, emitted from the two granddaughters sitting beside me, drew attention from the surrounding passengers, as the plane's engines ramped up from their low growl to a vibrating roar. The girls had not, within their memories, flown and were now exhibiting alternating waves of fear, squelched almost immediately by beaming smiles of exhilaration. And it seemed that we barely landed before we found days had passed, and we were briskly walking the concourse to make our flight home on time.

Newly minted mornings had melded into sun-soaked beachy afternoons, stealthily drifting quietly into early evenings on the streets of the quaint beach town. Sandy vacation warriors wearily dropped into bed, unaware of the passing of night and approach of a new day. There were too many things to see, so many shells to bag, too many shark teeth to glean from their beds of sand, and endless waves to tame on boogie boards. Time had yielded much too quickly before we found it was already "tomorrow".

We will awake to the startling passage of time in much the same way as the precious trip with my family. Events roll over us like the waves of the evening tide; some are ridden gracefully, while others bowl us over, dragging us across the painful sands of life. Time will stand amid the crashing waves of activity, then evaporate on the clouds of the ocean storm. Hours dissolve into days, days collapse into months, and years seem but a breath.

The passage of time, I recently read, was created to protect us, giving us increments of day and night, seasons and years. It is to break up the trials of our lives into bite-size pieces, the burdens into manageable loads. Our Creator was wise in His creating, and generous to His fragile creatures, endowing them with sleep and a limited number of hours each day. He limited our exposure to the demands of a world far beyond our capacity and cushioned our souls with allotments of time.

One day, there will be an ending to time, and in its Creator's presence, it will vanish with irrelevance. It, with death, will be vanquished. In the presence of Jesus, there will be no night, no shadows, no stress, nor fatigue. The city of God will shine with the brightness of His very Presence, and His peace will reign there. This earth will pass away, and as it does, we will joyfully find that it is already tomorrow, and will last for the rest of time, the time called eternity.

"As long as the earth endures, seedtime and harvest, cold and heat, summer and winter, day and night will never cease." Genesis 8:22

"The city does not need the sun or the moon to shine on it, for the glory of God gives it light, and the Lamb is its lamp. The nations will walk by its light, and the kings of the earth will bring their splendor into it. On no day will its gates ever be shut, for there will be no night there." Revelation 21:23-25

Chiggered

Don't ask how my yard was abundantly cursed with the nuisances, but chiggers have found a home in my grass, wood railings, and even the potted flowers. Living on this property for many years, no one ever encountered them until recently, and now they are everywhere! Like the mosquitoes, chiggers seem to be especially attracted to me.

They wouldn't be so annoying if their bites weren't so insidious. Unlike the mosquito bites, which last a few hours, chiggers make their way to "warm, moist" areas, burrow into the skin, and itch like microscopic, fire-breathing dragons. Not ones to give up easily, they linger for several days to a week. Since they burrow into the skin, there are not many effective remedies, either. The only preventive defense is to peel off clothing and shower thoroughly following any outdoor encounter.

Likewise, I have found my enemy to be just as strategic and insidious. The Bible says that he prowls in search of someone to devour. I think he is the one who invented chiggers; they share much in common. They both sneak up on you, totally invisible to the naked eye. They burrow into dark places. They both cause extreme discomfort, which lasts far longer than you think it should. They are both destructive and difficult to destroy. Yes, Satan's forces are like, and his weapons must include, chiggers.

Chiggers are a mysterious malady until you learn their ways, and I would say that is also true of our enemy. We are blindsided until we recognize some of his tactics, tricks, and strategies. He watches and patiently waits in the weeds until he knows us well enough to dangle the tastiest bait before our eyes, at just the right moment. He shows up in our secrets and bids us to keep them in the dark. He lurks in our losses and fatigue, whispering into our weaknesses, and echoing condemnation. He chants our sins over and over until our guilt is overwhelming, and his favorite barb is that we will never be good enough.

There isn't a great remedy for chiggers, but there is a remedy for the destruction and temptations of our enemy. His name is Jesus. The Remedy was not free; it came at a great cost. It cost the Father the life of His Son. He is the remedy, and repellent, to any plan Satan attempts to execute against you. His love was not extended to you as a one-time cure; it is an eternal-life cure, which includes your needs while on this chigger-infected earth. His price, the cost of "treatment", is your trust, just simple childlike trust. When life has "chiggered" you, His treatment will never fail, nor expire, and was personally formulated just for you.

"Cast all your anxiety on him because he cares for you." I Peter 5:7

"Come to me all you who are weary and burdened, and I will give you rest. Take my yoke upon you and learn from me, for I am gentle and humble in heart, and you will find rest for your souls." Matthew 11:28-29

There is nothing like a farm to impress the seasonal timing of life. From the birthings in spring to the mid-summer picking and canning; from the cool fall of slaughter and preserving meat, to the winter's season of resting and repairing. Preparing fields for planting, weeding before harvest, planning before doing; the inescapable rhythm of life, that in my youth seemed bereft of adventure, is now comforting. There is a time for everything under heaven, King Solomon stated, and I have come to recognize the truth of it.

For every human being, there is a time to be born and an appointed time to die. And what lies in between those markers is ordered by God, an ordained sequence of events, a march through the corridors of time. On the journey, we find that humanity has more in common than the differences on which we selectively focus. Go where you will in the whole world, you will find love and hate, smiles and tears, fatigue and sparks of energy, imagination, and deprivation, absurdly simple and outrageously complicated people.

Life is a swirling concoction of elation and bitter disappointment, gladness and suffering, confidence and despair, hope, and desperation. We all question our existence, question God, struggle against sin and evil, and search for answers to questions that have none. We deem everything unpleasant as a curse from God while embracing all that caters to our senses as blessings, yet God's wisdom is proven in the end. We hide from God, run from Him, and attempt to outsmart Him. We deny His existence, sovereignty, love, and power while striving to order our lives in a way that benefits our own goals, only to find He knew best all along. Yet all our longings are ultimately for Him.

These things I know well, having personal experience questioning God, and to my shame, trusting in myself much more than I should. Because I am human, this all comes very naturally to me, as for all human beings. But God, in His infinite grace and mercy, has revealed my folly and drawn me into increasing faith, trust, and knowledge of His truth and Presence. I can look over the years God has given me and see that His seasons, wisdom, and timing have been perfect, and what He said in His Word is true:

"There is a season for everything and a season for every activity under heaven...I have seen the burden God has laid on men. He has made everything beautiful in its time. He has also set eternity in the hearts of men, yet they cannot fathom what God has done from beginning to end. I know that there is nothing better than for men to be happy and do good while they live." Ecclesiastes 3:1, 11,12

"When times are good, be happy; but when times are bad, consider: God made the one as well as the other." Ecclesiastes 7:14

Storm Waves

The idyllic sailing on Lake Kerr began to show signs of disruption as the wind, previously soft and steady, gathered strength. Puffy white clouds exchanged their friendly countenances for gray angry faces, as they rapidly forced their way overhead. Our 18-foot catamaran began to pitch steeply, its bow plowing deeply into the coming waves. Lightning streaked vertically in rapid succession all around us, as thunder shook us to the bone. With one hand, I hung onto a rope, the other frantically clinging to a very panicked dog attempting to jump ship.

The mast suddenly snapped, barely missing my husband, and lay across the starboard and into the water. I felt we would all die if we did not get off that boat. Feeling somewhat relieved, I saw we were being blown toward an island, and a beach strewn with boulders. Regardless, we disembarked, climbing over the rocks just in time for another bolt of lightning to crack a nearby tree in half. As quickly as storms form on lakes, they also quickly pass. The tumultuous waves settled into calm waters. A passing boat came to our rescue and towed us back to safe harbor. Not long after that harrowing experience, the catamaran found a new home with owners who were not sailing novices.

Our mortality is never as apparent as when we are in dire circumstances. Our awareness is never so acute as when no one can help us, except God. Jesus asks each of us to walk on the water, like Peter, in the sense that where He asks each of us to go seems imposing, if not impossible. We see the obstacles, dangers, and barriers. He asks us to "Take courage!" and to trust Him, like Peter's invitation to walk on the water:

"But Jesus immediately said to them, 'Take courage! It is I. Don't be afraid.' **'Lord, if it's you,' Peter replied, 'tell me to come to you on the water.'** *'Come,' he said.* **Then Peter got down out of the boat, walked on the water and came toward Jesus. But when he saw the wind, he was afraid and, beginning to sink, cried out, 'Lord, save me!'** *Immediately Jesus reached out his hand and caught him. 'You of little faith,' he said, 'why did you doubt?'* **And when they climbed into the boat, the wind died down. Then those who were in the boat worshiped him, saying, 'Truly you are the Son of God.'"** Matthew 14:27-33

Notice the progression: Taking the first step onto choppy water, we believe in the possibility of the impossible. The second step is listening to doubts—"this really can't be possible!" The third step, we crumble, forgetting who is asking us to walk with Him in the impossible, crying out as we flail and sink. Then Jesus simply asks why we didn't trust Him, not with condemnation, just with a simple statement of the obvious lack of faith, followed by a question, "Why did you doubt?" Finally, Peter understood the obvious reason he could trust Jesus—"You are the Son of God!" When we begin to understand who Jesus is, faith to go where He is leading is no longer lacking, even into the storm.

Coca-Cola bottles sat in a weathered wooden crate, each nestled in its slot during transport. Once they arrived, it was my job to evenly distribute them in the massive, red, metal Coke chest. The bottles were chilled on a very large block of ice, delivered weekly. My grandmother's salon customers paid ten cents for the beverage, drank the cola, and returned the bottle to her. Each bottle returned earned my grandmother two cents, the container retainer she had paid in deposit for each one.

With their subtle green-tint, patented design Coke bottles, at one time, were all brand new, unscratched, and unmarred by use. As they were emptied of their sweet contents, they retained value because of the deposit paid for them. Like those beautiful, shining new bottles, full of life, so are we as we enter this world, becoming citizens of the human race.

Life is much like the Coke bottle, beginning full on the inside, and shiny new on the outside, contents under pressure, ready to explode into the world with great energy and vigor. Once the lid is off, life bubbles to the top, a bit more under control. As time goes on, the outside is less shiny, the inside less full of vigor. Some of us are tempered and mellowed with positive changes, but for others, life has sapped our strength and diluted our flavor.

Those of us who know Jesus have an advantage, though. As we experience the hardships and tumult of living, our external bottle may appear a bit scratched and worn, but we are containers for the eternal essence of the Holy Spirit. Our aging on this earth does not devalue us; our internal contents, while we remain earthbound, have the promise of being refilled, refreshed, and restored to brand new each day. We have a deposit of return through Jesus, a container retainer, promising that our deposit on eternity has been paid in full, and is collectible upon our departure, our return to our Creator.

To our heavenly Father, who is the God of restoration and relationship, our value is limitless, for we are made in the image of God, and viewed by Him in the image of His Son. The precious-beyond-our-imaginings blood, poured out by His Son in voluntary sacrifice is what defines our value. It is ours by His grace, wholly undeserved; it is ours to His glory, as we become more like His Son. By faith, we live; and by His life, we live again. God's "container retainer" is eternally redeemable, but only accessible in this life, until the day closes, and the bottle is empty.

"And this is the testimony: God has given us eternal life, and this life is in his Son. He who has the Son has life; he who does not have the Son of God does not have life. I write these things to you who believe in the name of the Son of God so that you may know that you have eternal life." 1 John 5:11-13

Setting out on our long trip, we left our dark driveway and headed east toward the mountains. The highway wriggled through the foothills like a piece of ribbon candy, the mountainside growing high on our left side. On our right was a drop-off, very steep and sudden. Beyond that drop-off lay a vast expanse of mountain range shrinking into the horizon, with still, quiet valleys nestled between. Fine veils of clouds hung in rings with the mountain tops regally floating above them.

Ahead was a high mountain blocking all forward view, save a piece of sky to the right of the top, which was layered with billow upon billow of golden-edged clouds. The sun was rising through them and shooting beams straight and true through the gaps, caressing the sides of the mountain in delicate golden rays. The clouds over the broad plateau and mountain range beneath us glowed as embers and shouted back to the rising sun.

As I praised God for this valuable gift of dark to glorious light, I also understood what I was viewing had hidden meaning. In these mountains, not only beauty but rustic danger lurked in the night, as large as rockslides and bears, and as small as ticks. Hidden from my eyes, also, was spectacular beauty as tiny as a red mushroom and gentle spotted fawn. The dark of night had turned to majestic light, shining over all the mountains. And it seemed that God was contrasting the pain and heartbreaks of life with the beauty of love and grace God lavishes upon us.

Sometimes I wonder if there truly are people who escape great pain and sorrows in their lives, living above the fray, untouched by tragedy or heartbreak. My life has certainly not fallen into those categories. For me, pain, heartbreaks, and life's uncertainties are a filter through which life was solidly jolted back into the right perspective; the darkness helps me appreciate the light, and the light helps expose what is hidden in the darkness. I avoid pain and discomfort at all costs, yet those are the times my conformity to Christ has been most intense.

Jesus promised His followers that trials and tribulations would afflict them in this world, but He assured them that He had overcome the world, promising them His Spirit's comforting presence in this life. In the next life, we enter a kingdom of light where darkness, pain, and sorrow are vanquished. With the Son shining His golden rays in dazzling brilliance all around us, eternity will stretch ahead of us like the ribbon candy highway. Death and tears, trials and tests will have done their work, landing us at the feet of Jesus in all His glory. We will have passed from dark to light, night to spectacular golden dawn in the radiance of His Presence.

"The heavens declare the glory of God; the skies proclaim the work of his hands. Day after day they pour forth speech; night after night they display knowledge." Psalm 19:1-2

"When Jesus spoke again to the people, he said, 'I am the light of the world. Whoever follows me will never walk in darkness but will have the light of life.'" John 8:12

Depth Defying

The water was clear and still, like a dark mirror, reflecting the puffy, summer clouds above it. Even in the midsummer heat, it remained bone-chilling cold. I never understood the desire to swim in the strip mine lakes—they terrified me! The mine lakes were bottomless, no one knowing exactly how deep they were, and they dropped off immediately with no gentle slope into the water. I much preferred my secure neighborhood swimming pool. There, the bottom was visible. And the only danger was that of mischief-seeking boys, stalking potential dunking victims.

A wooden platform was anchored in the mirrored water about 100 feet from the shoreline. Once we jumped into the water, there was no way to get there but to swim as if our lives depended on it, because they did! And there were no lifeguards. Pure adrenalin fueled my strokes, fearing the entire way that I would go under, never being seen again. The depth-defying event ended when I shot out of the water and climbed to safety on the bobbing raft, only to realize that I then had to swim back to shore.

My relationship with God has been like swimming in the strip mines, knowing how powerfully consuming He is, and how vulnerable and weak I am. He reflects the puffy, summer clouds, which make Him approachable, but His depths are unfathomable. He is dangerous beyond my understanding, yet loves me, who can barely swim the surface of His Being. He is the expanse I cannot envision, the vastness beyond my view. I am frightened at my own sense of control, my ego, and my pride. I am appalled that I can be so foolish, in contrast to His great wisdom, mercy, and goodness.

If not for the grace purchased through the blood of Jesus, I would sink immediately. Forgiveness in depth-defying measure abounds. He understands the weaknesses and frailty of my being. He provided, beyond my wildest expectations, for my salvation and continued relationship with Him. He sustains me, buoys me up, saves me from the depths of transgression, and gives me hope. He keeps every promise, speaks tenderly, and listens faithfully.

Many times, I have realized the fragility of life, and looking back I can see that He protected me all along. I wish I had known Him when I was swimming the mine lakes in fearfulness. Knowing Jesus, I would have been able to swim in peace, understanding that my life was in His hands. And now, I don't have to wonder if He is present; He always is. There is no need to fear the depths of life—I know this Lifeguard personally, and He hasn't lost one soul who placed trust in Him.

"Out of the depths I cry to you, O Lord; O Lord, hear my voice. Let your ears be attentive to my cry for mercy. If you, O Lord, kept a record of sins, O Lord, who could stand? But with you there is forgiveness; therefore you are feared. I wait for the Lord, my soul waits, and in his word I put my hope." Psalm 130:1-5

Wasps and hornets have abounded this summer. For unexplained reasons, they have begun nesting in my potted plants, behind my shutters, between rocks, and in my mailbox. They are relentless builders and invasive neighbors. Yesterday I observed one red wasp enter through the doors with a guest at a commercial building. Ascending to the second-floor balcony, it came to rest on one of its spindles. The first thought I had was, "This is where you will die." There would be no possibility of it finding its way out of the building, and it had flown into enemy territory—I know of not one person who considers wasps kindly!

The thought which followed was a bit more startling. "I am like that wasp, wandering through life, oblivious to when my end will be." From the moment we are born to our ending of days, humans presume eternity. The Bible, in Ecclesiastes 3:11, states that God "has also set eternity in the human heart". Instinctively, we believe we will not die. It is a traumatic event for us to confront death because it contradicts what God has set in our hearts. We were made for eternity.

We also grasp that illness, brokenness, darkness, and disease are not normal. All of them cause our souls to cry out, wondering out loud "Why, God?" We understand that these difficult places shouldn't exist, that we were created for perfection, our spirits longing for restoration and wholeness. What we fail to grasp is that in all of it, God has a plan.

Jesus entered our world, suffering at the hands of sinful men, to conquer sin and defeat death. And through Him, we have the ever-present help we need as we walk through this segment of eternity. He promises there is more to come, as well as His loving watchfulness over us here and now. He invites us to know and follow Him each step of the way, as He unfolds the path to eternity before us, even as we are oblivious.

"But Christ has indeed been raised from the dead, the firstfruits of those who have fallen asleep. For since death came through a man, the resurrection of the dead came also through a man. For as in Adam all die, so in Christ, all will be made alive. But each in his own turn; Christ, the firstfruits; then, when he comes, those who belong to him."
I Corinthians 15:20-23

"For the light and momentary troubles are achieving for us an eternal glory that far outweighs them all." 2 Corinthians 4:17

Layer upon Layer

The painting was never intended to be a painting, just a line drawing, pencil on paper. I could not walk away from it, magnetically drawing me back before I could even lay the pencil down. Each time I attempted to leave it, something felt lacking; I went over the pencil with ink, but it still felt incomplete. I over-laid just a touch of color with my watercolor brush, when to my horror, as I touched the brush to the paper, the ink began to run. It was not waterproof ink!

Quickly catching the run with the brush, I pulled the ink back to the edge, creating a "shadow" with it. Adding a shadow to another area, then another, and another the shell took shape and dimension before my eyes. I carefully added another layer of color and then filled in the darkest shadows, this time with waterproof ink. Layer upon layer, a beautiful shell came into view. To my amazement, it was pretty! But it was not finished yet. Framing would be its crowning touch, complementing the shell painting perfectly.

Every room I attempted to hang that painting was the wrong place for it; it did not fit anywhere. I finished decorating each room in our new house, with the master bedroom the last to be completed. That room became the "shell" room, centered on that painting. Every treasure I had gathered from years of visits to the sea became part of the loveliest room in the house. God knew what it needed long before it was completed, and in fact, we had not purchased that house yet when I painted the shell.

My life has been like the painting. It is constructed "layer upon layer", built by His hand, in His timing. He has been completing His work of art in me, too. With each layer, I know there will be incidents appearing as "accidental spills", but they will be no surprise to my Father; He will transform them into the dimension my story needs to make it beautiful in His eyes. What the world sees is only one layer at a time, but He sees me as complete in Christ, lovely, and valuable. He knows what is necessary to complete the painting of my life, layer upon layer.

"The Spirit of the Lord is on me, because the Lord has anointed me [Jesus] to preach good news to the poor. He has sent me to bind up the brokenhearted, to proclaim freedom for the captives and release from darkness for the prisoners, to proclaim the year of the Lord's favor and the day of vengeance of our God, to comfort all who mourn, and provide for those who grieve in Zion---to bestow on them a crown of beauty instead of ashes, the oil of gladness instead of mourning, and a garment of praise instead of a spirit of despair. They will be called oaks of righteousness, a planting of the Lord for the display of his splendor."
Isaiah 61:1-3

A straight, but bumpy, road cut through prime farm acreage, delivering me to one of my most happy places. The summer visits to my great aunt and uncle's house featured a wrap-around porch. Its gray painted wood floor sat high enough off the ground to accommodate the dogs, searching for cooler ground. I loved it because my feet dangled freely. On that porch, beans were snapped, June bugs captured, and if lucky, a cool breeze occasionally brushed my skin.

The family of seven children, all girls, to my great uncle's dismay, were mostly grown up and married, so the mouths to feed were vast on Sundays. Everyone migrated to the porch to eat, talk, and play games. Laughter was as gentle, and persistent, as the breeze rippling around the porch until my younger brother asked to ride the pony. A plump city kid on a pony was a bit too tempting for one of the male in-laws. After my brother was firmly seated in the saddle, he slapped the hindquarters of that pony with his hat.

That pony shot off in a full gallop around and around the farmhouse, with my brother wild-eyed and hanging on for dear life! A mixture of fear and laughter followed that pony around the porch. Some feared for my brother's safety (mostly the women), and some found the situation incredibly funny (you guessed it, mostly the men). I will never forget my grandmother laughing uncontrollably, while I wondered if I would have one less brother on the way home. When they were finally able to end his wild ride, my brother dismounted, white as a sheet, but never shedding a tear.

Some of us can relate to my brother's brisk ride on a runaway pony. Life slaps the rump of our horse with events unanticipated, and out of our control. We hang on for dear life and feel the ride will never end. Fear grips our hearts and we can see no way out; there is no rescuer in sight. And if you haven't experienced that kind of event in your life, it is only a matter of time before you do. Jesus himself promised that in this life we will have troubles, trials, and tribulation; if he didn't escape it, neither will you.

But here is the good news for runaway events in your life: God knows about it, loves you, and is ever-present. He wants His best for you, His best being a close relationship with Him. Is He waiting for you to ask Him for help? Is this event for your ultimate good? Is He teaching you to trust only Him? Only you and He can answer those questions. However, I do know that He always has a reason for the ride, and a plan for our rescue, if we will only turn to Him. God always has good intentions toward you, so take hope—all wild rides end eventually!

"So do not fear, for I am with you; do not be dismayed, for I am your God. I will strengthen you and help you; I will uphold you with my righteous right hand." Isaiah 41:10

"Do not be anxious about anything, but in everything, by prayer and petition, with thanksgiving, present your requests to God. And the peace of God, which transcends all understanding, will guard your hearts and minds in Christ Jesus." Philippians 4:6-7

Gram and Grandpa lived in a paid-off house, while also supporting my mother and four children as Mom finished college. Both of my grandparents continued to work until late in life. They lived frugally but well, took us to church with them when we visited, and to league baseball games Grandpa played. On Friday nights we always went grocery shopping, and every Saturday night, weather permitting, Grandpa grilled the best hamburgers I ever recall eating. Ice cream was served at 8 PM every night, so you can understand where my love for both my grandfather and ice cream, originate.

There was one odd thing about Grandpa, though—he ate jars of baby food at most meals. No one seemed to want to talk about it, so for the longest time, I didn't ask. Finally, one night I whispered to Gram, "Why does Grandpa eat BABY FOOD???" The painful secret was revealed to me. Asking the question brought back the not-too-distant memories of Grandpa's prisoner-of-war days, being starved nearly to death, resulting in stomach problems for the rest of his days.

Grandpa never once complained about having to eat baby food, or Gram's overly-pressure-cooked meat, that made it more digestible for him. He thanked God for the blessings of his home, family, and food every day, without fail. In that prison camp, he discovered a Savior who never failed, nor left him, for the rest of his life on earth. Grandpa was a humble man who quietly served a mighty God, a God who saved his life while in uniform, and ever after. To Jesus, he was eternally grateful in every way.

Everyone encounters adversity in life if we live long enough. Our first tendency is complaining, but it is through gratitude and trust that the overcoming Power resides. Ingratitude and complaining are obstacles of resistance to the Holy Spirit. Yet, when we yield to His ways, He brings peace to our hearts. Many are the blessings we bypass daily, simply because we do not honor and thank God for them. God is sovereign over everything, and through trusting His ability and acknowledging His good intentions for us, His power is unleashed, as evidenced in Grandpa's blessings.

"Be joyful always; pray continually; give thanks in all circumstances, for this is God's will for you in Christ Jesus." 1 Thessalonians 5:18

"Every good and perfect gift is from above, coming down from the Father of heavenly lights, who does not change like shifting shadows." James 1:17

"Now may our Lord Jesus Christ himself and God our Father, who loved us and by his grace gave us eternal comfort and a wonderful hope, comfort you and strengthen you in every good thing you do and say." 2 Thessalonians 2:16-17

Following weeks of busyness and much neglect, my lush tomato vines appeared a disheveled mess. Brown withered branches hung amidst sporadic dots of red cherry tomatoes in varying stages of ripeness. I was tempted to do away with the whole plant, but the promise of another harvest before frost beckoned me to prune and clean instead. An hour passed in the oppressive heat of the day, sorting through the branches, carefully separating the entangled mass to find the base of each dead or dying limb, without damaging the viable ones.

As I continued the process, it became easy to see that some branches, turning yellow, had borne their limit. The brown web of dead branches obscured the fruit in other places. Some branches were very green, but their fruit had already been harvested. At this point, I contemplated the role of the pruner; the time, care, and thoughtful consideration required to bring a maximum harvest to fruition. He must know what to prune, how to execute it, how severely to cut back, and when.

How careful my Lord is to gently and purposefully sort the vines in me, separating the strands of self, of a narrow, choked viewpoint, of a disease entwined heart. He gently strips them away while saving the fragile tendrils that please Him. His timing and skill are meticulous. He causes me to bear more fruit as He strips the dead branches away, diverting my energies to the fruit of His plan. God saw my potential to bear fruit long before any sign of blossoms. For the first time in my walk with Jesus, I desired pruning, truly desired to be useful in His Kingdom, to be all He created me to be, to His glory. I wanted to be productive, healthy, and useful to Him.

I realized something else I had never considered, that when the dead branches were pruned away, the fruit was suddenly visible and much easier to harvest. Perhaps, in a grander scheme of things, God's pruning in our lives is necessary to expose our fruit to view. The world can then see the fruit God intended them to see, bringing Him glory and making Christ more visible to them. It's not all about the branches, it's about the fruit, the fruit that others can taste and see, revealing that our God is good.

Pruning is not a one-time event. It is an ongoing process, especially for growing Christians. It is necessary for continued fruit production throughout the season of life. At times, the process of snipping is painful, and we cannot understand what God is doing, but we can trust that in His wisdom, each snip of the shears is purposeful, intentional, and ultimately good.

"No discipline seems pleasant at the time, but painful. Later on, however, it produces a harvest of righteousness and peace for those who have been trained by it." Hebrews 12:11

"I am the vine; you are the branches. If a man remains in me and I in him, he will bear much fruit; apart from me you can do nothing." John 15:5

A red-haired girl named Jenny was my "summer" friend, meaning I only saw her when I visited my grandparents in the summer. She lived in a house across the street from my grandmother's hair salon, and I would have lived with her if I had been allowed. There were few girls in my neighborhood at home, and I loved playing jacks and paper dolls at her house. I don't remember her family at all, probably meaning they were calm and pretty normal, which for me was a bit abnormal, living with three brothers. Jenny was the friend by which I measured all friends for decades to come.

We all have a mental picture of someone who immediately comes to mind when "friend" is mentioned. From casual to best, recent to lifelong, the word brings someone to mind. The most valued qualities of friendship seem to be someone who listens, understands, comforts, advises, is loyal, and would never betray us. Walking through happy times, as well as struggles together, solidifies the bond between friends.

My mother repeated the adage many times throughout my childhood, "To have a friend, you must be a friend." I have found that saying to be true over the years. I also realized there is often a high price to pay for any real and lasting friendship, payable in many installments over a long time. I discovered that there are preliminary steps in developing a friendship:

❖ Reach out but be selective.
❖ Confide, but in increasingly valuable increments over time.
❖ Give, but give generously only after trust has been established.
❖ When trust is broken, be prepared to forgive, but don't be foolish in repeating the process endlessly.

Not everyone is or should be your friend. Some "friends" are not capable of being friends, unwilling to give of themselves or their time. Others do not understand boundaries, and some are selfish; it's all right to say "no" to them. Friends have boundaries and respect each other, and friends are accountable to one another while allowing the freedom to be who God called them to be.

The best friend in the world will not be perfect. There is not one person in the friend pool who will meet all your expectations, but I know One who will. Jesus keeps all His promises, and never leaves nor forsakes us. He is closer than a brother and is ready to listen, comfort, and guide us at all hours, in any location. He paid a high price for this friendship; in fact, I am sometimes not a great example of a friend at all, but He still loves me. And, yet, He still calls me His friend.

"Instead, I have called you friends, for everything that I learned from my Father I have made known to you." John 15:15b

Air Borne

The Piper Cub skipped over air pockets, thumping me gently up and down in my seat, somewhat like an amusement park ride. The pilot must have noticed the smile on my face and viewed it as his personal challenge to wipe it right off. He suddenly took the little propped plane into a steep climb, then abruptly nose-dived into a free fall. I heard his voice over the engine noise, explaining the feeling of inertia and weightlessness I had just experienced. That was my first exposure to flight at age 11, quite the thrill and an unforgettable moment.

As I have flown since then, mostly commercial airliner flights, the danger of suddenly dropping out of the sky has rarely occurred to me. I love flying and it has become a normal experience, one I look forward to, not the cabin or the commercial aspect, but the actual flight. I love to gaze down upon the earth, and upward to the heavens, to be closer to the stars and fly through the clouds. I find it fascinating to watch the traffic shrink to microscopic proportions and view the cloud formations from their tops instead of bottoms. To witness the sun rise and set, casting its golden hues bouncing among the billows of clouds, is magical.

As I gaze backward, over my relationship with God, I am beginning to understand my dips and valleys, the soaring moments, and the occasional coasting. They are very similar to my flight experiences. The newness and thrill of first experiences with God brought heights of wonder and amazement. The ongoing relationship leveled out to expose new perspectives and the security of familiarity. I sometimes confuse that familiarity with distance, but it is not so; it simply means I am in need of an altitude, or attitude, adjustment. Jesus never changes, never distances Himself from me, and never leaves.

The greatest limitation an airplane has is fuel, only flying as far as the gas in its tank allows, before refueling dictates landing. The same principle applies to my relationship with God—I can only fly so far without refueling, filling up with His power and presence. I like to think I can do it alone, that I can live life without taking time to be with Jesus. I mistakenly refuse the refueling and attempt to go a little farther before stopping to commune with Him, to seek His wisdom and leadership. He has proven me wrong, as I have crashed and burned many times over in my neglect and pride. The only means of being "airborne" is to refuel in His presence daily, moment by moment trusting Him to power my flight.

"The Lord is the everlasting God, the Creator of the ends of the earth. He will not grow tired or weary, and his understanding no one can fathom. He gives strength to the weary and increases the power of the weak. Even youths grow tired and weary, and young men stumble and fall; but those who hope in the Lord will renew their strength. They will soar on wings like eagles; they will run and not grow weary, they will walk and not be faint."
Psalm 40:28b-31

Remember the Mirage

Rippling in the desert heat, the image is clear and seemingly real, as the mirage hovers before the thirsty man's gaze. Even upon approaching it, it can barely be distinguished from reality, ever-elusive, and just beyond reach. The illusion torments and taunts, unable to quell or satisfy the thirsty man; it is so real, yet totally unreal, a deception of the mind.

Part of Satan's great deception is to keep our sins ever before our eyes, persistently bringing them to our remembrance. He uses them to condemn and separate us from Jesus, dangling them as a mirage before our gaze. The opposite is true of the Holy Spirit's conviction of sin in our lives; He will firmly show us our guilt, but never condemns us to live in it. When we confess our sin, He forgives and casts it far away, remembering it no more.

There is no further condemnation for our sins once we are forgiven, but we often allow the mirage to be dangled before our eyes daily. We must determine that the mirage is exactly that, an elusive taunt from our enemy, unable to convict us before our righteous Savior. See it for what it is; an illusion with just enough truth to convince you it is real.

As a mirage can attract that thirsty man's attention in the desert, a spiritually thirsty man's attention can be focused on the sins and condemnations of the past, forgetting that the reality of those sins is no more. Satan would have us remember the sins; Jesus would have us remember the mirage.

"When you were dead in your sins and in the uncircumcision of your sinful nature, God made you alive with Christ. He forgave us all our sins, having canceled the written code, with its regulations, that was against us and that stood opposed to us; he took it away, nailing it to the cross." Colossians 2:13-14

"Therefore, there is now no condemnation for those who are in Christ Jesus, because through Christ Jesus the law of the Spirit of life set me free from the law of sin and death…The mind of sinful man is death, but the mind controlled by the Spirit is life and peace…" Romans 8:1

"The Lord is compassionate and gracious, slow to anger, abounding in love. He will not always accuse, nor will he harbor his anger forever; he does not treat us as our sins deserve or repay according to our iniquities. For as high as the heavens are above the earth, so great is his love for those who fear him; as far as the east is from the west, so far has he removed our transgressions from us." Psalm 103:8-12

Soft Serve July 29

The world of baseball gives an entirely different meaning to the term "soft serve" than waltzing up to the take-out window of an ice cream parlor. That means that the player "serving" the ball to the opposition is making it easier to connect; soft serving generally to someone just learning the game, not real competition. Having grown up with three brothers, I was rarely delivered a soft serve, as they seemed to delight in my struggles dealing with a league baseball.

That league ball was lethal when powered off a fully swung bat, and I did not relish the thought of being hit with it. I had fresh memories of being hit in the head with a flying bat, so the prospect of pain had been firmly imprinted, with the full force of a mild concussion, complete with proverbial stars. They did not expect me to play ball unless I could take the pain.

Life does not offer up soft serves often. Most life events knock the wind out of your lungs and leave you seeing stars. I have walked through several of those hardball plays that life tossed my way, staggering under the blows, not knowing which way was up. How I handled some of life's events before knowing Jesus and after knowing Him differed vastly.

The hard-hitting, gut-wrenching experiences without Jesus were largely hopeless, dependent solely upon my abilities to rectify the situation. They were lonely, filled with dread and a lot of fear. After I submitted my stubborn self-will to Jesus, the lonely events were less lonely, the fear subsided, and hope restored. I knew that He was present in my pain, loved me despite my failings, gave me strength in my weakness, and helped me recognize the blessings in the storm.

Life's painful experiences, God can soften. The mountains, He can level. The storms, He can quell. He knows me and has created me for this moment in time. He has prepared me with the experiences already passed. As I have grown, some of life's challenges have become greater. Others have been hit out of the park, out-of-sight and only a memory, as the flying bat is. But one thing remains constant, I know I can trust my Father to soften the blows when He sees fit or to remove them completely.

So, whether life is serving you a pitch that is too hot to handle, or a soft serve, you can know that your Savior is ultimately calling the play. He is standing for you, not against you; He is present this moment, not hiding from you. You were uniquely created to play on His team. More than you can trust any coach, you can trust Him with whatever pitch is thrown your way.

"Hear, O Lord, and answer me, for I am poor and needy. Guard my life, for I am devoted to you. You are my God; save your servant who trusts in you." Psalm 86:1-2

Fill 'R Up, Pete!

As we pulled into the gas station, Grandpa rolled his window down, smiled, and repeated the same instructions Uncle Pete had heard every Saturday morning, "Fill 'r up, Pete!" Uncle Pete owned a Texaco gas station in the same town where their mother lived, whom Grandpa visited every weekend at ten in the morning. But before we left to visit her, Grandpa spent an hour sitting with Uncle Pete, catching up on family news and the happenings of their tiny hometown.

As Grandpa chatted, I sat on the wooden bench near the door, sipping on a soda and nibbling on a candy bar. Grandpa paid Uncle Pete for the gas and treats, and we headed to his mama's very old farmhouse, a tiny home, painted white, surrounded by colorful flowers. I roamed the house, sat on the porch, and waited. I was the city kid on an old farm with nothing to do, except to avoid the bees and June bugs.

However, just being in the presence of my grandfather was enough for me. I loved spending time with him alone in the car, holding Penny, the small Toy Manchester dog, on my lap. I loved my grandfather and felt special in his presence, and I knew he loved me. He was my grandfather in name only, but he never treated me differently than his own kin. And that is how my Heavenly Father treats me; to Him, though I was not born into His bloodline, I was adopted into His family.

We are adopted through faith in Christ Jesus, and God loves us because of Jesus' sacrifice, as though we were born into His bloodline. The spiritual children born out of wedlock, abandoned, filthy, and ragged, He sees as clean, whole, perfect, and legitimately born into His royal kingdom. He doesn't treat us as distant relatives; He embraces us as dearly loved children. And this Father who loves His children so much is often brushed to the sideline, or the back of the line, of our attentions. I am guilty, as charged.

When I consider God's goodness, ponder His infinite mercy, and focus on His tenderness toward me, my heart cannot be still. I am so grateful for the man God placed into my life, who would imitate His love so meticulously; for the grandfather displaying unconditional love so matching my heavenly Father's love.

The most comforting place to be is in His Presence, to be aware of Him moment by moment, and be filled with His peace. It is no wonder that in God's Presence, Moses' face shone with radiance, that David danced, or that Daniel knew the mind of God. It is our blessing to know Him through His Spirit. As Grandpa requested of his brother, "Fill 'r up!", so we can request of our Father to fill us up with His Spirit and Presence.

"You have made known to me the path of life; you will fill me with joy in your presence, with eternal pleasures at your right hand." Psalm 16:11

Canning fresh produce is a thing of the past for me, but I recall the great satisfaction of "putting up", as my grandmother used to say, the freshly picked vegetables. During a bountiful season, preparing green beans and tomatoes for the canning process would take many hours. Snapping and cleaning, prepping the jars and lids, adding the salt, then standing over a very hot stove, the jars were then heated to the proper temperature. Finally, jars proudly sat lined up on the counter to cool, as we listened for the little popping sound each lid made as it suctioned itself to the rim.

When filling the jars, we were always careful to leave "head space", approximately a half inch of room, between the contents and the rims of the jars. Without that space, the jars could explode, not having room for temperature expansion in the canning process. Exploding glass jars are not exactly desirable, in case you were wondering.

That is not to say that I did not experience other "explosions" in my life. The pressures of living produce mounting steam for everyone. People tend to encroach upon each other's space, demands outweigh resources, and life just gets messy. At one point in my journey, my adult daughter suggested I read a book, aptly titled, "Boundaries". Feeling emotionally exhausted and out of control, I ordered the book. After reading it, I began applying the principles outlined, one of those being to build fences with gates.

The fences with gates are boundaries securing your right to allow entry to those who respect you. The gate opens and closes depending upon that respect. Of course, that works both ways and must be honored by both parties; it is not fair, or right to infringe on someone else's boundaries while expecting yours to be honored. It's like "head space", allowing a bit of room in your life for flexibility, avoiding a pressure build-up, which can result in a nasty emotional explosion.

Even Jesus, and I would point out, especially He, was our perfect example of setting boundaries. While thousands followed Him, and hundreds sought Him, Jesus allowed twelve to follow closely, only three within the inner "gates". He measured His time and energy wisely, spending much of it in prayer, communing with and listening to what His Father specifically directed Him to do. And He was obedient in executing only what His Father instructed, taking on no more than that. Seeking God's wisdom and direction in all we do, including setting appropriate boundaries, allows us "head space", resulting in a harvest of peace as we obediently walk in Jesus's example.

"Very early in the morning, while it was still dark, Jesus got up, left the house and went off to a solitary place, where he prayed." Mark 1:35

"Search me, O God, and know my heart; test me and know my anxious thought. See if there is any offensive way in me and lead me in the way everlasting." Psalm 139: 23-24

August

Sun Blind   August 1

Eight hours, from late May to early September, were occupied at our neighborhood swimming pool. They were divided between swim lessons in the mornings, afternoons on the diving boards, and evenings floating in the sun-warmed, softly lighted water. The sun reflecting off the water for hours on end, combined with the natural light sensitivity of blue eyes, caused me to find my way home one day, nearly blind, and with a severe headache. My mother called it sun blindness; the formal name for it is photo-keratitis, often known as snow blindness. I just knew it was painful and scary.

I don't know why my mother thought it a useful remedy, but I was assigned half of a lemon, sprinkled generously with salt to suck on. I was then led to a wonderfully dark bedroom, and a cold compress was placed on my eyes. I was thankful for the dark room, but not so wild about the lemon. By the end of the day, my headache had improved, and my vision began to return; Mom was right about that part. The lemon, however, added a new malady by stripping the enamel from my front teeth, causing acute pain for three days more.

There is another day, fast approaching when Son-blindness will affect every human being on earth. The Scriptures are very clear about the return of Jesus; it is not a mere possibility; it is an anticipated fact. Jesus will fill the sky with His brilliance, the very radiance of God Almighty in human form. Every knee will bow in His presence, whether they choose to, or not. His power, and all the glory of heaven, will pour forth in an ocean of magnificence, bending every knee in awe and fear.

His desire for me is that by faith, all my days ahead of His arrival will be filled, too, with His Light. The Holy Spirit was sent to us as the seal on that promise, and it is His desire for us to be "Son-blind", even as we walk this dark earth. Our Father's will is that we become blind to all but Him; to be so filled with Jesus, that His brightness begins to vanquish any dark recesses of my heart. Today, I pray that God will increase my Son-blindness.

"The sun will no more be your light by day, nor will the brightness of the moon shine on you, for the Lord will be your everlasting light, and your God will be your glory. Your sun will never set again and your moon will wane no more; the Lord will be your everlasting light, and your days of sorrow will end." Isaiah 60:19-20

"In his right hand he held seven stars, and out of his mouth came a double-edged sword. His face was like the sun shining in all its brilliance." Revelation 1:16

"We live by faith, not by sight." 2 Corinthians 5:7

Rocks and clay are the mainstays where I live, and topsoil is an afterthought. So, it is not surprising, as anyone who lives here can attest, to witness trees growing out of rocks. One must wonder at the variety of foliage adorning the stone faces that line our highways; ivies, trees, and vines are all on display within easy viewing for those of us who do not hike the rough terrain.

Considering the harsh conditions these plants withstand, it is a miracle that any survive. Despite the difficult growing conditions, their roots tenaciously form in any crack presenting itself to the sun. They sink searching fingers into the tiniest spaces, into little more than dust; and when they have grabbed hold, they send a shoot searching for sunlight.

As I marvel at the small tree stubbornly growing into a crack in the rock, I also wonder at the miracle of God's love reaching out, wondrously planting me into His kingdom. As a new Believer, I made the mistake of thinking it to be a cushy garden assignment, but that would soon turn out to be the farthest from the truth; being planted in rock is a more accurate description. The choicest growth would be found where the winds of adversity caused me to cling most tenaciously to His gracious love.

Just as the seemingly harsh winds sweep the cliffs, the winds of life are allowed by our Creator, testing, trying, and strengthening us. Each blast causes us to hug the unmovable Rock, sinking our roots deeper into a firm foundation, anchoring our faith, and proving His faithfulness. The tree's tender roots are fed in the dark places, and its leaves are spread open to receive the sunlight; so, we too, find our sustenance as we retreat to Him. We are taught trust, not in the strength of the rocks surrounding us, but in the strength of the One under us.

God develops these inspiring trees over many years; in their infancy, they are not strong, but those that survive the windswept cliffs are tenaciously anchored. Through our suffering, perseverance, and discipline, our strength of character and commitment are molded. Like those trees clinging to the rocks, we are conforming to the very image of our Savior and Lord. From the highway view, those who pass by will marvel at the miracles that we truly are, too; beautifully green miracles on God's stony, windswept cliff called life.

"He is the Rock, his works are perfect, and all his ways are just. A faithful God who does no wrong, upright and just is he." Deuteronomy 32:4

"But blessed is the man who trusts in the Lord, whose confidence is in him. He will be like a tree planted by the water that sends out its roots by the stream. It does not fear when heat comes; its leaves are always green. It has no worries in a year of drought and never fails to bear fruit." Jeremiah 17:7-8

Sandwiched somewhere between the scorching sun and deluges of rain, the sweet perfection of summer days perched. I have not remembered such a summer of blissfully beautiful evenings, with gentle breezes and airy clouds. The grass in mid-to-late summer is radiantly green and vegetation is reveling in the perfect growing conditions. Rabbits, turkeys, and Tree Swallows have reared their young and paraded them across the lawn, as if for review.

Every season requires trust in the Creator. Spring nips at the heels of winter in short bites of sunshine and warmth. I know that the buds will burst into leaves and flowers, but I cannot see them at spring's origin. Summer promises maturing fruit, but all I see at the beginning is a tiny leaf pushing through the warming soil. Autumn displays nearly spring-like colors in its early days, before yielding its full, riotous, color palate. And winter most often drizzles its way onto the calendar before white glory falls. Every step forward requires trust.

My life has been much like the seasons, with blissful days full of wonder like spring leaves budding, others burgeoning with the productivity of summer. There were dark days of loss like leaves tumbling to earth, so many at times, that I felt they were unending. Some were days of winter-like silence when I could not hear from the Lord, with no apparent answers to my cries for His help. The beauty of seasons, though, is that they each serve a purpose, to mark our time on earth, to point us to our Creator and His wisdom, and to transform us into the likeness of Christ.

So, whatever my "season", whatever my need, I am learning to ask, trusting Him to provide; and He has. When I have been desperate for a new relationship, He provided me with an unexpected friend. Needing approval, He sent word that I am a delight to Him. In loss and pain, He sent ministering in the form of Life Group "angels". In the face of financial ruin, He sent relief. In the face of decay, He sent windows I could never have replaced. Confronted with insurmountable obstacles, He sent a helper with a kind heart. In brokenness, He sent healing, both physically and spiritually.

I cannot tell you, honestly, that trust has come easily to me; it has not. God, though, has taken whatever trust I would yield to Him and multiplied it many-fold. That is His nature; what we give to Him, He always multiplies it, often in most unexpected ways. It is the immutable law of His creation—He is an extravagant Creator! He gives back to us more than we can conceive or ask. He repeatedly displays His affection for us, and He LOVES to prove His love, in every season!

"As long as the earth endures, seedtime and harvest, cold and heat, summer and winter, day and night will never cease." Genesis 8:22

"Find rest, O my soul, in God alone; my hope comes from him." Psalm 62:5

The sunlight glinted off the waves, sending laser-like beams in every direction. It was a beautifully clear day, with the repetitious sound of waters crashing on the beach, lulling me into a completely false sense of security. As I paddled on my belly away from the surf, the giggles and squeals of children playing at the water's edge grew faint, and I realized how far I had drifted. Caught in a cross current, struggling as hard as I could, I made no headway and began drifting farther from shore.

Panic began to seize my heart as I yelled for help, not knowing if I could even be heard. My husband must have panicked when he saw the danger I was in and began swimming hard in my direction. He was not a particularly strong swimmer, but adrenaline saved the day, and he was able to pull me to safety. I have an aversion, even now, to swimming in the ocean; I am a decent swimmer, but no match for an ocean current.

The problem that day was that I did not respect the underlying currents, nor the strength of the tide. I never considered anything but the prospect of having a good time and thought my own strength was sufficient. The dangers of that "fun" on the ocean began to settle into my head after I was reeled in by my husband. His life had been put into jeopardy by my folly. My own life had been at stake, and many others, especially my children, would have been affected.

How often I have found myself "in over my head" in life, too, believing myself sufficient for the task at hand, and never consulting God about my undertakings! Not until I found my plans decimated, my proverbial raft adrift, did I remember to ask the Lord what He wanted for me. Not until my safety was threatened or my health in danger, in some cases, did I bother to seek His will and not my own.

Most of us, most of the time, go about "our" business without consulting the God who made and loves us. We are paddling against the current of the world and expect to win the day on our own, devoid of our Father's input, and believing we have life under control. Many times, He shows up whether we consulted Him or not, through His grace forgiving us and providing for us. That's what grace is, helping us even after we do stupid, willful things. He pulls us back to shore, sheltering us with His love and protecting His oblivious children.

Life is overflowing with risks, dangers, surprises, and upheavals, few of which can we know in advance. Some are unavoidable, others preventable. But instead of calling upon Him as our last resort, I pray He will help us remember to consult Him first, before we find ourselves adrift.

"But I trust in your grace, my heart rejoices as you bring me to safety. I will sing to Adonai, because he gives me even more than I need." Psalm 13:5-6

The ferry launched from the dock, heading across the sound, a trip spanning approximately twenty miles. Traversing the choppy waves on a very gray and chilly day, we exited the vehicle and stood at the railing. My husband and I, my mother, and our little girl were on board As I gazed over the rough waters, my only thought was, "Please let us make it to land!" I was not fond of the sight of water as far as I could see.

I understood full well the survivability factor was very low in the middle of an ocean, floating on a vehicle full of other vehicles. Since that time, I have taken other ferries, all without incident, but I have not traveled by ferry boat such a distance since that trip, and thankfully, have not had the need to do so. There is just something unsettling about not being able to see my destination while on a boat.

It is quite the puzzle, though, when I compare my reactions to water. I have no reservations about boarding a jet without seeing my destination, until I am flying over a body of water. And being on the water without being able to see any land is quite the opposite. There is just something secure and comforting about seeing land, which is probably a perspective birthed from being raised in a landlocked state.

Faith is a bit like traveling by ferry boat for me. I am not fearful if I can see my destination but drop an ocean of uncertainty in front of me and panic begins to soak into the edges of my confidence. But faith is believing without seeing; it's traveling to the destination while having no idea how you will get there. It is trusting that the ferry boat pilot knows exactly what he is doing, and has the experience required to dock the boat precisely where it needs to land.

God requires that level of trust from us as He guides us over the rough waters of our lives. We may not be able to see the destination or even the means to get there, but He powerfully navigates every trough and crest until we arrive. He knows the way; He planned it before we were ever born, no, even before the world began. He made us, knows us, planned for our lives, and integrally fit each of us into His master plan.

It was a frightening thing for me to look over the waves and see nothing but more waves, as far as I could see. However, since that trek across the sound, I have learned much from this Pilot's character. He is the Master of the waves, the Commander of the ship, and the Voice who calms the storm. He merely speaks and the wind stills, the rain stops, and the waters flatten. And when He chooses not to calm the storm, I know I need not fear; He calms my heart instead.

"But he said to them, 'It is I; don't be afraid.' Then they were willing to take him into the boat, and immediately the boat reached the shore where they were heading." John 6:20-21

Switchgrass

As we stood next to the fence surveying his fields, the farmer informed me that "switchgrass" was a real issue. "If you see a field full of it, that means it has taken over, crowding out the original crop", he said. It is rather pretty, resembling ripened wheat, and when it has fully occupied the field, it sways like wind over ocean waves. In reality, it is insidious, destructive, and a wasteland.

I was reminded of the parable of the wheat and tares, which is essentially what switchgrass is, and I wondered, why do we live in a world that God made, yet we must endure evil alongside good? The answer is in the switchgrass. Until the wheat and the grass grow together and begin to mature, they look very similar. If the farmer acted prematurely by destroying the switchgrass, he would also damage the wheat.

There's a second reason, too. Since we have free will, we can change our choices as we live our lives. Some of us change our relationship with God through his Son, Jesus, at some point in our lives. Some will accept His kingship early in life, some midway, some not until the very end; and He alone knows if, or when, we will change our minds to follow Him. And we don't know how much time we will get to make that decision. For me, I did not know Jesus until I was 30 years old; had I been plucked out of this world before that, eternity would have been awful for me.

We don't see what God sees in each individual, and we don't have insight into their lifespans. We can only trust God's wisdom in allowing evil people to exist in this world. And we can trust that He always knows best, always loves us, and sees who will yet become wheat. Our job as followers of Jesus is to pray for those who do not know Him and show the love of Christ Jesus to a world where the field appears to be filled with switchgrass.

"'No,' he said, 'if you pull the weeds now, you might uproot the wheat with them. Let both grow together until the harvest. At that time, I will tell the harvesters: First collect the weeds and tie them in bundles to be burned; then gather the wheat into my barn.'"

Matthew 13:29-30

It was final—we were moving! It was final, but all the plans and details were not. We were leaving my beloved Bible study group who had mentored and loved me well, cared deeply for my family, and shown me the face of Jesus for the first time in my life. Cheraw, South Carolina, the place I had complained of moving to, in the beginning, was to become "where I moved from".

In the lonely time warp of Gary working out his last days in Savannah (the place to which we *thought* we were moving, until God intervened), it was up to me to carry the household, sell the house, and prepare for the transition to Tennessee, our new landlocked home. We hadn't even made the trip yet to find a house, which left me one option—lifting my concerns to my heavenly Father.

I longed for a newly built house, but we were taking a loss on our house in South Carolina, and the prices in Tennessee were higher. So, my hopes morphed from "new" to "whatever you want us to have, Lord, even if it is a barn". Days stretched into months; I waited, and prayed, and waited.

One day, I felt compelled to draw a seashell, then two more. It took all day to draw one, another day to draw the other two, and a third day to paint them and add ink lines. I truly felt that the Spirit had taken hold of my hands—I had never been able to draw or paint anything with this detail and was amazed by the end of the third day.

They now needed framing, even though I had no idea where they would hang. Parking my car in front of the frame shop, a man walked up to me and asked if I would like to have a Tiger Conch shell. He explained that he had been diving and had two, so I gladly accepted.

The paintings and that magnificent shell became the centerpieces of our new bedroom, in my newly constructed house, in my new city in Tennessee! My Father foresaw the depth of my longing for ocean days, of kids covered with sand, long quiet stretches with only the sounds of waves and chattering seagulls, thunderheads building on the horizon, and salt breezes touching my lips. The Tiger Conch shell was the prize never found in all our days of searching for treasured shells amid all the common, broken, and odd things the waves washed up.

Today, as I remember those things, I am in awe of an intimate and infinite God, who shows His love in meticulous detail. Providing exceedingly, abundantly more than I can think or ask, He blesses me. Jesus has become my treasure house in every way.

"But I trust in your grace, my heart rejoices as you bring me to safety. I will sing to the Lord, because he gives me even more than I need." Psalm 13:5

And They Moved On

Moving, as a teen, to Colorado, I felt I would never leave, but God had other plans for me. Living in Indiana, where most of my family was, I thought that would be my permanent residence, but again, it not where I was intended to plant my roots. North Carolina was my first exposure to Southern culture but was too brief. South Carolina was where I was sure I was staying until God gave His input. It was Tennessee where my roots were finally allowed to sink deeply into the rock-strewn soil, exactly where God's Spirit guided me.

I had become quite the seasoned mover and had the logistics of moving well in hand. Over my lifetime, I have moved to new locations eighteen times, living the longest in one location, for 32 years. I am happy to say that I have become quite rusty at moving. But my eighteen moves spanning several decades doesn't hold a candle to the moves required of the Hebrew children.

Forty times in forty years, the cloud of the Lord's Presence moved the newly freed slaves from place to place, before leading them to their Promised Land. When the cloud descended, they stayed; when the cloud lifted, it was time to follow God, as He led them where He wanted them to camp next. There was no plan, save God's plan for them.

They were completely dependent on Him for provision, protection, and guidance. Nor did they did take a day for granted. They were aware of God's Presence and watchful for His movement, constantly dependent upon Him for a place to rest their heads. And God never failed them. He supplied food daily, manna and quail, water in the desert, and their shoes and clothing did not wear out.

I would do well to learn from their experience, to not take today for granted, to be watchful for the Holy Spirit's presence and leading, and to listen to Him. I should have their confidence that God is real, powerful, and attentive to them.

God did not fail the Hebrew children, and for those who are His children by faith in His Son, He provides, as well. We should not live as the world lives, fearful and anxious about our needs. We have a very real God, a Father who loves and cares for us. Until we plant our feet on the soil of heaven, Child of God, following the "cloud" of God's Spirit, we move on.

"Neither the pillar of cloud by day nor the pillar of fire by night left its place in front of the people." Exodus 13:22

"Now choose life, so that you and your children may live and that you may love the Lord your God, listen to His voice, and hold fast to Him, For the Lord is your life, and he will give you many years in the land he swore to give to your fathers, Abraham, Isaac, and Jacob." Deuteronomy 30:19b-20

The wake of the larger boats crisscrossed in deep troughs and generated choppy water ahead of us. Everyone in our boat thought the pilot was going to take the smooth route, but surprising them, I turned the wheel heading toward it. I knew our boat was sturdy and could "jump" the wakes, and though bouncy, we made our way over them. The riders on the "tubes" had no idea that "Nana" was capable of piloting the boat. They were wearing paled expressions, but all made it safe and sound.

Life also pitches us against the waves, tossing us up and pitching us headlong into the turmoil, but God is our secure and sturdy boat. He carries us through the wake and over the rough waves. Each one is no surprise to Him. He sees the insurmountable waves ahead of us and knows the way to lead us through them. Because we are in His boat, we are secure.

But if you are having difficulty trusting Jesus, consider who He is. By His words, He stilled waves and crushed storms. By His touch, He healed those who had no hope of healing. By His presence, He gave hope. By His prayer, He provided food from nothing. He cast out demons, multiplied fish and bread to thousands, and raised the dead with just a word. He used saliva and dirt to restore sight to eyes that had never seen.

He knew what people were thinking before they spoke and saw what was in their hearts before they realized it themselves. He saw Nathaniel under the tree while Nathaniel sat alone. And He changed the hearts of all who followed Him. His ears beheld the words of favor from His Father, and His eyes the descending of the Spirit upon Him. He defeated Satan, overturned the religious order, and broke the chains of death.

So, do you think you can trust Him? Can He take care of you? Is He able to carry you when you are weary and broken? I can only tell you from my own experience that He is fully capable of it all. Nothing is beyond His reach, nothing. When you are facing churning waters, and waves you never believed could be so high, trust Him. Trust Him and rest in His boat peacefully, especially in your choppy waters.

"But this is what the Lord says---he who created you, O Jacob, he who formed you, O Israel: 'Fear not, for I have redeemed you; I have summoned you by name; you are mine. When you pass through the rivers, they will not sweep over you. When you walk through the fire, you will not be burned; the flames will not set you ablaze. For I am the Lord, your God, the Holy One of Israel, your Savior.'" Isaiah 43:1-3

"But when he asks, he must believe and not doubt, because he who doubts is like a wave of the sea, blown and tossed by the wind. That man should not think he will receive anything from the Lord; he is a double-minded man, unstable in all he does." James 1:6-8

Me Tarzan, You Jane!   August 10

Envisioning Tarzan, swinging through the jungle, vine to vine, he was usually off to rescue Jane, who fell into the hands of kidnappers, or poachers of Tarzan's animal friends. I watched many episodes growing up. My husband found it quite humorous when teaching our dog to lie down. Saying "Down, Tantor!" he was referencing Tarzan's elephant friend. Our children thought it was so funny! The fact is Tarzan was considered the king of the jungle. What Tarzan willed was carried out!

There will be days when you feel like Jane stumbling into quicksand. You can't seem to control the situation you are in; it controls you, and there appears to be no escape. Some days may feel like there was a stampede in the jungle, leaving you lonely and alone, in uncomfortable silence. Others may be akin to swimming in the river, seeing crocodile eyes suddenly come out of nowhere. Children may oddly resemble monkeys out of control in the trees, or your budget may seem like a waterfall, every drop going out and not enough coming in.

Those are the days to remember your Tarzan. No, it's not your husband, or for that matter anyone else you might look to for rescue. Your "Tarzan" is uniquely able to rescue you and His name is **Jesus**. Remember His reference to the vine? How you are to stay connected to it? Well, just translate that to jungle-eze! Trust Him to rescue you, to transport you through His power to the place of peace, provision, and safety.

Allow Him to comfort you and still your heart, control the beasts, stem the flood, protect your family, and provide for your needs. Feel yourself in the power of His trustworthy arms, as He transports you through the jungle canopy to your next destination. He is KING JESUS, King of this jungle, King of the world! And you are His most prized relationship and treasured child, simply by resting in His overwhelming grace. Rest, Jane, *rest*!

"I will instruct you and teach you in the way you should go; I will counsel you and watch over you. Do not be like the horse or the mule, which have no understanding but must be controlled by bit and bridle or they will not come to you. Many are the woes of the wicked, but the Lord's unfailing love surrounds the man who trusts in him. Rejoice in the Lord and be glad, you righteous; sing, all you who are upright in heart!" Psalm 32:8-11

The white striping on the road blurred together into one long string as we passed another car. Pulling into the right lane, our view shifted to the constant gray pavement, fascinating four children in the back seat. Our friend's car was old and built before seatbelts were required, so our view of the road was that of sitting on the floorboard, peering through a rusted floor, directly to the highway beneath its wheels. The hole wasn't big enough to fall through but certainly big enough to deliver healthy respect for pavement. Nevertheless, we were going places.

At the time, we, like many families, did not own a car. We walked to the grocery store, pulling a wagon to carry my youngest brother on the way; and coming home to tote the grocery bags. (This all sounds very alien to a culture where there is a car for each family member, something we all take very much for granted.) Several years following our close-up view of the pavement, my mother bought her first car, a VW bug, in which she sardined four children; again, the sandwiching of children was insignificant. We were going places.

How we travel is not as important to God as the attitude by which we travel. My attitude during parts of this journey through life has been unimpressive, and at times downright scary. It has been like looking through the hole at the pavement flying by. Some of the "transportation" God has provided on this journey I have balked at, and I have been prideful about some of the "rides" He gave me. But through my Father's patience, and despite me, together, we were going places.

My pride has been elevated when more humility should have prevailed. My gratitude has been lacking when it should have been overflowing. I could not see down the road God had me traveling; with much questioning, and little trusting, I felt pulled along, as in the wagon. After riding with God on this long but too-fast journey, I am finally figuring out that the vehicle is insignificant; the journey is all about learning to trust Him. I am seeing more clearly that all along He and I have been going places.

We cannot see the future nor change the past, and through the hole in the floorboard, we can see that life is quickly moving along. Sometimes it is slower, sometimes the lanes are changing, and sometimes it is all a blur. But the one thing we can count on is that God is in control of this "car" one hundred percent of the time. Going places with our Savior, we can anticipate an ultimate destination far beyond our imaginings.

"The Lord replied, 'My Presence will go with you, and I will give you rest.' Then Moses said to him, 'If your Presence does not go with us, do not send us up from here. How will anyone know that you are pleased with me and your people unless you go with us? …And the Lord said to Moses, 'I will do the very thing you have asked, because I am pleased with you and I know you by name.'" Exodus 33:14-16a, 17

On the Edge

One of the most harrowing experiences of my life was traversing a narrow, and I mean only wide enough for the Jeep to fit, "road" across the face of a mountain in Colorado. I could reach out on one side of the Jeep and almost touch the mountain. On the other side, I could peer over the edge, to a straight drop of hundreds of feet, to the valley below.

Our teenage driver, barely older than me, assured us of our safety, barely containing his laughter over his captive, city slicker's faces. Meanwhile, if there had been upholstery on the seats, my fingernails would have shredded it by the time we arrived at the other end of the torturous journey. It was one of those "Oh. No. I'm gonna die!" moments brought to me by the great state of Colorado.

Now, after decades of traveling mountain roads and highways, Rocky to Smoky, I whiz by the flat-landers with hardly a thought. I can well remember the initial insecurity of slopes, steep grades, and twisting pavement, so I give them a little extra room. I pass when the opportunity opens, recognizing that their fear and caution will eventually give way to confidence and familiarity. Having learned to respect the speed limits (for which there are good reasons on mountain roads) and giving proper regard to the laws of physics, mountains are less scary now.

The road we travel through life, though, often feels just as scary. Steep slopes, unexpected turns, and threatening drop-offs abound. Some of those highways are soaked in tears, others are shrouded in blankets of fog, and we cannot see the road before us. Occasionally, someone else is driving and we feel we are being carried along helplessly. Steep drop-offs pop into view, where we fear even peering over the edge of uncertainty. Another place in the road may be a dangerous stretch, fearing death itself.

There is One who stands ready in every situation, who understands the obstacles, and who empathizes with your mountainous journey. Jesus is always present and reminds us, for our protection, of the rules of the road in His Word. He is never surprised by our fear, asking only for our trust. He sees the road ahead of us and behind us; He knows where we have been and where we are going. And none of it is beyond His reach. Jesus loves us from the beginning of our road to the end, even when we feel we are driving on the edge.

"There is no one like the God of Jeshurun, who rides on the heavens to help you and on the clouds in his majesty. The eternal God is your refuge, and underneath are the everlasting arms." Deuteronomy 32:26-27

"For this God is our God for ever and ever; he will be our guide even to the end." Psalm 48:14

White Picket Fences   August 13

The mere mention of a white picket fence paints the picture of an ordered and perfect life, which is the aspiration of many a dreamy-eyed young woman. The foregone assumption is that the perfect man, woman, and children will live in a cozy but perfect home, with few problems and an abundance of solutions. The one time I had to paint a picket fence ruined forever my view of them, with its many slats and inside edges. Few objects in life are more hateful to paint than a picket fence.

And the reality of the white picket fence is that behind every one of them lives a flawed family of real human beings, each carrying a generation, or two, of sin into that home. People are broken, some are shattered, all are marred by sin. We may attempt to bury it, disguise it, dress it up, hide it in a closet, ignore it, or cry it into our pillows. It may be expressed in anger or silence, in manipulation or being manipulated, in aggression or withdrawal, but our flaws will always be present. We, mankind, are born in sin.

The white picket fence is but a symptom of our longing for what the world cannot give us, peace. Jesus said that in this world there will be many troubles, but He also stated that He came to give peace, not as the world gives it, but only as He can impart. He has overcome the obstacle of sin, bringing forgiveness and restoration to all who will receive Him. As we allow Him to walk through the gate of our picket fence and invite Him to live with us, He begins the transformation of our hearts and homes.

As Jesus lives in the home of our hearts, a new creation emerges. We no longer look for the white picket fence on earth but understand that it exists only in heaven. There, the fence no longer requires painting. The people of God have been made perfect; we reside in the house of His sweet Presence where fear and tears are vanquished. Our clothes will be spotless, there will be no evil, no anger, no harm. God's rule will not be threatened, there will be no challenges to His authority, and His Kingdom will reign forever. Until then, we receive His comfort, guidance, and peace as we trust Him with the home of our hearts, tucked behind the security of the white picket fence of His love.

"But to as many as did receive him, to those who put their trust in his person and power, he gave the right to become children of God…" John 1:12

"I have told you these things, so that in me you may have peace. In this world, you will have trouble. But take heart! I have overcome the world." John 16:33

"May the God of hope fill you with all joy and peace as you trust in him, so that you may overflow with hope by the power of the Holy Spirit." Romans 15:13

An Unexpected Gift   August 14

Cookbooks have been a personal weakness, a trait I trace to my mother and grandmother, or at least they are my excuse. Half a century of cookbooks, rarely seeing a page turned, finally beckoned me to thin them. Flipping through one before sending it to the Goodwill donation box, a paper hidden away for years fell to the floor. This is what it said:

"It was one of those perfect moments in time where I was surrounded by quiet. No one was up at 6 AM on Saturday except me, it seemed. I soaked up the delicious solitude and glanced down the vast expanse of lawn, thinking a deer may be silently grazing. Disappointed to find none, I glanced up at the sky.

The softly colored clouds hung loosely on a pale blue sky while diffused sunlight danced around their edges. Out of a clear blue hole spilled a rainbow, splashing a paint box of colors across the clouds below like a waterfall. Vivid pink, orange, blue, green, yellow, and violet in distinct bands arced from behind one cloud and over the others. And, off to the right, it was shadowed by another rainbow, arcing in perfect symmetry with its twin.

The irony of this is that we are in the middle of a drought! It was not raining this morning, not at our house nor in the distance. The clouds dangling on that clear blue sky were not rain clouds; other than low humidity, we could boast no moisture. The only explanation was that there was no explanation—it was a gift! Very few, if any, people received that gorgeous and rare gift this morning. It was withdrawn as quickly as it appeared.

Rainbows are symbols of promise and a new beginning. I am excited as I contemplate the day ahead, knowing that my Father gave me an unmatchable gift of double rainbows, double promise, double portion, double joy. His gift was delightful because, like every good gift which comes from God, it is His way of expressing His love."

God lavishes gifts upon us every day without fail and in many forms: A kind act, a compliment, a smile, food on the table, a pillow and blanket, transportation, a Bible verse, a song, a butterfly, a sunset, a friend, a spouse, a visitor, a listener, or shade on a sunny day. These are all unexpected gifts bestowed upon us if we will but see them in the light of His love, and with gratitude. Even day is an unexpected gift.

"And God said, 'This is the sign of the covenant I am making between me and you and every living creature with you, a covenant for all generations to come: I have set my rainbow in the clouds and it will be the sign of the covenant between me and the earth." Genesis 9:12-13

"Every good and perfect gift is from above, coming down from the Father of the heavenly lights, who does not change like the shifting shadows." James 1:17

Will I have it soon enough? Where will I get the money for it? What do I do next? No one was more entitled to worry than I. I could well justify my "concerns". Many types of loss were strewn across my past: abuse, abandonment, loss of provision and employment, illness, relational loss, loss of possessions, and deaths. I had plenty of justification for the insecurity I felt and the control I coveted. I hid my stress and worry, but the reality was that my desire to control the details of life was a spiritual addiction.

Only one thing disrupted my entitlement, God's Word. It was a heart-rending moment when I realized that to have a real relationship with Him, I had to be willing to give up all control, every excuse, and all reliance upon myself. He showed me that I had a choice to make; to let it all go and follow Him OR follow the ways of the world, elevating myself above trusting Him. Honestly, it was not an easy choice, though it should have been---He is GOD! What in the world was I thinking???

It is a choice God requires of each of us, regardless of our circumstances. We all tend to covet control of the world we touch. Whether people, things, or situations, we desire to control and manipulate our outcomes for our benefit. To submit every detail of my life to God's control is to yield the illusion of power that I have; it is all an illusion, ultimately. Daily choices can turn into a playground for my willfulness or opportunities to yield to His sovereignty. The irony, which God must feel great satisfaction in, is that yielding to Him, in turn, grants enormous freedom from the conflicts of control.

The enormity of responsibility was lifted from my shoulders as I complied with God's ways and direction. The magnetic draw to worry was transformed into the freedom and comfort of trust. My God is perfectly able to handle all my needs according to the riches at His disposal. It is not possible to have a need He is unaware of, even before it presents itself. My Father has proven trustworthy more times than I can re-count, a flawless record, which comforts me even as new challenges arise. The tools He has provided, prayer and His Word, through His Holy Spirit, are re-training me daily as a recovering addict of worry.

"Who of you by worrying can add a single hour to his life?" Luke 12:25

"Where can I go from your Spirit? Where can I flee from your presence? If I go up to the heavens, you are there; if I make my bed in the depths, you are there. If I rise on the wings of the dawn, if I settle on the far side of the sea, even there your hand will guide me, your right hand will hold me fast." Psalm 139:7-10

Sticky Flip Flops   August 16

Living eight blocks from the community pool placed us within walking distance, and for my single mother, also placed us within the range of sanity. Mom obtained the family discount membership, and as long as the pool was open, that is where you could usually find my brothers and me. Swim lessons began at eight A.M. in the frigid water, after which we went home for lunch. At 1:00 P.M., we were again diving, swimming, dunking, and splashing, then home for supper. From 6 to 8, the pool was quieter, soothing, and my favorite part of the day.

During that trek home for supper following the afternoon session, I vividly recall gripping my towel around my middle, listening to my sticky steps. There were no sidewalks, and homeowners along the way were not fond of having kids wearing paths through their yards, so the hot asphalt pavement of the street was our only option. The heat bled through our thin flip flops, scorching the soles of our feet and often suctioning our flip flops to the sticky tar. Occasionally, the thong would pull through, leaving my shoe behind me and no place to go with my bare foot. Let's just say it was an unpleasant experience, at the least!

I have found myself in similar situations in life, not stuck in tar but stuck in the muck and mire of selfishness and emotional upheaval—no, I will just call it what it is—sin. Selfishness is the cause, emotions are a symptom, and the result is upheaval. It seemed easier to be a victim than to take responsibility, making the changes I needed to make within myself. I have not been "responsible" for many of the things that happened to me but, I have certainly been responsible for my reactions and my lack of boundaries in the first place, often treading where God had not specifically led me.

In every facet of life, Satan and his forces use our flaws against each other, then he lays guilt to our charge "sticking" us to the tar of shame. We blame ourselves, blame one another, and hold on to it until we are bitter to the core. Instead, God calls us to lay our sins, weaknesses, and flaws down at His feet.

There, He cleans us up and sets us back on track with forgiveness and love. God does not lay guilt, blame, or shame on our shoulders; our enemy does. He expects as any good parent would, that we will learn from our mistakes, set new boundaries, and trust Him more as we surrender our "flip flops" to His control and presence, trusting God today more than we did yesterday.

"The thief comes only to steal and kill and destroy; I have come that they may have life and have it to the full." John 10:10

"Many are the woes of the wicked, but the Lord's unfailing love surrounds the man whose trust is in the Lord." Psalm 33:10

The Apollo 8 astronauts marveled at the earth as they viewed it from space, especially from the vantage point of a quarter-million miles away, perched on a globe of desert. Author Robert Kurson wrote about Frank Borman, Apollo 8 moon mission commander, saying, "The Apollo 8 astronauts wondered at the moon they could see outside their windows, but they also marveled at the Earth dangling in the distance." The earth against a field of deepest black, like a pearl on a jeweler's cloth, is beyond our imaginations.

In stark contrast, astronaut Charlie Duke recalls of the moon, "The surface was spectacular. It was the most dramatic desert I've ever seen...Just the stark contrast between the bright lunar horizon and the bright lunar surface and the blackness of space." Parched dust, languishing boulders, seas of nothing, and nondescript grays, reflect the sun like a distress mirror signaling to be rescued. Devoid of life, it has only expanses of brilliant neutrality.

Kurson also wrote, "Earthrise was the most beautiful sight Borman had ever seen, the only color visible in all the cosmos." Impacting me most is the phrase "The only color visible in all the cosmos," which causes me to wonder at the miracle that our planet is, and the Creator who conceived it. To grasp that every drop of blue, and every shade of green they saw teemed with life; every brown spot abounds with plants and animals even in those extremes. God gave mankind a garden, a planet bursting with living color, color so intense and amazing that it is visible from a quarter-million miles away!

It is a good practice to engage in wonder at God's creation, which we most often take for granted. When our eyes are open to it, we are drawn to the God of the Universe with restored vision, seeing the amazing character of our Creator. When we get a momentary glimpse of the immensity of His power and the expanse of His creativity, perhaps we may lay hold of a fragment of His vast love for us. His heavens and His earth are a display of His love—in living color.

"It is I who made the earth and created mankind upon it. My own hands stretched out the heavens; I marshaled their starry hosts." Isaiah 45:12

"The heavens declare the glory of God; the skies proclaim the work of his hands."
Psalm 19:1

"He is the image of the invisible God, the firstborn over all creation. For by him all things were created; things in heaven and on earth, visible and invisible, whether thrones or powers or rulers or authorities; all things were created by him and for him. He is before all things, and in him, all things hold together." Colossians 1:15-17

Magnifying Light

In the blackest of night, with summer storms roaring, I was racing as fast as the speed limit allowed to arrive home ahead of the rain. A whip of horizontal lightning zipped across the velvety, dark clouds, as if to open them so I could peer inside. Suddenly, at the end of the tip of lightning bolt, a stronger one flashed vertically, as if to place an exclamation point on it! I was so excited that I whispered a quick, "Thank you, Lord!" It was a more spectacular display than I had seen all summer, and it continued until I safely arrived home. I had beaten the storm, and watched quite the show, too.

Storms with their display of raw power are incredible reminders that the raging rains, crescendos of thunder, and voltage dancing through the clouds are but a glint in God's eye. Nature is our magnifying glass multiplying His wonders before our eyes, if we will be still and look. I don't think we, as humans, can even begin to grasp His greatness; God Himself if the only one who can reveal it to us.

In the book of Job, God gives a peek at His greatness as He describes to Job just a smidgeon of His power: **"Can you loose the cords of Orion? Can you bring forth the constellations in their seasons or lead out the Bear with its cubs? Do you know the laws of the heavens? Can you set up God's dominion over the earth? Can you raise your voice to the clouds and cover yourself with a flood of water?**
Do you send the lightning bolts on their way? Do they report to you, 'Here we are'? ...Who has the wisdom to count the clouds? Who can tip over the water jars of the heavens when the dust becomes hard and the clods of earth stick together?" Job 38:31-35, 37, 38

God reveals Himself in nature all around us, but I don't think He is ever so dramatic on a daily basis as He is in our skies. I once saw a display showing where on the map lightning was striking at that moment on the earth; it was truly mind boggling. Astronauts viewed spectacular lightning flashes, even from orbit.

There is no other event so frequent, or profoundly staggering, as thunder rolling, rattling, and shaking everything in its path. It is comforting to me, as it reveals a little of His power, reassuring me that He is big enough and strong enough to protect me, too. Awe is awakened in my soul as I consider Who is at the controls; Who commands praise but does not demand it. We will all fall at His feet one day. We will see Him in His majesty and consider the God of the Universe, the One who holds it all together, Jesus, the true Magnifying Light.

"In the past God spoke to our forefathers through the prophets at many times and in various ways, but in these last days, he has spoken to us by his Son, whom he appointed heir of all things, and through whom he made the universe. The Son is the radiance of God's glory and the exact representation of his being, sustaining all things by his powerful word."

Hebrews 1:1-3

Seated in a very open casual space, other lunch diners were easily within hearing distance. I was not conscious of them until I shared this statement with my companions, "God delights in me!" Those four words startled everyone at my table into a disquieting stare, and I could hear the cloak of quietness descend with a hush around us. I'm pretty certain they were all in shock that I could actually speak those words aloud as if a secret hidden for eons had been released from some dark cavern.

Most of us intuitively understand that we are, by our sinful nature, unworthy of that title. That is why it is so shocking for us to hear someone claim it aloud, never mind speak it of ourselves. Until recently, I could not imagine in my wildest imaginings that it was true, either. I couldn't have spoken it out loud even a year ago, and I have been a believer for decades.

Not having a father most of my formative years, required multiple layers of revelation to grasp the elusiveness of love never experienced. Waltzing their daughters upon their feet, observing loving fathers interacting with their daughters, I began to witness the provision, protection, and tender affection lavished upon them. I observed the fathers' delight in them as they grew up and the pride in their accomplishments even as adults.

So how can I brazenly claim this status of "delightful"? Jesus was proclaimed with God's audible words to be well-pleasing, the Son whom He loved. Since Jesus, in perfection, became the sacrifice for my imperfection, I became a delightful child to my Father in heaven from that point on. He sees me with only eyes of grace. It is with brazen faith that I am clean, perfect, forgiven to the utmost, boldly proclaiming, "My Father in heaven delights in me!"

So, you see, it is a secret breathed by God's Spirit from a very bright, pure place. It is the voice of all heaven rejoicing over every sinner who repents, each becoming the very child of God he or she was created to be, a pure delight to the heart of our Father.

"The Lord delights in those who fear him, who put their hope in his unfailing love."
Psalm 147:11

"The Lord your God is with you, he is mighty to save. He will take great delight in you, he will quiet you with his love, he will rejoice over you with singing." Zephaniah 3:17

"For you used to be darkness; but now, united with the Lord, you are light. Live like children of light, for the fruit of the light is in every kind of goodness, rightness, and truth---try to determine what will please the Lord." Ephesians 5:8-10

It Balances!   August 20

For two months I struggled, the ready-to-scream type of struggle, with my checking accounts, two of two that would not balance. Those of you who have ever attempted to keep a balanced account will understand my pain. Even when I assumed the bank had the correct balance, I could not reconcile the difference the next month. With great optimism and prayer, I sat down with checkbook registers in hand, believing God would show me the answers. And, at the end of each register calculation, I could finally express, with great thanksgiving and relief, "It balances!"

No less important, in fact, very much *more* important, is the state of my soul in my account with God. My account was out of balance, totally bankrupt, without Jesus. He is the one, through the cruel cross and His powerful resurrection, who paid my account in full to God. He is the payment for my overdraft of sin, the one who reconciled my debt with His Holy Father on my account. That account is now, and forever, balanced.

But there is another account to check daily, and that is the accounting of my soul's condition. Where am I today in my relationship with Jesus? Is my account full, or bankrupt? Is my account with God needing a deposit of trust, or relationship "currency"? Is there a sin I need to confess, or a worry nagging in the background?

Many times, when feeling unsettled, fearful, or out of balance, I have been able to trace my error back to my relationship with God. Somewhere in my "register", I have gone astray, not doing my part. Most of my errors can be traced to pride, willfulness, selfishness, or unwillingness to surrender control to God. An error in this account is the most painful of all, separating me from the fullness of what God has planned for my life.

Once I confess my error and make any necessary corrections, the Lord, in His loving grace, is willing and ready to forgive and set my account straight! Nothing is more important to Him than the relationship He desires with each of His children. And on that day, at that moment of my heartfelt correction, He smiles and stamps my "account" in big letters, "It Balances!"

"For the word of God is living and active. Sharper than any double-edged sword, it penetrates even to dividing soul and spirit, joints and marrow; it judges the thought and attitudes of the heart. Nothing in all creation is hidden from God's sight. Everything is uncovered and laid bare before the eyes of him to whom we must give account. Therefore, since we have a great high priest who has gone through the heavens, Jesus the Son of God, let us hold firmly to the faith we profess. For we do not have a high priest who is unable to sympathize with our weaknesses, but we have one who has been tempted in every way, just as we are---yet without sin. Let us then approach the throne of grace with confidence, so that we may receive mercy and find grace to help us in our time of need." Hebrews 4:12-16

Tempest in a Teapot August 21

Sunlight glinted a thousand times off the swirling crystals, as they raced the spiral to the top of the pitcher, and back down again. Tea is my family's beverage of choice. Making it, for perhaps the ten-thousandth time, I watched the sugar crystals sparkle in the sunlight as I stirred, then disappear as the water swallowed them up.

I considered how Christians are often tossed about and caught up in the tornadoes of life, mixed in furiously with the waters of the world. It is most often with a sense of helplessness and confusion that we face life's difficulties, looking to God with questioning eyes. As we seem to fade into the oblivion of the world, we wonder what good our lives have accomplished.

If the sugar was not stirred vigorously from the bottom of the pitcher, it would lay in the bottom, not flavoring the water at all. So we, if not stirred and shaken, tend to keep our "flavor" to ourselves, not allowing the unpleasant world to taste the sweetness of God. As we are swirled into the lives of others, the Son's light glints off each of us, producing the "sparkle" that makes this world a more beautiful place.

The sugar must dissolve to be of any value. It appears to be lost as it is absorbed by the water but tasting soon reveals its presence. We often feel in our struggles that we are being diminished, too, but we cannot see the effects of His presence, and how far His influence in our lives may ripple. We are oblivious to how our sweetness in Jesus reaches far and wide, rippling to places we will never personally touch. And when we are touching lives, even in our tempest-like teapot, God's flavor is apparent to those around us.

"May the God of hope fill you with all joy and peace as you trust in him, so that you may overflow with hope by the power of the Holy Spirit." Romans 15:13

"But I trust in your grace, my heart rejoices as you bring me to safety. I will sing to the Lord, because he gives me even more than I need." Psalm 13:6

"I have told you these things, so that in me you may have peace. In this world you will have trouble. But take heart! I have overcome the world." John 16:33

Limited Time Offer   August 22

As I browsed the website, a pop-up ad burst into view with a "limited time offer". I would most likely be shocked to know the number of ads I have been subjected to over my lifetime; I can only say, decisively too many. But the world seems to revolve around advertisements and limited time offers. I have come to deduce that most advertisements are rarely a great "deal", and the time before expiration usually too short. They barely impact me anymore.

God, too, has His own advertising agency, figuratively speaking, with the promise of unique, limited time offers. Offer number one, of course, is the offer of salvation through His son, Christ Jesus; that would be the offer of your lifetime, and His price cannot be matched anywhere else in the universe. Your redemption time is unlimited if you can predict when you will expire. Any minute prior to that grand event will do, but better that you take God up on His offer, sooner rather than later, since you do not know the day or hour.

There are additional offers available to us, also, which you will not want to miss. We can access a free suit of armor, spiritually speaking, which will protect us from the plots against us by our eternal foe, Satan. But wait, there's more! Freely offered, too, is the power of the Holy Spirit. And the living Word of God is part of the array of free offerings; it is an asset so vital that God calls it the Bread of Life, an alias Jesus Himself assumed. One of His best offers, though, in my humble opinion, is fellowship with Him through prayer---it is free to you, and granting you access to the throne of God, while walking the earth!

The offers of our Heavenly Father are all limited time offers, which we can choose to accept or turn down. We can hope for better deals from the world, but they can never equal the value of the offer God makes to us. The world's counterfeit deals are great in appearance, but neglect to deliver the goods in the end, always a deception in advertising. Real peace, joy, happiness, trust, and confidence come only through the genuine Product. These limited time offers are found in Jesus alone. But hurry! This offer may expire sooner than you think.

"How much more, then, will the blood of Christ, who through the eternal Spirit offered himself unblemished to God, cleanse our consciences from acts that lead to death, so that we may serve the living God! For this reason, Christ is the mediator of a new covenant, that those who are called may receive the promised eternal inheritance---now that he has died as a ransom to set them free from the sins committed under the first covenant."
Hebrews 9:14-15

"The Spirit and the bride say, 'Come!' And let him who hears say, 'Come!' Whoever is thirsty, let him come; and whoever wishes, let him take the free gift of the water of life."
Revelation 22:17

Moon Over My Shoulder

The Crowd of "Me" August 23

Their noxious cries were a bit unsettling when I first encountered the brashly chattering seagulls, dipping and diving around me as I walked the beach. They were loud, unruly, and frankly, a bit scary, especially if you have ever viewed the horror movie "Birds" by Alfred Hitchcock. Unfortunately, I had. Many visits to the beach ensued over the years, and I became accustomed to the brash birds. With each trip to the beach, the seagulls became less frightening and more laughable.

A children's movie accurately portrayed the comical birds as flying about, crying, "Mine, Mine, Mine!" as they competed for food. I always thought their cries to be, "Me, Me, Me!" but so close to reality were the content creators that I will not quibble. The gaggles of seagulls bear a stunning resemblance to people, which is perhaps why I found them eventually comical. Aren't we similar in our struggles to obtain what we think we should have or what we deserve? We compete so strongly for status, to possess that which we do not have, or recognized in a world of blank faces.

I have made enough trips to the beach to have made wonderfully pleasant memories, but I can retrospectively consider the seagulls in my life. All my dipping and diving, flying hard to catch the tiniest morsel, crying loudly, "Me, me, me!" wears me out and accomplishes little. Occasionally, I obtain enough reward to keep me flying, but I often have to ask myself if it was worth it. Of the things I wanted or believed I could not live without, I eventually discovered most of them counted for nothing.

Jesus encountered the crowd of "me's" every day in His ministry walking the earth, people starving for His attention, miracles, and answers. He fed them the Word of God. Some recognized the truth, some stayed for the food alone, a few took what He offered and left the crowd of "me". They surrendered "me" to the Son of the Living God. "Me", "mine", and "self", yield to "Yours", "Your will", and your assigned cross to carry. But in that yielding, what freedom follows!

God calls us to surrender, not to take away from or to deny us, but He calls us to surrender to have it all. In our surrender, we are given peace, life more abundantly, love unconditionally, and forgiveness without limits. In Christ alone we have the freedom to fly above the "crowd of me", to soar above the fray, even as we walk amid it.

"For my Father's will is that everyone who looks to the Son and believes in him shall have eternal life, and I will raise him up at the last day." John 6:40

"Jesus answered, 'I tell you the truth, you are looking for me, not because you saw miraculous signs but because you ate the loaves and had your fill. Do not work for food that spoils, but for food that endures to eternal life, which the Son of Man will give you. On him, God the Father has placed his seal of approval." John 6:26-27

Microwave or Crockpot?   August 24

The one thing I find most elusive in microwave cooking is flavor. Microwave "ovens" are not conducive to producing flavorful food, they are good only for expediency. For heating water, melting butter, reheating soup, or other elemental tasks, there is no rival for it. However, it is a "no contest" between a microwave and a crockpot when it comes to extracting flavors. The crockpot is the superior cooking method for blending flavors and producing a full-bodied meal, extracting flavors over hours instead of minutes, whole days as opposed to seconds.

Many times I have heard people say that we are a "microwave society", requiring instant gratification, instant meals, instant rewards, and instant service. We may also be categorized as "instant Christians". Stamp me as guilty right away! Weeping before God on uncountable occasions, I have not understood why He did not answer my prayers immediately, questioned Him during seasons of trial, and withdrew my trust when I could not see the answers. I agonized over why my spiritual growth seemed to proceed at the speed of a snail on ice. God's answers and methods can rarely be placed in the microwave category.

To extract the fullest flavor from our lives, our loving Father works more in a crockpot fashion, slowly blending the traits of our personalities and gifts, revealing our purpose and His plan in His own sweet time. It is often difficult for our finite minds to grasp that His ways are not our ways, His thoughts far above our thoughts; and His plan, spanning millennia, is exceedingly beyond our understanding. It is equally beyond our comprehension that we are infinitely valuable to Him, created as eternal beings to fellowship with Him.

Expediency is not God's way and no shortcut will produce the qualities He finds valuable. His greatest desire is for us to love and trust Him, and to follow His leading. He is faithful to accomplish all He has promised. The examples of the "slow cooking" method God uses to produce the character He desires are many: Moses, Joshua, Abraham, Joseph, Peter, John, and Paul became the men we admire after decades, not days. God perfected them through trial and trust, hardship and dependence; even Jesus was subjected to his Father's process of refinement. God does not have favorite children, but He does have a favorite process---slow, crockpot style.

"'For my thoughts are not your thoughts, neither are your ways my ways,' declares the Lord." Isaiah 55:8

"Show me your ways, O Lord, teach me your paths; guide me in your truth and teach me, for you are God my Savior, and my hope is in you all day long." Psalm 25:4

"How great is your goodness, which you have stored up for those who fear you, which you bestow in the sight of men, on those who take refuge in you." Psalm 32:19

Essentially Happy August 25

A tiny, white-furred face with big, round, black eyes had nudged the door open, just enough to see inside the bedroom. Her daughter, even smaller than she, was wedging her head between, both attempting to see if the coast was clear. They were not allowed in the bedroom I had just entered, and they were well aware of the rules. I knew they wouldn't be able to resist the temptation to peek, and this time, they restrained themselves to observing instead of invading.

Many times each day, my little dogs follow me to the bedroom, stopping at the door, sometimes peeking, and occasionally trespassing. Their scolding is severe when they place the first paw on the carpet, except at bedtime. They know when I open the door and say, "Time for bed!" that they have special access. Their path is direct, with no wandering in the room. Their bed, at the foot of mine, is their essentially happy destination. There, they rest peacefully, quite content for the night.

And now, you are wondering what in the world this dog-day scenario has to do with you and your relationship with Jesus, aren't you? Dogs aren't much different from people in that we both test boundaries in a willful sort of way. We know God laid down the law about our behavior, very literally and intentionally. His rules are clearly laid out in the Bible, and though we are not encouraged to be legalistic, the rules exist for good reasons.

When God instructs us never to build idols and to worship Him only, He's not joking. The golden rule, to love others as we love ourselves, Jesus made clear. To love Him, honor our parents, stay sexually pure within the bond of marriage, to not steal, to be truth-bearers, to be content with what He gives us, and not envious are all rules for our benefit.

Our Creator understood human nature and our inward leanings toward rebellion before He created mankind. Yet, He provided the solution before the first sin entered the mind of Eve. She, like my little dogs, couldn't resist the temptation to try the forbidden—and here we are today, grappling with the "one thing" the Spirit is telling us to step away from, whatever that may be in our lives!

A Savior was required to reverse the curse, and only by following Him in obedience are we essentially happy. His Holy Spirit guides us, and when temptation seems irresistible, He will always provide a way of escape if we will simply trust him. Through obedience, we are at peace with God. And instead of fear of punishment, He alone becomes our "essentially happy" place, just as He originally intended.

"No temptation has seized you except what is common to man. And God is faithful; he will not let you be tempted beyond what you can bear. But when you are tempted, he will also provide a way out so that you can stand up under it." 1 Corinthians 10:13

Promises, Promises   August 26

My childhood neighbor, Claire, loosely designated as a friend, was not very good at keeping her promises, often opting to throw me to the curb if a better offer came along. Her broken promises, and my often-broken heart, led my mother to ban Claire from my realm of friends; but it was not easy to let go of one of the only friendship options in our neighborhood, which was predominately boys. I learned, though, to choose healthier relationships over broken promises.

In our current culture, promises of faithfulness, paying our debts, keeping sensitive information to ourselves, and keeping our word are often mere illusions based on hope, not trust. Oaths are meaningless to most politicians, throwing their constituents under the bus at the first opportunity to discard their promise in exchange for wealth. Vows yield to convenience, serving self over others, all of the above predicted by Jesus. It shouldn't surprise us, but it always hurts when our hearts are involved.

God does not make idle promises, nor does He renege on His word. His promises are real, solid, and His resolve to keep them will not fade over time. When He makes them, we can bet our lives that His promises are true, lasting, for our benefit, and will come to fruition. I find it quite puzzling that I have had so much difficulty trusting God at times, doubting His word and forgetting His intentions toward me. I suppose I am not alone or there would be no need for Bible promise books.

Think about that: There are so many assurances from our heavenly Father that we can compile whole books containing just His promises. And they are profound promises. Here is but a small sampling: God promises never to leave or forsake us, to be present always, supply all our needs, give us peace, extend mercy, an eternal home in heaven, and adopt as sons all who believe in Christ.

And that's just the beginning! He also promises to give us rest, that He hears our prayers, has a plan, and changes hearts yielded to Him. But wait...there's more! He promises to direct our paths, instruct us, forgive our sins, and reward those who seek Him. He is our awe-inspiring, loving, merciful God, and through Jesus, all promises are kept; every single one. He is Faithful and True, the ultimate Promise Keeper, and if I will but trust Him who has never broken His promise, He will never let me down.

"The Lord is faithful to all his promises and loving toward all he has made. The Lord upholds all those who fall and lifts up all who are bowed down. The eyes of all look to you, and you give them their food at the proper time. You open your hand and satisfy the desires of every living thing. The Lord is righteous in all his ways and loving toward all he has made. The Lord is near to all who call on him, to all who call on him in truth. He fulfills the desire of those who fear him, he hears their cry and saves them. The Lord watches over all who love him, but the wicked he will destroy." Psalm 145:13b-20

Big Fish

"Gone fishin', Mom," said my son with pole and tackle box in hand. A friend had given him a new lure, a purple and white critter of undetermined species, the hook set in a tucked up, nearly hidden position. After a while, Trevor returned with a large green bucket (the one that had housed seven frogs the night prior), curious friends hovering and peering inside. Looking into the bucket, I spied a tiny fish and a BIG fish, a nice ten-inch Brim; we were informed it was the biggest one the owner of the pond had ever seen caught there.

Not wanting the fish to die, Trevor released it and set out to fish again. He later returned to inform me that the big fish had died, stating that every time he threw his line into the water, the same fish would latch onto that hook. Trevor would carefully remove it, set the fish free, and throw the line back into the pond. That fish would immediately take the bait again until finally, it swallowed the hook, the resulting damage fatal. The big fish could not resist that lure to the end.

The sad thing is I am not much different than that big fish in some respects. The similarities of the temptations I face should be clear as day to me, too, and I wonder at times why I seem to be so oblivious. So many times, I take the bait set before my eyes. Satan's forces don't create new temptations, he just employs the same ones over and over again; and I find myself falling for them, over and over again. Let's face it, he knows what works!

Temptation is effective because it exploits our lack of trust in God, implying that He is not able to meet our needs and that we must act or be left wanting. "Certainly, God does not love you, does He? Why would He care about you...look at the mistakes you've made..." whispers Satan. I find that my trust wanes as my notion of God's distance waxes. How much better off I would be if I could simply recognize that God desires good for me. If only I could see the bait of temptation and swim around it instead!

God's best always awaits those who place their absolute trust in His lovingkindness toward them. He promises to provide a way around temptation if we will but wait on Him. The temptations will never stop in this world, but our God has not forgotten His promises and never will. Unlike Trevor's big fish, I have the opportunity daily to be more trusting of my Father in heaven, and through that trust, I am set free indeed.

"No temptation has seized you except what is common to man. And God is faithful; he will not let you be tempted beyond what you can bear. But when you are tempted, he will also provide a way out so that you can stand up under it." I Corinthians 10:13

Turning Up the Heat

It was midsummer, and the sun sizzled through two small windows over the sink, adding to the already unbearable heat in my grandmother's tiny kitchen. Hot potato cubes awaited mashing, by hand, as meat finished frying and the steaming beans, seasoned with bacon and onions, added to the misery index.

Summer evenings were hot and humid living near the river, with sweltering long days and nights that would have been even more unbearable if not for the attic fan installed years prior. Living there only on summer vacations, I primarily remember the heat. By dawn, as the Mourning Doves cooed a sweet greeting, the heat had dissipated just in time to begin again.

As I survey the world I live in today, I am reminded of my grandmother's summer kitchen. The heat seems to be ratcheting upward with layers of discord in the world around me. The political landscape is intensely hot. Corruption, on many levels, is being systematically revealed, a recent tornado has ravaged our community, and the economy is precarious at best. A blip of good news occasionally finds its way through the turmoil. But for the most part, it is layer upon layer of unpleasant news.

Though my eyes see sizzling sun in a hot kitchen-of-a-world, my heart is calm like the morning breeze, not through any doing of my own, not by willpower or self-direction. It is as settled as the dew on Gram's roses because I know the Rose of Sharon. I know I can trust His character. I understand that I can trust Him as evil is exposed, layer by horrific layer. I believe I can trust Him in the storm and that He will bring me safely through to the parting of the clouds. I have His promises upon promises that He will care for me and will never leave me. Though the heat seems unbearable, He promises to carry me through.

Whether your world is heated beyond your comfort or tossed and turned beyond your control, you can trust that God knows where you are, that He has not abandoned you and will never forsake you. Those are His great promises, sealed by the holy blood of His only Son.

When in the heat and tempted to question "why", perhaps we should consider asking how; "Show me how to trust you more, Jesus!" It's not that we don't have *any* faith; it's just that sometimes we have *little* faith, faith that needs to grow. And the trials we face are the tools God uses to grow it when all around us the world is turning up the heat.

"Consider it pure joy, my brothers whenever you face trials of many kinds, because you know that the testing of your faith develops perseverance. Perseverance must finish its work so that you may be mature and complete not lacking anything." James 1:2-4

"Immediately the boy's father exclaimed, 'I do believe; help me overcome my unbelief!'"
Mark 9:24

Potato chips, fries, pretzels, hamburgers, popcorn; I love them all, and there seems to be no end to the craving once the grazing begins. Americans are addicted to snacks, junk food, and particularly, fast food; and I cannot claim an exemption. Recently, I began a diet to "un-do" too many years of past cravings, opting instead to permanently change my menu to real food instead of junk food.

Every day we are presented a menu with two categories on it, one side being "junk food", and the other "real meals". It is God's menu, and He gives us the freedom to choose our items for the day. The junk food side of the menu consists of worldly pleasures, distractions, swirls of activity, and a plate full of self-gratification. The real meals are intimate dining with the Creator, carrying on a conversation with Him, enjoying His presence, and feasting on His Word.

The key to today's menu is that you can choose as many items as you wish. When you choose junk food, though, the results are fairly predictable—the world and its attractions will leave you weak, weary, and malnourished, sluggish, and adding unwanted spiritual weight. There is short-term satisfaction, but nothing lasting.

On the real-meal side, too, you are free to choose as few or many options as you wish. You may desire a quick chat or a fleeting visit, but you also have the option to drink deeply, lingering in His Presence. You may pick at the crust of the Beef Wellington, or dive into the mouth-watering center of His "filet mignon" wisdom.

When we choose to focus on Jesus, we are never left hungry or thirsty. It is no accident that Jesus called Himself the Bread of Life; or that in Matthew 4:4 He says that man does not live on bread alone, but on "every word that comes from the mouth of God." He admonished the woman at the well to drink the living water He supplies. And He stated that whoever feeds on Him will live forever. The choice between life and death, starvation or health, is on the menu every day. And today's menu is free, courtesy of Jesus!

"This is the bread that came down from heaven. Your forefathers ate manna and died, but he who feeds on this bread will live forever." John 6:58

"…but whoever drinks the water I give him will never thirst. Indeed, the water given him will become in him a spring of water welling up to eternal life." John 4:14

Unforgettable August 30

A round mirror stood tall on the dressing table where my grandmother applied her make-up, and on Sundays, adorned herself with costume jewelry. It was one of my favorite places. I felt very special, as she allowed me to powder my face and play with the bulky faux-gemmed pieces. As a girl growing up in a household of boys, it was an unforgettable experience. And my grandmother knew I needed her encouragement and guidance.

We don't often forget the people who make us feel special, the ones who see deeper than the surface, who know our flaws but appreciate our assets more. They are the ones who can love freely, give generously, and forgive with little effort. These are the friends, and sometimes family members, who see us through life's trials, loving us more than we can love ourselves. They are like your first pink cotton candy experience, pleasantly sticking with you for life.

Thankfully, those people see the possibilities of a better future, a healed soul, or a changed spirit more than we can see in ourselves. For most of my life, I had little hope, less confidence, and fewer dreams. Until adulthood, encouragement and edification were rare moments in my life experiences, except through my grandparents. My viewpoint began to transition only as I grew up in Christ, as I trusted Him with how He had made me.

How I see "me" is not how God sees me, and how I see me affects how I see God. As I began to examine myself from the vantage point of God's mirror, I could not deny my worth in His eyes; my Father showed me that it was time to align my opinion of myself with His truth. Child of God, you may need to realign your view to your Father's, as well. Some of us think too much of ourselves, others much too little. The balance is in recognizing what God says, not what we think or feel. You, through Christ Jesus, are a child of Royalty, loved and treasured.

Jesus is the friend who sees us through life's trials, loving us more than we can love ourselves. It is He who makes us special, even while knowing our flaws. But He appreciates our assets more. He knows how we were created and what we were created to be. Only He is truly able to love freely, give generously, and forgive without effort. And in His eyes, you always were, and always will be—unforgettable.

"See what love the Father has lavished on us in letting us be called God's children! For that is what we are. The reason the world does not know us is that it has not known him."

1 John 3:1

"Now the Lord is the Spirit, and where the Spirit of the Lord is, there is freedom. And we, who with unveiled faces all reflect the Lord's glory, are being transformed into his likeness with ever-increasing glory, which comes from the Lord, who is the Spirit."

2 Corinthians 3:17-18

From the top step of my porch on a cool spring day, I sang praises to God while basking in the sun. A Mockingbird perched suddenly on the top of the basketball goal, only about ten feet from me, turning to question the song coming from my direction. I supposed it would soon flee, but it instead cocked its head as if to question whether I was another bird or not. Then, from my warm view, I observed two separate battles ensue.

The first battle erupted when a bold crow crossed the invisible boundary, trespassing into the kingdom of the Mockingbirds. It was scoping out the Mockingbird nests and their newly laid, most vulnerable, spring eggs. The tenacity of the swooping and dive-bombing Mockingbirds held the intruder at bay, and the marauder fled until a more opportune time.

The second battle ensued almost immediately, resulting from the encroachment of a rather large yellow stray cat, wandering into view from the shadows of the nearby bushes. I am no friend to the cats who covet my birds for their next meal. So, from my perch on the highest step, I mustered all the bravado I could, demanding its departure. Little good it did! But, as if on cue, a Mockingbird swooped down, diving at the cat's head. The devourer scooted away as if its tail had caught fire.

These were just two brief battles in the war for survival in nature surrounding me, a war I remain oblivious to most of the time. The world outside my door appears placid and serene, to most appearances, calm, lovely, and uneventful. But in that world, babies are born, some die, some are eaten, others grow up, and even yet become prey. Sickness occurs without my notice, and struggles ensue without my care. And that is the war of the world to which I am oblivious.

Daily, there is another war being waged against humankind, too. It is a war for our minds, spirits, and bodies. It is a war seeking to divide us from each other, our God, and the treasures He has for us. And our only hope of winning the war is found wholly in Jesus. He alone unites us with our heavenly Father, provides for our needs, and heals our wounds through His grace.

Our enemy may hate us to death, but our God loves us to life. In this war of the spirit worlds, an ongoing saga, we fight our battles and stand our ground until Jesus swoops in on the clouds, declaring victory. Jesus has already claimed it, but until He marches onto His physical territory with the hosts of heaven, we have been instructed to hold ground for the King. Let us not lose heart in the battles we fight in this war of the worlds!

"'Be strong and courageous. Do not be afraid or discouraged because of the king of Assyria and the vast army with him, for there is a greater power with us than with him. With him is only the arm of flesh, but with us is the Lord our God to help us and to fight our battles.' And the people gained confidence from what Hezekiah the king of Judah said."

2 Chronicles 32:7-8

September

Moon Over My Shoulder

Driving Me Crazy September 1

Not a patient driver, and admitting to needing vast improvement, I can truthfully say that traffic drives me crazy. As the Friday afternoon traffic choked the road before me, all lanes were backed up and almost at a stand-still as far as I could see. From my higher elevation on the hill, the cars strung out as on silvery chains across all the lanes, glimmering in the sunlight.

On such a bright day, even viewing the scene through my dark sunglasses, the road glittered with the reflections of hundreds of mirrors and metal parts. It looked as if diamonds had been sprinkled over the roadway before me. As it sparkled, it seemed almost alive, and I wondered if perhaps that is how God sees us. In a world of darkness, I believe we "glitter" as we reflect the radiance of Jesus to His Father.

Each of our lives, a tiny point of glimmering light, bounces back to Him as He sees us with the Creator's eyes, as the individuals He lovingly created in His image. Imagine the intensity of the light reflected as we mirror Jesus by becoming more like Him. As our lives model His, we beam Jesus's love into a fallen world, then reflect Him back to the Father. Every place on the globe must sparkle with His radiance as He gazes upon it, millions upon millions of His children shining through the darkness.

Considering that possibility gave me a whole new perspective on the drivers of those cars. They are God's children, each one loved and treasured by Him. His heart longs for their salvation and restored relationship with Him. Many of those drivers are my brothers and sisters in Christ, worthy of my patience and understanding. All of them are worthy of my forgiveness and gentleness toward them, worthy of the same patience God shows me.

I pray my heavenly Father reminds me of what He showed me each time I sit behind the steering wheel. When I am irritable with my fellow road warriors, instead of allowing them to drive me crazy, I pray I will rather show them His crazy, undeserved grace, the same grace He has abundantly shown me.

"We therefore were buried with Him through baptism into death, in order that, just as Christ was raised from the dead through the glory of the Father, we too may walk in newness of life." Romans 6:4

"Do everything without complaining or arguing, so that you may become blameless and pure, children of God without fault in a crooked and depraved generation, in which you shine like stars in the universe as you hold out the word of life…" Philippians 2:14-16b

Awakened by the reverberating crack of thunder, the pounding rain seemed to hit all sides of my house at once. It was a good day to stay home, except that it was Sunday. I glanced at the clock, realized an hour remained of my "cushion" time for a tad more slumber; it did not take but a minute to fall back into dreamland.

The next time I awoke, the clock had ticked off *two* hours, making my plans to go to the worship service appear rather tenuous. It was still dark gray, pouring rain, and extremely tempting to stay right where I was. I decided to trust God with the timing, preparing anyway, and amazingly, I entered the church door exactly on time.

Leaving the building, heading to my car after the service, I determined that I wanted all of Jesus, in all my life. I realized that the brokenness and desert I had been wandering through required making a choice; choose to keep wandering or choose to ask for restoration and follow the path God laid out for me. As that thought floated in my spirit, I glanced up at the dreary sky. Ahead of me were tiny cracks revealing blue sky in the west, though it was still very gray over me.

The choice was evident; abiding in His presence, in light, peace, clarity, and truth, or lingering in the grayness of oppression, depression, detachment, and brokenness. At that moment, and from that point forward, I chose the blue sky of Jesus over the clouds of brokenness. I asked Him to restore me in every way and, have since trusted Him to accomplish it.

Every day, no, every hour of the day, I am faced with that same choice: Do I choose the life-giving power that comes from loving God, listening to His voice, and clinging to Him; or, do I choose self-indulgence, fear, and clinging to the world for answers? God's best is found in relationship with Him, in the answers and examples of the Bible, and the leading of His Spirit. That sounds simplistic, but it is the world that complicates and misleads us; in Jesus is life, love, peace, and purpose.

Choosing to love my God, paying attention to what He says, and clinging to Him only is the profound purpose not only of my life. He is my blue sky. In Him, my "choice moments" are easier, my purpose clear; loving God is my place of confidence, trusting Him my place of rest.

"Therefore, choose life, so that you will live, you and your descendants, loving the Lord your God, paying attention to what he says, and clinging to him---for that is the purpose of your life!" Deuteronomy 30:19a-20b CJB

Unbridled   September 3

Though her parents will not be buying a horse, they have recognized the deep love Addie has for equines and are paying for riding lessons instead. My granddaughter shares that unquenchable love for horses with her grandmother, so as I watched one of her Dressage riding competitions, my heart melted. She was riding beautifully on the gentle but large palomino, attired in her riding habit, with her steed under her control as it circled the show ring.

Following her performance, one of Addie's classmates began riding into the ring. Her horse stumbled, taking both horse and rider to the ground. The audience and judges sat stunned at the unexpected turn of events for a fleeting second, then ran to her aid. The horse and rider were in a bit of shock but weren't hurt, walking out intact. But it reminded me how quickly injuries can happen when large animals with minds of their own decide to exert their will at any given moment.

Horses are controlled through the bridle that signals the horse to turn or stop as the rider directs. They are ineffective on untamed horses; it is a learning process. Tamed horses, trained to take the bridle and yield to the rider's direction, are far more valuable than the untamed and rebellious ones. And so it is with human beings.

When we accept Jesus, we are essentially "taking the bridle", accepting His leadership and direction. Our rebellious hearts are yielding to His right of control instead of running head-long under our own. Like a horse running unbridled in a crowded ring, the unbridled heart leads to injury, destruction, and death. Without Jesus, we are unbridled and untamed; with Him, we progress through stages of growth until fit for the heavenly "show ring". It is a process for people, as with horses, many years in the making.

For headstrong horses and people, whatever our stage of growth, submission is the basic requirement, and the most difficult. Yet when we yield our will to God's perfect will, submitting to His control, our growth is unstoppable. With His training, like a beautiful show horse, His light shines through. Every day is an opportunity to allow God's control in our lives, with many small opportunities to be obedient to His will and learning His ways. His is the gentle but firm hand on the reigns as He guides us step by step, under His bridle.

"During the days of Jesus' life on earth, he offered up prayers and petitions with loud cries and tears to the one who could save him from death, and he was heard because of his reverent submission. Although he was a son, he learned obedience from what he suffered and, once made perfect, he became the source of eternal salvation for all who obey him and was designated by God to be high priest in the order of Melchizedek." Hebrews 5:7-10

"If you love me, you will obey what I command. And I will ask the Father, and he will give you another Counselor to be with you forever---the Spirit of truth." John 14:15-16

Rush Limbaugh's radio show was the first time I remember a talk-show host opening the phone lines to listeners on Fridays each week, dubbing it "Open-Line Friday". It was interesting to hear each listener's question presented to Rush. He always listened patiently, while the nebulous figure over the airwaves often struggled to present a cogent question, some of which never materialized. Some petitioners seemed to like hearing themselves on the radio more than they wanted an answer.

Many of us are like those Limbaugh fans when we call in to speak with God. Some of us only phone in on Sundays, hoping to drop a courtesy call to God, fulfilling our obligation dutifully. Others are like the caller floating on the fringes as if suspended in the neverland of "hold"; they are hoping to randomly connect, or possibly collect a notable moment with the Creator of the Universe. Then there are the petitioners who simply want their questions answered and a possible blessing tossed their way.

But the "callers" God treasures most are His children who tune in the rest of the week, too. They are the ones who listen diligently, not because their requests will be fulfilled, but because they value each word their heavenly Father speaks. They primarily desire to know Him. These are the ones who understand God's will and strive to be obedient, not out of duty, but because of love and a desire for a real relationship with Him. Their thirst is satisfied by the river of wisdom poured out through God's word and their search for it is rewarded with pearls of truth excavated by inquiry.

We have the opportunity each day to connect with our heavenly Father, with no restrictions or permissions, no payments, and no waiting on hold. Through the blood of Jesus, the toll-free line is open twenty-four hours a day, with no one ahead of us in the queue. Full access was awarded when the tomb birthed a Savior, never to be restricted again. Love prevailed and reigns forevermore. Rejoice, treasured child of God! Open-line Friday is open every day. And the Host of Heaven desires your presence as His special guest; He is ready to take your call personally.

"Rejoice in the Lord always. I will say it again: Rejoice! Let your gentleness be evident to all. The Lord is near. Do not be anxious about anything, but in everything, by prayer and petition, with thanksgiving, present your requests to God. And the peace of God, which transcends all understanding, will guard your hearts and minds in Christ Jesus." Philippians4:4-7

"Jesus answered, 'It is written: "Man does not live on bread alone, but on every word that comes from the mouth of God."'" Matthew 4:4

My young daughter, Whitney, inquired one day, "Why did God make the stars?" I shared with her what I knew from God's account in Genesis 1: **"God set them in the expanse of sky to give light on the earth, to govern the day and the night, and to separate light from darkness."** In Psalm 19:1, there appears another compelling reason to have the stars, sun, and moon: **"The heavens declare the glory of God; the skies proclaim the work of His hands."**

As space probes beam their incredible photographs of deep space to us, they only confirm the wonders and glory of God. Galaxies of stars are strewn across the black vastness like marbles on velvet and are visible evidence of the creativity and care of God. The universe seems to suspend the earth in its optimal place for life, as distant orbs contrarily shine through eons of darkness. Who else could have conceived of hanging flaming globes in the cosmos to light our nights?

I firmly believe that everything created is meant to point us to our Creator. It is His displayed power in creation that encourages our hearts to seek Him, and His Spirit's work in our hearts which convinces us of His intimate love. The stars give us encouragement that our God is constant and enduring, His love never-ending and passionate, and His abilities far beyond anything we can imagine. And in stark contrast, He promises that though the heavens may eventually fall away, our Savior never will.

If the stars can be the spark for igniting faith in our simple minds, Jesus is its radiant completion through the Holy Spirit. His love for us is beyond our understanding and His sacrifice beyond our ability to fathom. **"Has not God made foolish the wisdom of the world?...for the foolishness of God is wiser than man's wisdom and the weakness of God is stronger than man's strength...But God chose the foolish things of the world to shame the wise; God chose the weak things of the world to shame the strong."** (1Corinthians 1:20)

Though this passage is speaking of Christ's death and resurrection, I believe it is safe to say that God's wisdom, displayed in every facet of the universe, puts us all to shame. The universe was created to that end—that God's glory would be on display, **"so that your faith might not rest on men's wisdom, but on God's power."** (1Corinthians 1:25) When the world around us does not make sense, I pray we will be star-struck, fully focused on the bright Morning Star, the Son of the Living God, the Light of Heaven.

"We did not follow cleverly invented stories when we told you about the power and coming of our Lord Jesus Christ, but we were eyewitnesses of his majesty. For he received honor and glory from God the Father when the voice came to him from the Majestic Glory, saying, 'This is my Son, whom I love; with him I am well pleased'....And we have the word of the prophets made more certain, and you will do well to pay attention to it, as to a light shining in a dark place, until the day dawns and the morning star rises in your hearts."

2 Peter 1:16-17, 19

Apple of My Eye

When the leaves began to paint their bright golds and reds against the autumn sky, our family knew it was time for its yearly trek to the huge apple orchard in the foothills of the Smokey Mountains. This orchard was famous for the delicious, green apple variety that they had developed over a generation. The Wooden Delicious apple, of all the varieties they grew, became the apple of my eye, the only apple for me.

How the apple became associated with the saying, "Apple of my eye", is largely unknown, but it is a phrase that has been around for many centuries. The pupil of the eye was thought to be a little round ball, like an apple; it refers to something of such affection that it fills one's eyes, allowing nothing else to be seen. Recently, I read the story of a couple who endured the pain of the loss of their first baby, and this euphemism applied, but not in the way I expected.

As the mother grieved the profound loss, her husband quietly, in pain of his own, ministered to her through small loving gestures. He tended to chores, made sure the lights were on when she came home, brought her favorite food, and held her tightly as she wept in his arms. He protected her in ways she did not observe; as her body and heart healed, he provided for her in every way he could, as his own heart hurt.

Jesus is the husband to a broken and hurting bride, a bride oblivious to the tender ways her faithful husband ministers to her needs. She takes very much for granted His gentle gifts of provision and protection. She cannot conceive of His enormous self-sacrifice, or the pain He suffered as He laid Himself down on the cross for her. She is self-absorbed, too lost in her pain, to know His; His pain cannot be calculated when she acts as though she knows Him not.

Tears well up as I consider that, as a wife, I was not all I should have been. Many times, I lacked understanding of the man I called my husband. But the tears flow deeper when I realize that I often treat Jesus the same way, going my way with little thought of consulting His wisdom. Taking His provision for granted, I ask, also, for protection I little deserve.

Thankfully, I do not get what I deserve. Instead, by God's grace, He gives me life to the fullest and eternal life in His presence. His grace prevails and I am forgiven. I live as a tiny part of the Body of Christ, but He loves me as He loves the whole body, the beneficiaries of His resurrected life. We are the Apple of His Eye.

"The Spirit and the bride say, 'Come!' And let him who hears say, 'Come!' Whoever is thirsty, let him come; and whoever wishes, let him take the free gift of the water of life. He who testifies to these things says, 'Yes, I am coming soon.' Amen. Come, Lord Jesus. The grace of the Lord Jesus be with God's people. Amen." Revelation 22:17, 20-21

A Stitch in Time

Its white fabric had aged to a mellow, pale, yellow but the pattern remained clean and tight, unchanged over a half-century. The stitches of embroidery outlined a black pony dancing across the border of the pillowcase, amid flowers, blades of grass, and a barking, brown puppy. How I loved creating pictures out of thread! The memories of learning each of the stitches from my grandmother suddenly flooded to the forefront of my mind, like a needlework time machine, as that memory created a "stitch in time" for me.

Reflecting on the subsequent needlework I did over the years, that is the only remaining piece I possess, and it is soon to find its new home with my eldest granddaughter. Two pieces, needlework samplers stitched by my mother-in-law, and her mother, will also find their way to my grandchildren eventually. They will likely grow up without an appreciation for the time or skill required in their creation, but they will, hopefully, sense the love each stitch represents.

Jesus created a similar tapestry with His life, weaving together a complete picture for us as He lived each day. In the deepest black stitch of night, the Son of God stepped into time. On that background, the radiance of His compassionate touch dotted the darkness with the golden light of His love. The foreground burst with miraculous blue hues, of calming waves, and water turned to burgundy wine.

In spotless pure white, His obedience to His Father shone in contrast with dark swirls of the sinful world. And finally, the brown stitches of the cross, stained with drops of pure red, ended His life residing in flesh. The unforeseen stitch, at just the right time, was the sparkling, radiant silver of resurrection to new life; Jesus was raised by the blinding, inconceivable, and brilliant power of God.

Never in our lifetimes can we imagine the depth of sacrificial love our heavenly Father felt, as He stitched together the tapestry of His only Son's journey on the earth. Each person He interacted with, each miracle He performed, was to reveal His Father to the beings made in His likeness, yet so rebelliously disconnected from Him.

The pattern of our lives, every stitch in time, is an opportunity to imitate His perfect tapestry of obedience, love, generosity, and relationship. As we lay our lives on His background of sacrifice, may each of our lives stand out in a completed pattern that mirrors His.

"Great are the works of the Lord; they are pondered by all who delight in them. Glorious and majestic are his deeds, and his righteousness endures forever. He has caused his wonders to be remembered; the Lord is gracious and compassionate…The works of his hands are faithful and just; all his precepts are trustworthy. He provided redemption for his people; he ordained his covenant forever---holy and awesome is his name."

Psalm 111:2-4, 7-9

Drips and Drops   September 8

While steeping the tea bags, my mind wandered to the many drops of water in the pan sitting on the burner of the stove. I have no idea how many drops it contained, but each drop of water would soon become tasty Southern sweet tea, innumerable drops consumed by my family over the years. Not one of those drops was significant to anyone by itself but offered on a hot day in a tumbler with ice, they combined to make a pretty impressive, refreshing treat.

My life has seemed to be like so many little drips over time, appearing insignificant in the world swirling around me, like the tea in the pot. I desire to make a difference, yet my inadequacies, in my own eyes, seem overwhelming. I want to make a difference for Jesus, to influence lives positively, and reveal His love to those around me. My intentions are wonderful, my actions intentional, but I often wonder if they are sufficient.

As I look at the historical recording of the lives of God's people in the Bible, I realize that God uses pretty ordinary people, nearly all the time. There are few records of great deeds done for God by the renowned in worldly terms. Aside from miracles, dramatic differences were rarely made in an instant, and their lives were lived in notable obscurity by the world's standards.

God called people in the past, and today, alike, to walk with Him one step at a time, or, if you will, one drip at a time. Many drips, falling over time carve channels; obediently following Jesus, many small acts at a time, also carve channels in this world. Each drop softens hearts and brings light, life, and hope into people's lives. His love is revealed to a hurting world, one at a time.

I have a quote written inside my Bible by Dr. Charles Stanley, "Be obedient, and let God be responsible for the consequences." I have found it to be good advice. As I listen for God's voice, am being led by his Spirit, and am obedient to His instruction, that is all He requires. He is faithful to use who He has made me, in touching the world He has made. It is a matter of trust, allowing Him to use me as He sees fit, as He brings restoration of relationship between Himself and a sadly broken world.

God's story is mine to tell, as He opens the way, one person at a time, one "drop" at a time. One drop can make a difference, but consistently, many drops certainly will. And as we flow together as the people of God, we are transformed into His refreshing, sweet nectar to those around us.

"But if anyone obeys his word God's love is truly made complete in him. This is how we know we are in him: Whoever claims to live in him must walk as Jesus did." 1 John 2:5-6

"I will sing of the Lord's great love forever; with my mouth I will make your faithfulness known through all generations. I will declare that your love stands firm forever, that you established your faithfulness in heaven itself." Psalm 89:1-2

But Wait, There's More

Most people can remember an infomercial selling the handy-dandy food gadget or instant shine product for your car. Near the end of the commercial, the on-air personality would enthusiastically pitch the line, "But wait, there's more!" There was always a bonus, a hook to entice you to buy the upgrade to another level and price. I was at a point in life where I was ready to give up but had a sense that God was pitching that line to me, in a good way, encouraging me to trust Him a bit longer.

Two events had left me feeling devastated, crushed, and beyond hope. One was the loss of a business in which we had invested every dollar we owned; the second was my husband's diagnosis of a debilitating and eventually fatal disease. My life, both times, felt it had officially ended. Both events happened between the ages of 35 while raising three children and 50, just after they had all left home. I could not see a future, and frankly, I was tired of looking for one.

That Easter Sunday, at a community worship service, the theme was, of course, resurrection. But the sermon took a twist when the pastor referenced the valley of dry bones in the book of Ezekiel, chapter 37. I had read the passage the week prior and now here it was again; dry, lifeless bones were being resurrected into living beings, a vast army of the Lord.

That army was raised to life to serve God, revealing His life-giving power to the world. That same message was spoken to me three more times in the following week, confirmation after confirmation that God had not abandoned me, and He still had a plan for my life. He was not finished with me, no matter how the circumstances felt or appeared.

Jesus's death was not an obstacle to God's mighty power, and there is nothing beyond His power even now. Though I had nothing on which to base my hope except Him, I could see that if God could restore flesh to skeletons and breathe life into their lungs, He could take care of my needs. I stepped out in trust, joining the ranks of God's army of believers, people who have surrendered and are willing to settle in His land. He is still in the resurrection business, restoring lives, lifting the hopeless, and bringing comfort to those walking in pain. God never runs dry of miracles. And just when you are ready to surrender, you will hear the words resound in your soul, "But wait, there's more!"

"Then he said to me, 'Prophesy to these bones and say to them, "Dry bones, hear the word of the Lord! This is what the Sovereign Lord says to these bones: I will make breath enter you and you will come to life. I will attach tendons to you and make flesh come upon you and cover you with skin; I will put breath in you, and you will come to life. Then you will know that I am the Lord.'" Isaiah 37:4-6

The one defining quality of my life, until recent years, has been fear—fear of lack, fear of loss, fear of death, fear of nearly everything. Jesus, the gentle Savior that He is, has been patient beyond measure as He has baby-stepped me into deeper and deeper trust, teaching His stubborn child about relaxing my fists and taking hold of His hand instead. As His child, my grip, also, has been weaker than I could ever imagine. And as a result, He has many times held onto me instead. Fear, or mistrust, is like a child attempting to pull away from its father's protective grip while crossing a busy street. It is his grip that changes everything, but it is the child's trust which makes the journey more pleasant.

One day, I re-discovered **Proverbs 3:5** and emphasized each of the keywords. "**Trust** in the Lord with **all your heart** and **lean not** to your own **understanding;** in **all** your **ways acknowledge** him and he will **make** your **paths straight.**" (Keywords emphasized)

A word study on this passage played an important role in changing my level of trust in the One so worthy of it: **"Put your confidence in the Lord with all your heart, and do not rely on your own discernment, good sense, or wisdom; in all your journeys, conduct, and way of life make him known, and he will make your manner and conduct right, and your path smooth and straight."** (Amplified Bible)

What I saw in this small passage is that God gives us wisdom, discernment, and good judgment, but we see within limits. We cannot trust the gifts themselves, but must ultimately trust the Giver, who sees far beyond our human limitations. He is always aware of where we are, who we are, and where we are going. He is the God of our today, Lord of our tomorrows, and Sovereign over our futures.

Jesus shared in our humanity so that by his death, he might destroy the devil, the power of death, and in doing so, free those whose lives are held in slavery by their fear of death. (Hebrews 2:14-15) As long as we fear not having what we desire, cannot shed our pride, or submit our willfulness in any area, we are not trusting God's sovereignty in our lives. Nothing escapes God's power; everything, including self, must surrender to Him.

In other words, my simplified interpretation is, "Trust in the Lord and be led by His Spirit, or I will mess things up." Holding His hand, trusting His grip, and walking *with* Him instead of in *front* of him, is the safest place of all. It truly is all about trust in Jesus and in His mighty love, displayed through God's power, that changes everything.

"Blessed is the man who makes the Lord his trust, who does not look to the proud, to those who turn aside to false gods. Many, O Lord my God, are the wonders you have done. The things you planned for us no one can recount to you; were I to speak and tell of them, they would be too many to declare." Psalm 40:4-5

The Art of Self Defense September 11

The martial arts, though I have passed the age of learning it is a fascination to me. I can fully appreciate the training, but when well done, it is more than a skill; it is an art form. The beautiful lines formed in kicks and the balance and rotation of the body, are to me, a form of dance. It is captivating to watch, in all its varied forms, from Taekwondo to Brazilian Jiu-Jitsu, Judo to Karate.

The martial arts in their original forms all center to some degree on self-defense, more than the destruction of an opponent. In addition to the self-defense aspect of learning these arts, they also develop self-discipline, respect, and diligence.

However, it occurred to me that though I don't practice martial arts, I have become well-practiced at self-defense when it comes to my relationship with God. I should know better by now, but I will confess that when my Father asks me to do something I don't want to do, I still become self-defensive. When I know God is directing me, calling me to do something I find difficult, as in forgiving someone, I have tried to hide. When He has given me a tedious assignment, I found myself procrastinating.

One very difficult and hard-learned lesson had to do with computer skills; I hated every single minute of the three months that God had me in training. I cried, begged, pleaded with God to release me from that assignment, but the only reply I got from Him was to "finish". Little did I understand at the time that this lesson would apply to finishing an assignment to write a book, taking more than two years instead of three months.

I was self-defensive before ever becoming a follower of Jesus. Self was who I protected at all costs. And I innately knew that if I accepted His invitation, I would also have to follow where He led, that I could no longer protect myself from Him. If I could go backward in time, I would show my old self that there was nothing to fear, that He only wanted His best for me, nothing more.

Slowly, ever so slowly, like the learning of martial arts, I am learning to be open to the changes God has asked of me. The funny thing about God's "request" for our cooperation and acceptance of change is that He really must find it entertaining at times; I have surely provided an array of interesting sidesteps. Learn this lesson early rather than late: Resisting God is a self-defense measure that never works out well. He knows that eventually, suffering enough self-inflicted pain, we will comply.

"If you love me, you will obey what I command. And I will ask the Father, and he will give you another Counselor to be with you forever---the Spirit of truth...Whoever has my commands and obeys them, he is the one who loves me. He who loves me will be loved by my Father, and I too will love him and show myself to him." John 14:15

All through the day, I had wept, grieving the loss of a friend I had known for a quarter-century, layered upon the recent loss of one of my best friends, and my husband. I struggled through the day, debating whether to drag myself out of the house, not feeling much like being with people or attending Bible study. But I changed my clothes dutifully, took the dog outside, and finally willed my car out of the driveway.

The dark clouds had hung over me, both literally and figuratively, all day. As I drove west on the highway, beams of sunlight were casting a flashlight-like ray through a minuscule hole in the clouds. Gray, thick, shadowy clouds cast a singular beam of light down upon "someone"—And it broke like that shaft of light, in my mind—Amid the darkness, "someone" is being shined upon.

By the time I arrived at my destination, my perspective had radically shifted from mourning to joy, as I realized that God's grace was quietly shining down upon me, also. Often, our view is obscured by thick clouds, sorrows, and troubles of life obstructing the light. When needed, though, we can trust that God will break through the darkness and shine a golden ray of His loving grace upon us. He doesn't require a very big hole, just the tiniest of openings to break through our gloom.

We must each decide to receive His Light or deny it, to allow God's love into our day, or to remain in the darkness. Let's face it, sometimes the darkness is comfortable, self-pity satisfying, and lingering in its shadows is attractive, but that is not where we are to stay. Our hearts are in danger when the darkness becomes too appealing or when grieving overcomes healing. God calls us to His Light for regeneration and transformation, to a certain hope of His promises fulfilled.

On that Interstate highway, under clouds of gray, I decided that I wanted to be the "someone" whom that beam of God's light shone down upon. Most of the time, I notice the clouds and forget to look for the sun. Likewise, I forget to look for the Son in the course of my day. Today I pray that God opens my eyes to the wonders surrounding me, to everything that testifies of His lovingkindness toward me, no matter how I feel. I want to be that "someone" the Light of Jesus shines on, "light" hearted, and searching for evidence of His abounding goodness toward those who love Him.

"Though I have fallen, I will rise. Though I sit in darkness, the Lord will be my light."
Micah 7:8b

"For God, who said, 'Let light shine out of darkness,' made his light shine in our hearts to give us the light of the knowledge of the glory of God in the face of Christ."
2 Corinthians 4:6

"From the fullness of his grace we have all received one blessing after another." **John 1:16**

Better Together

The river-tour boat lazily echoed the San Antonio guide's voice, as it bounced softly off the water's surface, to the crowds wandering the walkways. On the hot pavement, under the afternoon sun, I received my first hug from Elizabeth, our newest grandchild. Freshly adopted into our family was a happy, sweet four-year-old, but the most memorable part of the day was her beautifully clear voice. And thinking no one noticed, she sang to herself quietly when not engaging with the family.

Our musically gifted girl has since learned to play the violin, piano, and is now learning guitar. I don't think she will ever realize how many precious notes have flowed to our ears, or how many blessings radiate from her God-given gift. I cannot imagine this lovely child not being part of our family, as if she has always been, and ever will be. She does not fear, nor should she ever, that she will be cast out. With Elizabeth, our family is better together, no matter what trials come.

Not so, in God's family. Many of us fret and fuss, living fearfully, wondering when God will expel us, and over what infraction. In my own life, a profound lack of trust from an underlying fear of abandonment was revealed; but I have realized, this same fear is rampant among Christians. We have no peace living in His household, as our Father's adopted children. Most do not bask in the love of their Father, nor do they live daily in His peace. They avoid, out of fear, the very God and Father who loves them most, who has promised never to leave or forsake them.

God provided a standard for adoption in ancient times, one which would mirror His strict standard. If a child was adopted, it was permanent, even more so than a natural-born son. It could not, by God's law, be undone. Through Christ, that spirit of adoption lives, one of permanency. No matter what happens, there is no turning back, and a new heir is seated at the family table.

The adoption into God's family is open to all. We are entitled, without question, to God's grace and love. It is permanent, and every sin is forgiven. The most beautiful thing about God's family is that there is always room for one more, and we are, in His family, better together.

"In love he predestined us to be adopted as his sons through Jesus Christ, in accordance with his pleasure and will---to the praise of his glorious grace, which he has freely given us in the One he loves. In him we have redemption through his blood, the forgiveness of sins, in accordance with the riches of God's grace that he lavished on us with all wisdom and understanding." Ephesians 1:5-8

"And I will ask the Father, and he will give you another Counselor to be with you forever---the Spirit of truth. The world cannot accept him, because it neither sees him nor knows him. But you know him, for he lives with you and will be in you. I will not leave you as orphans; I will come to you." John 14:16-18

A turn of the key ignited the starter, sparking the resultant low rumble, followed by a roar of power as the gas pedal opened the throttle, and a thrill surged through my body. There was a well-tuned engine under the hood, an engine sporting more than enough horsepower to coast the highways at speeds well above lawful limits. Practical people question why so much power is needed in cars when excessive speed is denied its expression, but those of us who enjoy the power under the hood will tell you that it is simply because of the power itself.

Sneering at the super-engines, or anything prized by someone else, we can feel superior. In anything, we can feel we are in control, self-sufficient, and capable of handling whatever crosses our paths. We can become arrogant, smug, prideful, eventually disdaining of others who are in periods of upheaval or weakness, denying our weaknesses and shortcomings. It is not a coincidence, it is human nature, and without humility, inescapable.

Humility is simply acknowledging that the power we require to function in life comes not from our self-worth or efforts, but from the Lord. A humble heart recognizes that we are not the ones in control, not the ones who supply all our own needs, and not the ones who can work our way to heaven. It is not about the works we do, the privilege we claim, or the birth-rites we possess. It is, in fact, all about our need for our Creator and Savior.

Jesus spoke to this tendency towards pride when confronting the people of greatest privilege, education, and position of His culture, the Pharisees and Sadducees. **He said to them, "Are you not in error because you do not know the Scriptures or the power of God?" (Mark 12:24)** And I will admit that when I slip into any error in my ways, especially pride, it always boils down to this very passage, forgetting what God's words say, or forgetting the power He has to change me, or any circumstance in my life.

It is not my power that matters, nor my influence in the world, nor my position, or possessions. The power of humility begins by acknowledging God's power, ability, and sovereignty. This is the real rumble of power under our hoods. Christ's position of authority and our submission to it are the fuel that yields the fruits of His Spirit, producing peace, patience, kindness, love, faithfulness, joy, gentleness, and goodness. Listening for His Holy Spirit to lead us through the day is the key sparking the ignition. Walking in His will opens the throttle, and He becomes the rumble of our engines, the full Power under our hoods.

"But the fruit of the Spirit is love, joy, peace, patience, kindness, goodness, faithfulness, gentleness and self-control. Against such things there is no law. Those who belong to Christ Jesus have crucified the sinful nature with its passions and desires. Since we live by the Spirit, let us keep in step with the Spirit. Let us not become conceited, provoking and envying each other." Galatians 5:22-25

The Princess Bride

The girls gathered on a blanket in front of the television for the crowning event of the day, one of their favorite movies. Of all the films our family has viewed over the years, "The Princess Bride" has become an endearing classic in our family, and for all the right reasons. It is a story of grand promise, tortured loss, colorful characters, and carefully revealed sub-plots. Fantasy, romance, danger, betrayal, and fierce loyalty intertwine in particularly unexpected and often humorous ways.

The best feature of the script is the hero answering the love of his life with the words, "As you wish", an expression of self-sacrificing love. His "true love" doubted, they, of course, had misunderstandings, and conflicts abounded as the plot unraveled. Buttercup, the heroine, was eventually won over by Wesley's tenacious and sacrificial love. Both were rescued from certain death, as the whole room sighed in relief. As expected, the characters rode white horses into the night.

I pondered an even more outlandish storyline. This story begins with the Creator of the entire universe fashioning creatures resembling Himself, then turning them loose on an orb full of tasty treats. Instead of eating to their heart's content and living happily ever after, they rebelled. The Owner expelled them but loves them despite themselves, so much so that he decides to enter enemy territory, eat the poisonous fruit Himself, and die in their place. After defeating their enemy, the Owner forgives their rebellion and gives them a new kingdom. In it, there is no more enemy, pain, or poisonous fruit. Ever after, they get to live as princes and princesses, becoming His true love, His Princess Bride. They then ride off together on white horses into eternal bliss.

As Christ-followers, we are the colorful characters in God's story, still living in enemy territory but bought and paid for by Jesus. Riding happily into the sunset is not an option just yet, but we have not been abandoned here. God provides for us, protects us in the battles we face, strengthens, and encourages us. He is coming back for us, but until we leave this planet, we are to occupy with courage, trusting the One who loves us from the beginning of the story to our very last scene. We are His Princess Bride, destined to marry the Prince of Peace. After all, the Author was the King of Glory, who wrote the real happy ending from the very beginning.

"Christ redeemed us from the curse of the law by becoming a curse for us, for it is written: 'Cursed is everyone who is hung on a tree.' He redeemed us in order that the blessing given to Abraham might come to the Gentiles through Christ Jesus, so that by faith we might receive the promise of the Spirit." Galatians 3:13-14

"The king is enthralled by your beauty; honor him, for his is your lord." Psalm 45:11

Interior Designer September 16

My daughter, Blair, became what I had always wanted to be, an interior designer, and is quite talented, with an eye for all things design. My path was a career I did not like and a subsequent hodge-podge of creative substitutions. I had been pressured by my mother to select a "reliable" career path. It was reliable only for the short time we lived in cities. When we moved to a sparsely populated area, my occupational security was nowhere to be found.

Interior design has never left my heart; it just morphed into other modes of creativity. It has taken many forms over the years, beginning with photography, then spilling over into cake decorating and painting. Basket weaving, needlework, pottery, sewing, and floral arranging found their way into my repertoire over the decades, as well. Dog grooming (yes, an art form!) came with having a Maltese in the show ring.

But for all the design forms I learned, I could never put my finger on the unrest in my soul. Even after meeting Jesus and surrendering my soul to Him, I knew something was amiss. My heavenly Father knew all along that Jesus was who I needed to fill the empty space in my heart, but He knew there was more that I was missing. I was badly in need of healing yet didn't realize the extent of my wounds. My emotional damage was so deeply rooted that I had no idea from where my dysfunctional behavior stemmed. Thankfully, my Father sent His most talented interior designer to my rescue.

When an interior designer steps in, space needs to be cleared of all the old furnishings before renovation begins. Some rooms can be redesigned with the simple rearrangement of furniture, while others need to be completely gutted from the foundation up. I was the major remodel in need of a complete overhaul. But God did not tear everything out at once; He methodically removed the old, one piece at a time, no matter my impatience or insistence that He accelerate the process. One step at a time, over many seasons, He is still completing His work.

And that is the beauty of the Holy Spirit! He knows when to speed up the design process and when to take it slowly. He will not work against our will and patiently waits for us to submit to His transformation. Sometimes, He will allow us to walk through the fires of change and testing of our faith, but it is never for our destruction; it is always for our transformation into the reflection of the perfect Designer, Jesus. He is the interior designer who takes us from shattered and broken to functional and beautiful—and always in perfect timing.

"Now the Lord is the Spirit, and where the Spirit of the Lord is, there is freedom. And we, who with unveiled faces all reflect the Lord's glory, are being transformed into his likeness with ever-increasing glory, which comes from the Lord, who is the Spirit."

2 Corinthians 3:17-18

Like Father, Like Son   September 17

Considering how my son obtained his optimistic and traditional values, I had to consider how like his father he is. They both loved the old cowboy shows, and I mean the really old ones! They were Roy Rogers-kind-of-old; and Gunsmoke, The Rifleman, Rawhide, and The Lone Ranger, too. Neither of them could watch enough. Both, as children, played cowboy, a lot! And both shared optimism and a sense of fairness. Father shared with son, and the son became like his father; "like father, like son".

The cowboy stories they loved were generally very similar. Their adventures featured adversaries of all kinds, from rattlesnakes to renegades, thieves to con-men, and bank robbers to cattle rustlers. Their heroes were almost always ordinary men, set with the task to preserve decency and rule of law, against all the evil schemes, and to finally arrive at a happy ending. The good guys always won, the bad guys were well defined, and always brought to justice. And it is no accident that the good guys always rode the white horse.

It is, surprisingly, the story we individually live every day. We face down worldly challenges, struggling to preserve decency and order in a chaotic life. We strive to uphold God's rules and laws and to arrive at a happy ending. We are taught in God's word to seek truth, focus on what is right and good, and strive for purity and honesty. Though His values are contrary to the world's values, God enables us to stand through His Spirit.

However, the best story always has a villain. Our adversary shows himself in many forms, as well. He whispers the temptation of a little lie, to take what does not belong to us when no one sees, or to puff ourselves up to more than we deserve. His tools are wide in scope and lay hidden behind rocks we never expected. He is prepared to ambush us in our weakest times. But God is our cavalry and hero, who appears at just the right time, and in just the right way, exactly as needed, when we entrust our problems to Him.

Jesus is the ultimate "good guy", the proverbial white hat cowboy, the Perfect One on the white horse. He is the very picture foretelling the return of Jesus on the clouds of heaven. He arrives at the end to save the day, rescuing us from the final destruction set for the Evil One. And when He does, all heaven and earth will see that, like Father, like Son, the resemblance cannot be mistaken. Neither can ours as we become more like Him every day.

"If God is for us, who can be against us? He who did not spare his own Son, but gave him up for us all---how will he not also, along with him, graciously give us all things? Who will bring any charge against those whom God has chosen? It is God who justifies. Who is he that condemns? Christ Jesus, who died---more than that, who was raised to life---is at the right hand of God and is also interceding for us." Romans 8:31b-34

The Great Divide

Our family of six eagerly exited the vehicle, spilling onto the parking lot at the landmark for the Continental Divide in Colorado. That six-pack was ready for adventure following our thousand-mile trek, mostly over plains---very boring plains! At that stopping point, I found my first Colorado acquaintances. A family of chipmunks popped their inquisitive heads up, then darted into their homes. It was also my first experience with a mountain stream, running ice-laced ripples over my bare feet.

The Great Divide is the ridge of the Rocky Mountains where the water runs west to the desert slopes and east to the greener basin. It is also what stops the clouds, creating the billowing eastern rains, and leaving the western mountains varying shades of grays and browns instead. The Continental Divide determines where the waters flow.

There is a great divide in my soul, as well. It also determines where the nourishing waters flow. On one side of the mountain, I struggle to squeeze out every bit of control I can. On the other side of the mountain, I "allow" God to guide and help me with the things which have become obviously too difficult for me to handle. Everything in my life becomes divided into "my control" and "His control".

Naturally, as naturally as being born, we arrive at the top of the mountain, demanding our independence from our Creator. And, just as naturally, we divide our lives into "mine" and "His". Our propensity to wrest control from His hands is always to our detriment. How sad we must make our Heavenly Father when we refuse to depend on His assistance of every kind in our daily lives. How different might our grey and brown lives be, how much more lush and green, if only we would look to our Father throughout the day, relying on and trusting Him instead of hoarding control.

Just as the waters flowing to the eastern slope of the Continental Divide nurture the lands they reach, so we can trust our Father's ability to care for us, producing green pastures of rest and peace. Or we can choose to dwell in the desert lands, watered sparsely by our own hands. As certainly as the waters flow over the Great Divide, east and west, so will our Father's blessings flow when we allow God's direction through His Spirit, placing *all* under His control.

"Trust in the LORD with all your heart and lean not on your own understanding; in all your ways acknowledge Him, and He will make your paths straight." Proverbs 3:5-6

"I write these things to you who believe in the name of the Son of God so that you may know that you have eternal life. This is the confidence we have in approaching God: that if we ask anything according to his will, he hears us. And if we know that he hears us---whatever we ask---we know that we have what we asked of him." 1 John 5:13-15

Squirrel!

Talking with Asher, my teenage grandson, is akin to chasing squirrels. Just when I think he is going in one direction with the conversation, his sharp wit abruptly changes the perspective, often in a most humorous twist. He has been gifted with an unusual ability to think creatively and uses dialog to flip the norms, cleverly and brilliantly. It is an enviable gift to me, who is slow-of-wit with the spoken word.

Following a lifetime of self-criticism for not being quick on my feet, I finally recognized that slowness is my strength. Where words dance in riotous order, only to spill out of Asher's mouth in awe-inspiring ways, words instead waltz through my brain, slowly and rhythmically, only onto paper. Ours are opposite gifts, apparent to everyone when we open our mouths.

Our Creator distributes natural and spiritual gifts to each individual with His ultimate plan in mind. And I have come to realize that is the beauty of God's gifts; they are magnified when we find their value through Him. And as the clay does not dictate to the potter what to make, neither should we consider ourselves unfortunate when we are not the instrument of our imaginings.

God's gifts are intended to prosper His kingdom, not our egos, nor our competitive bent, though He will sometimes use competition for our development. When we strive to be something we are not intended to be, how our Father's heart must grieve. But as we develop the gift our Father endowed, as He leads and guides us, our joy increases as our talents grow.

Through the process of growth, discipline, and refinement, God will lead us to the opportunities He desires for us. Along the way, He challenges the intent of our hearts and increases our ability to listen, learn, and grow. And I can testify that age is insignificant in the use of His gifts; as long as we are alive in Christ, we are here for His purpose and to accomplish His will through those gifts and talents.

Will we waste those gifts while chasing worldly wealth and fame? Or will we use those talents to reach those who do not know Jesus? Will we focus wholly on the One who saved us, using what we have received to bring Him honor? Or will we allow ourselves to be distracted by the squirrels, the shiny objects the world dangles in front of us? Each day has an expiration date, and the answers are in the minutes we have. Are you chasing squirrels today, or using your gift to do your Father's will?

"There are different kinds of gifts, but the same Spirit. There are different kinds of service, but the same Lord. There are different kinds of working, but the same God works all of them in all men." 1 Corinthians 12:4-6

"Each one should use whatever gift he has received to serve others, faithfully administering God's grace in its various forms." 1 Peter 4:10

As dogs are prone to do, Coco took off running as soon as she found a crack to squeeze through, onto the porch, then into the unfenced open spaces. The allure was too overwhelming, and call as I might, the wayward Maltese bolted toward the street. I called her name and took off running— the opposite direction! There was a method to my apparent madness, and sure enough, she changed course, chasing me as I ran toward the house. Though she believed she was running wild, she was actually running toward safety.

As I am prone, like every human being on earth, to do, I also tend to attempt squeezing through the cracks of boundaries God sets for me, aiming for the wide-open spaces of independence. Control is the insidious fruit we each covet, and God's boundaries, even of barest restriction, are sufficient temptation; and any open door of opportunity will suffice.

The Holy Spirit will sometimes chase me down, occasionally bringing me down in a full tackle, and still other times, lure me home ever so gently. But He will always pursue me, whether by whisper or by storm, returning me to the safe confines of His pasture. He does it jealously; the purest desire for my safety and security are His greatest concerns. There is no distance He will not traverse, no depth He will not plumb, nor temptation He will not reveal for what it is.

The enemy sets traps, and the Spirit exposes them; facades which appear solid, He will tear down. There is only one reason for Him to go to such lengths—love. Jesus expressed that love by laying His body on the cross, willingly, knowingly, purposely. He saw my need for a Savior, a rescuer, and a protector for this sheep who wanders obliviously or intentionally, in rebellion or blindness. And His grace covers it all.

Like Coco, who does not know the hawk's threat or the coyote's hunger, I rarely consider the dangers of sin, or the evils lurking in the darkness of my wanderings. Only a little smarter than my ten-pound dog, I would do well to recognize my propensity to wander. The older and more seasoned I become, I "come home" quicker, running toward His safety. Thankfully, my heavenly Father knows how I am made, calls me back faithfully, and keeps me from running wild when it counts the most.

"So, if you think you are standing firm, be careful that you don't fall! No temptation has seized you except what is common to man. And God is faithful; he will not let you be tempted beyond what you can bear. But when you are tempted, he will also provide a way out so that you can stand up under it." 1 Corinthians 10:12-13

"But each one is tempted when he is drawn away by his own desires and enticed."
James 1:14 NKJ

The Employer

My employment began at 12 years old with babysitting. At 14, I was cleaning empty apartments; and 16 squarely placed me in my first real job as a dental assistant—in training. A driven perfectionist, this was probably a poor choice, but solidified my determination early on; I did not want to be a dental assistant. It is a job requiring precision, timing, and acute anticipation of the next steps in the procedures. It also required a steady hand and a bit of confidence. A significant tolerance of blood and saliva is helpful, too. I had none of the requisites.

Dr. Roberts was an absolute saint throughout my two-year employment, perhaps sensing my need for a stable influence more than my need for a job. He gently corrected, carefully instructed, and patiently waited. His corrections were firm and clear, and his expectations defined. Above all, he was known for being kind. He was the best example of a Christian man I had witnessed in my life up to that point.

Having many jobs since then, I have been blessed that many of my employers were fair, honest, and decent people, most of them Christians; none of them perfect. There are no perfect people, but there are saints. Followers of Jesus are never perfectly completed in this lifetime; they are perfectly completed by it. Employers and employees all qualify for the process of perfection, but none attain it on this earth.

I was so blessed to have Dr. Roberts, who seemed nearly perfect in my young eyes, as an early employer, setting an example of balance and integrity. I am grateful for each of my later employers and the lessons I learned through them along the way. We all have much to learn from one another as God leads us on the paths He ordains. I am grateful to God for His plan, and presence in my life through work and employment, through the people I have met, and how God pieced it all together.

The real saint is simply a believer in Christ Jesus who acts upon that belief, who imitates Him, becoming increasingly like Him day by day. Praise God for those who willingly submit to the ultimate Employer, the perfect pattern for all employers. Jesus instructs and oversees the perfecting of our faith, weaving His plan together through imperfect people, by the power of His love, wages paid in grace.

"Whatever you do, work at it with all your heart, as working for the Lord, not for men, since you know that you will receive an inheritance from the Lord as a reward. It is the Lord Christ you are serving." Colossians 3:23-24

The Power of "Then"

A financial decision I had entrusted to the Lord years prior had worked to my benefit. However, financial times since had become more difficult and the opportunity to change my leverage was gone. I spoke aloud the desire to change that decision to the Lord. The opportunity which had been entirely impossible came in the form of a letter just three days later. I was incredulous, though I shouldn't have been. I was in awe that God would pull off such a miracle and that His timing was so impeccable.

Later, facing the finality of the decision, I was floundering. Wrestling, questioning, and doubting had me in turmoil, yet I had to acknowledge that this was exactly what I had requested. Still, I had no answer. My future finances depended on my decision. Yet, the financial world around me was unstable, with no way to reasonably predict where it would land. The only thing certain in the world at the time was uncertainty!

That morning, I stumbled upon notes from a sermon eighteen years ago, a study on Ezekiel 37, where God raised a living, breathing army of men from a valley of dry bones. Verse 14 says, **"I will put my Spirit in you and you will live, and I will settle you in your own land. <u>Then</u> you will know that I the Lord have spoken, and I have done it, declares the Lord."** I had the word "then" underlined in my Bible. And I understood at that moment that God had given me this opportunity for a reason. My "do-over" was evidence of His power and His intervention in my life. It was intended to reveal His active love and provision for me. I only needed to trust Him implicitly for direction, taking steps as He led, waiting when He said wait, acting only on the prompting of His Spirit.

Ezekiel had to decide whether he would speak to a valley of absolutely desolate bones—can you imagine how easy it would have been to doubt God??? After they stood up, it says God breathed life into them, *after* they stood. Notice that in the middle of verse 14 God says, "and I will settle you in your own land." He didn't just raise them to new life; He settled them in their own land, providing for them, too. I realized that to doubt God is to live in the valley of dry bones. On the contrary, trusting Him is to witness impossibilities overcome, new life breathed into our circumstances, all to His credit and glory.

How easy it is, in our limited understanding of God, to confine Him to our expectations. Yet He has no natural or supernatural boundaries and is contained by nothing on earth or in the heavens. When we trust God for what seems impossible to us, we are acknowledging His sovereignty, power, wisdom, and good intentions toward us. His truth will forever prevail, and His love for us will never end. His intentions toward us are always good. The real power of "then" is displayed only after we trust God and before we can see the outcome in our valley of dry bones.

One of my favorite frying pans is stainless steel with a copper core, that evenly transmits and retains the heat. It has no synthetic handle but is a "real chef's pan" with a sturdy, smooth, long handle of the same steel as the body. Once the pan is searing hot, every part of it is too hot to handle. I found out the hard way the first time I used it that an oven mitt is required to successfully lift, relocate, or turn the pan.

Like a stove-top full of piping hot pans, too many to count have been the blazing hot trials in my life. In every crushing experience of life, there was always someone who would quote the proverb, "God will not give you more than you can handle." My response to the comment was always agreement, until one day the truth settled in my soul; God will never fail to give me more than *I* can handle, and for good reason. He is not being mean, nor does He take joy in my suffering.

God knows full well that if He gives me only things I can handle, pride soon rises like the steam from the hot pan. It whispers a sultry message in my ear, "You can do this. You don't need God's help. You are in control." It is the very same message Satan whispered into Jesus's ear during His temptations. That day, the thought occurred to me, quite the revelation, that God seemed to always give me more than I felt I could handle. And I thanked Him for it.

I thanked Him because pride is the hot handle that burns deeply every time. It draws us away from our Father who loves and cares for us. God detests prideful hearts which believe they can operate independently of Him. It nudges us to act independently of Him, apart from His wisdom and rules. Pride hurts us, leading to our destruction.

From that day forward, my response to that well-intentioned comment has been, "God won't ever give me more than *HE* can handle." God desires my dependence on Him, knowing my frail condition and weaknesses as He does, and He highly esteems my trust in His abilities to provide for His children. He is not distant, but always near in our troubles. So, when life becomes too hot to handle, I try to remember that my Father acts as my oven mitt, shielding and protecting me, as only He can.

"Now I, Nebuchadnezzar, praise and exalt and glorify the King of heaven, because everything he does is right and all his ways are just. And those who walk in pride he is able to humble." Daniel 4:37

"Blessed is the man who makes the Lord his trust, who does not look to the proud, to those who turn aside to false gods." Psalm 40:4

"For I am the Lord, your God, who takes hold of your right hand and says to you, 'Do not fear; I will help you.'" Isaiah 41:13

Pinky Promise

One of my favorite aspects of parenthood has been the ability to give my children gifts, specially chosen to suit their interests and personalities. Trevor, being the only son, required stretching my imagination and journeying into realms I am not naturally inclined to explore. Some of his gifts were: Lego blocks, a real bow with flint-tipped arrows, a hobby horse and cowboy hat, a pocketknife, video games, and books about castles. On one particular birthday, gifting centered on an empty aquarium and his desire for a hermit crab.

Let's just say that my enthusiasm for the crab was nowhere near his level of interest. Allowing plenty of time to plan his special day, I arrived at the pet store a week before Trevor's birthday. I paid a deposit on the hermit crab, a sort of "pinky promise" asking that they hold it until the big day, which they happily did. When I arrived one week later to transport our newest resident to his happy new abode, I paid the balance, keeping my promise, and brought it home for Trevor's special day.

Choosing Jesus as our Savior, God has a very rare, priceless gift in mind for His children. He gives us His Holy Spirit, a deposit on the gift of eternal life through Christ Jesus. As I did for Trevor's gift, placing a deposit as a promise of return, His Spirit is deposited in us as evidence of our family membership, sealing us with His love for all time. He, who paid the price in full, gives us all the benefits of living in the Family of God, a promise kept, and payment fulfilled.

He gives natural gifts from birth, such as musical ability, athletics, inventing, writing, mechanical, etc. But He also gives us spiritual gifts intended for the building of His Church, the body of believers. He is thoughtful about each gift He gives His child, every gift tailored to the personality and plan He has purposed for us. One has the gift of speaking, someone else the gift of encouragement, one of preaching, evangelism, mercy, or healing. It delights God to give us all good gifts and delights Him more to see us use them for His glory.

Just as Trevor could not know his gift until the deposit was followed with full payment, we receive the gift of the Holy Spirit in anticipation of Jesus's return. His Spirit is the ultimate "pinky promise" of more to come.

"He anointed us, set his seal of ownership on us, and put his Spirit in our hearts as a deposit, guaranteeing what is to come." 2 Corinthians 1:21b-22

Well acquainted with fear from a young age, life didn't have to heap a large serving of challenge on my plate to trigger it. I thought for most of my life that I was pretty decent at hiding it. But as I peer down the corridor of time, I realize that may not have been accurate. I just found convenient ways to cover it up. When one of my grandchildren began dealing with fearfulness, I understood that it doesn't take a devastating trauma to instill fear. The world is well equipped to instill it in any child, without great cause, and children are inclined naturally to put their imagines into over-drive.

I thought about the fears I had had as a child, fears that lingered well into adulthood. As I look backward, some were very well-founded, but most were completely irrational. I also considered what ways my fears had lessened; some receded because experience proved them baseless, others tenaciously clung to me until, later in life, I found my solutions in Jesus. Writing my observations down, seven truths emerged:

1. *My emotions are not the truth—God's words are THE truth. Emotions can lead me astray.*
2. *My thoughts steer my emotions—Those thoughts need to be trained to align with what God says.*
3. *I can hold ANY thought, which is not the truth, captive to the power of Jesus, and He is perfectly able to destroy it!*
4. *This feeling will pass, this time will pass, this circumstance will pass.*
5. *Because Jesus supplies my needs, I can be and do who He made me be and do.*
6. *Jesus is a promise keeper.*
7. *I am deeply loved by God.*

While it takes little effort to be fearful, it seems to take quite a lot of focus and diligence to overcome fear. Learning God's word and using it to reinforce these principles has proven critical for success. Memorizing key verses is a potent weapon against the spirit of fear. The world displays a vast array of reasons for insecurity and all-out fear. However, God tells us not to accept that as our standard. When we trust His promises and believe His words, He stands up for us. When we whisper His name, however many times it takes, He shows up to calm our hearts and quiet our souls. With discipline and diligence, those seven truths become the power of Christ to overcome fear.

"So, do not fear, for I am with you; do not be afraid, for I am your God. I will strengthen you and help you; I will uphold you with my righteous right hand." Isaiah 41:10

"We demolish arguments and every pretension that raises itself up against the knowledge of God, and we take captive every thought to make it obedient to Christ." 2 Corinthians 10:5

Land of Opportunity

Growing up as a United States citizen, I have heard the description, "Land of Opportunity", all my life. It has been the vision of many an immigrant, that as a natural-born citizen I have taken much for granted. I never doubted that the "American dream" could be achieved; I saw bountiful examples in my neighborhood as I was growing up. Many were first-generation Americans with immigrant parents from Italy, Ireland, Germany, Cuba, and Poland. Most came with very few possessions but had big dreams and a willingness to sacrifice to achieve them.

Those who had dreams of success did everything within their power to capture them. They worked longer than normal hours, sacrificed time with their families to provide for them; they slept less, had fewer recreational times, no vacations, and difficult work conditions. But they assimilated to the culture, had faith in God, learned the language, and persevered. Most overcame their hardships and were able to provide well for their families, but it took a lifetime to "succeed".

God also offers an extraordinary opportunity for those who will accept it. He has offered restoration of relationship with Him, through the blood of Jesus, the sacrifice we so often take for granted. Jesus Himself stated that the faith of a little child would accomplish this great feat, such an utterly simple act; yet, many of us find it so simple that it does not make sense. Pride alone stops us dead in our tracks, refusing submission and surrender, and with them, we forfeit the peace our Father offers. Once we cross the border, though, into His kingdom, our land of opportunity is opened wide for our success.

If I made the same sacrifices for my relationship with Jesus that I witnessed immigrants make to establish new lives, my spiritual land of opportunity would overflow with blessings, as well. Time spent with the Spirit in God's word, time talking to and listening to Him, a life more focused on being like Him in action and deed, and diligently following His leading would inevitably bring success in God's kingdom.

Most of us take the easiest path, the one with the least resistance to our faith, instead of pushing forward in our new land of opportunity. What few realize is that this new life in Christ was never to be a cushy assignment. The rewards are great only when we have the courage and diligence to lay our desires and dreams at His feet, and the willingness to sacrifice all we are for all He is. Simple faith is all that is required for entrance, as the visa to enter the country; but the great success of following Jesus is achieved by discipline, persistence, and a lifetime in His land of opportunity.

"Find rest, O my soul, in God alone; my hope comes from him." Psalm 62:5

"To this end I labor, struggling with all *his* energy, which so powerfully works in me."
Colossians 1:29

On the perimeter of our property, providing a lovely backdrop for our modest home, stand many trees. The prickly cedar, an also-prickly holly, a beautiful Red Bud, a lot of pine trees, and a Corkscrew Willow are tucked into the corner—our yard is full of trees, though one would not think so at first glance. There is a giant Tulip Poplar that stands out among them all.

The Tulip Poplar towers above the rest of the tree line, making it the most conspicuous of all the trees in the yard. Its bright green, broad leaves, shaped like mittens reach in all directions, begging to be the center of attention. It was planted thirty years ago by my husband and son, anchoring its place, through storms and sun, ice and wind. When stepping into our yard, it is the one tree you will see before noticing the rest.

Adam and Eve had every kind of tree in their yard, as well. However, instead of focusing on the trees with exquisite fruits, exotic flowers, interesting shapes, and eye-popping colors, they focused only on one tree, the one forbidden to them. They could not resist the only one in thousands of trees they were not to touch. Like our Tulip Poplar standing out from the rest, they could only see one tree.

Temptation is like that one tree, seemingly irresistible, and just out of our reach. A nagging voice insists that God has something He will not share, that He is withholding something very good and desirable. Our temptation problem is a form of fear, fear that we cannot have what we want or find essential. It is an allure to take a shortcut to get what we believe God will not give. It is a mistrust of God's provision and goodness.

Every tree in the Garden was pronounced "good" by God, not one of which was denied Adam and Eve, except that one tree. The tree of knowledge of good and evil was also good, just not what God allowed for that time. God may not deny something because it is bad for us; it may simply not be the right timing. So, what do we do when God says "no"? We shift our focus from the one tree to the many. We can generally find many "trees" to be thankful for, and many blessings to focus on. And if you need just one tree, focus on Jesus Himself, the one which stands above them all, and be thankful.

"No temptation has seized you except what is common to man. And God is faithful; he will not let you be tempted beyond what you can bear. But when you are tempted, he will also provide a way out so that you can stand up under it." 1 Corinthians 10:13

"Be joyful always; pray continually; give thanks in all circumstances, for this is God's will for you in Christ Jesus." 1 Thessalonians 5:16

The Never-Ending Story September 28

I believe that it is part of our spiritual DNA, a gift from our heavenly Father, to be strongly attracted to stories. Through a well-told story, we learn the value of protecting others, building character through enduring hardship and trials, and about love. Stories, real or fictional, inspire, mold our character and expand our understanding of the world. They give us perspective on our humanness yet propel us with the hope that we can be better.

Stories have danced on musical notes, been recounted on far-sailing ships, and whispered around campfires. They have been enacted on city stages, cast among towering trees, narrated in school plays, and re-told in prison cells. They are formulated in the imaginations of children, dreamed by young men, told, and re-told countless times by the aged. Stories are treasures created by dads and moms at bedtime and passed down through generations. They last a few seconds in an advertisement, a few hours in a book, some requiring a lifetime to complete.

There is only one story that encompasses all the common threads of ours, the life story of Jesus. Jesus was conceived, God and man joined in flesh at the perfect time. He grew up in a family full of siblings, a household spilling over with joys, sorrows, hardship, and struggles to make ends meet. He experienced good memories and close ties, strained relationships, weddings and funerals, rejection, and betrayal. He learned to work in His father's carpentry business, the only carpenter in history who was also the Son of God.

He struggled against the powers of this world, lived perfectly to the end, and died the cruelest of deaths. Like every good story, His did not end there. The villain cannot win, though he may deceive, harass, and convince us to believe the lie that God is not powerful enough to save us. This happy ending had been written before time itself. And we are so precious to Him that He wrote His story with the ink of His blood. And resurrection is now credited, through His shed blood, to all who receive Him.

Often, the "happy ending" doesn't appear to be a happy one on this earth. As Christians, though, we already know the end of the story—Jesus won, therefore we win! He is the initiator of our stories and guides each plotline; He is present at our beginning and throughout our stories until the final word. And the story that we write with our lives is treasured by the One who authored each of them. In every way, His story intentionally directs us to our Father and a happy ending-without-end, heaven.

"Jesus did many other things as well. If every one of them were written down, I suppose that even the whole world would not have room for the books that would be written." John 21:25

"You yourselves are our letter, written on our hearts, known and read by everybody. You show that you are a letter from Christ, the result of our ministry, written not on tablets of stone but on tablets of human hearts." 2 Corinthians 3:2

Life on this planet has its glimmers of heaven, days when the sun shines, rainbows abound, picnics have no ants, and gain comes without pain. Then, there are the days when the rain seems never-ending, your picnic is eaten by the ants, and there is great pain with little gain in every task. There are days, and weeks, and months, and, heaven forbid, even whole years when my wisdom failed, and I found myself flat on my face.

I have had my fair share of those days over my lifetime, finding it much too tempting to look down instead of up, forgetting too easily that my heavenly Father waits to guide me. Self-pity was too easy, inward focus too enticing, and watching my own feet too captivating. I am continuing to learn the concept of "the beginning of wisdom"; it is to be found not in gazing downward but in looking up.

The beginning of wisdom is marked by a starting line, a day when the realization dawns like the sun. God defines it as "fear" of Him, a similar concept as teaching a child through loving discipline, healthy boundaries, and respect. It seems that I return to that starting line, over and over, stubbornly refusing to learn from my Father's discipline and determined to walk in my obstinate direction instead of His.

I have found that knowing Him and knowing *about* Him are worlds apart. We can know about Him from what others tell us, but the only way to *know* Him, the pattern of relationship He instituted in the beginning in the Garden of Eden, is to spend time with Him. Through His Holy Spirit, He speaks to us as we explore His letters to us in the Bible, listen to His promptings, and talking to Him through prayer. He teaches us who He is and the principles He desires us to learn.

As I have grown to know Him, these are a few of His characteristics I have come to love: Our Father is a binder of wounds, forgiver of sins, and friend to lost and forgotten sheep. He is the perfect father, provider, protector, and encourager of broken hearts. He is our shelter in storms. He treasures little children, strangers, and travelers. He is the whisperer of dreams, God of second chances, and our ultimate hope. He is just, kind, and lovely in every way.

Our Father is the birther of imagination, creativity, innovation, and dreams. I see Him in colors and numbers, music and art, the giant Redwood and tiny pearl, yet spinning a universe upon His fingertips. He is unimaginable power, all-mighty, and commands vast multitudes of angels, yet tenderly moves men's hearts. He is complete, needing nothing and no one; He does not need my love; I need His. And at His feet, gazing into His face, I find the very beginning of wisdom.

"The fear of the Lord is the beginning of wisdom, and knowledge of the Holy One is understanding. For through me your days will be many and years will be added to your life." Proverbs 9:10-11

"I keep asking that the God of our Lord Jesus Christ, the glorious Father, may give you the Spirit of wisdom and revelation, so that you may know him better." Ephesians 1:17

Anna's Friend

Anna's invisible companion, the proverbial imaginary friend, has been, for most of her young life, not just one friend but gaggles of them. She has played with them as though everyone around her lived in that imaginary realm, not understanding how her siblings and parents could be unaware of them. Carrying on conversations with these friends, her facial expressions indicated the emotion of the moment as she played "alone". Most of the imaginary friends are now outgrown, but Anna retains a vivid imagination. She carries on lively conversations with real people in great exuberance, a joy to behold.

As I contemplated how real Anna considered her imaginary friends to be, I felt I had experienced something similar in my relationship with Jesus. Jesus sometimes seems like an imaginary friend who shows up when I need Him, like a figment of my imagination. The rest of the time I keep Him hidden away in a cloud somewhere. Though we cannot see the spirit realm, it is perhaps more real than the world we can see with our eyes. When Jesus walked the earth, He demonstrated, over and over again, the reality of that truth, tearing back with His own hands the veil separating the two realms.

Spirits of darkness were cast out of people, and men, women, and children were raised to life by the very hand of God! The lame walked, leprosy, and every conceivable disease was healed; sins were forgiven, and lives were transformed by the power of God. Satan was defeated by way of the cross; Christ rose from death and tomb, splitting the curtain of the Temple from top to bottom, obliterating the barrier between God and man. He is so real!

Jesus is real whether we acknowledge Him, or we don't, whether we are aware of His presence or unaware; but oh, how much better to be aware! To be cognizant of His presence, we only need to utter His name, that powerful and wonderful name of Jesus. He is available to us all the time, not only when we "feel" it, and our fellowship can be as it originated in the Garden. There is peace in His Presence; joy and strength at His feet.

Anna is not aware just yet of this special Friend who awaits an intimate relationship with her, but I pray that she finds Him soon, the One who is not far from her at any time. I pray He will be the love of her life and the friend she was searching for all along. I pray that we, too, will each be acutely aware of His presence and friendship today.

"In the presence of the disciples Jesus performed many other miracles which have not been recorded in this book. But these which have been recorded are here so that you may trust that Jesus is the Messiah, the Son of God, and that by this trust you may have life because of who he is." John 21:30-31

"And the Scripture was fulfilled which says, 'Abraham believed God, and it was accounted to him for righteousness.' And he was called the friend of God." James 2:23 NKJV

October

Catch Me, Dad!

One of our pastors recently delivered his oldest son to the dorm of his new college. While waiting, he and his seven-year-old son walked around the campus. Discovering a high, brick, retaining wall edging the sidewalk, the boy could not resist walking the top span of bricks. His dad shadowed him on the sidewalk below when suddenly his son exclaimed, "Catch me, Dad!" He leaped into the air, flying into his father's startled arms. What he didn't know was that his father, looking up, was gazing suddenly into the sun, unable to see him at all! Amazingly, he was still able to catch him.

The child trusted in his father's ability to safely retrieve him from mid-air. That level of trust must delight our heavenly Father, as well. It is reassuring to know that our actions never surprise Him; He is never caught off guard. We, as humans, tend to limit God, seeing Him as we are, not as He is. When we read about God in the Bible, stories don't seem possible or real, but archaeology and experience will bear them out as truths and principles, revealing the character of God the Father, who intervenes in the lives of His creation.

Over seven billion people inhabit the planet and He knows each one, not solely by name or appearance, He *knows* each one. He knows the number of hairs on our heads, our thoughts before we think them, our words before we speak. He understands our weaknesses and has endowed us with our strengths. He guides our steps, establishes kings, and subdues nations. Planets and galaxies retain their places, meteors swim in an ocean of stars, and black holes reside where He has ordained. An infinite, ordered, majestic-beyond-our-imaginations God is in meticulous control, but His defining quality is love for those created in His very image, mankind.

Why does He care...why should He? I won't ever understand or fathom the answer, but I can guess that it is because God's creation of this dimension is very personal. He loves that which He conceived, created, and cares for, us who were made in His very image. We were created by Him and for His pleasure—it's personal, and it's called love; so much love that He would enter this realm, living and dying as one of us. It is love so personal that He invites us to call him "Abba, Father". When I call to Him, "Dad, catch me!" my needs will never catch Him off guard. He is the Father who loves me, and I can trust Him without fail.

"The Lord is gracious and righteous; our God is full of compassion. The Lord protects the simplehearted; when I was in great need, he saved me." Psalm 116:5-6

"You will keep in perfect peace him whose mind is steadfast, because he trusts in you." Isaiah 26:3

"For I am the Lord, your God, who takes hold of your right hand and says to you, do not fear; I will help you." Isaiah 41:13

Perfect Vision

Six months prior, I had canceled my eye surgery, intimidated by the prospect of anyone, highly qualified or not, operating on my eyes. Fear had ruled the day as I considered the horror stories of acquaintances past and talked with all-too-confident surgeons of the present. The prospect of my vision being permanently affected was daunting. Now, my vision was truly being negatively affected, and the choice loomed before me once again. With some reservation and prayer, I chose to have the surgery.

The day following my first surgery for cataract removal, I marveled at the spot of light shining on my wall. Cautiously closing my now cataract-free eye, the spot was dark and yellow-tinted. Closing the eye with the cataract intact and peering at the same spot of light, the difference startled and amazed me! It was clear, crisp, beautiful white light, and in that eye, I now had perfect vision. Instead of wishing to postpone my next surgery, I asked my surgeon if I could move the date up.

Fear had nearly robbed me of clear and perfect vision, something I had not had in twenty years. But it was not the first time I had been robbed. I can see that there have been many times in my life that I relied on my wisdom and strength, trusting my plans without consulting God about His. There were times when I was afraid of being hurt, pulling away from relationships before giving them a chance; there were relationships I should have abandoned when they were unhealthy, not trusting the nudges the Spirit of God prompted.

Fear stops us from pursuing the best God has for us when we see only our limitations. It robs us of blessings when fear overcomes trust in Him. Fear is walking in our vision instead of walking in God's perfect vision. Often, we believe that He is not involved, or is not capable, of protecting and directing us. We are saying to God, however indirectly, that He is not perfectly loving or trustworthy, setting ourselves up as more capable to make our own decisions in life than He is. And oh, how we suffer under that delusion.

We serve a magnificent God through Jesus Christ, our Lord! He is infinitely patient with His obstinate children, longing to help us, and yearning to pour out His loving kindness upon us daily. Our eyes are filled with worldly cataracts, discoloring and darkening our world, but He desires our trust and obedience so that He may remove what obstructs our view of Him—no surgery necessary for perfect spiritual vision.

"'Though the mountains be shaken and the hills removed, yet my unfailing love for you will not be shaken, nor my covenant of peace be removed, says the Lord, who has compassion on you.'" Isaiah 54:10

"This is what the Lord says: 'Let not the wise man boast of his wisdom or the strong man boast of his strength or the rich man boast of his riches, but let him who boasts boast about this: that he understands and knows me, that I am the Lord, who exercises kindness, justice and righteousness on earth, for in these I delight,' declares the Lord." Jeremiah 9:23-24

The mind of man is forever seeking shortcuts and, as I can testify after many ventures, I am not an exception. My brain seems to specialize in finding the shortcuts and solutions, and in the process, learning new skills. I have solved problems as minute as to how to hand feed a hummingbird, and as large as how to run a business, some solutions a resounding success and others a dismal failure.

One day I was completely at a loss. The website I was building crashed with every single change I attempted to initiate. Depending on the number of changes I made each day, the site crashed that many times. In one day, I tried over fifty times, spanning hours, before utter frustration caused me to cry out to God, "Why do I have to do this???" His words came in response within my spirit immediately, "You must learn to finish."

I had been excellent at initiating projects up until that point in my life, but not so hot at finishing them; I instantly knew what I was being taught. I persevered and finally came to the resource I needed, discovering that my website had been assigned to an incorrect server, which was not able to process my changes. A few weeks later, the website was complete and functional.

There is always a lesson in our delays, and the obstacles we have to overcome, our testing and trials. Most often it is an ongoing lesson that refines our characters, defines our faith, or molds us into an image quite contrary to the one the world intends for us. There are, however, rarely shortcuts to God's plans for our lives, and certainly little peace in shortcuts taken without His direction.

God's goals for us culminate in conforming us to the image of His precious Son, and we humans do not yield readily to that process. With God, the solution to our problems is Jesus; the answers to life are found in Jesus; our purposes are in Jesus; and eventually, our focus becomes only Jesus. We will find no other shortcut to heaven, or peace, without God, and there are no answers that He cannot provide.

"Jesus answered, 'I am the way and the truth and the life. No one comes to the Father except through me. If you really knew me, you would know my Father as well. From now on, you do know him and have seen him.'" John 14:6-7

His divine power has given us everything we need for life and godliness through our knowledge of him who called us by his own glory and goodness. Through these he has given us his very great and precious promises, so that through them you may participate in the divine nature and escape the corruption in the world caused by evil desires." 2 Peter 1:3-4

The Road Ahead October 4

The morning sun hadn't burned off the low-hanging dense "smoke" ahead. As it enveloped my car, I eased off the gas and slowed my descent into it. Visibility was nearly zero, but I crept ahead, not much faster than I could have walked. Suddenly, the fog lifted, and a clear road was before me. Such is travel through the foothills of the Great Smoky Mountains!

Tennessee foothills are renowned for being "smoky", which is a pleasant description for 'clouds of moisture rising at inconvenient times, especially when driving. It is a fascinating phenomenon when sitting on a porch overlooking the hills. It becomes a deadly cloak of gray when driving the curvy roads, happening at unexpected times. It is only the sun that disperses the stubborn clouds clinging to the densely foliaged hills.

Many are the days I have also been bewildered by the fog obstructing my path, as I have traveled my spiritual road with Jesus over the years. Life seemed to run unhindered, then suddenly a roadblock appeared; my path was unclear and progress, in my eyes, slowed to a crawl. Many of those clouds were unpleasant at the time, but I can say that each one taught me to be more dependent on Jesus. Each taught me that He is trustworthy, loving, and strong enough to meet my needs.

Recently, three of my grandchildren were baptized. I wondered what message I could give them about following Jesus. This is my conclusion: When the road ahead of you is dense with fog and uncertainty causes you to balk, back off the gas a bit and trust the Guide, to whom you committed your life. The Son can lift the fog; and if not, He has a reason for slowing your plan. Watch closely, listen softly, and follow Jesus intimately. It is the Son who disperses the fog and brings clarity to our lives on the road ahead.

"But I trust in your grace, my heart rejoices as you bring me to safety. I will sing to the Lord, because he gives me even more than I need." Psalm 13:6

"Find rest, O my soul, in God alone; my hope comes from him." Psalm 62:5

"When Jesus spoke again to the people, he said, 'I am the light of the world. Whoever follows me will never walk in darkness, but will have the light of life.'" John 8:12

"This is a test of the Emergency Broadcast System..." The announcement interrupted the song on the radio, followed by the high-pitched squeal, signaling that the actual broadcast test was commencing. Breaking into the regularly scheduled programming on radio and television, the test assures the readiness of the Emergency Broadcast System; established by the government to alert citizens of a natural disaster or national emergency.

God reminded me that He also uses a test system, utilizing daily tests and trials to prove our character and willingness to follow Him. He tells us specifically in 1 Thessalonians 2:4 that it is He who tests our hearts. It reminds us that God tested Paul in his travels, Moses as he led rebellious people for a generation, and even Jesus in the desert. He tested Joseph in prison, Abraham's resolve to leave his home as God directed, and Noah's steadfast obedience as he followed the instructions for the ark. God tested kings and prophets, priests and shepherds, warriors and women.

The purpose of the test is to purify our hearts and motives. It can be to prove our trust in our Savior, and sometimes, even to show us the strength of our faith. The bottom line of God's emergency testing system is to reinforce our trust in a Sovereign Lord who can use any circumstance in our lives to grow and refine us, molding us into the image of His precious son, Jesus. Testing is one of God's ways of teaching us to focus our attention on Him.

As we face the tests of today, the difficulties, trials, and hardships, let us keep our focus on the One who can deliver us, if necessary. But let us also trust that if we are not delivered immediately, our Father may have a purpose through the pain. Today, quietly whispered in your spirit, you may hear, "My child, this is a test..." Just remember that though the place of testing is sometimes lonely, He never leaves us alone in it.

"The crucible for silver and the furnace for gold, but the Lord tests the heart." Proverbs 17:3

"I know, my God, that you test the heart and are pleased with integrity." I Chronicles 29:17

"But he knows the way that I take; when he has tested me, I will come forth as gold." Job 23:10

"On the contrary, we speak as men approved by God to be entrusted with the gospel. We are not trying to please men, but God, who tests our hearts." I Thessalonians 2:4

Under Fire

Any day's news cycle is mostly bad news, but on this day, it seemed especially so. Bibles were being burned in Portland, a hurricane was skirting up the east coast, and voices advocating truth were being silenced. Churches in some states were banned from opening, which I never expected to see in the United States in my lifetime. Riots continued for months in major cities, murders and suicides were escalating, Humanity itself appeared to be under fire.

In my lifetime, all these things have never occurred simultaneously and globally. And the aforementioned events don't even include the natural disasters happening globally in the past few months. Massive thousand-year record-breaking floods, volcanoes, earthquakes, fires, and billions of locusts in devastating swarms have frequented the continents. Significant numbers of travelers have been stranded away from home and country, my son included.

Reminding myself that these sorts of things have happened throughout history is little consolation. Though indeed true that these events have always been part of a broken world, a new intensity that I have not witnessed in my lifetime is clear, and I have lived through more than a few wars and pestilence. I found myself discouraged and losing hope. And that was the telltale sign that I had placed my hope in the world more than the Savior.

Finding my hope in Jesus, rather than a fallen world requires me to shift my focus from the events around me to the One who has overcome them. My "center", my peace, and hope are found in my God and King, Jesus. No matter what storm swirls around me. I can rest in the knowledge that Jesus Himself predicted that this would all take place. Still, He offered us His peace and presence in it, and in the end, I remind myself that I am not alone, that God loves me and is adequate to meet my needs, even amid upheaval and turmoil. I can stand strong in my faith, offer hope to others, and help where He shows me to help. I can be strong, not because I am but because He is. His orders to His followers have not changed: Have faith and trust in Him, reach others with the Good News. We are to hold our ground, even while under fire.

"How great is your goodness, which you have stored up for those who fear you, which you have wrought for those who take refuge in you, before the sons of men! You hide them in the secret place of Your presence from the conspiracies of man; you keep them secretly in a shelter from the strife of tongues." Psalm 31:19-20 NASB

"For our struggle is not against flesh and blood, but against the rulers, against the authorities, against the powers of this dark world and against the spiritual forces of evil and the heavenly realms." Ephesians 6:12

A perfect mother I was not, but I never wished away one minute of my time with my babies, not once in all the night feedings, sickroom fevers, or temper tantrums. Neither in preparing their meals or tending to mountains of laundry did I long for them to be grown. With their scraped knees, bicycle accidents, surgeries, and tears I didn't yearn for them to advance to independence more quickly. You may not believe it, but I longed for school vacations to stretch a bit longer, for time to slow ever so slightly, so that I could savor the time I sensed would soon dissipate.

I didn't hurry them to grow up, neither did I attempt to hinder or hold them back. There was an innate sense of limited time with my children. I loved these little personalities God had entrusted to my heart and hands. We cannot understand the rapid passing of time until we are on the opposite side of it, glancing furtively back at what we can never retrieve.

Growth and maturity are God's plan for children, and babies are, by nature, intended to grow up. It is a parent's privilege and responsibility not only to meet the physical needs of their children but to provide an environment of challenges and support that brings them to full maturity. Children grow into functioning adults, able to handle the challenges of life, making mature decisions, marrying, and having children of their own. This is a family following God's original pattern.

As Christians, we follow a similar pattern: We are born again into God's kingdom through Christ Jesus, nibble on baby food as spiritual infants, graduate to table food as we grow a bit, mature into youth as we understand God's word more, then multiply as we share Jesus with others. God does not leave us as babies any more than a loving parent would wish to constrain her baby in infancy. He desires for us to stretch and grow, maturing into adulthood.

Many of us expect life in Christ to hold fewer obstacles, trials, and burdens. We expect a smooth path and a level road. It is not so, nor was it intended to be. God knew even before I was born that a path like that would have yielded a spoiled, self-centered brat, poorly representing my heavenly Father in this world. Each trial, each disciplining, and every hurdle has been carefully calculated to strengthen and refine this strong-willed child. Though not quite "all grown up", I better understand, as most adult children do, the sacrificial love of my Father's patient and kind heart, as I am transformed to resemble Him more each day.

"Endure hardship as discipline; God is treating you as sons. For what son is not disciplined by his father? If you are not disciplined (and everyone undergoes discipline), then you are illegitimate children and not true sons. Moreover, we have all had human fathers who disciplined us and we respected them for it. How much more should we submit to the Father of our spirits and live! Our fathers disciplined us for a little while as they thought best, but God disciplines us for our good, that we may share in his holiness. No discipline seems pleasant at the time, but painful. Later on, however, it produces a harvest of righteousness and peace for those who have been trained by it." Hebrews 12:7-11

Framed

Dreading trekking about in the rain, I finally flipped the hood of my raincoat over my head and dashed to my car. Slipping my amber-lensed sunglasses on, the autumn colors popped alive as if magically activated. As I drove the twisting, hilly roads, the colors of fall, mediocre this year, were now washed clean of the lingering dust of drought and intensified by the rain. The vivid crimsons, golds, and tangerines adorned branches hesitant to release them to winter coming.

As I rounded each bend, my mind was framing photographic possibilities with each curve. One of the last curves on my trip homeward revealed a particularly interesting frame. Of the many trees, one shadowy, dark, tree reached an extended branch over the road, completely to the opposite side, as if narrowing my view to the exquisite colors beyond it, intensifying the beauty of the road before me. That tree became the frame, with no leaves of its own, to the beauty beyond, glistening in the soaking rain.

What a lovely and peaceful picture it was! I sighed as I drove slowly beneath that sheltering limb, reluctantly surrendering the view to the rest of my day. I marvel at the simple gifts God gives me in a day, and they are many; but it is so easy to miss them, to overlook the gifts because they are in the rain. God is generous and good, even in the dreary days when we are hurried, and not much in tune with the blessings of beautiful views. He is merciful and kind, even when I am unappreciative and quick to move on with my plans.

Perhaps, because I am a photographer at heart, my mind sees photographic opportunity in many ordinary everyday activities. What a blessing I have found that to be! Each "frame" becomes a chance to be grateful, to thank God, and acknowledge those little gifts revealing His beauty and creativity. With whatever talents He has given us, I believe we are given opportunities to know Him better through them, to see the world uniquely through that viewpoint. It is all intended to bring God glory and honor, praise for who He is. He is infinitely creative and wonderful, generous, and loving to all His creation.

"Give thanks to the Lord, call on his name; make known among the nations what he has done. Sing to him, sing praise to him; tell of all his wonderful acts. Glory in his holy name; let the hearts of those who seek the Lord rejoice." 1 Chronicles 16:8-10

"Shout for joy to the Lord, all the earth. Worship the Lord with gladness; come before him with joyful songs. Know that the Lord is God. It is he who made us, and we are his, we are his people, the sheep of his pasture. Enter his gates with thanksgiving and his courts with praise; give thanks to him and praise his name. For the Lord is good and his love endures forever; his faithfulness continues through all generations." Psalm 100

The transmission towers for our electric grid are not difficult to spot in the area surrounding our city. Quite a swath must be cut through the dense foliage to erect them, and they are unavoidably visible on the forested hills. Carrying high-voltage electricity, they span the distances between the power generation plants and customers, for which I am very grateful. A blight on the landscape at heights around 100 feet or more, those lines become a blessing when powering up my appliances and lights.

The power, made available to us through those lines, marks the dramatic difference between "have" cultures and "have not" cultures. Electrical power determines job availability, food preservation, communications, hospital operations, and nearly every facet of our daily lives. We use it to dry our hair, wash our clothes, cook our meals, entertain our imaginations, pay our bills, and light our nights. Try living without it for just a few days, and you will soon discover your total dependence on it.

Considering the power of an electric switch, I marvel at my reluctance to use what is at my fingertips, sometimes working in low light, oblivious to the electricity at my disposal. I find myself doing the same thing with God, often resisting calling upon Him. It is as if I will waste His power on something trivial, or worse, believing I can get by without His power.

Often, I find myself in utter denial about His abilities to help me, subtly denying His power to alter circumstances; or rejecting His power to change me, heal me, or to speak to me. I have, in the past, run from His power to forgive me, and hidden from His power to enable me to do what He has called me to do. My power line is often cut by the very one who needs it most, me.

Unlike the power of electricity, which pales in God's presence—like a July 4th sparkler in the vastness of deepest space—God's power is unlimited. It is always available to those who love Him and seek to do His will. Most often, we do not have because we do not ask, believing God is impotent, or unavailable; few of us grasp that all things are possible to him who believes. Accessing His power requires knowing the Heavenly Father through Christ Jesus but is granted through the power line of asking and trusting.

"I keep asking that the God of our Lord Jesus Christ, the glorious Father, may give you the Spirit of wisdom and revelation, so that you may know him better. I pray also that the eyes of your heart may be enlightened in order that you may know the hope to which he has called you, the riches of his glorious inheritance in the saints, and his incomparably great power for us who believe." Ephesians 1:17-19a

"' But if you can do anything, take pity on us and help us.' '" If you can"?' said Jesus. 'Everything is possible for him who believes.' Immediately the boy's father exclaimed, 'I do believe; help me overcome my unbelief!'" Mark 9:22b-24

The Gold Standard

A flash of brilliant yellow caught my eye as I passed the window. Immediately, I backed a few steps to recapture the glint of gold, discovering two American Gold Finches perched on a dog run-line outside the glass. The female busily explored the pulley, turning nearly upside-down with curiosity, pecking at the line, while the more beautiful, brightly colored male sat patiently watching. I marveled again at the brilliant color of the male with his clear, bright yellow body and bold black markings. He was quite the contrast to the drab olive green and dull yellow of the female.

I inquired of God, as I have innumerable times, asking like a small child, why. "Why, Lord, did you make the males so outstanding and the females so plain?" The answer came at once, shocking me with its swiftness, "The male's daring color enables him to draw attention to himself, and thereby protect the female." They are perfectly created to suit their roles on this planet.

God made all creation perfectly, and we can barely imagine its original splendor. What a contrast this sin-ridden world must be to the lush, exquisite garden of beauty God originally designed and constructed! Yet, what we have in store for us in Christ Jesus causes all else to pale in comparison, even to the original Garden of Eden. Imagine that one day there will be no need for a male to protect a female, or a female to protect her offspring. There will be no tears, no sickness, no sadness, and no sin.

It will be a world restored to perfection, new and without blemish. It will be a world possible through the life, death, and resurrection of the King of Glory. It is a future home so incredibly beautiful and perfect that without risen bodies, we could not withstand the glory of it. It is a home bathed in the light of the Risen Lamb. It is the gold standard of all God's creation, glistening in His glory, and vibrant in His Presence. It is the home awaiting each child of the Father, born in Christ.

Thank you, Lord, for the perfection of your plan and the beauty of your creation, now and in the world to come! Thank you for your "gold standard", your risen Son, Jesus.

"Then I saw a new heaven and a new earth, for the first heaven and the first earth had passed away, and there was no longer any sea. I saw the Holy City, the new Jerusalem, coming down out of heaven from God, prepared as a bride beautifully dressed for her husband. And I heard a loud voice from the throne saying, 'Now the dwelling of God is with men, and he will live with them. They will be his people and God himself will be with them and be their God. He will wipe every tear from their eyes. There will be no more death or mourning or crying or pain, for the old order of things has passed away. He who was seated on the throne said, 'I am making everything new!' Then he said, 'Write this down, for these words are trustworthy and true.'"   Revelation 21:1-5

Protected and Perfected

In a mere six months, countless challenges seemed to arise, from having the flu to our neighbor's tree unexpectedly landing in our yard. Flooding of nearly every variety saturated my home on four different occasions, my dog died, and my son was stranded in a country halfway across the globe. My car was whacked with a stray golf ball, a pandemic galloped across the globe, and a rather large snake visited where it was not welcome. There was more, but you get the picture—my year had its challenges!

A day of discouragement ensued, and I wondered whether God heard my pleas for help, knowing full well that He did. Then I read a passage I had written in my journal years prior: "Today, as so many times before, You have shown me that you are always listening to your children, that You are all-knowing, and that You do communicate with us. It has happened too many times to be coincidental or even accidental. Your ears, Lord, are perfectly attuned to the prayers of Your children.

Thank you, Lord, that even as I prayed, pouring forth the ugliness of my doubt, condemned by guilt over the attitude of my heart, you did not condemn me. As I prayed, I knew I needed someone to confess these things to, someone who would understand, and You brought a face to mind. At that very moment, that precious friend called! You had spoken my name to her, Lord, and she responded obediently. You are compassionate, as your Word says in Psalm 145:8, 'The Lord is gracious and compassionate, slow to anger and rich in love.' Thank you, Lord, for Judy."

Through all the trials challenges we face, our heavenly Father does not condemn us but reaches out to us through His Holy Spirit, seeking to give guidance and comfort. He asks us to persevere and not give up, but He never leaves or forsakes us. He sends help when we need it, listens when we are struggling, and encourages us when we are lonely. And along the way, He allows us to face challenges, because we cannot grow in grace or trust without them.

Life often feels like more than we can handle, even with the help of others, and especially when no help seems near. But God is faithful to hear our pleas and send, even unrequested, assistance; just as He heard my cry and sent Judy, nothing is beyond His ability or timing. He is compassionate and kind to His children, even as He is protecting and perfecting us.

"The Lord is gracious and compassionate, slow to anger and rich in love. The Lord is good to all; he has compassion on all he has made. The Lord is near to all who call on him, to all who call on him in truth. He fulfills the desires of those who fear him; he hears their cry and saves them." Psalm 145:8-9, 18-19

Fine China

The home in which I grew up had nothing resembling "fine china". The everyday dishes were used whether we had guests or not. Setting up my new household after marriage, we were given a few pieces of china, which were never enough for more than two guests; therefore, rarely used. My opinion of china at that time was that it was pretty useless, but that changed as I entered my later mid-life crisis, believing I had missed out on an important rite of passage—that of selecting a china pattern that I couldn't live without.

So, for many birthdays, Christmases, and Mother's Days, my family would contribute to my wish list, aka registry, from the local china dealer. In but a few years, my reserve would easily accommodate place settings for up to twelve people; and lovely china graced the table for a short time. That was until grandchildren arrived in sufficient numbers to outpace china's usefulness. Paper and plastic once again ruled the day. My all-important china remained stacked in place, awaiting the Christmas Eve dinner celebrating Jesus' birth and the Easter dinner proclaiming His resurrection.

In retrospect, though I enjoy those events and still find my china a pleasant thing to have, it was silly to desire such a temporal and unnecessary thing as that. However, when I contemplated selling it, I just couldn't do it. Each piece of that china had been a gift of love, something valued because of the giver, not so much the gift itself. So, I hang on my wall the beautiful plates and now use them more frequently, not just when company comes to dine. Its lovely butterfly-patterned pieces grace my table every season. Its memories are priceless, and it continues to have special uses in my home.

Contemplating my china, I reflected upon what Paul wrote in 2 Timothy; that if we keep ourselves pure, we are special utensils for honorable use, ready for the Master's good work. Like fine china, we are set apart for special purposes, God's work. The everyday dishes are useful, but it is the china that is handled with special care.

And who would set the table with dirty china??? It would go back to the kitchen for cleaning before being set on the table of the Master. In such a way, we too strive to keep our lives free from sin so that we can be used for God's purpose. Wherever He has placed us on His table, we reflect His love, mercy, and forgiveness. We are God's fine china in a broken world.

"In a wealthy home some utensils are made of gold and silver, and some are made of wood and clay. The expensive utensils are used for special occasions, and the cheap ones are for everyday use. If you keep yourself pure, you will be a special utensil for honorable use. Your life will be clean, and you will be ready for the Master to use you for every good work."
2 Timothy 2:20-21 NLT

There seems to be an app for everything lately, and one of the most interesting yet popped up on my phone recently. On it, the armies in the world are on full display, touting the lethal capabilities of their special forces. These days, even local police departments have their elite division of specially trained officers, tactical teams functioning more like paramilitary instead of police. I never hear much about their negotiating skills, but their impressive weaponry is always on display, and their willingness to use it, never questioned.

Potential enemies are never in short supply! In this world, even for those of us who abide lawfully, finding an enemy is never too difficult. We don't even need to look as far as nations, in most cases. An enemy can pop up through a misunderstanding or an unintentional affront. Our neighborhoods can become battlegrounds. Playgrounds and school hallways can give rise to bullies. We can discover an enemy even in our own families.

The fact is that this world is neither fair nor good. People cause friction, division, and sometimes wars; the truth is rare, deceit rampant, and selfishness abounds. People do unkind, occasionally even intentionally unkind things to upset or wound us. Even our own minds can deceive us into slapping the "enemy" label on someone who has offended us, whether the offense was real or not.

The unseen enemy, Satan, is the most dangerous enemy the world has ever known. He is the thief who comes to kill, steal, destroy, and by any means possible. His forces of hell delight in creating division, pain, and suffering; he especially takes great pleasure in pitting people against one another. We are all, at some time in our lives, victims of the war. But in the end, the forces of evil are no match against God's power.

In a time of strife, it is difficult to remember that the forces coming against us pale by comparison to the overcoming power of God's love through Christ Jesus. Whether our enemies are small or large, imagined or real, there is only one Special Force who can guide us through the conflict, heal our wounds, and comfort our souls. The final sentence in Romans 12 succinctly summarizes the solution God offers to the evil we encounter: "Don't let evil conquer you but conquer evil by doing good." And remember above all: God wins in the end, but He is also our Special Force in the middle!

"Do not repay anyone evil for evil. Be careful to do what is right in the eyes of everybody. If it is possible, as far as it depends on you, live at peace with everyone. Do not take revenge, my friends, but leave room for God's wrath, for it is written: 'It is mine to avenge; I will repay,' says the Lord. On the contrary: 'If your enemy is hungry, feed him; if he is thirsty, give him something to drink. In doing this, you will heap burning coals on his head.' Do not be overcome by evil but overcome evil with good." Romans 12:17-21

From the sidelines, I watched as two-year-old Hannah probed her mother's skirt for the pockets which were not there. Hannah voiced her request, "Give me candy!" Her mother replied that she didn't have pockets or candy. Her demand for the sweet treat before supper had failed.

Persistent two-year-old that she was, she targeted her dad next and trotted into the kitchen. Her daddy's leg received a firm tug as he talked on the phone. "Me want candy!" she demanded, but daddy's response was worse than mama's; he ignored her completely. Her persistence deepened to an all-out war for candy, as she cried, appealing for reconsideration. I am happy to report that Hannah lost to the wise counsel of her parents.

My observation of this event brought me to an unsettling conclusion, despite the happy ending, for everyone but Hannah. I often find myself approaching my heavenly Father the same way, persistently and selfishly asking for what *I want*. I focus on situations and things instead of admiration for *the One* who gives *all good things*. He is also the One who withholds them when it is not in our best interest, or timing, to have them.

Hindsight is certainly a valuable tool, in this respect. Many times, I have made petitions for God to supply a need, but felt God left my prayer unanswered; looking back, I can see that the answer I desired would have been detrimental at the time. The answers to other petitions were longer in coming than I had wished, but in the grand scheme, ended up perfectly timed. Other prayers were never apparently answered at all, like the prayer for healing up until the day of my husband's passing; only in eternity will I see God's hand in that denial of my request.

We do not possess God's omniscience, nor His wisdom, to determine which requests should be granted, or in what timing. His plan for each of our lives is His secret, one which is only revealed to us as He deems appropriate. God the Father gave all authority to His Son, the son who loved us with His very life. We can trust His judgment and wisdom, rest in His timing and love; or insist on our way, like two-year-old Hannah. The candy "on-demand", may seem sweet for the moment, but the meal is far more satisfying in the end.

"I keep asking that the God of our Lord Jesus Christ, the glorious Father, may give you the Spirit of wisdom and revelation, so that you may know him better. I pray also that the eyes of your heart may be enlightened in order that you may know the hope to which he has called you, the riches of his glorious inheritance in the saints, and his incomparably great power for us who believe." Ephesians 1:17-19

"I know what it is to be in need, and I know what it is to have plenty. I have learned the secret of being content in any and every situation, whether well fed or hungry, whether

living in plenty or in want. I can do everything through him who gives me strength…And my God will meet all your needs according to his glorious riches in Christ Jesus."
Philippians 4:12-13, 19

Cup without a Handle

One of my favorite cups is a straight-sided, thin-walled porcelain mug with colorful thin stripes set in a vertical pose, sporting a perfectly balanced handle. It fits snugly into my hand, adequate without excess. It usually remains hidden away, saved for special moments. It is not a cup of great worth except that it does, simply by its existence, make the ordinary moments special to me. Its twin met its demise a while ago when its handle was broken, rendering it useful for practically nothing but a pencil holder.

Considering the difference between the two, I concluded that I had little use for another pencil holder and discarded the damaged cup. The remaining twin resumed its place of honor on the top shelf, out of common reach or thought. And here is where my day intersected with God's design. The cup without a handle had other uses, but its uses became limited, its value in my kitchen lessened, while the intact cup took the place of honor.

Such is the kingdom of God. The cup is each person, equipped with a special purpose in life by his Creator, fit for a place in God's plan for this world. By rejecting redemption through His Son, we remain broken. God doesn't discard us, but we disqualify ourselves from use in His kingdom when we reject His plan. His desire is for us to come to Him in our brokenness and find wholeness.

The "cup" yielded to Him finds special warmth and favor through Jesus, and in the working of the Holy Spirit, a place in God's family and plan. It is a position the world scorns, but God values highly, a place of honor on the highest shelf, treasured and adored. The heart yielded to Him recognizes that it was purchased by the King of Kings at an excruciating price and with unfathomable love, such as the world cannot grasp. The cups on the King's shelf have purpose and fit exquisitely into His plan of use, none wasted or neglected.

Our cup may not appear perfectly suited to the Kingship of Jesus to those around us, but in His eyes, there is only tenderness, acceptance, and wholeness. Our broken parts are mended without trace of a flaw when viewed under His gaze. What we bring to Him, surrendering to His hands, is used to His glory. You may appear to be a cup without a handle to some, but to God, your surrendered heart and unique creation transform you into the cup perfectly suited to His taste.

"May God himself, the God of peace, sanctify you through and through. May your whole spirit, soul, and body be kept blameless at the coming of our Lord Jesus Christ. The one who calls you is faithful and he will do it." I Thessalonians 4:18

"The Spirit of the Sovereign LORD is on me, because the LORD has anointed me to proclaim good news to the poor. He has sent me to bind up the brokenhearted, to proclaim freedom for the captives and release from darkness for the prisoners…" Isaiah 61:1

A highly dysfunctional young woman from a very dysfunctional family had graduated high school and was entering college. She wasn't entering college as much as she was running away from home, and college was the most reasonable place to hide. Her wounds persisted throughout college and followed her into marriage, pushing her new husband to the brink of abandoning her, as she was certain he would. Three babies later, they barely held their family together. This runaway, emotional train wreck, strewing ruin in her wake, was me.

And this is what changed: When I accepted Jesus as my God and Savior, His peace settled into my soul. Hope arose, and despair gradually evaporated. There was only one "catch" as I understood it, and that was that He required total surrender. A pretty big "catch"! Clinging to past excuses was taboo, fear of lack was not allowed, and complete trust was essential. Gradually, I would come to experience the unconditional acceptance I could not imagine as a runaway. Fear, of every sort, was eventually subdued.

Here is the caveat: All the changes; all the growth; the depth and subtleties of a relationship take time. I felt frustrated with my progress, not satisfied with myself or my Father until I realized that I had all the time in the world, at least God's time for me in this world. The transformations of discipleship are nuanced, and the modeling of spiritual children into adults, just as with natural children, are executed over many years. I am in a hurry, but He is not.

My temptation is to run away and to hide from God as Adam and Eve did, but that is not what God desires for us. Running from God leads to our destruction, not restoration to our relationship with Him. This Father God who loves us so much is not limited by time, not put off by our past; He does not dwell on our imperfections or reject us because of our sins. Jesus did not run away from sacrificing Himself for us. He walked to the cross and willingly laid Himself upon it for the sake of this runaway child. He runs *to* us in our deepest needs.

So, when you feel you are broken, not good enough, have wounds beyond healing, or sins beyond forgiving, say this out loud, like I do: "I am not worthy, but Jesus is. And because He loves me, I will not be rejected. I will not run away, either." Running to my Father's arms, this "runaway" has run home instead.

"Now this is eternal life: that they may know you, the only true God and Jesus Christ, whom you have sent." John 17:3

"The Lord is righteous in all his ways and loving toward all he has made. The Lord is near to all who call on him, to all who call on him in truth. He fulfills the desires of those who fear him; he hears their cry and saves them. The Lord watches over all who love him, but all the wicked he will destroy." Psalm 145:17-21

When the world portrays God or His kingdom, one can be sure that it was inevitably distorted, and angels are no exception. The world's portrayal of angels would have us believe they are babies, or distinctly feminine; harmless creatures whose function is cute and inoffensive, imaginary, and speechless. How contradictory to God's word I have found the world's perception to be!

With only a limited study, I was able to find a lengthy list of characteristics these "mighty creatures who do God's bidding" possess:
Angels are mighty (Revelation 10:1) **and strong** (Acts 12:7). **They take their directions from God** (Numbers 20:16), **relay messages and commands from the Lord** (1Chronicles 21:18). **Angels attend to the affairs of heaven and do the will of God.Angels have supernatural powers** (Acts 12), **are charged to protect** (Psalm 91:11), **rescue people** (Acts 5:19), **and bring comfort** (Luke 1:30), **but they are not all-knowing** (1 Peter 1:12).**Angels can speak to people** (Genesis 16:9) and **appear to people** (Luke 1:26-37, and many more). **They have names** (Luke 1:26). **They are spirits** (Hebrews 1:14), **they were created by God and belong to Him** (Matthew 16:27). **They are holy** (Acts 10:22) **and are before the Father in constant praise** (Psalm 103:20, 148:2).

With all that angels are, there are also some things that they are decidedly not:
Though God's angels are imitated by Satan and his forces (2 Corinthians 11:14), **angels all originated in heaven. Satan and his followers rebelled against God's authority and were cast out, what we recognize as demons** (Matthew 25:41, Psalm 78:49). **Angels are of two camps, God's and Satan's, and cannot act independently of their directives;** one loves and serves God, the other is evil and hates God. **Jesus did not come to save the angels; their fate was decided long ago and cannot be changed. He came to save mankind** (Matthew 25:41, Hebrews 2:14). **They cannot separate us from the love of God in Christ Jesus** (Romans 8:38).

By no means can I deduce that angels are passive, un-directed, child-like beings. On the contrary, they are mighty, powerful creatures who act only upon directions from God, and they serve Him for the welfare of men. And this is where we would do well to pay close attention; we have an enemy who wages war against us with utmost hatred simply because God loves us. Though we cannot underestimate the power formed against us, we should gain strength knowing that God's power always prevails.

Conquering death, Jesus defeated Satan's power over men. He alone is the reason good will prevail against evil in the end. I long for the day of Satan's eternal bondage, the collapse of his kingdom, and the day the reign of the Lord will be complete! And, for those of us who live in Christ, how thankful I am that God directs these wondrous creatures for our welfare while we live in enemy territory. Jesus's death and resurrection power are what set the two worlds apart.

Her great-great-granddaughter, Bryn, was gifted with a lovely voice, but my grandmother was not. Every Sunday when we went to church with my grandparents, snickers multiplied as Gram sang the hymns with all her heart. We children were hard-pressed to contain our outright laughter, I am now sad to admit. It never hindered Gram in any way, though, as she boldly sang what rested in her heart, praise to her Savior. She may have exuded pride in her appearance, but she sang with humility, loudly.

Gram did not allow the opinions of others, or the view of herself, to get in the way of her relationship with Jesus, not that I could see. Saturday evenings found her sitting on her bed with her Bible and Sunday school lesson spread across her lap, preparing her heart. Every day of the week for her and my grandfather was a lesson in prayer, generosity, and helping others. They lived humble, quiet lives with steadfast service, not for themselves but to God.

I will admit to pride hindering me greatly in the past, not for my beautifully gifted voice, which I have not. Pride's pitfalls for me have been connected to people-pleasing, that insidious tendency to allow their opinions of me to shape my decisions. I don't believe any of us desire to be marginalized, belittled, or looked down upon but eventually, the realization dawns that pride is world-dependent, while humility is God-dependent.

Centering my sense of worth on what anyone on this earth thinks of me places me in a very tenuous position. In doing so, I place my trust in someone other than God, essentially elevating that person to the status of God. Eventually, I understood that it is far preferable to suffer weakness than to walk in arrogance and pride. In my inadequacies and dependence on Him, God promised to lift me up in His timing, while walking in pride assures my downfall.

Asking the Father to reveal pride in my life has yielded rather startling revelations, eyes opened wider to my own, and other people's pride. I cannot say that I have thoroughly learned it yet, but in yielding to and trusting God, progress marches ahead one step at a time. Only through the Gospel of Jesus, and understanding the humility of God becoming flesh, can we find a humble heart. The only Voice that matters is the still, small Voice in which He whispers His love to our hearts.

"How blessed the man who trusts in the Lord and does not look to the arrogant or to those who rely on things that are false." Psalm 40:5

"And those who walk in pride he is able to humble." Daniel 4:37

"When pride comes, then comes disgrace, but with humility comes wisdom." Proverbs 11:2

Highest Frequency October 19

Not an expert in electrical frequencies, I cannot explain why sitting in my office chair, I can swivel slightly left and hear a buzzing sound, then swivel right and hear silence. After closing my eyes and trying again, I got the same results, and many times since. The current flowing through the overhead light becomes audible to me, a steady drone that is barely audible as I sit still in my chair; and so consistent that it goes unnoticed throughout the day.

It is common for all creation to tune out that which is not important, like that audible drone. Now, I am not comparing God in any way to a "drone", but I find that many times during the day I tend to tune out His voice in favor of the activity at hand. My frequency is attuned to the world around me; I am too busy with "important" things to pause, listen, and turn my attention to what His Spirit is speaking to my heart.

We presume a lot with God. I am convinced that we miss much of the relationship God desires with us because of our presumptions. It is too easy to believe that God cannot possibly be interested in the mundane details of our days; that He is too busy to take interest in the seemingly insignificant workings of our lives. We act as if He is interested in only "religious" interaction, yet Jesus related to everyday people on a very personal level, during everyday activities. We attempt to restrain God according to our perceptions of Him.

What I have found instead is, that while God is vastly greater than all we can imagine, He is also vastly more intimate than we can imagine. He is desirous of an unimaginable closeness with His people, more than we can fathom. Jesus Himself said that His Father would send the Holy Spirit to tell us about *all that belongs to the Father*. His greatest desire is for us to *love* and *know* Him, and that "knowing" goes far beyond what religion can provide. As we yield our minds, wills, and hearts to Him, He interacts with us very personally in our daily lives, as much as we will allow. In tune with Him, our lives are lived on His "frequency", the highest, and most desirable, frequency of the universe.

"But when he, the Spirit of truth, comes, he will guide you into all truth. He will not speak on his own: he will speak only what he hears, and he will tell you what is yet to come. He will bring glory to me by taking from what is mine and making it known to you. All that belongs to the Father is mine. That is why I said the Spirit will take from what is mine and make it known to you." John 16:13-15

Untangled October 20

It was nearly midnight and I was exhausted. As I prepared for bed, I started to put my earrings away, along with a piece of jewelry my brother had given me. It was valuable to me since it had been my mother's, so I thought it best to put it in a safer place. I rarely go to my jewelry box—priceless gems are not in great supply at my house—so it hadn't been opened in several years. I was surprised to find what was inside—a tangled mess!

It wasn't just one necklace with a knot in the chain, it was *four* very fine chains tangled together in a combined knot about the size of a nickel. What a mess! I vaguely remembered giving up in exasperation and closing the lid on them years earlier. As I gazed wearily on that tightly woven knot, I thought, "That's me—one tangled, ugly mess." And the words I heard in my spirit were, "Untangle it."

Midnight is not my best time of day and I only wanted to climb into bed, but I began...gently lifting, separating, draping strands delicately over several fingers and making little headway. I heard Him say, "Keep going."

Memories from each strand began bobbing to the surface: This was the one Gary added beads to on each of my birthdays. This was the one he gave me on an anniversary when we had little money. This one came from a store I opened. And as the memories flooded back, I realized how broken I have been; everything on the outside looked fine to those around me, but they couldn't see the knotted mess hindering me inside. I asked again, "God, please heal me!"

The words came immediately, "This is what I have been doing in you. You couldn't see it, but I have been gently untangling the knot. Keep going! Don't give up! Trust me." Many times, over what seemed like an hour, I heard myself saying, "I won't give up—Lord, heal me!" And another strand moved closer to freedom. In only ten minutes all four delicate strands lay perfectly on my sheet as tears streamed down my cheeks.

It was no accident that my final entry in my now-full journal was one asking for emotional healing. Today, I wrote this prayer in my book, "The Power of Right Believing" by Joseph Prince, which has been instrumental in guiding me to a better place in my life:

"I've never seen myself as 'enough' for anyone to love and accept me. Lord, please help me understand, truly understand, your love and acceptance of me, your redeeming power. Heal my emotions, the damage from my youth. Show me how to fully accept all you've done for me on the cross, the healing power for every part of me that I am powerless to change. Show me, too, what I can do, that you want me to change."

Suddenly, I realized I am enough. I am enough not because of me, but because Jesus loves and cares for me, because my life was not an accident. I am enough because when I accepted and trusted Jesus, He became my "enough". Right now, it is my job to remember that and trust Him with the "knots".

Healing is rarely instantaneous; most often it is a process. Our Father is the one who ultimately guides that process and in His infinite wisdom and mercy determines its path. Wounds deeply buried, like my necklaces hidden for years, need to be exposed to the light and air, healing in layers over time.

This passage from Joseph Prince's book, The Power of Right Believing, expresses the healing I long for: "Because you are in Christ, having a blessed future is not contingent on how much you strive to be perfect or how hard you work at changing yourself. It is contingent on the person of Jesus. It is not about whether you deserve to be blessed, favored, and victorious. The question is, does Jesus deserve to be blessed, favored and victorious?...This is what being in Christ Jesus means."

He also gave these instructions for finding that healthier balance:
- Believe in God's love for you.
- Learn to see what God sees.
- Receive God's complete forgiveness.
- Win the battle for your mind.
- Be free from self-occupation.
- Have a confident expectation of good.
- Find rest in the Father's love.

I can look forward to the untangling process with confidence in the One who is able to complete it. That work was done already through the work of Christ on the cross. Will it be painful? Healing most often is. Will it be worth it? Healing always is. Will it be finished here on earth? Probably not, but that is our hope, isn't it? Perfection comes when we are in the presence of our perfect Savior in the perfect place, heaven. Until then, He is in control of the untangling process and wants us to access His power in our lives. We just have to being willing to be untangled.

It's all in the Name   October 21

Shopping for clothing with my pre-teen girls was a challenging endeavor, as we attempted to stay on budget and in step with the current name brands. There was a real premium, and an expensive one, at that, on the designer jeans, in particular. You know, the ones that are in vogue; the "outside our family budget" style. They are the ones that produce tears of regret and backward glances as you pass them by. Heading for the "jeans you can afford" requires all the strength one mom can muster.

Once the girls obtained a few more painful years and began working part-time jobs, they were welcome to spend their own money on the designer names. And it was just amazing to me how those all-important names became so much less important! My daughters matured into quite balanced and relatively frugal young women, realizing that the name on the label was only as important as what they were willing to spend on it.

On the opposite end of the name-value scale, like my daughters, I also matured into realizing the value of the name brand—of God. It puzzled me that God had a proper name of Yahweh, which He had expressed to the Hebrews; God instructed them to call Him, "I AM".

Jesus' name in Hebrew is J'shua meaning "salvation", but I could not find a proper name for the Holy Spirit other than "Helper". For quite a long time, I inquired of my heavenly Father as to the name of the Holy Spirit. One day, it occurred to me to simply link the names He had given me, and this is what resulted: "I AM Salvation and Helper". That is a pretty awesome name!

That simple combination, "I AM Salvation and Helper", expresses so much of who our God is. I do not know how many individual descriptive names God gives Himself in His written word, but they are many. Each is a hint at the fullness of His personhood and character, His power and might, and most awesome sacrificial love. There is no name above His name, no name invoking power and glory like His, and no other name under heaven by which men can be saved. In the end, it really is all in the Name!

"God said to Moses, 'I AM WHO I AM. This is what you are to say to the Israelites: "I AM has sent me to you."' God also said to Moses, Say to the Israelites, 'The Lord, the God of your fathers---the God of Abraham, the God of Isaac and the God of Jacob---has sent me to you. This is my name forever, the name by which I am to be remembered from generation to generation."   Exodus 3:14-15

"She will give birth to a son, and you are to give him the name Jesus, because he will save his people from their sins."   Matthew 1:21

"But the Advocate, the Holy Spirit, whom the Father will send in my name, will teach you all things and will remind you of everything I have said to you."   John 14:26

Window Dressing

The jobs I have had have been varied and many, but one of my favorites was creating window displays for a bookstore. Retail stores use their street-side windows to present their very best in a way that invites us into their world. Usually a seasonally themed display, they are designed to visually invite customers to comfortably enter the store and explore. Advertising online is intended to do the same digitally. Window dressing, as it is called, is all about the image and the invitation.

As Christ-followers, we wear our window dressing. It's not about the clothing we chose. The most beautiful example I have ever seen is a greeter at the worship center door on Sundays; my eyes are immediately drawn to her smile and bright blue eyes, radiating her peaceful spirit. The outpouring of gentle love and kindness she displays distracts completely from the clothing she chose that morning. The loving smile she wears every week is the perfect church attire.

Our calm demeanor, peaceful radiance, and bright spirit are the window dressing that the world sees first. And it is most often noticeable during difficult times, the storms in life, where the calm is unexpected, and the peaceful spirit a shocking abnormality. It is genuine love, which can only come from God, His peace oozing out, even in trying events. In tragedy, when our spirits are crushed with grief, still, there is His peace. Walking in this dark world, still, the light of His Spirit never leaves our eyes.

We are, essentially, God's window dressing. We are the invitation He extends to those living in darkness, to comfortably enter and explore a relationship with our King. We are the living examples of His work in progress, of His power and love poured into imperfect vessels. He does not demand perfection; He knows all too well that we can never, without Him, achieve it. He doesn't demand sacrifice; He already gave it. He wants our love and obedience; He paid the price for it. He asks us to follow Him and then lead others to the ultimate gift, Jesus. We are His window dressing, inviting others to the greatest Gift.

So, as you dress for the day, put on the character of Jesus. Drape yourself in His love and grace. Top it off with eyes that smile as you walk out your door and into the world today. And be God's window dressing, on display, an invitation to the world to know the One you know and love.

"For we are God's handiwork, created in Christ Jesus to do good works, which God prepared in advance for us to do." Ephesians 2:10

"Here is a trustworthy saying that deserves full acceptance: Christ Jesus came into the world to save sinners---of whom I am the worst. But for that very reason I was shown mercy so that in me, the worst of sinners, Christ Jesus might display his unlimited patience as an example for those who would believe on him and receive eternal life. Now to the King eternal, immortal, invisible, the only God, be honor and glory forever and ever. Amen." I Timothy 1:15-17

Recently I discovered a list I had made a couple of decades ago. Always having been a fan of lists, I enjoyed ticking off the boxes, with a sense of accomplishment. Sometimes, the boxes became more important than the actual items comprising the list, a reward for doing the menial tasks which would never rank on my bucket list.

This list was broken into three headings: 1. Trials of the past year, 2. Unpleasant realizations, and 3. The results. Under the heading of "Trials", these events languished: losing a business, losing a job, a grave illness, a wedding, and an emergency appendectomy. Under the heading "Unpleasant realizations" the gory details emerged, nothing to be proud of. It included pride, self-reliance, unbelief in God's faithfulness, and failure to recognize Satan's lies and deception. More accurately, an epic failure!

The third heading, though, surprised me. Thinking it to be three items long, I turned the page to discover "The Results" to be another entire page, an additional 18 items. Some of them stunned me as I read them, not realizing what a beneficial era it had been; I remembered the hardships but had forgotten the blessings. A few follow: Learning to finish a task; dying to self; increased peace; recognizing God's character more and His refining of mine; trust in His provision; learning to walk in greater freedom through Christ; and being faithful to my promises, even when it hurts.

The backward view caused me to realize the importance of writing down these milestones in my life, because I would never have remembered that list of 21 Results. It is not beneficial to look back unless it is profitable to my growth in the present; but examination without lingering there can propel me forward, with increasing confidence that God is refining and molding me into the image of Christ Jesus.

Thankfully, He does not comprise a list of sins, shortcomings, weaknesses, and flaws. Instead, He "casts my sins as far as the east is from the west" when I confess them, instantly washed away by His blood, shed just for this reason. Jesus is the ultimate "checklist" to which I can attain. Joyfully, I can endure trials as He refines my character, replacing the "unpleasant realizations" with endurance, peace, patience, love, forgiveness, and trust. Thankfully, too, the checklist He keeps has only one item on it: Child of the Most High God.

"For as high as the heavens are above the earth, so great is his love for those who fear him; as far as the east is from the west, so far has he removed our transgressions from us. As a father has compassion on his children, so the Lord has compassion on those who fear him…"
Psalm 103: 11-13

"For you did not receive a spirit that makes you a slave again to fear, but you received the Spirit of sonship. And by him, we cry, 'Abba, Father.' The Spirit himself testifies with our spirit that we are God's children." Romans 8: 15-16

A photo flashed onto the display, a black and white screen capture of an intricate highway cloverleaf, with multiple levels. Cars, trucks, and busses, all frozen in time, were suspended loftily above the cityscape. I realized that real people were in each vehicle, a freeze-frame of their lives at that moment in time. Likely, they were men, women, and children from various parts of the city, distant neighborhoods, counties, and even countries; all were there at the same split second, and most of them unlikely to be passing each other again. I thought how unique each one was and wondered at what would have been their differences, and what they held in common.

We all flow through life with mostly black and white snapshots of other people, perceptions with variations of gray, of those with whom we are not likely to interact. They are to us much like the cars on the highway—anonymous and nondescript, until we are nudged together through circumstance. We normally don't bother to look beyond the screen capture.

God invites us to see our co-inhabitants of planet earth a little differently. As we dare to look beyond the shades of gray and interact with individuals, we begin to appreciate their unique qualities. Some surprise us as we recognize traits in them that resemble their Creator; and through them, we recognize more of His character as well. Every human being bears the DNA of God. That means that they are valuable to Him, and if to Him, then also to us. Human beings are the Father's treasure.

He shows me their personalities, quirks, talents, and value in ways I could never have known, or appreciated, without taking the risk of getting to know them. And those people have, in turn, colored my life in ways I never could have imagined. It is as if the cars in the photo of the highway were each, in turn, being propelled to living color before my eyes.

As our world becomes more disconnected in a time of social media "connection", we need more than ever to purposefully interact and know one another. I will admit that for me, an introvert, this is a tall order; it requires me daily to lay aside my fears, inconveniences, and preferences, and reach out to people. As I trust God increasingly with my relationships, He begins to "color" people for me. He opens my eyes to see them in a different way, not as a flat, gray screenshot, but perhaps, in some small glimmer of what He sees and loves, in the "living color" He intended them to be.

"Yet to all who received him, to those who believed in his name, he gave the right to become children of God---Children born not of natural descent, nor of human decision or a husband's will, but born of God." John 1:12, 13

"A new command I give you: Love one another. As I have loved you, so you must love one another." John 13:34

As I drove away from the airport drop-off area, I glanced back to see my son entering the terminal doors. I had just sent him off on his trip halfway across the globe to meet his bride overseas. It was a three-week trip, which seemed so long at the time. Sixteen months, and counting, he is still stranded there due to the pandemic, which has shut down the world. There are moments when my heart aches; weighing on my spirit is the realization that it still may take many months more for his return. The world is in upheaval, my son is in a foreign culture, and I am helpless to help him; he is out of my hands.

My two daughters live in cities opposite directions from me, in towns close to a hundred miles away. My heart aches to see them, just as much as it does my son; they "own" all of my grandchildren, and selfishly, I don't see them often enough. Their welfare, daily lives, the children's activities, and growth are elusive in the busyness of life. They are one of the last treasures to be taken out of my hands.

The removal of tiny idols began long ago, and there has been a progressive loosening of my fingers ever since. The first to go was obscure and deeply hidden, but there was no mistaking God's firm directive; it was the idol of "excuses" and the pain of my past that He was requiring me to deny. He would be my only Source from that point, and from there, He asked me to remove others from my focus. Jobs, homes, vehicles, food, and friends rounded it out, until the next step of progression.

That was where religion, also, fell to the chopping block, one of the strongest of all. I came to realize that it is the opposite of my relationship with Jesus and was one of the most difficult idols to surrender. Following rules is the easy way out for humans, who notoriously drift away from the Living God. It is much more challenging to listen, to identify His voice, and to patiently follow Him when the rules aren't so clear. Little by little, His voice became easier to define, my love became stronger, and His ways easier to understand, though not always easy to obey.

Our Father loves us too dearly to allow idols of any persuasion to occupy places of prominence in our hearts and lives. One by one, He will root them out, exposing them to the fatal Light of His Presence and Power. He is the Living God, deserving of every molecule of respect, every breath of our praise, and every submission in worship. Little by little, sometimes lots by lots, He weans us from this world and self. Every form of idol He will expose, gently, or firmly if need be, transferring it out of our hands, and our focus back to the One who is worthy of it.

"What agreement is there between the temple of God and idols? For we are the temple of the living God. As God has said: 'I will live with them and walk among them, and I will be their God, and they will be my people.'" 2 Corinthians 6:16

"God is spirit, and his worshipers must worship in the Spirit and in truth." John 4:24

While my mother attended college, our weekends were transformed into treasure hunts in the state arboretum for the sake of her botany class. Following the clean-room inspection, she packed a picnic lunch for us, loaded four kids and a picnic blanket into the car, and headed to the forest. There we would spend the afternoon searching for the identity of trees she needed to complete her class project. As an adult, I gained a head start in my horticultural projects thanks to my mother's botanical quests that year.

Gazing over the landscape recently, one giant oak tree stood out as it towered above most of the other trees. I couldn't help but wonder about its age and how much of history that tree had weathered. It suffered some damage through the storms, as evidenced by its fractured limbs, but remained steadfastly fixed in its place; never giving way to the wind or rain, roots deeply clutching the clay-like soil. Its crown has thinned like the graying hair of an ancient man, though it still stands tall as it looks out over the heads of the surrounding trees, remaining a regal specimen on display.

My mother searched out the best specimens for her botany projects, and I doubt my old oak tree would have fit the parameters of the project. It has suffered many trials of blazing hot summers, ice storms, soaking rains, and punishing winds. Tornados have vaulted over its head, minor earthquakes have shivered its roots, vines have twisted through its branches, and rivers of fleeing waters have circled its base. Yet, it stands.

Grief, disappointment, heartache, illness, and loss of every kind have waged their attacks upon my life. In those days, Jesus has been my strength, my hope, and my joy through the storms. In all my days, I would like to be known as an oak tree in God's kingdom. I want to stand amid the other "trees", trusting Him, not bending to the world's demands. I want my roots sunk deeply into the Word of God, and to be resilient when disappointments assail. I want to find my nourishment in Him through the droughts, and my stability in His love. I want to be found praising Him with my crown lifted high, a planting of the Lord on display, and a reflection of His splendor.

"And provide for those who grieve in Zion---to bestow on them a crown of beauty instead of ashes, the oil of gladness instead of mourning, and a garment of praise instead of a spirit of despair. They will be called oaks of righteousness, a planting of the Lord for the display of his splendor." Isaiah 61:3

"I have set the Lord always before me. Because he is at my right hand, I will not be shaken." Psalm 16:8

What's in Your Wallet?   October 27

The tanned leather pockets were worn around the edges, discolored from thousands of touches of my fingers. I carefully removed my driver's license, my voter registration, photos belying the age of the wallet itself, a debit card, and several business rewards cards. Relationships with my family were evident by the emergency contacts list. A minimal amount of cash, a few coins, and several postage stamps were the only "valuables" I could claim. In that wallet, my whole identity rested, as far as any bureaucrat was concerned.

The contrast between my wallet's identification of me and how I perceived myself became suddenly stark as I asked myself, "Who am I?" I wrote my answer down on a tiny piece of paper, not giving the question much consideration, just a quick thought. When I finished it, in under a minute, I shocked myself; it didn't contain any of the information in my wallet.

This is what it said: "I am an artist, musician, singer, dancer, writer, encourager—precious child of the Most High God—I am a holder of hands, speaker of truth, a match lit in the darkness, explorer, and seeker. I am a protector of innocence and promoter of relationship—born in brokenness and born again—a precious child of the Son of Man, Immanuel, God with me. I am temporary and eternal, poor yet rich, blessed and favored in every way. I am young in heart and old in age. I am nobody special yet special because of Jesus. I see God everywhere, in everything around me, and He is everything to me."

God's incredible timing was evidenced as the song which played on my radio at that moment was "Everything" by Toby Mac, speaking to that very sentiment that God is everything to those who desire Him. It is staggering when God reveals Himself to us in such a personal way. When we come to understand that He is not impersonal, but in a crazy inconceivable way, He is intensely personal. Just as the things in my wallet identified me but gave no reasonable indication of who I essentially am, we look at God the same way, as a description of His data, but not His persona.

God is not going to ask for our personal data for admittance to heaven, and the information in our wallets will not give us a pass. Nor will our accomplishments or status, our earthly connections, or our influence. Only one thing matters: What did you personally do with Jesus? Did you consign Him to a fold in your wallet, a membership card to a church; or did you surrender the "real you", with all your flaws and shortcomings, entering a real relationship with Jesus? Ask yourself, "Who am I?" and see where Jesus fits into your identity. It won't be found in your wallet.

"I pray that out of his glorious riches he may strengthen you with power through his Spirit in your inner being, so that Christ may dwell in your hearts through faith. And I pray that you, being rooted and established in love, may have power, together with all the saints, to grasp how wide and long and high and deep is the love of Christ, and to know this love that surpasses knowledge---that you may be filled to the measure of all the fullness of God."

Ephesians 3:16-19

The Good Fight

Mixed martial arts gained traction worldwide in the sporting arena over the last decade, something I cannot bring myself to watch. Boxing, mild by comparison, was more than I could handle. Growing up with three brothers and no father in the home to guide them, their tendency toward fights brewed under the surface, erupting as teens and young adults. I became the peacemaker when possible, quietly retreating to safety otherwise, totally a wimp. Tempers flared up often and with little restraint.

It was not until many years later that I understood, in some small measure, the value of a good fight; that boys need proper training to become men. My son had to educate me. Making life easy is detrimental to growth. Experiencing the rough and tumble "hard knocks" in a safe place, they learn to persevere, stand up for themselves, and protect others. They also learn when to fight and when to back away and good strategy, and logical thinking. With wise instructors, they become mighty in spirit and resolve.

Until Jesus returns, there will be people who are not "nice", nor kind. Wars will rage in pursuit of power; there will be revolutions and violence, whether we like it or not. To do nothing is to surrender countless souls to the poverty of mind, soul, and body; to slavery, bondage, and death. I am learning to be less timid, bolder in my faith; a warrior in spirit instead of running for shelter.

If we do not protect the innocent, weak and downtrodden, and do not stand for Godly principles, do we believe the relentless enemy of our souls will slink away in defeat? No, he will not; his mission is to kill, steal, and destroy, and he cares not what methods are employed. While called to love our enemies, God does not require us to allow evil to prevail without challenge. We are to be people of peace as far as possible, but we are not to fear, knowing that the Spirit of God leads, guides, and strengthens us.

Ultimately, we are called to fight the good fight, to put on the armor of God. We are called to grow up in Christ, resist the forces of evil, and stand up to the enemy of our souls. Battles are long and exhausting, drain our resources, emotions and resolve, but we must learn not to surrender to evil. Trusting God above all, we stand in the gap for the treasure of His heart, people. The Commander of God's armies is calling us to duty, training us to fight the good fight for the sake of the Kingdom of Light. Take heart, warrior, in this war, the winner has already been declared, and His name is Jesus.

"Fight the good fight of the faith. Take hold of the eternal life to which you were called when you made your good confession in the presence of many witnesses." I Timothy 6:12

"This is love for God: to obey his commands. And his commands are not burdensome, for everyone born of God overcomes the world. This is the victory that has overcome the world, even our faith. Who is it that overcomes the world? Only he who believes that Jesus is the Son of God." I John 5:4,5

Six words stood out at the bottom of a page I had written in my very first journal eons ago. At first, I dismissed them, and then they made me angry! Who was I to make such an awful statement, one that was so careless and exhibited such a cavalier attitude?!? They were inscribed at the beginning, too, cheapening the thousands of words written in that and subsequent journals. Six careless words, "No literary awards here, for sure!" Reading them one more time, I grabbed a pen and drew a big red "X" over the "no", emphatically eliminating it.

I had written those words, discounting the power of God through my writing and the consequential effects on lives that could be encouraged to seek a deeper relationship with Him. My calling, by a great and awesome Father, to write those hundreds of pages was certain. Yet, I so easily discarded the value of it, thinking it could not be possibly true that God would use me in a significant way. Who am I to take that calling so lightly?

I do not believe I am alone in such actions. Most of us dismiss any great calling from God because we do not believe that God could possibly expect it of us; or that He is uninvolved with our lives. For some, they are even hoping He keeps His distance. Boiling that sentiment down to its essence, we doubt that God can accomplish anything great of us. With such limited faith or unwillingness to trust our Sovereign and Mighty God, it is most probable that nothing great will be done. At the worst, many will die without knowing Him. But the smallest of faith, followed by obedience, He will honor and use in ways unimaginable.

Just before those six red-x ugly words, these had been written: "You are my life, Lord, even in the fog of my confusion, in the desert of my doubts, in the draught of my pride, in the tides of despair, and the winds of the world. You are my steadfast anchor, my wisdom, my peace. Thank you that when I can't hold on any longer, your grip has never failed." His plan will prevail, and I will cling to His blood-soaked cross with all that I am, trusting Him to bring about His purpose in my life. Nor will I doubt any longer that, with Him, all things are possible for those willing to walk where He leads, not for my glory, but His.

"For we do not preach ourselves, but Jesus Christ as Lord, and ourselves as your servants for Jesus' sake. For God, who said, 'Let light shine out of darkness,' made his light shine in our hearts to give us the light of the knowledge of the glory of God in the face of Christ. But we have this treasure in jars of clay to show that this all-surpassing power is from God and not from us." 2 Corinthians 4:5-7

Eyeglasses and contact lenses have enhanced visual clarity for many people, but I can tell you the pitfalls of both, having utilized them over the years to increase my visual acuity. Glasses, even after proper adjustments, tend to slide down my nose as reliably as rocks succumb to gravity. This also means that as I continually nudge them back to their starting line, smudges invariably attach themselves to the lenses.

Contact lenses have their own set of problems, becoming invisible unless I am wearing my glasses. And you can see, no pun intended, what a challenge that presents. They must be removed periodically and cleaned or replaced, and I am here to tell you that they are not inexpensive little rascals. Those tiny pieces of plastic make sizeable dents in my plastic, if you know what I mean.

My spiritual eyes are even more of a problem. I have been spiritually blind since entering this world, and until I met Jesus, I could not discern His work in me or the world. Even following Him daily, the path is sometimes difficult to discern, my vision clouded with concerns, and my mind battered by doubts. How do I discover the direction God wants me to go, the choices He would have me make?

Caught up in my imagination, picturing the possibilities, but not knowing what tomorrow will bring, I can be fearful of what is to come and dreading things that have not even happened. Panic can well up in an instant if allowed, and dread can paralyze me in the decision-making process. What if I make the wrong choice? What will the consequences be? How will I know if I made the right decision?

We are all faced with moments when outcomes are uncertain and consequences unpleasant, forgetting that God is present. He can rescue us when the need arises and is perfectly able to provide clarity and peace amid of all of the circumstances we face. He will speak to our hearts through His Word, wise counsel, and His Spirit. Our job is to be yielded to His will at every moment and in every decision.

This is the prayer I have prayed when faced with difficult or confusing decisions: "What do I do, God? Speak clearly to me, Lord, unplugging my ears and uncovering my eyes. Help me be bold enough to dream, daring enough to follow you, and tenacious enough to cling to your best plan for me. Let me not be deceived—keep my heart yielding and tender toward you. Keep my eyes wide open, recognizing your hand is directing my path." Clarity of vision always results when I leave it in His capable hands and timing.

"Trust in the Lord with all your heart and lean not on your own understanding; in all your ways acknowledge him, and he will make your paths straight...My son, preserve sound judgment and discernment, do not let them out of your sight; they will be life for you, an ornament to grace your neck. Then you will go on your way in safety..."
Proverbs 3:5-6, 21-23a

Fascinated, as I sat on the edge of his bed watching, Trevor sat on the floor with thousands of tiny building blocks strewn in front of him. He quietly studied the instructions and carefully placed each block, layer by layer, as the LEGO castle began to take shape. Halfway into the building project, he threw down the plan book and the castle construction halted abruptly. He explained that there was a discrepancy of one minuscule block, an error in the plan, and as I inspected it, there surely was.

As we made adjustments and attempted to finish the structure, we found that one tiny block affected the rest of the design. After many revisions and consequent frustrations, we finished it, though it did not look exactly like the picture. The project was painstaking, but I was proud and surprised that my young son would see it through to the end, despite hours invested and all the difficulties. Trevor didn't disassemble that castle for a very long time, unlike other LEGO builds.

God created a plan long ago before I was born, and as I grew, He began putting the pieces together, pieces that did not seem to fit. It appeared that the plan had some obvious errors. I attempted to make alterations in the structure to accommodate the pieces which were uncomfortable, even ugly. But as I observe the structure of my life, I can see that God's plan was perfect after all. There were no "misfit" pieces and no errors in the Great Engineer's plan. He had, and has, a strategy that will not be discarded until the structure is complete and perfect, all in His timing and not mine.

Until then, even though it is difficult for me to envision at times, I am already complete and perfect in my Father's eyes. That perfection is not visible to the earthly realm, but it is a completely solid reality in the spiritual realm. I belong to Jesus, bought and paid for by His broken body and blood, sealed in His resurrection by His Holy Spirit. There was no flaw in His plan for my life, no mistake in His calculations, not one error in timing.

The evil intended for me worked in the end for my good, and the hopes for my destruction became my help to prosper. And if I appear as though I have nothing to offer this world, the world would be mistaken; I have a Savior so perfect in love, so amazing in His grace, and so matchless in His glory that He transforms anyone He touches.

God takes our pieces and plans, edits them in His wisdom, and tenderly places them one piece upon the other, until He builds us into the image of His precious son, Jesus. It is the best and most perfect plan ever assembled, and not one block, when viewed from eternity, will have been a mistake.

"For every house is built by someone, but God is the builder of everything. Moses was faithful as a servant in all God's house, testifying to what would be said in the future. But Christ is faithful as a son over God's house. And we are his house, if we hold on to our courage and the hope of which we boast." Hebrews 3:4-6

November

Fog on the Mountain

The white blanket of cloud with fringe-like edges, draped over the distant mountain as if it had just been gently laid over a comfy bed, fluffed and softly hanging perfectly in place. Its appearance was tenderly inviting, peaceful and calming, until I considered the people who lived under that puffy mountain blanket. When it encompasses you on the mountain, the dreamy beauty of distant fog becomes the very near horror of a nightmare.

Having personally experienced the deadly nature of fog on the mountain, I am familiar with the uncertainty of navigating the tight turns along steep drop-offs. Without guard rails, and only trees as barriers to a plunge into the valley below, fog won't lull you to sleep, it will wake you to maximum awareness. Those who have experienced it most of their lives can little understand the terror of the newcomer.

I have, myself, become a seasoned navigator of fog on the mountain, both physically and spiritually. There have been many moments of uncertainty, as I have traveled the steep and winding paths of life. When the fog seemed to obscure the way, God appeared hidden and far from me. The fog was dense, especially as I sought Him, and I wondered why He would leave me to such a lonely path fraught with danger. The truth is He never left. Not once. I could always look back and see where He led.

Through each wandering trial, His words have as surely settled in my heart as the fog settled on the mountain. His words encouraged trust. His words spoke softly of comfort, words of reassurance of His presence and tenderness. He is faithful to give assurances along the way, and His purpose of building trust in my heart has become more apparent in each phase of my growth. He continues to speak those words of guidance and affirmation as I seek Him today.

He never leaves us to wander through the fog on the mountain alone. He is ever-present, always guiding, whispering His direction to our hearts. And if we will slow our pace and listen intently for His voice, He will speak through the fog on our mountain.

"The Lord replied, 'My Presence will go with you, and I will give you rest." Exodus 33:14

"I will instruct you and teach you in the way you should go; I will counsel you and watch over you." Psalm 32:8

"For we walk by faith, not by sight." 2 Corinthians 5:7

"Show me your ways, O Lord, teach me your paths; guide me in your truth and teach me, for you are God my Savior, and my hope is in you all day long." Psalm 25:4-5

Just Keep Swimming

The sizable snail lazily dropped from the water's surface, landing squarely upon the back of the lemon-colored catfish diligently scrubbing the bottom of the tank. Rudely interrupted in foraging for its supper, it became agitated, shaking the wayward snail off. Abruptly turning away, as if casting a rebuke of side-way glance at the culprit, it continued its narrow focus of food finding.

Like the oblivious snail that was so unlikely to "target" that yellow bottom dweller, the interruptions and disruptions in our paths are generally not intentional. However, agitation arises, and our spirits bristle at the audacity of said interruption. Annoyance seems to be the universal reaction to disruptions. And whatever interrupts the tranquility of our personal space, whether mental or physical, becomes the object of our wrath.

I am well acquainted with this reaction, especially when I am in the middle of accomplishing "good" works. The reality is that often, the task at hand has become *my* work and *not* God's. I know He must be smiling right now as I admit this; countless times my Father has shaken my world with a disruption with the intent to redirect my focus from the creation back to the Creator.

God allows disruption in our corner of the universe to remind us that He is in control and we are not. Those moments expose my self-centeredness. Sometimes, I can sense that His goal appears to be to teach me to "let go and let God" handle the situation. Most often, it is to redirect my focus to Him. Turning my eyes from a focus on self, to a focus on Him benefits not only me; but also, the ones He loves who live within my sphere of influence.

When our focus is solely on "things below" we are caught off guard, flinching and fighting the interruption, directing our ire at the subject of it, just as the lemon catfish did. However, we can trust that everything placed into God's capable hands will be treated with His loving care. Anything we attempt to withhold is to deny God's capability and character. Attempts to restrict His control in our lives are a signal that our motives and focus need tweaking.

When our sight is focused on "things above" all disruptions become less annoying. Trusting Jesus, we can shake off the surprises. As we "just keep swimming", trusting Jesus, all pressure is removed; and we become conquerors through Christ Jesus in all things.

"The king was overjoyed and gave orders to lift Daniel out of the den. And when Daniel was lifted from the den, no wound was found on him, because he had trusted in his God." Daniel 2:23

"Since, then, you have been raised with Christ, set your hearts on things above, where Christ is seated at the right hand of God. Set your minds on things above, not on earthly things." Colossians 3:1-2

Unseen Cargo

Wedding cakes, floral arrangements, dogs, people who are ill, and most recently, live fish have been transported in my vehicle. It is problematic when slow turns or stops are necessary. The drivers behind me have no idea why I am creeping, like a slow-growing vine, across the intersection. I see their expressions of displeasure; and I often wish I could just show them what is in my car, so they could understand and exercise a little patience with me.

We are all a bit like my car, transporting unseen cargo, commonly described as "baggage". Some are loaded down by so many wounds that their frames are scraping their tires. Others carry fragile cargo, and an unexpected curve will throw them into a panic. Many keep adding to their loads as they rumble through life, picking up one here, and another there, until the car is so full that pain is jumping out of their windows.

The point is that you may not see the cargo someone else is carrying until they have lost control of their vehicle. There is usually a reason for the way they are driving, and they may not be aware of the effect their cargo is having on them. Those who have learned to unload their cargo along the way are the ones who reach their destination with the least damage to themselves, and those around them. The unloading is achieved through forgiveness, and healing through trust in Jesus, but we don't all see how to unload our problems onto His shoulders in the same ways, or time.

So, I am learning to remind myself, when encountering another "driver" who is not traveling at the speed I approve, (or is holding up traffic, or appears to have socks hanging on their mirror) to give him or her a little extra room. I simply have to trust that God is at work, because I may not be able to see the cargo in the trunk. My own unseen cargo is more than enough to occupy my attention, anyway.

"Therefore, as God's chosen people, holy and dearly loved, clothe yourselves with compassion, kindness, humility, gentleness, and patience. Bear with each other and forgive whatever grievances you may have against one another. Forgive as the Lord forgave you. And over all these virtues put on love, which binds them all together in perfect unity."

Colossians 3:12-14

Cold Feet

Crossing the threshold, my bare feet met the vinyl floor, and the change in weather outside became immediately evident inside. The outside temperature had dropped significantly and was now stealing the warmth from my floor; the closer I walked to the outside wall, the cooler the floor felt. My cold feet were the direct evidence of the falling temperatures, a very unpleasant reminder that winter was fast upon us.

At that moment of realization, the Holy Spirit spoke clearly to my heart concerning the coolness of which I had just complained. "Why have you felt so cold to the things of God lately?" The quiet, convicting answer was immediate. The magnetic attraction of the world had subtly drawn my heart away from my first love, its warmth stolen away by the cares of this world.

Our God is so loving, so compassionate, so jealous for our love to be returned to Him, that He will not allow us to wander too far before tugging gently, but firmly, at our hearts. He will ever be consistent in His efforts to bring us back into closer proximity, like the interior floor's warmth, to His wisdom, guidance, and compassionate love. Anything we suffer is insignificant compared to losing our relationship with Him; it is to our everlasting detriment to wander too far from our Shepherd.

I am thankful that my God never allows me to become too comfortable with this world and that He is a jealous God. He does not tolerate trivial competition; everything this world offers is trivial, in comparison to a relationship with Him. This God, *the* Almighty God, glorious beyond imagining, King of the Universe, powerful beyond conceivable measure, is our sure Foundation. He is the Sacrificial Lamb, Resurrected One, Savior of the World, our Hope, Truth, and Eternal Life.

In a world where every tree dangles desirable fruit before our eyes, Jesus is God's unspeakable gift, and the Holy Spirit is our Counselor and Comforter. The world's fruit promises to anchor our hopes, and fulfill our dreams; what it produces is a cool distraction from the God who loves us the most, who is truly equipped to fulfill our dreams, and to provide the foundational security we seek. As we step away from the "cold feet" influences of this world in increasing measure, we are stepping toward the warmth of His presence and the security of knowing Him in full measure.

"We know that we live in him and he in us, because he has given us of his Spirit. And we have seen and testify that the Father has sent his Son to be the Savior of the world. If anyone acknowledges that Jesus is the Son of God, God lives in him and he in God. And so we know and rely on the love God has for us. God is love." 1 John 4:13-16

"Has not God made foolish the wisdom of the world? For since in the wisdom of God the world through its wisdom did not know him, God was pleased through the foolishness of what was preached to save those who believe…For the foolishness of God is wiser than man's wisdom, and the weakness of God is stronger than man's strength."
I Corinthians 1:20b-23, 25

The view through the huge windows, gracing an entire wall, spread before me, layer upon layer. Lake Michigan spanned the horizon with a cloudy haze blanketing its northern edge. The beach nudged its curve into a close hug of the businesses along Lake Shore Drive, as the taller buildings of the city stretched upward as if to break the notorious Chicago winds rolling off the lake. I felt as if I was on top of the world in this first exposure to the posh restaurant, replete with maître de, on my fifteenth birthday.

Since that special and unexpectedly lavish birthday, I have dined in a governor's mansion, been a guest of influential people in their homes, and traveled to many places I never expected. I have skied pristine mountain slopes, sailed a catamaran, soared in a hot air balloon, and walked on a glacier. The truth is, I never deserved any of these blessings, and never imagined in my most daring dreams that I would have opportunities to experience any of them. Only by God's grace and plan for me did they come to pass.

Though I did not deserve any good thing God gave me, He loved me anyway and has been so generous that I have often felt overwhelmed. None of us "deserve" God's mercy or grace; we are rebellious against Him by nature and determined to wrest control from His hands through our delusions. Yet regardless of our inward tendencies, He does not hold it against us when lavishing His blessings upon us, raining on the good and evil alike; He is merciful, especially when it is undeserved. He loves us so much that He paved the way to reconcile Himself with His creation through His precious son, Jesus.

No matter the circumstances, no matter the place I am or what I have at the moment, I am content. God has already brought me through so much. He has taken me to so many unimaginable places. He has shown me so much grace, even following awful judgment and mistakes, that I cannot doubt His love, provision, or plan.

He has taught me to find contentment, like Paul, in having much or having little, being grateful for whatever comes from His hand, and trusting that He has my best interests at heart. He places me in the paths of those needing encouragement, leading them to the Lord of Life. On this earth, whether we sit on top of this world or not, if we know Jesus, we will sit there with the King of Kings when this life ends. And He sits daily at the top of my world.

"He causes his sun to rise on the evil and the good, and sends rain on the righteous and the unrighteous." Matthew 5:45

"I know what it is to be in need, and I know what it is to have plenty. I have learned the secret of being content in any and every situation, whether well fed or hungry, whether living in plenty or in want. I can do everything through him who gives me strength." Philippians 4:12-13

Passengers lined the deck of the Department of Wildlife boat in eager anticipation as it chugged across the gray lake waves in early November. The shore was vacant, the trees naked of their summer foliage, and the waiting list had been long. Now, we were hopeful, everyone scanning the treetops and sky in search of our target, American Eagles nesting in the wild. As our guide rotated, pointing to the outcrop of rocks and bare trees, we fixed our binoculars on an eagle, perched on its nest with wings up.

As it launched itself overhead, it circled high momentarily. Suddenly losing altitude and flattening against the wind, it swooped over the water, low and close. The wingspan of better than six feet carried it just enough above the water for its feet to snag the fish it had in its sight. How exciting it was to see that beautiful, graceful eagle on-wing, close-up in my lens.

It is just as powerful and beautiful for the Lord to witness our reliance on Him. But in our weak moments, trying times, and periods testing our souls, our wings can hang limply at our sides, our confidence shattered, and our souls weary. We feel we may never fly again, wounded and confined to a nest of pain.

Sorrow overwhelms our souls. Rejection and failure drain our courage, rendering us hopeless and without direction. But if we will peer over the waters of our pain, looking to Him, we will see that God has placed our sustenance in it. Eagles live for flying, but they live *through* fishing; both require perseverance and training. Jesus calls us to lift our wings, offering Him the situation, then trusting Him for the rest.

When we cannot understand the next step, keep flying in the direction in life that He has already revealed. When we cannot see a clear direction, wait for the next "fish". God looks ahead of us and will always show His eagles the way to go; He will give us strength when it is time to launch out on His capable wings.

Adult bald eagles can fly above the rain clouds, up to 10,000 feet high. And as we lift our wings in trust, our Father in heaven will enable us to fly to whatever height He has called us. He alone knows all He has planned for us and will give us the strength and ability to do it. Do not doubt; just fly. Trust Jesus. Wings up, child of God!

"Why do you say, O Jacob, and complain, O Israel, 'My way is hidden from the Lord; my cause is disregarded by my God?' Do you not know? Have you not heard? The Lord is the everlasting God, the Creator of the ends of the earth. He will not grow tired or weary, and his understanding no one can fathom. He gives strength to the weary and increases the power of the weak. (Emphasis mine) **Even youths grow tired and weary, and young men stumble and fall; but those who hope in the Lord will renew their strength. They will soar on wings like eagles, they will run and not grow weary, they will walk and not be faint."** Isaiah 40:27-31

An announcement was being made by the President of the United States in a Rose Garden ceremony, where Senators, dignitaries, and the Vice President's family sat in anticipation. As the camera panned those seated, it occurred to me that each person had been specially invited, checked off by security, and seated in a carefully planned arrangement. Important people attended that event. They were the highest officials of our country, exclusively selected, and present by invitation only.

It brought back a distant memory, the singular "invitation only" event of my lifetime, so far. We had been invited to the governor's mansion as delegates to an electoral convention. As we arrived for dinner at the mansion, we were required to present the formal invitation; absent that special envelope, no entry was permitted. The seats of power and influence in this world are not readily accessible to most of us.

However, there is a King who has granted me immediate access, unlimited time, and freedom to enter His presence at a moment's notice. I do not have to wait for a special invitation, either. My invitation to enter my heavenly Father's presence was obtained at extraordinary cost; my royal invitation was inscribed by the blood of His beloved Son. It is sealed with the royal seal of the Holy Spirit, delivered into my hands when I placed my faith in Jesus. There is no other invitation so exclusive, or holy, in all the universe, no other name above His name.

The Holy of Holies opened in heaven the day Jesus breathed His last breath on the cross. As the temple veil split from top to bottom, our heavenly Father broadcast His invitation to all humankind; access to the Father now came through faith in His Son alone, to anyone who would accept God's ultimate invitation. Free access, an unimaginable opportunity to connect with the Living God, was now available on that one condition alone.

I will be the first to admit that I do not take advantage of His invitation often enough, even believing I should not take "trivial" matters to Him. He is not pleased when I underestimate His influence and power, or that I would withhold my requests for His assistance. But no matter how I feel; whether I have drifted from Him or even sinned against Him, His grace prevails. There is an open invitation to return to His arms, an exclusive invitation for the children of God in Christ Jesus. And though this incredible relationship is by invitation only, everyone has been invited, any time, any place. Just come as you are, and don't delay—come now. The King is expecting you!

"And when Jesus had cried out again in a loud voice, he gave up his spirit. At that moment the curtain of the temple was torn in two from top to bottom." Matthew 27:50-51

"Let us then approach God's throne of grace with confidence, so that we may receive mercy and find grace to help us in our time of need." Hebrews 4:16

Love AND Like

A vague irritation, floating just below the surface of my consciousness, pricked at me all day. It was a physical discomfort, a tag inside my shirt rubbing tender skin. It was not enough to demand my immediate attention, but enough to be irritatingly present. The solution was simple, requiring nothing more than a pair of scissors, and a few seconds. As I pushed the nuisance into the background of consciousness, I read this passage in Bruce Wilkinson's "Secrets of the Vine":

"If you were to list the qualities of your best friend, I expect you would note things like 'She accepts me,' 'He always makes time for me,' and 'I always leave her presence feeling encouraged.' What you appreciate in a best friend is precisely what God offers. He is trustworthy and patient. When He looks at you, He does not call to mind the sins you've asked Him to forgive. He sees only a beloved child, a worthy heir. . . If we really abided in His love, we would come away feeling so nourished, so cherished, so liked that we would rush back to Him whenever we could."

The irony of that passage made me laugh out loud and kept me smiling long after. But this was the bombshell: "If our need for this relationship is so deep and constant, why do few of us fervently pursue it? One of the primary reasons, I'm convinced, is that we don't really believe God likes us," he (Bruce Wilkinson) said.

Bam!!! Target acquired and hit! I had felt distant in my relationship with God for months but was not able to place my finger on the reason. I had already repented, asking for forgiveness for everything that came to mind. Still, I felt hopeless, empty, and unliked. I wandered through my day feeling vaguely irritated, and not understanding why.

After reading the passage by Bruce Wilkerson, I laughed, and wondered at my God's sense of humor! Like the irritating tag, where all that was required was the simple act of excision, it was also time to excise the wrong belief. God created me and loves me, but even more, He LIKES me! How amazing to realize this for the first time in my life! My heavenly Father did not randomly create me but gave me the personality and traits He wanted me to have.

When I accepted Jesus as my Savior, He accepted me as though I came with zero baggage of sin and brokenness. Jesus cleared all my debts on the cross, my weaknesses and burdens gone, never to be seen again. The burdens I carried were not mine to carry after all. Ever since that day, I cut tags out before they irritate me, and take worries to my Father before they become constant companions. And I'm still smiling over His amazing love AND like!

"Therefore, humble yourselves under the mighty hand of God, that He may exalt you at the proper time, casting all your anxiety on Him, because He cares for you." I Peter 5:6, 7

Congratulations! You just won an all-expense-paid trip, with one caveat—I get to choose your destination! I am escorting you to the boarding ramp, and only the pilot and I know where you are flying. Are you considering the possibilities yet? You may disembark in Hawaii or the Bahamas; you could be hopeful, but by no means certain. Your destination may be the Antarctic, the Sahara Desert, or the jungles of the Amazon. You would have to trust my character to choose the best destination for you. And how would you prepare for such a journey?

Many people are flying through life without knowing their destination, ill-prepared, uncertain where they are heading, and attempting to navigate the turbulence on their own. On the other hand, on my flight I have trusted my Pilot, and overcome the turbulence of life through faith in Christ. When I have lost altitude, my engine sputtering, and my faith waning, I have had to ask forgiveness and make many adjustments in my course and attitude. But my destination has never changed.

Those of us who know our destinations are looking forward to our landing, trusting that God has kept his promise of a home in heaven. We are preparing for that destination, excitedly anticipating our welcome and entrance into God's very presence. How can we imagine it? While we struggle to know details other than the descriptions in God's word, we can trust His goodness and promise.

For example, if I have been to Hawaii and attempted to describe it to you when you have never seen it, never viewed photographs of the volcanoes, flowers, or waterfalls, you would have no idea what I was talking about. Heaven is like that; there is no adequate description without seeing it ourselves. We are accepting it on trust, but, like Hawaii, it is real. God's presence, holiness, unimaginable beauty, and power are beyond our comprehension. And what He has in store for us upon arrival will be worth any sacrifice made on our journey.

For each of us, our plane will inevitably land, sooner or later, and we do not know the exact time. Our destination will be determined by the choice we made in accepting Jesus as our Savior or refusing the ticket to life's ultimate destination, by rejecting the Son of the Living God. For us who received Christ, our citizenship is in heaven, and our final stop is in the presence of Jesus—home, at last!

"But our citizenship is in heaven. And we eagerly await a Savior from there, the Lord Jesus Christ, who, by the power that enables him to bring everything under his control, will transform our lowly bodies so that they will be like his glorious body." Philippians 3:20-21

"But as it is written, 'No eye has seen, no ear has heard, no mind has conceived, what God has prepared for those who love him---' but God has revealed it to us by his Spirit."
1 Corinthians 2:9

Absolutely, Positively!

This message was absolutely, positively what I needed to see. A page in one of my journals was inscribed "God has a dream for my life," and it was dated for New Year's Eve. Its valuable message reminded me to dream, something in which I have never excelled. I daydream wonderfully and have a vivid imagination, too vivid at times, to be honest. But dream? I could never put my finger on exactly what my "dream" was.

The notes on that page outlined some great advice to those with an actual dream: "Dream big, and don't limit God! Run with other dreamers; but get ready to run alone, since most people won't be excited about your successes. Dreams are accomplished first in our hearts, but tempered in our experiences, testing us, and promoting growth; regularly check your attitude and learn from the tests. Resist mediocrity. Lastly, help someone else achieve their dream along the way."

And when you are finally closing in on the realization of your dream, I would add, don't give up. Most people give up their dreams too soon; it must be a basic universal law because it seems to happen to nearly everyone. Dreams, like babies, die prematurely if the process of birthing them ends before its time.

That is all sound advice when you realize what, exactly, your dream is. I have recently discovered the dream my Father prepared for me since I was born, so this advice is exactly what I now need to hear every day, too. I am attempting to pursue my late, but not too late, God-given dream, the one I never thought possible. I have discovered that the dream I want is the dream God desires for me; it is not the dream that fulfills me, but the one that fulfills His purpose for me.

He has a perfect plan for you, too. It is tailor-made for the individual He created. He is asking you to trust Him, to go where He leads, persevere, and listen to Him. You were designed to be, and accomplish, that for which your Creator tailored you. At exactly the right place and precise time, absolutely, positively perfect through Christ Jesus, He is bringing His love to those around you, in His custom-made vessel—you!

"Many are the plans in a man's heart, but it is the Lord's purpose that prevails."
Proverbs 19:21

"For you created my inmost being; you knit me together in my mother's womb. I praise you because I am fearfully and wonderfully made; your works are wonderful, I know that full well. My frame was not hidden from you when I was made in the secret place. When I was woven together in the depths of the earth, your eyes saw my unformed body. All the days ordained for me were written in your book before one of them came to be." Psalm 139:13-16

"For I know the plans I have for you," declares the LORD, "plans to prosper you and not to harm you, plans to give you hope and a future." Jeremiah 29:11

Fred, a missionary to Africa, lifted articles from the table one by one, explaining how each was used by the native tribes. The wooden pillow caused visible grimaces to ripple throughout the crowd. The hippo tooth brought vivid images of the weak-eyed animal's dangerous demeanor.

The next item was a metal ring, worn by a tribe on their necks and extremities. The rings were added liberally until the entire neck was covered by them. When tribal members left the village to live in the city, they shed the "heavy metal". The problem was that their neck muscles had atrophied over time and rendered their necks very weak and unable to support their heads. Eventually, their muscles strengthened and supported their heads once again. The missionary's point was that Jesus frees us from bondage, just as those rings removed free the tribal member.

But, there's more to it. Jesus frees us from the bondage of sin, but He doesn't leave us on our own to figure out how to become stronger. He sticks with us through the process of strengthening our spiritual muscles. New Christians may look a bit wobbly as they are released from their bonds, but given time and encouragement, Jesus will grow them into the fullness of His image, too.

What a wonderful thought! Jesus frees us, but He does not turn us helplessly loose to fend for ourselves. He is lovingly present and aware each time a muscle is tried and tested, stretched, and strengthened. He does not abandon us in our weaknesses, but He supports us in His gentle, but firm hands. In Christ Jesus, there are no bobbleheads, just opportunities to grow in faith!

"For He Himself has said, 'I will never desert you, nor will I ever forsake you.'"

Hebrews 13:5b

"So do not fear, for I am with you; do not be dismayed, for I am your God. I will strengthen you and help you; I will uphold you with my righteous right hand." Isaiah 41:10

Be Prepared! November 12

These past few years have seen quite an uptick in natural disasters, from earthquakes to floods, and fires. Most people have discounted them as normal and natural, especially when they are not personally affected. The phrase, "has been happening since the beginning of time" has rung a bit hollow in my ear. I know better. I have lived long enough to have witnessed many disasters and been blessed enough to have personally experienced only a few floods, two real draughts, several tornadoes, and a hurricane.

Deciding to do a bit of research, I found my perspective to be accurate. Natural disasters have been recorded in history for hundreds of years, so statistics are not that difficult to dig up. Even though I expected to find an increase in events, I was startled to find that in the past century, the average number of 1 to 5 per year increased to an average of over 400 per year by 2018! (And the numbers are not increased due to better reporting, or media. They have been recorded by governments worldwide for the past hundred years.) Floods, drought, earthquakes, extreme weather, and epidemics were the primary causes of death.

Our government sponsors an entire month as, "Emergency Preparedness Month", in October each year. Should the supply chain collapse in the event of emergencies, much time is required for help to arrive, if it ever does. If you are caught unprepared to meet the urgent needs of food, water, medications, warmth, and shelter, you may be risking your life and the lives of those you love. The Boy Scout motto, "Be Prepared", would serve us all well.

Even more urgent than our physical safety and provision, is our urgent need for rescue from the original "natural disaster" of sin. Only the Lord Jesus Christ can rescue us from eternal ruination, separated from God for eternity. Neglect of our spiritual growth, of our relationship with Jesus, leaves us destitute in spirit and vulnerable prey for our enemy.

It is easy when faced with dire situations to run to God, and we should. But we are also responsible for prepping ahead of the hard times by tending to our relationship with Jesus. As we face trials of many kinds, we become confident of His presence, protection, and provision. We are building endurance and spiritual maturity for the duration of life. Being prepared is simply being equipped to do what God has called us to do, in season and out of season. And that can only be accomplished by spending time with Him, ahead of the inevitable upheaval and disaster life serves us.

"Therefore, prepare your minds for action; be self-controlled; set your hope fully on the grace to be given you when Jesus Christ is revealed. As obedient children, do not conform to the evil desires you had when you lived in ignorance. But just as he who called you is holy, so be holy in all you do; for it is written: 'Be holy, because I am holy.'" 1 Peter 1:13-16

Lover's Leap November 13

Starved Rock State Park, in northern Illinois, was a family picnic favorite. It was a getaway outside the city where my brothers and I could run off steam. One of the sites in the park was a high cliff overhanging the rock-lined riverbed, hundreds of feet below. A beautifully spectacular view, it was mysteriously named, "Lover's Leap". The name was a puzzle to me, simply because I could not imagine how those two words connected. Why would anyone do that, especially if they loved each other???

There was, of course, a legend behind the name. Supposedly, a young man and woman from warring tribes fell in love but were forbidden from marrying. Embracing, they threw themselves over the cliff to their deaths on the rocks below. I never could wander the top of that cliff without thinking of the tragic loss resulting from forbidden love, wondering if there couldn't have been another way.

The story of another young maiden emerges as I contemplate that scene. She was condemned to death with no rescuer in sight, no hope of a future, and a ransom so high that it could only be paid with her life. She had nothing of value to offer. Her reputation was wrecked and life in ruins—all was lost, until a young man of regal birth learned of her plight. At just the proper time, he pledged his own riches for her; then plunged over the cliff on her behalf. She was now free.

The Son of the Living God, a life inconceivably precious, paid my debt with His life. What He did was, in many ways, far worse than falling over a cliff to instant demise; instead, He allowed His own creation to torture Him to death on a tree that He grew. He sacrificed Himself to depraved, sin-sick men, arrogant, drunk on power, and blind to the authority of the Son of God. And Jesus allowed it, knowing that all the armies of heaven were at His disposal. He ransomed me, giving me hope and a future, wrapped me in His arms of grace, and raised me to life with Him in eternity.

I, from a warring tribe, in full rebellion against a Holy God, found my reconciliation through the love of Jesus, the warrior Lamb, who reunited me to my Father through His sacred blood. His was the leap of true sacrificial love. It is a bond I dare not consider lightly; a love too priceless to consider trampling underfoot by rejecting it.

"Anyone who rejected the law of Moses died without mercy on the testimony of two or three witnesses. How much more severely do you think a man deserves to be punished who has trampled the Son of God under foot, who has treated as an unholy thing the blood of the covenant that sanctified him, and who has insulted the Spirit of grace?...It is a dreadful thing to fall into the hands of the living God." Hebrews 10:28-29, 31

"Be imitators of God, therefore, as dearly loved children and live a life of love, just as Christ loved us and gave himself up for us as a fragrant offering and sacrifice to God." Ephesians 5:1-2

Unstoppable November 14

There exists no greater test of a young man's love than to wreck his pride and joy. At some point, I became aware that I was not it, at least not in the same way. This love was reserved for his newly purchased dream car, his worked-long-hours-and-saved-for car. It was Gary's "finally replacing the college junker" car. When he proudly drove up in the newly polished, bright red Dodge Charger, he was ecstatic, as he revealed his newly claimed steed.

And when he allowed me, the inexperienced driver, to drive it, alone for the first time, the powerful engine had its way with me. It landed his pride-and-joy squarely embedded into a telephone pole. I was fine, but the car was not, requiring a substantial restoration. Gary's love passed my unsightly driving test, he was able to look past the event, and our love was, ever after, unstoppable.

Many years hence, I would come to realize another unstoppable love, that of the love of God. Our sin, my sin, wrecked God's pride and joy, too, destroying His only Son. The pinnacle of perfection and power, the Prince of Heaven came to earth in human flesh, only to be wrecked by our sin. Just as Gary allowed me the free will to drive his new car, God allows us the free will to decide whether we will follow and love Him, or not. He does not coerce obedience, nor demand love, but shows us His love first, though we do not deserve it.

Jesus came to die in my place, sacrificing Himself so that I could be restored to relationship with the Father through Him. He did not have to do it, and it was not accidental; he did it willingly and intentionally, as He followed God's only plan of restoration, Self-sacrifice. When I had lost control of the car, I realized the cause of my accident was my pride and sense of power, and I felt great remorse toward Gary. It was somewhat akin to the remorse I felt for my willfulness and sin against my heavenly Father later.

Just as Gary forgave me and the car was restored, God forgives, forgets, and restores so much more. When we come to Him in honest repentance, with sincere hearts of sorrow for our deeds of rebellion against Him, no matter how wrecked our lives, He forgives. There is not a "broken" that He cannot repair, a "lost" that cannot be found, or a "wreck" that cannot be salvaged. That is what grace is---your fault for sinning, but your relationship with God restored at His expense. Grace is God's restoration power, undeserved, but bestowed because His love is unstoppable.

"And this is the testimony: God has given us eternal life, and this life is in his Son. He who has the Son has life; he who does not have the Son of God does not have life."

1 John 5:11-12

"For it is by grace you have been saved, through faith---and this not from yourselves, it is the gift of God---not by works, so that no one can boast. For we are God's workmanship, created in Christ Jesus to do good works, which God prepared in advance for us to do."

Ephesians 2:8-10

As a Christian, one of the most frequent questions I have heard is, "Why does God allow evil people in the world?" The only answer I found was, "We simply trust in God's wisdom and plan." Until now, that was good enough. But if salvation through Jesus is real, permanent, and rewarded for eternity, I still wondered, "Why did God allow people, who He knows will never come to Him, to live on earth, where they cause pain, sorrow, and live in denial of Him?"

Once this life ends, there are no second chances, no changing the choice made, and no begging for a stay of execution for our sentence. The choice is a forever one, and "always" never ends. The gravity of it grieves my spirit, and I realize that my spirit is, most days, not grieved *enough* by it. So many people have not yet heard, or not yet chosen salvation through the priceless Son of God. So many people live lives of sweet oblivion, their time ticking down, their choice unmade, and heaven unsecured with Jesus right outside their door.

My next question is, "Is it possible that God allows people to live on earth, knowing them fully since the world was established, knowing that they will reject Him and His offer of eternal life through Jesus?" Just as He has fore-known each of us who would accept Him, in His infinite mercy, will God have given them a brief reprieve to enjoy the earth? Is this the best they will ever know? Their prospects, even the most wretched life on this earth, will still be far better than what they have ahead of them, in a place of never-ending torment, loneliness, with the total absence of God's goodness.

God loves each one, and that eternity is not what God wants FOR them; He sent His treasured Son, Jesus, to die for every one of us. We each hold that choice in our hands: the Gift of Life chosen and the Key to heaven's access granted, or the Gift of Life refused, and passage through the gates of heaven denied. We can choose to look forward to the jubilation of Christ's return as Sovereign Lord; or dread the death knell of His re-entry to the world that condemned Him.

If God, in His mercy, allows the wicked to live on the earth for a season, it is all the more evidence of His compassionate love; God's invitation will be the "always and forever" invitation the unsaved will wish they could reclaim.

"But Abraham replied, 'Son, remember that in your lifetime you received your good things, while Lazarus received bad things, but now he is comforted here and you are in agony. And besides all this, between us and you a great chasm has been fixed, so that those who want to go from here to you cannot, nor can anyone cross over from there to us.' He answered, 'Then I beg you, father, send Lazarus to my father's house, for I have five brothers. Let him warn them, so that they will not also come to this place of torment.' Abraham replied, 'They have Moses and the Prophets; let them listen to them.' 'No, father, Abraham, he said, 'but if someone from the dead goes to them, they will repent.' He said to him, 'If they do not listen to Moses and the Prophets, they will not be convinced even if someone rises from the dead.'" Luke 16:25-31

"For God so loved the world that he gave his one and only Son, that whoever believes in him shall not perish but have eternal life. For God did not send his Son into the world to condemn the world, but to save the world through him. Whoever believes in him is not condemned, but whoever does not believe stands condemned already because he has not believed in the name of God's one and only Son." John 3:16-18

Since practically the beginning of time, ear-piercing stood as a common practice, but my mother stood firmly against it. No amount of begging was effective, and all negotiations failed. She would have no change of heart during my teen years, and her negative view of the act was held with firm conviction. I would not be pierced for life under her watch.

Just after being married, I headed to the local mall with my new husband, and while he looked on, the job was done. I could not believe how much it hurt! But 43 years later, as I dressed and put on a pair of earrings, I considered how much I had enjoyed wearing them every day. The pain was a small price to pay in the long run. Comparing the price against the benefit, there was no contest. And not five years later, my mother had her ears pierced!

Over the course of a lifetime, ear piercing is such a minuscule event. And I believe heaven will be like that, as we look back at the suffering and trials of our lives. In the span of eternity, they will seem tiny in comparison to living in the presence of God. However, one piercing will penetrate all time, as the point dividing all history, and all people, into "before" and "after". That point in time is the cataclysmic death of the Son of the Living God. The piercing of his side by a Roman spear spilled the blood of the Lamb of God, and divided time into "B.C." ("Before Christ"), and "A.D." ("anno Domini", "after Christ's death").

The piercing of His hands, feet, and side pierced my heart when I understood that He had suffered beyond my comprehension, for my apprehension. His life saved mine and will weigh in as the ultimate, and an eternally memorable price paid for my unbreakable bond to Him; my debt was paid in full. He was pierced for life, pierced for my freedom from sin and death, a price unimaginable. And as He views eternity, I know Jesus will say that the pain He suffered was worth every soul redeemed, because He loves us that much.

"But he was pierced for our transgressions, he was crushed for our iniquities; the punishment that brought us peace was upon him, and by his wounds we are healed…For he bore the sin of many, and made intercession for the transgressors." Isaiah 53:5, 12c

Priceless

Her big, brown eyes opened widely as she searched my face for a hint of weakness, and I knew I had made a mistake. Five-year-old Abby had noticed, as five-year-old girls always do, the jewelry adorning my wrist and a matching ring. Noticing that she had noticed, I relinquished the baubles to Abby as the Sunday morning service continued, also realizing that retrieving them would not be a simple task.

To Abby, my jewels were priceless treasures. And I was whisked back in time to my grandmother's side, playing with her rings and bracelets, sitting in Sunday service together. I daydreamed among riches that were not valuable at all, but in my eyes, they were priceless. At the end of the service, as her mother gently removed the jewelry from her little limbs, the bright, brown eyes sank into a river of tears. As we walked through the playground, Abby's expression, as she looked up at me, hinted that I had been forgiven.

At that moment, I saw myself again, not as a young girl, but the woman I had become, and who, ever since those days sitting beside my grandmother, has been attracted to the glitter of worldly baubles. The seduction of all things "valuable" in the eyes of the world had begun at an early age and had not relented since. Slowly, though, but profoundly God began to expose their true worth as I walked with Him.

How much I resemble Abby in my Father's eyes! I am so attracted to the world and all it has to offer. It is all so very appealing until it is exposed for what it is—a cheap imitation. The real value is found in the riches of knowing Jesus. Every treasure on earth is His to give, but being the good Father He is, He knows when and what to give. His are the gifts that build our character, instilling trust in Him, and all are in His perfect timing.

He patiently allows me to explore this world, and as He does, He knows I will eventually find it empty and completely lacking. He will also remove from my hands anything I become so dependent upon that my perspective becomes unbalanced, anything that I have made my idol. The real priceless treasure is not found in the glamour of the world, it is produced through love and obedience to a Savior who sacrificed the riches of heaven to die on a cross. And because of Jesus, through His grace, the King's coffers are always accessible and overflowing for His children, with the true priceless treasures.

"Command those who are rich in this present world not to be arrogant nor to put their hope in wealth, which is so uncertain, but to put their hope in God, who richly provides us with everything for our enjoyment. Command them to do good, to be rich in good deeds, and to be generous and willing to share. In this way they will lay up treasure for themselves as a firm foundation for the coming age, so that they may take hold of the life that is truly life."
1 Timothy 6:17-19

A wide chasm separates the people we have known for a lifetime from those who have the honor of being "life-long friends". Winnie-the-Pooh comes to mind, he with his circle of colorful but common friends, all residing in the neighborly plot of forest called the Hundred Acre Woods. I wonder how his friendships aged beyond the storyline of Christopher Robin growing up.

Did Piglet remain Pooh's closest friend for life, or did he become so brave that he struck out in an adventure beyond the neighborhood woods? Roo certainly had to grow up and venture out into the world. Tigger may have impulsively bounced himself right into a new relationship, and Kanga may have had more Roos. Let's face it, life changes; and to a certain extent, people we love and care for change, too. Some friends come, some go, and a few endure for a lifetime.

To have a lifelong friend is truly special, and though I cannot count even one, God has graced my life with precious decades-long relationships, people who are like family to me, and I am exceedingly blessed. But the friend who has stood by me is the one I call Savior. It is Jesus I count on when no one else can hear my sighs, wipe my tears, and mend my heart. It is Jesus who understands my pain, my struggles, my failings, and none of those cause Him to retreat.

Jesus is the one who is closer than a brother, wiser than a father, more tender than a mother, and more compassionate than a sister. He is not jealous, resentful, or dominating. He is patient, caring, loving, and concerned for my welfare like no one else on earth. And though He doesn't expect me to look to Him exclusively for friendship, He is the friend to top all friends.

Friends can spend a great deal of time together or be separated for lengths of time, but they experience deep ties that bring them back into deep fellowship. Jesus does not rebuff me when I have neglected Him for a time; He always forgives, always desires a restored relationship with me. My guilt is dissolved by His grace, and we begin anew. There is no insecurity in my relationship now, proving Him faithful many times over. We are friends for life.

Winnie-the-Pooh had wonderful adventures with his friends in the Hundred Acre Woods, and I am as blessed to have similar friendships. They are honest and sincere friends who care for one another without judgment and condemnation. And I am confident that, if Pooh Bear had known my Jesus, he would have made Him his friend for life, as well.

"A man of many companions may come to ruin, but there is a friend who sticks closer than a brother." Proverbs 18:24

"My command is this: Love each other as I have loved you. Greater love has no one than this, that he lay down his life for his friends. You are my friends if you do what I command. I no longer call you servants, because a servant does not know his master's business. Instead, I have called you friends, for everything that I learned from my Father I have made known to you." John 15:12-15

Bread Alone

No larger than six pounds, black with white accented chest and chin, Ebby sat gazing up at me as I brushed my teeth. When I finished, I spoke very lovingly to her, telling her what a good dog she was and how much I loved her. Her black face visibly softened. Her dark eyes warmed at my loving praise, and her body relaxed as she eased into a peaceful pose. At that moment, I understood the words Jesus spoke in rebuke of Satan's temptation; **"Jesus answered, 'Man does not live on bread alone, but on every word that comes from the mouth of God.'"** (Matthew 4:4)

The realization struck me that Jesus was countering Satan's temptation with more than a statement about bread, more than physical food. The word "comes" is not past tense, it is present tense. God doesn't speak to us only in the past, but today, in every moment. His speaking is continual. How amazing it is that God speaks to us now!

I am everything to Ebby. Dogs, like people, need companionship, a relationship, a "pack" of support, and interaction. Ebby can eat all the food her body requires, but if she has no interaction with me, she cannot be happy. She will become anxious, destructive, sick, and eventually die without me. Ebby waits for, anticipates, and longs for interaction with me.

How much more do we depend on our heavenly Father who loves, cares for, and provides for us! He has provided for an intimate relationship with us through His Son, Jesus; yet when we neglect that relationship, unpleasantness follows. Often, we do not hear what He is speaking to us because we are inattentive, slow to hear, distracted, believing it not possible, and certainly not likely. We were created for a relationship with the Father, and no substitutions, no other "bread" will sustain us. It is food available only from one Source; the substitutions of the world will leave us empty, sick, and dying.

As we sit expectantly, as Ebby did, waiting to hear our Father speak to us, we are nourished by His forgiveness, love, and acceptance. He is the Supplier of every need, the Giver of Life, the Love we long for, the peaceful Presence in which we flourish. Jesus is the bread, His body broken, to make that relationship possible. His priceless sacrifice enables us to sit peacefully in God's Presence. Gazing into His face and drinking in every word He has for us, we understand that we cannot live on bread alone, but on every word that proceeds from our God.

"For to you I call, O Lord my Rock; do not turn a deaf ear to me. For if you remain silent, I will be like those who have gone down to the pit. Hear my cry for mercy as I call to you for help, as I lift up my hands toward your Most Holy Place…Praise be to the Lord, for he has heard my cry for mercy. The Lord is my strength and my shield; my heart trusts in him, and I am helped. My heart leaps for joy and I will give thanks to him in song." Psalm 28:1,2,6,7

Thirty-eight states, to date, have welcomed and bid me farewell as I traveled the United States of America. A stunning display of needlework, with each state represented, also traveled the country; its winner was chosen from the contest within its respective state. Their craftsmanship was a work of art and a testimony to the diversity and beauty of the country in which I live. It was as though I was sightseeing, virtually traveling the country again.

Meandering the exhibit, memories resurfaced of my travels. Magnificent waterfalls, the unimaginable brilliance of sunrises over the oceans, and the first glimpses of majestic mountains inspired awe. Sprawling concrete cities, with only dots of greenery, made me feel lonely. Mighty rivers, vast oceans, brisk mountain ice melts, and lazy streams flowed through my memories. Towering glaciers, skyscrapers, and underground cities fascinated me. Signs, lights, inventions, and historic sites illuminated my mind and ignited my imagination.

The United States includes many cultures within its borders. But wherever I have gone, I have observed that we are all simply human beings with the same basic needs. And the greatest basic need is that of reconciliation with our heavenly Father. Every heart knows that singular hunger instinctively; it is embedded in our hearts from our first breaths.

We marvel at man-made wonders, but God marvels at the stunning beauty of a heart surrendered to Him. We rave over the sunset and forget the Maker of it. We make icons of bridges, but He built the only Bridge supported solely by love, the bridge of reconciliation laid across the chasm of sin. Our heavenly Father's focus is on our dire need of Him; and all that has ever been or ever will be in His Creation hinges on the center of His attention, mankind.

In all the world, only one sight is worth seeing. There is only one sight that God, our Father, wishes to see more than any other. It is that of one of His children opens his heart, surrenders all, loves, and submits to Him. He searches for a heart that desires to go where He leads, to do as He asks, and to follow His heart instead of its own. The human heart, humbled and submitted to God in love, is the most beautiful sight in the world to its Creator and Redeemer.

"But the Lord said to Samuel, '…The Lord does not look at the things man looks at. Man looks at the outward appearance, but the Lord looks at the heart.'" 1 Samuel 16:7

"We live by faith, not by sight. We are confident, I say, and would prefer to be away from the body and at home with the Lord. So we make it our goal to please him, whether we are at home in the body or away from it." 2 Corinthians 5:7-9

Coming Home

One of the most difficult times as a parent was when my teenage daughters were dropped off at band and gymnastics camps. For the first time, our son was also leaving to be a camp counselor. I recognized profoundly, on the return trip home, that we were in the upheaval of teen growth. The preparation for leaving home was underway, with unending change on our horizon and stretching into the near future. The way home was poignant with the silent acknowledgment that an empty house would soon be our new normal.

The new experiences we all encountered would entail great times and new relationships, uncertainties, insecurities, trials, and a certain amount of pain. And from that point on, I would stand helpless, unable to protect them. They had always belonged to the Lord, but now, I had no choice but to entrust Him with the responsibility for their complete well-being and growth.

When each teen walked through the door, I could barely contain my excitement to have them home safely, to hear all that happened while they were away, and to know how they felt about their experiences. At that point, my family was once again complete, and my heart content, but I knew their exit would approach faster than my heart was prepared to accept. Home is truly where the heart is, but not necessarily its permanent residence.

As I later read the verse, **"Precious in the sight of the Lord is the death of his faithful servants," Psalm 115:16**, I questioned the use of the word "precious" until I considered it from my Heavenly Father's perspective. As my children's coming home from camp was precious to me, so is it precious to receive His children home again. There is no more precious time than welcoming home the son or daughter who is dearly loved, and who has been away too long.

To touch them, feel their closeness, search their faces, and watch their expressions in person cannot be duplicated. To enfold loved ones in your arms, knowing they are finally safe in your embrace is matchless, and this is our Father's heart. Our coming home is truly precious in His sight, for there is no one in this world who loves us more, and no place more filled with His expression of love than heaven itself.

"Now we know that if the earthly tent we live in is destroyed, we have a building from God, an eternal house in heaven, not built by human hands. Meanwhile we groan, longing to be clothed with our heavenly dwelling, because when we are clothed, we will not be found naked. For while we are in this tent, we groan and are burdened, because we do not wish to be unclothed but to be clothed with our heavenly dwelling, so that what is mortal may be swallowed up by life. Now it is God who has made us for this very purpose and has given us the Spirit as a deposit, guaranteeing what is to come." 2 Corinthians 5:1-5

Walking through the lobby, a fundraising sign caught my attention reading, "You Are Not Alone". The organization promoted by the sign was speaking to the isolation resulting from brain deterioration in the aged. I am quite experienced with the process, having witnessed first-hand the torments of it in more than one family member. I have been a caregiver and can attest that suffering is personal; no one else can alleviate our pain and grief.

There has only been one person in my life possessing the capacity for healing my pain and sorrows, only One, who suffered even more than I could ever comprehend. He walked that path Himself, witnessing profound loss, pain, and suffering, and He was angered by the futility of it. He is the God who formed us, the Healer who touches our pain.

He is the Son of Man, acquainted with grief and sorrow. He is Jesus, who wept at the grave of Lazarus, even knowing that He would soon call him forth from the dead. He too felt alone in His suffering, even knowing that His Heavenly Father knew all He was going through. He asked His disciples why they had abandoned Him to lonely prayer in the darkness of the garden; but even in that dark olive grove, He was not truly alone, and neither are we.

Our omniscient, all-knowing Father witnesses every tear, holding us tenderly in an invisible embrace, assuring us we are not alone. To whisper the name of Jesus aloud, to speak it tenderly if only within our own hearing, is the access code that activates His living presence. He will never ignore those who call His name in faith, and who trust Him in their trials.

Jesus promised never to leave or forsake those who trust Him, never to turn away any who come to Him in pain and need. Whisper His name, trust His love, quietly surrender your will to His, and walk with confidence where He leads. Rest, knowing His very Presence, the Holy Spirit and Comforter, will hold you securely. No matter what your reality is, whatever suffering, pain, or sorrow, you are not alone.

"Praise be to the God and Father of our Lord Jesus Christ, the Father of compassion and the God of all comfort, who comforts us in all our troubles so that we can comfort those in any trouble with the comfort we ourselves have received from God. For just as the sufferings of Christ flow over into our lives, so also through Christ our comfort overflows."
2 Corinthians 1:3-5

"If you love me, you will obey what I command. And I will ask the Father, and he will give you another Counselor to be with you forever---the Spirit of truth. The world cannot accept him, because it neither sees him nor knows him. But you know him, for he lives with you and will be in you. I will not leave you as orphans; I will come to you." John 14:15-18

Used Up

"Turn your eyes upon Jesus. Look full in His wonderful face, and the things of earth will grow strangely dim, in the light of His glory and grace." This song by Helen H. Lemmel, written in 1922, immediately came to mind. I felt weary, drained, poured out with barely a drop of strength remaining. Every morsel of "me" had been used up.

"Am I never to find a place of contentment and belonging??? I reach out to so many people. I'm too busy to have friends, and too involved to be involved. Demands consume me. Everyone is ready to take what they need but has nothing to give." Some of you may immediately recognize this for what it is, weariness giving way to self-pity. Others may recognize the need for boundaries in my life, which I later recognized, too. What I saw was an unexpected revelation about Jesus. This was my conversation with Him after my whining:

"Jesus, I guess this is all very familiar to you. You said You not only know how I was made, but You intentionally made me. And You lived everything I am going through. You reached out to thousands more than I, yet separation bound You on every side. You were on the outside of many more circles than I will ever know. You were too busy to have friends because You were training disciples. Everyone was ready to take what they needed from You, having little to give You. You knew all the demands before the moment You were born but came because you knew how much we needed You."

The spiritual gift of encouragement is a sword that cuts both ways. Because it is a gift, it delights my soul when I can offer uplifting and sincere words to anyone who is hurting, wounded, and broken. Because it is a gift, it can also be taken without gratitude and used up without replenishing. On the days when I am completely stripped and drained of any crumb of encouragement for myself, I find myself crying out to the Lord in something that resembles a temper tantrum.

Jesus reminds me that when I am feeling exhausted and weak, my acceptance is wrapped up in the wrong packaging, and tangled in "people" string. We are all broken, all needy, and demanding of others when we lose focus of our Savior. But we can never use up all that Jesus has for us. Like a man starving for food, the acceptance, the food I crave, is only to be found in Him. I am learning that when I cannot feel His presence, when I feel all used up, He is the only one who can refill me.

"I know how to live humbly, and I know how to abound. I am accustomed to any and every situation—to being filled and being hungry, to having plenty and having need. I can do all things through Christ who gives me strength." Philippians 4:12-13

The magnetic attraction of digital gaming has not been lost on me, and I find it exceedingly difficult to break away once I begin playing word games, particularly. The best excuse I have heard and used myself is that "playing games keeps my mind sharp". I believe that is a good debating point, yet to be definitively proven. I would argue that mind games play games with our minds.

One conflict I have observed with individuals playing electronic games is that he or she becomes so engrossed in play that anything interfering causes irritation. Self-absorption is one of the common denominators of gaming of all kinds. And recently, another perspective dawned on me—the games are intended to keep us engaged, so much so that they become addictive.

God's purpose for creating human beings was companionship and mutual love; an intimate relationship was intentional. Our fallen spirits have played with our minds, shifting our focus from "He Who Is Worthy", to we who are not. The greater revelation is that our enemy (the real one, not the ones in the games) has a deeper purpose, with anything keeping us self-involved, a highly useful tool in his arsenal.

We were created for our Father's good pleasure, not to focus solely on our own. The games to which we glue our attention can obscure our focus and obstruct our purpose. Life becomes "all about me" instead of "all about Him". This is not to say that every pleasure should be thrown on the dung heap. God bestows good gifts on His children, but they are never given as His replacement.

Digital gaming, like any good gift in excess, can easily run headlong into manipulation by our enemy. We can become not only distracted but also deceived. If anything distracts us from a relationship with our Father, drawing us away from Him, the moment has arrived in which we must question, "Is this a wise choice, or is it a tool of God's enemy?"

The games meant to improve our minds may be the "mind games" he is attempting to use against us. They are intended to steal our most valuable assets, moments with our Creator. Moment by precious moment, we can choose to turn our attentions to a Divine relationship, purchased with the priceless blood of the Lamb of God. God doesn't play the mind games of His enemy, He demolishes them.

"Praise be to the God and Father of our Lord Jesus Christ, who has blessed us in the heavenly realms with every spiritual blessing in Christ. For he chose us in him before the creation of the world to be holy and blameless in his sight. In love he predestined us to be adopted as his sons through Jesus Christ, in accordance with his pleasure and will---to the praise of his glorious grace, which he has freely given us in the One he loves."
Ephesians 1:3-6

It could not have been a mere coincidence that the daily reading in my Bible fell upon Exodus 16. Or that today, after many failed attempts at making sourdough bread, the most exquisite loaves emerged triumphantly from my oven. It had taken many months of experimentation, frustration, and starting from scratch again ten days prior. This batch rose high and light, the cinnamon swirled tightly throughout, with the light flaky crunch of a crust, delicately browned. I have never tasted a more perfect loaf.

As I savored every bite, I read the chapter laid out before me, Moses's account of the Israelites grumbling about their lack of bread and God's miraculous solution: **"The Lord said to Moses, 'I will rain down bread from heaven for you. The people are to go out each day and gather enough for that day.'"** (Verse 4a) God rained down bread! Manna, as the people called it, was white like coriander seed and tasted like wafers made with honey, making me think of the sweet cinnamon bread in my mouth. Moses told the people, "It is the bread the Lord has given you to eat."

God also provided the meat they complained about lacking. He drove enough quail into their camp to cover the ground. But the best part was, there in the desert, the glory of the Lord appeared to them in the cloud! All this was done for them even as they complained against God about leaving their place of slavery and bondage. What an impression this made, as I finished my delicious bread and complaining for months about my failures!

The bread had not been my only complaint, though, and I realized that I had done my share of grumbling about circumstances I found unfavorable. In finances, stressful relationships, and employment challenges, I never considered the depth of my ingratitude to my heavenly Father. I sounded just like the Israelites in the heat of the desert, delivered and set free, but blinded by the desert sun in my personal wilderness.

God provided meat and bread, despite the bitter complaints of His people, and He continues to do so today. Above all, God sent into our desert the Bread of Heaven, the Son of God, the sweetest, and most perfect life-giving bread of all. Jesus is the sweetness of God's mercy and the bread of His grace; He is inviting us to come, taste, and see, that it is He who is truly the bread from heaven, giving life to the world and life to my soul. God was present with the Israelites in their desert, and He is with us in our own.

"Jesus said to them, 'I tell you the truth, it is not Moses who has given you the bread from heaven, but it is my Father who gives you the true bread from heaven. For the bread of God is he who comes down from heaven and gives life to the world…I am the bread of life."

John 6:32-33, 35a

"The Lord said to Moses, I have heard the grumbling of the Israelites. Tell them, 'At twilight you will eat meat, and in the morning, you will be filled with bread. Then you will know that I am the Lord you God.'" Exodus 16:11-12

Broken, but Not Destroyed November 26

Perfectly enveloped in a half inch of crystal ice, the Crepe Myrtle berries adorned the ends of the laden branches. The dim light from the low hanging, snow laden clouds did not hinder the glistening of the jewel-like berries in their translucent encasement. An ice storm the night before had laid its heavy blanket on each branch, and now the branches bowed their heads gracefully to greet the ground.

The River Birch did not bend as gracefully beneath its burden. One by one, its ice laden bows snapped and laid in the cold grass below. Half of its original mass remained. However, what remains will grow again, defying the attempt at its demise when spring peers over the winter horizon.

What the two trees have in common is resilience in the face of trial. For a Christian, resilience equates with trust in our Father's good intentions toward us. It is trusting that whatever trials we face in this life, we serve a God who is capable of changing our circumstances. And if He chooses another method, He is wise and good anyway. He is a God of infinite new beginnings.

When our new beginnings upon this earth are exhausted, another and final new beginning awaits. Our journey on this earth may end in exhaustion, perhaps broken and spent, but the last new beginning will be nothing short of spectacular. It is the ultimate display of the power of God through resurrection life.

We may appear bent under the weight of our trials, crushed and defeated. But just as the ice magnified the beauty of the Crepe Myrtle's berries, so Christ magnifies Himself as we trust in Him. As the River Birch bent under the weight and damage ensued, we can flourish again as we trust in the One who is the God of renewal and rebirth. We may feel broken, but through Jesus we are not destroyed.

"But we have this treasure in jars of clay to show that this all-surpassing power is from God and not from us. We are hard pressed on every side, but not crushed; perplexed, but not in despair; persecuted, but not abandoned; struck down, but not destroyed. We always carry around in our body the death of Jesus, so that the life of Jesus may also be revealed in our mortal body...Now we know that if the earthly tent we live in is destroyed, we have a building from God, an eternal house in heaven, not built by human hands. Meanwhile we groan, longing to be clothed with our heavenly dwelling, because when we are clothed, we will not be found naked. For while we are in this tent, we groan and are burdened, because we do not wish to be unclothed but to be clothed in our heavenly dwelling, so that what is mortal may be swallowed up by life. Now it is God who has made us for this very purpose and has given us the Spirit as a deposit guaranteeing what is to come...We live by faith, not by sight." 1 Corinthians 4:7-11 and 5:1-5, 7

Leftovers

Thanksgiving and Christmas holidays are the pinnacle of "leftover" bliss. Cooking everyday meals is hard work, but cooking for the holidays, when expectations soar and the number of mouths to feed doubles--or triples---is exhausting. It is a labor of love and rewarding to know that the meal served was satisfying and that it spoke to each heart of my care for them. But on the holidays, chefs and home cooks alike have my respect.

Not only do the meals require preparation, but after every guest has waddled home, the kitchen once again becomes the arena of labor; packaging of foods, washing dishes, and returning the kitchen to a recognizable and familiar space. Leftovers are the equivalent of recovery time for the cook. Throughout the year, I have come to depend on the leftovers. While sustaining me, they also grant me a smidgeon of extra time.

And leftovers were elevated to a high status in the Bible. Really! Leftovers were used   by Jesus to illustrate God's provision, as evidence of Jesus' authority from the Father. Two different times Jesus miraculously provided meals to thousands of people, not in fancy kitchens but in isolated areas where no food was available, aside from a child's snack. Following both meals, the disciples were instructed to collect the leftovers. When the meal ended, I don't know how many of the crowd noticed the initially empty baskets now full, but His disciples did; they knew the impossible had taken place.

I am certain that many scholars have evaluated these miracles performed by Jesus from every perspective. But in my humble opinion, it is God's simple illustration of His thrill in surprising us with the magnitude of His generosity. Food is elemental to life, yet He provided more than they required. Jesus didn't meet the minimum standard; He exceeded it. He stamped the event with His special touch. The leftovers were proof that God provides abundantly, when we trust Him, with even more than we ask or can imagine.

Every day that we have food to eat is a testament to God's provision. Whether in abundance or just enough, whether leftovers come from it or another meal requires preparation, I am rarely as thankful as I should be. Nor do I recognize often enough my God's generosity, benevolence, and mercy. Overlooking my ingratitude daily, He continues to bless me beyond what I deserve. Today I am thankful for His grace and provision--including leftovers!

"Then Jesus directed them to have all the people sit down in groups on the green grass...They all ate and were satisfied, and the disciples picked up twelve basketfuls of broken pieces of bread and fish. The number of the men who had eaten was five thousand." Mark 6:42-44

"Then Jesus declared, 'I am the bread of life. He who comes to me will never go hungry, and he who believes in me will never be thirsty.'" John 6:35

Convergence

Recently, I learned that I am in the life stage called "convergence". Convergence is the stage where all the rest of your life supposedly begins to make sense, the age of 50-ish to 80-ish, so I am right in the middle. I have been at a loss for years to define it, though I could sense a different perspective on life, having lived through much purifying and cleansing, transformation, and mellowing.

I've seen birth and death, loss and gain, dishonor and honor, wonder and revelation. Living through all those experiences brought me to the doorstep of convergence, my place of influence. By sharing my experiences, I have been able to offer encouragement to others; but more importantly, it has landed me squarely in God's presence, the very place He desires me to be.

"I sense there is a major reason I am still here but cannot see it yet. All in His time..." was what I had written in my journal. And, two weeks later, I felt strongly impressed that it was time to begin this book. Keep in mind that 30 years earlier I felt I was to write a book, and in all that time it hadn't happened. The timing was always off. I simply lacked direction and couldn't bring myself to do it. Convergence was the missing element, or more accurately, God's timing was of greater importance.

At any stage of life, we can become anxious and fretful, struggling to find our "purpose", but God is the one who reveals it in His timing. God has timing for everything, whether seasons in nature or seasons in our lives. Nothing happens without His purpose. True convergence, the ability to see past experiences with contentment and peace, can happen anywhere along the timeline of our lives. When we walk in simple gratitude for the gifts and talents God has given us, utilize them in the place He has planted us, and walk in His Spirit, that is the ultimate "convergence".

The revelation of how God formed you to be an influence in His world can be realized in two days, two weeks, or two decades; but the revealing is ultimately God's to give. Trust that you are where He has you this moment for a reason, that He will guide you as you yield to Him, that He loves you, and He has a plan and purpose for your life. You will know "convergence" as God reveals it.

"For I know the plans I have for you,' declares the Lord, 'plans to prosper you and not to harm you, plans to give you hope and a future.'" Jeremiah 29:11

"Humble yourselves, therefore, under God's mighty hand, that he may lift you up in due time. Cast all your anxiety on him because he cares for you." 1 Peter 5:6-7

As a young believer, I found it difficult to trust the Lord's control over my life, as I tenaciously grasped my "right" to retain that control. I greatly resembled the proverbial two-year-old child, stubbornly refusing to yield her favorite toy, or insisting that I don't want to go to bed yet, all the while falling asleep. A typical human being, I am.

Humans in general are quite deluded by darkness and believe we are in control of life on this planet. Our free wills lead us to believe the lie. I have personal knowledge verifying that fact from my own experience. Here are some areas of expertise I cannot claim to control: My heart beating and my lungs breathing—God owns the number of my days, the seasons, governments of the world, secrets small and large, the stars and moon, day and night, and the movement of the Spirit.

Many things can change *through* God, through prayer and petition, and by His Spirit. But by my will alone, they won't. It is humbling, and should be, to realize the Lord is God, and I am not. My pride is exposed when the curtain is pulled back and my delusion is exposed to full view. God is in control, and I am finding peace in relinquishing what was not mine in the first place. I am replacing the illusion with a deeper understanding of who Christ is—the One who holds the universe, and my life, together.

It has not been easy to yield my out-of-control self into His patient and knowing hands. Years have passed, with many opportunities to loosen my grip. I have had, by His grace, ample do-overs; and He has been a kind and gentle, but a firm teacher. I can now walk more calmly next to my Lord, trusting His control, direction, and His purposes. My world is more peaceful when my will is submitted to His plan. My fears are more subdued, though I always have room to practice and grow.

But isn't that the beauty of knowing Jesus as our Savior, and God as our heavenly Father? When we are willing to confess our prideful bent, relinquish our control to Him, and acknowledge that He is God, and we are not—that is the beginning of a beautiful relationship. The balance of power is unmistakable; it has been His all along.

"Then the Lord spoke to Job out of the storm: 'Brace yourself like a man; I will question you, and you shall answer me. Would you discredit my justice? Would you condemn me to justify yourself? Do you have an arm like God's, and can your voice thunder like his? Then adorn yourself with glory and splendor and clothe yourself in honor and majesty. Unleash the fury of your wrath, look at every proud man and bring him low, look at every proud man and humble him, crush the wicked where they stand…Then I myself will admit to you that your own right hand can save you.' Job 40:6-12,14

"All a man's ways seem right to him, but the Lord weighs the heart." Proverbs 21:2

Steve stood before us describing his struggle of seeking God and wrestling with his faith. He said that he knew the Lord dwelt within him, likening the situation to having a pilot light burning inside. Though the light was small, it still burned; his faith existed, but he desired for it to burn more brightly. This man, with his incredibly passionate and sensitive spirit, seemed always to burn brightly to me, so it came as something of a surprise. But as I considered my walk with God, it was not surprising at all. I had walked the same path, and have many times since, feeling my flame flickering weakly.

Pilot lights on gas burners are fed by a gas source, and the length of flame is dependent upon the volume of gas coming through the line. It is regulated by the valve, allowing greater flow, and hence, larger flame, or reduced flow, producing a smaller flame. The "pilot light" in us is the Holy Spirit, the seal of redemption received when we yield our lives to Christ Jesus. Our power source is God Himself. We have, by our wills, some control over the valve, allowing God to work in greater measure through trust and obedience, or by suppressing His work with doubt and disobedience as we resist His Spirit.

As we yield to His will and direction, the flame burns brighter. God has ultimate control over the power source and the flame of the pilot light, but it cannot be extinguished; we cannot be "unsealed" by His Spirit. Those He has marked since the beginning of time, set aside and redeemed, will never walk on this earth without His light burning within them.

Even when we feel alone, struggle with our expectations, or face unfathomable loss, we are not abandoned, and His fire is never extinguished. When we feel we have failed Him, when we understand we can never be "good enough", even then we are never rejected, and His fire still burns. When we have difficulty comprehending His directions, and we cannot see the way before us, He is faithful to gently reveal Himself to us, and His flame burns on.

Though the fire sears the mountaintop of Moses or lifts the chariot of Elijah, it is the same fire that inscribes God's love on our hearts. He is the Alpha and Omega, beginning and end, and everything in between. He is Faithful and True, pouring out His grace, sustaining us with His power, and burning within us. His is the pilot light that cannot be stamped out, smothered, snuffed out, or quenched. Turning up the valve and allowing His fire to burn its brightest within us, the world recognizes His glow even before they recognize our Power Source.

"And you also were included in Christ when you heard the word of truth, the gospel of your salvation. Having believed, you were marked in him with a seal, the promised Holy Spirit, who is a deposit guaranteeing our inheritance until the redemption of those who are God's possession---to the praise of his glory." Ephesians 1:13-14

December

Cross-Eyed Christmas   December 1

The mono-focus contact lens in my left eye was fitted for distant vision, and the one in my right eye was fitted for near vision. A very cross-eyed Christmas resulted, as the battle for dominance in my brain proved a very real struggle to see clearly. The only benefit I found to donning the opposing lenses was that the Christmas lights were beautifully blurry and sparkly.

Christmas presents another version of dual vision in the Nativity story itself. One character was short-sighted, attempting to maintain his throne and power through devious methods. King Herod's sneaky way of finding the newly born Messiah, through the deception of the three Magi, masked his intent to kill the infant King. His order to slaughter all the male children revealed what was really in his heart.

The other character, Jesus, was far-sighted, maintaining a lifetime of focus on His Father's will. His goal was to bring the broken human race to a relationship once again with His Father, the true King. Jesus, the Prince of Peace, did all that his Father told Him, in complete submission and humility, never demanding a place on the throne, but trusting His Father for it. He trusted His heavenly Father's will, and His ability to accomplish it.

A similar struggle for dominance exists in each of us. We can choose to act as Herod, or as Jesus, at Christmas, and the whole year through, recognizing the same inclinations within ourselves. We can choose to be the near-sighted king of our own lives, like Herod, controlling and manipulating life to obtain what we desire. Or we can choose to be far-sighted and focused, like Jesus, on trusting our Father in submission and humility, living in His power instead of our own. We can insist on our way, or we can insist God have His way.

We can avoid choosing altogether, resulting in a truly cross-eyed Christmas, our path in life blurred and awkward. We will find ourselves at the mercy of the "king" who reigns forcefully, usually the king of "self", who is a brutal master. Or we can submit to the true King, finding that He rules with love, mercy, and unmerited grace, pouring out His blessings beyond what we can hope or imagine. Which king have you chosen to follow this Christmas? I pray your Christmas is not a cross-eyed one, but one focused on the only One who brings clarity and light to the world.

"When King Herod heard this he was disturbed, and all Jerusalem with him. When he had called together all the people's chief priests and teachers of the law, he asked them where the Christ was to be born. 'In Bethlehem in Judea,' they replied, 'for this is what the prophet has written: "But you, Bethlehem, in the land of Judah, are by no means least among the rulers of Judah; for out of you will come a ruler who will be the shepherd of my people Israel… Then Herod called the Magi secretly and found out from them the exact time the star had appeared. He sent them to Bethlehem and said, 'Go and make a careful search for the child. As soon as you find him, report to me, so that I may go and worship him.'…And having been warned in a dream not to go back to Herod, they returned to their country by another route."" Matthew 2:3-8, 12

Christmas songs were rehearsed beginning in early November, with the buzz of activity ramping up immediately following Thanksgiving. Christmas was special and anticipated nearly as soon as the school year began. Our excitement built as we crafted Christmas decorations for our classrooms, rehearsed performances of Nativity plays, and sang the sacred Christmas carols. In our classroom Christmas parties, it was not unusual to find the baby Jesus, or Holy Stars of Bethlehem, atop the cupcakes.

All these activities were within the public school I attended near Chicago. The candle-light worship services and Nativity displays were the only events that were separately held at churches. "Merry Christmas!" was the standard greeting on the street, and "Happy Holidays" the rarely used generic. Slowly, over decades, the norms changed in our culture, Jesus replaced by safer terminology.

Without Jesus, Christmas has no Christ, no Savior, and no hope. Without the Prince of Peace, we find no peace, and without the holiness of the day, we simply have a vacation day. Without Immanuel, God with Us, we simply have a party without the guest of honor. Without the Baby in the manger, life is business as usual, life without meaning.

The trappings of our celebrations can mask His importance or enhance it, but the truth of Christ's entry does not change. Christmas forever proclaims the birth of the King; the announcement by angelic throngs heralded the royal entrance of the eternal God into His creation. The Ancient of Days became a babe in flesh; the Timeless One was birthed into time. The Owner of all things became the Heir to all things. The Only Wise God became the Author of Salvation. *The* Invisible God became the Image of the invisible God. The Builder of the Universe became the Sure Foundation of our faith.

"Christ"-mas honors the exquisite gift of unimaginable cost, God's gift of love to those who least deserve it. To a world groveling in sin and despair, with no hope of grasping God's approval, the Heavenly Father offered the gift of His only Son to you and me. So, I wish you a truly blessed "Christ"-mas; "Happy Holidays" just doesn't come close to wrapping up this Gift!

"The people walking in darkness have seen a great light; on those living in the land of the shadow of death a light has dawned. You have enlarged the nation and increased their joy, they rejoice before you as people rejoice at the harvest, as men rejoice when dividing the plunder. For as in the day of Midian's defeat, you have shattered the yoke that burdens them, the bar across their shoulders, the rod of their oppressor...For to us a child is born, to us a son is given, and the government will be on his shoulders. And he will be called

Wonderful Counselor, Mighty God, Everlasting Father, Prince of Peace. Of the increase of his government and peace there will be no end. He will reign on David's throne and over his kingdom, establishing and upholding it with justice and righteousness from that time on and forever. The zeal of the Lord Almighty will accomplish this." Isaiah 9:2-4, 6-7

It was the first time I had done it, and it would be the last as well. I had tiptoed into my mother's bedroom, quietly opened the closet door, and found the stash of Christmas gifts for my brothers and me. I lifted the lid of a very small box and gently pulled back the tissue. A tiny porcelain statue of a perfect, gray, and white Arabian foal was revealed; I knew the gift was intended for me. It would become my most prized possession, as well as a profound reminder not to pry into secrets. The surprise was ruined, but the gift was priceless.

For some people, gifts are not very important, but I realized recently how meaningful they are to me. The gifts my mother gave me over her lifetime bring loving memories. Some of the priceless gifts I received were a flannel nightgown made by my grandmother, and a trip to the ball field concession stand with my grandfather. There was a surprise wedding shower given by my soon-to-be sister-in-law, bags of groceries during a job loss, and tender words at the passing of my husband. Tickets to my favorite musical, handmade cards from my grandchildren, and a precious necklace for my birthday; they all grace my memory. A yard mowed by an anonymous neighbor, and meals delivered by loving hands have warmed my spirit. I have been extraordinarily blessed, as evidenced by these and other numerous gifts. Each gift cemented the giver into my heart and memory, as they expressed their care for me.

When I became a believer in Christ Jesus, I learned that God had gifts to give, too, and I earnestly desired those gifts. A bit of a late bloomer at thirty, I felt in a rush to receive what God had for me. I began pleading with Him to show me my gifts. At forty, I was a bit disillusioned, but still searching for evidence. At fifty, full-blown panic set in, believing I had been left off the gift list. At sixty, I focused on Moses and Abraham, who were much later than me in receiving their calling at 80.

Today, I realize that I had my gift all along, the gift of relationship with the Sovereign and Holy, King of Kings. Yes, He is my gift, and through that revelation, I am uncovering the other gifts I could not recognize, until it was His time to reveal them. I have the gift of encouragement, the gift of vision to see His traits revealed in His creation, the gift of insight, and sharing through parables. I am overwhelmed now by the gifts I thought so elusive; they were simply hidden until He deemed the time ripe. Realization dawned, that the Giver of the gift **is** the gift of a lifetime! The rest follows according to His plan, not mine.

"Humble yourselves, therefore, under God's mighty hand, that he may lift you up in due time. Cast all your anxiety on him because he cares for you." I Peter 5:6-7

"We have different gifts, according to the grace given to each of us." Romans 12:6a

In High Definition

The difference between our old tube television and the newer, high definition, HDTV screen, yielded crisper images, nearly lifelike color, and amazing clarity. The details jumped out, the colors popped, the sharpness of images made me feel as though I could reach out and touch them on the screen. Short of being there in person, high definition made all the difference in creating lifelike broadcasts. High definition was a vast improvement, as well as a profoundly exciting experience.

Similarly, I am not equipped to see myself in high definition the way God does. I see myself through "tube vision", which is a bit warped, not too detailed, and a tad out of focus. My colors are muted, a bit darkened by life, and the sharpness of my picture is not all that great. In many ways, I am like the aging technology that is seen by the world as useless and disposable, lacking the vibrancy of youth, the colorful energy of newness gone, much sooner than expected. My shelf-life has been much too short.

God, however, does not see me that way. His eyes see with high definition, with the ability to gaze past the aging surface and see who He originally created me to be. His eyes view me in vibrant living colors of personality, with the gifts He bestowed upon me. He sees me as the eternal creation He made for a purpose on this earth and a specific place in heaven, even giving me a name no one else has yet heard. I am uniquely colorful and bright, and He sees every detail of my life without despising me for my weaknesses and frailty.

My heavenly Father's eyes see me as He sees His beautiful and pure Son, and bestows the same mercy and grace on me as on Jesus. In my Father's high-definition view, I am endlessly beautiful and pure, spotlessly cleansed. I am not warped; I am highly detailed, fit for the King's viewing. No eye has seen, nor ear has heard what God has in store for His children, and because of Him, I have endless possibilities ahead of me. There are people to bless, new ways to love, and words of encouragement yet to be spoken. I am determined to live the high-definition life God has called me to live.

"But the LORD said to Samuel, 'Do not consider his appearance or his height, for I have rejected him. The LORD does not look at the things people look at. People look at the outward appearance, but the LORD looks at the heart.'" 1 Samuel 16:7

"No, we speak of God's secret wisdom, a wisdom that has been hidden and that God destined for our glory before time began. None of the rulers of this age understood it, for if they had, they would not have crucified the Lord of glory. However, as it is written: 'No eye has seen, no ear has heard, no mind has conceived what God has prepared for those who love him' but God has revealed it to us by his Spirit." 1 Corinthians 2:7-10

Background Noise December 5

A pad of notepaper and a pen were positioned on my grandmother's lovely wood buffet cabinet, the location where Christmas cookies, candies, and desserts were traditionally set out. The seven grandchildren were asked to jot down any memories they had of "Nana Camp", times when they came to my house for my themed events.

Some were listings I remembered well, "Nana's Famous Cinnamon Rolls", "Nana's Famous Parking Lot Tour", "Nana's Famous Art School", "Nana's Famous Cooking School", and "Nana's Famous Extra Cheesy Scrambled Eggs". Of the several items listed, one particularly made me smile, and think; the one that surprised me was "Nana's barking dogs". Three of my grandchildren have grown up without any inside animals and it never occurred to me that the barking of my three, little loud-mouth dogs would qualify as a memorable impression.

Their barking doesn't bother me most of the time. It becomes background noise, easily deciphered by the voice of each dog, and the level of and type of alarm they are conveying. Most of the time, when alone with the dogs, I listen, then tune out; when they know I am seriously giving a command to stop, they stop. Now that I think about it, I can understand how unsettling it could be to children who were not accustomed to it.

Background noise can become so easily tuned out that we no longer notice that it even exists, and so can bad habits, or "little sins" we allow to play in the background of our lives. They become so familiar and comfortable that we no longer notice them. They become pets who know how much latitude they can get by with, pushing us just to the brink of doing something about, until we nudge them down, postponing the eventual reckoning. God cannot let any sin be permissible; all are an affront to His holiness.

In my own life, God has brought my pet sins to the forefront, asking that I release them into His hands, and confessing their hold on my affection. I have come to realize that it is an ongoing process, a fine-tuning in my soul. The Holy Spirit shows me the distractions and noise and asks me to eliminate anything that keeps me from hearing His voice and realizing His presence. The background noise of my "little pet sins" has become less obvious as each demand for my attention is exposed and dealt with, but, like my dogs, requires constant vigilance and discipline.

"Catch for us the foxes, the little foxes that ruin the vineyards, our vineyards that are in bloom." Song of Songs 2:15

"So then, dear friends…make every effort to be found spotless, blameless, and at peace with him. Bear in mind that our Lord's patience means salvation…" 2 Peter 3:14-15a

"If we confess our sins, he is faithful and just and will forgive us our sins and purify us from all unrighteousness." 1 John 1:9

The Nutcracker Ballet performed in Denver, Colorado long ago, was my first professional ballet experience. I was mesmerized from the prelude to the finale. How could anything be so incredibly beautiful? The story was a bit confusing at first, only because I could not unfasten my gaze from the costumes and prima ballerina. Sets glided into and out of place as if on magical cue, and live toy soldiers danced their precision steps. My favorite, "Waltz of the Flowers", concluded the dazzling array of leaps, pointes, and dancing on tiptoes.

Incredibly graceful, poised, and controlled, I am impressed each time I see a ballerina pivoting on toe shoes, appreciating the amount of skill, discipline, and training required. But it takes an entire production company to bring those ballerinas into the spotlight. What would a ballet be without sound? Where would the toy soldiers be without uniforms? What of the background set? The director? Or the producer raising the funds? The makeup artist who defines the expressions? The technical crew who weaves it all together through lighting and special effects?

There was a time in days past I would have compared myself to that prima ballerina and felt like a failure. Because I could not boast such a grand achievement by the world's standards, I felt I had somehow failed at life. That is the problem with comparisons—there is always someone who has accomplished something you haven't. And our culture would have us believe that if we have not risen to the "top", we have failed. I have learned to recognize the lie, asking instead, what would God have me do and be?

Eventually, I could only acknowledge that what God had for me was not a spotlight, but a backlight. The funny thing is that once I was content to be wherever He wanted me, peace followed. I began to be the encourager He intended, listening more, talking less, observing, and praying. I am not the prima ballerina and am relieved to finally be who God created me to be, one of the supporting cast instead.

God has a place for each of us, for some in the spotlight, and others in the background. Stress and fear result from striving where we should be resting, warring for our place in this world instead of trusting Him who holds our place for us. God will move us from the place we believe we should be to the place *He* knows we need to be. He guides us to the sweetest place, that place of ultimate trust in Him alone. That place will involve all He has endowed us to be, but we are not created to be the audience; we are to be part of His grand production of salvation and redemption, through Christ to the world.

"Many are the plans in a man's heart, but it is the Lord's purpose that prevails."

Proverbs 19:21

"If the Son sets you free, you will be free indeed!" John 8:36

"You will show me the path of life; in your presence is fullness of joy; at your right hand are pleasures for evermore." Psalm 16:11

Learning to cook at an early age created a culinary daredevil of sorts, willing to take risks and make substitutions of ingredients freely. By the time I married, I had a decent amount of experience behind me. However, cooking for someone with a different cultural experience played havoc on my culinary skills. My background had many foreign influences, and my husband was all-in rural Midwestern.

My substitutions sometimes took a turn for the worst, yielding the occasional meal nearly inedible. Gradually, I learned what substitutions were desirable in the new recipes, and even began creating my own. Winter Bean Soup has turned out to be a real hit, my corn casserole recipe has made its way to a state far away, and I was ahead of my time with my Chocolate Cloud Mousse.

Most of the flops are long forgotten, but the one that lives on is my Chocolate Rum Torte. It was created over ten years of trial and error, though the errors were never bad enough to toss out. At one point, my husband named my icing "Budge". I had kept adding powdered sugar until the icing was nearly un-spreadable and became fudge; it could barely be scraped from the bowl. He wouldn't allow me to throw it away and ate every bit, though.

That perfected secret recipe is a family Christmas tradition now, harboring more than one ingredient for which there is no workable substitution. There is, however, a substitution that has dire consequences daily, and most of us make that replacement with little thought. We find it natural and normal to substitute worldly things for a relationship with the Creator of the Universe.

An attempt to substitute things, people, or experiences for closeness with God has yielded many a broken heart, resulting in a thoroughly disordered world. Many times, God has allowed me to choose the substitution, if only to prove His worth by comparison. How messed up we become when we opt to replace a relationship with God for all the world has to offer, finding emptiness and darkness instead of His peace and acceptance. He desires for us is to live in the fullness He intended, and that cannot be found in making substitutions.

"So now we can rejoice in our wonderful new relationship with God because our Lord Jesus Christ has made us friends of God." Romans 5:11

"When Jesus spoke again to the people, he said, 'I am the light of the world. Whoever follows me will never walk in darkness but will have the light of life.'" John 8:12

"So then, just as you received Christ Jesus as Lord, continue to live in him, rooted and built up in him, strengthened in the faith as you were taught, and overflowing with thankfulness." Colossians 2:6-7

The retail industry has generated many occasions for gifting, with Christmas being the crown jewel of gifting seasons. Of the many hats of employment I have worn, one of my favorites was being a retail display designer. It was an exhausting job mentally and physically, especially at Christmas, as the whole store required new displays.

Wrapped "gifts" often graced the designs, all being empty boxes and bags adorned with lovely dressings. The designs helped customers imagine what they could do with the wraps and trimmings; no one cared that the containers themselves were empty. They were "dummy" boxes and bags, and no one expected that there were actual gifts inside.

Unlike the elaborate displays I assembled, the most valuable gift of Christmas came, not prettily wrapped in elegant, expensive trappings, but in a very plain and humble wrapping of rough cloth. In the darkness of night, highlighted by smelly, dirt-encrusted shepherds freshly arriving from the fields, baby Jesus was tenderly cradled in a cattle manger.

He was the gift the wise kings from the East recognized, and the angels of heaven proclaimed. But this once-in-eternity Gift went largely unnoticed by the sages, scholars, and kings of the day; save one king named Herod, who wished to kill him. The gift of Christmas, God in flesh, King of Glory, Son of God, and Son of Man was the gift to mankind which mankind largely ignored.

Other than the angelic host, there was no grand display of power. There was no spotlight, save the star undimmed. Until three kings arrived in Nazareth, there was no royalty in attendance.

Jesus' entry into the world He had created by His own spoken Word would, by all appearances, seem to be the "dummy box" event, empty and disappointing from the world's viewpoint. But from God's perspective, the heavens roared riotous exaltations surrounding this unmatched gift, of God giving Himself human form.

The world would have us believe that the bright, shiny, fancily wrapped gifts on the shelves of our lives are the gifts of worth. However, they always prove to be empty, and devoid of life and peace. The gift of Jesus, however, is the favor and pardon of God Almighty upon mankind. He is the gift *of* the ages, the gift *for* all ages. He is the gift of incalculable worth but free to all who will accept it. Ironically, the "dummy box" the world saw as God's gift became the priceless Gift not one of us could afford.

"For God so loved the world that he gave his one and only Son, that whoever believes in him shall not perish but have eternal life. For God did not send his Son into the world to condemn the world, but to save the world through him." John 3:16-17

"For the wages of sin is death, but the gift of God is eternal life in Christ Jesus our Lord." Romans 6:23

"**D**ear Kathryn, Here's a special 'remembrance' gift to remind you of your 8th Christmas and all the good feelings of Christmases past! I'm sorry we didn't keep the original Barbie when we moved to Colorado, but I'm sure she brought happiness to little girls at the orphanage. I hope you have many good memories of your childhood because they are precious, and we live our whole life with them—ornery brothers included! Enjoy Barbie—I recognized her with her fur stole, long white gloves, and beautiful pink gown—see, memories linger— Love you and hope for all the best things in life for you. Love, Mom"

"Dear Mom, I opened your gift, having no idea what it could be. As I peeled the packing material away, I think I was just as excited as the day I received her on my 8th Christmas! As I read your note, I hugged the box, as tears began streaking my cheeks faster than I could brush them away. The words were a most precious gift and the doll a beautiful remembrance of your love for me. I know I'll never be able to express how deeply this affected me, nor how much I appreciate your gift.

So, with all my heart I say, 'Thank you, Mom!' Thank you for returning a piece of my childhood to me. This time is better than the first because this time I see more than the gift, but also the love that sent it. I thanked Jesus for the mother He gave me; I will always be thankful for you. The children in the orphanage got my Barbie, and I don't regret that—I had you! I love you, Mom! Kathryn"

"Dear God, I received your gift, and with all my heart I want to express to you how much I appreciate your love and sacrifice in sending your only beloved Son, Jesus. I have only scratched the surface of knowing how wonderful He is, but have already received such love and acceptance, unworthy as I am, that I am overwhelmed by it. Thank you for planning to purchase me with His blood since you set time in motion. It is a gift I can never begin to repay.

Thank you that you adopted me into your family without hesitation, though I was thoroughly undeserving of such honor and riches. Thank you for being ever-present in my life, even when I don't realize or acknowledge it, and for your Word which has penetrated my heart and restored my life. You have forgiven me when I did not deserve such mercy and poured out abundant grace upon me. I love you, Father! Kathryn"

"**But because of his great love for us, God, who is rich in mercy, made us alive with Christ even when we were dead in transgressions---it is by grace you have been saved. And God raised us up with Christ and seated us with him in the heavenly realms in Christ Jesus, in order that in the coming ages he might show the incomparable riches of his grace, expressed in his kindness to us in Christ Jesus.**"   Ephesians 2:4-7

Lost and Found

The weather was suddenly changing, with temperatures dropping from the sixties down into the twenties, within the span of a few hours. Wrestling with the downdrafts of the chimney as he attempted to build a fire, my son did not notice my six-pound, half-blind, thirteen-year-old wayward Maltese dog wandering out of the door. Upon arrival home from work two hours later, the temperature had dropped to 40 degrees and it was dark. That was when I noticed that Tiffy was gone. My heart sank as we searched the house and found no trace of her.

My son and I began the search outside, under bushes, under the deck, around the drainage ditch—to no avail. I knew the conditions were not conducive to survival; she had no spare fat, a short coat, was wet, nearly blind, and in the dark. She had been gone almost three hours already, so I was nearly without a crumb of hope. Flipping the switch of my flashlight off, I walked back into the house, resigned to the loss. At that moment, I experienced a strong impression to check under the shed, which I relayed to my son. Watching as he maneuvered the beam of light from one end to the other, Tiffy was not there.

Suddenly, he stood up and walked around to the back of the shed. There, a very large opossum greeted him, and a rabbit; then a little, white dog wandered toward the shed where he stood. As he enfolded the wet, shivering animal in his arms, carrying her into the house, I was in awe that she could still be alive. And I was in awe of my God, who preserved that tiny dog for hours, protecting her from predators and exposure to the deadly elements. As I sat in front of the warm fire drying her, I could only thank the God who cared so much for me that He would bring Tiffy back, returning her to my arms. Just twenty hours prior, I had lost Molly, Tiffy's best Maltese friend, to complications from surgery.

I couldn't help but compare myself to Tiffy, wandering away from a secure home with God, battered and drenched with sin, cold and shivering with no hope. Jesus sought me out, cradling me in His strong, secure arms, and carried me home to the Father. If Tiffy had not wandered toward the shed, our last hope, she would have died, exposed, alone, and in the darkness. I am so thankful that when Jesus called me, I finally listened and found His saving arms, too.

Following a warm bath and good night's sleep, one would never know how harrowing a plight Tiffy had experienced. She will probably forget it ever happened. I, however, cannot forget my plight without Jesus; I need to forever remember what it was like to be without Him, lost with no hope, and condemned to death. To remember is to be grateful, forever grateful, to the One who seeks and saves.

"For the Son of Man came to seek and to save what was lost." Luke 19:10

Traveling Light December 11

With worn corners, and dirty smudges front and back, my faithful suitcase is beginning to show its mileage. The bright red color of its heavy canvas has darkened, and its handle has developed a glitchy sort of catch in it. It has been thrown into the bellies of planes and heaved onto luggage belts too many times to count. It has been stuffed to bursting point, then gathered dust in seasons of patient waiting for the next trip. The one thing it has never seen in its lifetime is light travel; it is just not my style.

My packing list is formulated by anticipating every conceivable possibility. Not until everything on the list is checked off, do I question what *has* to be left behind. And, my packing for every emergency has been found justified on too many trips. You may not consider taking moleskin with you on every trip, but it has more than once come to my rescue; the one time I did not have it with me, the tops of my feet sported a blistering sunburn, and a side trip to the drug store ensued.

No matter how I anticipate my needs while away from home, it is certain that I will find myself lacking something. But the one thing I can attest to, in all my adventures, is that God has taken care of every need that has arisen. From being stranded in an airport to sitting in a plane on the runway for hours; to finding after I arrived home from a trip to Alaska that I had had appendicitis while a thousand miles from home. Even unknowingly walking between two men transacting a drug deal, oblivious to the danger, God protected me.

Traveling light means that you may sacrifice some amenities that would have made life a tad more comfortable, but the only essential necessary is Jesus. Whatever I needed was, in one way or another, provided. The two things I have never lacked were God's provision and protection.

It doesn't mean that things will always turn out the way we want, but it does mean that they will always turn out the way He sees fit. Whether on the road, in-flight, floating across an ocean, or boarding a high-speed train, He is present. Wherever we are, He is there, regardless of our preparations, or lack thereof. The Holy Spirit resides within us, His angels do His bidding, and God is never moved from His throne; wherever we go, we can travel lightly with confidence.

"O Lord, you have searched me and you know me. You know when I sit and when I rise; you perceive my thoughts from afar. You discern my going out and my lying down; you are familiar with all my ways…Where can I go from your Spirit: Where can I flee from your presence? If I go up to the heavens, you are there; if I make my bed in the depths, you are there. If I rise on the wings of the dawn, if I settle on the far side of the sea, even there your hand will guide me, your right hand will hold me fast." Psalm 139:1-3, 7-10

Recently, I found myself wondering when storytelling began, and why stories resonated so strongly with human beings. In my contemplation, I realized that history is filled with stories—of adventure, romance, and relationship, challenges embraced, good facing down evil, and conflicts resolved. And every person also has their own story to tell.

Stories are formulated in the imaginations of small children, dreamt by young men and women, and repeated many times by the aged. Stories have been shared on ships and around campfires. They have been told by kings in castles, on stages for royalty, and beggars. Stories have been shared among trees, in prison cells, and lands far from home; some for generations. Stories ring out through song, movies, books, sign language, on TV, and even in advertising. Stories can last a few seconds, a few hours, and some take a lifetime to complete.

The Bible, too, tells the stories of many very different, and very real people, from Moses and Abraham, to Rahab and Ruth. Jesus promised that Mary Magdeline's story would be retold throughout time. King David's story still brings hope for those who have made very poor choices, repented, and came back to God. Daniel's story encourages us to be faithful, as he trusted God to take care of him, even in the face of very real, and very hungry, lions. Joseph's story of betrayal, false accusations, and imprisonment leaves us cheering with his release, vindication, and promotion.

I believe the best stories are patterned after God's creation of man, the greatest love story ever told. God personally walked the Garden of Eden with Adam and Eve, the main characters, and they loved and had personal fellowship with Him, the Hero of the story. That relationship was severed by their sin, (the enemy slithering in on cue) sin that required a blood sacrifice. God's plan of reconciliation was fulfilled through Jesus, as He carried the sin of all God's creation upon the cross, the climax of the story. It became the darkest hour of God's story. Raised in resurrection power, God's story has a happy ending, with the Hero and main characters reuniting.

The original story is the basis of our longing for stories that follow the same pattern. Our eternal spirits find hope for the present and the future, knowing that in the end, God and goodness prevail over the brokenness, enemies, and trials. Jesus says He is the author and finisher of our faith. I believe the word "author" was very intentional; He is the initiator of our story and writes each of our timelines. He is there at our beginnings and guides us until the very last word of our personal stories is written. From the very first word to the very ending sentence, He is with us. The original story was His all along.

"Let us fix our eyes on Jesus, the author and perfecter of our faith, who for the joy set before him endured the cross, scorning its shame, and sat down at the right hand of the throne of God." Hebrews 12:2

Flying from Anchorage to Juneau, Alaska, the aerial view from the small, twin-prop plane was one of the most interesting of all my flights. It was low enough to gaze over the reflections of the rugged mountains on the surface of the glaciers, and high enough to skim the clouds. The pilot pointed out something fascinating midway up one of the mountains on our right side. A small, very small, clearing hung on the side of the mountain; and sitting in that clearing was a picnic table!

There was no road to it. The only way to access that picnic table was by foot and required quite the trek. Whether from the top or the bottom, access was not easy, since it sat at the halfway point. The mountain goats we saw were the only visitors that day. I marveled at the builder's possible reason for constructing it there, and it was left a mystery, lingering still. My romantic guess is that a man's wife requested a picnic table; and he surprised her by building it, overlooking the spectacular valley below.

Jesus, our Savior, has prepared a special place for each of us from the time we place our trust in Him. It is a place of close relationship with Him, a retreat from the noise and rush of the world. It can be found only in the quiet space of our heart, as we focus our attention solely on Him. The way is not easy. It requires us to lay down the cares of the world, the demands of the day, and consciously make our way along the rugged path. To find that place of solitude, we must follow His voice to the quiet of the mountainside.

You may carry your burdens with you, but when you come into His presence, they will be lifted from your shoulders. There, you can speak freely, knowing that He will not be shocked, surprised, or condemning. He knew you before you came to the mountain retreat. He watched as you made the effort to come to Him, and He loved you already. He is faithful to forgive, His love is unfailing, and special access is never denied.

"The mind of sinful man is death, but the mind controlled by the Spirit is life and peace."

Romans 8:6

"My sheep listen to my voice; I know them and they follow me." John 10:27

"Fear not, for I am with you; be not dismayed, for I am your God. I will strengthen you, yes I will help you, I will uphold you with My righteous right hand." Isaiah 41:10

It seems to me that God has many rebukes, gentle and otherwise, for the arrogance of human beings. It is probably no accident that humility is a constant theme throughout the Bible, and perhaps a hint to each of us as we navigate life. Pride always, with emphasis on always, raises us in our own eyes above the object of our comparison. It belittles those who are not just like us and lowers them to positions beneath us. It is one of the favored tools of our enemy, Satan. He understands pride best and was the first to succumb to it in his attempted elevation above God.

Perhaps my aversion to arrogance is, in fact, the reason I find the book of Job so fascinating. I love the end chapters where God calls Job to account for "speaking of things he did not understand". But even more so, I appreciate God's reprimand of Job's friends for their arrogance, assuming Job had sinned. We are so limited in our perspective, so oblivious to God's workings, yet so filled with opinions! I know I am. God has humbled me more than once over my pride in believing what was not so or judging on worldly appearances.

We are all prone to pride. It separates us from God, as we believe with little hesitation that we do not need Him and that our decisions can be made on our judgments. We believe control rests in our hands until God allows our vulnerability to be exposed. Those who have encountered humbling under God's hand, are not so quick to make such judgments. Not through higher intellect or education, but personal contact with the God of the universe through Christ Jesus, are we taught to be wary of wresting that control from His wise hands.

Our "counterintelligence" of trusting God goes against the world's understanding. Our pride submits itself to the One who reigns with power and authority. And He levels every mountain of arrogance. God is no respecter of persons; and He will hold all accountable in due time. His ways are far above our ways, His thoughts far above our thoughts, and He can be trusted for perfect judgment, counter to our intelligence.

"Then Job replied to the Lord: 'I know that you can do all things; no plan of yours can be thwarted. You asked, "Who is this that obscures my counsel without knowledge?" Surely I spoke of things I did not understand, things too wonderful for me to know.'" Job 42:1-3

"As the heavens are higher than the earth, so are my ways higher than your ways, and my thoughts than your thoughts." Isaiah 55:9

Over six months, our neighborhood transformer blew up at least ten times, so many that I lost count. Raising tropical fish, several generations perished during the outages. We waited for restoration of power fearing our refrigeration was compromised. Flashlights just don't serve as adequate replacements for overhead lighting, and cooking was out of the question. Getting ready for work, we discovered, is also power-dependent.

The power company finally corrected whatever was at fault in the frequent failures, and the transformers are behaving themselves once again. However, we found ourselves in "top of mind" mode for a while, knowing it could be an issue daily. But when the kilowatts hummed through the lines unabated, we quickly took that power for granted once again.

I find myself in similar situations with God, trusting He is in the background so long as my plans flow freely in the direction of my comfort zone. When things go awry, I pout and question. I have even been known to express the horrid phrase, "Where are you when I need you?!" I take His gifts freely and without hesitation, barely noting to thank Him most of the time; ingratitude abounds until pain steps upon my path.

Other times, I find myself in pure awe of God's power flowing throughout the universe, His unbridled and raw power. I find comfort and encouragement in His displays of lightning and hearing the deep roar of thunder reverberate through the clouds. His displays of power remind me that He is bigger than my problems, transforming them with just a spark from His fingertip.

Jesus came to the earth, God in flesh, to prove that even in the smallest measure, God's transforming power can accomplish big things. Miracles upon miracles are recorded for our benefit, to remind us how unlimited God's power is. It may flow in the background unnoticed, or surge to the surface of life at any moment; we can choose to see it, or ignore and explain it away. He is always present, always loving, ever merciful, always generous beyond what we deserve. He is the Transformer that we can connect with and access freely, the One whose power transforms our lives. He is Jesus, the true power line of life.

"And without faith it is impossible to please God, because anyone who comes to him must believe that he exists and that he rewards those who earnestly seek him." Hebrews 11:6

"Can you bind the beautiful Pleiades? Can you loose the cords of Orion? Can you bring forth the constellations in their seasons or lead out the Bear with its cubs: Do you know the laws of the Heavens? Can you set up God's dominion over the earth?" Job 38:31-33

Elon Musk has become quite well known for his technological advances in rockets. Most recently his company, Space X, launched a rocket carrying a payload of mini satellites to form a communication grid just above the earth's atmosphere. It is fascinating to imagine the details of planning, experimentation, checking and rechecking systems, and making thousands of adjustments and calculations. As a result of all the planning, the restraints broke free and the rocket lifted off, belching fierce flames in the upward push.

Spaceship launches have been part of my personal history, from their advent in the 1960s to today. We ordinary people simply take it all for granted, never worrying whether a rocket lifts off, escaping the force of gravity and blasting into the inhibitions of space. The details are far above our heads, as the rocket takes its proper trajectory and a successful launch is taken for granted.

Our lives here on planet Earth greatly resemble Space X's launching pad for its prized rockets. There is a very detailed plan in place, one far too complex for the ordinary mind to comprehend. The details are far above our heads; however, they are not beyond the understanding or execution of the ultimate Mission Commander, our heavenly Father. His ability to perform the many checks and adjustments, control the variables, and track the constants is unrivaled. He has never lost a "rocket" to His poor planning or untimely execution of the plan.

While the earthly mission God lays out for us is a simple one, we often complicate it. God's basic plan is to display His love and glory through our relationship with Jesus, yet the execution of that plan remains challenging to most of us. We become distracted from God's plan by the "launch details" of life, veering off into the complicated "schematics" of the world, or are sidetracked by the minutia of daily tasks. But our mission is simple: God loved us first and wants our love in return, and we are to share it with others, inviting them to the Father.

One day, our mission on this earth will be complete, our spirits lifting off and propelling into the spiritual realm, our destination heaven, standing before Jesus. The trials and hardships will fade from view, and the complications and details will be forgotten. Our possessions will remain earthbound as we become heaven-bound, and our relationships will cease outside of Christ. Space X will seem like a Tinker Toy as we view from God's perspective all His preparations, interactions, and loving calculations for our successful launch into His loving arms. Three, two, one...counting down!

"For just as the Father raises the dead and gives them life, even so the Son gives life to whom he is pleased to give it...I tell you the truth, whoever hears my word and believes him who sent me has eternal life and will not be condemned; he has crossed over from death to life." John 5:21,24

Monopoly

The Monopoly game I played as a child was revealing of my personality in many ways, now that I reminisce. One of the game pieces was a Scottie dog, and it was my favorite; my love of dogs reflects that early attraction. An interesting fact about the Monopoly game recently came to my attention, too. It was created in 1933 and put on the market by Parker Brothers in 1935. By 1944, during World War II, Monopoly games were smuggled into POW camps inside Germany, with a little "extra" tucked inside; escape maps, files, and compasses found their way through security checks by way of the board game. Often, they included real money hidden inside the packages of Monopoly money to aid escapees once outside the fences! Those Monopoly games contained the ultimate, and literal, "get out of jail" card.

We have another "get out of jail" option and we don't have to wait until it is drawn by chance. Each of us has a choice to claim that card through Jesus. It is a choice of relationship with Him or eternity in the absence of His love. Jesus had more to say about hell than heaven—it is real; it is not folly, nor a fairytale. If we choose darkness and death, eternal separation from God, we have lost everything, but that is not God's will for us. His will is that everyone would come to Him through Jesus and that no one would be lost.

We can choose spiritual life or spiritual death, and God has given us free will to choose; no one else can determine our fate. In our stubbornness, we can push Jesus away, hoping for another turn, another roll of the dice. We hope that something other than Him will set us free, but there will come a day when the game of life will end, and our turn will be over. Without Jesus, an eternity in darkness and the absence of God's love awaits.

I claimed my "get out of jail" card many years ago, never once regretting my decision to follow Jesus. Once He was invited into my life, the freedom and forgiveness He gave changed everything from the inside out. It did not happen instantly, but the changes were significant for me as He became my shelter, strength, and peace. When He states **"Peace I leave with you; my peace I give you. I do not give to you as the world gives,"** in John 14:27, it is difficult to understand until we experience it. But I have taken Him at His word and His promise has proven true.

We can claim our rescue, or we can stay in jail; we can be set free in this life and the next, or live in bondage, sin, and pain. Jesus holds the monopoly on heaven; I've played my card, how about you?

"Jesus said to her, 'I am the resurrection and the life. He who believes in me will live, even though he dies." John 11:25

"For the Son of Man came to seek and to save what was lost." Luke 19:10

The Perfect Gift

This particular Christmas was the first where I was truly alone. It was Jesus and me, so I was not totally alone but had no one else with whom to share it. I had two gifts to open, one from my dear friend Sandy, the other from my daughter, Whitney. As I opened Sandy's gift, tears began to well up as an embossed leather journal came into view; I love my journals—my heart lights up as I turn each page and caress its cover.

Though I would see my daughter in just a week, she had mailed my gift so I could open it on Christmas Day. Still teary, I cut the tape on Whitney's package. Inside were multiple wrapped gifts, tagged "Something New" (a gift card), "Something Old" (glittery bracelets), "Something that Smells Good" (an essential oil), "Someplace to Go" (movie pass), and "Something Good to Eat" (cookies and other treats). Each gift was a thoughtful and loving consideration of my personality.

God's gifts are like these thoughtful gifts—He knows our hearts, tailoring each of His gifts for us—but we may not recognize everything He gives as gifts. Some are wrapped in sorrow, and some are delivered as disappointments. Others may have fancy paper, elevating our expectations but letting us down when we look inside. His gifts often come in unexpected forms, through grief and loss, through misunderstanding, and what we would consider mistakes.

I have experienced all forms of them, and though I could not see the gift in the circumstance at the time, I can say that the gift of great value eventually became clear. The gifts presented themselves in the forms of greater compassion, learning to forgive even when I did not want to, having empathy for others who are suffering, and exercising generosity amid my own pain. Each gift led me to a Savior who understands my tears, delights in my gratitude, and calms me in the storms. He gifts me with peace during turmoil and heals my hurting heart when there seems no comfort elsewhere.

If we can indeed be thankful in every circumstance, Jesus is faithful to meet us where we are and reveal the hidden treasures in His perfect gifts. I am thankful for my first Christmas alone, though I naturally would have chosen to have my family with me. But God's presence was more than enough. The gift He gave me in this experience was a deeper understanding of those who spend the holidays alone, who do not know that they really are not alone.

"Let the peace of Christ rule in your hearts, since as members of one body you were called to peace. And be thankful. Let the word of Christ dwell in you richly as you teach and admonish one another with all wisdom, and as you sing psalms, hymns, and spiritual songs with gratitude in your hearts to God. And whatever you do, whether in word or deed, do it all in the name of the Lord Jesus, giving thanks to God the Father through him."
Colossians 3:15-17

Rabbit Cookies

My grandmother's house was a six-hour journey. It was an annual event we eagerly anticipated partly because of one thing, Rabbit cookies. Immediately upon arrival, Gram and Grandpa got hugs, immediately followed by a mad dash for the dining room. There were only two pieces of furniture, one being the dining table with accompanying chairs; the other was a massive buffet piece. Under the buffet lay the treasure we were all seeking, sugar cookie cutouts of rabbits dressed in pastel icing with chocolate chip eyes.

Gram's sugar cookies were legendary in our family and among our friends, who benefited from their generous distribution during Easter and Christmas. They were transformed at Christmas into stars but became generically known year-round to be "sugar cookies"; and a generation later, both were known as "Rabbit Cookies" ever after.

The following two generations attempted to duplicate them using Gram's recipe, and though ours were good, they weren't Rabbit cookies yet. I stumbled upon the secret one holiday season as I searched for a container to store the treasured treats in; I resorted to a discarded cookie tin in place of my Tupperware plastics. The subtle difference in flavor confirmed the fact that Rabbit cookies tasted best when hidden away in tin containers.

There is also a mystery of being hidden in Christ, which brings about a subtle difference in our "flavor". Jesus likened it to being salt, having a flavor that seasons not only us but those whom our lives touch. Our flavor determines how we influence the world. Salt can be corrosive if not used correctly; it can even lose its saltiness. However, when it is used in the right places and amounts, it enhances sweet dishes, even Rabbit Cookies. There is not anything else that can adequately replicate the flavor and benefits of salt.

God's love tucks us away with Christ, His secret recipe that He never intended to keep a secret. It is available to all who will run to Him and seek it. The world cannot duplicate the recipe of God's "Rabbit Cookies"; we are the children of Light who follow Jesus. The subtle difference is produced when we are hidden in Christ and abide in that secret place alone with Him. Yielding to His influence and spending time in His Presence, knowing his Word, and loving Him, we can then influence those in the sphere He has placed us. We become God's Rabbit Cookies, sharing His love with the world.

"How sweet are your words to my taste, sweeter than honey to my mouth!" Psalm 119:103

"Taste and see that the Lord is good; blessed is the man who takes refuge in him."

Psalm 34:8

The signs hung on the doors may have simply stated, "Full", or have stated, "No Vacancy". Whether Joseph had to knock on the door of each inn or had wandered the streets searching for a sign for a vacant room, it was to no avail. The best he could procure, in the end, was a stable for Mary and their heir-to-the-Kingdom-of-God baby.

The inn was full, and that meant the stable, too, was full of traveler's animals. They did not bed down with one donkey, one cow, and one sheep, as most nativity sets include. I am pretty sure there were far more animals present than people, and the innkeeper was pretty pleased with the night's business. But can you imagine the innkeeper's realization one day as he stands before God? He had ushered the King of Glory to a stall instead of a room. He conducted great business that night with a packed hotel, but there was no Jesus in it, for he had shut Him out.

We cannot fault the innkeeper too much, though, because we all reside in the hotel but ignore the stable until God transforms our hearts. We can celebrate Christmas without Christ in our celebrations, or we can humbly walk to the stable, in awe and wonder to gaze upon the face of Innocence, too soon sacrificed for our sakes.

Dr. Tony Evans once stated, "If the written Word does not lead you to the Living Word, it's just another word," meaning that the Bible will always lead to Jesus, to an intimate relationship with Him if we will open our hearts. The three kings who visited Jesus following His birth sought the ultimate King, yet Biblical scholars who knew the prophecies of where Jesus would be born refused to search for Him at all.

We can lock Jesus out of our lives, stubbornly holding the "No Vacancy" sign out with both arms, emphatically inviting Him to keep His distance. Or we can hold our arms out and invite Him into the room of our "inn". We can go about our business, as usual, ignoring Him, and isolating Him from our affairs and concerns. Or we can marvel at the miracle of all miracles, God with Us, and intimately know Him.

Today, as we celebrate the Christmas season, we have the choice of turning on the "No Vacancy" sign of our hearts, denying the Prince of Peace a room, or we can welcome Him with the honor He deserves. What a beautiful sight it would be if we could turn off the "no vacancy" signs, and in their places erect signs reading, "Occupied by Jesus", Christ in us, the hope of glory—a truly Merry Christmas!

"While they were there, the time came for the baby to be born, a son. She wrapped him in cloths and placed him in a manger, because there was no room for them in the inn."
Luke 2:6-7

"You diligently study the Scriptures because you think that by them you possess eternal life. These are the Scriptures that testify about me, yet you refuse to come to me to have life.'
John 5:39-40

It's a Wonderful Life   December 21

George Bailey had so many problems that he was thinking about ending it all—and it was Christmas Eve! As George was about to jump from a bridge, he instead found himself rescuing his awkward guardian angel, Clarence. As Clarence revealed to George what his town would have looked like, if not for all George's diligence and good deeds over the years, George began to see life for the gift it is, even with its challenges. "It's a Wonderful Life" has been a Christmas favorite in my family for four generations and will happily be passed on to the fifth and sixth, if possible.

Though the film "It's a Wonderful Life" debuted in 1946, it remains universal in its message of love, hope, and persistence in the face of evil, dashed dreams, and tragedy. Each time I watch it, the revelation that life is indeed worth living is the treasure I walk away holding. Like George Bailey, feeling inferior, dejected, or comparing myself to others is an indulgence in self-pity; and like him, a feeling of worthlessness and destruction will surely follow.

The second takeaway is not to judge others, nor envy too quickly. Their point of view has many influences, just as mine does. Though we may live similarly, even then, God has endowed each of us with unique experiences and gifts. He created us to fill a place in this world where we interact on His behalf in love, mercy, and grace. We are, after all, made in our Father's image and tasked with loving each other as He loves us, through self-sacrifice and doing what Jesus taught.

Thirdly, trusting God trumps everything else. Having a "wonderful life" depends upon our view of God, as we trust our moments and days to Him. No matter how glum life appears, there is joy to be found in the birth of the Son of God, and because of Him, miracles can and do happen. God delights to reveal Himself to us when we take the leap of faith that He bids us to take, just planting one toe on His promises and inviting him, in that small faith to act on our behalf. He is a God of riotous giving, lavishing His love on His children at every opportunity. Because of Jesus, it is a wonderful life!

"But after he had considered this, an angel of the Lord appeared to him in a dream and said, 'Joseph son of David, do not be afraid to take Mary home as your wife, because what is conceived in her is from the Holy Spirit. She will give birth to a son, and you are to give him the name Jesus, because he will save his people from their sins.' All this took place to fulfill what the Lord had said through the prophet: "The virgin will be with child and will give birth to a son, and they will call him Immanuel---which means, 'God with us.'"

Matthew 1:20-23

Two Japanese chef's knives, a Christmas gift from my son, had far more meaning than I ever could have imagined. As I examined their razor-sharp edges and admired the beautiful patterns of their Damascus steel blades, he reminded me to exercise extreme caution while using the potentially dangerous knives. From that day on, I have been almost as fascinated with beautiful Damascus steel as he is.

Damascus steel is characterized by patterns created in the steel itself, not printed on the blade. It is resilient and strong, with an inability to shatter. It is most interesting to me that it is forged under more fire than any other blade. In between every step in the process, the Damascus steel is heated, and reheated, beaten, and reheated, folded, fired, and beaten again. It is a process of intense labor.

Each blade is a mystery, created with intense heat, beginning in a crucible and ending with an acid cleaning. And no two Damascus knives are alike. Each knife is one-of-a-kind, and valuable as an individual work of art; they, like us, are forged to produce an intricate pattern in the steel, forged for strength and beauty. This is how God molds us into the beautiful pattern of His son, Jesus. We are chosen, not for our perfection, but in our imperfect state, and then thrown into the fire.

Our imperfections often become our very strengths, just as the carbon in the steel gives it strength. Our beauty is molded through the heat of trials, our imperfections smoothed out with the wise strikes of His hand on the hardness of life's anvil. Layer by layer, He folds and tucks the steel of our resistance back into the heat. We often fear the process. But God's wisdom is complete, His vision clear, and His knowledge of what is to come, unobstructed. That very painful process is what He uses to prepare our hearts for the use of the blade, yet unseen.

Faith in the Lord is a lifelong process of tempering, testing, and trial. It is hard-won, and though each blade is different, the process is similar. A truly valuable blade cannot avoid the fire, nor evade the testing. The Blade-Smith knows His metal; He can see the imperfections that our eyes are not trained to and knows all too well what will be required to finish the blade for fit use. He will spare no effort to train it, as He knows what will bring out its best. He will never test it needlessly. With tender loving care, He places each of us in the forge of fire, only long enough to produce the Master's blade, a work of art.

"I can do all this through him who gives me strength." Philippians 4:13

"Do everything without complaining or arguing, so that you may become blameless and pure, children of God without fault in a crooked and depraved generation, in which you will shine like stars in the universe." Philippians 2:14-15

Our culture calls it Christmas, I call it Unfathomable. As hard as I try, I cannot plumb the depths of the vastness of God, poured into the body of a baby. Nor can I grasp the reduction of the King of Heaven to earthly flesh, a helpless and poor infant, born in poverty with nothing to His name but love. He was birthed in the rawest form, in a stable, to an inexperienced young mother and shell-shocked father, far removed from family and friends. From Creator to being created in the womb, I cannot fathom.

From untold glory, He stepped into human flesh with only a brief angelic proclamation. From speaking the stars into existence to not being able to speak a word, leaves me speechless. From the Light of the Universe to the pitch-black darkness of night, He came with a single beacon of light in the sky pointing to His majesty. From the Son of the Almighty God to son of a lowly carpenter; from Him Who Holds All Things Together, to Him who holds nothing. From Him who wields all power in heaven and on earth, to become a baby, powerless and vulnerable in every way. From spanning all time and eternity, His life would span only 33 years; and for the first time, He would feel the effects of time.

The God receiving lamb sacrifices would now become the sacrificial lamb. The One demanding obedience would now learn obedience. He who loved His children would now become the child. From overthrowing the proud, He would assume the most humble of human forms. Being perfect in every way, He came to a future of marring pain, scars, and sorrow. Receiving unending praise and worship in heaven, He subjected Himself to ridicule, doubt, and shame; and from acclamation, He would submit to shouts of condemnation.

In all the days He walked among us, He never once doubted His Father's love or plan, resolutely following it to the end, for my sake. I can only grasp fleeting moments of the intensity of His love, and the complexity of His plan. I can only acknowledge, humbly, that His ways are far above my ways, and His thoughts high above my own. I can only, and meagerly at that, love and obey Him in return, as imperfect as my offering is.

Is there any praise or sacrifice I can offer which is worthy? How can I do anything but worship and praise Him? The unfathomable occurred, Immanuel, God with Us— God with me!

"Today in the town of David a Savior has been born to you; he is Christ the Lord. This will be a sign to you: You will find a baby wrapped in cloths and lying in a manger." Luke 2:11-12

"The Word became flesh and made his dwelling among us. We have seen his glory, the glory of the One and Only, who came from the Father, full of grace and truth." John 1:14

"The virgin will be with child and will give birth to a son, and they will call him Immanuel---which means 'God with us.'" Matthew 1:23

It had been a very long and harrowing journey of nearly two years through the desert, over the mountains, and into the Promised Land. The unusually bright star had guided them every step of their travels, finally positioning itself over this humble house. A young woman held a squirmy, curious toddler in her arms, while her sturdy husband stood between the visitors and his family. Three men were seated regally atop their camels, accompanied by their vast entourage. They were out of place in the village, unexpected and startling visitors to a common carpenter's home.

The kings from the East did not have to inquire as to the King they sought. As they gazed into the face of the young child, they understood that they had found the King of the Jews, and so much more. They began their journey with the intent of worship; then they kneeled, overjoyed in His presence, praising God, and offering the precious gifts they had guarded so carefully. They tenderly laid the silk-covered box of gold at Mary's feet, followed by the rare incense of worship, and finally the myrrh, which they could not understand just yet. "Why burial spice for the young King?" they all wondered silently.

And in a dream that very night, they were instructed to avoid King Herod and return home by another route. As mysteriously as they appeared, they were now gone. Mary pondered the event, Joseph wondered, and the neighborhood was dazed. Immediately the wise men, who were warned in a dream not to return to report to Herod, returned to their homeland. Also warned in a dream, Joseph left in the middle of the night, moving his little King and beloved wife to Egypt. Herod was not happy.

"When Herod realized that he had been outwitted by the Magi, he was furious, and he gave orders to kill all the boys in Bethlehem and its vicinity who were two years old and under, in accordance with the time he had learned from the Magi. Then what was said through the prophet Jeremiah was fulfilled: 'A voice is heard in Ramah, weeping and great mourning, Rachel weeping for her children and refusing to be comforted, because they are no more.'" Matthew 2:16-18

The three kings from the East made the journey of a lifetime to worship the Lord of Life. Their decision to find Jesus came with a great sacrifice of their time, riches, and relationships. Today, I look back over my journey, so thankful that I also searched for and found Him; so thankful that He first found me. I can testify that no gift will ever match His priceless love and His sacrifice on the cross of Calvary for my sake. And there is no gift worthy of Jesus, nothing I can offer but the gift He desires most, my heart, wholly paid for by His priceless blood. For wise men, the journey to a relationship with Jesus is still worth any cost.

"For my Father's will is that everyone who looks to the Son and believes in him shall have eternal life, and I will raise him up at the last day...Everyone who listens to the Father and learns from him comes to me...I tell you the truth, he who believes has everlasting life."
John 6:40, 45b, 47

The Christmas Table

Weeks ahead of Christmas, cookies were baked, decorations for the celebrations hung, and Christmas carols welcomed through car speakers, sung with great enthusiasm. Gifts were thoughtfully gathered and gracefully wrapped. But the Christmas Day table was the crowning glory of our celebration, our finger food bounty, laid out all day to graze upon without more labor than adding or subtracting lids. However, my favorite part of Christmas had already passed. It is Christmas Eve that stirs my heart.

Christmas Eve is my "holy time", the most extravagant meal of the year set on the table, even if I eat it alone. The best plates and silverware come out only on that day. The meat is the best I can afford, and the side dishes cooked for that day alone. Dessert is a cake created over decades of refinement in my kitchen and eaten only once a year. And it is all done to remind me, that there was one day that God gave the One closest to His heart to save my own.

It is Christmas Eve. It is the mysterious Light birthed into darkness. It is an eternal King born into poverty. It is a mother and father, first-time parents, seeing the face of their son, with wonder at how God could reside in such fragile form. It is the Prince of heaven's passage from glory into obscurity, adored by donkeys and sheep instead of angelic beings. It is God's holiness and purity confined to a world of degradation, and dirty shepherds straight from the fields. It is the poignant moment in time that divides history from "God afar" to "God with us".

That baby was born to die, not because He had sinned, but because I did. He was born that I may live. The gift of God's Son is one to a world of darkness, death, misery, and hopelessness, to even those who hate Him. It is the very invitation to approach His table of peace, laden with all the celebratory feast of His kingdom. The choicest fare awaits all who will accept His forgiveness, to any who will repent.

At the Father's table, the feast of Christmas is overflowing. At His table, He invites us to linger in His presence, indulge in His Spirit, to taste and see that He is good. He has overlooked no detail at His table. And He invites us to the celebration of the real Christmas gift, a lifetime, an eternity with Immanuel, God with Us.

"Therefore, the Lord himself will give you a sign: The virgin will conceive and give birth to a son and will call him Immanuel." Isaiah 7:14

"For to us a child is born, to us a son is given, and the government will be on his shoulders. And he will be called Wonderful Counselor, Mighty God, Everlasting Father, Prince of Peace." Isaiah 9:6

The Dog Ate My Homework

Somewhere within the murky past of excuses, one little boy's dog really did eat his homework. I suspect that the explanation was sufficient for his teacher, who then gave him extended time for a "re-do" or granted complete amnesty. This is all my supposition, but I believe the excuse, and reprieve, was impressive enough to become a folk legend in the arena of students vs. teachers ever since. It has been perpetuated through generations, with the resultant wink accompanied by, "Sure it did".

Mankind is infinitely creative with excuses for our poor choices and behavior, the dog being only one of a vast array of scapegoats. I would have to confess to having mastered the art, at some level, never finding it very appealing to suffer the consequences of my choices, consequences being generally unpleasant and embarrassing, as they are. And people haven't changed one iota from the time of Creation; Adam roundly accused Eve of being the problem and Eve tossed the blame right back at him.

When the accountability of our choice concerning Jesus comes home to roost, there will be no one waiting on the sideline to step in for us, no blame to be shifted, and no excuse solid enough to stand. It will be a simple yes or no answer to the question, "Did you accept my Son's sacrifice for your sin, or did you reject him?" God already knows, but I will be required to give the pre-recorded answer. Eternity will hang in the balance, as the throngs of heaven anticipate, with suspense, the word I will speak. For me, that answer is "yes", and at that word, the citizens of heaven will cheer!

If your honest answer would have to be "no", there is still time to change it, before your deadline, and it is called a "deadline" for a reason. Today is the day of salvation. Lay aside the excuses, stop deferring to other people, and quit stalling for time you may not have. Today, choose whom you will serve. Today, this moment, know that a Savior awaits your surrender, holds out His arms to receive a child whose excuses have been as ludicrous as "The dog ate my homework". He already knows all you have done, who you have been, and He still loves you more than you can comprehend. His name is Jesus, and I hope your name is "Child of God".

"See to it that no one takes you captive through hollow and deceptive philosophy, which depends on human tradition and the basic principles of this world rather than on Christ. For in Christ all the fullness of the Deity lives in bodily form, and you have been given fullness in Christ, who is the head over every power and authority." Colossians 2:8-10

"For since the creation of the world God's invisible qualities---his eternal power and divine nature---have been clearly seen, being understood from what has been made, so that men are without excuse." Romans 1:20

Fear Factor

It seems people didn't have quite enough fear in their lives, so a great deal of it was manufactured through reality television shows for over a decade, marketed as "entertainment". The lineup generally included things like eating bugs and buckets of who-knew-what, usually blindfolded, and the more disgusting the better. The producer's goal was obviously to make viewers empathetic, and fearful, hence the name.

Not many people on this planet will be able to avoid a pandemic, or a cataclysmic volcano spewing us into an ice age, or an asteroid gone awry. Humans are subject to the drastic changes of a fallen and decaying world. Tragedies abound and change is more than inevitable—it is an absolute certainty, and an unavoidable collision with reality absolute. There is no dialing back the effects of the Covid19 pandemic; my life, and that of 7 billion others, will inexplicably change, and it's scary but not an excuse to be fearful.

God did not endorse the release of this plague, nor any disaster that affects human beings, the creation He loves. We have a spiritual enemy who is powerfully evil, who delights in deceit and destruction, and whose only goal is to destroy the objects of God's love. There is a war raging in the heavenly realms between God's forces and those of our enemy, but we can be confident that God is ultimately in control.

Through the bitter death and powerful resurrection of the Son of God, this war has already been won. God allows pain, uncertainty, change, and hard things; they are a part of His work that we cannot understand. And humankind has suffered them before us and will after we are gone, but God promises that **nothing** can separate us from the love of God in Christ Jesus. He will never leave or forsake us, and He is able to handle any obstacle that falls across our paths.

Fear can propel me to remember who my God is through His word, writing His words down, and posting them in front of my eyes. I need to speak them aloud and remind myself of how great and mighty He is. As we sing His praises and speak His name, the fear factor is greatly diminished, our trust in Christ rises, and our focus shifts from our circumstances to a steady and trustworthy peace in Jesus. Praising the One who tells us to fear not is the lasting antidote to the fear factor.

"For we wrestle not against flesh and blood, but against principalities, against powers, against the rulers of the darkness of this world, against spiritual wickedness in high places."

Ephesians 6:12

"Who shall separate us from the love of Christ? Shall trouble or hardship or persecution or famine or nakedness or danger or sword…No, in all these things we are more than conquerors through him who loved us. For I am convinced that neither death nor life, neither angels nor demons, neither the present nor the future, nor any powers, neither height nor depth nor anything else in all creation, will be able to separate us from the love of God that is in Christ Jesus our Lord." Romans 8:35, 37-39

One of the greatest wonders of God's creation is that human beings are formed in His very image, not one of them lacking the fingerprint of the Creator. From the moment of their birth, I watched and waited for the indicators of what my children and grandchildren would become. The shared traits notwithstanding those common to mankind, are canceled out in my mind. Instead, I searched with intensity for the specific talents which will deem them uniquely suited to the God-given purpose He had in mind all along. Those qualities will show up in their lives during the intentionally appointed seasons He sets.

Jeremiah, the prophet, was yet a child when set apart by the Lord for immense tasks that only God could empower him to do. Jeremiah 1:5 says, **"Before I formed you in the womb I knew you, before you were born I set you apart; I appointed you as a prophet to the nations."** When Jeremiah objected, saying he did not know how to speak, God responded by touching his mouth. His assignment was to speak God's own words to the nations, and not back down no matter what happened.

Jeremiah was a youth who seemed average to all around him, but not to God. God had unique plans for him, just as he has for each of us, endowing each individual accordingly. There are no age limits, young or old. No worldly qualifications or specific experiences are required. No prerequisite theological training is needed; trust is the only requirement.

God has exceedingly, abundantly more for us than we can think or ask, but without asking or trusting, we will stagnate where we are. Decay is inherent in this world and the antithesis of growth; it is a universal principle we will not escape through complacency or avoidance. Speaking from experience, the journey can be overwhelmingly difficult; but I can also speak to God's faithfulness, love, and trustworthiness, bringing beauty from ashes and renewal from ruin.

God is not withholding the destiny He has for you. He is waiting for you to embrace it in faith, trusting Him to lead you in His wisdom. *Relationship with Him is where we discover the plan from Him.* Every resource you need in fulfilling your unique destiny in God's plan, He will provide, often in shocking ways! God seems to delight in surprising us. He opens doors we never expected, pouring opportunities into our hands when they are open to receive, not what we think we need, but open to His perfect wisdom and timing.

"'Ah, Sovereign Lord,' I said, 'I do not know how to speak; I am only a child.' But the Lord said to me, 'Do not say I am only a child.' You must go to everyone I send you to and say whatever I command you. Do not be afraid of them, for I am with you and will rescue you,' declares the Lord." Jeremiah 1:6-8

What a painful and frightening thought! Writing a book, A BOOK! Where would I even begin??? My friend, Lori, had nudged me a week earlier, asking if I had started yet. Ever since she asked, I had avoided writing even one word. The prospect of taking on such a project as a book scared me senseless! Years later the book you are holding came to pass, and though I could not envision the ending, God considered it done.

It is not as if I had no hints of God's direction for me. I had spoken at a Christian women's conference, and as I greeted people afterward a woman approached, asking for my book; I smiled graciously and promptly discarded the request. Another lady asked for my poetry. Yet, I convinced myself I had nothing to offer, which hadn't already been said; I was not confident that God had a plan for me and that I had to be perfect before He would. Frankly, I was afraid of what I knew God was asking me to do.

Over twenty years, God has had me in training, teaching me to listen more closely to His voice, to be led by His Spirit. I was afraid, so fearful of opening my life and spilling it onto the pages of a book, exposing my flaws and fears, my views and experiences. I struggled, pitched fits, resisted His direction, and finally, trusted. A decision, an absolute resolution to follow Him, was necessary while trusting that He would shield and protect me. I needed to trust my Father's direction and that He would tie it all together with His ribbon of grace.

If God has shown you what He desires of you, and you are afraid, peal that fear off like a hot, heavy coat in summer! Allow Him to take you, too, down a sweet path of trust. Don't look for the rocks before they appear or the steep incline before reaching the hill. God is faithful. God is loving. God is capable. One step at a time, in His timing, just consider it done.

"And we know that in all things God works for the good of those who love him, who have been called according to his purpose." Romans 8:28

"For the Lord gives wisdom, and from his mouth come knowledge and understanding. He holds victory in store for the upright, he is a shield to those whose walk is blameless, for he guards the course of the just and protects the way of his faithful ones. Then you will understand what is right and just and fair---every good path. For wisdom will enter your heart, and knowledge will be pleasant to your soul, discretion will protect you, and understanding will guard you." Proverbs 2:6-11

In the darkness, and even on some sunny days, the moon is quietly present. It was created with the sun, a provision for light in the night, shining softly, not interfering with sleep but enhancing it, a nightlight in the sky. It is a timepiece to mark the days and months, a guide to mark events in our lives. It is the silent companion of the boisterous sun and yet a reflector of it. The sun warms our spirits, and the moon calms our fears. The moon is hidden for part of the month, yet it is never gone.

I would never have chosen the moon to describe God's presence in my life. The moon seems too tranquil and passive, yet it is the gentler revelation of Him, which was necessary to soothe my crushed spirit and allow Him into my night. Many moments in my life were marked by His quiet presence and tender beckoning. He was my provision during the dark events and became my night light. When I could not receive His brilliant presence, He sent it by softer rays into my soul. When I could not understand His ways, He simply calmed my fears; and though He seemed mostly hidden, He was never gone.

Many Christians have little understanding of the God they proclaim and acknowledge. But I would challenge each reader to embrace Him, run into His outstretched arms, and search His face for expressions of His love. He is not distant, nor haughty; He is humble, kind, forgiving, and accepting. Thankfully, He is also patient and merciful. My heart grieves for those who know not how dearly they are loved. He is not an exacting taskmaster, nor a tyrant, not a slave master, nor a harsh boss. And though He may be the strong sunlight to some, I find that He is mostly the moonlight that hurting and weary souls seek.

So, I invite you to step in closer, whisper His name, and allow Him to envelope you in His loving arms. Allow Him to be the tender Presence you have been seeking. You will find His peace there, and He will be your night light, too. I cannot fathom life without Him—He has been the Moon Over My Shoulder all along.

"When I consider Your heavens, the work of Your fingers, the moon, and the stars, which you have set in place, what is man that you are mindful of him, the son of man that you care for him? You made him a little lower than the heavenly beings and crowned him with glory and honor." Psalm 8:3-5

"The day is yours, and yours also the night; you established the sun and moon. It was you who set all the boundaries of the earth; you made both summer and winter." Psalm 74:16-17

"Come to me, all you who are weary and burdened, and I will give you rest. Take my yoke upon you and learn from me, for I am gentle and humble in heart, and you will find rest for your souls. For my yoke is easy and my burden is light." Matthew 11:27-30

Happy New Year! December 31

Wool coats and jackets of all sizes, in dark winter colors, deep and warm, layered the bed. All the trappings of winter garb became my retreat when the New Year's Eve party waxed into the late hours of the old year, and the wee hours of the new one. My mother was graciously invited to her college friends' houses for parties, kids and all. As they played cards, laughed, and snacked on our much-coveted homemade sugar cookies, I drifted into sleep among the caress of coats. It was time to go home when I felt the coats gently pulled free of the sleeping me, Mom usually one of the last to leave.

New Year Eves since have found me in many diverse places, but I found that the best place to be was at home in my bed. My husband, night-owl that he was, had no problem with the midnight hour, but it was torture for me; he worked late shifts, but mine began early in the morning. For years I forced myself to wait for the last stroke of midnight. Bidding farewell to the passing year, excitement for the new eluded me as I escaped as quickly as possible to my warm blankets.

For me, the present moment is far more important than memories past or future hoped. I found I could do nothing to change my past; focusing on the future only compounded my propensity for stress. In a way, I feel arrogant counting on the future; Jesus Himself even stated that we do not know what tomorrow will bring. And it is He who walked alongside me in my past, He I can count on today, and He who will be with me in the future.

I love how God numbers our days but did not give us insight into the count ahead of us. Attempting to control and manipulate every one of them would be the result. But in God's great wisdom, He reserved that control for Himself. I have proven Him correct in His judgment many times over. I have bungled my way through decades of do-overs, finding that God knows perfectly well what will ignite my transformation into a greater resemblance of Jesus. His long-term goal, His resolution for the ages is that of refining me into the image of Christ.

So, I will take each day as it comes, looking forward to what each hour brings, fully recognizing that tomorrow may begin eternity. Today I spend with Jesus; tomorrow I may be in His very presence! The celebration truly began the day I accepted Christ as my Savior, and the party hasn't stopped since. Every day is a new beginning. Happy New Year!

"For a thousand years in your sight are like a day that has just gone by, or like a watch in the night…Teach us to number our days aright, that we may gain a heart of wisdom…Satisfy us in the morning with your unfailing love, that we may sing for joy and be glad all our days."

Psalm 90:4, 12, 14

It Is Finished

Your old year has passed. You lived long enough to see it completed, and now you are anticipating that which is ahead. But I would strongly urge you to pause and consider, not what you can do, or who you will see, or where you will go, but rather, the state of your soul. Life will continue to surge ahead. Will you drift along on its tide or consider a better path?

If this book has done nothing else, I pray you have realized your need for Jesus. His work on the cross was for you. His life was spent for you. He died for you. When He cried out, "It is finished!", it was for you. The blood, suffering, and pain were for you. He came to die so that you could live. You may have "head knowledge" of this, but do you **know** Him? He completed His mission on earth so that you could find Him and know Him.

If you have never made a conscious commitment to Christ, I hope that you will do so right now. He asks you to bring nothing because He already gave everything. But He does ask you to yield everything; because in doing so, you gain more than you can conceive. To surrender to Him is to take up your cross and follow Him, and that is the ultimate freedom. Because of His love, grace, forgiveness, and compassion, He longs to embrace you, to bring you into His fold. It is simple but profound; a simple prayer and a surrendered heart are all He asks of you.

My suggestion for a simple prayer of salvation:
"Father, here I am. You love me and know me; you know what I have done that I am not proud of. You know the rebellion of my heart. I cannot save myself and pay the debt I owe for my sin. I am coming to you to thank you for saving me, for paying the penalty for me. My life is now yours, Jesus. Show me how to love and follow you. Lead me in the path you have for me."

Now, it is finished! I rejoice with you in your newfound love and eternal life. Welcome home! Praise be to God the Father, Jesus the Son, and the Holy Spirit!!! Amen.

If you prayed this prayer today, talk with your pastor, or someone you know who walks with Jesus faithfully. It is an important step and will solidify your resolve. There is power in speaking aloud what took place in your heart. Please let me know that you are a new member of the family of God (at MoonOverMyShoulder@protonmail.com). It would be an encouragement to me, and an honor to pray for you.

ABOUT THE AUTHOR

Kathryn Powell has the gift of translating the beauty of the world around us into written parallels of God's love and faithfulness. She has lived and traveled throughout the United States and is a skilled speaker, photographer, and artist. Mother of three adult children, she lives in the rolling hills of Tennessee.

By *Whitney Powell Williams*

ACKNOWLEDGMENTS

A special thank you to **Gwen Paul** for editing, technical support, and a wonderful friendship.

Thank you to **Cindy Wilson**, **Amy Key**, and **Abbey Key** for your love, prayers, and support, and for inspiring me to be more like Jesus by your examples. A very special thank you to Abbey for your patient technical support and editing.

Thank you to **Christopher Ricci** for taking this newby under your wing. And to **Michael Mishoe** for fielding a barrage of questions and helping me cross the finish line of publishing. Thank you both for believing in me.

Thank you to **Frances Albury** for technical support and seeing me through the trials, my fellow author and friend.

To **Pam Blair**, **Mary Lu Kirchner**, and **Jay Ann McDonald**: Without your love, support, and admonishment to keep every page intact, this book would never have existed. Thank you for your loving friendship.

Thank you to **Steve and Kathie Smith** for your diligence, above and beyond duty, as well as your friendship and support.

And to **each of you** who read very rough drafts and still offered your kind support and encouragement, thank you.

Credits

Cover artwork: Kathryn Powell ©2021 All rights reserved.

Cover photography: Jordan Steranka, Unsplash.com

Author photograph: Steve and Kathie Smith, Smith Photography

Scripture quotations marked (NKJV) are taken from the New King James Version

Scripture quotations marked (NLT) are taken from the New Living Translation.

Scripture quotations marked (NASB) are taken from the New American Standard Bible.

"Everything", by Toby Mack, produced by songwriters Toby McKeehan and David Garcia under the label Forefront Capital CMG. Released on July 18, 2018

Moon Over My Shoulder

Moon Over My Shoulder

Made in United States
Orlando, FL
19 August 2022

21288073R00220

The Tribe of Tiger

CATS AND THEIR CULTURE

The Tribe of Tiger

CATS AND THEIR CULTURE

Elizabeth Marshall Thomas

Illustrated by Jared Taylor Williams

G.K. Hall & Co. • ISIS Publishing Ltd.
Thorndike, Maine USA   Oxford, Great Britain

This Large Print edition is published by G.K. Hall & Co., USA and by ISIS Publishing, Great Britain.

Published in 1995 in the U.S. by arrangement with Simon & Schuster, Inc.

Published in 1995 in the U.K. by arrangement with The Orion Publishing Group Ltd.

U.S.   Hardcover   0-7838-1169-1   (Core Collection Edition)
U.K.   Hardcover   1-85695-092-1   (ISIS Edition)

The text of this Large Print edition is unabridged.
Other aspects of the book may vary from the original edition.

Set in 16 pt. News Plantin by Ginny Beaulieu.

Printed in the United States on permanent paper.

British Library Cataloguing in Publication Data available from the British Library

Library of Congress Cataloging in Publication Data

Thomas, Elizabeth Marshall, 1931–
    The tribe of tiger : cats and their culture / Elizabeth Marshall
Thomas ; illustrated by Jared Taylor Williams.
        p.   cm.
    Includes bibliographical references.
    ISBN 0-7838-1169-1 (lg. print : hc)
    1. Cats — Behavior. 2. Cats. 3. Tigers — Behavior.
4. Lions — Behavior. 5. Cats — Anecdotes. 6. Large type
books. I. Title.
[SF446.5.T48 1995]
599.74'428—dc20   94-37502

For Stephanie, for Ramsay

About the Title

The title of this book is from a poem called "Rejoice in the Lamb," written sometime between 1756 and 1763 by the English poet Christopher Smart. The poem is long and rambling to the point of incoherence, a product of the confusion the poet experienced and for which he was kept in solitary confinement in a madhouse. A more frightful setting than a rat-infested madhouse of the eighteenth century would be hard to imagine, as would the loneliness and despair that Smart must have known during his eight-year ordeal. His torment was mitigated, however, by the presence of a cat, Jeoffry, who became the subject of one section of the poem — some seventy-five radiant lines that are today well known and much beloved by cat fanciers and that often appear as a poem in their own right, usually under such titles as "Of His Cat, Jeoffry"

or "Jeoffry" or "For Jeoffry, His Cat." The rest of the poem is virtually lost, known only to a handful of scholars of English literature.

My book is but one of dozens, perhaps even hundreds, of books about cats that take their titles from "Jeoffry." Almost anyone who reads the fragment, even those who are unaware of Smart's confinement and suffering, can share the strength of his feeling. In the following lines, for example, one feels the poet's prayerful gratitude for Jeoffry's company in the echoing asylum during the black, terrifying hours of night:

For I will consider my cat, Jeoffry.
For he is the servant of the Living God, duly and daily serving him.
For he keeps the Lord's watch in the night against the adversary.
For he counteracts the powers of darkness by his electrical skin and glaring eyes.
For he counteracts the Devil, who is death, by brisking about the life.

One feels how the cat touched the poet's heart:

For having considered God and himself, he will consider his neighbor.
For if he meets another cat he will kiss her in kindness.
For when he takes his prey he plays with it to give it a chance.
For one mouse in seven escapes by his dallying.

And one feels the poet's inspiration:

> For he is of the Tribe of Tiger
> For the Cherub Cat is a term of the Angel Tiger.

I chose to take a title from the poem mainly because it represents a powerful link between a person and an animal, and also because the poem expresses the sanctity of an animal who the poet feels is serving God by his wholesome behavior and is keeping the devil at bay. I also chose the poem for its excellent and touching insights, made centuries before anyone thought that animals were deserving of good observation. To call the light brushing of noses between two cats a kiss, for instance, is to describe perfectly the greeting of cats who know each other (suggesting, incidentally, that there may have been a cat population as well as a rodent population in the asylum) while the observation that Jeoffry lost one mouse in seven because he played with his prey is worthy of a modern field biologist. But most of all, I chose the poem because it expresses something that is intensely true of and important about cats — that their tribe is the tribe of tigers. As the cherub is to the angel, so the cat is to the tiger, and although today we tend to put the relationship the other way around, saying that tigers are a kind of cat rather than that cats are a kind of tiger, the fact is that cats and tigers do represent the two extremes of one family, the alpha and omega of their kind.

9

Introduction

One summer evening at our home in New Hampshire, my husband and I were startled to see two deer bolt from the woods into our field. No sooner had they cleared the thickets than they stopped, turned around, and, with their white tails high in warning, looked back at something close to the ground as if whatever frightened them also puzzled them. We were wondering aloud what might be threatening the deer when to our astonishment our own cat sprang from the bushes in full charge, ears up, tail high, arms reaching, claws out. The deer fled, and the cat, who fell to earth disappointed, watched them out of sight.

Our cat is a male and at the time was just two years old. He weighed seven pounds and stood eight inches at the shoulder, in contrast to his two intended victims, who weighed more than a hundred pounds apiece and stood three feet at the shoulder. Even so, the difference in size and the difficulty of the task seemed to mean nothing to our cat. We realized we hadn't known him.

In truth, most of us don't know our cats. Hunting, if we stop to think of it, should of necessity be topmost in their minds. Not that the obsession always shows for what it is — sometimes its manifestation is obscure. As an adolescent, this particular cat, for instance, became enormously excited by a winter storm. Eyes blazing, he tore around in circles through the whirling snow, leaping high to catch the flying leaves that the wind was ripping from the oak trees. In addition, he forcefully tackles just about everything that comes his way, including a large loaf of Italian bread my husband had removed from a shopping bag and placed on the kitchen counter. To our amazement, the cat came hurtling up from the floor, landed on top of the loaf, bestrode its back with his claws dug deep into its sides, and instantly delivered what should have been a killing bite to the "nape" of its neck on the left side. When the loaf took no notice, the cat swarmed all over it, slashing at it with his claws and biting it deeply all over its body. Still the loaf ignored him. Suddenly the cat stopped short, stared down at his prone quarry, and then, perhaps reasoning that the loaf was dead after all, quickly scratched around it as if covering it with leaves, as wild cats hide the uneaten portions of large victims from competitors.

But there were neither leaves nor competitors in the kitchen. Abandoning the idea, the cat turned back to the loaf and rubbed it twice with his lips, swiping first to the left and then to the right. Then he jumped down from the counter and without a trace of confusion or embarrassment strolled from the room, head and tail high. Later, I photographed the badly mauled loaf of bread with the killing bite still showing on the nape — the very place, according to field studies, where most man-eating tigers, such as those of the Sundarbans in the Ganges Delta, seize their victims.

The cat has a tiger's name, Rajah (in just about every collection of zoo or circus tigers, one is named Rajah), and formerly had been called Rajah Tory Peterson because of his interest in birds. But after he proved himself willing to hunt everything from deer to loaves of bread, we dropped the surnames. Later it became clear that Rajah was not the only cat in our community to hunt so ardently — not five miles from our home live other cats who also hunt deer, and have done so long enough that the resident deer have lost all fear of them. At the sight of little cats staring up at them from the long grass the deer whistle and stamp their feet in angry warning, but to no avail. The moment they lower their heads to eat, the determined cats creep nearer.

Like Rajah, these cats are well cared for by their owners, whose homes they share and whose affection they return. Not one of these cats must catch his own food in order to eat. What then explains the obsessive hunting? The answer to that question is the subject of this book — a story of cats and the cat family.

PART ONE

The Animal

The story of cats is a story of meat, and begins with the end of the dinosaurs. Before their mysterious disappearance, the dinosaurs had reached a sort of climax in the art of meat-eating, which had begun simply enough, almost with life itself, when the early swarms of small aquatic creatures had little else to eat except one another. For these early swimmers, plants as we know them were not an option, since plants had not evolved. As life became more complicated, hunting and meat-eating became more complicated too. Most of the vertebrates were meat-eaters — certainly most of the fish ate other fish, as did the first amphibians, who in turn became food for the emerging reptiles.

During Permian and Triassic times, predatory dinosaurs crowded out most of their meat-eating forebears, ending the long reign of the big carnivorous amphibians. From Jurassic times onward even the largest dinosaurs had predatory dinosaurs trying to kill them, with more dinosaurs waiting to scavenge the remains. The mammals had no chance to mount any kind of challenge. As a result, when after 130 million years of highly successful predation the dinosaurs vanished, they left behind a most unusual situation — a world newly free of carnivores of any appreciable size.

Even as recently as the Paleocene, sixty-five million years ago, only two groups of mammals could have been called carnivorous, and by today's standards, or indeed by the former high standards of the predatory dinosaurs, neither of these would have seemed particularly adept at hunting. The first group, called the creodonts, were not built for speed and probably specialized in carrion, and the second group, called the miacids, ancestors of the modern carnivores, were for the most part very small and possibly specialized in insects; in other words, despite the new situation, both groups continued to eat what they had been eating when the dinosaurs were still around.

Thus, there was no one to molest the millions of large, hairy, milk-fed animals who soon evolved to roam the fertile forests left them by the dinosaurs, browsing the trees and bushes without much fear of predators. The early herbivores became a vast, slow-moving food supply which eventually even they themselves could not ignore. A few of them, including an enormous hoglike, bull-sized creature called *Andrewsarchus*, gave up leaves for meat. The largest carnivorous mammal ever to have lived on land, this minotaur with a carnivorous habit probably lacked the delicate sensibilities of a true carnivore such as a dog or cat or weasel and surely must have been the most frightening predator the world has ever seen.

By all that is sensible, the creodonts should also have been developing themselves to better exploit the world of meat. Surprisingly, however, they went into decline. Their eventual extinction seems puzzling — not only had some of them grown to the size of bears, so that they were much heftier than their insect-eating competition, but they were in the very act of evolving larger brains and learning to run faster. Even so, they disappeared.

And thus, a way opened for the modern carnivores. Encouraged by the magnificent opportunities and in the absence of rivals, the former little insect-eaters grew and changed. From them emerged two bloodlines, sometimes known as the Vulpavines, or Fox Tribe, and the Viverravines, or Mongoose Tribe. (Students of Latin should simply ignore the fact that *viverra* means ferret, since a ferret is not a kind of mongoose at all but a kind of weasel and belongs with the dogs in the Fox Tribe. Also best ignored is that *viverra* comes from *wer,* the Indo-European root word for squirrel. Squirrels aren't carnivores, of course, and except as prey have no place in this story.) During the Oligocene, members of the Fox Tribe started turning into the dogs, the bears, the raccoons, and the weasels. Members of the Mongoose Tribe became the modern mongooses, the hyenas, and the cats.

While these new carnivores became the hunters of the plains and forests, and also, by Miocene times, hunters of the sea as walruses, sea lions, and seals, many of the Fox Tribe secured for themselves a place close to the evolutionary middle ground. Although they were carnivores, they may have slowly weaned themselves from their insectivorous habits by eating some vegetable matter too. Insects and plants, after all, are so intermixed that they can almost be called two parts of the same thing, and go together like franks and beans, so to take a bite of one is often to nip a little of the other by mistake, especially if whoever is eating has a big mouth. If, like most animals, you have no hands to pick up your food but must put your mouth directly on it, when you snap up an insect, you sometimes can't help biting off a piece of the plant it was sitting on. Conversely, if you eat the plant, you often chew up some insects accidentally. (Allegedly it's hard to tell the difference. A man who ate a caterpillar in a desperate, failed effort to impress a woman said later that the caterpillar had tasted like the plant he'd found it on.)

To the early Fox Tribe, the ability to eat vegetables proved very helpful in times of meat shortages. Today some of its members — the raccoons and bears, for instance — can eat almost anything. This allows them to exploit a wide range of habitats. Others, such as the dogs and modern foxes, can endure a decline in their usual meat supply by varying their diet to include fruits, legumes, insects, and other forms of nourishment. One very early member of the bear family, the bamboo-eating giant panda, has passed right through meat-eating into vegetarianism again and thus has become, paradoxically, a vegetarian carnivore.

The cats, however, took a riskier path. In general, the descendants of the Mongoose Tribe eat fewer vegetables than do decendants of the Fox Tribe, and the cats eat almost none. A cat might eat the chyme that had been in a victim's stomache, or take a little catnip as a recreational drug, or chew some leaves for vitamins, or swallow a few sharp blades of grass as a scour, but cats can't extract enough nourishment from these or other vegetables. Well-meaning human vegetarians notwithstanding, cats must eat animal protein or they slowly decline and eventually starve. Not for them the comfortable middle ground, eating meat one day and berries the next, and no carrion either. Fresh meat killed by themselves or by their mothers is virtually the only item on the feline menu. The cats have chosen the edge.

Survival at the edge is no easy matter. The food of cats is not found at the tips of branches, waiting aromatically in the sun to disappear down someone's throat. Fruit, after all, is the reward offered by a plant to anybody willing to swallow its seeds, soften the husks, and eventually put them on the ground, securely packed in fertilizer and too far away from the parent plant to offer any competition. In contrast, the food of cats is frightened of the cat and is dedicated to its own survival.

It is intelligent, brave, fast moving, often well armed, and sometimes much larger than the cat who wants it. So to live at the edge, the cats were challenged to become highly skilled as hunters.

And this they did. Hunting preoccupies a cat almost from birth. The behavior of kittens at play is hunting behavior and nothing else. Because a cat can hunt without eating but cannot eat without hunting, hunting means life to cats, so much so that the process of hunting matters more than the resulting food. A cat of ours, named Orion because of his unquenchable hunting (and also because he seemed to say "Orion" when he gave his ringing, far-traveling call), brought no fewer than thirty chipmunks into our house during just one summer. Head high, pace determined, jaws bulging with the chipmunk who was forced to ride, feet forward, in his mouth, Orion would hurry to the living room, put down his victim, and step back.

Of course, once the poor creature got its bearings it would try to escape, and Orion would chase if from room to room. Up and down the curtains the chipmunk would run with the cat leaping after him, up and down the stairs, over the beds, under the sofa, over the kitchen table, through the sink and out into the hall. The moment my husband and I would hear what the cat was doing we would of course join the chase in hopes of rescuing not only the chipmunk but also our things. Even though we almost always managed to catch the chipmunk and let it out, thus depriving Orion of his sport and his prey, he nevertheless seemed to enjoy our participation, possibly because we added to the excitement, or possibly because housecats (contrary to what many people believe) do in fact hunt cooperatively when the opportunity arises. They don't cooperate as well as lions do, but they cooperate to some extent — a practice that seems to have developed from the tendency of kittens to follow their hunting mothers, trying to take part as best they can. At any rate, perhaps in hopes of our participation, Orion released chipmunks again and again, to the point where we hated to hear the cat door slam because we knew what was coming.

Interestingly enough, our area could not possibly have sustained the thirty chipmunks captured by Orion. At most, ten or twelve might have lived in our woods and stone walls. This meant that Orion was catching some chipmunks for a second or third time. One chipmunk lost a tail, and two were slightly wounded by Orion's inconsiderate games, but only three of his victims died. And not from any lack of hunting ability on the part of the great Orion, who enjoyed his sport for one summer and then gave it up for reasons of his own but not from a lack of chipmunks.

Had he been cruel? Well, yes, by human standards. But human standards mean little to the cats. Furthermore, incredible as it seems, chipmunks are hunters too — not as skilled as the cats, of course, but equally cruel. Once one of the above-mentioned chipmunks caught a wood frog and ate it, swallowing one of its legs and packing the rest of it, still feebly struggling, into his cheek pouches. The frog was almost half the size of the chipmunk, so it didn't fit in easily. Three or four times the chipmunk was forced to drag the dying frog out of his mouth, turn it around, and repack it. So Orion, who may have captured this same chipmunk once or more than once, seemed almost kind by comparison.

Throughout the cat tribe, many individual cats can kill without benefit of experience or education, contrary to an often-stated belief that killing is a skill that mother cats (but not father cats) teach their young. Mother cats certainly are teachers, but exactly what they must accomplish with this teaching is imperfectly understood, at least by human beings. A female puma, for instance, who was born in a zoo and knew less than most of us about the ways of the wild, instantly killed an unfortunate young male elk whom her keepers had found injured by the side of a road and, in order to make a video of their puma killing something, had shoved into her pen.

Even more revealing, perhaps, is the account of a puma named Ruby, who was born on a fur farm but rescued as a tiny kitten by her owner, a wildlife rehabilitator, Lissa Gilmour. Except for her first few weeks of life, Ruby had always lived with Lissa at Lissa's home in Colorado, and was completely uneducated from a puma's point of view. Thus it was impressive to learn how much information on hunting was already in Ruby's head.

One evening, Lissa was giving a lecture on the puma at the Denver Museum of Natural History, with Ruby scheduled to make an entrance after the slides had been shown. Friends had offered to help by keeping Ruby occupied until the time came for her to join Lissa, at which point they were to bring her to the lecture hall. The kindly people were doing exactly that, and Ruby, restrained by her collar and a leash, was patiently padding along beside them through the dark, deserted halls of the museum, when in one of the dioramas she spotted a stuffed deer. Instantly she sprang at it, whisking the leash out of her handler's grasp. Alas, she crashed into the glass and dropped to the floor, so the experience, for her, must have been quite bewildering. Yet for the rest of us it must be considered extremely illuminating, since Ruby had never done such a thing before. She had never seen any animal killed, let alone a deer. Furthermore, the deer in the exhibit certainly hadn't moved to attract her, nor had it given off a tempting sound or odor. No — Ruby had reacted to its appearance only, and her reaction had been sure and strong.

These episodes show something important about the cat family — that meat-eating is deeply ingrained in their nature. Consistent meat-eating explains much about all cats, from why, except for size and camouflage, there is very little difference among the thirty-two species of the family to why they seldom mark with feces but frequently use urine, which they spray.

In short, cats resemble each other because, so far, they have had no reason to change. Good hunters since the lynxlike Ur-cat of the Miocene from whom the modern cats descend, the cats have had no need to adjust their bodies or their diets in response to major changes in the world's climate. Why not? Because, unlike the diets of other animals, the diet of cats didn't change. The vegetarian menu listed everything from bananas to pecans, from seaweed to eucalyptus leaves, items so different from one another that completely different organisms were required to find, chew, and digest them, but the cat menu listed only one item: meat. From a cat's point of view, the difference between a bird who eats cherries, a fish who eats algae, and a giraffe who eats acacia thorns is mainly one of quantity. All three are meat, and a cat can benefit from any one of them if he can catch it. So while the glaciers came and went, while the vegetarians struggled against all odds trying to digest new plants and adapt themselves to overwhelming global changes, the cats simply kept on hunting, waiting to pounce on whoever managed to survive into the next epoch. The limber cat body that hunted successfully in the Pliocene hunts just as successfully today.

Hence, meat-eating has formed cat bodies, beginning in the mouth with daggerlike eyeteeth suitable for fastening their owner to a victim, and with strong, triangular cheek teeth, capable of severing

26

the victim's spine and shearing his flesh into bite-sized chunks for passage down the cat's throat. Meat-eating has caused the shortness of the cat's intestine, since meat is easy to digest and doesn't require a long, heavy gut that would weigh a cat down and keep him from accelerating quickly — a basic requirement for the feline lurk-and-leap style of hunting. Meat-eating explains the short digestive period, the rapid passage of food through the cat, and the nutritional residue in a cat's feces, which is why dogs forage in cats' litter boxes and why cats mark with spray. A spray is not as visible as a scat, perhaps, but at least it will still be there when the owner returns to check on it. Thus, finally, meat-eating even explains why a cat can twist his penis. Like a gardener spraying roses, a cat can direct his urine upward to moisten the undersides of leaves where other cats will find it and where rain won't wash it away.

The most important fact about meat-eating, however, is that it explains a cat's emotions, or some of them. Many expressions of a cat's feelings seem deeply related to the capture of live prey. An excited, happy, or much relieved cat may ambush and pounce upon whatever triggers its pleasure — something worth considering before getting a large cat all worked up.

One moonless night when Lissa was out for the evening, Ruby escaped from her pen. Finding herself at large on the isolated homestead high in the Colorado Rockies, Ruby must have felt anxious and unsure of herself while she waited for Lissa to get home and straighten things out. When Ruby heard Lissa's car, she crouched low beside the house, and as Lissa groped her way through the almost prehistoric darkness that surrounds her mountain fastness, Ruby joyously sprang on her from behind and bore her down. It was her way of expressing relief.

I have occasionally witnessed similar episodes, the most touching involving a tiger, whose version of a free-floating predatory dream was displayed backstage at an outdoor circus one very hot day. The tiger grew increasingly excited at the approach of her trainer, then abruptly stopped leaping and spinning and quickly crouched low to hide behind a solid partition in her cage. When the trainer passed the partition, the tiger sprang at him with her fingers stretched and her claws out. Especially touching, I felt, was the fact that the trainer had not come to feed this tiger but to squirt her with a hose to cool her, and she knew it. The prospect not of food but of cool water, and the joy of playing in it, had fired the tiger's excitement so high that she saw herself leaping from ambush. That her concept of climax was to seize her trainer — as she surely would have done without the bars to stop her — is simply a meat-eater's way.

Conversely, a committed meat-eater may express affection and even gratitude toward his or her prey — a touching and thoroughly appropriate emotion in a creature for whom captured animal protein is the only source of food. Or so that emotion should seem to us, since in many human societies people do exactly the same thing when thanking or venerating an animal who has been killed for food. In a tender scene I happened to witness on the African savannah, a lion and some lionesses were rendering the carcass of a female kudu. The lion took the intact but severed head of the kudu between his paws and, holding it upright so that she faced him, slowly licked her cheeks and eyes intimately and tenderly, as if he were grooming her, as if she were another, beloved lion. Rigor mortis had not yet stiffened her muscles — under his tongue her eyelids opened and shut in a lifelike manner. An infant lion pushed up under his father's elbow and helped to wash the kudu's face.

Even more touching was a scene that aired on public television several years ago. Shot through such a long lens that the image appears flat and blue with distance, the film shows a large male puma who evidently has just killed a large male bighorn sheep. The sheep is lying dead on his left side. The puma lies down full length on his right side, face to face with the sheep, gazes fondly into the sheep's eyes for a moment, then reaches out his paw and tenderly pats the sheep's face as a kitten might pat its mother.

Finally, meat-eating, and meat-eating alone, accounts for a cat's sense of fun, of play. The only forms of amusement ever attempted by any of the cats are simulations of hunting, whether with toys, with each other's extremities, or with live prey. All three of our cats bring live prey into the house, to release and chase, either singly or together. When we see the three cats lined up, peering under a radiator or a bookcase, we know what we'll find there. So, too, do we know what we'll find when we hear creatures rushing about in the dark, banging and thumping. My husband and I have great sympathy with the need of cats to hunt, so except to put the bird feeders very high, we don't interfere with our cats as long as they hunt outside, but it hurts us to watch them torturing their prey, and when a cat comes inside with her head high and her jaws bulging, we rescue her victim.

Considering the great behavioral similarities found among the different kinds of cat, and considering the number of actions that cats appear to perform while on automatic pilot, it seems paradoxical that they show so much individuality. Although every cat lover has seen astonishing deeds done by cats, I offer a few observations of my own, mostly because, as examples of what cats do that cannot be preprogrammed, they seem spectacular. A few cats, for instance, understand their owners' feelings — or to put it differently, many cats may understand their owner's feelings, but a few cats seem to want to affect them. I was told of a cat who, upon finding her owner lying exhausted and weeping on a bed, lay down beside her with her belly curled over her owner's face and, putting her front paws around her owner's head, enfolded her owner as she would have enfolded a kitten.

Cats also appear to understand the use to which human beings put their things. A cat of ours who brings mice and birds into the house has on several occasions put her victims on plates or in bowls. Many cats know what doorknobs are for and can manipulate them successfully. And unlike dogs, who, as everyone knows, are apt to regard toilets as drinking fountains, many cats understand the use to which people put toilets, and a few can even figure out an appropriate technique for using one without falling in.

Housecats are not the only cats with such abilities. Evidently pumas have them too. One night, again at the Denver Museum of Natural History, Lissa was bringing Ruby from her place of confinement to the lecture hall. Ruby tugged so hard toward the ladies' room that Lissa assumed she wanted to drink from a toilet and didn't refuse her. In the restroom, however, Ruby forced her way into a stall, clambered onto the toilet, and, with her four feet on the seat and her tail aloft, she defecated into the bowl. What a cat!

My grandmother, Bessie Merrill, had as a young wife a similar experience with a cat. Much to the delight of members of the family, this cat was often seen using the toilet. In those days, indoor plumbing was relatively new, and a toilet was considered too intimate an object to discuss openly, so the talents of this cat were not celebrated outside the immediate family. If my own cats would do the same, I'd tell the world shamelessly, but they haven't quite got the technique of perching on the edge of the seat, tail high, front paws together, rear paws spread. They know what a toilet is for, though, and they occasionally relieve themselves around the base of the pedestal. This attribute of cats is particularly remarkable in light of the fact that cats in the wild don't seem to have formal dung middens, where everyone in the local population defecates. Cats do spray where other cats have sprayed, or in the same area, but the object of this is almost certainly territorial. Nor is the traditional use the only use to which cats put toilets. Our cats cling to the seat while leaning low to drink from the bowl. But our son's cat dips his left front paw down into the bowl while clinging hard to the seat with the others, then licks the water from his paw. Finished, he jumps down, shakes his paw dry, and walks away.

Finally, cats understand many words of their owners' language, although they often don't seem to. I happened to notice this when my black cat, Wicca, would sleep on top of my word processor. As her body absorbed the heat from the monitor her tail would dangle in front of the screen. "Your tail, Wicca," I'd say, and push it aside. One day I was saying "Your tail" just as the phone rang. Wrong number. When I turned back to clear my view of the screen, I was surprised to see that Wicca had already moved her tail. So the next time her tail dangled, I didn't touch it but just asked. Eyes shut as if fast asleep, Wicca simply moved her tail so that it folded around her body and didn't hide the screen. And from then on, all I ever needed to do was to say, "Your tail."

Wicca, who specialized in hunting birds, died tragically in the claws of a bird, a great horned owl. One of her successors is a cat named Christmas, who also sleeps on my monitor and also dangles her tail. To my surprise, it turned out that Wicca wasn't the only cat who understood the meaning of words. If asked, Christmas sometimes also moves her tail. However, Christmas seems to want something in return for doing me so great a favor. Seizing my hand with both of hers, claws out, she brings it up to her head so that I can scratch her.

Finally, I offer the doings of a cat named Wazo, who lives in Massachusetts with my friend Margie Born. An intelligent, mature male, Wazo is interested in dogs, whom he manipulates. As in many households with dogs and cats, Wazo is fed on top of the refrigerator so that the dogs won't eat his food. When he eats, the dogs eye him from below. From time to time he picks out a kibble, puts it at the edge of the refrigerator's tablelike top, and flips it over with his paw. A dog finds it on the floor and eats it. At one time, Wazo also fed the dogs from bowls of candy that had been left on a table, but as he saw it, candy was fit only for dogs. He himself didn't partake of it, although the dogs ate it wrapper and all.

Yet there is a reciprocal aspect to the relationship. Wazo is a very territorial cat who values his space and hates to see another cat intrude upon it. Nevertheless, in his community, which is urban, many other cats are always prowling about. When one comes into his yard, Wazo goes into the house and somehow manages to communicate the presence of a rival to the dogs, who then burst out the door and chase away the stranger. Margie doesn't know how her cat communicates his problem to the dogs — but communicate he does. In the wink of an eye, the dogs are out of the house and the strange cats are gone.

Most species of cat have never been studied, to be sure, but because cats as notably different as tigers, pumas, and housecats show surprising amounts of individuality, it is probably not unreasonable to guess that the other kinds of cat might too. It is as if Gaia has said to the cats: Here, my beauties — the information you need in order to hunt, mate, fight, yowl, be cautious, raise children, is safely packed in the back of your brains. Save your forebrains for whatever creative inventions may strike you; use your wits to amuse yourselves and me.

Scientists sometimes divide the cat family into two taxons, big cats and small cats. The big cats are the lions, tigers, jaguars, leopards, snow leopards, and clouded leopards. The small cats are all the others, twenty-eight species in all. But what is the basis for the division between big and small?

Not size, evidently, since the smallest of the big cats, the clouded leopard, is smaller than the biggest of the small cats, the puma. And not the old adage that big cats can't purr and small cats can't roar. Well, perhaps small cats can't exactly roar, since they haven't got the bodily mass for it, and at the base of their tongues is merely an ordinary tongue bone, the hyoid bone, where big cats have a flexible cartilage, possibly to help produce the deafening vibration. But big cats purr or hum. Leopards certainly purr. And I once heard an interesting story about a lion purring. Admittedly, the story is anecdotal and unsubstantiated, and I don't even recall the source, since I heard it over thirty years ago, and at that distance my memory is faulty. Nevertheless I brazenly repeat it anyway. Years ago, in the country that was then the Bechuanaland Protectorate and is now Botswana, a lion is said to have seized a missionary by the nape of his neck and his shoulder and, straddling his body, dragged him into the shade. Before the mission students could drive the lion away and rescue their teacher, the missionary believed he felt an ongoing vibration in the lion's body which he took to be purring. Also interesting was that the missionary reported feeling neither pain nor fear but rather a trancelike detachment that helped him endure this very trying experience. One cannot help but note that cats purr when they are very ill or in pain, and that purring supposedly is related to the release of endorphins. Could the purring vibration in the lion have had that desirable effect on the missionary? Could purring help to soothe other victims? It would help a cat a lot if his victim ceased to struggle and simply accepted fate. But that evolution could promote the reaction seems unlikely to say the least.

Purring is a communication. Enough cannot be said about this fascinating feature of the cat tribe. It is probably the first and most important link between a mother cat and her kittens. They feel the vibration with her warmth as they smell the milk in her breasts, and they grope toward her body. Small cats purr to people probably for the same reason that they purr to their mothers —

a reassuring sound that means to the cats what a smile means to people. Interestingly enough, purring affects the human psyche just as smiling seems to affect the feline psyche — our signals, in this case, cross and are mutually understandable. Also very interesting is that no person has yet been able to pinpoint the purr conclusively. A veterinarian and cat specialist, Dr. Richard Thoma, trying to locate a cat's purr with a stethoscope, found that the sound was equally loud all over. Several theories of purring have been advanced — one holding that it is the product of turbulence in the blood stream traveling up the windpipe and into the sinuses. More accepted is the theory that the purr results from a complex interplay involving the voice box and air pressure in the throat. However, another veterinarian, Dr. Richard Jakowski of the Tufts University School of Veterinary Medicine, suggests that the organ of purring may be the soft palate — the thing that shuts when we swallow so that food doesn't get into our lungs. Dr. Jakowski finds that a cat's soft palate is much longer than necessary if its function were merely to separate air from food, and it contains the kind of muscle that is controlled voluntarily. In other words, a cat can will his soft palate to flutter.[*]

Possibly the reason that the big cats are presumed not to purr is that they tend to reserve the communication for their children. People are

[*] *Catnip* (Newsletter of the Tufts University School of Veterinary Medicine), vol. 1, no. 9 (December 1993).

seldom present on such occasions and so don't often hear it. And no cat purrs unless someone is around to listen. Those fortunate enough to have heard a lion purring report the sound as a hum. Like the purr of the small cats, the hum or purr of the big cats is produced in the throat, not in the mouth, and seems to be related to the sound of greeting made by some of the big cats when they chuff, or do *prusten,* a sound like a discreet Bronx cheer which a person can replicate by blowing through the lips. As the purring of small cats can be either soft or loud, so the chuffing of big cats can be with or without vocalization — as small cats purr loudly when their feelings are strong or when the person (or cat or other creature) to whom they're purring is relatively far away, so big cats add voice to the chuff for emotional emphasis, if they're really glad to see whoever it is they are greeting. Our cat Rajah, realizes that his beloved owner, my husband, is slightly hard of hearing, and he raises the volume of his purr until he knows my husband can hear him. Even from afar, a listener can tell when the cat and my husband are together because the purring is extra loud.

The main difference between the sociable vocalizations of the big and small cats seems to be that big cats chuff only briefly, whereas small cats purr on and on. The tale of the lion and the missionary is further complicated by the fact that lions don't seem to chuff or purr in greeting but rather give a high, discreet moan. If in fact the lion was purring when he dragged the missionary, was he expressing gratitude to the missionary for what he, the lion, believed he was about to receive? A queer thought, but not at all impossible — like the puma who patted the face of his victim, cats of all sizes express their satisfaction at the immediate prospect of food.

One characteristic that seems to distinguish small cats from big cats is the manner of eating. A small cat typically crouches over its food, all four feet neatly on the ground, in the familiar posture of a domestic cat eating from a dish. A big cat, on the other hand, typically lies down to eat and holds its food with its front paws. A small cat often begins eating at the head or neck of its victim, while a big cat usually starts at the haunch or belly. Even so, the form of eating has more to do with the size of the food than with the size of the cat — a tiger given a small piece of meat does not normally lie down for it but simply laps it up off the ground in passing or crouches directly above it, housecat style. Or if such a bit of meat is tossed to him, the tiger may catch it with a snap of his small front teeth — his incisor teeth — and then push the morsel into his mouth with the back of his wrist or with the side of his paw.

All cats tend to pluck some of the fur or feathers before eating. Lions and tigers remove the quills from porcupines, and housecats pluck or partly pluck birds, if only of the tail and pinion feathers. Here, small cats show a further behavioral division: cats with origins in the New World are said to tear the feathers off cleanly, with a strong, upward sweep of the head, while cats of the Old World tear off the feathers with a shaking motion, a motion that rids their lips of feathers and that they begin almost as soon as their lips touch the corpse. Small cats characteristically remove the viscera as well as the hair or feathers, a fact which the owners of free-ranging housecats hardly need to be told, as these viscera are the squashy little things we step on in the dark or find on the floor in the morning. Big cats tend to eat the viscera, but first they cut the silagelike cud from the rumen (if the victim had a rumen) and then they clean the gut by dragging it between their clenched incisors to pop the feces out.

Is this all that distinguishes small cats from big cats — table manners and a hyoid bone in place of cartilage? One might point to a few minor differences, such as the fact that big cats usually sprawl when they lie down, while small cats often tuck their tails around their bodies and fold their paws under their chests. Also the sheathing of the claws is more symmetrical on big cats than on small cats. But these are not major differences.

The fact is, the important thing about big cats and small cats is not that they are different but that they are the same. And like so many other truths about cats, their sameness is due to their diet and their hunting. So perhaps the greatest measure of the cats' success is that the basic cat body, with very little change in shape, comes in so many different colors and sizes. Even the basic call, *meow*, seems to be shared among species, for when a cat wants something (if she sees a bird through the window, for instance) the *meh, meh, meh* of her call is the first part of the *meow*, and when a tiger wants something (another tiger, for instance) the booming *eow, eow* of her call, the moan, is the last part of the *meow*.

A result of the range of feline size has been that, until very recently in evolutionary terms, few if any land animals were too large or too small to escape cat predation. Diminutive cats caught the mice and the butterflies, while giant saber-tooths caught the elephants and the rhinos, with other cats of assorted sizes catching the animals in between. Today, one of the largest carnivores on land is a cat — second only to the polar bears and grizzlies is the Siberian, or Altai, tiger, a huge but silent deer hunter of the ice and snow, who can measure sixteen feet from nose to tail and weigh over eight hundred pounds. Two species of cat could claim to be the smallest — *Felis rubiginosa*, the small, rusty-spotted cat of India and Sri Lanka, and *Felis nigripes*, the even smaller black-footed cat of the African savannah. Adults of either species can measure just fourteen inches from nose to tail and weigh two or three pounds. These cats, of course, can live on worms, insects, and the smallest mice and birds.

However, that they can doesn't mean that they always do. Even these tiny cats can also prey successfully upon creatures much larger than themselves. The black-footed cat has been reported to kill sheep, something I for one did not believe until

41

Rajah, the housecat, began to hunt white-tailed deer. But is this really so surprising? Male American bobcats, who weigh about fifty or sixty pounds, regularly hunt and kill deer that outweigh them by a factor of three. And Daniel Boone and his brother reported seeing a puma killing an American bison, which would have been eight times heavier than its assailant. (Complaining that it was a gruesome sight, the Boone brothers, who themselves were hunting the same bison, shot the puma.)

As cats changed size to better exploit the bountiful smorgasbord of prey animals, they also changed their camouflage and thus can hide or hunt in a wide variety of habitats. The cats of northern climates are often soft colored and grayish, since they must match the background during all four seasons, which is particularly difficult to do in snow. People who work with fabrics know that colors mixed with gray seem to blend.

In contrast to the cats who live in snow, cats of the tropics are often brightly striped or spotted to match the dappled sunlight falling through the leaves. Cats of the savannahs are plain colored, usually tawny, and match the dry grass. Interestingly enough, they often match the green grass too, to the extent that their coats are often the same tone and intensity of color, so that even if the grass is new after a rainstorm the cats vanish into it easily. Some animals are color blind, so would be particularly disadvantaged by the ability of red cats to merge with green grass, but even birds and primates with acute color vision have difficulty in spotting a red object in a green field, or vice versa, if the tone and intensity of the colors are the same.

Even more interesting are the cats that could be considered exceptions — the cheetah, say, who is a savannah dweller if ever there was one but who is spotted nevertheless, and the puma, who has successfully occupied all habitats, from the taiga forests of northern Canada to the pampas of Chile and Argentina, and has spots only in infancy. How so? Probably because, in the case of the cheetahs, camouflage isn't too important, since the cheetah spots his prey from afar and dashes after it. In the case of the puma, since no single camouflage could match all the habitats, perhaps a generic camouflage has emerged. Or perhaps pumas were colored to match their main prey, the deer. Where the deer hide, so do they.

To be unseen and undetectable is a state that seems to suit the cat family. Frequent grooming removes much personal odor from the small cats (although the grooming itself produces a faint odor — an observant friend, the late Susanna Schweitzer, once pointed out that few things smell as delicate, as lovely, as a freshly groomed cat). Furthermore, cats walk so quietly that they are inaudible. In this, they are of course in dramatic contrast to many other animals, including us. We move forward as if by falling, saving ourselves at the last moment by quickly extending a stiffened leg, heel down. As inertia carries the body onward over the extended foot, the rest of the flat sole slaps the ground. Almost instantly we start to rise up on the toe, casting ourselves forward, and repeating the noisy process over again.

Cats walk differently. A cat lifts out each paw like a person offering to shake hands, then gently places the paw, outer edge first, very carefully on the ground before shifting any weight onto it. A very interesting observation on the footsteps of cats was made by the forest ecologist Susan G. Morse, who is also a tracker, and is the only person, as far as I know, ever to notice what is probably the single most important difference between dog tracks and cat tracks.[*] Most people believe that dog tracks can be distinguished from cat tracks by the claw marks, because cat claws are retractable while dog claws aren't, so that claw marks are said to be diagnostic. But this isn't always so. My husband's dog, for instance, manicures his own toenails by biting them, keeping them so short that on one rather embarrassing occasion his tracks passed briefly as puma tracks. And one of our cats, Silent Spring, for reasons best known to herself, would sometimes walk with all her claws out, leaving tracks that could almost pass for a dog's if they weren't so tiny. A more reliable distinction, Sue Morse suggests, is that a dog's second and third toes are almost perfectly symmetrical, while a cat's paw is like a human hand in that the middle finger is almost always a bit longer than its

[*] Susan G. Morse, personal communication.

44

neighbors. Thus an asymmetrical print not only distinguishes a cat track from a dog track but also distinguishes the left paw from the right. Yet perhaps the most interesting observation ever made about dog and cat tracks was also made by Sue Morse, and is this: that a dog walking on a soft matrix such as dust, mud, or snow leaves a tiny ridge of the matrix between the toes and the large pad, as if between the tips of the bent fingers and the forward edge of the palm if a similar print were made by a human being. In other words, a dog grasps the earth as he walks, squeezing up some of the matrix if it is soft enough. A cat, in contrast, lays down his foot very smoothly, gently, leaving no mark but the faint dents of his pads and only then if conditions are optimal, such as after a dusting of fresh snow. To me, Sue Morse's observation is as moving as it is insightful and original and shows a basic emotional difference between dogs and cats — that cats tend to hold back, approaching life with reserve and caution, while dogs tend to be a little anxious or eager, always pressing, however slightly, always a little tense.

It also explains why cats walk so quietly, and it even explains why cats, more than any other animal of similar size, often walk without leaving any tracks at all. Thus, many of the wild cats manage to live among us without our being any the wiser. We don't see them, we don't hear them, and we don't find their tracks.

On several occasions when visiting Lissa Gilmour, owner of the puma, Ruby, I searched for

45

tracks and other sign in Ruby's pen. I wanted to find clues to the presence of a puma, clues that I might recognize later. And I did. In the dust of the pen I saw part of a road-killed deer that had been hidden in leaves; farther on I saw puma hairs, puma scats, and a puma scrape; beyond these I saw a well-worn puma trail, and at the end of the trail, on top of a kennel, I saw the puma herself, pretty Ruby, who had been watching my progress with big yellow eyes. But I saw not a single footprint anywhere.

Even the puma herself didn't stay visible for long. When Lissa playfully called out "Yoohoo! Mountain lion!" Ruby crouched low and vanished in seven inches of grass. Quite literally, she was gone. We couldn't see her, at least not for what she was. She had made herself so flat that only the curve of her back showed, like a sand-colored stone or a dry patch of Colorado earth.

For a moment, nothing moved. Then Lissa turned and started running, and suddenly the enormous puma materialized as if from nowhere and came hurtling through the air. In two bounds she was on Lissa. Down they went, with Ruby's mighty paws clutching Lissa around the body and her daggerlike eyeteeth very close to Lissa's head. All this was accomplished in absolute silence. In a moment, Ruby stepped back, averted her eyes from Lissa, and sneezed lightly. Lissa got up and brushed off her clothes. But as the three of us smoothly strolled toward Lissa's parlor, where, in pleasant congeniality, we would soon take tea together, I couldn't help but notice that although this strenuous activity had produced a few scrapes from Lissa's sandals, not a trace could be found of the puma.

So much for the theory that no tracks means no cats. If the experts and authorities say differently, then they cannot be called experts or authorities.

Yet there's more. Where wild cats are hunted, they don't like to leave footprints, which in fact may be the most compelling reason for our failure to find tracks. In African game parks, lions trudge heedlessly along the dusty roads leaving long trails of footprints just as if they were people, but in the New World, pumas, lynxes, and bobcats who commonly use dirt roads as thoroughfares will quite consciously keep to the parts of the track where the dirt is hard packed so footprints won't show. On snowy ground this is particularly dramatic, especially when the cat comes to a patch of snow too big to walk around or to jump over, and can't help leaving a footprint, showing that he's been there. Otherwise, he threads his way around the patches of snow, keeping to the bare earth, even if this forces him to go out of his way.

Why so discreet? The almost perfect discretion of the cats who depend on stealth is part of their camouflage, their secrecy. An animal who understands hunting, either because it hunts or because it is hunted or both, as is the case of the New World cats, is very well served by discretion in all forms. That is why one can live among cats without realizing they are present, a state which was probably as true in the Miocene as it is in Ruby's pen in Colorado, or even as it is in the New England woodlands today.

Most books on cats include a chapter on the cat body, and this book is no exception; however, this book will not repeat the obvious, that cats keep themselves clean, say, and have retractile claws. Rather, here I will focus on two features rarely mentioned in cat literature: the awesome strength and the highly developed senses that are found in every cat alive.

Pound for pound, cats are by far the strongest animals many of us ever encounter. When my husband and I recently tried to wash our cat, Rajah, for example, it took our combined strength just to keep him in the washbasin, and we really needed a third person to put on the soap. All we had sought to do was to rid Rajah of fleas, but both of us got seriously scratched in the process, and the bathroom got drenched from ceiling to floor. In the confusion, poor Rajah escaped, dried himself off, and had nothing to do with us for days thereafter.

When one projects the strength of that seven-pound cat into a seven-hundred-pound tiger, one gets some idea of the animal's might. So it's a good thing that tigers bathe themselves, or so says the science writer Sy Montgomery.

The sense organs, too, are developed to a degree we find hard to imagine. Cats have six kinds or more, if, as some people feel, psychic powers are also present. Cats have whiskers, teeth, and skin to provide the sense of touch; eyes, ears, and nose for sight, sound, and smell; the tongue for taste; and a nearly invisible system of pits or pores known as the vomeronasal organ in the upper gum and palate for detecting the presence of certain chemicals in the environment. Among other signals picked up by the vomeronasal organ are the estrus pheromones.

Of all the senses, the sixth is least understood. The sea mammals and the higher primates were thought to be the only mammals in which this sense was missing, although some of the higher primates such as ourselves were thought to have it vestigially — the vestige was supposedly the little lump in the roof of the mouth. Or so it seemed until 1993, when a paper was published announcing that the vomeronasal organ in human beings may be functional after all. Exactly what purpose the organ serves for us has yet to be determined.

To use the organ an animal stretches his or her mouth to expose the pores in an act known as "doing flehmen." A tiger doing flehmen grins a terrible grin that stretches out her tongue. A housecat makes a tight little smile, with her front teeth covered by her upper lip, which is stretched tight. Cats often do flehmen, for instance, when they encounter the urine sprays of other cats. Our cat Lilac, mother of the hunting housecat Rajah, slowly and deliberately does flehmen when she encounters a glass of white wine. Other cats scratch dirt over wine and beer, as if covering pools of urine. Why? No one knows. Probably the answer lies in the chemical properties of the alcohol and additives, which are such that most if not all tiger trainers abstain from alcoholic beverages before a training session or a performance. Tigers are said to so deeply dislike the smell of alcohol on someone's breath that, given the opportunity, they will shred the drinker.

Perhaps a cat's most important sense is sight. To understand the impact of eyesight on cats, it is useful to contrast the way dogs and cats respond to films and television. Many dogs seem well aware that what appears to be in the TV set is an illusion and unreal, yet some dogs respond anyway, usually to sound, particularly to the sound of other dogs barking, but sometimes to the image as well. Usually this happens to naive dogs. Once a dog of mine named Koki, a sled dog who began life on the end of a chain in a village in northern Canada, reacted with restrained excitement to the image of a deer in someone's home movie. She leaped eagerly into a chair to better see the screen, but quickly realized that whatever she was looking at was an illusion, and quietly got down. On another occasion, when a television set was placed on the floor, a young female dingo named Viva became very taken with an ad for pet food in which a little team of horses ran through a room and disappeared into a cupboard. Viva tore around the set to catch the tiny horses when they ran out the back. But Viva and Koki were exceptional, probably because of Viva's youth and Koki's rustic origins. As a rule, not much experience is necessary for dogs to ignore the images of television. Koki soon realized her mistake, and young Viva, ashamed, was never fooled again, although I and other loudly laughing people tried everything we could to get her to repeat the mistake.

In contrast, cats seem drawn to the flickering screen. At bedtime, our three cats appear as if by magic to lie at the foot of our bed to watch the evening news like an audience in the front row of a theater. Videos made especially for cats are particularly popular with them. When Rajah was shown a video of fluttering birds made expressly for cats, he couldn't get enough of it — squarely in front of the screen he sat, his eyes huge, his ears in silhouette against the light, his whiskers straining. Every now and then the image would prove too much for him and he'd fling himself against the glass, only to drop to the floor. Reality. At that point, he might leave the room for a while, but soon he would quietly return to the enthralling spectacle. He quickly learned the sound of it, and the twittering of the sound track would draw him from elsewhere in the house. At the time of this writing Rajah still watches the cat video even though he knows it's an illusion, and his excitement is nearly as strong today as it was the first time.

Christmas has also learned to watch this particular video. Now and then she leaps at the screen, and so involved is she with the images that after leaping she sometimes looks down at herself, backing up as she does — she believes she has caught the bird but has lost it again, and is checking to see if it has escaped underneath her, as mice sometimes do.

Certain people might offer the anecdote of these cats and their video as evidence of cat stupidity. Not so. The anecdote merely illustrates the nature of a cat's hunting instinct. And if cats are proved stupid by having such an instinct, why then, so are we. One of the most important observations I've ever encountered concerned the human hunting instinct and was made by Ken Jafek, a hunter and professional outfitter in Malta, Idaho. It will ring a bell with anyone who loves the natural world. Ken said that the intense excitement that accompanies the sighting of a wild animal does not diminish with repetition or with familiarity or with time. Although Ken is now a grandfather, he gets the same rush when he spots a deer (or other wild animal) as he did when he was a youngster, although in his capacity as a guide and a hunter he by now has encountered wild animals hundreds or even thousands of times. I'm sure this important reflex is found in many of us. It certainly is in me. And here we share something with the cat tribe after all — the stimulus to our hunting instinct in both cases is visual.

A cat's sense of smell, in contrast, seems to have relatively little importance as a hunting tool but is more than useful as a way of learning about other cats. Unlike most hunters, including wolves and human beings, the big cats (those whose habits are known) sometimes ignore the wind when hunting, even though they surely know of their own strong personal odor. Some cats are just as apt to stalk their prey down the wind as up, not always to advantage.

A cat's weak response to airborne scent seems particularly interesting in light of the fact that cats use their sense of smell to find things and to identify other animals. I watched an example of the latter skill at our home in New Hampshire after an elephant and her trainer, who is an acquaintance of ours, had walked past our house. Our cats had been locked up with the dogs in a detached, windowless garage while the elephant was present, and after they were released and were gladly making their way back to the house, they stopped dead when they crossed the elephant's trail. Whoa! They didn't know what the smell was — they had never seen or smelled an elephant — yet they wanted to know! Hair bristling, they lingered long over the footprints, pressing their nostrils to the earth, audibly snuffling. The dogs, in contrast, ran right past the scent trail, much to my surprise. But then I realized that they would have been catching whiffs of the elephant during their imprisonment, so the smell would not have come as a shock.

Their respective reactions were as typical as they were informative. The dogs wanted most of all to join us, their social group, after being kept from us while something as strange as an elephant was present, while the cats cared less about their group and more about their surroundings. They wanted to know what strange thing had visited their home. Furthermore, if it is true that my dogs had caught the scent before the cats did, I take that not as evidence of cats' lesser ability but rather as a sign that they do not give airborne odors the same credit that dogs do. After all, every year at Christmas these same cats use olfaction to detect our family's hidden hoard of Christmas presents, then to find their own presents in the pile, then to remove and open these packages. Our cats are never wrong; they open only their own presents and no others. Obvious? Not really. Why does a cat who can find catnip not search for odors in the wind? I think that cats experience odors as pools, not as trails, as dogs do. A kitten finds his mother by entering the pool of her scent, then finds his own personal nipple by sniffing through the fur of her belly. What this must mean to a cat is suggested, I believe, by the preference cats show for their owners' clothes. To lie on one's owner's sweater, in a cloud of one's owner's scent, must awaken secure and pleasant feelings.

For cats, intraspecies communication is probably

the most important function of their sense of smell. Cats have tiny scent glands on their faces — on their lips, chins, cheeks, and at the base of their whiskers — which they rub on us, on each other, and even on objects, mixing their odors with the odors of other cats in a gesture of unity and bonding. Similarly, cats have scent glands on their backs at the roots of their tails with which they perfume other, familiar cats and objects in and around their homes. When a cat arches its back and rubs against you, it is probably marking you with this friendly odor. Cats also have glands between the toes and inside the anus which leave secretions that may carry a hostile message. Cats bury their feces when at home, perhaps to mute the message. But when far from home cats purposely leave scats on top of rocks or hills or other conspicuous, windswept locations for the information of other cats. Thus scent also serves as a Keep Out sign.

The entire face of a cat, including the lips, the fine hairs inside the ears, the points of the eyeteeth, the tips of the whiskers, and perhaps even the surface of the eyes, is an area of extreme sensitivity, and perhaps functions in the same way that facial vision functions for blind people. As a cat walks, his whiskers point forward — forward and down if he's calm, forward and up if he's anxious or excited. A circus tiger often enters the ring wide-eyed and with his whiskers pointed far forward, as if unsure of what will meet him as he emerges from the chute. Usually, the cause of concern is another tiger already in the ring. If the newcomer reaches his seat unmolested, he may feel more confident and will await his first cue calmly, with his whiskers to the side. If his trainer then comes to speak to him, or if he happens to be seated beside a tiger whom he likes and who likes him, he may chuff and bow his head in greeting, with his whiskers flat against his cheeks. But if he is then expected to do a trick that's difficult for him, his whiskers come forward in advance, as he gathers himself to perform. Interestingly enough, human beings can replicate these emotions by moving the skin around the mouth in a comparable manner, pursing our lips when unsure (an act which, if we had whiskers, would push them forward) blandly smiling when serene (to lay the whiskers back against the cheeks).

Using his face and all its senses, a hunting cat keeps his whiskers forward, his lips very slightly parted, his ears up and his eyes very wide. Even his eyeteeth are fitted with nerves, making the tips of the teeth highly sensitive, so that when the cat grabs his prey by the neck and bites down, his eyeteeth feel his victim's vertebrae, finding the spaces between the bones where he can cut through the spinal cord. If the cat is a small cat, he may then shroud his victim with his whiskers to learn through them whether any vibration remains in the victim — in other words, to learn if it's still living. Usually, the small cats don't start eating if the victim is living. So perhaps through his sensitive whiskers a cat learns the moment when eating may begin.

Since all cats are basically so similar, what force produced their thirty-five different species? Probably their habit of roaming. Sometimes we have difficulty imagining how far it was possible to roam during prehistoric times because we wrongly see the earth's dry land as, essentially, two huge islands, with the New World floating on one side of the planet and the Old World floating on the other. This image is of European origin, whereby the Atlantic looms large. And so it should. The first land mammals ever to cross the Atlantic were the Vikings.

The Pacific is much bigger, but the Pacific could sometimes be crossed if one knew where to find the bridges and the stepping stones. We would picture the earth better, therefore, if we saw the earth's dry land as a single continent, like a horse-shoe bent around the planet. If we stood at one end of this continent — on the coast of Scotland, say — and instead of looking west over the Atlantic and wondering how to sail across it we turned our backs on the ocean and began to trudge east, our biggest problem would be to cross the English Channel, which on occasion has been little more than a stream. Once on the east side of it, we would tramp onward through Europe and Asia. Eventually we would reach the Bering land bridge, which may be under water today but not so long ago was a cold and windswept tundra and may be so again. Crossing the land bridge, we would wander eastward across Alaska and Canada into Newfoundland, where we would again reach the Atlantic. And once there we would have to stop.

Near the beginning of the voyage, we could have made a lengthy side trip down into Africa, and near the end of the voyage we could have made a similar trip into South America. Thus, most of the earth's dry land was accessible to creatures who roamed over it on foot, at least during certain phases of its history. And roam is exactly what the cats did, not just once or twice but countless times, traveling in all directions.

Like their distant relatives the modern lynxes, the lynxlike Ur-cats, *Pseudaelurus*, probably lived in forests. No one can say for certain what they ate, but one can easily imagine them hunting large rodents and ground-nesting birds. However, the pressures of different habitats were working on the Ur-cat's body, and eventually the animal began changing to better exploit the various parts of its range. In South America about ten million years ago, the ocelots branched from the parent stem and, along with other little spotted mousers of the New World jungles, became known as the ocelot lineage.

Meanwhile in the Old World, wildcats appeared. Colored to blend into the shadowy forests, they were tabbies, with a large, long-haired form, *Felis sylvestris*, for the forests of Europe, and a smaller, short-haired form, *Felis sylvestris lybica*, for the forests of North Africa.

The forests of North Africa? Yes, North Africa was verdant until the Neolithic, when people domesticated many of the ungulates, invented the concept of wealth, and began to display their status and their social importance with the size of their herds. The Book of Job records, for instance, the generous compensatory damages awarded to Job for his suffering — 23,000 head of livestock, far more than Job would ever need. With all these animals, Job must have been one of the richest and most powerful pastoralists of his time or indeed of any time, a man of great importance, overgrazing with the best. According to Scriptures,* only 13 percent of Job's animals, the cattle and donkeys, were water dependent, while 87 percent, the sheep and camels, were desert tolerant, suggesting that whoever organized the gift seemed to have known how best to exploit a dry and overgrazed pasture. The preference for sheep and camels further suggests that livestock had been chewing up the suffering landscape long before

*Job: 42:12.

60

Job's animals put their lips to it. The result was desert, from the Negev to the Sahara.

Still camouflaged for the nonexistent forests, the African wildcats stayed on after desertification, hunted mice in the granaries of North Africa and Asia Minor, and became housecats, *Felis sylvestris catus.* Thus, just as we originated in Africa, so did our cats, and today the wildcats and their domestic cousins are known as the domestic-cat lineage.

Meanwhile, something must account for Siamese cats, Himalayan cats, Burmese cats, and their relations. So, undoubtedly, the Asian version of the wildcat, *Felis sylvestris ornata,* had not been idle. Perhaps penetrating the granaries of India and China, the gracile cousins of the African cats seem to have ingratiated themselves with the human population there as well. Unlike the Egyptian cats, they didn't gain civil rights or get themselves deified into an Asian version of the goddess Bastis. Even so, they became the treasured pets of monarchs and to this day, for whatever reason, are often accepted by fanciers as a higher order of cat. This, of course, is a human concept and has absolutely nothing whatever to do with excellence or competence, which both the Asian and African versions of the housecat seem to have in equal shares, depending not on the ancestry but on the individual.

Another big step in cat evolution was the rise of the pantherines. There is still some disagreement as to how the ancestral forms relate to one another, but at least one version puts the pantherines in the New World with a wildcat ancestor, probably a wildcat who had padded across the land bridge in fits and starts. This ancestor took its time in becoming a true pantherine, with many experiments along the way. Perhaps the simplest experiment was to grow very large. Not too large, though — the saber-tooths were already the big cats of the New World, preying on the big herbivores and probably living in prides. Better to stay mid-sized in the face of such competition, big enough to hunt deer when circumstances allowed but small enough to hunt rabbits when the deer were gone. The result was the puma, really nothing but a small cat grown to large proportions, who is still counted as a small cat and who keeps a small cat's ways. Pumas purr loud and long like housecats, for instance, and crouch above their food. Soon, pumas had spread over the entire New World, from the estuaries of Maine to the coastal forests of the Pacific, from the peaks of the Rockies to the swamps of Louisiana, from the evergreen taiga of Canada's far north to the open savannahs of the Argentine.

Few animals are as capable or resourceful as pumas or have been as successful. Even today, after having been exterminated throughout much of their former range, pumas are returning in eastern Canada and New England, where their habits seem to differ somewhat from the habits of western pumas in that they are even more shy. Nevertheless, they are here and are seen more and more often.

Was the ancestor of the pumas also the ancestor of the cheetahs? The two cats have much in common. Like pumas, cheetahs roamed the New World. Also like pumas, the cheetahs preyed on deer and other deer-sized ungulates and in hard times could, like pumas, turn to rabbit-sized prey. But the cheetahs hunted by coursing their prey on the open plains, whereas the pumas hunted by stealth in long grass and in thick forests. Thus these cousins avoided competition and could live together in the New World.

Perhaps because cheetahs are thought of as African and pumas as American, the two are seldom compared. Even so, powerful similarities exist. For instance, pumas and cheetahs sound alike; both make trills and chirps like birdcalls and sharp, clear whistles that sound like a person whistling with two fingers in the mouth. In fact, these whistles are made with the voice and are extremely thin, high-pitched *meows* used for communication between mothers and kittens or between pumas or cheetahs and people or other creatures with whom the cats have a positive relationship. The thinness of the sound ensures that it doesn't travel far, which helps to keep the whereabouts of the loved one or loved ones a secret.

Both cheetahs and pumas have pupils that stay round and don't form slits like the pupils of wildcats and housecats. Both cheetahs and pumas have long hind legs that tilt their hindquarters upward and give them a graceful, ankling walk. Both cats have long, heavy tails to give them balance. Both cats can move almost faster than the eye can see, although cheetahs sustain the movement far longer and are said to be the fastest mammals on earth. Yet it is hard to imagine any animal much faster than a puma — in support of which I offer an observation of Ruby, Lissa Gilmour's puma, on Lissa's handsome carpet, amusing herself one quiet afternoon. Seemingly half asleep with boredom, Ruby lay on her side while her yellow eyes followed the circling of a fly. Suddenly her forepaw made a blur and the fly vanished. She had snatched him from the air, not with her fingers but with her palm. Idly, she turned her paw over, palm up. Clasped in a single crease that had appeared across her leathery pad, a crease that a palmist might have called her lifeline, the fly kicked his tiny legs, struggling.

Soon Ruby's paw relaxed. The fly turned over and soared away, unharmed. Ruby watched him without seeming to watch him, as if the fly might be frightened by her stare. When he came near, her paw blurred again, and again she had him. What other animal could do the same?

Both cheetahs and pumas rely on long-distance vision for much of their information, and both use lookouts — high places from which to survey the passing scene. Both cats give birth to three or four kittens at a time, usually in a hidden nest or a cave in the rocks, and both cats breed at any time of year. Year-round breeding may not seem so unusual in cheetahs, since they live in warm climates where many other animals also breed year round, but it seems astonishing in pumas, who are rare if not unique among indigenous wild North American mammals in having such an ability.

The fate of pumas and cheetahs diverged somewhat when cheetahs crossed the Bering land bridge into Asia and became a global species, ankling along to India, to the Middle East, to Africa, and to Europe. Farther, no cat could go.

Why didn't the equally successful pumas follow? The answer probably lies in meat, as usual, and, if so, also explains why tigers didn't come the other way. These cats probably couldn't have crossed the land bridge — a tundra without trees or cover — because being stealth hunters they almost certainly couldn't have hunted there. Plenty of animals would have grazed on the tundra, but these were migratory animals such as bison, elk, and reindeer (caribou), who would have visited the land bridge in high summer. Like reindeer today, the migratory herds of long ago probably used the windblown snowfields as sanctuaries from the Arctic's terrible mosquitoes and biting flies. Coursers such as the cheetahs and group hunters such as the cave lions (and probably also the sabertooths) could have fed themselves on the open tundra, just as lions and cheetahs feed themselves successfully in broad daylight on the open plains of Africa. Smaller cats such as the wildcat who gave rise to the puma could also hunt on open tundra — even short grass hides the smaller cats. And, indeed, the wildcats and the lynxes crossed the land bridge many times. But tigers and pumas need good hiding places, and on the exposed plains of the land bridge these larger cats would have been too visible. On similar open plains farther south in America and Asia, the pumas and tigers could have caught their prey at night, but on the land bridge in high summer there was no night. Darkness didn't come until autumn, but by then the migratory herds would have been on their way to treeline, to their sheltered, winter ranges. In contrast, the little voles and lemmings that fed the small cats didn't migrate seasonally. Rather, they sheltered in grass tussocks or in burrows under the snow and thus provided food for wandering wildcats and lynxes all through the year.

So perhaps the most interesting members of the pantherine lineage are the lynxes, heirs to the cat family's ancestral size and habits. Numerous lynx types have appeared over time, some in Africa, others in Europe, still others in Asia. One in particular, an Asiatic lynx, spread both east and west, the westward travelers arriving in Europe to meet previusly established European lynx, and the eastward travelers arriving in Canada to encroach upon another established lynx, an earlier immigrant, the bobcat.

Today in Canada and the northern United States the two kinds of lynx live side by side. The more recent immigrant, known as the Canada lynx, is adapted for the far northern snows with huge feet and heavy fur frosted with white (perhaps because he had come more recently over the Bering tundra and simply stayed in country he had grown used to); the earlier arrival, the bobcat, has faintly dappled spots, which give good camouflage in wooded, brushy habitats from Canada to Mexico. Thus have these two cats of similar size and appearance divided the lynx-size feline's share of the New World.

Invariably, two similar animals dividing a habitat find ways to diverge, so that they become less rather than more alike. The two kinds of lynx were no exception, but interestingly, one point on which they diverged seems to have been personality. Why this is so, no one can say. Yet Canada lynxes are said to be calm, even gentle, while bobcats are supposedly spitfires. Perhaps their different lifestyles suggest the reason — the main prey of many lynxes is the snowshoe hare, for which they are particularly well adapted, while many bobcats must hunt deer (or so they have evidently been doing, at least in the northeast, since the rabbit population declined). Probably only large male bobcats are capable of killing deer, which must be extremely difficult even for them and must put a premium on courage and aggression, or at least on the ability to overcome fear and charge right into the task at hand. Perhaps the ferocity of bobcats is the by-product of centuries of hardship. No one knows, of course. And very few people care. The studies we choose to finance on the subject of bobcats relate mainly to their role as furbearers so that vain and selfish women can parade around wearing scraps of hide torn from these capable animals. Other than facts that help us trap them, we know so relatively little about the daily lives of cats in the wild that we have few mechanisms even for approaching the more complex questions that could be asked.

The lynx family gave rise to the so-called big cats: the lions, tigers, ounces, leopards, and jaguars of the genus *Panthera*. Like the lynxes, all the big cats are spotted, at least for part of their lives, except for the tigers, who are born striped and whose coats, unlike the coats of lions, say, don't change from childhood to adulthood. But are tigers truly striped? Maybe not. A tiger's stripes are actually elongated spots, a secret that is betrayed by certain individual tigers whose stripes are conspicuously open in the center, so that each stripe is shown for what it is: a leopard's rosette greatly elongated, like a stretched rubber band.

Beginning about two million years ago with the appearance of the clouded leopard (bearing the beautiful name of *Neofelis nebulosa*), the big cats evolved in increasingly larger sizes to hunt increasingly larger prey. Today, the biggest animals hunted by cats are probably wild cattle such as the African buffalo and the Asiatic gaur, with the cats dividing these populations so that tigers get at them in the forests and lions get at them on the plains.

Most of the big cats were highly successful as colonizers. In the Old World, the leopards were widespread, with the ounce *(Panthera uncia)* and the leopard *(P. pardus)* in much the same relationship to each other as the Canada lynx is to the bobcat — the ounce adapted for snow-covered mountains, and the many races or subspecies of the leopard adapted for the jungle and bush. In the New World the jaguar managed to colonize most forested parts of the Americas except in the far north, thus competing for the deer-sized prey with its older and more gracile cousin, the puma.

Few animals, however, have ever been as successful as the lions. The most recent of the *Panthera,* lions evolved on the African savannahs only 700,000 years ago, probably to the consternation of our ancestors, and soon thereafter — long before our ancestors thought of doing anything similar — the lions colonized the rest of the planet. Until very recently lions were almost everywhere that glaciers were not. They lived in North and South America, all across Asia and down into India; they lived in Europe and on the British Isles; they lived in the Middle East and throughout the continent of Africa, where of course they remain to this day. (Australia and the Pacific Islands were about the only places the lions hadn't found.)

In keeping with the tendency of animals to be

very large in the northern parts of their ranges, the northernmost lions were enormous. These were the cave lions. Having survived the Ice Age, their hair would have been longer than the hair of their southern relatives. They may have been quite fluffy. Only recently extinct, they certainly coexisted with people in Europe, Asia, and the Americas and may have been observed by at least one Chinese painter, who made a scroll showing a huge, fluffy cat — tigerish but not a tiger — whose pale fur was plain except for some stripes around its tail and knees. Perhaps this painting shows a cave lion. If so, it would not be the only cave lion image left by people, by any means. In some Magdelinean sites in Europe, Paleolithic artists carved large bas-reliefs of lions to lurk in the darkest recesses of the caves.

Today we think of tigers as Asian and lions as African, but this is a misconception; the two species coexisted in Asia from the Caucasus to China and from Korea to Iran. A few Asiatic lions still live in zoos, and a tiny relic population remains in Gir, one of India's national parks, where each one of them knows and is known by each of the park rangers personally.

Lions and tigers are so much alike in size and shape that it is difficult to distinguish their skeletal remains. They can even mate and produce young (the tions and ligers bred for zoos, circuses, and private menageries). That the two cats don't interbreed in nature is due in part to the habitats they seek and even to the times of day they sometimes favor, the tigers tending to be nocturnal forest dwellers and the lions, if perhaps to a lesser extent, diurnal plains dwellers.

By the middle of the Pleistocene, cats of all sizes lived all over the world except in Australia. However, the cat was so well designed and so successful that the Australian marsupials created a cat of their own. Called *Thylacoleo carnifex,* or "marsupial lion executioner" (literally "meat-maker"), the animal evolved, touchingly enough, from possums. These possums, in making their own version of a lynxlike creature, adopted the cat family's most popular size — small enough to subsist on mouselike animals but big enough to tackle deerlike forms. But while a true cat's longest teeth are the eyeteeth, this possum-lion's longest teeth were the front teeth, or incisors. His threats would have looked like a squirrel's, or like Dracula's. *T. carnifex* supposedly went extinct long ago but nevertheless is believed by a handful of optimists to exist to this day, and in that extremely unlikely event would be clinging to life somewhere in the far reaches of the Outback.

Meanwhile, as the true cats spread themselves over the earth, they managed, for the most part, to adjust so perfectly to one another by keeping their distance, by hunting different prey, and by moving around at different times of day that now different kinds of cats can coexist on the same bit of ground. Three square miles of national forest in Idaho might, for instance, support a puma, a bobcat or two, and perhaps a few feral housecats, with the puma hunting deer and the bobcats and housecats hunting birds and small rodents and keeping well out of the puma's way. A few square miles of tropical rain forest might similarly support a jaguar, a puma, an ocelot or two, and one or more varieties of the smaller spotted cats. In a European forest, to the consternation of roaming housecats, a lynx's range might also support some wildcats, and in the Asian jungles, a tiger's range would probably support a leopard and possibly one or more kinds of the small, rare, and beautiful jungle cats. Finally, the range of a pride of lions on the African savannah could support up to five other feline species, most of them in slightly different settings. One might find a black-footed wildcat, a serval (Africa's version of the ocelot), and perhaps a caracal (Africa's version of the lynx). Larger cats might live there, too, perhaps a leopard to hunt in the long grass and thickets and a cheetah to course the open plains. Such cats are competitive and mutually hostile; they seek and destroy one another's kittens but otherwise avoid one another at all costs. Even so, by overlapping the distribution of their species, the cats have so perfectly arranged themselves that virtually everything that creeps or flies or walks can be used by one or another of them in almost every situation. Or at least, that's how it was before habitat destruction, the pet trade, and the fur trade took a heavy toll on the cats.

Cats are well known for their homing instincts. At a recent Christmas party in our town, one of the guests boasted that he had successfully rid his family of their housecat by driving her to Concord, the state capital, some thirty miles away, and tossing her out of the car. Shocked, other guests asked him why he had done it, wondering, I'm sure, why he hadn't taken the cat to our local humane society, which costs nothing, does not euthanize its animals, and is much nearer than Concord. But the man misunderstood the question. He had been forced to go all the way to Concord, he explained, because he had already tried abandoning his cat at shorter distances, and each time she reappeared.

The cat hasn't returned from Concord, at least not as far as is known, suggesting that the owner's enormous and callous cruelty was greater than his cat's ability to home. Meanwhile, the disturbing episode raises a question: Why did the cat keep trying to return to those people?

The answer is that many cats care more about their homes than their owners. Housecats feel for their homes strongly and obviously, but other kinds of cat do too, and many cats, both housecats and wild species, have made some very impressive journeys using navigational skills that are hard to explain. A radio-collared puma, for example, whom researchers had transported in a closed box by plane for relocation in a new environment, evidently didn't like his new surroundings and headed for home, arriving there four months later after a journey of three hundred miles.*

Why is the pull of home so powerful? Again, the answer lies in meat. Every cat must live amid a population of prey animals, whether mice or bison, in a place where there is suitable feed to keep the prey from wandering away. Every cat also needs water, and every cat needs shade or shelter, particularly if she is female, since she will need several hidden nests in case she must move her kittens. To meet these requirements, each cat tries to establish and hold a territory which, of course, varies in size according to the species of the cat and the habitat of the prey animals. The size of a territory also varies by the sex of its owner. Female cats of most species tend to own adjacent

*Maurice Hornocker, "Learning to Live with Mountain Lions," *National Geographic*, vol. 182, no. 1 (July 1992), p. 52.

or almost adjacent territories of relatively modest size. These fan out through a jungle or drape down a mountainside, sometimes overlapping very slightly, sometimes touching at the corners like the petals of a wild rose. A male cat tends to own a larger territory that may partly overlap the territories of several females or may encompass the territories of these females. If their territories are the petals, his is the rose.

When a cat finds a place with the necessary requirements, he or she marks out the boundary with scratches, perhaps placing a few scats on high places, and squirting out a great many sprays. Some if not all species of cat even have two types of spray for the purpose, one like the jet from a water pistol, the other like the mist from a plant fogger. At least to a human nose the two kinds of spray seem different, one being more odoriferous, so perhaps the cat mixes the secretions of a gland into its urine when spraying but withholds the secretion when merely relieving itself.

Hence, except for the fact that most cats tend to change their territories rather often, the boundaries of cats are for all the world like those of human beings, although set in claw marks and urine rather than in fences and surveyor's tapes. Yet in both cases, the boundaries have a psychological effect on members of the same species. Not many people can genuinely ignore a No Trespassing sign. Even if they trespass, few do so without some twinge of conscience and most must overcome a certain amount of reluctance. Cats are the same. Coming upon the sprayed urine of a property owner, a cat will stop and sniff and grimace, and perhaps back off to think for a while. It may then go forward, but only after having made up its mind.

Thus cat properties are like ranches. The space enclosed by the cat's boundaries is actually the grazing land for livestock, whether deer or deer mice, which belong to the owner and to no one else, and which the owner does not disturb except to harvest.

When new land is difficult to find, mother cats often share with their children, keeping their sons with them until they are full grown and keeping their daughters or some of their daughters even longer, sometimes even dividing the ranch with one or more daughters. Lions and housecats carry the practice to an extreme, so that the members of a pride — really a group of females who are related to each other, grandmothers, mothers, daughters, sisters, nieces, and grandchildren — own one enormous ranch together. The area owned by a pride of lionesses can be hundreds of square miles, particularly in southern Africa, where game is sparse, while the area owned by a group of housecats is usually someone's farm, particularly the barn and its surroundings, where most of the mice are. Female cats share nests with their sisters and help to birth, groom, feed, protect, and teach one another's children.

Cheetahs are something of an exception to the paradigm of cats as ranchers, since female cheetahs seem not to own land. Male cheetahs do, though, and form coalitions, sometimes of brothers, but sometimes just friends, who together own a territory. From time to time a female cheetah joins them on it. If the males are successful, they defend the territory against takeovers by other males and offer the female a safe place to raise her children.

Thus, if the need to eat meat explains the cat body, so the need for a ranch on which to raise the meat explains cat society. The social organizations of cats are so different from ours that we seldom recognize them for what they are. Even so, they are there, very important to the cats, who with some exceptions merely practice different variations of the family theme. To us, lions in a pride on a savannah seem to be organized very differently indeed from solitary tigers in a forest, and yet from a cat's point of view the organization of the two species could be very much the same. Imagine, for instance, a limp balloon with spots painted on it to represent a pride of lions. When the balloon is inflated, the same spots could represent a community of tigers or other so-called solitary cats. The distance between group members might be different, but the relationships of the individuals might be the same.

Because cats are otherwise so much alike in their needs and habits, their social similarities are perhaps not surprising. For example, contrary to what many people believe, tigers not only have recognizable social units but also sometimes live together in small groups, usually consisting of a mother and two or three of her full-sized but still subadult young. But even mature male tigers sometimes join these groups. A 1989 newsletter of the International Union for the Conservation of Nature and Natural Resources (IUCN) reports that in Kanha Park in India the filmmaker Belinda Wright observed the meeting of a mature male tiger with a mother tiger, her two small cubs, and her full-grown son from an earlier litter. The five animals greeted each other with enthusiasm and affection and eventually departed in a group.

Therefore, that all cats don't live in prides may have little to do with their social inclinations but much to do with the type of food available to them. A tiger, after all, is roughly the same size as a lion and eats about the same amount at a sitting. Yet in many localities the prey available to the two kinds of cat differs greatly in size. Out on the savannahs, any one of the large African antelopes provides a meal for many lions together and may encourage their cooperative hunting and sociability. But deer and pigs are the mainstay in many tiger habitats. Scattered in dense forests and too small to feed many tigers together, the potential prey may encourage tiger solitude.

Still, the mystery remains. What explains the apparent paradox of areas where lions are found living singly at least part of the time even where large game is plentiful? The question may have to do with water and will be considered further on. Like many other questions about animals, the problem is as fascinating as it is complex.

Is the concept of cats owning property far-fetched? I don't think so. All wild cats need territory — that's why they establish home ranges. But where does the concept end? This question, I think, has no simple answer but should not be ignored. Why own a home range if no food can be found on it? I submit that the cat who owns the property also has a proprietary interest in the food supply. In fact, to keep the food source for himself or herself is the single most important reason for the cat to claim the property in the first place. In this spirit, housecats display a proprietary interest in their owners, marking them with wipes of the lips, rearing up to incise their legs with claw scratches, occasionally spraying them and their belongings and defending them from the advances of other cats. Why? Because a supply of food issues from a housecat's owner in much the same way that a supply of wildebeests issues from parts of the savannah or a supply of

80

Arctic hares issues from a few square miles of taiga forest.

A human paradigm can be found in hunter-gatherers — the Ju/wa Bushmen, for instance — whose sense of land tenure very closely resembles that of certain other species and for exactly the same reasons: people must have access to food and water and must protect these commodities from takeover by other people. The ability to control access to one's food supply is life itself. This is so obvious it scarcely bears mentioning, and is as true of any other territorial species as it is of us.

If asked, a group of Ju/wa Bushmen might not say in so many words that they owned a stretch of land. And they don't own land in the way we own land. They don't buy it or sell it or transfer ownership in anyway, since land is not a commodity. Rather, they own land like we own air. As we might say we had the right to defend the purity of our air so that we could all breathe safely, a group of Ju/wasi might say that they had a right to hunt the game in a certain area, to gather the wild vegetables, and to drink the water, and that any newcomers who might wish to do the same would have to ask permission. "For everything?" you might ask.

"Yes, that would be right," the Ju/wasi might answer.

"Even to hunt hyenas?" you might ask. "Do I need permission for that?"

"Oh, no, not for hyenas," the Ju/wasi could say. "Hyenas are *chi dole*, worthless things. We wouldn't care. You could kill as many hyenas as you wanted. It's amusing that you would think to ask permission for that!"

So hyenas aren't part of the deal, you say to yourself. "Elands, then," you ask. "And kudus. What about my hunting elands and kudus?"

"Ah well — elands and kudus," answer the Ju/wasi. "It is better to ask permission before you start killing the game. Kudus and elands are useful animals, hoofed animals. People care about them."

In this scenario, then, did the Bushmen *own* the elands and the kudus? Not according to our standards, to be sure, by which someone could buy or sell or even rent those animals. But the Bushmen owned them by another standard, by the standard of land tenure and land stewardship, by the standard of a territory as a place complete with flora and fauna where one could live without unwholesome competition from others of one's species, and where one stood ready to dispatch other predatory species, nuisance competitors of about one's own size such as cheetahs, leopards, and hyenas. In short, ownership as the Bushmen experienced it was of an ancient standard that held as long as the owners lived in the old way. In this way the cats, too, own land and the game animals upon it. The lionesses of a pride own, say, the wildebeests on their territory for as long as the wildebeests stay.

Ownership of a ranch, whether communal or individual, often makes the difference of life or death to a cat. Not only does the ranch provide the cat with shelter, food, and water but the land and its inhabitants become familiar to the cat in great detail, which is extremely helpful to any hunter. Cats often rest where they can view their holdings — they watch the movements of their livestock and can assess the condition of each animal they see. In all likelihood, they even know some of the prey animals personally, so they know who is aging, who is sick, who has calved or has been bested in a battle or weakened by ticks. Such knowledge combined with knowledge of the cover and topography cannot help but contribute to successful hunting. Once in an Idaho forest I was shown the carcass of a deer killed by a female puma who obviously had known that a deer trail led through a certain heavy growth of trees and had reached the area by creeping through a shallow draw. Chance could hardly have brought her there just at the exact moment when a deer was passing. Rather, she had obviously planned the hunt in advance, had crept along where she knew she could hide, and had perhaps been waiting for the deer. After killing it, she had eaten her fill, and then, covering the carcass with leaves to hide it from birds, she had gone off to rest at a little distance. But she had kept her food under surveillance and had returned to eat from it again and again until all the meat was gone. We found only the shins with hooves and scraps of hairy hide, the parts that pumas usually discard when preparing their food before eating it. A year later, these parts still lay near the edge of the draw as a tribute to an excellent hunter, a Diana of the douglas firs who understood not only her prey but also the topography.

In contrast was another Idaho puma, a young female with four kittens, perhaps her first litter, who seemed homeless. I was able to briefly trace her fortunes with the help of Ken Jafek, whose expertise and whose marvelous hounds enable an ongoing puma study. Ken had found evidence of this young puma a few days before I joined him. Because the young female had not previously been noted by the study, when Ken first found her tracks near an old, abandoned farm he felt sure that she had come from afar. At her heels trailed her four children, onely three months old, still fluffy and spotted. Why had she chosen the coldest part of winter for her travels? Why had she come to that barren valley where no deer stayed? No puma who realized that the place offered so little game would have chosen it for a new home. So surely her presence there meant that in her former home something had gone wrong. She had chosen the valley because she didn't know where else to go.

Still, a stream ran through the valley with thickets growing along the banks, so the puma and her children had drinking water and small amounts of food in the form of hares and other little creatures. Soon, Ken found that she had managed to kill a porcupine, which she and her children had eaten, leaving nothing but quills on the scraped and frozen skin. By the time I arrived and was shown the scraps, the young mother had covered them with snow, as if to save them for later.

Very soon after her arrival, the researchers set a dog to chase her up a tree so that they could fit her with a radio collar and monitor her doings. But this panicked stranger didn't climb a tree. Instead, unfortunately, she kept running, followed by her kittens. The little family ran right through a grove of fir trees that would have saved them and up an open, snowy slope where the dog overtook them and caught one of the kittens. Nothing could be done — the kitten was dead before the researchers, far behind, could intervene.

That night it snowed, and the scattered family had regrouped but had not left the valley. Instead, the mother had brought her surviving children to an old, long-abandoned farmhouse that stood crumbling beside a little road. When Ken and I came looking for this puma in the predawn hours of an icy morning, we found her tracks in the snow, showing how the mother and her children had hurried toward the house, not in single file, as they normally would travel, but four abreast, as if all had welcomed the sight of it.

Inside, they took shelter from the bitter night under the broken boards of the living room floor. We tried to approach quietly in hopes of seeing the pumas, but the mother heard us. Once again she fled with her kittens behind her, out the back door as we approached the front. The departing tracks told us that here the kittens had run behind their mother, following in her footprints.

Wanting to identify them for the study, Ken loosed a dog — not an experienced old warrior like the dog who had killed the kitten but a tender little pup only a few months older than his quarry. Nose to earth, and amazingly professional for one so young, the puppy quartered the willows by the stream, his tail waving briefly with each encouraging odor. This time, two of the kittens hurried up a tree, and the third, a female, climbed into a bush that didn't seem high enough or strong enough to keep her aloft very long. But the youthful dog barked "Treed!" and we came scrambling. The mother was long gone.

We spent the day there, tying the dogs to trees and sending for the researchers in Pocatello, who arrived hours later, to tranquilize, measure, and radio-collar two of the kittens before letting them go. (They would have collared the third as well but had brought only two collars.) I thought, from the changing orientation of the tied-up dogs, that the mother might be circling, and on her behalf I tried to keep the kittens warm and safe until the drug wore off. They weighed about twelve pounds apiece, which spoke well for their mother's care-giving ability, but they seemed surprisingly light, almost cloudlike, and I couldn't quite make out their edges under their long, fine, soft fur. Yet it was the paws of these kittens that I found most surprising. Huge, like soup plates, these paws seemed out of proportion to the little bodies. And when I gently pressed the velvet toes, great daggerlike, horn-colored claws eased out, strong and curved like an eagle's talons. One, caught in my parka, slit the heavy fabric like a razor in silk. These twenty great weapons on each kitten are a promise of the cat to come.

When the kittens were themselves again we put them safely into a tree and left, revisiting the place in the morning to learn how they had fared during the night. The mother must have watched our departure from the bushes — she had come for her kittens almost immediately and had led them far away. Judging from the direction she had taken, she was heading back to the place she had come from.

We stopped at the abandoned house to see what we could learn from it and found the fur, heads, paws, and paunches of two small raccoons that the pumas had eaten, not much food, perhaps, but lots better than nothing. We also found the print of the young mother's body in snow that had drifted through the open door. She had lain in the doorway keeping watch through the night, as any parent would do.

This fragment of observation suggests, I think, how disadvantaged an animal is when in unfamiliar country, let alone when in a place where food and comfort are in short supply. Mule deer were plentiful about two miles distant — we later saw a distinguished herd of them, fifty or more, making their way up the side of a high hill. But the young mother didn't seem to know about these deer. Nor did she know where to take shelter or where to hide. Ken Jafek has loosed his dogs upon dozens of pumas (exclusively for scientific research in recent years), and he tells of pumas evading the dogs by such tactics as climbing rock faces, showing that they knew the countryside and all its refuges — in other words, those pumas were at home.*

But the young female wasn't at home. A stranger in a strange land, she had fled aimlessly when the dogs first chased her, and after her second experience with a dog, she had moved elsewhere, surely to continue her search for a place to live and raise her remaining children.

Her story is typical of many if not most of the wild cats today, whose dwelling places are thoughtlessly destroyed or invaded by people. When we think of cats or indeed of any animals, we comfortably assume that they belong in the woods, and if that is where we find them, why then, they must be in good shape. Yet even the animals that eat grass and leaves have very real, even rigid requirements, so that one place is not just the same as another but depends for suitability on many factors, including the food supply. Just as some parts of a city are vastly different from other parts, so that a New Yorker in Sutton Place would

---

*Hunting pumas or, for that matter, any of the mid-sized cats with dogs is by and large a safe procedure. Except in rare instances, a cat pursued by dogs merely climbs a tree, and the dogs bark up at him from below. If the human hunter doesn't shoot at or otherwise injure the puma, or chase him out of the tree so that he must confront the dogs, he simply waits until the excitement is over, then climbs down and goes on about his business, and no harm is done.

experience life differently from a New Yorker in the South Bronx, so the natural world is not monolithic. Most human beings, especially those in Western and Asian cultures, are so isolated from the natural world that they lack all feeling for these truths.

When I was in my late teens and early twenties, I was privileged to be a member of a series of anthropological expeditions to the Ju/wa and /Gwi Bushmen who lived in a vast, largely unexplored part of southern Africa. I went there with my parents, Laurence and Lorna Marshall, and my brother, John, to record the Bushmen's way of life. While traveling in one of the most remote parts of the desert, we met a little group of ten people — two men, three women, four boys, and a baby — who, like the young puma and her children, had no suitable home. As Bushmen, these people were hunters and gatherers, deriving their entire livelihood and all their possessions from the natural world just as our ancestors had done long ago and just as all wild animals today continue to do. During the dry season, in the way of the savannah from time immemorial, the people would go to live near permanent waterholes, and during the rainy season when water was generally available they would move out over the veldt to take advantage of the foods that grew there. The Bushman people had distributed themselves fairly evenly in those days, and evidently had been doing so for a very long time, so that each waterhole and the surrounding land did not become overcrowded with more people than the land could feed. People therefore experienced hunger no more and no less than the other creatures. They would suffer during prolonged droughts, of course, but they escaped the frightful devastation of famines that result in other parts of the world today. In contrast to what the so-called civilized people erroneously believed about the Bushmen, who were wrongly described as nomads and wrongly assumed to wander aimlessly over the veldt in search of food, they, no less than the other creatures of the savannah, had territorial claims which apportioned the area's resources among their population in a way that gave everyone the necessities of life.

Living in the old way, by the old rules, the /Gwi people in those days experienced life very differently than we do now. Their cultural experience was much more like the experience of the other creatures with whom we still share the earth. Therefore, when the group of ten people lost their home, they suddenly found themselves cut off from their dry-season water supply and in a desperate situation. How had they lost their home? They lost it just as many animals do — their holding happened to be on land that had been taken over by a European farmer. Naturally, he didn't recognize their prior ownership; after all, they had never farmed the land and had no deed or other written claim to it.

At first he didn't need exclusive use of the waterhole, and he tolerated the presence of the /Gwi family just as we might tolerate some foxes, say, or other wild things whose ways didn't particularly interest us. But when he decided that he needed the water for his own use, he drove the people off just as we might drain a swamp or forget to fill a bird feeder, never dreaming that such a deed would cause anyone any harm. After all, the people were Bushmen who lived wild, in the bush. Why should he, a busy farmer, concern himself with them? Why couldn't they disappear into the bush and go on about their business?

What happened to the /Gwi family was exactly what happens to many other creatures who lose their homes — they did not go to some other place to live because there were no suitable places available to them in the dry season. They knew that, but they tried anyway, departing for a place they formerly had used only in the rainy season, relying on their people's greatest skill and art to draw liquid from some unexpected sources in the desert. When we met them deep in the interior in the middle of the dry season, they had no water at all but were doing without it. Yet for all their knowledge and skill, life in the driest part of the desert in the hottest, driest season eventually proved too precarious even for them and they returned to their old place. Still the farmer didn't let them stay, so their family disintegrated. They went where they could, good luck did not follow them, and a few years later, only three were still living. A statistical look at survivors from other mammals in similar straits would have predicted who these three would be: the young men. The women, the old people, and the young children perished. This situation has occurred more times than anyone could ever imagine, both to animals and to human hunter-gatherers, and is exactly what had happened and was still happening to the little puma with her surviving, cloudlike children.

Although cats are no less social than many other species, we tend to think of them as solitaries, probably because whenever we see a cat he is physically far enough away from the other members of its group as to seem alone. Celebrating the concept of cats as solitaries, Rudyard Kipling described the cat who walked by himself, waving his wild tail in the wet, wild woods. In fact, however, even when spread out on their ranches, cats are highly social. If they weren't, they wouldn't need the vast repertoire of vocalizations, scent glands, or tail and body postures to convey an almost unlimited number of emotional impressions to other cats. Nor would they need their highly mobile facial skin — their delicately muscled ears, eyelids, lips, cheeks, and whiskers — to produce a wide variety of changing facial expressions. The faces of cats are more mobile even than dog faces or our faces. The unsocial animals, by contrast, don't need facial expressions

93

and hence their faces seem stiff.

My husband and I saw the importance of facial expression in cats dramatically illustrated by our cats after one of them, our beautiful white Aasa, went blind. We had no idea that anything was the matter with this cat. Her blindness was caused by an inherited condition that we were unaware of and that had come on gradually. Because Aasa had known our house and its surrounding land from childhood, she managed to get around almost perfectly even after she became blind, so that the only changes we noticed were that she seemed very quiet and subdued, that she had developed a strange way of getting onto a bed — never jumping but reaching stealthily with her paw and feeling the surface before clambering up — and that there were fewer little corpses of mice and birds being brought into the house.

But the other cats noticed big differences. Perhaps the most important was that Aasa's response to them wasn't right and wasn't the same. Even to us, her gesture of feeling a surface before jumping up to it seemed eerie, disconcerting, perhaps because she seemed to do it stealthily, without looking at us and without changing her facial expression even when we were right there watching her. Undoubtedly, her failure to do the right thing at the right time provoked the other cats very deeply and caused them to persecute her. They seemed to be especially hard on her when we were away from home. We would return to find no sign of Aasa except piles of white fur that the other cats had torn from her skin. After long searches, we would find her hiding, usually in some dark corner of the basement. We would call her, and she would come part way toward us, moving very slowly, very carefully, particularly when crossing a part of the crawlspace that contained a deep, open well. Looking back, picturing where she would stand and how she would move in the crawlspace, I can see that she remembered the well and was being careful to stay far away from it.

Eventually we would catch her and carry her upstairs. Sometimes the three other cats would then chase her, and in flight she would often narrowly miss a doorway and run into the wall. Even then we didn't get it. We knew that something was terribly wrong, but we had no idea what. Before long, we had to section off the house, putting Aasa in one part and the rest of the cats in the other. But still the other cats stalked her, peering at her through an interior screen door. She had no way of knowing they were looking at her and therefore failed to respond to them appropriately, which to them was inflammatory behavior and only made them try to get at her all the more. Because we didn't know what the matter was, we weren't able to observe what mistakes she made that brought on the attacks, but my guess is that because she was a junior female in our household's cat group, she didn't realize when a senior cat was looking at her. She couldn't meet the other cat's eyes, nor could she avert her own eyes, a very important social requirement for lower-ranking cats. Nor could she solicit affectionate rubbing — another feline gaffe. The other cats must have felt a cat's version of the idea that Aasa was deliberately trying to frustrate them, something that a normal cat would never do.

At last, we decided to find her a new home. There, her blindness was discovered by the wonderful, thoughtful people who adopted her. They are Peter Schweitzer and his late wife, Susanna, cat owners extraordinaire. So the strange persecution was finally explained. Aasa now knows her way around Peter's house and is on good terms with an adolescent cat who also lives there and, being younger than the blind cat as well as her junior in the household, is in no position to take offense at any possible mistakes.

Why don't we recognize cat society? Probably because, at least superficially, it differs so greatly from ours. In contrast, we recognize caste in dogs because we rank ourselves by the familiar dog system, a ladderlike social arrangement wherein one individual outranks all others, the next outranks all but the first, and so on down the hierarchy. But the cat system is more like a wheel, with a high-ranking cat on the hub and the others arranged around the rim, all reluctantly acknowledging the superiority of the despot but not necessarily measuring themselves against each other. Farm cats and cats of other closely knit groups usually seem egalitarian. But it is my impression that they may actually have a cat's version of the social ladder, not like that of dogs and people with one individual per rung but rather with several cats on each rung. Even then, the signs of hierarchy in cats are displayed so subtly that our poor powers of observation can barely detect them. A cat expresses soft, submissive feelings by lightly rubbing his face on the faces of those whom he would please: his feline superiors or dogs or his owner — anyone close who he feels is not a rival and who is above him socially. Likewise, a vertical tail can be a sign of superiority in housecats, as is a curved "scorpion" tail in leopards, tigers, and lions. It is important to note that a raised tail in a cat is not the same as a raised tail in a dog, because in dogs the raised tail means higher rank, and thus when two dogs meet, Dog One raises his tail while Dog Two holds his tail low. When two cats meet, however, both may raise their tails, with Cat One raising his higher, perhaps because he feels more confidence. My cats usually go out into the fields with their tails low and usually come home with their tails high — they are coming home to other cats, as well as to the dogs and human members of the family.

In a delightful encounter in 1993 in Harvard Yard in Cambridge, a certain cat who had been hunting birds in the bushes noticed me watching him, gave up his hunt, backed out of the bushes, and purposefully strode right toward me, lifting his tail to the sky and his gaze to mine as he drew near. As our eyes met, he *meowed* once and kept on going. *You have disturbed me so I'm leaving this place,* his gesture said. *But since you are a human being, I'll greet you anyway. Hi there.* Sometimes, though, the tail shows nothing. Two cats simply eye each other and both know who is who.

If the social arrangement of cats differs from ours, so does their social behavior. Here again, human beings are more like the dog family, whose social inclinations we have no trouble recognizing. As an example of the difference I offer my own three dogs and three cats, who each morning choose to follow me to my office in a detached garage. I don't ask them to come with me and I don't feed them when I get there; they are free to come and go via many dog doors. In short, I offer no incentive other than my company. When I start for my office, the dogs crowd out the kitchen door with me, squeezing past my legs and almost upsetting me, never bothering with a nearby dog door because in the morning they are feeling sociable and want to be close. Meanwhile, nothing is seen of the cats. However, by the time the dogs and I are halfway to my office we notice that the cats are also outdoors and heading in the same direction. On we go, the dogs and I exchanging looks, words, and touches, while the cats apparently ignore us and each other. But soon after the dogs and I are inside the office the cats materialize there, too, just as interested in being together as the dogs are but expressing themselves in a different way.

So it is my impression that cats seem unsocial to us only because we aren't good at recognizing the signals of other species. We interpret cat signals to tell us, for instance, that they don't care about us and don't miss us when we're gone. If people were giving off similar signals, we'd be right. But they're not people, and we're wrong. When my husband and I take a trip, we leave our three cats in the house with plenty of food and water. We take the dogs to a kennel, but the cats may not know that, because we drop the dogs off on the way to the airport. As far as the cats are concerned, we and the dogs depart together, leaving the cats at home. And evidently the cats mind this.

No wonder. The cats depend on the people and the dogs, whether they show it or not. When thunderstorms gather, for example, the cats come indoors to be together with me or my husband. If neither of us is at home, the cats stay with the dogs, preferably with my husband's dog, Sundog, who is Dog One in our family. Even though Sundog doesn't like the cats, they look up to him, believing that when cosmic troubles threaten, he'll know what to do. Thus they feel truly abandoned when we go away, taking Sundog and the others but leaving them, the cats, alone in the house. As we leave they retire to the upstairs rooms to lie on the beds, tails tucked and paws neatly folded, where they become unresponsive, a demeanor that resembles human pouting or sulking and may be an emotional withdrawal from an unpleasant situation. If called, they won't answer and won't come.

But when we return they have heard the car

and are waiting at the door, tails high, to curl themselves around our feet and lift themselves to brush
lips with the dogs (but not always with Sundog,
who keeps them at a distance by showing them
the tip of an eyetooth and watching them out of
the corner of his eye).

I once watched a group of four male cheetahs
crossing an African plain, not one behind the other
in the way of most land mammals but scattered
like crows about fifty feet apart, each finding his
own way. These cheetahs had formed an alliance
to own a tract of land, and therefore it seemed
to me — enclosed as I am in primate sensibility
— that they ought to glance at each other every
once in a while. In a similar situation we primates
would glance at each other, perhaps to see if our
companions were in agreement as to where to go
next, or perhaps merely to reaffirm our bonds.
Dogs, too, would glance at each other. But cheetahs evidently don't feel the need. With their chins
high and their half-shut eyes looking at the hills,
the woods, the sky, the horizon, anywhere but
at each other, they slouched along in bland oblivion. My first impression, stupid as it now seems,
was that none of them realized that the others were
there. When as if by chance they all reached the
edge of the plain together, each chose his own path
as they sauntered off among the trees.

As for Kipling's cat, being of the same cattish
mindset as the cheetahs, he probably never thought
he was walking by himself. On the contrary, he
may have thought he was walking with Kipling

and, waving his tail aloft as a beacon, was probably trying to lead the author out of the wet, wild woods.

Perhaps the most dramatic evidence of cat sociability is their vocalizations — a logical means for animals whose economic needs drive them apart even as their emotional needs draw them together. People who have both dogs and cats can verify the statement: when called, the common response of dogs is to come, and of cats is to answer.

Lions certainly answer. During a period in the 1950s when I was in Nyae Nyae, in the Kalahari Desert of southern Africa, the lions kept in touch by roaring. One would roar, and after a short while another lion, very far away, would reply. On certain nights the lions would spread out through the bush in a line perhaps a mile long or even longer and seemed to keep their line straight and in order by answering in turn. The farthest would roar, then the next and the next, until six or eight had made themselves known. This way they could tell if all were present and if their line was reasonably straight. In the rainy season, these lions even answered thunder. I loved that: a dark night, the endless, rain-soaked bush, a flash of lightning, a cosmic crash of thunder, a little pause, and then, faint and far, a lion's roar!

"WHERE ARE YOU, MY LION?"

". . . (me?) . . . I'M HERE!"

Among all mammals, and indeed among most other vertebrates, the basic social unit is a mother and her children. But the so-called social animals form strong and fundamental alliances far in excess of the bare-bones maternal tie. Among dogs the unit is the pack, classically a mated pair with their young from several litters. Among people the unit is the extended family, a hunter-gatherer band. But among cats, at least among the species whose ways are known, the unit is the polygamous marriage.

Lions practice a form of polygamy that is also practiced by people in, say, parts of North Africa and the Middle East. In it, a man and his wives and children might occupy a common residence. Such a family would commingle on a daily basis and could travel together as a group. These same conditions could just as well apply to a pride of lions.

The so-called solitary cats are fully as polygamous as lions but with different living arrangements. Theirs resemble, say, those of certain families in Idaho and Utah, wherein a man provides a separate residence for each of several wives and their children and then moves himself from one household to the other, living with each wife in turn. Thus a male puma, say, or a male tiger maintains a large range that he patrols to guard against incursions by other males, a range that overlaps or adjoins a number of smaller ranges that belong to his wives.

Once, in the mountains of southern Idaho, as a short-term participant in a telemetric study of pumas, I found it very heartening and also moving to compare a family we were monitoring on the shoulder of a mountainside with a family in the valley below. The family on the mountainside belonged to a polygamous puma. He himself was probably not present during our period of study, but two of his wives were there with five nearly adult youngsters; one female had twin sons about a year old, and the other female had eight-month-old triplets — a daughter and two sons.

The family in the valley belonged to a polygamous man who had set his homestead right in the middle of the national forest. He, too, was evidently not present, but members of his family were there inside the widely scattered cabins and trailers — the dwellings of his wives.

All day the seven pumas above us slept near one another (actually the two mothers were a quarter of a mile apart with the youngsters scattered between them, which is sardinelike compression for pumas); all day their radio collars were silent — evidently the cats were resting in the shade behind some large boulders. All day the people below us stayed indoors, each woman with her children in her cabin or trailer. So well did each group mind its own business and keep to its daily routine that the only time we became aware of any of them, other than from empirical knowledge, was when a formation of F-111 jet fighters from a nearby airbase came zooming so low overhead and with such a roar that I, for one, thought I was being sucked up by the wake. The two polygamous families also reacted to the disturbance — all the startled pumas immediately raised their heads — not that we could see them, but the action set their radio collars signaling — and several people ran out of the cabins to look up. Of course by then the jets were gone, so the pumas let their weary heads sink down again and the people went back inside. Nothing else moved for the rest of the day except the sun, which slowly crept down to the horizon.

But when darkness gathered and stars came out, the people and the pumas changed activities. Several of the people, who had spent the day apart, came out of their cabins, got into a pickup, and drove away together, while the pumas, who had spent the day together, got up and moved apart. Heading west, the mother of the triplets followed a contour into the next valley. Heading south, the mother of the twins climbed the ridge and vanished over the top. And as each mother chose her own separate hunt, each was trailed at a distance by her children. Big as they were, they hadn't yet perfected the skills of hunting, and they padded youthfully after their mothers, knowing that the mothers would provide.

Since we saw none of the pumas in this instance, but knew them only by the faint beeping of the radio collars around their necks, how did we know the configuration of their relationships or even who they were? In truth, except for the mother-child and sibling relationships, we didn't know for certain. Bits of tissue, snipped from the poor creatures at the time of their collaring, had been sent to the National Institutes of Health in Bethesda, Maryland, for a study of the DNA that would provide clues to their relatedness, but the researchers were still waiting for the results. One time, the senior scientist on the project told me that the two females were probably mother and daughter, but another time he told me that he guessed their ages, which he would have tried to determine when collaring them, to be about the same. He said, however, that mother and daughter seemed the most likely, and I think most people would agree. The study gave no indication of a male puma in the picture.

Even so, I thought a big male puma was around somewhere, or had been until recently. Why? Because I thought that his image, his shadow, lay over the other pumas. Here, two female pumas lived virtually side by side, yet the kittens of one

were three or four months older than the kittens
of the other. Since male cats are infanticidal and
kill kittens who are not their own, the father of
the second, younger litter, the triplets, was probably the father of the twins as well and also was
probably the dominant male puma of the area. As
to his whereabouts, he could have been elsewhere
on his range. After all, the range of a male puma
can be ten times bigger than the range of a female
puma, so perhaps he was at the far side of his
holdings, perhaps on patrol to check his perimeters, perhaps to visit other wives.

But that he was somewhere in the picture
seemed likely, or at least, it did to me. There seem
to be few other possibilities. If the father of the
younger kittens had been a newcomer to the area,
he would, in all likelihood, have sought out and
killed the older kittens as soon as he arrived.

Why would a cat do something like that? Because
he would be forced to. What Gaia expects of male
cats makes a dramatic, complex story that begins
with the fact that the various cats, unlike many
other animals, have two different reproductive
strategies, one for the males and another for the
females. The social organization brings the strategies into harmony.

Unlike people — or unlike Americans, anyway
— and unlike many other animals such as geese,
young adult cats of the opposite sex do not meet,
pair off, start a family, and hope to live happily
ever after. Male cats are more like the Year Kings
of Eleusis, who after a period of wandering would

supposedly arrive at a land dominated by women, under the reign of a temporary king. A newcomer would fight the resident king, and if he won, he would take over. His reward for victory would be the crown and the favors of the women, yet his fate would surely be that of his predecessor, so no king could expect to remain with the women for long. One wonders what beneficial genetic effect the Year King system might have had on the population of Eleusis, or at least upon its royal family. The practice has certainly contributed to the strength of the cat family, since virtually every male that comes along gets tested by the resident, and the better of the two gets to father the next crop of children. By making themselves available to the victor, the females constantly upgrade their children's genes.

The price of cat excellence is therefore paid largely by the males, and the life of most male cats is difficult indeed. The best beginning a male cat can have is to stay with his mother as long as possible so that she can provide him with sufficient nourishment during his growth and teach him all she knows. As long as he's in his mother's home, and as long as the resident male is his own father, he's likely to stay put until he's physically and mentally ready to seek his fortune. In some cases, his own father tolerates him for a surprising length of time, especially if the youngster lives discreetly, doesn't challenge his father, doesn't advertise himself by yowling (if he's a small cat) or by roaring (if he's a big cat), and doesn't spray or mark. But sooner or later his young male heart prompts him to do some of those forbidden things anyway, and when he does, his father forces him to leave.

Off he goes, to roam where Fortune takes him, in search of females and a place of his own. Now comes the difficulty. His species, after all, has been populating the earth for a million years or more (700,000 years if he's a lion), and his kind has had plenty of time to fill every habitat available to them. Cats have been known to go to breathtaking extremes to overcome this difficulty — a housecat in New York City, for instance, bravely made his way along a hazardous trail of narrow ledges on tall buildings in order to look through a sixth-floor window at a certain female cat named Bubastis. (Sad to say, when Bubastis noticed him looking in at her, she became a bottle brush and spat at him.) Perhaps on the vertical surfaces of skyscrapers in Manhattan, a cat could establish a territory without having to face down too many challengers, but under most circumstances, if the population of the male cat's species is healthy, all suitable homes are occupied. Each is patrolled by a big, experienced tom, a tom who has put scratches on the trees higher than our young male can reach at present, and whose spray drips off the undersides of an astonishing number of leaves. The young male learns that no home is open to him.

So for a while he lives at the edges of other cats' territories, keeping to the parts they use the least, where their scratches are blurred, their feces dry, and their sprays of urine stale. After he has been surprised by one or two of them, perhaps after he has been mauled a few times, he learns to be even more careful. He tries to leave no tracks, he buries his feces, he urinates discreetly downward into holes he has dug for the purpose, and he never, ever sprays. Of course he must keep on hunting, otherwise he will starve. But he doesn't stride around the countryside looking everywhere for animals as his father used to do. Instead, he learns to hunt secretly, crouching patiently near mouse holes (if he's a small cat) or by game trails or in the reeds around waterholes (if he's a big cat), waiting for his prey to come to him. That way, the cat or cats who own the property and whose game he is poaching are less likely to become aware of him. He knows all about them, of course. After all, they spend a lot of their time patrolling, checking the perimeters, constantly on guard against intruders such as he. He may even see one of them go by, since they walk openly and boldly and don't need to hide like he does, at least not from other cats. At night he hears them yowling (if they're small cats) or roaring (if they're big cats). For a while, he manages to elude them. Possibly they suspect his presence, but they can't prove it. Sooner or later, though, he yowls or sprays, too, or is glimpsed by one of them, or otherwise makes a mistake so that they're sure he's around. They then get all excited and hunt him down.

Because cats have such dangerous teeth and claws, they can inflict enormous damage on each other in a fight, and consequently they are inclined not to fight, even in a territorial encounter. Instead, they put their facial expressions and bodily postures to use, each conveying the emotions stirred by the sight of the other. Often, this is enough to end the challenge and frighten the newcomer, who runs away as fast and as inconspicuously as possible — ears flat, tail and belly low to the ground — never to return but rather to try his luck at poaching on other cats' land.

One day, however, our youngster may find a piece of land without a male owner and claim it as his own. Or while he is roaming around or living as a squatter, he may notice, say, that the marks of the owner are not as high on the trees as his marks, suggesting that the resident cat is shorter than he. In this case, he may well seek a confrontation, and because on this occasion both cats have a great deal at stake, a fight may result. How so? Because the young challenger, seeing his chance at a future, has everything to win by fighting, a state fully as compelling as that of the established cat who will fight because he has everything to lose, including his life and his children.

So let us say the two males fight and the young cat wins. Slowly starting to lick his wounds, the young hero keeps his round eyes on the departing form of his bleeding, defeated rival. And then he begins his hunt for the old cat's wives. These may be mothers and daughters, and (if the cats are lynxes, say, or jaguars or ocelots or bobcats or tigers or pumas) their lands may adjoin each other in the cat family's wild-rose configuration. One after another, the young male will locate these holdings and find the nesting places if he can. He has plans for the females, but his plans do not include the kittens of his defeated rival. He is searching for kittens, and when he finds them, he kills them, often with bites to the back of the neck.

By this time, the females know all about him. Any female with kittens fears him. She won't leave her kittens alone any longer than she must, and she fights if the new male finds her nest. Some females manage to drive him off. Most male cats wouldn't fight too ferociously on such occasions — if one observes housecats during male take-overs, one gets the feeling that the marauding male prefers to back off and try later, when the mother cat is absent, rather than to engage in battle and risk injury. Anyway, he undoubtedly wants her goodwill later and would thus prefer to play a waiting game rather than confront her. So despite his greater size and superior strength, the first few times he tries to get to her kittens she usually manages to drive him off.

Still, she knows he'll be back. So if the kittens are small enough, she almost invariably moves them, carefully carrying them one by one to a new hiding place. Most nesting cats keep several possible den sites in mind against just such an eventuality. But when she leaves for the new place dangling a kitten, she may return to find the others limp and still, their spinal cords severed in the neck. And while she bends over them, licking them, trying to revive them, the male may be back-tracking her to her new nest to kill the last survivor. Touchingly, when threatened by a tomcat, even a very small kitten seems to understand what is happening and tries to resist, staring and hissing at the marauder.

If the kittens are old enough at the time of a takeover, the mother may try to lead them far away. Her own home range may not be big enough to give sufficient distance from the killer — she may strike out for places unknown. This is not an unrealistic effort, since kittens are amazingly strong. Ken Jafek discovered the trail of a female puma who for reasons unknown had decided to move her three six-week-old kittens through deep snow to a place more than three miles away, a move which by rights should have been impossible for the kittens: the snow was over their heads and too heavy for them to plough through. Yet they completed the journey. True, their mother had done some of the heavy work for them by breaking trail, but their legs were much shorter than hers, so their strides were shorter than her strides. Her footprints were the size of saucers and their footprints were the size of silver dollars. Even so, as Ken's photographs show, the kittens had followed all the way in the trough made by their mother's body, bounding from one deep footprint up over the snow and down into the next footprint; up, over, and down; up, over, and down; repeating this exhausting maneuver no fewer than five thousand times, or once for each yard-long stride their mother had taken.

If kittens are adolescent at the time of a takeover they may strike out on their own. Feeling the menace, the young sons of the defeated ruler may simply decamp as fast as possible. Some of the young daughters, on the other hand, may try to stay with their mothers, but if they do, their fate may depend on how their new stepfather sees them. If he sees them as wives, he won't disturb them. But if he sees them as children, then they, too, may be in danger. George Schaller in his book *The Serengetti Lion* tells of a mysterious observation made by G. Dove that in my admittedly inexperienced view might pertain to this phenomenon. Near Lake Lagaja, Dove watched a lioness approach a feeding lion. At first she walked, but when she got near, she crawled, as if she were begging for the lion's good will. The lion got up from his meal, attacked the lioness and, after a brief scuffle, killed her with a bite to the back of the neck. He then returned to his food. When he was finished he walked over to her and lay down to rest companionably beside her still body.

As Schaller himself has pointed out: "An observer seldom knows the history of an animal he sees, yet its behavior and the responses of others toward it are often influenced by what has happened in the past." Dove's haunting story makes one wonder if the lioness could have been a subadult, a daughter of the pride, trying to appease a new stepfather.*

How long can a male cat control his territory and protect the kittens that, shortly after his conquest, he fathers on the bereaved females? This, of course, depends on him. If he is to make his genetic contribution, however, he must stay long enough not only to father some kittens but also to defend them from takeovers by other males at least until the youngsters can fend for themselves, which is, very roughly speaking, about nine months to a year for most of the small cats, perhaps fourteen to eighteen months for mid-sized cats, and at least two years for large cats. Of course this does not mean that the youngsters are full grown so quickly — lions and tigers, for instance, take three or four years to reach maturity — it just means that some of the youngsters may be able to support themselves if conditions are favorable and if the necessity arises — a minimum age, so to speak. Hopefully, a resident male will be able to dominate an area long enough so that his wives can raise his children to an age when they will surely be able to manage on their own, so that his daughters can settle on or near their mothers' ranches and his sons can go voyaging as he once went voyaging, to start their own families and perpetuate his lineage. Sometimes a resident male can dominate an area long enough for

*George Schaller, *The Serengetti Lion* (Chicago: University of Chicago Press, 1972), pp. 55, 189.

114

his wives to raise more than one litter. However, like the Year Kings, the average male cat will probably reign relatively briefly, with the length of his sojourn depending on his intelligence and strength and his skill at fending off challengers. And if he is not killed when a younger, stronger stranger finally defeats him, he again becomes a vagabond, a voyager, camping temporarily on the holdings of other cats, poaching their game, trying to escape their notice.

This should result in a large population of homeless male cats who are past their prime, and yet no such population seems to exist. For the relatively few species of cat who have been studied, the old male cats who are homeless may be fewer than ordinary attrition would suggest. On the other hand, homeless youngsters are numerous. Surely a possible explanation for at least some of the discrepancy is the amount of fighting the older cats are forced to do, against not one challenger but many. The battles are exhausting, and since cats are such dangerous animals, severe wounds invariably result. Yet in contrast to a young up-and-coming cat who, if he finds himself outgunned, can retreat to fight later at a time of his choosing, the old landowner must put up a full-blown defense against each and every serious challenger, ready or not, and can never indulge in the luxury of retreat. In my opinion, two possible reasons for the apparent scarcity of older, landless male cats may be that they tend to get killed during successful takeovers and that those who survive the final battle are made more vulnerable to ordinary hazards by exhaustion, depression, and their wounds.

Once I was privileged to examine the skull of a saber-tooth. A relic of the La Brea tarpits near Los Angeles, the skull had belonged to a male *Smilodon fatalis,* one of the largest cats the world has ever seen. The skull's mass alone was impressive, but the famous eyeteeth were awesome — strong, curved, pointed, and almost six inches long. The eyes had been large and the chin small, which must have made even this great face somewhat catlike. Beyond that, though, the bones of his lower jaw were fairly narrow, and the bony processes at the corners of his jaw were tiny, just two points, really, so that nothing stopped the jaw from dropping straight down like a trap door.

Other cats have lesser gapes, the result of heavier jaws with wider hinges to anchor the muscles that clench the teeth. But the smilodon didn't need to clench his teeth. What he needed from his lower jaw was that it drop out of the way to let him deploy his sabers. A number of reconstructions* suggest how he might have done this, and although these reconstructions differ on how he mounted his attack, all agree that he drove his eyeteeth home not by pushing up against them with his lower jaw as other cats do but by plunging them down

*In Andrew Kitchener, *The Natural History of the Wild Cats* (Ithaca: Comstock, 1991), pp. 29–34.

116

into his victim, driving them home with the vicelike force of his neck and shoulders and indeed with the whole curl of his body. Considering the size and strength of that body and the length of those teeth, to be bitten by a smilodon must have been a terrible experience. If he had attacked a person, and he could have, since in those days our species shared the New World with his species, his teeth could have speared right through his victim like toothpicks through a little pork sausage. Rightly was he named *fatalis!*

While thinking such thoughts, I had been looking at the skull from the top and sides and had, for a few moments, postponed looking into the face straight on. I wanted to be ready for the experience because I expected to get a chill. I expected to look into the face of Death, into the gaping mouth and empty eye sockets of the Great Devourer! But to my surprise, when I put my palms under the sabers to lift and turn the heavy skull, the sense of awe was cancelled immediately by the points of the teeth, which almost pierced my hands.

What had we here? These teeth were perfect, even after ten thousand years in tar! No dings or dents or furrows marred them as they could mar, say, the teeth of a mature African lion. Here was not the Face of Doom — here was the face of a young male cat who had met with a tragic and fatal accident. And since cats don't grow from kittens without plenty of help, two or three years of his mother's care and effort had been necessary to raise this smilodon to his present giant size. Her warm thighs had sheltered his little body from the glacial winds. The back of her long heels moving through the grass had been his beacon as he stumbled along behind her. Why had her efforts gone for nothing, and how had a fine young creature like himself ever gotten into a tar pit?

One can't know, of course, but judging from a census of the corpses found together with this youngster, the tar was a magnet to smilodons. With the possible exception of dire wolves, more smilodons fell in than any other animal. Why this happened is not perfectly clear. My own guess is that a tar pit is exactly the sort of peril that would challenge young smilodons off on their own, away from their mothers for the first time, and prone to accidents. Their huge young bodies would have needed lots of food. Small-sized prey would not have nourished them. To get enough to eat without, as it were, overspending their energy budgets, young smilodons would have had to tackle fairly large animals. Certainly, large animals were what they would have learned to hunt from watching their mothers. Even so, hunting very large animals isn't so easily done, especially by a neophyte hunter. Surely the difficulty increased as the populations of the bigger North American mammals dwindled toward extinction — an event that occurred before the disappearance of the smilodons. Furthermore, because smilodons are believed to have lived in prides like lions, a male takeover could have resulted in the cubs of more than one litter suddenly finding themselves on their own in rather close quarters, giving one another plenty of local competition for the easily captured prey. How tempting it must have been to a hungry youngster to come upon an animal evidently standing in a shallow lake, obviously in distress and crying or struggling!

What happens to female cats at times of takeovers? How do they feel about the challenges to their resident husband? It is my impression that female cats have mixed feelings, as is shown by their actions. Among housecats, at least, but surely among some other kinds of cat, too, the females sometimes pitch right in and fight beside their husband when defending against a marauding male, particularly if he comes near their nests and kittens.

But if the newcomer keeps his distance, perhaps staying at the periphery but calling to the females, they may go out to learn more about him and eventually reach familiar terms. If he is a barn cat, he may set up a territory at the edge of the woods, at some distance from the main cat scene at the farm, and lure a female or two over to see him, perhaps even to mate with him. This the females often do quite willingly, an act which is in their best interests in the event that the newcomer should mount a successful assault on the resident male and take over. If the newcomer has been enjoying sex with the local females, he will remember them after his victory. And if his new, promiscuous wives have long been giving him reason to think that their kittens are also his, his interests are served by sparing these kittens when he finds them.

In my early years I lived on a farm where barn cats flourished and where male takeovers must have been reasonably common. The basement of the farmhouse was accessible to the outdoors through gaps in the fieldstone foundation, and through these gaps cats would come to wait for skim milk from the milk separator when, every night, we cleaned and sterilized the machinery. The following is a reminiscence, not an observation, since it happened so long ago. I remember one evening after hours that we heard someone singing in the basement. A strange male cat had arrived and was calling. Never before had I heard such a hauntingly beautiful song. Because he sang for a long time, I learned his song and could sing it to myself for years thereafter.

The door to the cellar stairs was open a crack, and one of the female tabbies slipped down to see him. I followed her and in the dim light saw one of the other females, a tricolor, crouching under the water tank, looking out with round eyes. The strange male was hiding and fell silent when I came. But when I left he began his song again in the dark basement of the farmhouse. A cat Orpheus.

For a while after that, we kept glimpsing the marmalade stranger at the edges of the fields and in the shadows of the outbuildings, and two nmonths later, the tabby and the tricolor females had litters containing marmalade kittens who lived to grow up under the nose of the resident despot, a black cat with a white chin, a white shirtwaist, and four white socks, a cat who in fact looked like the famous Socks, the presidential cat at the time of this writing, but was battle-scarred and more massive. Who had fathered the marmalade kittens? Marmalade coloring is the male version of tricolor and was so common that it could not be diagnostic of paternity, so no one knew. But in a way, actual paternity may not have mattered. What mattered was that neither of the male cats killed the kittens, since each had consorted with the mothers and may have felt that the kittens could have been his.

Do cats love each other? They certainly seem to. The wives of the black-and-white tomcat lightly lifted their faces to his when they met him and seemed to want to be near him, especially when at rest. On cool mornings, he would choose the roof of the pickup, or a sheltered corner where the white barn reflected the sun, and, wrapped in his tail, would lie on neatly folded legs, his ears and whiskers relaxed, his eyes almost shut. Around him at various distances, perhaps on the hood of the pickup, one or two of his wives would lie in similar positions, not touching him, not even looking at him, but oriented toward him nevertheless and very much in his presence.

Not so our current cats, who today live in the

same place — Rajah the deerstalker; Lilac, his mother; and Christmas, his mother's half sister. If the pattern above had no special meaning, one might expect that all cats would mindlessly copy it, and that Lilac and Christmas would orient to Rajah, to sleep where he sleeps, neatly curled and far apart but oriented to him nevertheless. But they do nothing of the kind. Although he is much larger than they, he is their junior, their son and nephew, not their husband. With spits and blows, they chase him away from their favorite places, and they respond with anger if he tries to chase them.

So I have come to believe that the male/female bond has much importance to cats. Female cats have their own ideas of what makes a good husband, and they exercise these ideas when choosing and supporting their mates. After all, the stronger the tomcat, the more successful he will be in defending his kittens, so that the mother's efforts to bring them into the world will not be wasted. When a cat family is settled and in place, with no males lurking on the periphery to threaten its safety, its members are relaxed and loving. In the population of barn cats that I knew best as an adult, the cats who belonged to my son's family in northern New Hampshire would usually greet each other, tails high, by fondly brushing noses when they met, a greeting initiated by the lower-ranking cat. The young cats grew up under a benevolent male despot, Rollo, who, although he was neutered and was not their father, functioned in place of their fathers. Their real fathers must have been several intact males from neighboring farms and households, but such was Rollo's presence that he kept these males at bay. Perhaps his lowered testosterone level smoothed things out, letting him refrain from fighting them when they appeared on the scene. The arrangement was excellent for the females, who got to raise their kittens without having to worry about marauding males. And, like many cat fathers, Rollo was excellent with the kittens, whom he groomed from time to time and allowed to play with his tail.

The impression that cat fathers mean much to their families was borne out by later studies of some British cats,* who did what the farm cats of New Hampshire had done so long ago. While the British male was confined in a crate for unexplained reasons, the females did not forsake him but spent the night lying on top of the crate. Where he was, there they wanted to be also. Housecats similarly orient to their human owners or sometimes to the empty clothing of their human owners, showing a sense of oneness even if to the dog family and to the primate family it seems underdeveloped and vague.

Considering the affection that cats in groups show for one another, one might almost consider

*D. W. Macdonald, P. J. Apps, G.M. Carr, and G. Kerby, "Social Dynamics, Nursing Coalitions and Infanticide among Farm Cats, *Felis catus*," *Advances in Ethology* (Berlin: Paul Parey Scientific Publishers, 1987).

it the tragedy of the cat family that whether they want to or not, most young cats sooner or later move away from their group. Practical considerations drive them away. Except around farms, where the presence of stored grain keeps mice and rats in sufficient numbers and where the farmer supplements the food supply, the cat's diet doesn't encourage life in groups. Spacing is essential, and cats feel it. They don't need a hostile stepfather to make them move — sooner or later they'll be forced to move anyway. We were able to experience this with our own cats in a way that surprised me — they saw developments in our household that impelled emigration, while we, the human beings, saw nothing at all.

Our cats all came from that population that lived in and around our son's house and barns. These cats were all related to each other through the female lineages, with neighboring males arriving to father new litters every once in a while. Our first cat, the white male Orion, had been born to our son's high-ranking cat, the matriarch Manas, which may have enhanced Orion's status in the group. His high rank may have explained his unusual confidence. Even as a kitten he dared to climb to the barn rafters in pursuit of swallows — he was the only kitten in that population ever to climb so high.

When he came to live with me and my husband, he was our only cat, and he made our house his house, spending all his time with us except when he went out to hunt, which he did by means of a cat door. About a year later, we also adopted his half sister, the inky Wicca, who at the time was about four months old, a lanky adolescent. Orion was older than Wicca and much bigger, and we expected that Orion would dominate her. But to our surprise, she evicted him. Within a week or so of her appearance he had abandoned the house except at mealtimes and had claimed as his territory the building that houses my office, a barnlike structure that we also use as a garage, tool shed, wood-storage area, and home to several communities of mice. We might have gone on this way indefinitely, with Orion in the outbuilding and Wicca in the house, but we were given a third cat, the young Aasa, a cousin of the others although she had never met them. Aasa was the youngest and smallest of the three, but she took over the house in the same way that Wicca had done, and Wicca, by now a mature and very capable animal, moved into the outbuilding with Orion.

What motivated these emigrations? Not sex, since all our cats were neutered, which meant that reproduction played no role whatever in their territorial arrangements. Cat behavior is so strongly motivated by individual choice that we at first tended to shrug off their arrangements as personal preference — another cat mystery that human beings cannot solve. But then visitors came to stay with us, bringing their cat, and Aasa moved out. When the visiting cat left, Aasa moved back. Clearly, something was happening that the cats understood and that we did not.

At last it came to me what the cats might be doing, how the situation might appear to them. Possibly they saw me in the role of mother cat. If so, each new cat might have seemed like the kitten of a new litter, a signal for the older kittens of the previous litter to strike out on their own. What makes this phenomenon most interesting is that wild or feral kittens sometimes stay to share space with the mother. And when they do, they almost certainly have been invited by the mother. But what might constitute an invitation, I didn't know. So I didn't give it. So perhaps my cats, in a very typical barn cat manner, moved to the outbuildings to give me and my "new offspring" plenty of room. There they stayed for the rest of their lives, although we tried everything, including imprisonment, to keep them with us in the house. They'd stay as long as we prevented their moving, but the moment the chance came, they'd go, leaving our house to young Aasa. Barn cats from a world of fields, barns, sheds, and outbuildings — they did what they knew to be right.

On the island of Cyprus, in connection with a human habitation, archaeologists discovered the remains of a cat that dated from 7000 BP,* making it older than the earliest known domestic cats of Egypt. No wildcats lived on Cyprus even in those days — this cat had gone by boat. He was a big individual, wildcat sized. Was he merely tame, or had the domestication of cats gotten started? No one knows, of course. All that can be said for sure is that his relations with the boatmen were such that when they set sail for Cyprus, they brought him along.

How did we ever manage to domesticate cats in the first place, let alone so long ago? With their promiscuous ways and polygamous marriages, their intolerance of leaders and their exclusive living habits, cats are quite unlike our other animal

*Juliet Clutton-Brock, *Cats Ancient and Modern* (Cambridge: Harvard University Press, 1993), p. 26.

slaves. Ironically, the only cat that could be said to meet, however superficially, the ordinary requirements for domestication is the lion. Yet before we rush to domesticate lions we might ask ourselves why most circuses that train big cats mostly train tigers only. Why so few lions? The answer is that 700,000 years of group life have made lions highly assertive, the feline response to competition in close quarters. Lions are to the feisty and difficult bobcats what tigers are to the emotionally more restrained lynxes. Trainers prefer tigers over lions because tigers are more tractable. Furthermore, as trainers are quick to point out, lions tend to band together against you, not with you, which makes them extremely poor candidates for servitude.

Of course, there are exceptions. For example, I know a trainer whose lionesses came to her aid when a male tiger tried to attack her during a show. Possibly the lionesses helped out because the trainer was also a female and was to some extent a group member — certainly more so than the aggressive male tiger could ever have been. Or the lionesses may have seen the difficulty in the ring as a potential threat to themselves and merely wanted to nip trouble in the bud. Whatever the reason, though, the event would not have encouraged anyone seeking to domesticate a lion, because cooperative aggression is not a quality people want in their slaves.

So how did we manage to domesticate a species of this improbable family? The answer is that we didn't. Today, it is true, cats are fully domesticated, showing the usual characteristics of reduced size, reduced brain capacity, and an increased tolerance for crowding. But cats came by these qualities by accident, because the domestication of cats was an accident, a by-product of the domestication of grass.

Yes, grass. When we learned to harvest some of the grains, which of course are the seeds of several kinds of grasses, we accidentally harvested an entire little part of the ecosystem with them. Like grass seeds everywhere, the seeds of our ancestral grains would have provided natural food for a host of small species, among them the local species of murids, the rat and mouse family. Not surprisingly, when the grains were harvested, the local mice and rats followed their food indoors. And who should follow the mice and rats into the granaries but their natural enemy who had been hunting them all along, the local wildcat, *Felis sylvestris lybica*, soon to become *Felis catus*.

Domestic grains then spread throughout North Africa, Asia, and Europe. Along with the grain came the mice and rats. Behind them crept the cats, probably encouraged by the people, who by then had surely learned that cats are not only better mousers than dogs but also are cleaner and quieter and don't steal most kinds of human food. Certainly, cats didn't eat the wheat products that were becoming a main source of nourishment for the people and their livestock. The same could not be said for dogs.

In time, people invented ships and began to trade, using grain not only as a provision but also as an item of barter, and the mice and rats went along, once again followed by the cats. In this way, still linked after thousands of years, a food chain that began in the grasslands to the south and east of the Mediterranean Sea has spread to all corners of the world.

Today, like little islands, our homes preserve that food chain. Grain born in Asia Minor makes our bread. The house mice and the brown rats and black rats who feed from that grain live in our walls and basements, very different animals in behavior and in appearance from the wild mice and rats who live in the woods and fields. And the former wildcats sleep on our beds. Even the old names have followed the cats on their journey from their grassy plains so long ago — the word *puss* seems to be a version of Bast, the Egyptian goddess; the word *tabby* seems to come from the Turkish *utabi,* a striped cloth; and the word *cat* seems to come from the Arabic word for the animal, *quttah.** Yet much has changed. Mice and rats have grown bigger and stronger over the centuries, and cats have grown smaller and weaker, which shows, I think, what natural selection has done for the rats, and what the softening, minimizing process of domestication has done to the cats.

*F. E. Zeuner, *A History of Domesticated Animals* (New York: Harper and Row, 1963), p. 390.

A very informative study done at Johns Hopkins University on the feral housecats of Baltimore showed that the streetwise cats of Baltimore made a real distinction between rats who lived in the city parks eating grass seeds and other wild foods and rats who lived in the alleys eating garbage. The park rats were wild, so to speak, and as such received only average nourishment. Of normal size, they were perfect victims for the feral cats. The alley rats, on the other hand, were nourished beyond all expectation by the uncollected garbage provided by the people of Baltimore and were so massive and strong that the cats cringed away from them. *

The same was surely true of the rats on the New Hampshire farms when I was a girl. Like most rats that infest our habitat, ours were Norway rats — actually not originally from Norway but from eastern Asia. Grain for the livestock was stored in closed wooden bins which the rats opened with their teeth, gnawing holes in the rear where the people wouldn't see. Then the rats ate so well that they grew enormous, too big for the undernourished farm cats to tackle. Ferocious in defense of their well-ordered society, secure in their system of trails and passageways inside the barn walls, the rats seemed valiant and could be genuinely dangerous. Even the dogs were wary of them. In

* James Childs, "And the Cat Shall Lie Down with the Rat," *Natural History*, June 1991, pp. 16–19.

this context, humans often found the cats less than satisfactory.

On the other hand, the human beings on the farms weren't always entirely satisfactory to the cats. Farm cats, after all, are neither pets nor livestock. They have no monetary value whatever and are tolerated with mild amusement as long as they intrude only by occasional visits to the dairy at milking time to beg for milk. Barn dwellers, these cats were traditionally the province of the men, not of the women, and few male farmers had much commitment to them. At least, they didn't in rural New Hampshire, in the areas known to me in childhood. Barn cats were seldom fed by human beings; they were never neutered or spayed, never given any immunization shots, never taken to the veterinarian (who in those days in rural communities specialized in livestock, and whose duty was to maximize a farmer's income, not to coddle his animals — the veterinarian of our community, for instance, pioneered the notion that anesthesia was a necessary part of surgery, to be included in the charge, and was no longer to be seen as an optional frill). When the cat population got too high for a farmer's liking, the cats were simply put into bags and gassed or drowned. To care for a group of animals for a time, and then to suddenly round them up and dispatch them without warning, is after all what farming is all about.

But if our relationship with cats has been only partly satisfactory to both sides, the relationship has also been less rigidly controlled than our re-

132

lationship with our other domestic animals. All the others originally lived in highly structured groups with leaders. In animals with leaders, the leadership system is self-promoting in that good leadership benefits the group, resulting in a higher rate of survival than would be found in groups with incompetent leaders. Imagine a herd of wild goats living in the mountains under the leadership of a wise doe who knows about avalanches and who, on the spring migration to higher elevations, can lead her younger sisters, daughters, nieces, and grandchildren across steep slopes by knowing when to walk on the dangerously tilting snow. Saved from being swept off the mountain, her kindred will show a high rate of survival, and if the tendency to obey a leader is transmitted in the genes, the wise doe's kindred will pass the tendency down through the generations.

In order to domesticate such animals as the goat — as we did early on — all that we human beings needed to do was to insinuate ourselves into the position of their leaders. Our enslaved subjects, the animals, had been primed by their own excellent leaders to follow and obey.

But except for lions, members of the cat family don't follow leaders in the same way. Kittens follow their mothers, to be sure, but after that cats make their own plans and decisions, each individual taking full responsibility for himself or herself, with no one else to show the way. An adult wild cat may get some help from her mother in the form of a gift of land and even in the form of baby-sitting services and personal protection, but the normal day-to-day decisions a cat makes on her own. What, then, ties cats and people together?

In fact, cats and people are tied in several ways, the most important probably being the simplest — that of ownership. We own cats as we own all other property — they are ours to do with as we please. A few mild laws protect them from our tendencies to cruelty, yet these laws are easily evaded and are seldom enforced. Interestingly enough, however, as we own cats by human rules of ownership, so cats own us by cat rules of ownership. As a wild cat owns a territory and the rights to hunt the mice or the deer thereon, so a housecat owns a human dwelling and the rights to the people. People are not prey to housecats, it is true, but we provide food even more readily than would a mouse population. This is why cats mark our homes with spray and lightly rub their scent glands on our bodies. *Mine,* say the delicate odors, and other cats keep off. My husband's cat, Rajah, has staked out my husband's office where they both spend the day (unless my husband is away or Rajah is out hunting), and Rajah has claimed my husband's side of the bed, where they both sleep. Rajah has also staked out my husband, who by cat law belongs solely to him. One of our other cats, Christmas, who is Rajah's aunt, keeps far away from my husband. Even at suppertime, even in a snowstorm or a rainstorm, even at dusk when the cats come in for the evening, she won't come to him when he calls. To her, Rajah's territorial claims far exceed my husband's wishes in importance. Rajah's claims even exceed her own need for food and shelter. The other cat, Rajah's mother, also respects her grown son's property but sometimes overrides his wishes and visits my husband anyway. I, in turn, am shared by the two females, one of whom owns the house and the other the outbuilding that contains my office. They both share my person and take turns sleeping on my side of the bed. Rajah is very nice to me, very cordial when we meet, but since I evidently belong to his aunt and his mother, he maintains a respectful distance most of the time. He is more likely to visit me when my husband is in the same room, or when my husband is away altogether. Interestingly enough, the three cats share the land around the house among themselves, so that any one of them may hunt anywhere. Cats from other households very seldom intrude, but if they do, they are driven off by the dogs.

A second tie between people and cats is probably the most basic, that of parent and child. Many people treat cats like children, and therein must lie much of their cats' appeal. An ordinary housecat weighs six to nine pounds, is soft, warm, and yielding, and when held against the chest feels very much indeed like a human baby, or at least it does until it puts out its claws. But the tactile resemblance isn't the only resemblance. Like a human baby, a cat has a high voice, a small chin, large eyes, and a head of short hair that stands on end.

Such powerful auditory and visual stimuli trigger atavistic care-giving behavior in our kind.

And if we treat cats as children, they treat us as parents. The length of an adult human being from the knees up is about three times that of the body of an adult cat, or, in other words, is in roughly the same proportion to the body of an adult cat as the adult cat's body is to a kitten. And people, too, are relatively soft and yielding. No wonder cats orient to people who are lying on their sides or sitting in chairs with their feet up. The curve of the human body must remind a cat of old times, of comfort and security in the warm curve of its mother's body with siblings all around. Many if not most cats enhance the effect by pedaling or kneading with their front paws, a well-known phenomenon sometimes known as "making bread" that kittens use to stimulate the flow of milk in their mothers' breasts and which they accompany by purring.

Even being fed by a person must seem like old times to a cat, because of the person's manner of delivering food. A person characteristically puts down a dish of food and moves away from it, offering plenty of space, which invites the cat to approach and eat. In the same way, a hunting mother cat puts down the dead bird she has brought, backing away from it to show that she will not compete for the carcass and that her kitten can approach. This system of food delivery is totally unlike the wolf-style dog system, whereby the providing adult lowers his or her head and heaves up a stomachful of chopped food while being mobbed by the puppies who eagerly lick the provider's mouth. Thus, the feeding method of the wild parent explains why dogs are ready to gobble when their howls of food hit the floor, while cats tend to hang back and approach slowly.

Yet the paradigm of a family in which the human being is the parent and the cat is the child is only half of the story. As cats see it, they, too, play the role of parent while their owners play the role of child. Many cat owners relate how their cats have saved their lives, accounts which I, for one, was at first reluctant to believe. Some of the accounts hold that the cats wakened their sleeping owners because the house was on fire or for other environmental emergencies. These accounts seemed reasonable, but the altruistic motives ascribed to the cats seemed unconvincing. If the house was on fire, why wouldn't a cat wake its owner? How else could the cat get out?

Then I heard an account that seemed impossible to discredit — that of the scientist Lisa Rappaport, who not only is a biologist but who had been hired by an important zoo to make observations of animal behavior. It seems to me that if her account cannot be trusted, none can. One night in her apartment, her cat prevented her from entering a room in which an intruder was lurking. Lisa tried to go around the cat but the cat persistently blocked the way. Lisa would have had to physically remove the cat to get by her, which she wisely decided not to do. That cat had clearly assumed the role of parent/protector, not the role of child.

Perhaps in the role of parent or educator, cats may sometimes try to teach us. Our Lilac tried to discipline my husband when he shifted his position on a sofa, accidentally squeezing her. Calling out sharply to get his attention, Lilac cocked back a front paw, and when my husband turned in surprise to look down at her, she hit him. Interestingly enough, her claws were out, but not far out. She meant to prick him, not to tear his skin. He was wearing a heavy sweater and didn't even feel the blow but was impressed nonetheless and has been more careful since.

Our son's cat, Rollo, tried to punish our granddaughter Zoë, age five, whose habit was to stroke Rollo's tail when she passed him, asleep, on his shelf above the radiator. Evidently Rollo didn't like this, but he tolerated it anyway, until one day he decided he'd had his fill. Down from the shelf he sprang, right on top of Zoë, and began to slash at her with both front paws, pummeling her like a boxer. She screamed and her parents came flying, chased off the cat and picked her up, but found not a mark on her entire body — Rollo had sheathed his claws.

Cats may be assuming the role of educator when they bring prey indoors to their human owners. Perhaps they want to feed us. Perhaps they want to teach us. Dead prey suggests feeding, but live prey suggests teaching in a number of ways. A mother cat starts teaching her kittens from the moment they start following her. They first learn from watching, crowding right up beside their mother if she lets them (a behavior that can lead to cooperative hunting), and later she gives them hands-on practice by flipping victims in their direction, exactly as a cat does in play. Mother cats even bring live prey back to their nests or dens so that their homebound kittens can practice, especially if the prey is of manageable size. So perhaps cats who release living prey in our houses are trying to give us some practice, to hone our hunting skills. I am speaking, of course, of the endless series of birds, mice, bats, voles, shrews, moles, snakes, frogs, toads, salamanders, hornworms, dragonflies, and other broken, twitching victims that our cats bring inside and set free.

Meanwhile, the practice itself raises some interesting questions. If, for instance, cats really see us as kittens, how old are we supposed to be? Not tiny kittens, surely, as these are fed with milk. Cats rarely lie on their sides and offer their breasts to human beings. No — we must seem like adolescents unready for life on our own. And if so, no wonder. Certainly we must seem unskilled if not downright clumsy, and we must seem impolite as well, since we show cats few of the courtesies that they show to us and to each other.

When our male cat, Rajah, had already grown much bigger than his mother, Lilac, he hadn't yet seen that as a reason to give up his perfect childhood. So at night he would curl himself comfortably beside my husband on the bed while his mother went out hunting. For our benefit he would purr loudly, but he would also pause from time to time and wait, ears up, listening for his mother's return. At last, in the darkest hour of the night, from the farthest corner of the house, he'd hear the quiet click of the cat door closing. Very alert, head high, he'd wait, still listening. Soon his mother would call him, with a booming, echoing *meow*. Before the echoes died, he would have launched himself off the bed with a powerful backward kick against my husband's body and would bound down the stairs into the dark kitchen where he'd find his mother beside the little corpse. Then she'd step back and he'd crouch down and polish off his food. Sometimes he'd even growl, evidently at her, the only living creature near him. But, in keeping with her indulgent mothering, she never objected.

It was at this time in her life and in this context that she brought food to my husband and me. She also brought food to our adolescent dog, Pearl, who had grown up with Lilac in our son's household. Three times Lilac fed young Pearl, each time placing a dead mouse in Pearl's bowl. Twice the bowl was on the floor, but once it was on the kitchen counter waiting to be filled at mealtime. Perhaps Lilac found the experience rewarding. Unlike Rajah, Pearl didn't growl at her, and unlike me or my husband, who tend to shout in disgust when provisioned by cats — we throw their gifts in the garbage — the dog ate Lilac's delicacies gratefully.

PART TWO

The Old Way

"Animals have no culture," wrote Konrad Lorenz. If an ethologist of his stature believed that animals have no culture, how many other people must think so too? But on the contrary, animals most certainly do have culture. We fail to realize this for no better reason than that our experience with populations of wild animals is so severely limited we are not often in a position to see much evidence of culture. Worse yet, we have been conditioned to believe that if we have seen one group of elephants, say, or lions, we have seen them all, so we don't even search among wild populations for cultural differences. But in fact, many if not most kinds of animals have culture just as we do, often very easily observed.

What is culture? Not what a professor of English critical of my claims once suggested. "Animals don't write poetry," he insisted. "They don't play musical instruments or attend the ballet." True, and they don't extend their little finger when they

143

hold a cup of tea. But the concept of culture that I have in mind is more like what an anthropologist might offer — a web of socially transmitted behaviors. Dictionaries usually assign this definition to human beings only, but dictionaries are not the voice of God and will change their definitions eventually, as evidence unfolds.

Culture in animals comes about in precisely the same way that it comes about in human beings, by each generation learning from the generation before. A cultural solution to a certain problem gives the cultural participants the benefit of their ancestors' experience. Thus, culture makes life a little easier. Because everybody doesn't have to solve every new problem for himself or herself, but instead can look to his or her elders and colleagues as role models or for advice, culture functions much like instinct, benefitting its participants by smoothing the way. Naturally, cultural solutions to the problems of any given species, whether human or nonhuman, vary considerably from place to place. This variety creates cultural enclaves, and these make up the cultural units that we human beings perceive among ourselves. What we don't perceive so readily is that other species have cultural units too.

Many scientific studies tease away at the question — a landmark study in Great Britain, for instance, showed that two populations of chaffinches from two different areas sang two different songs. And chaffinches from one area who were raised in the presence of chaffinches from the other area sang the song appropriate to their foster home, rather than the song that their close relatives would be singing far away.

Culture in social animals is relatively easy to understand and to observe — wolves in different areas, for instance, show marked preferences for different kinds of prey. In some areas, the wolves are deer specialists, and in others, moose or caribou specialists. In still other areas, the wolves specialize in the difficult task of hunting beavers, even though other prey animals abound.

Culture in cats, supposedly solitary animals, is less obvious, yet it is there just the same. I witnessed an excellent example in my own cats, which came about quite by accident but could not have been more apt an illustration of culture if it had occurred by design. As I have noted, all our cats come from the same population, the population that lives in and around our son's home. Over time, all but one or two of our son's cats were spayed, but not surprisingly, from time to time the unspayed cats had kittens. Some were kept by the family, and some were placed in good homes elsewhere. But now and then the family would feel that it had a cat too many, and would ask us to take the extra one. These cats were so healthy, so loving, so capable and intelligent, that we seldom refused. They may well have had different fathers, but they all came from the same lineage of females and thus are not radically different genetically, or not different enough to explain, in my opinion, divergences in their behavior.

As I have mentioned earlier, in the past whenever a new cat arrived from our son's household, the cat who happened to reside in our house made way for the newcomer by moving to an outbuilding, which was unnecessary in our household, but would have been very sensible behavior on a farm. Or at least this was what happened as long as our son and his family lived in New Hampshire.

But after a number of years, our son moved his family to Boulder, Colorado. On moving day, to the surprise of some of his neighbors (customarily farm cats are simply abandoned), he and his family took all the cats — loading them into carrying cases and boxes and putting them into a trailer which the family pulled behind the car (having carefully vented the exhaust with a hose, so as not to asphixiate the animals). All arrived in excellent condition, and all adjusted well to Colorado. There were still occasional kittens, and from time to time we adopted one. Our gray cat, Christinas, came to us from Boulder as a young subadult, and at our house met her relative, Aasa. In keeping with the old farmyard tradition, Aasa seemed to feel displaced, and moved to the periphery.

But there the practice stopped. More cats have been added to our family, but never again did a new immigrant cause an older cat to move away. Why not? Probably because Aasa was the last cat to come from the old barnyard culture. Although all the new cats came from the same population as the old cats, that population was by then solving its problems in a very different setting. No longer did their property include barns and outbuildings. Rather, all the cats born to that particular population after its transfer to Colorado grew up in and around a suburban house, with no more land than a back yard, and no outlying place to take shelter without venturing beyond the group's territory. As a result, when the newer litters of kittens reached adolescence, if they weren't given to new homes, they simply stayed on. And when one of them found himself or herself in a new setting, such as our house, he or she kept the customs learned from kittenhood, from observing the behavior of the older cats. A minor matter, perhaps, yet it wouldn't seem minor to the cat family, since one of the most significant acts in a cat's life is to leave its natal setting and find a new home.

Nowhere is cultural difference more evident than in pumas, who in certain areas have learned to leave livestock alone.* The Idaho pumas I was privileged to observe, for instance, spent their days in the presence of unsupervised livestock on an open range. From their high lookouts the pumas could actually watch not only the adult horses and cattle but also their very tempting, easily captured foals and calves. Even so, simple as it would have been for these pumas to help themselves to some of the livestock, they passed them by and instead hunted deer. Moreover, a rancher whose livestock grazed safely within the sphere of such abstinent pumas would enjoy their protection, since in de-

*Personal communication from Ken Jafek.

fending their own territories the pumas would keep possible killers of livestock away.

Supposedly, this should have contributed to the survival of abstinent pumas, since the ranchers, in theory anyway, should have realized that they weren't losing livestock to pumas, and appreciated what was going on. But American ranchers are notoriously indifferent to and ignorant of these matters, so that Idaho and Utah have lengthy hunting seasons for pumas, and the game wardens make only feeble, ineffective efforts to inhibit poaching. Hence the pumas lose their lives to hunters anyway.

How does one observe cultural change in a cat population? Probably the best way is to revisit a population over a period of time. I was privileged to revisit the lions on the Namibian side of the Kalahari Desert, first in the 1950s and later in the 1980s. Originally I was a participant in an ongoing study my family made through the courtesy of the Ju/wa Bushmen who live there. Although the focus of the study was to learn about the Bushmen, my own interest was in the lions. I had little time to indulge that interest in those busy days, but lions are hard to ignore, so I was able to learn something about them. But the big revelation came when I returned to Nyae Nyae in the mid-eighties, only to find that while the people had changed greatly, the lions had changed even more, so that many of the things that I thought I had learned about them no longer held true. Also, the old lion population has been divided. Where there was one lion population, now there are two, each as different from the other as they are from the population I had known.

All this had happened in just thirty years, or, from a lion's point of view, in less than two lion lifetimes. Plenty of lions still living could have been reared and educated by lions who had known the old days, and there had not been enough time, by any stretch of the imagination, for the lions to have undergone genetic adaptation.

In the 1950s, the lions and the hunter-gatherers were the most formidable beings in the Kalahari. This fact was widely recognized. "Where the lions and the Bushmen ask for your pass" was a synonym for the Kalahari in apartheid times, when passes were required of black South Africans and when non-Bushman people seldom ventured beyond the limits of the farms and the towns. In those days, the Kalahari Desert was a vast wilderness, unexplored by anyone except the Bushmen. No safarists, no travelers, no farmers, no white or Bantu people had ever stayed in the roughly ten thousand square miles of dry bush savannah that formed the most remote parts of the western desert. The Bushmen were the only people ever known to have lived there. Few non-Bushmen had even passed through it. Most of it had not been mapped. There were no boot marks in the dust, no roads across the plains, no jet trails in the sky, no satellites among the stars. In those days the western Kalahari was still whole, a delicate

149

ecosystem of enormous antiquity. The plant communities, untouched by modern man and his domestic animals, were drought adapted and in balance. Their size and composition were controlled by time, by soil conditions, by rainfall and fire. The populations of animals, in keeping with a dry savannah, were not large and crowded, as they are in most African game parks today, but sparse and highly varied. Showing the ancient relationship between this place and some of its inhabitants, the antelopes who lived there had become independent of water and could range throughout the great dry areas of the western Kalahari, getting enough moisture from dew and from little wild melons called tsama melons. In those days, water-dependent ungulates such as rhinos, elephants, zebras, and buffalos were not present in the western Kalahari except as occasional visitors during the rains. But all the large southern African carnivores were generously and widely represented — an indication of the health and stability of the ecosystem.

The only primates in the western Kalahari were the people, the Ju/wasi. When we visited these people, they were living in the old way, as hunters and gatherers, getting their food, their clothing, their tools and their shelter from the savannah. Tobacco, small pieces of metal, and tiny glass beads were the only exotic materials they had, and they got those from the neighboring Bantu-speaking peoples by trading animal skins. The Ju/wasi smoked the tobacco in pipes made of animal thighbones, and they cold-hammered the metal into knives and arrowheads, gradually replacing their old style implements and bone arrowheads with the new material, though the implements remained unchanged in usage and design. Otherwise, like the Kalahari itself, Ju/wa technology was stable. The most recent innovations seemed to be the bow and arrow and an extremely powerful arrow poison made from the grubs of *Diamphidia* beetles and their parasites.

No one knows how long the Ju/wasi or any other people have lived in the western Kalahari. No one knows whether the modern Bushmen are descendants of an ancient population or are newcomers in a series of occupying populations. Needless to say, in the 1950s no archaeological work had been done on them. Excavations in bordering areas have since unearthed encampments containing artifacts of hunter-gatherers — encampments that were occupied more than thirty thousand years ago. That figure was determined while the excavations were in their early stages. At the time of this writing, the depths of the encampments have not been reached nor the antiquity of their occupancy established.

Although these archaeological findings will certainly be important to our understanding of human prehistory, they may be unimportant ecologically. What mattered to the integrity of the environment was that human hunter-gatherers had been there long enough to count as ecologically indigenous. Human beings, after all, evolved on the African savannahs. Fossil evidence from sites such as Olduvai Gorge places some of the earliest hominids just a few weeks' hike to the north. So people and their ancestors could have been gathering the groundnuts and wild melons of the western Kalahari for a very long time.

During that time, the human populations were governed by the same forces that governed the populations of other living things. The ecosystem absorbed the impact of our species just as it absorbed the impact of, say, the lions. As a result, the hunter-gatherer economy as it was practiced by the people in the Kalahari will probably prove to have been among the most successful human economies ever practiced on earth, if duration and stability are any measure of success.

Even the plants of the Kalahari seem to have adjusted to our kind. Although plants have been adjusting to animals since the time of the dinosaurs and before, their adjustment to fire may have been furthered by people, at least on the African savannahs. In the Kalahari only people and lightning can set fires, and lightning sets only a few. The rest, the fires whose smoke used to redden the sunsets at the end of the dry season, were of human manufacture, set from time immemorial by hunters to induce the new green grass, which draws the game.

To some Westerners, the practice of casually setting a fire and then letting it burn on to travel where it will throughout the dry season until the rains come and put it out might seem destructive.

Yet in fact, at this point in its evolutionary history, the Kalahari's vegetation profits from the fires. Without fires, a certain kind of thornbush takes over. With fires, the grass is renewed and many plants germinate. The fires help the vegetation, which in turn helps the animals.

Although the people of the Kalahari got more of their food from gathering than from hunting, and thus were very different from the other carnivores, the animals saw the people as hunters and acted accordingly. As the antelopes responded to lions by signaling warnings or by positioning themselves to keep the lions in view, they responded to people by staying beyond bowshot — a distance most antelopes seemed to know. In fact, some animals seemed to know a lot more about arrows than just their range; many giraffes knew to keep the branches of a bushy tree like a shield between their chests and a person. That defense would do nothing to help against any other predator or against any other weapon, but against the small, lightweight arrows used by the Bushmen it worked very well. Lacking the right kind of tree, a giraffe would move farther away from a hunter.

So much knowledge and such highly developed safety strategies on the part of the game meant that the human hunters and the other hunting species faced the same difficulties: the game was almost but not quite a match for them; they were pushed to the limits of their skills. In terms of hunting success, it seemed to me, the Ju/wa men were probably more or less equal to the other large-sized hunters of the Kalahari — especially those who hunted large-sized game cooperatively. In those days, the most important of the other large-sized cooperative hunters in the western Kalahari were, of course, the lions.

Whatever large animals the people hunted, the lions also hunted. Unlike the many predators who have no choice but to kill old or young or sick or wounded animals, the Bushman hunters simply killed the nearest animals. So did the lions. The people tended to favor giraffes and the larger antelopes — hartebeests, gemsboks, kudus, and elands. So did the lions. Even the hunting technique of the people resembled that of the lions. In contrast to other large-sized coursing hunters such as cheetahs and members of the dog family who have the stamina to run down their prey, the people for the most part crept near their victim through some kind of cover and then sprang out for the kill, just as cats do. A lion springs from hiding onto his victim's back and, twisting its head around, clamps shut its windpipe, stifling it, while a person springs from hiding and throws something, or shoots a poisoned arrow, but although the actual kill is achieved differently, the underlying lurk-and-spring method is the same.

Perhaps these shared preferences aren't surprising; both people and lions needed the same kind of victim for the same reason — to feed a group. Most of the time, the people preferred to stay in groups of twenty or thirty, while the lions apparently preferred to stay in groups of six or seven.

Hence, in a way, the group size was the same: the people were more numerous, but the lions were larger. Each group would have weighed about three thousand pounds, so on a cosmic set of scales the groups would have balanced each other. A meat meal big enough for the people was also big enough for the lions.

Perhaps partly for this reason, the lions and the Ju/wasi helped themselves to each other's kills. Once, I was present when Ju/wa hunters robbed some lions. As we were walking along in the bush, the hunters noticed vultures coming down out of the sky. When we went to the place where they were dropping, we found white-backed vultures in a tree above a rack of red bones that once had been a hartebeest. Since white-backed vultures are not birds who delay gratification, their sitting in the trees meant that lions were very near. Realizing this, the hunters approached slowly. The lions must have been watching from the bushes, but they didn't object. The hunters picked up the carcass bit by bit, deliberately and confidently, if mindful of the lions. No lion showed herself to challenge them.

Another time, my brother, John, was present when lions tried to rob people. He and four Ju/wa hunters had been following a wildebeest that one of the hunters, days before, had shot with a poisoned arrow. When, at last, they caught up to the wildebeest, it was lying down on folded legs in a clearing in heavy brush, very ill from the poison and surrounded by an unusually large pride of lions and lionesses — about thirty of them. Some were subadult, but many were mature lionesses in their prime. Back in the bushes was at least one mature maned lion. The four Ju/wasi took in the situation, then slowly advanced on the lionesses. Speaking firmly but respectfully, they announced that the meat belonged to people. The lionesses rumbled unpleasantly. Some stood their ground. But others turned tail and retreated to the bushes. And then, although the bushes seemed alive with huge, tan forms pacing and rumbling, the Ju/wa hunters descended on the wildebeest, tossing clumps of earth at the lionesses, speaking firmly and respectfully as they did so. At last, the lionesses slowly, unwillingly, backed off. As soon as the lions and lionesses were screened by the bushes, the Ju/wa hunters seemed to give them little further thought and turned their attention to the wildebeest; they surrounded it, killed it, skinned it, and cut it into strips to carry home, leaving nothing behind but a green cud of partly chewed grass.

These days, this story must seem incredible, so it is fortunate that the event was well documented. My brother, a filmmaker, had a loaded camera with him and filmed everything. Yet at the time, I saw nothing remarkable about a group of four Ju/wa hunters and my brother, armed only with clumps of sod, chasing thirty lions from their intended prey. I was taking my cues from the Ju/wasi, to whom the encounter seemed almost a matter of course. Naturally, I was deeply impressed by the courage of the Ju/wa hunters —

only another Ju/wa hunter could take that for granted — but I should have been equally impressed by the lions.

I thought we were finding out about lion nature. I thought that this was how lions would behave anywhere if approached as the Bushmen approached them, with firm but respectful requests, without fear. After all, the Bushmen had seen nothing unusual about the event and had known what to do immediately. Nor were the lions unusual, for that time and place. We all knew, of course, about lions who might have acted differently — for instance, the lions who lived at the edges of the Kalahari where Bantu people kept cattle. But at the cattle posts, because the lions hunted cattle, the people hunted the lions. One of the Ju/wa hunters explained the different behaviors by saying, "Lions are dangerous only at the cattle posts. The lions around here don't harm people. Where lions aren't hunted, they aren't dangerous. As for us, we live in peace with them."

That was certainly true, but it was not the whole story. Rather, it was the Ju/wa side of the story, which in those days was the only side ever given any consideration by any human being. All of us assumed that the people, not the lions, determined the events.

But the lions also had a share in shaping the relationship. A truce if ever there was one, the people-lion relationship wouldn't have worked unless both sides had participated. Yet how and when the truce started, and what the lions gained from it — and therefore what they put into it — have never been precisely determined.

The beginnings would have been very deep in the past. Our ancestors evolved on the African savannahs in the presence of lions, who themselves had been in southern Africa for 700,000 years. Perhaps we were too small to interest them as dietary items. We were most certainly too small to take any kind of commanding tone with them in the manner of the four Bushman hunters' attitude toward the thirty lions as witnessed by my brother, and we were too small to chase them away if they wanted our food. If there was robbery in those days, the lions, not we, were the perpetrators. Obviously, by the 1950s, something had changed.

It is often assumed that such a change in the relationship between people and animals is due to the development of weapons, but the Bushmen's weaponry wasn't necessarily superior to the lions' in a combat situation. The Bushmen had their spears and their bows and arrows, marvelously designed for hunting, yet all but useless in self-defense. The Bushmen's spears were then, and still are, lightweight and barely four feet long — or about the length of a lion's reach — far shorter than the formidable nine-foot heavyweight spears that the East African pastoralists used when testing their manhood against lions. Bushman bows and arrows are also very small and light. To do its work, a Bushman arrow does not need to pierce a vital, inner organ but needs only to pierce the skin, to inject a drop of poison anywhere at all inside the body. But a drop of poison could take several days to kill a lion. Meanwhile, the hunter might find himself in considerable danger if not torn to shreds. In short, Bushman arrows are about the worst possible weapons for self-defense.

So if not arrows, what? No one in his right mind would think of going up against a lion with a knife. Nor would fire be a useful weapon. The Kalahari animals are accustomed to fire; they evolved in the presence of fire, and they are not afraid of it. Anyway, the normal bushfire in the Kalahari has little to burn except grass, and isn't very hot. If caught by a fire, animals and people alike merely wait for the fire to come to a patch of low grass and then step over the flames.

Also significant is the fact that, unlike the East African pastoralists, the Bushmen have no shields of any kind, and never have had, as far as anyone knows. A shield, after all, suggests that the owner is expecting trouble. The warfaring, lion-hunting Masai, for instance, carried enormous shields. The Bushmen, in contrast, seemed to expect no trouble. Skinning knives, lightweight bows and arrows, short, lightweight spears — hunting tools all — were the only weapons the Bushmen had or felt they needed.

A better explanation for the truce — the only good one I can think of — is that the people, who were not combative with each other, were also not combative with animals. People hunted, of course, but hunting isn't a form of combat — or at least it wasn't to the hunter-gatherers. Hunting was merely a method of obtaining food and clothing. Most animals, as a rule, avoid conflict when they can because conflicts cause injuries, and injuries impair survival. For most of our time on earth, our kind, too, had to abide by the practical considerations that govern other animals. And the Bushmen in the 1950s lived in the old way, by the old rules.

Yet the observation of a truce did not imply that the Bushmen took lions lightly. On the contrary, the Bushmen thought of lions as they thought of no other animal. The Bushman hunters whom we knew deeply respected the hunting ability of lions and even said that lions are better hunters than people because they understand teamwork, in contrast to the Bushmen, who hunt singly and only work as a team* when tracking an animal after it has been shot with a poisoned arrow. Teamwork, said the Bushmen, allows the lions to exploit the tendency of hoofed animals to circle back for a look when followed by a hunter. With a team, one hunter could position herself (if she were a lion) or himself (if he were a person) to be waiting where the prey animal turns back.
Also, the Bushmen recognized a supernatural quality in lions. The word for lion — *n!i* — like the name of God, could not be uttered in the daytime. And people attributed human qualities to

*There is no word for *team* in !Kung — the phrase used was *//ue //om,* "do it together."

lions. Certain lions, for instance, were thought to be sorcerers, a belief that may have come to the Bushmen from the Bechuanaland Protectorate (Botswana, after 1966), where certain people were said to take the form of lions by night, but to be unaware of the transformation. When lions formed a line at night and kept in touch with each other by sequential roaring, the Bushmen sometimes said that the roars were emitted by a single supernatural lion sorcerer, a werelion, who took great leaps through the air, giving a roar each time he touched the ground. A lion could even cause an eclipse of the moon, said the folklore. He would cover the moon's face with his paw to give himself darkness for better hunting.

The success of the Bushman/lion truce seemed truly remarkable. While we were in the Kalahari in the 1950s, we knew of only one Ju/wa person who had been injured by a lion — a man who had been mauled while helping a group of Herero ranchers hunt a cattle killer in the Bechuanaland Protectorate. Being a Bushman and a servant, he had been conscripted as a foot soldier in the Herero-lion wars and during the advance on the lion had been forced to the front with the dogs. There the lion had mauled him. We knew of no one who had been killed by lions. This fact became all the more impressive in light of a genealogical study made in the early 1980s by my brother and a colleague, Claire Ritchie. The study, which attempted, among other things, to determine some of the causes of death among Ju/wa Bushmen, took in more than three thousand people and went back about a hundred years. Naturally, people remembered deaths by unusual or violent causes very well, and among such deaths they recalled several caused by animals, mostly snakes and leopards. But among fifteen hundred deaths recalled by the hundreds of people whose testimonies I was able to examine, only one was said to have been caused by a lion. The victim in this account was a paraplegic — a young Ju/wa girl. My daughter, also a paraplegic, is a source of intense interest to captive lions and tigers and has only to roll her wheelchair through a zoo to get the big cats bounding in their cages. She proposes that the girl's motion — slow, uneven, and low to the ground — caused lions to regard her differently from the way they regard able-bodied people.

Furthermore, throughout the world attacks on human beings by the cat family are most often made on people who are low to the ground — people squatting to relieve themselves are well-known targets, as are children. The sight of a head peeking up above cover such as grass has a mesmerizing effect on all cats, as our cat Rajah demonstrated recently while I watched a televised educational program about the sea. On the screen, a seal's head broke the surface of the water. Rajah, who had been watching the screen very closely, as if he knew that something was about to happen, flung himself at the head the moment it appeared, although he had already learned from many sad experiences with his cat video that televised images are not real. But he evidently preferred to take a chance on being wrong than on missing so golden an opportunity.

A head above a surface has equal appeal to lions, as a certain film company learned to its sorrow. Preparing for a shot of the underside and vanishing hindparts of a lion as it leaped over the cameras and ran for the horizon, the film company had dug a trench as a workspace for members of the camera crew, whose heads, moving back and forth just above the ground, gave the temporarily restrained lion something compelling to watch and to think about while waiting for his cue. When the lion was released, instead of jumping over the trench, he (not surprisingly) jumped at one of the heads and mauled the person badly. Fortunately, the person survived and evidently is still working as a photographer.

Even people with very inconspicuous disabilities are quickly zeroed in on by cats: once at a tiger act attended by some two hundred people tightly packed in a north-facing amphitheater, the entering tigers stopped in their tracks to stare into the sun at someone they had spotted deep in the crowd. Following their gaze I finally found what they had noticed immediately: a child with Down's syndrome sitting quietly and (to me) inconspicuously amid his family.

Just as the Nyae Nyae lions respected the lives of the Ju/wasi, so the Ju/wasi respected the lives of the lions. Although poisoned arrows are not the ideal weapon against lions, the Ju/wasi would certainly have used them without hesitation if it had become necessary to rid themselves of a problem lion. Keeping out of the lion's reach until it collapsed would have been inconvenient but by no means impossible. No — only the fact that the lions gave the Bushmen no cause to want to harm them explains the forbearance. The lions kept their side of the truce.

In contrast with the lions were the other members of the genus *Panthera*, the leopards, with whom the Ju/wasi seemed to have a somewhat different relationship. I attended one leopard robbery, during which the Ju/wa hunters simply collected a leopard's kill without showing him any respect, not even a cautious approach — they just picked up the carcass and left without so much as a backward glance. But the leopard had kept himself discreetly hidden during the robbery and therefore hadn't required respect.

Leopards seem to have a somewhat ambivalent relationship to people. Shy creatures who tend to live in social isolation except for the usual mother-child families, they lack the boldness of lions even in areas where no one molests them. Even so, they are formidable animals, and they know they are frightening.

The fact that the Ju/wasi grouped leopards with hyenas and other predators who merited no special treatment was in itself interesting, because it suggested that the purpose of the respect shown to lions was not necessarily to mollify them. On the contrary, if the Ju/wasi had wanted to mollify an animal, the leopard would have been the logical choice, for among all the large animals of the Kalahari, leopards were the most dangerous to people. While we were there, we heard of several people who had been killed by leopards, and the survey made by Claire Ritchie and my brother revealed several more.

Leopards are smaller than lions and, unlike many lions, live alone or in very small groups; therefore, leopards are more apt to be satisfied with small and mid-sized prey. Size of prey is of real importance to the cat family, even to housecats, particularly as the object of a hunt. A housecat, say, will catch a beetle and may even chew it up and swallow it, but only as a snack; the same cat would probably not start his hunt with a beetle in mind as his quarry but rather would be envisioning something larger. Why waste energy hunting something too small?

A sad fact for human beings is that our size makes us almost perfect prey for leopards, a characteristic which the leopards have not ignored. Leopards haunt the camps of human beings, and this habit has led to their scavenging people's temporarily unburied dead. Sometimes, during an epidemic of terrible illness such as smallpox, all the people of a group would be stricken at the same time. No one would have the strength to bury the dead, and thus the bodies would have been available to scavengers. According to Ju/wa eyewitnesses, the practice of scavenging seemed to lead leopards into watching camps in which many people were ill and, in a few instances, into taking the very ill shortly before death. Possibly this habit also led some leopards into entering camps in which no one was ill — something they may have done in the past and may still do today, killing people and, if possible, carrying them off. In the most recent episode I know of, which was in 1987, the leopard didn't even wait to choose someone who was asleep but took a man who was sitting by a fire. His wife beat off the leopard and saved him. We didn't hear of anyone's being taken by a leopard in any other way than from a camp at night; no one was stalked or ambushed while gathering roots or berries in the bushes, or while crouching down to urinate in long grass (a practice which in the interests of privacy is used by Ju/wa men as well as women), or while crouching down to get water in the tall, thick reeds that surround some of the waterholes. Leopards everywhere hunt other animals by those methods, and some leopards in other areas hunt people by those methods. So the restriction of man-hunting to campsites at night was apparently a cultural feature of the western-Kalahari leopards — leopards whose traditions went back to epidemics of the past.

Why didn't the lions do likewise? Didn't they, too, have the opportunity to learn of a possible food resource in the camps of sick or sleeping people? Hungry lions should by rights refuse nothing, and in many places man-eating by lions is well known. On certain roadsides in East Africa, for instance, lions occasionally wait for drunken people to come staggering home at night from bars. Because man-eating is so often practiced by single lions, by old or young male lions who evidently lack the advantages of pride membership, it is my opinion that man-eating is a lion's solution to the problem of landlessness. A lion without land must poach on the territory of other lions. If the nomadic, landless lion captures one of us, the resident lions won't mind as much as if he had captured an animal such as a kudu or a gemsbok that they, too, could most likely have eaten some day. Thus a nomad's wish to avoid competition, to avoid attracting the negative attention of other lions, could make human beings seem like tempting prey.

Not in the Kalahari of the 1950s, though. Not in that deep and perfect wilderness. No one can explain the truce because no one understands it. The truce was simply taken for granted, as most situations involving animals are simply taken for granted. Animals are assumed to be static in nature. So even today, with both the human and the animal populations stressed and damaged, few people realize the difference between how things are now and how things were then.

During the years that we stayed in the Kalahari, we often lived near a waterhole called /Gautscha. One of three permanent waterholes in the area, it lay in a rocky outcropping in a thicket of long reeds. For much of the year, /Gautscha was the only source of water in nine hundred square miles of very dry country.

On a rise of ground a few hundred feet east of the waterhole, in the shade of a grove of little trees, the group of Ju/wa Bushmen camped in shelters made of bent branches sparsely thatched with grass. We camped nearby in tents. To the west of the waterhole lay a great clay pan, /Gautscha Pan, which formed the bottom of a shallow lake during the rains but was a bare, cracked mud flat in the dry season. In a dry bank to the northwest of the pan, perhaps a mile or two from the waterhole, were the dens of some spotted hyenas. Somewhere nearby, until someone killed him, lived a brown hyena. On a neighboring grassland lived a cheetah. In the vast bush southwest of the pan lived a leopard. And in the (to us) featureless bush to the southeast lived a pride of lions. Its size varied, but there were never fewer than ten. We never found the lions' resting places, nor did we try to find them, but we thought we knew where they were because we sometimes heard lions there in the morning, when lions tend to gather together, and in the evening, when, after a day's rest, lions begin to move around. So in an area of a few square miles lived about thirty people, ten or more lions, a cheetah, a leopard, and at least five hyenas, or approximately fifty large, predatory creatures, all of them hunting the same antelope population, all of them drinking from the same waterhole.

Helping to minimize the chance of meeting was the habit of the different groups to use the area and its resources at different times — the people and the cheetah by day and the other predators by night. Time of day was particularly important for the people and the lions because the people needed daylight for hunting and also for gathering, and the lions, who couldn't hope to hunt if they couldn't conceal their large bodies, preferred darkness. The grass was seldom long enough or thick enough to hide them by day.

As one group spread out to forage, the other group would gather together to sleep. Further limiting the chance of meeting was that neither group started the day's or night's activity quickly. The lions began their hunting not at dusk, when the people might still be on their way home, but long after dark; the people, on the other hand, delayed leaving their camp until the day was well along and thus never met the lions — or, for that matter, any nocturnal predator who might be finishing a night's hunt in the dawn.

Yet, for all the factors that kept the groups apart, we often did meet the other predators. For instance, we often heard or saw the hyenas. Watching at night by the waterhole, I would see them when they came for a drink. Unlike the hyenas in game parks, these were not used to vehicles, and, eyeing my jeep with great suspicion, they would stalk around it like cattle who have seen a dog. But they were not shy about visiting us. One night, while poking stealthily around our camp, one of them very cautiously put her head into my little backpacker's tent. I was reading with a flashlight and looked up to see her sensitive nose just inches from mine. Our eyes met. "What is it?" I asked. Unsure, she drew back. We would also see hyenas when we went by their dens, which had been dug, like caves, into a vertical bank. One hyena, a large female with breasts, would stand half in, half out of her doorway, watching us with an unfriendly, almost twisted facial expression, as if she found us repugnant.

Occasionally, we would see the leopard stretched out upon a certain rock, his thighs loosened, sunning his furry white loins. We would often see the head and shoulders of the cheetah above the grass when we went to his flat grassland. But we never, in all the miles we traveled on foot or in vehicles, on all the nights we spent watching for nocturnal wildlife by the waterhole, chanced upon one of the lions.

I used to ask people what would happen if someone met a lion in the bush. If that should happen, I would be told, one should walk purposefully away at an oblique angle without exciting the lion or stimulating a chase. Several times, people showed us how to do this. But at /Gautscha we never met a lion. Although among us we spent at least parts of more than fifty person-years in the bush there, we never once had occasion to use the technique we had learned.

We saw it used, though. One day, in the close quarters of some heavy bush in the farthest waterless reaches of the Kalahari, my brother and I met a lion. He was all golden in the sunlight, with a golden mane. He seemed very large and, unlike many Kalahari animals today, he was in beautiful physical condition: he had no scars or scratches and had plenty of flesh on his bones. Stupefied, we gazed at him, in awe of his presence and his beauty. He stood still, gazing at us. How long we might have stayed this way I don't know. My brother and I were too dazzled to do anything. So the responsibility fell upon the lion. Moving calmly, confidently, purposefully, keeping us in view without staring at us aggressively, *he* walked purposefully away at an oblique angle. The effect of the encounter on us — or at least on me — was memorable. The lion was only a few feet away, and I could have become afraid for my life. Yet his intentions were so clear and his demeanor was so reassuring that I felt absolutely no fear, not even alarm — just interest and wonder. By his smooth departure and his cool, detached behavior, the lion apparently intended to save himself the risks of an unwanted skirmish. A man acting in a similar way under similar circumstances would have been considered refined, gentlemanly, polite. In our species, too, reassuring manners can bring desirable results, for exactly the same reasons.

That was the only time, as far as I can remember, that any of us saw a lion by chance. But it was not the only time we saw a lion. In fact, we often saw them. That, however, happened at their discretion, when they wanted to see us. Usually this happened on the first or second night we spent in a new area, or upon returning to a familiar area that we hadn't visited for a long time. As animals who keep close watch over all that happens in their sphere, the lions would inevitably come to check us out.

These days, my own three cats remind me of the Nyae Nyae lions whenever an unfamiliar vehicle stops in our driveway. At first, the cats scatter, perhaps to await developments or to consider the situation while remaining out of sight. After a while, they emerge inconspicuously from hiding, then discreetly advance upon the vehicle. Before long they are sniffing its tires, and when they have satisfied themselves about the odors thereon, they jump to the hood or the roof and simply stand there for a time, neck long, ears up, tail down, hindquarters low, hind legs bent at the knee as if waiting to see who will come to challenge them. They do this in all seasons, day or night. It seems to me that the cats are intrigued by the height, and wish to experience the vehicle as a high thing, the way that one of us might climb on a pile of lumber or a mound of hay. Later, if the door is open, the cats go inside and explore the interior. It is as if they are asking themselves what difference the vehicle is making to their world. We try always to ask visitors to close the doors of their vehicles when no one is in attendance, lest a cat get shut inside and driven away. (This has never happened to us, but it has happened to our neighbors. They were lucky — the owner of the van, an electrician, realized whose cat he was transporting and very considerately drove him home again.)

Our first encounter with lions was on our first trip, at the edge of the Kalahari, far to the west of /Gautscha, just after we had camped for the night. With us was a young Afrikaner man, a former smallpox-control officer, who had come to show us the way to a place where he once had found and vaccinated some Bushmen. (In those days, almost no non-Bushmen had contact with the Bushmen, or even had any idea where they were.) In the dark, a group of five lions came quietly up to us. Beyond our fire we saw their shining eyes, which were so high above the ground that we thought at first we were seeing donkeys. When I realized that we were seeing lions, I was overcome with excitement and ran around the fire to see

173

them better. Just then, a bullet whizzed by my ear, shots rang out, and the eyes vanished. Before anyone realized what the young Afrikaner was doing or could stop him, he had shot two of the lions.

That was all he did, too. He wouldn't even go to see if he had killed them. When the rest of us found tracks and splashed blood but no dead lions, we realized the extent of the problem created by the young man — two wounded lions nearby in the dark. We asked him what he was going to do about it. Nothing, he said. It was, after all, nighttime. It would be dangerous to follow up the lions. So the task fell to me, my brother, and a man named William Cam, who had come with us as a mechanic.

We set off on foot in the starlight, moving very quietly so that we might hear the lions breathing or the low, mumbling growl that a wounded lion might make. We also tried to catch their scent. At last we heard a soft moan. We followed the sound, turned on the flashlight, and found a lion — a male, full grown but still too young to have a mane or to have left the pride. Badly wounded, he was lying on his side, unable to get up. He was evidently in pain, for he had been biting the grass. We had to shoot him several times before we could kill him and each time a bullet hit him he cried. One of the worst moments of my life, that scene is as fresh in my mind today as it ever was, and as painful. The lion turned his head aside, to look away from us as we stood over him and shot him. I wonder now if by averting his gaze he was hoping to limit our aggression.

We couldn't find the other lion, and after many hours of searching we gave up, to try again in the morning. When the sky grew pale, at the place where the lions had been when the young man fired, my brother and I found the tracks of a lion who had taken a great leap. Not fifty feet from camp, at the end of the next leap, lay the body of a lioness shot through the heart. She, like the lion, seemed young: she still had spots on her white belly. Her fur and the grass around her were cold and wet with dew. Or mostly cold and wet with dew. Right beside her we found a warm, dry place where the grass lay flat. Looking around, we saw a dark trail through the grass where something had knocked off the dew. Then on the trail we saw a grass stem starting to rise after being pressed down, then another, and another, and under the slowly lifting grass stems we found the round footprints of an enormous lion, who had left only moments before. So we knew that while the dew fell, this huge lion or lioness had stayed beside the dead lioness, within sight of our camp, listening to all our comings and goings, listening to the shots and cries. During the night the watching lion or lioness had groomed the body of the dead lioness, turning her fur the wrong way.

Our next encounter took place on the first night of our second trip to /Gautscha. We had come in vehicles after much hard traveling. We were too tired to pitch tents so, about fifty feet from the Ju/wa encampment, we threw down our sleeping bags and without even bothering to build a fire went immediately to sleep. During the night, we heard the Ju/wasi saying some strong words to someone, but we didn't pay much attention. We were too tired. In the morning, we found the footprints of lions all around us. Several lions had come to investigate us as we slept and had even bent down to sniff our faces. We found the huge, round prints of lions' forefeet, toes pointed at us, right by our heads.

Afterward, the lions had gone on to the Ju/wa encampment and had stared over the tops of the little grass shelters at the people there. Unlike us, who stayed awake all day and slept all night, the Ju/wasi took naps during the day and got up often at night. Hence they were virtually never all asleep at the same time. Even in the depth of night someone would be awake, getting warm by a fire, having a snack or a sip of water or a chat with someone else. When the people who were awake saw the burning green eyes, they got smoothly to their feet and firmly told the lions to leave. Since the Ju/wasi would hardly take a low, commanding tone with one another, the unusual voices woke everyone else. At first, the lions didn't want to leave, but the people insisted, and at last shook burning branches at them. Eventually, the lions went.

On several occasions, lions seemed to have strong feelings about us, about something we had done or were doing. As I look back, the interesting thing about the episodes is not that they were frightening, which they were, or dangerous, which they could have been, but that the lions seemed to be trying hard to communicate with us, perhaps simply to give expression to their feelings, perhaps to make us do something.

Unlike the lions, who correctly understood, and even obeyed, the spoken and gestured commands of the Ju/wasi — words and gestures that were designed for other human beings and then merely applied to lions — we human beings were not able to understand the lions. Not even the Ju/wasi understood them, and they knew them better than anyone else. Why could the lions of /Gautscha understand the requests of the people but the people not understand the requests of the lions? Are lions better than people at understanding interspecific messages? Are people better than lions at conveying messages? No one really knows. It came to me, however, that our kind may be able to bully other species not because we are good at communication but because we aren't. When we ask things of animals, they often understand us. When they ask things of us, we're often baffled. Hence animals frequently oblige us, but we seldom oblige them. Elephants are different, but then, elephants can motivate people as no other animals can. Once, an elephant who didn't want me near him threw gravel at me so hard it felt like buckshot. I understood at once what he wished to communicate, and thereafter I paid scrupulous attention to his boundary, which was, incidentally, not the bars of his cage or the edge of the sidewalk but a creation of his own mind and seemed to be expressed by an unchanging but invisible line.

Of course, each time an animal tries to communicate with a human being, the animal is pioneering, since there are no established ways. Sometimes the animal tries something that is familiar and that works with his or her own kind — a dog who wanted something might, for instance, bark or stare or whine, all ways in which he might successfully communicate with another dog. But not all animals are satisfied with the familiar. Cats are particularly inventive in communicating with human beings, and most of us can see plenty of examples in the efforts of our own cats. Our cat Orion, perhaps having noticed that at night I would investigate noises on the stairs, once jumped hard from step to step, and repeated the procedure so successfully that I thought the sound was being made by a heavy person, and I got out of bed to investigate. Orion had, I saw, been jumping on the top three stairs only, and when he got to the third step from the top, he would go back up and do his jumps over again. He was just starting over for the fourth or fifth time when I arrived. He then looked at me and *meowed*. He had food, he had water, he had a cat box. In short, he lacked nothing that I ordinarily would provide for him. It occurred to me that he wanted to go out, and needed me to open the cat door for him. But we had long since begun keeping our cats indoors at night, for fear of a coyote, and I couldn't oblige him. I said aloud, "I'm sorry, but I can't let you out." His eyes lingered on mine, as if he were taking in what I had told him, and then he turned his head and went on down the stairs in perfect silence. Did we communicate what I believe we communicated? Had he really wanted to go out? Had he understood my remark, or some of it, and deduced the rest from the tone? Possibly — he was certainly communicating something, and I may or may not have picked it up.

But in my experience, the most dramatic episode involving a cat's attempt at communication took place one hot, moonless night in the rainy season at /Gautscha, when a lioness came to our camp. Most of our people and also many of the Ju/wasi were elsewhere. I happened to be alone in a tent in our camp, and my mother and brother happened to be visiting people in the Ju/wa camp, about thirty yards away. I was working on my notes by lantern light. At the Ju/wa camp, about six small fires burned. We had been in residence there for almost a year and in no sense could be considered newcomers.

At about ten o'clock that night a lioness suddenly appeared between the two camps and began to roar. The loudness of lions cannot be described or imagined but must be experienced. My body was so filled with the sound that I couldn't think or breathe, and in the brief silences between roars my ears rang. The earth and the walls of the tent seemed to be shaking. Terror-stricken and confused, I tried to collect my wits. There was no-where to go that gave more protection than the places we were already in — I in a very flimsy tent but at least not completely exposed, the other people all together beside fires. Climbing a tree was out of the question — there were no trees whose upper branches the lioness couldn't reach by standing on her hind legs. At last, with trembling hands, I carried the lantern outside the tent, partly so that its light would shine on the tent rather than through the tent, to make the fab-ric seem solid rather than transparent, with me quivering inside like a shadow puppet. I also wanted to illuminate the lioness so the other people could see where she was, because her roars were so deep and so loud that they gave no direction. To judge from her roars, she was all around all of us — anywhere, everywhere.

She seemed to have in mind something in the Ju/wa camp, since she was looking in that direc-tion. She seemed not to notice the lantern. With her ears half up and turned sideways, with her tail taking great, full sweeps, she seemed angry and edgy, a lioness whose patience was at an end. Sometimes she would pace back and forth, and once she leaped out of the lantern light, only to leap back into it again. It is sometimes claimed that lions roar at other creatures to confuse or stampede them, making them easy prey. That night, such an explanation seemed improbable. Long ago, natural selection would have removed from the general population any people unwise enough to leave their fires and weapons and scatter in the dark, especially at the urging of a lion. Even Western people don't necessarily stampede under such conditions. Not knowing what to do or where to go, they simply remain rooted to the spot with terror. That was what happened to me. As for the Ju/wasi, the lioness certainly got their attention but perhaps didn't frighten them as badly as she frightened me. Cool but alert, they awaited developments. Anyway, there wasn't anything anyone could do. The lioness certainly didn't seem in the mood to consider a firmly spoken request from the Ju/wasi, and that night they didn't offer any; they maintained a tactful silence. It seemed to me terribly important to notice how long the lioness stayed there, so I timed her. She roared intermittently for almost thirty-five minutes. Then she left, with swift, impatient strides. And there the episode ended. She never came back, or not in any obvious manner, and no one ever knew what it was she had wanted of us.

Another time, lions combined their investigation of newcomers with unexplained roaring. The event took place on the second night my mother and I, along with some of the Ju/wasi, spent camped at Tsho//ana, a Kavango cattle post by a ravine about fifty miles north of /Gautscha. Up the ravine and into our camp came a great group of lions, and they began to roar in unison. Some began to roar as others ended, so that no gaps appeared in the appalling sound. Again the earth shook and the tent rattled. Noise so loud literally robs the breath and stuns the senses. We were paralyzed. At last, as suddenly as the noise began, it stopped. Then came a long silence, more terrifying than the roaring. The lions must have been listening, surely to learn the effects of their aggressive bellows. I held my breath and tried to keep my jaws apart so the lions wouldn't hear my teeth chattering. The lions apparently heard nothing and began to roar again.

As frightened as I was, I couldn't help pointing my flashlight's quavering beam around in the hope of sighting some of the lions. But they were right behind the tent, where I couldn't see them. Instead, out of the night, out of the deafening, thundering din, came one of the Ju/wa men. He had been on the far side of the ravine when the roaring began and, armed only with his little spear, he had crossed the ravine to be with his wife and children. Walking silently on bare feet, he had actually woven his way among the roaring lions in the dark.

What was the importance to the lions of the truce between them and the people, and what did the lions have to do to keep the truce? To consider the question, one must consider lion life. Probably the ideal situation for a lion is to live in a pride that owns a territory. Next best, perhaps, is to live with other lions in a nomadic, landless band. Least desirable, it may be, is to live alone as a nomad, although that is often done by young adults and by displaced males. But since a solitary life is possible, since a lion can hunt for himself or herself and, if alone, doesn't need to share food (to judge from the way lions fight when they eat, they seem to hate sharing), why do lions prefer groups?

Surely one reason is that, like housecats, they care about each other. Mealtime behavior notwithstanding, like housecats lions rub faces lovingly when they meet, sleep near each other, groom each other, and keep in touch by voice when far apart.

There are also many practical and economic advantages to group life. George Schaller, in his 1972 study *The Serengetti Lion*, reports that under certain circumstances lionesses hunting cooperatively in groups of five or six were more than twice as successful as lionesses hunting singly. And no wonder. A team of lions can hunt more effectively than a single lion, and while the carcass must then be shared by all the hunters, so that no lion gets nearly as much at a sitting as she would get if she hunted alone, she nevertheless gets to eat more often. All in all, by providing moderate meals at reasonably regular intervals as opposed to enormous meals at rare intervals, teamwork is the better way.

Nor are lions the only cats to hunt in groups. In fact, other cats do, too, probably for many of the same reasons. Housecats sometimes hunt together, with at least rudimentary cooperation if not with the disciplined teamwork of lions. As I have mentioned, my cats even hunt cooperatively with my dogs, or at least they tolerate the presence of the dogs, since the cats usually initiate the hunts and the dogs join in when they see what's happening. (Such hunts are often quite successful, since two animals limit the avenues of escape, thus entrapping the little quarry. Usually the cat makes the catch but then relinquishes the corpse to the dog, who eats it, just as a lioness might relinquish her victim to a lion.)

Like housecats, lionesses cooperate in child care. It is not unusual to see a lioness striding along with cubs of different ages stumbling behind her.

Lionesses nurse one another's cubs as cats do and even teach one another's cubs. My brother once came upon a lioness holding a struggling warthog in her front paws while two large cubs and two small cubs looked on, very interested. From the bushes, a second lioness watched. In short, as long as food is available, there are few disadvantages to group life for lionesses and virtually none for lion cubs. Even if a mother is away for long periods, she can know that her infants are safe, held close between the warm thighs of their aunt or their grandmother, fed by her four black nipples, and protected by her brave lion heart.

Some lionesses live alone as nomads, but do so probably because group life is not available to them. Such a lioness was Elsa, in *Born Free*. When George and Joy Adamson, who reared Elsa, tried to get a pride of wild lions to accept her, no pride would take her — any more than a family of hardworking people would take in a homeless stranger simply because the stranger was of the same species. The saddest thing about Elsa was that as far as she was concerned the Adamsons had been her group and, from her point of view, they forsook her.

A male lion also derives many advantages from a group. Although he begins life in his mother's group, he leaves when he reaches young adulthood as all cats do, probably driven out by a new stepfather. The young lion's task, then, is to find a group that will accept him, a pride in which the lionesses will not be his mother, aunts, and sisters but his wives. Finding such a group is not easy, if for no other reason than that most groups already have a resident male or males. Until the young lion can find a group whose resident male is missing or is too old or too disabled to defend his lionesses, the young lion lives as a nomad. Yet occasionally some find vulnerable groups, defeat the resident male, and take over. In return for the sexual and hunting services of the lionesses, the lion guards their territory, if they have one, and fathers their children until other young males appear and defeat him. Then, if he survives the battle, he must once again become a nomad, squeezing out an existence at the fringes of other lions' territories until he dies. It is easy to see what great advantages a male lion can derive from a companion — another male to join his battles, to share his responsibilities as well as his wives. Normally, young males — sometimes littermates but sometimes just friends — find themselves pushed out of their group or groups around the same time. Joining forces, they find new lionesses. Together they defeat the resident male or males, together they defend a territory and father the cubs. In fact, a group of males provides a much more stable situation for the rearing of cubs than a single male can hope to do, since the group members can better defend their position. Not easily can newcomers take over from them.

With all the advantages to be had from group life, it is surprising that some lions live singly even where game is plentiful. Solitude seems to be the choice of some lions in the desert reaches of the southern Kalahari and in the sand dunes of the Skeleton Coast. Could the determining factor be water?

Water is seldom considered as a possible factor in the size of lion groups, for in many parts of Africa lions are known not to drink water. The moisture they need evidently comes from the bodies of the animals they kill and also from dew and from tsama melons. Even so, I believe that water as well as the alternative forms of moisture may be more important to lions than we now suppose. Lions are not like the antelopes, whose special physical mechanisms enable them to tolerate great heat and to limit their bodies' water loss. Lions are like us — they must cool themselves. Just as we lose moisture when we sweat, lions lose moisture when they pant, and they must replace it. For a possible answer, we may look once again to the Kalahari hunter-gatherers, whose group size at certain times of year may have been related to the availability of water. During the dry season, in places where there was no water, where the people got moisture from plants and from the bodies of animals, the groups were small. Where there was water, the groups were much larger. Almost seventy Ju/wasi had communal rights to the waterhole of /Gautscha, and although the food supply didn't encourage so many to live there during the dry season, more than that number would meet there for periods during the rains.

In contrast were certain people who, perhaps

more than any other people on earth, were attuned to desert life: the /Gwi Bushmen. Before we went to /Gautscha, we visited the group of /Gwi Bushmen mentioned earlier, the people who were living without water. They had no hidden spring, no secret sip wells or buried ostrich-eggshell water containers — not even a pool of stale rainwater in a hollow tree. Like desert lions, this particular group of two men, four women, three teen-age boys, and one baby got liquid from a number of different kinds of watery plants and from the bodies of animals. From the latter these people were past masters at collecting every drop. On one occasion, when we were able to measure the amount of liquid, we found that they collected about five gallons from the rumen of an adult female gemsbok, one of the large antelopes of the Kalahari. To do it, they made a bowl of the gemsbok's skin, so that no liquid escaped. This technique gave each person several good drinks. Many more people could have eaten from this gemsbok, but not many more could have satisfied their thirst.

In the same way, the availability of water may have affected the size of the lion group at /Gautscha. With only the liquid in melons, meat, and dew, the lions might have had to scatter or live in small groups. So the waterhole may have enabled them to live together. And they seemed to want to be together, as their pride of thirty shows. On the day that my brother and the Ju/wa men drove the thirty lions from a wounded wildebeest, the lions were far too many to have met by chance. That day they were together by design, and not as an aggregate but as a community. The appearance of a staggering, weakening wildebeest had surely focused them, but if they had been widely scattered, the Ju/wa hunt would have happened too suddenly to draw them from afar. They had to have been near one another when the wildebeest came along. And they weren't together for hunting; in fact, they were about twenty-five too many for efficient hunting. They had been brought together by some other impulse — a lion's impulse — and the water may have let them indulge it.

In the western Kalahari, since there were only a few sources of permanent water in the dry season, the vast savannah was not as vast as it seemed. Whoever wanted to drink water had to live within reasonable distance of a waterhole. In the case of the /Gautscha lions, that was the /Gautscha waterhole, and probably no other. We believed that there were lions associated with the other dependably permanent waterholes, which were many miles distant from /Gautscha. Other prides had surely established lion ownership of those waterholes. So it seems possible that the lions at /Gautscha, knowing that the source of water was unique, maintained a low profile around it. To mismanage their public relations so as to endanger their access to water could have altered their social opportunities. The lions contributed to the low profile by using the waterhole very late at night. They also came and went quietly. They didn't roar near it. They never lay near it, viewing it all day, as the lions in some game parks now do. And no lion ever left a scat by the water.

What do scats mean to lions? That might depend partly on their cat nature and partly on their particular culture. To me, the discretion of the /Gautscha lions about leaving scats near the water was reminiscent of certain housecats who won't use litter boxes that are placed too near their feeding areas. Perhaps these cats don't want to mix food or water with feces. Or perhaps scats mean more than simple waste to these cats. After all, most cats use scats as hostile signs. And scats seem to carry a negative message for lions as well. A resting lion, for instance, gets up and leaves the vicinity of its sleeping comrades if it wants to move its bowels. But under most circumstances, most lions seem to view scats with indifference. In places frequented by lions, including the waterhole areas of game parks, their scats are many and obvious. But the /Gautscha lions were different. Perhaps they wanted to safeguard the cleanliness of the water. Perhaps they wanted to avoid leaving negative messages. Yet whatever their reason, they viewed the waterhole area as an unsuitable place for feces and never soiled it. The lions knew why. We didn't.

The people, too, used the waterhole with care. They didn't pollute it or sit around it but drew water and left, usually at about the same time of day and never at night. And, just as the lions owned the water from the point of view of other lions, the people owned the water from our point of view. Other people wishing to use it needed permission. Thus, with respect to water use, the people and the lions had much in common, although neither group, perhaps, would have seen it that way.

In the 1950s, the lions of /Gautscha belonged to one continuous population, a single lion nation occupying a more or less undivided country. At the eastern edge of this lion nation were the cattle posts of Herero, Kavango, and Tswana ranchers. A Kavango family maintained such a post at Tsho//ana, where a lioness had worked out an amazing technique to secure cattle.

In response to the threat posed by the lions, the Kavango family had built a fortress of heavy poles, each about six inches in diameter and about twelve feet long, all planted in a deep circular trench that held two or three feet of each pole below ground and left nine or ten feet above. It would be hard to devise a more substantial, safer kraal. Yet in 1955 at least one lioness removed cattle from this kraal. How she did it was not exactly understood. Of course, her method didn't interest the Kavango family as much as her banditry did. She was seen only once, by torchlight, at the top of the fence, scrambling out with a heifer over her shoulder.

Was there only one lioness who could leave the kraal carrying a heifer? Were there several? Since only one lioness did it at a time, or on any given night, and since no human beings really knew much about the pride or its membership, no human beings knew or ever will know what actually happened. I feel safe in assuming that the lioness preselected her victim. She couldn't easily have made her choice while flying through the air, so almost certainly she studied the herd ahead of time, probably through the cracks between the poles. She would choose a mid-sized animal, perhaps a yearling heifer — not a large cow, which would be too big to carry, and not a little calf, which would be so small as to make the risk and the effort wasteful. Then this formidable lioness would leap from the ground to the top of the fence, wedge her forearms between the points of the uneven, tapered poles, and brace herself with her hind feet, her claws dug into the wood. From there she would probably locate her chosen victim. A quick scrabble would put her over the top and into the crowd of cattle, who, of course, would raise an appalling alarm, bringing out the Kavango men with weapons.

In among the dangerous sharp hooves and horns of the frantic cattle, the lioness would seize her heifer and, leaping to the top of the fence, would scrabble out again, bearing the entire weight of the heifer with only her shoulders and her mouth.

It is hard to appreciate such a mouth: one must hold a lion's skull, taking time to admire the huge, arched, buttressed, deep-rooted eyeteeth and the wide, bony anchors for the massive jaw muscles. Two men together, using their entire bodies, could just barely carry what one Tsho//ana lioness picked up with her mouth.

A somewhat different situation pertained at the village of /Kai /Kai, a Herero cattle post about fifty miles east of /Gautscha. /Kai /Kai had been a Herero settlement for a long time, how long I don't know. If at first it was a place of Bushmen, a rich Herero found and took it, using it as a place to keep part of his vast herd. He seldom if ever came to /Kai /Kai. Instead, a few poor Herero families with their Ju/wa servants tended his cattle for him. The kraal at /Kai /Kai wasn't as strong as the kraal at Tsho//ana, although the people kept more cattle. Yet at /Kai /Kai, perhaps because the people were merely the guardians and herders, not the owners of the cattle, they put up less resistance to the lions, who had long been coming in groups to help themselves, until they had grown so bold that they would walk through the village in broad daylight while the people shut themselves in their mud and wattle houses. Only the village dogs — starved, beaten skeletons almost too weak to walk — regularly put up any resistance to the lions. When the lions came the dogs would rush at them, barking, and sometimes would actually succeed in chasing them off. Sometimes the lions wouldn't leave, though, but instead would chase the dogs. The dogs well knew the lions could kill them, so they tried to stay out of reach.

For the most part the people did little to stop the lions, but how could they do more? /Kai /Kai was in the Bechuanaland Protectorate, and in pre-independence times the protectorate government forbade black people to have rifles or bullets. At /Kai /Kai the Herero men had to defend themselves with a muzzle-loading musket, for which they couldn't always get powder. But one day they had powder, so the gun was ready, loaded with nails, when, according to a Ju/wa participant, the lions strolled into town.

Armed with the gun, the people came out to confront the lions. The dogs barked as usual, but this time, encouraged by the people behind them, they broke with custom and rushed right up to the lions. Surprised at this change in the rules, the lions suddenly charged the dogs. The dogs turned tail and ran headlong for the protection of the people. Between the people's legs they scurried, with the lions right behind them. Most people were forced to scatter. But the man with the musket stood his ground and fired. The blast and the pattern of nails turned the lions' charge. The lions left and, as far as I heard, never came back in the daytime. No person was hurt and no lion was disabled that anyone knew of. Only a dog had failed to escape, a dog whose back had been broken by a heavy blow from a lion. A few people had noticed her, a paraplegic in a seated position, slowly dragging herself by her front legs. She didn't last long — she certainly wasn't there when I visited later. A few people remembered her predicament with amusement, but as to what became of her, no one knew or would have cared, except the other dogs.

In the 1950s, the lions around Tsho//ana and other cattle posts in the area had large, prospering territories that happened to include cattle pens that they visited only because they chose to. As time went by, however, the peripheral areas of what had once been the lion nation were slowly taken over by ranches and farms. In the Bechuanaland Protectorate, some years of drought tended to concentrate the huge herds of cattle in the few places where grazing could still be found. In other areas, farmers expanded their holdings or changed their style of farming, giving up the old-fashioned, un-mechanized methods for more efficient, mecha-nized, commercially oriented methods. Gone were the days of a few sheep sent out to graze in the care of a dog and a child; in place of such inef-ficiency, large herds of livestock were guided through cycles of rotational grazing by men in ve-hicles. The end product, which had once been milk, a little cheese, and a little mutton for the farm's dependents, changed to commercially raised beef and hides for the export markets.

As a result, the peripheral areas of the lion nation became more precarious. The lions who lived there became the unfortunates of the population — the poor. The antelopes were quickly hunted out by the ranchers and farmers, for sport, for meat, for disease control, and to eliminate competition for the grazing. As the grassland was denuded and the once delicately balanced savannah became, in places, a moonscape with dunes, even the peripheral areas contracted. Then the lions had no other place to go and nothing else to eat: they were forced to hunt livestock. Of course, the farmers demanded the eradication of all lions. And the lions seemed to understand. Apparenlly in an effort to save themselves, the lions who lived on the periphery stopped roaring: the roaring alerted the people, who then hunted them more intensively. How did the lions know not to roar?

When I was in northern Uganda, where a similar situation prevailed, the former lion range had in just two lion lifetimes been invaded by the powerful Dodoth, a Maasai-like people with big herds of cattle. As the cattle began to displace the game, existence became increasingly hard for the lions. They couldn't emigrate to better country because to the south, east, and west were crowded farmlands, and far away to the north, in a game reserve, where there was good, rolling country and abundant game, other lions already owned every inch of space.

Fugitives in their own home, the lions of Dodoth county tried to adjust to the presence of dangerous people by living as discreetly as possible — by leaving cattle alone except for strays, by staying out of sight, by moving only at night, by seldom even leaving their footprints on the roads, and by never roaring. Lions don't roar when they are trespassing on the territory of other lions, and for the same reason: the trespassers don't want the owners hunting them down. Therefore the Uganda lions acted toward the people as if the people were lions and as such were the rightful owners of the land, and as if they, the resident lions, were not the residents at all but were deposed lions or interlopers, although they were the only lions there.

To stop roaring must have been a real deprivation to the lions because the cat family in general and lions in particular do much of their communication by voice. To try to understand the probable cost to lions of not roaring, it seems useful to compare cats to dogs and to ourselves. The reason to communicate may differ with each species, but the benefit is the same. As a general rule, dogs come when called but cats answer. Dogs therefore follow the pattern set by their ancestors the wolves, who range very widely with the sun or the stars as their beacon and the pack, wherever it may wander, as their home. When called, a dog realizes that the caller may be afoot and moving and, rightly fearing permanent separation, hurries to join the caller, to catch up. An adult cat, on the other hand, is sure to be firmly ensconced on some kind of spot — his spot, however temporary — and he sees a call as a query, not as a summons. If he feels safe, he'll answer, which will disclose his whereabouts, but he probably won't feel the need to join whoever called. We, too, have atavistic feelings about calling and being called. We, too, feel the need to call to the members of our group when we're apart, and if we are called we feel impelled to come and also to holler "Here!" or "What?" Very few of us lack this response; it's a rare person who for no reason just stands there dumbly with his mouth shut. So when one thinks of one's own need to communicate and of how it feels to keep silent when one normally would call or answer, one can perhaps see what enforced silence cost the lions. Housecats, too, keep silent when they are frightened, and don't wish to be found.

As for the Uganda lions, their silence was worthwhile. To some extent, the low profile maintained by these lions helped them to survive. People didn't hunt them and hardly even thought about them. Not infrequently in northern Uganda, my own bad planning would force me to grope my way over long distances through the wildest country in the middle of moonless nights, usually alone, seldom with a flashlight, never with a rifle. Occasionally on these dicey journeys I worried about a certain leopard who haunted our camp and was evidently contemplating my children — age two and four — but I never worried about lions.

Once I almost met the leopard. It was a dark, overcast night, and as happened embarrassingly often I had gotten lost without a flashlight and had spent about an hour groping around in the dark bush until I finally recognized the silhouette of a hill against the sky. It seemed to be the hill we had camped upon, and as I was making my way up a trail that I hoped led to my camp, the leopard coughed loudly ahead. "Waugh!"

He was, I realized, on the trail. He had coughed, I reasoned, to reveal himself, to show his presence, to give me plenty of warning so that I wouldn't come on him suddenly in close quarters. I think his idea was that I should change direction and go around him. He certainly didn't want me walking up to him, getting surprised and all upset and perhaps involving him in some impulsive reaction at close quarters.

But I couldn't oblige him. I couldn't get off the trail, since without the trail I would gave gotten lost in the dark again and then would have been wandering vaguely in deep bush with a leopard close behind me. No — the alternative was to keep going, even though it meant making straight for him, which I did. For just a moment, he said absolutely nothing. Then, sounding startled, as if he couldn't believe I was simply going to ignore him, he coughed again, much more forcefully. *"WAUGH! WAUGH!"* He thought I hadn't heard him!

But my own situation remained the same — I was in the wild, dark bush very near to a leopard and I didn't dare leave the trail. I had to reach my camp and my children about two hundred feet beyond him, so I still kept going. The leopard fell silent to listen. He would have heard my steps falter (because I so badly wanted to do as he said), but then he would have heard me stride forward with renewed determination. So he said no more. Instead, still in absolute silence, he stepped off the trail and let me go by. How near he let me come to him I never learned.

The Ugandan lions, in contrast, kept out of the way of people so well I never had a close encounter. Occasionally at night when I would be driving to my camp in a Land Rover, I would come upon the entire pride sitting in the road. Like a flock of pigeons they would fly off in all directions to escape. It might have been interesting to see what, over time, the lions would do about their new situation, but most of the lions, the leopards, and the other large predators are gone, gunned down for sport, first by the King's African Rifles, again by the Uganda Rifles, and yet again by Idi Amin's army and the invading armies that came in his wake. I suspect that any lions who may be there now are recent immigrants from the Sudan.

Between the late sixties and the mid-seventies, more lions of Botswana and South-West Africa (now Namibia) were displaced, for the same reasons that the lions of Dodoth county in Uganda were displaced. In the developing commercial farmlands of South-West Africa, almost all the lions were hunted out. But not quite all; some lions were still able to cling to life on remote farms as lone, cattle-killing fugitives. One, a big male with a black mane and distinctive footprints, made a name for himself — Jakob — for his near-human powers of reasoning and his exceptional elusiveness. Over the years, all the white hunters and most of the ranchers and farmers shot at Jakob, but the bullets didn't hit. The failures seemed sinister to the would-be assassins: they didn't see his breathtaking escapes as possible indications of Jakob's education or intelligence, rather, seeking the explanation in their own minimal educations, they attributed Jakob's escapes to Satan, his alleged protector.

Sad to say, Jakob was killed in 1986, though not by any of the loud-voiced, beer-swilling hunters and farmers with their incredible lion stories, their high-powered rifles, their hollow-point bullets, and their telescopic sights. No, Jakob was killed by a Bushman with a thirty-six-inch bow and a quarter-ounce poisoned arrow — with just one shot. Only a Bushman hunter would know how to stalk a lion like Jakob in the moonlight — or have the nerve, for that matter.

No one knows what happened to most of the displaced lions. Perhaps some of them managed to invade the territories of lions in areas that were only lightly disturbed. If so, the general lion population might have declined even more. When a lion population is in a state of flux and movement, with territories being invaded and prides of lionesses being gained and lost, the infant mortality rises. And when the dust clears after the battling and the infanticide, any given territory left to lions holds roughly the same number of lions it has always held. That is true of any animals who must own land.

In what was the western remnant of the lion nation, by now separated from the eastern section by a belt of farms and settlements about a hundred miles wide, an effort was made to preserve some of South-West Africa's wildlife by the creation of Etosha National Park, which was formally established in 1958. To the eternal credit of the government, the need for a park had been recognized much earlier — mainly because of Etosha Pan, which the park encloses. A national landmark on the order of Old Faithful or Niagara Falls, Etosha Pan is an impressive, shimmering white salt flat in the dry season and a shallow lake during the rains and has for some years been an international attraction. By the early seventies, farms surrounded much of Etosha Park, which had become a wildlife preserve of about 8,600 square miles of mixed bush desert, grassy savannahs, and mopane forests with widely spaced, scrubby little trees.

Because the park was created on a map with a pencil, its existence as such wasn't noticed at first by its original occupants. They, of course, were the Bushmen and the game. While farms were laid out around the park, life within its boundaries went on as before.

But after the Second World War, the park authorities took notice of the Bushmen and reasoned that Etosha would be a better, more natural place without a human population. Nothing much was done for a time — in the early fifties, many Bushman families still made their homes near the waterholes of Etosha — but as tourism began to grow, as tourist facilities were built and roadbeds were scraped so the tourists could drive to view the animals, the Bushmen became undesirable. They begged from the tourists and they hunted the game. It wasn't nice to be sitting in the privacy of your car, enjoying the majestic elephants and getting the feel of the wilderness, only to see tapping at your window a half-naked Bushman smiling hopefully and pretending to puff the tip of his finger as he begged for a cigarette.

By the 1960s, almost all the Bushmen had been evicted but not necessarily resettled. Apparently, little attention was paid to where they went or what they did. Since they had no formal education, vocational or otherwise, since they spoke none of the European languages, and since they were generally unfamiliar with Western customs and with money, alcohol, machinery, buildings, vehicles, roads, cities, and farms, their futures were grim. Only a few Bushman men remained in the park as trackers and camp servants to the white personnel. A few Bushman families became laborers on neighboring farms. But all the other Bushmen, perhaps five hundred or so, seem to have disappeared. So ended the old way in Etosha.

By 1986, when I visited Etosha, the Bushmen had been gone so long that their former presence was beginning to seem romantic. At least one young white park official had begun to reconstruct the old hunter-gatherer past. Although some of the evicted people were surely still alive somewhere, the official ferociously enjoined visitors to the park from disturbing any of their old campsites because these, he said, could have archaeological value. The official had also written a paper in which he gave translations of the old place names. But not convincing translations. In his paper, a waterhole that might have had a simple, classic name such as Gu Na (Big Waterhole) became something like The Place from Which You Can See if Anyone Is Coming from Keitseb. This young park official had as his servant a Bushman in his mid-fifties, a man who was almost certainly one of the people who had lived in the old camps. Because he was about my age, and because when my family first visited in the 1950s we had traveled to the Etosha area, I wondered if I had ever met him. But I didn't get a chance to ask. The official did not favor interracial fraternizing. Wherever the official went in his pickup, he took along his servant, who rode in the back, as if in apartheid times, uncomfortable and possibly in danger, looking ragged and threadbare among the prosperous tourists and very much alone.

In the 1980s I went to Etosha for a reason that had nothing to do with the Bushmen, or even with lions. I went because a friend named Katharine Payne had made the important discovery that elephants make calls too low for people to hear — calls that travel great distances and by which elephant herds that are far apart can keep in touch. Before Katy's discovery, people jokingly spoke of "elephant ESP." Since her discovery, hardly a reference is made to elephants that doesn't mention their infrasonic calls. While Katy was working to prove the existence of these calls, she invited me to join her research team. The work, sponsored by the National Geographic Society and the National Science Foundation, brought us at last to the wild elephants in Etosha, where we spent two seasons.

At first, we worked at a waterhole in Etosha called Gobaub, beside which Katy and her research team built an observation tower. Gobaub, which was far from the areas that tourists were allowed to visit, reminded me of /Gautscha. A wide, flat plain like the pan at /Gautscha surrounded the waterhole. The plain seemed to be the bottom of an ancient lake. Around its edge the old lakeshore rose to a rolling sandy expanse of heavy bush and mopane forests. The waterhole itself was a wide pool formed by a spring bubbling out of a ledge. The pool and its runoff provided drinking places for many animals, and their long trails approached it from all directions, like the spokes of an enormous wheel.

One night, as Katy and I were leaving the observation tower to go back to camp, we heard a great ruckus of roaring and screaming and of pounding, running feet. I shone a flashlight beam and saw, at a distance, a herd of about ten wildebeests facing a group of four lionesses, three of them ranged in a line behind the fourth, for all the world like three backfielders behind the center forward. Like soccer teams on a playing field after the whistle has blown, both sides were at a standstill. Whatever had happened was over, and the wildebeests were still in the game.

Remembering to be careful lest some predator who had watched us go up the ladder was waiting for us to come down, we left the tower, got into our van, and started slowly for the camp. At the first bend of the track, in a patch of heavy sand, the headlights shone on two full-grown but still adolescent male lions sitting very still and very straight, intently watching the place where the disturbance had been. Not wanting to alarm them, I dimmed the lights as the van labored slowly around them. They turned and looked at us.

Then, suddenly, to our astonishment, they launched themselves at us and, tails high, began to chase us, one on each side of the van. Bounding along like two huge dogs, they seemed to be snatching at the tires. Fearing that we would soon be wobbling feebly on the rims while two adolescent lions tried to pull us through the windows, I floored it. The struggling van lurched forward, the lions fell behind, and in the rearview mirror I saw the distance widening. In my last glimpse of them they were standing in the road, somewhat crestfallen but still much interested, watching us go.

I was flabbergasted. I, who had spent so many nights sleeping on the open ground in the Kalahari and so many more nights lost in the bush in Uganda, had never dreamed of being chased by lions. No such thing would ever have happened at /Gautscha. The Ju/wasi would not for one moment have tolerated being chased or played with or harassed in any way by lions — not in the past and not today.

Then I saw how stupid I had been, and how deeply I had misunderstood Gobaub and Etosha. The beautiful, dry country, the white grass, the clear sky, and the sight every evening of the setting red-ball sun had all misled me. I had been seeing everything as if I were still in /Gautscha thirty years earlier. But it wasn't the same at all. The animals of Etosha didn't know people. Perhaps never before had that population of animals known so little about people. But the people who would have taught the animals were gone.

The people were gone, and the old way was finished. If the authorities had decided that the park would be more natural without lions and had removed them, their absence would not have been more glaring than the absence of human hunter-gatherers after half a million years. As soon as I realized that, I no longer saw the similarities between Gobaub and /Gautscha but, rather, the differences. At /Gautscha, time and rainfall had managed the ecosystem; in Etosha, as we soon learned, the ecosystem was managed so thoroughly by the Department of Nature Conservation that the place sometimes seemed like a farm. The populations of animals were continuously monitored and controlled. The lion population was controlled to some extent by means of long-lasting contraceptive devices implanted under the skin of some of the lionesses. Those lionesses had grown old without having offspring, and after the drug wore off they might be too old to raise and educate offspring. If so, the experience of these lionesses would be lost — a situation more serious than might at first appear, for a lion needs to know a great deal to be able to meet the challenges offered by the environment, and especially the challenges, such as serious droughts, that happen only rarely. In such circumstances, the guidance of an experienced lion can mean the difference between life and death, not only at the time but for lions of the future, who, like links in a chain, will someday also benefit from and carry imparted information. For learning to take place, informed and uninformed lions must share an experience — for learning to take place about human beings, an inexperienced lion would have to watch the reaction of an experienced lion when a human being appeared. If the chain breaks — if there are no human beings to provide the occasion for instruction — the experienced lion has no way to pass on the information, and the information is lost. This important truth about the cat family (and indeed all animals who learn from one another) can be seen in housecats, if the human observer compares the overexcitement of adolescent kittens testing a new prey item on their own with the eager yet respectful manner in which the same kittens keep back and out of the way while an experienced mother cat shows them how it's managed.

In the case of the Etosha lions, it is impossible to guess the age of the imparted information that has now been lost. But a population of lions on the same land for generation after generation could have been passing information that might have been exceedingly old — hundreds or even thousands of years.

Much of the park's intense management was directed toward research, with the animals, of course, its subjects. In keeping with the hard-science trend in behavior biology, the park, which has in the past permitted invasive research on the animals, generally disapproved of unstructured observation, considering the results not measurable and therefore not worthwhile. Katy's work required complex equipment and had a "hard" aspect, in that we collected measurable sounds, and this contributed to our being allowed to work there. We were ordered never to name the elephants we studied, lest we appear sentimental; we were told to number them instead — a strange conceit along the line of white lab coats for scientists, evidently conjured to make scientists appear to be more scientific. Wild animals have no names, it is true, but they certainly have no numbers either. With this in mind we named the elephants anyway, despite the warnings, because names are much easier to remember than numbers.

On the shortwave radio that we had been ordered to keep on so that we would be in constant contact with the park authorities we couldn't help hearing, day and night, the doings of the park biologists as they darted, biopsied, branded, and tagged the game — especially the lions. If under the old way the lions and the hunter-gatherers had kept their distance from each other, under park management the people took such an interest in the lions that any lion could expect to be physically invaded sooner or later by a diagnostic procedure or a telemetric device. For the lions, that meant sudden, probably bewildering intrusions: a drug experience almost certainly followed by pain — the lingering burn of a brand, perhaps (not that pain seems to be much of a problem to lions). Most lions experienced such handling only rarely and hence had little need, or even incentive, to adjust. So the presence of the park personnel, though it changed the lions' lives, probably didn't make a difference that lions would recognize. Nothing that I could detect in the lions' attitudes suggested that they gave much thought to the presence of the park personnel.

What I did detect in the lions' attitudes was that they had no concept of the hunter-gatherers. After we moved our camp to a second, remote waterhole called Dungari, we found ourselves under intensive observation by the Dungari lions, who apparently didn't know what we were but wanted to find out. Like mice in a cattery, we could do nothing without first checking to see whether we were safe from them. Three of us — Katy, her daughter Holly, and I — first visited Dungari to learn if elephants used the water, which at Dungari was provided by the park in a large concrete trough kept full by a solar pump. Dungari was just a place in the woods, really — not a great flat plain with a natural well like /Gautscha or Gobaub. Nevertheless, lions were there, as we began to notice after dark, when, in the van, we started a twenty-four-hour vigil. With me in the driver's seat, Katy in the passenger's seat, and Holly in the back seat, we thought we were watching carefully and seeing everything, so we were more than surprised when the face of a lioness suddenly appeared by Katy's shoulder, framed in the right front window. How had so big a creature managed to creep up on us?

A lion had come with her, we soon learned, but

of the two she was the more curious. He was more or less hiding and seemed to be waiting for her to do something. What that might be we weren't sure. We suspected that she might be hunting us, though; it seemed that every time we looked out the window her head would pop up beside the van.

Of course, after we realized she was around and was probably hunting us, I kept trying to find her with the flashlight. I picked up the eyeshine of many other animals, and I often spotted her large, tawny form near at hand, but very seldom could I spot her blazing green eyes. At first, I couldn't understand why. But then it came to me that she might be concealing her eyeshine by averting her eyes. Because she was usually facing us when I spotted her, I began to think she was catching us in her peripheral vision and consciously avoiding a direct look. But why? Do lions know that their eyes shine? Lions' eyes shine in moonlight and even in starlight. Moonlit eyeshine can be by far the most conspicuous feature of a lion at night, especially of a lion hiding in the grass. If a lion should see another lion's eyes shining, could it then infer that its own eyes might also shine? The fact is, we haven't the slightest idea whether lions could make such a deduction.

My own feeling is that they can and do, because cats know so much about eyes, eyesight, and visual perception, as the following observation of a housecat demonstrates. One evening, our son, Ramsay, was sitting on his livingroom sofa when he noticed his cat Buster on the far side of the room, creeping along the wall. Because Buster sprays at night, he is put outside, but because he sprays to claim for himself the parts of the house that he fears will fall to his rival, the family's other male cat, Eddy, he wants to stay inside where he can stand up to Eddy. Therefore, when darkness gathers, to avoid being put outdoors Buster tries to elude the human members of the family. So Buster was creeping along because he had seen Ramsay and was trying to cross the room without being noticed.

At one point, an armchair in the middle of the room blocked Ramsay's view of the cat, and at that point, the cat vanished. Because the armchair was in the middle of the room and the cat had been ten feet away against the wall, Ramsay grew puzzled. Where was the cat? Very quietly Ramsay stood up so that he could see over the chair, and to his surprise saw the cat crouched against the wall, ears low, craning his neck to peer in Ramsay's direction, like a cat in hiding, peeking around a corner. And it came to Ramsay that the cat was indeed hiding from him, using the distant armchair as a screen.

The episode shows very clearly that the cat knew where his body was and how it could be hidden, and had calculated Ramsay's line of sight accurately and from afar without benefit of eye contact. A person in a comparable situation would have felt exposed.

The lions began a more intensive investigation

of us when we came to stay at the Dungari waterhole, and they were later joined by two other lionesses. I was quite moved to realize that their investigation of us resembled ours of them. At night, through the fence of a horse camp that the park authorities had urged us to use, the lions watched us sleep, just as during the day we watched them sleep. As we examined their sign, they examined ours, following our tracks to our various latrines, which they unearthed. Our sign meant something to them: frequently, they left their scats beside ours and squirted their marks over the traces of our urine. In other ways, too, they seemed to do what we did. One day, I was sitting near the solar pump at Dungari watching a lioness who lay by the water. She was near enough that I would need to get to safety if she stood up, so I was trying to be careful and not forget her. She was watching me in an equally casual manner. But the day was warm and the air was soft, so it was hard to sustain anxiety. In time, I yawned. To my amazement, without taking her eyes off me she also yawned. Was it a coincidence, her enormous red gape? Was it empathy? Fascinated, I deliberately yawned again. She yawned again! I yawned again and again. But I had done it too quickly. She simply watched me through half-shut eyes. I waited two or three minutes and then yawned once more. She yawned right away. More than excited, I called the other people so that they could see what was happening. One last time, the lioness obliged us with an empathetic

216

yawn. Then, seeing that several of us had gathered to stare at her, she suddenly seemed to get self-conscious; looking irritated, she got up and left.*

Perhaps this lioness had been studying me. Not long afterward she stalked me. Once, when I didn't think she was around, I walked several hundred yards from the safety of our study area to collect some equipment. As I circled through the heavy bush, someone in the study area noticed the lioness creeping stealthily toward me and called to me to come back. So I did, remembering to walk as the Ju/wasi had taught me, and here I am to recommend the method.

If she had caught me, would she have killed me? Quite possibly, but not necessarily for food. Cats after all learn much about their future prey by playing with the first few specimens they acquire. They learn how much stamina their victims have, whether they bite, and how fast they move, among other interesting facts. So to pursue her observation of our kind, the lioness probably would have played with me, which could have injured me pretty badly if it didn't kill me.

That same season Katy had an experience that must be unique among field biologists who study

---

*She was not the only large felid to engage in empathetic yawning. A young white circus tigress named Taji in New Jersey did the same thing in response to an accidental yawn from me. I yawned, she yawned, we paused, time passed, then she yawned hugely and watched me closely, perhaps wondering if I'd keep it up. For some reason I didn't, but I wish I had.

large animals. It happened at night in a tourist area of Etosha, near a waterhole that is illuminated by floodlights like the stage in a theater, where in reverent silence the tourists watch the comings and goings of the game. On one side is an area where visiting researchers are allowed to make their camps, and there Katy had put her sleeping bag right next to a length of fence made of light-weight wire. Katy is one of the most sensitive people I have ever known, as fully attuned to the natural world as Ju/wasi. In the middle of the night she woke and looked up into the face of a huge maned lion, who was sitting on his haunches, intently looking down at her. He was on the far side of the fence, but right up against it, and could easily have jumped over it or gone around the end of it or broken through it. He could also have walked through a large gap nearby, where two sections of fence had come unjoined. He looked and looked at Katy. She looked and looked at him, hearing the wet noises of him swallowing his saliva and settling his tongue. He was thinking of eating. Cats are famous for their patience — the big lion watched Katy while the moon slowly rose behind him, shone through his golden mane which the wind was stirring, slowly climbed to the top of the sky, and shone down on both of them. All this time Katy held his gaze and lay perfectly still. The lion continued to think of eating. Eventually, he drooled. Moonlit strings of saliva stretched from his tongue to the ground. Still Katy lay motionless. The sky began to get light. For the first time, the lion looked away. Then he looked back at Katy, then he slowly stood up and turned sideways. Stiff from sitting so long in one place, he stretched. Then he walked away.*

Did the fact that Katy held the lion's gaze save her? Possibly so. Eye contact has much meaning to the cat tribe, as foresters in the Indian Sundarbans discovered through efforts to protect local woodcutters and honey hunters from the Sundarbans' notorious man-eaters. The foresters found that the tigers wouldn't attack a person wearing a mask on the back of his head. Ordinarily, the tigers would attack from behind, leaping on the person's back and seizing him with a death bite to the nape of the neck. But no tiger would attack head-on. Thus the staring eyes of the mask inhibited the tigers, some of whom followed the woodcutters and honey hunters anyway, snarling at them as if angered to be cheated of their prey. According to the science writer Sy Montgomery, who has done some astonishing research in the Sundarbans,† the tigers soon learned that the masks were an illusion and began to attack people anyway.

Katy's interpretation of her experience is illuminating, or so it seems to me. "I kept trying not to move, but of course I knew the lion must have been aware of my breathing," she says. "I

*Personal communication from Katy.
†Sy Montgomery, *Spell of the Tiger* (Boston: Houghton Mifflin, in press).

got cramps all over from trying to hold still and knew I wasn't succeeding. So I knew that if I survived, it wouldn't be because the lion was deceived but because he understood that I respected him."

Was he the same lion who, at the age of twelve in 1993, killed and ate a tourist? At the same waterhole, in the floodlit tourist area, a young man from Germany had, like Katy, been sleeping on the ground when a lion and a lioness killed and ate him. According to statements issued by the park authorities, the incident was the first of its kind, and in a way it may have been, since the young man was probably the first *tourist* to be killed by lions. But according to information given to me in the 1980s, he was not the first person to be attacked or killed, by any means. In 1986 or '87, a SWAPO guerrilla trying to penetrate Namibia from Angola was allegedly killed by lions and may not have been the only guerrilla to lose his life in this manner. (Another possibility is that he was killed by people, maybe by the police in an effort to extract information from him, and the killing was blamed on lions.) Whatever happened, the lions were generally credited with maintaining the park as a military-free zone, although that, too, is hard to believe, since SWAPO guerrillas would have carried weapons. The other lion victims of Etosha were park employees who for one reason or another had had to travel on foot through the dangerous bush. Foot travel is strictly forbidden to everyone, to park personnel as well as to tourists. Tourists are enjoined to stay in their cars no matter what happens to them, so any foot travel is undertaken only by park personnel and only on the rare occasions when their vehicles break down.

The absence of the hunter-gatherers from Etosha showed in the habits of lions as well as in their obvious unfamiliarity with people. Many a waterhole in the park, for instance, was the headquarters of a pride of lions. The Etosha lions had the misleading reputation of being waterhole hunters, with the implication that they needed only to wait for their prey to come for a drink. This wasn't so, of course; never stupid, the prey animals don't drink where they can't see, don't drink at night, and would drink elsewhere or forgo drinking if they had reason to think that lions would seize them at the water. No, the lions of Etosha had to hunt the hard way, like lions everywhere. So no one really knows why they liked to stay near the waterholes. Yet lions are excellent observers, and observation is important to them — hence their empathy. Other cats learn by practicing; for instance, the hunting skills of kittens of cheetahs and housecats are sharpened by their mothers, who bring them live animals to kill. But lions learn mainly by following their mothers, aunts, and grandmothers and watching how it's done. The warthog lesson observed by my brother was an exception. Most of the animals hunted by lions are too big to be transported and too dangerous to be released for the cubs.

So from childhood onward, observation is a useful tool for lions, as it is for all the cats, and perhaps explains why lions station themselves at waterholes, where they can't help but observe the herds that pass by. Perhaps they preselect victims. They certainly get to know the animals individually; their techniques of observation are not that different from the techniques of field biologists whose job is also to know individuals well. Perhaps, however, lions merely note the general condition of the herd and its direction of travel. Anyway, whether or not the practice of waterhole viewing helps lions with hunting, the practice of sitting near a waterhole means that lions don't have to walk far for a drink. Even this could mean a lot to lions, since, like most animals, they suffer from dehydration and need water when they exercise in hot weather.

That's why lions mostly stay still by day. But they can't always. Once near the waterhole at Gobaub we watched a lion and a lioness having sex. Hour after hour they went at it, experiencing one climax after another that would wring from the lion a touching, high-pitched *meow*. The lioness, though, would bellow out a thundering roar, then would twist herself around and smash the lion in the face with the full strength of her powerful arm. As her blow snapped his head to the side he'd shut his eyes, grimacing. After several hours and well over fifty climaxes (I was keeping score but had to stop because elephants approached and we needed to collect some data) both lions got up, walked side by side down to the water, and refreshed themselves with a drink. Although he started drinking before she did, by the time they finished, their tongues were touching the water synchronously. Then they walked together back to their spot, where she raised her hips, frowning; he mounted, thrust, and *meowed;* she roared, turned, and hit him, and they were off again.

The truly interesting thing about waterhole viewing, as I saw it, was not so much that the Etosha lions did it but that the /Gautscha lions hadn't done it. Just as at /Gautscha the presence of the hunter-gatherers' camps appeared to keep the animals at a distance from the water, so in Etosha the absence of people's camps may have allowed the animals to come near. From the archaeological sites that the young official had forbidden us to touch I learned that the hunter-gatherers of Etosha had favored the same kinds of places as the hunter-gatherers of the /Gautscha area. That was perhaps not surprising. What was surprising was that those sites were also favored by the lions. Sometimes the lions of Gobaub chose the very spots where people once had lived. Sometimes the lions chose spots that people would have chosen. In fact, I soon found that as often as not I could locate the lions of Gobaub, even in that vast space, merely by looking around for places that I felt the /Gautscha people of the old days would have liked. I would search with my field glasses for a shady place without too many stones and screened from view on the raised ground around the edge of the plain. There were many such places near Gobaub, and in most of them, at one time or another, we might see a pair of round ears above the grass or spot a sleeping lion. What did it mean? It meant, I think, that the lions had taken over those good places soon after the people had gone.

Seeing that, I felt that I was looking through a window at the distant past. Long ago, in the northern hemisphere, cave lions would have used the same good caves that their human hunter-gatherer rivals used and would have competed for these caves in much the same way as the Gobaub lions competed for the good campsites with the Bushmen. Good caves are scarce, and the lions would have needed them as much as the human beings, for exactly the same reason — any mammal with altricial young in the far north during glacial times needed meaningful shelter, a place where helpless infants could be kept warm. To be sure, the campsites of Gobaub were not as essential as the caves of the north — life for either species could have gone on in less attractive campsites. But cats and people have similar tastes in residences, or cats perceive the good qualities of our residences, so that all over the world there are many examples of cats trying to share with us. The humble female puma of Malta, Idaho, for instance, brought her three surviving children to a long-abandoned farmhouse and took shelter in the empty kitchen. And in India today, the palatial hunting lodges at Ranthambhore built centuries ago by the maharajahs of Jaipur have since changed ownership. Abandoned by their princely owners and overgrown by jungle, these palaces now lodge certain tigers, the original emperors of those forests, who have taken the shady palaces as their residences and stretch out on the cool stone floors.

Long ago, around the southern shores of the Mediterranean, little African wildcats took shelter in people's dwelling places, probably finding the supply of mice and rats and the escape from heavy rains much to their liking. There they stayed. Perhaps they even liked the warmth of people's fires. The earliest cat known is from Jericho (now Israel) nine thousand years ago when one of the few amenities that people had that might attract a cat was fire.

I saw an example of this attraction in 1989 in Bushmanland after I had been there quite a long time and thought I knew most of the creatures of the area, certainly the domestic animals — the cattle and dogs, the horse and the donkey that had become part of Bushman husbandry. I visited the Bushman village late one cold night and was amazed to see a black-and-white housecat crouching by someone's campfire. The Bushmen don't keep pets, and forty miles of empty veldt separated the village at /Gautscha from any other human habitation. So who was this cat? And where was he from? No one knew the answers. He belonged to no one; he was feral. Few people ever even saw him, except on those rare occasions when he crept out of the night to get warm.

My heart went out to the Etosha lions, although their size and might, combined with their naiveté about our species, could be frightening. Once, I was charged by a lioness, and then I felt in awe of the hunter-gatherers who, so long ago, had commanded the respect of lions. I was charged while doing just what the Ju/wasi would have done to move a lioness; she had been sitting right beside some of our equipment, which I had come in our van to collect, and when she wouldn't move I got out and slowly picked up a pebble. Then, speaking very respectfully because I could already see displeasure in her eyes, I gently tossed the pebble as I asked her to please leave. *Whap!* She charged! In the blink of an eye she had covered the distance between us. Luckily I had gotten out of the driver's door, which slammed, rather than the side door, which slid. How would the early hunter-gatherers have wrested respect from an animal like this? And without vans to jump into? If the lions of long ago had in any way resembled the lions of today, their respect would have been hard to come by. The lions in Etosha seemed to respect nothing but other lions.

And of course, elephants. The Etosha lions kept away from elephants much as the /Gautscha lions had once kept away from the Ju/wasi. In Etosha, if lions and elephants met, the lions became more than respectful — or most of them did. One night, one of our group saw an adolescent male lion, tail high, rushing an elephant, but the lion probably wasn't entirely serious, because he gave up quickly. In an East African lion story — the personal communication of a reliable witness — a certain lion once crouched down in the grass to hide from elephants coming from his right. Apparently, he hadn't seen that they were on their way to greet other elephants, coming from his left. Before he could decide what to do, he was surrounded. He then threatened an elephant to try to make her back off and give him a way out of the closing circle. All the elephants were startled to see a lion in their midst, and they roared, screamed, and threatened him. In the excitement, he felt forced to attack, so, leaping at the nearest elephant, he clung to her head. She plucked him off, dashed him to the ground, and killed him — the only possible outcome, really, of a conflict involving a lion and an elephant.

I saw only one encounter between the Gobaub lions and an elephant. The encounter ended very quickly and as encounters go was minimal — a nonevent, really. Yet it stayed with me. Probably I would have learned nothing at all from it if I hadn't first seen the same lions in the same place with a rhino. The rhino was a rather belligerent female, who, with her large child at her heels, often came to drink soon after dark. One moonlit night when the lions were relaxing in the open near the runoff, the rhino seemed to take exception to their presence and she charged. The lions seemed hardly to notice. To my amazement, they did nothing at all until the rhino was almost on top of them, and then, very casually, they got to their feet and, with unbelievable aplomb, moved gracefully toward her, stepping aside at the very last moment to let her charge through. As soon as she was among them, they seemed to flow around her like water around the prow of a boat, to reassemble behind her armored rump. Seeming not to know what had happened, she cantered on for a while before she realized that no one was there. The lions barely glanced at her, as if they had hardly so much as a passing thought for her. They looked, in fact, as if they already knew much about this rhino, as if they had developed their coordinated, dancelike tactic just to avoid her and had practiced the maneuver many times before.

In contrast was the encounter between these lions and an elephant. One evening soon after the lions had been charged by the rhino, they were lying in the same place, a pile of tan bodies behind a fallen log which hid them from the plain. I was watching some of them peer over the log at a zebra who was considering drinking from the runoff when I saw them stiffen, then get up and move apart. Far away, elephants had appeared at the edge of the trees. It seemed to me that the lions recognized these particular elephants. A big adolescent male elephant, about sixteen or seventeen years old, left the others and strode toward the lions with his head high, his ears wide, his tail and trunk up. Although he was at least fifty yards from them, the uneasy lions were watching him intently. For just a moment, the maned lion stood his ground. Then, with his legs braced and his head high, he gave a roar. The elephant answered with a roar of his own. The lion roared once more, which brought the elephant onward at a run. This was more than enough for the lions. Without a sound, they turned tail, scattered like a flock of sparrows, and vanished. In the same way — if not, perhaps, as quickly — would the Kalahari lions once have disappeared before an advance of the Ju/wasi.

Today, even the Bushmanland lions don't give ground to people in the same way as before. The respectful behavior once displayed by the people toward the lions cannot be depended upon either. This is surely because the old way is fading in Bushmanland, and neither the lions nor the people are sure of their positions anymore. Typical of the new way was a recent photo in a Windhoek newspaper showing two white people, a lion biologist/conservation officer, and his most recent girlfriend, posing astride a dead or anesthetized Bushmanland lion under the caption "The wild pair."

Today, after a wrenching period of transition from their former lives as hunter-gatherers, many of the Ju/wasi are trying to live as subsistence farmers in permanent villages with cattle. Such a village, with about sixty cattle, stands on the eastern rim of /Gautscha Pan, above the waterhole. In the veldt around this village, the lions are trying to live too. To do so, they seem to be changing their culture.

The /Gautscha people became aware of this one dark night — oddly, at about the same time I was charged by the lioness in Etosha. On that night, two Ju/wa men and my brother, John, who since 1978 had been spending most of his time living at /Gautscha to help establish Ju/wa farming, were returning to the village in a pickup when the headlights caught the eyeshine of ten or fifteen lions in a patch of heavy thornbush just across the road from the cattle pen. Not liking the look of such a large group of lions so near the cattle, my brother stopped the pickup and everyone got out. As in the old days, he and the Ju/wa men moved slowly and purposefully toward the crouching, staring lions, thinking to get them up and moving.

However, these lions didn't react in the old way. Instead, one — a lioness — began to roar. But rather than give a deafening shout, as if to say "Back off!" she began a very loud, prolonged, classical series of roars, such as one might hear from a lion at night, far away — something like this: *Uuuuuuwaugh. Uuuuuuuuuuuuuoooooooooowaugh. Uuuuuuuuuoooooooooh! Uuuuuuuuoooooooooong! Uuuuoooowaugh! Uuuoo, uaooo, uaooh, ooogh, ooogh, aangh, unh, unh.* But the most interesting thing was that just before the earsplitting climax, as the roars rose to a series of deafening bellows and earth-shaking hollers, other lions joined the first. Many lions roared in chorus. They were like the lions at the Kavango cattle post, whose choral roaring had so badly frightened my mother and me many years before. Needless to say, my brother and the other men stopped in their tracks. In the terrifying, echoing silence that followed, the men stood motionless. Suddenly, the roaring began again, first one voice, then a chorus. Again came a profound silence, and again the roars. Four times, one lion started the roaring and other lions joined the chorus while the men stood absolutely still. After the fourth chorus, the silence lasted so long that the men began to inch back toward the pickup. When they got inside and turned on the headlights, the lions were gone.

Why were the modern /Gautscha lions so different from their predecessors? To loiter at the village as if they didn't care who saw them, and not to move off at the approach of the men, showed that they had changed their ways. Yet the choice of meaningful vocalizations instead of physical violence showed that they were forming customs of their own, different from those of the Etosha lions. Why?

The choral roaring could have been intended to show the size and solidarity of their group, which a listener would ascertain from the volume and the number of voices. A massive choral assault might be useful when two groups of lions meet if the ownership of a resource is in question. Almost certainly, the /Gautscha lions meant to show my brother and the Ju/wa men that the human claim on the area, with its resident cattle, would no longer go unchallenged. In contrast to the silent

Uganda lions, who showed their deference to human territorial claims by refraining from roaring, as if they were fugitives on the land of other lions, the /Gautscha lions made it clear they would not leave without protest just because some people wanted them to go. Yet the old days weren't quite forgotten; evidently the lions had enough feeling for the ancient truce not to savage the men, as any of the Etosha lions almost certainly would have done.

But the Etosha lions were in a stable situation — at least from their point of view. For them, the past was lost. In contrast, the /Gautscha lions were in a period of transition. The old way must have lingered in the memories of the older lions, memories that they seemed to use when trying to cope with the violent economic and social changes that threatened to overtake them.

Since the late 1960s, in the eastern section of Namibia's Kalahari, the area now called Bushmanland, enviromnental productivity had been diminishing. By the seventies, Bushmanland had lost two of its three permanent waterholes to Bantu pastoralists and had lost its western territory to farms. In the remaining portions, overgrazing by livestock, ruts made by vehicles, and the prevention of fire had reduced the vegetation in some places to thornbushes on hard sand. Legions of South African hunters with automatic rifles and all-terrain vehicles had all but eliminated the wild populations of many water-independent grazing animals to make jerked meat, or biltong. Gemsboks had become rare, and elands had virtually vanished. Factories to process the meat and skins had become a big business around the Kalahari. And hundreds of miles of fencing had prevented thousands of grazing animals — giraffes and wildebeests in particular — from reaching their sources of seasonal water. They died trying, and their dry corpses lie beside the fence.

After our first season of elephant research in Etosha, I went to /Gautscha. Unlike the rest of my family, who had continued to work there, I hadn't been back for thirty years. I came alone from Windhoek in a rented pickup, a drive of three hundred miles, and stopped for gas at the only gas pump in Bushmanland. It stands at the edge of the Kalahari, before the track leads to the interior from the administrative center called Tsumkwe. But the gas pump was closed, so I had to wait, and as I waited, I looked around.

Once Tsumkwe was just a tree in the middle of an endless wilderness, a huge baobab that still dominates the town. Almost forty years earlier, my father and his friend Claude McIntyre had made the track that led there from the last place within the farming area, the town of Grootfontein. They had mapped the area, and they had dug a well. Since then, the current administrator had built his house in the shadow of the tree and had capped the well, thus dominating the only evident source of water in many miles of hot, thornbush savannah. Remembering the water from long ago, and noticing a faucet where the well had been, I got a cup from my pack and went to drink from it. But evidently there were rules about that faucet. A German guest of the administrator's emerged from the house to tell me that the faucet was private and that I couldn't draw water there. Very surprised to be refused water in that arid climate, under the blazing sun, from a well dug by my own father, I left, still thirsty.

It gave me a strange feeling to stand alone in the middle of the road, part of which I myself, at the age of nineteen, had pioneered in a jeep. Now, a few widely spaced, boxlike houses stood far back from the extra-wide road, which went straight for the horizon where the wind stirred dust devils. Thornbush and sand were what the herds of government livestock had made of that segment of the Kalahari. The barren landscape was hung with dust.

As I waited, a few people passed by. All of them looked at me. Some were young Ju/wa people on foot; others were white people in vehicles. Of course, no one knew me — in fact, some of the whites looked at me with considerable suspicion. And perhaps not unreasonably — I was a gray-haired woman alone, wearing dusty clothes, seated upon what passes these days for a running board, and there was no reasonable explanation for my presence. No one spoke to me, although every

Ju/wa person met my eyes, serenely checked my face to see if it held racial rudeness, and upon finding my expression acceptable, nodded kindly. Apparently the administration had not been able to erase the intense, humanitarian courtesy that the Bushmen had practiced in the old days. In contrast, the whites — or my own people, so to speak — stared scornfully once they realized that I was a stranger.

At last the hour of siesta came to an end and the storekeeper returned to the store and opened the pump. As he filled the tank of my pickup, I heard a scraping sound and noticed in the distance a Bushman man, dressed in a coverall, beginning to rake the yard of one of the administration buildings. Every few minutes he would stop raking and look at me intently. And then, as I watched, he let the rake fall and began to walk toward me. On and on he came, not following the road but walking straight across the intervening yards, paying so little attention to the white government's innovations that he passed right between two of the whites themselves — administrative personnel who were waiting near their vehicle for a turn at the gas pump. They might have been a pair of posts. A few feet away from me, the Ju/wa man stopped, looked me right in the face and said, "You're Di!ai."

And I was. Thirty-seven years before, Di!ai had been the name the Ju/wasi had given me. But who was the man? And how had he recognized me at all, let alone from such a distance and over all the years? I had had no way of telling people I

237

was coming, so it wasn't that anyone had been expecting me.

What little of the language I had ever known had more or less deserted me, but I began to grope for words. Realizing this, and seeing my amazement, he laughed. Then, very carefully, in a sort of pidgin baby talk suitable to my incapacity, he told me his name and his parents' names, and, after racking my brain to put all this together, I realized that when this man and I had last seen each other, he had been a little child.

Ever since I had been in the Kalahari, I had thought about the Ju/wasi I had known, remembering them, speaking of them, often dreaming about them, always wondering what this or that individual might be doing and what was happening in their world. But never once had I thought about the very young children. In those years, before my maternal instincts had rightly gotten started, children under five or six seemed devoid of interest and were little more than scenery to me. What an injustice I had done the Ju/wa babies! I laughed. Then I cried, probably because I had learned so much about life in the intervening years but evidently not everything. Then I laughed again. The man waited, smiling. I told him where I was going. He said he'd go with me.

Remembering the rake, I said I'd wait for him to finish what he had been doing. He said that wouldn't be necessary. So we got into the pickup and banged the doors and together drove to /Gautscha.

A large number of elephants had come to live in Bushmanland, where before there had been none. Vitally all were males between the ages of fourteen and fifty. Most of them seemed to know one another, and many had bullet wounds in their bodies or bullet holes in their ears. No one — neither the Ju/wasi nor the government's conservation officers — knew who these elephants were or where they had come from, since no elephants had ever been more than transient, seasonal visitors to Bushmanland before. In my opinion, the bullet holes suggested that the elephants were refugees from war, culls, or poaching, and the fact that very few females or young were with them suggested that they had made a difficult journey from very far away. Even more moving and more interesting, if possible, is that they materialized in Bushmanland very inconspicuously. Elephants had not been seen roaming at random through farms and towns, searching aimlessly for

239

somewhere to stay. These elephants had known about Bushmanland and had zeroed in on it. How so many of them knew where to go is less clear.

Bushmanland was not a haven for them, no matter how far they had come or how difficult the journey had been. Their presence quickly attracted a repulsive hoard of millionaire hunters, mostly men from North and South America and Europe who were eager to pay immense sums of money to the Department of Nature Conservation, which, incredible as it seems considering the endangered status of elephants, sells licenses to rich sportsmen for the pleasure of killing the elephants. The department encouraged these hunters to buy licenses to kill as many different kinds of animals as possible, so these sportsmen shot lions too.

Loss of habitat, shortages of food, and being hunted were some of the general problems faced by all the lions of Bushmanland. However, the /Gautscha lions also had to cope with a change in their water supply. The waterhole was never meant to supply the sixty cattle that by 1982 were in /Gautscha. Two years later, halfway through a severe eight-year drought, the waterhole was dug out in an effort to increase the water supply. After that, a deep well was drilled at a distance, fitted with a pipe, a pump, and a trough. The new well was accessible only to human beings. Meanwhile, elephants began to haunt the waterhole — by the time I visited, six or seven huge male elephants would be at the edge of the pan every evening, waiting for dark before moving their enormous,

240

conspicuous selves out of what little concealment the bushes gave them and coming to the water to drink. But the cattle, who drank from the waterhole in the afternoon, would have used all the water, and nothing but mud was left. So the huge, thirsty elephants, who needed about forty gallons of water apiece, would stand all night by the waterhole taking little sips as the water oozed in. It hurt to watch their subdued desperation. And it hurt to see that not much water was left for any other creatures.

Nor was it safe to approach when the elephants were drinking. At the time of my visit, two huge male elephants, one in musth, also haunted the pump by the cattle trough, trying to work out some way to get water from it. One night a young man, a foreigner who had been working with the Bushmen, thought to chase them off. Knowing how dangerous a musth elephant can be, I and other people of the small community at /Gautscha beseeched the young man to leave the elephants alone, especially since the tents, the vehicles, and the little mud houses, which were the only shelter any of us had, would offer no protection whatever against an angry elephant. But even though all of us were vastly more experienced than this young man, and even though I for one had just partic-ipated in a long-term study of elephants and could point out the symptoms of musth exhibited by this stupendous individual, the young man paid no at-tention to our warnings or appeals. Instead, he got out a police whistle, flounced busily up to the elephants, and blew an annoying blast.

Whatever had made this young man think that an irritating noise from a little primate like himself could frighten away a monstrous, experienced male elephant twice his age, an elephant with bullet holes in his ears, desperate with thirst, and revving on testosterone? Bellowing out a terrible roar, the elephant charged. The young man turned and ran straight toward us.

An elephant runs at thirty miles an hour. A person runs at fifteen miles an hour. The outcome of the chase seemed clear. The only question was where the once arrogant young man would be by the time the elephant caught him. If I had a rifle I know I wouldn't have shot the elephant. I love elephants, and this one wasn't at fault. But I might have been tempted to drop the young man before he led the elephant up to us. From reading Ernest Hemingway's "The Short Happy Life of Francis Macomber" for a course in American literature in college, I had learned that such crimes are not always punished. Anyway, by the time the elephant had finished with the young man, no one would have been able to find the bullet hole.

But the elephant was more merciful than I am. He wanted to frighten the young man, not to kill him. With no more effort than a person makes to swat a fly, he could have pulverized his tormenter, but he didn't. Towering above the running man, he suddenly stopped short, gave a snort, flapped his ears, and then, turning on his heel, he walked back to the pump where he could smell, but not drink, the water.

As for the lions, even in the face of so much change, they seemed to be keeping some of their old customs. Perhaps they were trying to keep the structure of their lives unchanged. More than many other animals, cats value sameness, and possibly lions resemble their little relatives in this preference. Sameness, after all, has enormous value to animals whose lives are close to the edge, whose food is unpredictable, and whose enemies include their own kind. Sameness helps a cat to remember things, and to a certain extent to predict the future. For example, by monitoring a certain cattle boma (corral) while patrolling his territory, a Kenyan leopard figured out the farmer's routine of visiting the boma for the purpose of collecting the calves who had been born during the month and moving them to safer quarters. The farmer habitually did this on the first Tuesday of the month, so the leopard made a point of visiting the boma on the preceding Sunday or Monday, and helping himself to a calf. Thus the leopard not only understood the farmer's complicated routine, but had developed his own routine in response, and by leaving as many days as possible for calves to accumulate in the boma, he minimized his chances of being discovered while maximizing his chances of finding a calf there to eat.*

*Mizutani, Fumi, "Home range of leopards and their impact on livestock on Kenyan ranches," in *Mammals as Predators*, N. Dunstone and M. L. Gorman, eds. (Oxford: Oxford Science Publications, 1993), pp. 425–39.

Housecats, too, value routine even if they realize no direct benefit from it. Our cats come home in the evening — a skill we taught them by rewarding them hugely for compliance. To us, their early homecoming has an advantage — at night our area is dangerous because of owls and coyotes — but the cats aren't afraid and would never come home because of predators. And they no longer come home because of the snacks — careless cat owners that we are, we have gotten used to their regular evening appearance and we usually forget to offer them even a single drop of cream. No, they come home for no better reason than habit. They even nudge me at dusk if I'm working in my office. It's time, they say.

Sameness is security to the cat family, especially if the sameness involves group activity. To our housecats, assembling at night means drawing together. Once indoors, they disperse, and would eventually go back out again if we let them. But their frustration at being confined all night does not outweigh their satisfaction in keeping the routine.

Like all cats, the /Gautscha lions probably valued sameness, which helps to explain why even after many years, some parts of their lives seemed unchanged. Their group, for instance, numbered thirty, the same as the group long ago. Also, the modern lions apparently rested in some of the old places — shady thickets in the bush southeast of the pan. And the lions still used an old game trail (on which, by the eighties, the tracks of vehicles had been superimposed) to travel between their resting places and the waterhole.

Some of their customs were new, however. For instance, they had apparently changed the size of their hunting parties. Although we didn't really know the size of their parties in the old days because we never saw them, we did find tracks and heard calling and answering that suggested that the lions favored groups of four, five, or six. In the eighties (albeit on somewhat impressionistic evidence), the lions seemed to prefer hunting in pairs. At least, this was so in any sightings. Perhaps the reason for this practice was the available prey. Although most of the large antelopes were gone, there were still kudus. Few were big or had long horns, as in the old days. Most were medium sized or smaller, but there were plenty of them, perhaps even more than before.* Duikers and steenboks were also present in reasonable numbers. But that was about all. Since there was little else to hunt, these small-to-mid-sized antelopes provided almost all of the food of the modern /Gautscha lions, who were thus in a situation similar to that of many tigers. Three lions could eat from a medium-sized kudu doe. Two lions could possibly make do with a steenbok or a large duiker. But if more lions were present, some might go hungry. Better to hunt in smaller groups to take the best

---

*Unfortunately I know no explanation for the kudu population; perhaps the kudus flourished in the absence of competitors, or perhaps the altered vegetation favored them.

advantage of the reasonably large supply of small-to-mid-sized prey.

Housecats are quite capable of changing specialties. In his early years, our cat Orion specialized in birds and would jump straight up, six or seven feet into the air, with one paw extended like an outfielder, to catch them as they flew down to a feeder. He later stopped hunting birds altogether and for one summer, as I have mentioned, took up the sport hunting of chipmunks. Toward the end of his rather short life (we believe he was killed by a coyote) he had shifted again, this time to mice and voles. If housecats can change their hunting preferences so readily for no apparent reason, why couldn't lions, especially lions with an excellent reason?

If a change in the food supply swayed the lions into adjusting their hunting style, the change in the water supply also caused new behavior. On the very first night of my visit to /Gautscha, I saw something I had never seen before: lions at the /Gautscha waterhole. Just a few hours after dark, six or seven lions appeared on the ledge of rock above it. But the waterhole was empty. Two elephants had drained it dry and were waiting for it to refill. On the ledge, the lions wove back and forth as if wondering what to do, then left all together, abruptly. I next saw them at the empty trough by the well where people had pumped water for the cattle in the afternoon. Although the trough was empty, the lions at last found water where the village dogs found water — in the muddy footprints of the cattle. They drank these dry, then left on the road.

Surely the biggest change in the environment, from a lion's point of view, was the introduction of cattle. When the cattle arrived in 1982, the lions, of course, killed some of them. But they didn't kill very many. For this there is no easy explanation. Although all cats are somewhat traditional in their hunting preferences, and though the cats seem to have different techniques for different kinds of prey, it simply does not seem possible that the lions didn't consider hunting the cattle from the moment they first became aware of them. One whiff of that dizzying, grassy scent would have set a lion's mouth watering. Nor were the cattle protected by the people — or, at any rate, not by day. By day, the cattle wandered far from the village under their own recognizance and came home each night of their own accord to a dung-filled pen fenced with a few strands of wire. Even I, in late middle age, could almost have jumped that particular fence; a lion would hardly have noticed it. By rights, considering the size of the pride, the absence of other food, and the cornucopia of opportunities, the lions should have killed a cow every few days. Yet for five years they didn't; they kept scouring the bushes for steenboks and duikers and, except for some very unusual instances, they left the cattle alone.

To me, this restraint was almost incomprehensible. While it is true that cats specialize in prey items, true that the leonine culture of the

/Gautscha area wasn't focused on cattle, and true that certain kinds of hunting techniques must be learned, lion populations have nevertheless responded to invasions by new species in far less time than five years. When in 1898 the Kenya Uganda Railway was built between Mombassa and Lake Victoria, certain lions of Tsavo learned to hunt the railroad workers soon after they had bridged the Tsavo River, and showed tremendous ingenuity in obtaining more than sixty of these unfortunate men. As housecats open gates and cupboard doors, the lions even opened the doors of railroad cars at night and crept quietly inside in quest of preselected victims.* Lack of ability is not a characteristic of lions, or indeed, of any of the cats.

And yet, in a way that I couldn't precisely define, the restraint of the lions seemed like the old days. Did the lions recognize the cattle as part of the human domain? A dog would. Are lions, those acute and empathetic observers, who in their own culture recognize certain kinds of ownership, less able than dogs to recognize ownership in other species? Unfortunately, we still know too little about lions (or any other animals) to answer these questions in any meaningful way.

Not everything was mysterious, however. The

*M. F. Hill, *Permanent Way* (East African Railways and Harbors, Nairobi, Kenya — no copyright notice — c. 1949), pp. 172–74. See also Lt. Col. J. H. Patterson, *The Maneaters of Tsavo* (Macmillan, 1927).

cattle themselves had much to do with their relative immunity from lion predation. When the pen was opened in the morning, the two or three cows who provided leadership wouldn't just start walking, as American cows might do, but instead would stand among the others for a while, as if waiting for something. Because they had long since eaten the grass near the village, the cattle might have been contemplating a number of grassy places a mile or more away. Eventually, they would choose one of those places and start walking toward it, always taking several precautions. At least when I was there observing them, they usually varied their direction, thus making their whereabouts unpredictable. They never left before the sun was high and always returned long before sunset, thus avoiding the times favored by the crepuscular lions. They always traveled in single file, especially through heavy cover, as infantry soldiers are taught to do in jungle warfare. And finally, they always stuck together. Once, when a young cow missed leaving with the others, she became panicky until, casting about, she found their scent and ran after them with her nose to the earth, like a hound.

To the Ju/wasi, accustomed to animals who knew what they were doing, the enterprising attitude of the cattle seemed to be the natural order of things — the old way. Might this not also have been true of the lions? The few times they had hunted cattle, the technique they had used was reminiscent of the past; a lioness came at night to roar repeatedly outside the pen, which caused the cattle to panic and lunge at the fence until they had jumped out or broken through, whereupon one of the lions killed one of them. The episode reminded some of us of the lioness whose roaring had frightened us long ago, because the roaring was of the same type — not the classical roaring that rises in a crescendo and falls away to grunts but a series of similar, loud, steady roars. I wondered if the lioness really intended to panic the cattle. Perhaps something else had induced her to roar. The cattle pen was precisely on the site of our old camp, and she had arrived from exactly the same place as her predecessor of thirty years before — from the trail that led from the southeast to the water. She also faced the same way while roaring. Was all this just coincidence? Or could the place itself mean something? On the plain, it was the high ground. Might that make it a good place to roar? We didn't know — we just listened nervously, as we had decades before. In response, the Ju/wasi built a thick thornbush barricade around the wire pen, but not with the thorns turned out against the lions, as one might expect. Instead, the Ju/wasi turned the thorns in against the cattle. That was to discourage stampeding and seemed to confirm the thought that the cattle had only themselves to blame if the lions caught them.

When I visited /Gautscha after our second season of research in Etosha, an event escalated the cattle killing by the /Gautscha lions. A new, young, farm-raised bull was brought to /Gautscha. There he met the enormous resident bull, Boesman (Bushman) — so named by his Ju/wa owner because of his impressive size and his unruffled demeanor. The new bull couldn't avoid being squeezed into the pen with Boesman during his first night. But in the morning, out of respect for Boesman and unaware of the danger of lions, the new bull stayed far behind the herd. That same morning, a pregnant cow began her labor. Because of the people's laissez-faire attitude, nobody noticed her, so she, too, went out with the other cattle, and she, too, lagged behind the herd. The cows who led the herd chose an unusual direction that morning — southeast, to the area where the lions sometimes spent the day. There the laboring cow began to give birth and soon caught the attention of two lionesses. They attacked her. The knowledgeable, experienced cattle left the scene immediately, but the new bull apparently tried to help the cow whom the lionesses were killing. The lionesses killed him too. They ate their fill and then went into the bushes and fell asleep.

That night, no one noticed at first that the cow was missing. But when the new bull failed to come home the people began a search. In the morning, they found the partly eaten carcasses — about half the cow, one little foot of the calf, and most of the bull. The people at once built a fire, cut a lot of the meat, and cooked it for a nourishing feast reminiscent of many such feasts inadvertently provided by lions in the old days. A party atmosphere prevailed. Afterward, the people cut the rest of the meat into strips and carried it home.

The lionesses, it turned out, were only about seventy feet away all the while, but, in the old way, they said nothing.

That evening the young man whom the elephant had chased persuaded some of the Ju/wa men to let him drive them to the site. He would provide light so that when the two lionesses returned to look for scraps the men could shoot them from the vehicle. Although the idea was that the Ju/wasi would stand in the open back of the pickup while the young man sat safely in the front seat, the Ju/wasi agreed, since they are fearless (and did not realize that the act would be illegal). But when the lionesses became vaguely aware of the poisoned arrows whispering by, they crept into the bushes uneasily. Later that night, I saw them trying to drink at the waterhole. A few days later, I went home. It was September.

The rest of the story was told to me by my brother, who was present. The rains had been scanty the year before and the drought was felt in October. Then a bad fire to the north, south, and west of /Gautscha Pan burned most of the grass. All the grazing animals were hungry, but the wild ungulates could leave the area and go to search for better grazing. The cattle, however, had to stay at /Gautscha, and they were especially hungry. One morning, a Ju/wa herdsman took the cattle to the southeast, where, perhaps because the cattle had been hesitant to venture there since the killing, some grass was still standing. After delivering his charges, the herdsman went hunting. Soon the cattle attracted the attention of the lions, who that day were all together, thirty strong. Among them, undoubtedly, were the two cattle-killing lionesses, with the memory of their September success fresh in their minds.

The cattle, too, would have remembered the episode. They presumably hadn't wanted to go back there in the first place. Anxious to leave, they split into two groups. So did the lions, apparently in order to follow the two groups of cattle, which went separate ways. That in itself was somewhat unusual. More unusual was the lions' method of attack. Evidently, instead of concentrating as one team upon killing and eating a single victim, many lions or teams of lions suddenly attacked many cattle simultaneously. Perhaps some lions or teams of lions slaughtered many cattle in the first group and then moved on to the second group, or perhaps each group of lions slaughtered many of the group of cattle it had been following. Whatever happened, the veldt was strewn with corpses — eight together in one area and four more about a mile away. The next day, the people backtracked along the path taken by the surviving cattle and found twenty lions with the group of eight corpses and ten lions with the group of four. My brother, who was concerned about preserving the livelihood of the Ju/wasi, shot and killed two of the lions.

He suggests that the drought, the fires, and the resulting lack of grass made an unusual set of circumstances that caused the wild game to go elsewhere, leaving the lions no choice but to kill cattle.

He has no explanation for the method of killing — the massacre — and wonders if it will be repeated. As for the lions, they will long remember the details of their achievement, even though at the time it was apparently a lion excess, an exception to the rule. Indeed, they may try another massacre someday, even though the first cost two of them their lives. After all, they aren't cowards. So far, however, that hasn't happened. Even before the rains came and the grass grew back, the surviving lions returned to their customary abstemiousness. At the time of this writing, they kill cattle only rarely and only by their former desultory methods. No one knows why.

PART THREE

New Ways

Born of the Eocene, cats have picked their delicate way into all continents except Australia, arranging themselves around the world in their fluid, rose-shaped territories, surviving in all climates except at the poles. Creatures of the edge, skilled hunters whose only food is meat they or their mothers kill, most cats are rare wherever they are found. Pressure from the burgeoning human population makes many kinds of cats much more rare; pressure for space crowds them from their homes and a rapidly growing market for their body parts is eliminating many of their species.

This is particularly true of the spotted cats and tigers. Spotted cats such as ocelots, marbled cats, black-footed cats, and margays fall victim to the fur trade, while a recent survey provides the shocking truth that despite the success of Project Tiger — a major campaign mounted two decades ago to save the species — less than four thousand tigers remain alive in the wild outside of the Sundarbans, where the world's last viable tiger population still clings. Most of the other tigers have been slaughtered by poachers and their bones have been ground up and sold as medicine in many Asian countries. Today the human population of these countries is close to two billion, meaning that the Asian buyer/wild tiger ratio is five hundred thousand to one. In other words, for every individual wild tiger from Sumatra to Siberia, there are a half million people who may think they need a piece of him.

One of the most important roles that concerned people can play in tiger conservation is to push hard for sanctions on countries that ignore the illegal trade in tiger parts. Another is to help support the forest guards in reserves where wild tigers are still found. Still another is to help support the captive breeding plans of the Species Survival Commission, a branch of the International Union for the Conservation of Nature (IUCN).

Four thousand tigers are extremely few, even if all belonged to one subspecies, or to one continuous population. But these four thousand represent all the living subspecies of tigers, from the big, northern Altai tigers to the slender, gracile tigers of Sumatra, and most of them live in tiny, relic populations on little reserves scattered here and there like islands. These populations have no communication with one another, and are now almost as threatened by inbreeding as by the Asian trade in tiger parts. Taking a leaf from the book of the farmer, scientist and game management officials are now trying to manipulate breeding through the artificial insemination of wild females in these island populations with semen from captive males, or from wild males of other island populations.

The process is only now being developed and is not without difficulty. Who, after all, dares to extract semen from a wild male tiger? The tiger must be tranquilized and his semen must be extracted by a process known as electroejaculation. His semen must then be transported to a wild female who must also be tranquilized and artificially inseminated. Hopefully, she will own her own ranch so that she is self-supporting, and hopefully she will be capable of teaching her skills to her children so that they, too, can survive on their own when the time comes. The male, on the other hand, can be from anywhere, even a zoo. His subspecies and genetic history are what matter, not his skills.

Tigers whose birth results from electroejaculation are far better than no tigers at all. But in the future, scientists will be making the choices that tigers traditionally made for themselves. Thus, as genetic intervention becomes the way of tiger reproduction, the participants will perhaps not live in cages but neither will they be wild.

Even then, in the foreseeable future, it seems very likely that the majority of the world's tigers will be found in captivity, either in circuses or in zoos. Under almost all conditions, tigers, like housecats, breed easily and well. And here, the problem is eerily similar to that of wild tigers. Zoos and circuses cannot provide homes for all the tiger cubs born annually in captivity. Places are found for the lucky ones. What happens to the rest?

The answer depends largely on the ethics of the zoo's management. Short lives are the fate of many of the tigers who participate in breeding programs for endangered species. As a rule, most breeding tigers are allowed to contribute relatively few kittens to the gene pool of their subspecies. After they have done so, their usefulness is over. They drain the zoo's scarce resources and waste precious cage space, so they are sold to other zoos or killed to make room for new genetic contributors.

Zookeepers would prefer, of course, to find good homes for these tigers, and responsible zookeepers are unwilling to sell them to just anybody, first because in the United States (if not in all countries) the laws pertaining to the private ownership of big cats are, fortunately, very strict, and second, because the zookeepers are well aware of the fate of tigers who fall into the wrong hands. Some unwanted tigers are sold to purveyors of Asian folk medicine who grind their bones into powder. Other tigers are sold for their hides. Still others are sold to game farms where people calling themselves sportsmen slaughter them for excitement. The young tiger is taken in a truck to the scene of his execution, where, as the sportsman waits, his weapon raised, the back of the truck is opened, people with sticks poke the tiger and the frightened animal comes cringing out. *Ak ak!* The tiger lies dying and the would-be sportsman has become a tiger hunter — a regular Jim Corbett in his own eyes.

Rather than encourage a trade in tiger bones and hides or provide easy thrills for lazy or inept sportsmen, many responsible zoo managers feel that euthanasia is a better end for unwanted tigers, sad as it seems. At least the bodies can then be studied for the benefit of the species, especially for the captive breeding programs. The people who run the breeding programs are well aware of the moral dilemmas stirred by captive breeding and fully realize the consequence to individual tigers of the effort to keep the subspecies alive. In short, in a situation where all solutions to the problem of breeding tigers are fraught with sadness and difficulty, the zoo managers have probably found the least pernicious.

Few people would deny the necessity of zoos. In a world where contact with nature is no longer available to most people, zoos are the only place where we can have even the most minimal experience with other kinds of creatures. Beyond that, captive breeding programs are the only possible way to keep many endangered species and subspecies on the planet. That we have come to this point in our ongoing ecological disaster is not the fault of the zoos, which should be encouraged and supported, no matter what the consequences may be to some of the individual animals involved.

A fortunate few of the captive-born tigers get

to live out their lives. What is the quality of those lives? Some zoos now let their tigers spend their days in large, open, outdoor enclosures. The ambience is therefore more pleasant for the zoogoers, who prefer to watch tigers sleeping on grass in naturalistic settings rather than on concrete floors behind bars. How the tigers feel about the difference is less certain. When recently I spent a few days watching a pair of tigers in a major urban zoo, I was impressed with the size and beauty of their pen but was struck by the fact that the two tigers hid all day behind some bushes, resting quietly in the only place that could conceal their large bodies. When evening came, they bounded to a hidden door on their hillside and waited eagerly to be let into the tiger barn where, in small cages, they would spend the night. Out of the public view, where no one would shout at them or explode flashbulbs in their eyes, they could communicate with their keepers and with several other tigers — much more pleasant for them than the outdoor enclosure with its ever-present, anonymous crowds. The tigers would enjoy a relaxing but informative night on shelves in their little cages, and in the morning they would again be driven outdoors with threats and shovel banging to face another day of stressful tedium. I found their preference both interesting and touching, especially since it was not food related. The tigers were fed outdoors.

In contrast to the zoo tigers are the circus tigers. Mostly, these are generic tigers who have been bred as most housecats are bred, by a chance meeting of the parents. Hence, as a housecat can be, say, part Siamese, so a generic tiger can be part Siberian. On the other hand, some circus tigers are very fancy indeed. As nothing stops cat breeders from raising hairless cats or cats who flop over as if dead when they are handled, so nothing stops many tiger breeders from breeding tabby tigers or white tigers. The former supposedly have distinctive stripes and the latter are merely an aberrant form in which white replaces the usual orange color, often with the undesirable side effect of an intractable personality and seriously crossed eyes.

White tigers are merely freaks, not an endangered species, as some breeders claim. That a white tiger is (at the time of this writing) the main or only tiger in the National Zoo should not be taken as an endorsement of the phenomorph — her presence is merely a tribute to the zookeepers, who won't dispose of her just because her color is abnormal. They keep her in spite of her color, not because of it. In contrast, two men in Las Vegas have produced what seems to be a pure white tiger with no stripes. It is hard to imagine that such a feat of manipulated inbreeding could be achieved without much trial and error and without the births of many, many kittens. Where are those kittens now? Rumored to have been deprived of his claws and his eyeteeth, the all-white tiger is part of a white-tiger menagerie that is utilized in a nightly spectacle put on by the two men. The eerie abnormality of the creatures and their life on a glittering stage in Vegas bespeak the ultimate degradation of wild animals in the modern world.

However, the personal lives of these animals, or some of them, are rumored to be rather pleasant. Supposedly the favorite tiger lives in his owner's house and has a room of his own. Do big cats want to live with people? I have no information that could answer for the Vegas tigers, but I heard of a lion in similar circumstances — though far less opulent, to be sure.

The lion in question was a large, black-maned Kalahari male. He, a man, and a male dog — a Great Dane — tried to make their living by performing throughout the South at local events such as mall openings. But something had gone wrong. Perhaps the trio couldn't make ends meet. At any rate, they had been forced to disband. What then happened to the dog and the lion is unclear. When I met the man, he was working as a security guard in Florida at a small circus museum and was very much alone. An animal lover, he mourned his former companions, with whom he had shared a trailer. Struck with the picture of spending a night in such close quarters with a loose lion, I asked if the lion hadn't had a cage. "Of course he had a cage," the man answered sadly. "But he preferred to sleep with me and the dog in the trailer."

What, then, is the best life for a captive lion or tiger? Strange as it seems, the answer may be that the best life for a large captive cat is that of a circus performer. A fortunate circus tiger, in my view, might share a cage with another, compatible tiger, in a collection of ten or twenty fellow tigers whose owners not only train them and perform with them but in all ways share their lives. Needless to say, a collection of tigers can seldom be trusted to caretakers other than the owners, no matter how experienced or well meaning the other caretakers may be. Therefore the owners and the tigers are almost always together. If the tigers are the prisoners of the owners, the owners are also the prisoners of the tigers, in a state of communal existence that can last for many years.

When on the road, both the people and the tigers live under conditions that seem uncomfortable and even severe. The owners live in small trailers and the tigers live in traveling cages on wheels, each cage about twice the length of the tiger who inhabits it. Sometimes nothing better than a large tarp or the edge of a circus tent shelters these little groups of people and tigers, just barely protecting them from wind, sun, and rain. Most of the time the people manage to eat seven days a week and to feed the tigers six days a week (even in the best zoos tigers fast for one day a week — supposedly a day without food is good for them). But, again because of the all-meat diet required by the cat family, life on the road is sometimes marginal — one tiger can eat $300 to $400 worth of meat a week, and the distributors and slaughterhouses from which the owners buy the meat don't always extend credit, certainly not to circus people who may be here today and gone tomorrow. So some days the tigers might not get full rations. Even so, if I were a tiger I wouldn't mind the circus life, even with the long hours and the hardships.

To be sure, the circus wouldn't be my first choice. First, I'd like to be a successful, high-status wild tiger on a large well-stocked ranch of my own in India. But afrer that, I'd choose the circus, assuming decent treatment. Third, I'd choose to be a less successful wild tiger, perhaps one in an overcrowded community or in a managed island population. My last choice would be the zoo. Even if the zoo were an excellent zoo like the Minnesota Zoo or the Brookfield Zoo in Chicago, which would put it high above the marginal roadside zoos, I'd find the boredom difficult. And the tigers do too.

One of the most moving facts about tigers that I've ever heard comes from Dr. Ronald L. Tilson, biological director of the Minnesota Zoo and senior editor of *Tigers of the World.* During a long-term study of tiger reproduction, essential if tigers are to be saved, numerous tigers lived in a busy laboratory in rather small cages, where they were immobilized regularly so that their blood could be drawn. One might think they would suffer. But they liked the life! Perhaps they didn't like the needles, and perhaps they got angry when tranquilized with darts, but they liked the activity. They could observe the goings-on — observation is a favorite recreation for all cats — they could interact with the people, and they could interact at least visually and vocally with the other tigers.

The relatively smaller cages didn't bother them — they lay calmly on their shelves and didn't pace but spent their days participating, sometimes as the audience, sometimes as the players, in the very active scene of the tiger lab. In short, they had a life. Dr. Tilson pointed out that all through the study the tigers had a very healthy aura about them. Their mood was high, so they looked well. Their coats were smooth, their eyes were bright, their gums were clean, and their teeth were shiny. In fact, their overall health was better than the health of the tigers in exhibits. Best of all, from the point of view of the scientists, was that the blood chemistry profiles of these tigers gave positive proof of their well-being.

Perhaps it is possible for us to imagine the differences in the life-styles of captive tigers, or at least to imagine what life might be like for us under similar circumstances. Comparable to a tiger's life in the wild would be the normal life of a person who has a home and family and who goes to work every day to put food on the table. In contrast, prison is the only life lived by human beings that even remotely compares to life in a zoo — prison, or the room with the yellow wallpaper made famous by Charlotte Perkins Gilman. To better imagine zoo life, you might picture yourself living with your brother (if you are male) or sister (if you are female) in a department store's window display that looks like a luxuriously furnished home. Satin drapes shroud the French doors, white woolen upholstery encases the armchairs and the sofa, and a thick silk Oriental carpet covers the parquet floor. But the doors lead nowhere, the books on the shelves are fake, the TV doesn't work, the radio has no innards, and the only magazine, a copy of *House Beautiful* on the coffee table, is dated 1980. Anyway, you have read it so often you now know it by heart. Long ago you and your sibling have resolved all your differences. You have little to say to one another and you no longer think of escape. You have forgotten your freedom and have accepted your fate. The building is your prison, and both of you realize that you will never leave it alive. To forget the boredom and the crowds of people going freely wherever they please, who gather each day outside the glass window, oohing and aahing at the luxury that surrounds you, you and your sibling lie down behind the sofa, where you escape into dreams. You don't wake up if you can help it, not even when people in the crowd notice your feet poking out beyond the sofa and bang on the glass to rouse you. You dream of the night, which you spend with three or four other prisoners shackled to the chairs in the employees' lounge. At least you and your fellows can talk all night without wild-looking faces staring at you.

But imagine yourself in a circus. You are often cold, you are sometimes hungry, and your quarters are no bigger than the inside of an automobile. But you have plenty of pleasant, friendly communication with your keepers; you have plenty of interplay, friendly and otherwise, with all the other prisoners, and you always find a lot to watch — people and animals constantly coming and going. Most of all, you know that three or four times a day you will be called upon to do demanding work that requires both mental and physical skills. True, crowds of people watch you do this, but the crowds look like a dim wall far away, a wall that breathes and vocalizes every once in a while but doesn't bother you. And at the end of the day when the work is done, you know you'll sleep in peace, secure in your own small space where no one can get in to harm you.

And thus, incredible as it may seem, as far as tigers are concerned, the circus is not a bad way of life. Contrary to some erroneous statements put out by well-meaning but seriously misinformed animal-rights activists, many circus tigers like their lives. They have meaningful work and are not tortured or hurt in any way by their trainers. This, too, is contrary to what the animal-rights activists would have us believe. But in fact, punishment is an ineffective way to train almost any living creature, and the good, skilled trainers don't use it. Training is best achieved by encouragement, practice, and rewards. The more sensitive the trainer, the easier the job. Many animals are very fond of their trainers and look forward to sessions in the ring.

All this is not to say that no trainers are cruel. Some certainly are. And some caged tigers are kept in appalling conditions. I once learned of a man and his wife who got tired of their menagerie of tigers and simply abandoned them. Taking their household items, the couple got into their car and drove away for good, and the tigers slowly died of thirst and starvation in their cages. However, that such things can happen is certainly not a reason to prohibit animals from performing in circuses, a remedy that some animal-rights activists advise. Terrible things happen regularly to pets and farm animals, but no one suggests that we abolish pet ownership or farming. Better to spend time and effort preventing the abuse. Anyway, at present, it is much easier to catch and punish a cruel tiger owner than a cruel farmer or pet owner, at least in the United States, since all captive tigers must be registered and since the conditions of captivity for all large carnivores are governed by a number of federal and local laws. The laws are designed largely to protect the public, but not entirely, and the effect is often the same.

Yet it is the tigers themselves who attest to their good treatment. I have watched an uncounted number of circus acts and over a four-year period have spent much time observing the training sessions and performance sessions of nine trainers and their tigers and/or lions. I've watched little traveling menageries as well as such giants as the Ringling Brothers Barnum and Bailey Circus. Usually the tigers in question stand patiently by the doors of their cages waiting to go into the ring for a practice session. Sometimes their faces brighten in anticipation when their trainer enters the barn.

This is not to say that tigers are never frightened

before entering the ring. Often they are, but the cause of their fear is almost always another tiger or an unfamiliar piece of equipment. On one occasion that I know of, it was a large collapsible pyramid, and on another, it was a huge mirror-spangled globe on a rotary turntable that groaned as it revolved. On their first encounters with these mechanical horrors, the tigers shrank in fear to the far side of the ring. It was then the trainer's task to accustom them to the machinery, which in both cases he did by luring them forward with little bites of meat. By the third or fourth session, the tigers were walking up to the machinery voluntarily, and by the fifth or sixth session, they were using it.

Fear of being out in the open is another cause of tiger malaise, and indeed of malaise in all cats. Tigers try to overcome this by skirting the edge of the ring. Fear of other tigers is probably not so easily assuaged. The tigers with which I was most familiar could become quite frightened of each other, but not consistently so, which showed, I thought, an ongoing but unstable relationship. In each case the trainer took great care to watch the threatening tiger carefully, so that the threatened tiger didn't feel called upon to defend himself or herself. A feeling of give and take existed among these particular tigers, so that no one tiger seemed to dominate the others, or not consistently, or for long. In contrast, these same tigers — even the biggest and fiercest of them — seemed in mortal fear of a certain lion who belonged to another trainer but was sometimes quartered with them. Never did these tigers and this lion get into the ring together, yet the mere presence of the lion in the tiger barn could get the tigers bouncing off the walls of their cages. Why? No one knows why. The lion had never been caged together with any of the tigers and had never harmed one of them. But he looked frightening and he acted frightening. Probably he wanted to seem frightening. And who could blame him? As the male of a species whose best strategy is to live in pairs, with either a brother, a littermate, or a friend, this lion lived all alone in a roomful of tigers. They must have seemed to him to be in a group, and he wasn't. If the cages were opened and they all came out, they would number in the dozens, but he would have been all alone. Perhaps that is why he always assumed an intimidating demeanor. He never walked into the barn if he could charge in. He seldom hummed or moaned, but he often roared. One day he roared every fifteen or twenty minutes, thirty or forty times each session. The tigers hated to hear it and stayed absolutely still.

Also he sprayed. His cage was on the corner with two sides exposed to the room, one side exposed to the runway, and one side exposed to another cage which was empty because no tiger wanted to live next to that lion. The first day I observed him he had just arrived and was making sure that everyone knew he was present. On two sides, from the floor almost to the ceiling, the walls were dripping with urine. And as I was standing there scribbling notes and wondering why he felt compelled to spray so frequently, my glasses suddenly went blank, like a windshield when the car before you speeds through a puddle. And my clothes and hair were wet — he had sprayed me!

But I've never seen a tiger show fear of a trainer. Nor have I seen a trainer show fear of a tiger. On the contrary, most trainers enter the ring carrying only a pole and a wand. The pole has a point on the end and is used for delivering small bites of meat to the tiger's mouth, and the wand, to which a length of string is often tied, is whisked under the tiger's chin to get his attention or, because he draws back from it, to persuade him to lift himself up. The wand is certainly not used to beat or whip the tiger, since one of the important bits of information that a trainer must impart to his tigers is that a training session is for pleasure, for success, and for many little snacks of meat, not for confrontation or fighting. In the former atmosphere, it is the trainer who prevails. In the latter atmosphere, it is the tiger.

In short, training often pleases tigers because, along with the snacks, it gives them something to do, which explains why many circus tigers seem vastly more alert than many zoo tigers. Circus tigers are also more responsive, more expressive, and more vocal. And they seem to live longer than zoo tigers.

Perhaps this is only because they are kept longer. A good, cooperative, well-trained tiger with long experience and ever-increasing skills is even more valuable in old age than in youth, something that cannot always be said of a zoo tiger who has contributed his genes and is simply taking up cage space. But probably circus tigers live longer than zoo tigers because they are happier and more stimulated. Except on rest days, circus tigers rarely pace or enter the comatose state that seems to be the norm for zoo tigers. Circus tigers are entertained and have a reason to live. Most zoo tigers are bored, and they show it.

My own brief and very informal survey of tiger longevity revealed a small but perhaps significant difference between zoo and circus tigers. In zoos that did not participate in the endangered-species breeding program (of necessity a life-shortening affair), the average age of large zoo cats was nine. But in one circus act, the average age of the tigers was thirteen, and in another, eleven. Recently deceased zoo tigers whom I happened to hear of had lived only eight to ten years and then had died of unstated causes. In contrast, numerous circus tigers were still going strong at fifteen and sixteen, with some continuing in good health into their twenties. A circus lion, Ace, lived for twenty-seven years as the much-beloved partner and companion of the trainer Klaus Blaszak. The relationship between Ace and Klaus was such that Ace would sit next to Klaus at mealtimes and steal food from his plate. When I met Klaus's wife, the trainer Ada Smieya-Blaszak, and their son, Brunon Blaszak, also a trainer, they had in their collection a number of elderly tigers including a tigress named Rowena, who was seventeen, and a tiger named Harry, who was fifteen. Despite her age, Rowena was the most agreeable of creatures, but being no longer young she would get tired late at night. By the time the last show started at 11:00 P.M., this elderly tigress would be asleep in her cage. When the music would start for the tiger act, she'd wake up and come willingly into the ring, since she was a loyal and veteran performer, but she couldn't wake up as well as she once could, and she would sometimes doze on her stool. Her eyelids would close, her head would droop, her thighs would loosen, and her knees would slowly spread. At last, even her tail would lose its tension and would hang straight down. The trainer and the other tigers would then exchange a glance. All would realize that the act was about to continue without Rowena. Sometimes she'd start to topple and would wake with a jerk, and if her cue was coming she'd try to stay awake to do her part, but once back on her chair she'd doze again. When the act was over and the spotlight had moved to the next arena, Rowena would rouse herself and trot appreciatively off to her cage, there to sleep until morning and to wake refreshed and ready for a new performance.

Harry was exactly the opposite. Age had made him angry and disagreeable, so that he was much too dangerous to perform. Very few people were willing to get into a ring with Harry. Nevertheless, the Blaszaks did not kill him or sell him but instead took him wherever they traveled, giving him good care and an extra large cage because, unlike the other tigers, he didn't get his exercise in the ring. A large red, white, and blue tarp draped his cage to protect his privacy. Behind the tarp he would lie on his side with his raised head relaxed against the wall of his cage, blandly taking note of everything.

It is hard for most of us even to imagine a unit like the Blaszaks and their tigers, a unit that consists of four highly skilled people — Klaus and Ada and Brunon and his wife, Marita — and eight highly skilled tigers, each species cut off from contact with its own kind by the needs of the other species, all individuals closely linked, voyaging together through space and time like astronauts, like a wolfpack, like members of a combat platoon, or like a family.

To keep their tigers, the Blaszaks of course must accept the best of the jobs that come their way, which often forces them to live in some pretty bad surroundings. I met them at the Jolly Roger Amusement Park in the noisy city of Ocean Beach, Virginia — a triumph of strip development on which bars, hotels, motels, convenience stores, gas stations, and fast-food restaurants are jammed together by the thousand. To the east lies a beach, if you can find it underneath the tons of human flesh piled on the sand, and to the west lie the dirty waters of an oil-streaked harbor on which rafts of garbage gently bob. Perhaps the unusually large amount of garbage is due to an eerie absence of birds, particularly gulls and other scavengers — these, together with their nesting sites, have been systematically destroyed as part of a beautification program allegedly conceived by the chamber of commerce.

Not in this setting would one expect to observe tiger behavior. Yet in this very place I had the honor of watching a fascinating interplay between one of the tigers, Rajah, and his trainer, Brunon. Rajah was focused upon a nearby cage holding several pacing tigresses whose erotic moans bespoke their sexual receptivity. Rajah kept answering, needless to say, meanwhile trying different ways to reach the tigresses through the bars of his cage.

In the course of his daily routine, Brunon would pass by these cages, readying the equipment for the first show, strewing fresh shavings, feeding and watering the tigers. One would think that Brunon was showing the tigers only kindness, only every time he passed, Rajah would leap at him, jaws wide, showing the length of his teeth and bellowing a horrible challenge. Why?

According to Ada, Rajah and Brunon had been youngsters together, and now that both were adults, Rajah saw Brunon as a rival for females. To put it very simply, Rajah was ascribing tigerish motives to a human being and was afraid that the young and powerful Brunon would take his women. Meanwhile, the behavior of the tigresses could only have further agitated Rajah. Whenever Brunon passed, the tigresses chuffed at him and lovingly rubbed their cheeks and chins on the bars of the cages.

Rajah repeated his threats all morning long, right up to the time he and the moaning tigresses were supposed to join Brunon in the ring for the first show. But amazingly, at that point Rajah's behavior changed completely, and his performance was adroit and smooth. Many people would not have been as professional as Rajah was that day — nothing in his bearing or his manner gave any hint of his differences with Brunon or of his feelings for the tigresses, for that matter. In fact, his good manners were such that when during the performance he felt the need to relieve himself, he stepped discreetly down from his stool and, while the performance swirled on around him, went to the edge of the ring, where he squatted, curved his tail upward, and defecated. Brunon and the other tigers ignored him, as polite people ignore a person who has excused himself to visit a bathroom. Finished, Rajah buried his scat with shavings by very slowly and deliberately scuffling, first with his right hind foot a few times, then with his left hind foot a few times, then with both feet alternating a few times. At last, in all dignity, his timing unblemished, he clambered back up onto his stool and waited for his next cue.

Scratching up the shavings may have said much about Rajah and his perceptions of his trainer, since he possibly saw himself as being on home turf in the presence of a more dominant male animal. Rajah might challenge Brunon vocally, but he evidently wasn't ready to stake a claim with a scat. If he had been, he would probably have left the scat uncovered. Equally interesting is that Rajah saw the ring as his home, even though over the course of time the tiger act would move from one place to another. Evidently the layout of the ring and cages and the dynamics of the act were what mattered to Rajah, not the larger setting. Other circus animals and circus people feel the same — witness the frequently told story of the ringmaster's dog who buries a bone under a circus wagon. The circus moves to a new town and sets up again in the same pattern as before, and the dog can't understand where the bone has gone when he looks for it under the wagon.

Traditionally, the cat act in a circus has had the appearance of a show of force, Man against Beast, whereby a man armed with whip and pistol subdued a beast armed with teeth and claws. To call these performances confrontational would be putting it mildly. But all that is changing. Today a more typical circus act is that of the trainer Eddie Schmitt, whose tigress, Natasha, has learned to ride the aforementioned rotating spangled contraption. Up she sits, her forepaws crossed and delicately lifted while, accompanied by lyrical music, she rides the slowly turning globe as thousands of tiny mirrors drench the audience with sparkles. The message is not that Natasha is dangerous but that she is beautiful.

Actually, however, she is both. This is what

makes her so interesting. I think that many people, myself included, once found the confrontational style of cat act gripping, if only because the trainer seemed less like a tyrant coercing helpless animals than like a small person outnumbered by powerful creatures over whom he was keeping only minimal control. Yet even more gripping was the underlying message, that the entire spectacle was a performance, and that the trainer and his big cats were acting. There were just too many big cats in that ring for the snarling and whip cracking to be real. If the cats had wanted to maul the trainer, they would have mauled him, anyone could see, even if they themselves sustained a few casualties in the process.

So the modern circus message isn't really as new as it seems. Meanwhile, the old message undergoes its own metamorphosis. In recent years, every evening at sunset on a pier in Key West, Florida, a wonderful trainer named Dominique La Font performs with four graceful little housecats who open their own cages, leap fluidly onto their stools, and perform a series of breathtaking tricks, while Dominique, a chair in one hand and a whip in the other, pretends to keep them at bay as if they were lions. After the last performance, man and cats stroll off together, the cats to their carrying boxes, the man to his large RV in which they all live amid a pleasant domestic clutter of coffee cups, cat kibbles, and litter pans.

Zoos keep people and animals apart. Circuses unite them. In the Ringling Brothers Barnum and

Bailey Road Show a man and a tiger mount an enormous double ferris wheel, the Wheel of Death, which lifts them higher than the aerialists, a process that evidently fazes this particular tiger not at all. Quite amazing. But for me, the most impressive moment of the circus comes just before, when the lights go down, and the tiger, leaving the center ring where the traditional tiger act has just been performed, goes to the ferris wheel. Loose, with nothing between him and the audience, he pads to his next act unrestrained and unguided except that his trainer walks at his side. This particular tiger wears a collar, and possibly is on a little leash, but the leash would mean less than nothing to a tiger of this size without the tiger's consent. He might as well be loose. Together the small trainer and his big colleague walk the length of the arena in the dark, the picture of professionalism. The lights go up when the two reach the ferris wheel. They both get on it, and the show goes on.

Rarely, the act itself illustrates the bond between an animal and a trainer. The most stirring circus act I ever saw was performed in the 1960s. The trainer was a beautiful woman with black hair, and the animal was a handsome lion with a black mane. These two also walked side by side and unrestrained from the door of the arena to a big swing, which they mounted. The lion sat on his haunches while the woman stood astride him, and then, in perfect silence, they began to swing. Higher and higher they swung until they were fly-

281

ing out over the heads of the audience. And at the limit of each arc the lion roared.

Do captive cats understand their circumstances? They want to. They try to. And with their awesome intelligence and their formidable powers of observation, they often succeed.

Perhaps the world's largest collection of captive tigers — up to seventy at a time including kittens — is kept in northern Illinois in a compound of barns and trailers enclosed by a heavy security fence. The facility is known as the Hawthorn Corporation, and in it, dozens if not hundreds of tigers are raised and trained to perform in circuses. The owner, John Cuneo, lives about twenty miles away, in the state's lake district, and was not present during my first few visits, but plenty of other people live within the compound walls — the grooms, the custodial staff, and the trainers, all under the direction of Roelof de Vries, who with his wife, Elke, have come from Holland especially for this purpose.

The tigers live in two huge barns in rows of roomy cages, one for each adult. Usually some of the interconnecting cage doors are open so that, except at mealtimes, two or more tigers can be together. The young adult tigers, especially those who are littermates, get along well and enjoy one another's company. Some of the older tigers, especially the older male tigers, prefer their solitude and are allowed to keep it. Many of the cages have access to outdoor pens where the tigers spend time in good weather. Each cage is also equipped with a high shelf where the occupant likes to rest, so that there is one shelf for each tiger.

Because these tigers have meaningful work which they seem to enjoy, so that most of them readily enter the ring for the daily rehearsals — eyes open, tails aloft and ears and whiskers forward — they are alert and lively creatures who assume the comatose state of zoo tigers only in the dead of night, when the barn is closed and all activity halted. Otherwise they are up and around, reacting to each other and to the ten or twelve grooms and trainers whose entire workday is spent in caring for them. The tigers, of course, know these people well and have pronounced personal relationships with each of them. The normal state of the tigers by day, therefore, is to be awake and alert, standing or walking through interconnecting cages, relating to neighboring tigers or to the people at their tasks, whom the tigers approach to greet, bowing their heads and chuffing as they do when greeting other tigers.

During my early visits to the Hawthorn Corporation I was of course a stranger, so the tigers seemed particularly interested in me, and whenever I entered the barn to visit their cages they would stop whatever they were doing to gawk at me. One day, therefore, I was mildly surprised to enter the larger of the two barns and see that the nearest tiger was high on his shelf, evidently watching something in the far corner so intently that he didn't notice me.

Accustomed to being greeted, I chuffed at him,

but he merely glanced quickly to learn who had made the noise and then turned back, ignoring me completely. How strange. The tiger in the next cage didn't look at me at all, nor did the third. When I climbed a ladder that led to the top of the cages to see what was engrossing these tigers, I saw that all the tigers in the barn were on their shelves, all in the same position on their sides, all propped on their elbows, their heads high and their ears up. Quite obviously, all were alert to something in the far corner.

What was it? I couldn't see and didn't really like to climb to the walkway on the top of the cages, since whenever I had done so in the past, the tigers in the nearest cages would try to catch me — not that they could get their paws through the heavy wire net, but they almost could, and their efforts were unsettling.

The scene was most unusual. In the many hours I'd spent among these tigers, I'd never seen them do anything even remotely like this before. Yet I had seen enough of them to know what they were *not* seeing — I knew, for instance, that whatever they were looking at wasn't an animal such as a dog or a horse that would make them think of hunting. If so, some of them would surely have been crouching, tails twitching, and all would have been in different states of excitement. And I knew they weren't watching for their daily food, large slabs of meat which they had already eaten and which always arrived on a cart from the opposite direction. And they weren't witnessing the arrival of the lion or of another, strange tiger, since the arrival of a tiger would have had them on their feet, moaning and pacing, and the arrival of the lion would have had them bounding off the sides of their cages. Realizing that the nearest tigers, like all the other tigers, were so intent on watching whatever it was that they wouldn't come after me, I climbed higher and I saw — what? Just a group of four men standing together, talking. Three I knew — one was a groom and two were trainers — but the fourth was someone I had never seen before. Yet from the tigers' behavior I suddenly guessed who he was — John Cuneo, their owner.

That the tigers had been watching Mr. Cuneo was confirmed when he left the building. Although the other men stayed, as soon as Mr. Cuneo was gone the tigers turned from their vigil, got off their shelves, and resumed their normal activities. Immediately, the tigers nearest to me began trying to reach me through the bars. Later I was introduced to the man, who was indeed Mr. Cuneo. But I felt I already knew him.

I was deeply impressed by this episode. Considering all the people who go in and out of the barns and who deal every day with the tigers, why had they singled Mr. Cuneo from all the others for such rapt attention? Although Mr. Cuneo is an accomplished trainer, he doesn't train the tigers, and the tiger grooms, not Mr. Cuneo, feed and water them and clean their cages. So the tigers weren't getting their clues from any direct experience with him. Nor is he the only visitor who rarely appears yet is nevertheless very important to the facility. The veterinarians would also fit that description. No — how the tigers knew the importance of Mr. Cuneo has no easy explanation, but involves a process of fact finding and deduction on their part that is far beyond our present capacity to understand.

In contrast to wild tigers, and indeed, to most wild members of the cat family, especially in the Old World, certain populations of cats in North America are doing surprisingly well. Partly this is due to repopulation efforts, although not all of these have been successful. A scheme to reintroduce the lynx to the Adirondacks met with failure, presumably because Alaskan lynxes, who traditionally have enormous home ranges, were chosen to replace Adirondacks lynxes, who traditionally had quite modest ranges. Evidently the Adirondacks were not big enough for most of the Alaskan lynxes, who, when released, hiked far away. On the other hand, perhaps they merely wanted to return to Alaska. If so, they would not have been the first cats who tried to get home.

But perhaps the most dramatic recovery of the cat family in the New World has been the puma, who in parts of its former range is making an extraordinary comeback. Nowhere has this been more evident than in Colorado, in the Front Range of the Rockies, where pumas had been exterminated. Their demise had taken place at the turn of the century, the negative consequence of a gold rush with its swarms of prospectors and miners who, living off the land while working their claims, had in a very short time quite literally killed all the elk and all the deer and had eaten them. Of course the pumas, who were already besieged by Colorado's bounty hunters, couldn't live without their natural food, and they, too, vanished. Years later, more elk and more deer were imported and released so that the Colorado sportsmen would have something to shoot at, and the imported populations multiplied and eventually grew big enough to support a puma population too. Then the pumas returned.

The subsequent recovery of the puma population was enhanced by a change in the human demographics. The mountain men, who hunted, had been replaced by suburbanites, who jogged. And in keeping with the new consciousness along the Front Range, the state rescinded the bounty on pumas and instead levied a fine for killing them without a license or out of season. Under such favorable conditions, the puma population grew. Meanwhile, the suburbs of Denver and the outskirts of Boulder also grew, creeping along the canyons and up into the foothills of the Front Range into areas the pumas were also occupying. So today Front Range pumas appear in unexpected places and are even turning up in cities and towns.

Pumas are also returning in New England, to everyone's amazement. Officially, the eastern subspecies of puma, *Felis concolor cougar*, was eradicated over a century ago to make New England safe for farming. And according to many wildlife experts, the nearest surviving puma population is almost a thousand miles distant. Where, then, are the New England pumas coming from?

At first, the experts suggested that someone was releasing captive pumas. And because no responsible institution would do such a thing, the finger of suspicion pointed to pet owners. Yet to some, myself included, the release of pet pumas seemed more than unlikely, if only because no puma without claws could survive in the wild, and no puma with claws could be tolerated in a household. Like a housecat, a puma will sharpen her claws on furniture, but while a housecat would need to pluck for several years to complete the destruction of, say, a sofa, a puma could render a sofa to fluff in a matter of hours.

Even so, the New England authorities have generally denied the return of pumas and at the time of this writing continue to do so, albeit with difficulty. After all, New Englanders keep seeing them. So the only reasonable conclusion that can be drawn is that with or without the acknowledgment of the wildlife authorities, pumas have been here all along.

The early sightings of pumas in New England were discredited just as often as are the present sightings. During the early 1940s, many people in rural New Hampshire, myself among them, believed that a strange animal lived in the woods. Numerous people reported seeing a black panther, which eventually became known as *the* black panther. Since panthers were supposed to live in India or Africa, the individual in our woods was assumed to have escaped from a zoo. That the only zoos were far away in Nashua and Boston troubled nobody — being urban centers, Nashua and Boston were the source of everything exotic, and the idea of a panther from the city didn't seem at all strange. Still, not everybody believed there really was a panther. So sometimes someone brave enough to report a sighting was accused of poor judgment if not of drunkenness or downright misrepresentation. Probably a dog, probably a coyote, probably an otter, probably a housecat, the smug listeners would say.

With the death of the New England farm, and with the resulting armistice in New England's war on wildlife, reports of the panther grew more numerous and more far flung. The animal would have had to wear seven-league boots to get from one sighting to another. Anyway, by then the panther would have been over forty, or nearly twice the age of the oldest big cat known. At this point, it became clear that the creature people had been seeing hadn't been an escaped zoo animal after all but in fact had been several pumas.

The amazing thing is that there ever was any confusion. Pumas are huge animals. A full-grown male can weigh two hundred and fifty pounds, stand thirty inches at the shoulder, and measure nine or ten feet from nose to tail. And pumas scream. A dismal howl, a trilling wail, an unearthly scream, a low moaning cry, a loud wailing scream, a wild screaming cry, a loud weird cry, a loud penetrating scream, a queer half-human cry, like the scream of a terrified woman, like the scream of some woman in trouble, like the agonized voice of a boy or a woman, like someone screaming from the pain of surgery — these are some of the images that came to mountain men and other early settlers whose puma stories were compiled in 1946 by the early wildlife biologists S. P. Young and E. A. Goldman.* Why do pumas scream? They scream because they live far apart in the woods where trees prevent most sounds from traveling. If they don't scream they won't hear each other. So who would have guessed that any question would remain about the presence or absence of such a large, vocal animal?

Eventually I became so interested in the panther controversy that I went to New Hampshire's Department of Fish and Game in Durham, which, while denying the presence of pumas in the northeast, nevertheless maintains records of the sightings. There, in two thick files, I found accounts of more than a hundred sightings, beginning with the report of a puma killed in 1895 and ending with a sighting that had taken place just a few

*S. P. Young and E. A. Goldman, *The Puma: Mysterious American Cat* (New York: Dover, 1946).

weeks before I read of it. Most of the accounts seemed reasonable and accurate, often mentioning features that are field marks of pumas, such as the account by one observer of a large cat with a long tail "as thick as a child's arm." That is an exact description of a puma's tail, and is especially telling because the only other cats that could be called large — lynxes and bobcats — have short tails. From 1980 to the time of this writing, no year has passed without at least one sighting. In 1985 there were seventeen reported sightings. Certain sightings seemed to cluster, as if several people were seeing the same puma, but even while allowing for this, the sightings increased slowly with time, probably an indication that a puma population was growing.

Even more fascinating were descriptions offered by observers who didn't understand exactly what they had seen. Often the fresh eyes of such an observer made the sighting particularly convincing, such as an account from 1984 in which the observer reported a puma being followed by a "little spotted dog." At first, the observation seemed flawed. Except for one or two rare and costly miniature breeds, there are no little spotted dogs. And such a dog would probably have more sense than to tag along behind a puma; if not, it would be killed. However, the description exactly fits a puma kitten, and the fact that the observer didn't know this made the observation all the more convincing. Furthermore, the presence of a kitten suggests two adult pumas and therefore some kind of community, not just a wandering stranger from afar.

Sightings continue, and the list of witnesses now includes a biologist with the U. S. Fish and Wildlife Service; also the former president of Radcliffe, Dr. Mary Bunting Smith; and finally — confirming a sighting in Connecticut — none other than Dr. George Schaller himself, perhaps the best and best-known wildlife biologist in the world, whose eminence began with his landmark studies of tigers and lions.

The testamentary evidence of such prominent people would have been quite enough for me, yet more was to come. On February 3, 1992, from my home in New Hampshire, I myself saw a puma in my own field. It was tawny, or deer colored, the color that was mentioned in most of the reports of sightings, and it was chasing something small that dodged. Around in a big circle ran the puma, then it vanished in the direction from which it had come.

Because I had just been writing about the controversy that swirls around pumas, and then had looked up from my desk to see one, I would have assumed I was merely hallucinating if Pearl, my dog, hadn't seen it too; she even seemed to know what it was, because she didn't rush out the dog door to launch herself at it as she would have done if it had been almost any other animal. Rather, she wisely stood rooted to the spot, but with her nose flattened against the glass window, her ears up, her eyes wide, and her body trembling with the strength of her emotions. An immediate search of the area by dogs and humans yielded nothing — the ground was frozen solid but was bare of snow.

More than excited, I telephoned everyone I thought would be interested, and we organized a real search party. Sue Morse, the forest ecologist and tracker, came down from Vermont to help us, bringing a pair of rubber puma feet to show the rest of us what to look for in a track. Ably assisted by many dogs, we combed large tracts of forest but found nothing, and the lures we set out — fish, musk, and catnip, promising the puma a chance to eat, have sex, and get high all in one place — did not, as far as we could tell, convince him. Through a friend of Sue's we even obtained a flask of puma urine (taking care that the donor was healthy and had been vaccinated so as not to make the local wild cats sick), but all we succeeded in doing with the urine, which we sprinkled in the woods, was to upset a certain bobcat, who, objecting violently to the perceived intruder, left his own emphatic scrape on top of the puma urine and marked the place with a scat. As a desperate, final measure, I bought a predator call, a device that makes an ear-splitting shriek like a captive rabbit's, but, alas, even this did not produce the puma. Evidently, however, the puma was still around. A few days later a neighbor came by to say he'd seen a big, tawny, catlike creature in his field.

In contrast to the extreme shyness of the eastern

pumas is the extreme boldness of the western pumas, who these days come right into the cities and towns. The newspapers of Denver and Boulder regularly carry accounts of pumas hunting people's dogs and cats, eating pet food left out on people's sun decks, and hiding in the dense, exotic shrubbery that people cultivate in their yards. In 1992 I made a study of the puma sightings that had occurred that year within the city limits of Denver and Boulder and came to the conclusion that the wanderers were young animals, probably off on their own for the first time and not coping well. The lack of a cultural taboo against our species, combined with inexperience and bad judgment, had brought them into the towns. Or so it seemed. In nearly every case, I had no difficulty figuring out where the youngster had come from or why he or she had chosen the place in question. All the places were at the edge of the foothills on the plains, and in all cases, I thought, the youngster, when starting his or her journey, probably would have had no choice but to travel east. West led back into the mountains, where, it seemed fair to conclude, the adult members of the growing puma population had acquired all the good territories. Surely big and powerful pumas already sat in the lookouts and patrolled the boundaries of the numerous Eastern Slope puma habitats and would chase any young newcomer away.

In fact, I could think of only one question that wasn't readily answered by topography combined with human demographics, and that was why the young pumas came so fearlessly straight into the towns when they could have slipped around them. In order to guess at an answer to that question, however, all I needed to do was to go up into the hills and see for myself what the youngsters must have seen as kittens. East of the foothills in the Denver-Boulder area, the Colorado plain is more or less a continuous urban sprawl, thick here, thin there, and from almost anywhere along the Eastern Slope one looks east at a sea of buildings with glittering windows, surrounded by streams of cars. The scene is sufficiently remote that sirens and horns and other urban sounds aren't audible; the scene contains, in short, nothing alarming when viewed by day. But viewed by night, it becomes positively entrancing for members of the cat family. Boulder, for instance, becomes a vast array of lights, some moving, others spinning, still others flashing, a scene so visually appealing to the cat family that it might have been designed just for their pleasure. As housecats watch television, not really caring what the program is about but thrilled by the irregular, jerking movements, so the young pumas in their mothers' lookouts in the Rockies might have viewed the flitting lights below.

The next step for the outward bound youngster is to start down the mountainside, toward the by now completely familiar landscape, which he or she has been viewing nearly every day and night since emerging from the den. The first human installations the young puma would encounter on the eastward journey would be the widely spaced homes of well-to-do suburbanites, who each year build houses ever higher on the slopes. Since, presumably, the appeal of such neighborhoods is their remoteness and their privacy, the human residents tend to be as quiet and as circumspect as the pumas themselves — after ten o'clock at night these neighborhoods are silent and dark, and most people are inside the houses. Often at night I've quietly walked through these neighborhoods just to learn what a puma might encounter, and the answer is: nothing. Needless to say, I wasn't furtive — on the contrary I walked in the middle of the road. But not one person ever saw me. No one even realized I was there. The dogs knew, of course — once in a while one of them barked, but usually from inside a house. In no case did anyone investigate, and sometimes the people even shushed the dog. So it seems that from the start a passing puma could expect no opposition.

Pumas like paths and follow them whenever possible. They have their own puma corridors, and they also follow our paths, trails, and roads, as well as riverbanks and canyons, much as we would. In consequence, most of the pumas who entered Boulder seemed to have come (or so I thought) along relatively few pathways. An informal and cursory survey yielded four possible routes into town that I thought I could identify: two of the routes came down canyons and two followed the banks of brooks. Each canyon route led into an upscale neighborhood with neon green lawns and a puzzling maze of fences, but the brooks became unkempt, forgotten ditches and thus remained wild-looking even deep inside the city, which was where many of the sightings took place.

In most cases the puma wasn't sighted until afternoon. Then, the people who discovered him usually got excited, in contrast to the young puma himself, who usually remained perfectly calm. That, too, seemed disconcerting to his discoverers. A puma who shows no fear of people seems sinister, dangerous, especially when the people are so much afraid of him. However, the reason for the puma's calmness could also be surmised by traveling his likely route. Being of a crepuscular species, the puma would most likely start out on a journey sometime in the evening, after resting all day, just as we might start a journey in the morning after resting all night. That timing would bring a traveling puma into the city in the middle of the night, when the streets were empty and all was quiet. If a puma had tried to travel through the city by day, people would have seen him, with the resulting fanfare of police and emergency vehicles, inevitably ending in disaster for the puma.

So the puma surely arrived before dawn and found himself deep inside the city by the time the city woke up. Then all of a sudden, doors began to open and people and their dogs began to come out. Soon traffic filled the streets and the city was once again alive and busy. Surely the puma was taken aback, and surely he felt he had no choice but to hide as best he could. In the sightings that

I investigated, most of the pumas had chosen to hide in bushes or long grass surrounded by open space — the most dramatic example being a puma that hid all day on the grounds of the school where my grandson, David, was attending seventh grade. From afar, that particular school must have looked wonderful to the young puma — set against a hill too steep for building, the school is surrounded by fields where the grass is long and golden, like wild grass. Best of all, a tangle of bushes grows at the edge of these fields. Hidden in these bushes, the young puma could watch the doings of all the people while hoping that none came too near or threatened him. After a day of watching warily as children swarmed around him, playing soccer and generally making lots of noise, he must have lost most of his fear just through acclimatization, and when in the afternoon someone noticed him, perhaps because he got up for a drink or to move into the shade, he had undergone about ten hours of city life during which nothing bad had happened to him. By then the busy school ground must have seemed somewhat less scary. Such was not the experience of his astonished discoverer, however, who probably had never before given much thought to pumas. No wonder the man was frightened when an enormous tawny cat calmly appeared from nowhere on the school grounds.

I didn't learn what happened to that particular puma. Possibly he was killed by the wildlife officers or by the police, although the attitude of the Boulder citizens is so favorable to pumas and, in fact, to most wildlife that the policy followed by the Colorado Division of Wildlife is to tranquilize the pumas and transport them back to the hills. Even so, the Division justifiably fears lawsuits and undoubtedly has to kill many straying pumas simply because of the vast number of litigious people who would view any encounter as a bonanza and sue the state.

Fear of lawsuits sealed the fate of a young puma who, in August 1992, somehow got himself into the heart of Denver. He had followed a dwindling watercourse to the intersection of Hampton and Monaco, two swarming thoroughfares lined with shopping malls and roaring with traffic. A worse place for a puma can scarcely be imagined. Even so, early one morning he entered a neighborhood next to these streets and hid there until eight o'clock at night, when a dog saw him and chased him into a tree. He had probably been trying to resume his journey. When the owners of the tree saw why their dog was barking they called the police. With the police came firemen, reporters, an entire television crew with vans, cables, lights, and cameras, and, eventually, an officer from the Division of Wildlife. The excitement drew a large crowd of passersby, who, much taken with the sight of the young puma peering down at them, begged the authorities to spare his life. The wildlife officer wanted to tranquilize the puma and move him out of town, but when the dart hit the youngster, he panicked and jumped out of the tree in a dash for freedom. The police opened fire and killed him.

He must have seemed enormous, at least to some of the reporters present. An early edition of one of the papers gave his weight at two hundred and fifty pounds. In fact, he was hardly more than a kitten, and in his starved condition probably weighed between sixty and seventy pounds. A photo in another paper shows him lying dead, his gaunt little body curled at the feet of the district wildlife officer.

After this sad drama appeared on the local television news, some people chose not to report sightings lest other pumas suffer the same fate. Such was the decision of a young couple in Boulder late one night when their dog, Bailey, chased a young puma up onto the roof of a toolshed. I met these people while investigating another sighting in the same neighborhood, and they told me that when they saw the puma looking down at the dog, they assumed it was trying to hunt him. In this they were surely mistaken. If, in fact, the puma behaved as they described — they said it had crouched on the roof for fifteen or twenty minutes looking down — it had been treed by Bailey and was afraid, nothing else. Yet, even believing as they did, the young people were generous to the puma and did not call the police. Instead, they brought Bailey inside and left the puma alone. In the morning, it was gone, perhaps headed back to the hills, and no harm was done.

Are pumas dangerous? Some are and some aren't. The pumas who find their way into cities have so far hurt no one, although dogs, cats, and chickens have evidently fallen victim to some of them. Even so, pumas do attack people. Pumas look for all the world like exceptionally beautiful housecats, so it is hard to believe that harm could come of them. Yet the fact that people are almost exactly the same size as deer cannot be lost on pumas. In other words, people are the perfect size to be prey, just as voles are exactly the right size for housecats, and attacks do take place. One June day, two pumas attacked a Boulder woman, after which one of them may have moved on to attack a young man. The Boulder *Daily Camera* of June 4, 1990, reports the first event, telling of the young woman who, while jogging in the hills near the city, saw a puma crouch low and come toward her. She threw a stone, but the puma kept coming. At that point, the woman noticed a second puma creeping up on her from behind, so, with great presence of mind, she made her way up an embankment and climbed a tree at the top. On her way up the tree, she felt pain in the calf of her leg, and looking down she saw that the pumas were climbing after her, one behind the other. The nearer of the two, the one who had scratched her, was looking up at her with its paw on her branch.

At this point, according to the *Camera*, the woman expected the pumas to kill her. However, refusing to give up without a fight, she stomped on the head of the nearest puma. That puma dropped to the ground. The other puma then climbed higher, snarling at her as she tried to drive it back with a branch. (An uncooperative attitude on the part of the prey sometimes angers a feline attacker — Rajah the housecat hissed and spat at a mouse whom he had carried indoors to play with, but who then evaded him by running into the toe of an overturned boot.) Eventually, though, the second puma also dropped to the ground. For a while the two paced back and forth under the tree; then they went off to drink from a stream and finally disappeared for good. The courageous young woman climbed down from the tree and ran a quarter of a mile to a group of houses.

A few weeks later, about twenty-five miles away, a puma who might have been one of the young woman's attackers killed a young man. He, too, had been jogging at the time of the attack, which came from behind. Searchers found his partly eaten body a short distance from the road; he had been dragged there and then covered with leaves by the puma as if he had been a deer. Eventually the searchers noticed a puma crouched at a distance, watching them. Later, this puma was hunted down and killed. It was a young male, about two years old, weighing about one hundred pounds. His stomach contained fragments of the young man's body, proving that the hunters had found the right animal and that a man-eater did not remain at large.

How many people have been killed by pumas? A variety of figures exists. The actual number, whatever it is, is very much less than a thousand, which was the number of pumas killed during the decade of the 1950s by one Robert McCurdy, a guide and bounty hunter in the Southwest whose tedious bragging is preserved in a blood-soaked biography called *Life of the Greatest Guide*. In virtually all countries, but certainly in the New World, far more people are killed by ordinary, domestic dogs than are killed by any kind of cat, still more people are killed by insects, even more are killed by lightning, and very many more are killed in sports-related accidents, to say nothing of the people killed by other people, especially by those with guns or automobiles. In contrast, we are surely the primary agent of death for all members of the cat tribe. For many if not most cat species, our depredations must surpass accidents, disease, and even starvation by a considerable margin.

Ironically, the very policies of game management, which in parts of the West combine a lax attitude toward poaching with a prolonged hunting season that encourages the killing of male cats, actually may contribute more to man-eating than any other factor. Why? Because Fish and Game biologists generally fail to recognize the social systems of the cats. Rather, many Fish and Game personnel cling to the superstitions that the wild cats are asocial and that male cats kill kittens indiscriminately. The fallacy of this belief cannot be overstated — if it were true, there would be no wild cats. In fact, the presence of a big male puma or bobcat or lynx or jaguar almost certainly serves to stabilize an area, because if he's already there, he is probably the owner, he has probably already committed the necessary infanticide, and at least for the near future he will probably keep any male newcomers away. Under his protection, the kittens he fathers will grow up and will stay with their mothers long enough to learn the necessary skills for survival on their own. Thus, under the protection of a resident tom, the cat population stabilizes or rises.

Many kinds of animal regulate their own populations, as of course they have done since their species began. This is particularly true of the carnivores. Yet the opposite belief, that human beings must control the populations of wild carnivores lest they overrun the food supply, persists like religious dogma, is a favorite recitation of furriers, and is even taught in certain low-quality biology classes. Thus the hunting of the wild cats continues, often on public lands where the game belongs to the federal government and is supported by taxpayers all over the country, not just by the hunters from the state. The big toms are shot by hunters and poachers, the once-protected ranges of these toms are opened to intruders, the intruders kill or disperse the dead tom's children, and the population drops.

Yet the fact that some of the dispersing orphans venture into cities does not suggest, even remotely, that most dispersing pumas cause problems to people or their pets. Most cats of any species and all ages remain shy and circumspect, even at the cost of their own lives. This is particularly true of young pumas. In just one year I learned of three different pumas, two females and a male, all between the ages of six months and eighteen months, who were found starved to death in the presence of mule deer and jackrabbits, not very far from human settlements. If these three were found at random, how many more had died that year who were not found? All were alone, and investigation showed no ailments, no injuries, nothing to explain the deaths except that they had not been eating. One, a young female, had the two wing casings of a beetle in her stomach. All three seemed to have been orphans, and all had died lying curled on their sides in long grass or under sheltering bushes, where, evidently, weakness overcame them.

Attacks on human beings by pumas were studied by Dr. Paul Beier from the University of California, who presented his findings at a conference on pumas sponsored by the Colorado Division of Wildlife in Denver in 1991. His study examined fifty unprovoked attacks that had taken place in twelve western states and in two Canadian provinces over the past hundred years. The most astonishing attack happened on Vancouver Island, which in itself was interesting, since the pumas of Vancouver seem more inclined to attack people than pumas anywhere else, suggesting, once again, a cultural bent. Also significant is that the inclination refutes a generally held belief that pumas are less bold where they are hunted. On Vancouver, pumas are heavily hunted by sportsmen, yet the pumas of Vancouver are said to be very bold indeed, and Vancouver continues to be the scene of an ongoing series of puma attacks on human beings. What, if anything, hunting has to do with this is unclear.

In the Vancouver attack, which was reminiscent of my friend Lissa's puma, Ruby, jumping at the deer in the diorama, a puma jumped through the large glass window of an isolated cabin, knocking over the only lantern and seizing the cabin's owner, a telephone linesman who was preparing for bed and had undressed to his underwear. In the dark the brave man, with the puma biting him, fought his way into his kitchen where he got a knife and stabbed the puma until it let him go. Running outside, he slammed the door behind him, closing the wounded puma inside and himself outside on a bitter winter night in the snow. Although badly injured, the nearly naked man got into his boat and rowed six miles against a strong wind and a heavy sea to a neighbor's cabin, where, since no one was at home, he broke in. By then close to death from shock and hypothermia, he had to huddle under a blanket for several hours before he could dial the telephone. His rescuers found and shot the puma, who was still locked in the cabin. Like most other pumas who have attacked people, this puma was a young male.

Of the fifty unprovoked attacks discussed by Dr. Beier, two-thirds were made on children. In eleven cases the child was alone, but in sixteen cases other children were present, and in eight cases an adult was present, all of which reinforces the notion that the size and age of the intended victim, rather than the presence or absence of another person, were significant to the puma.

In spite of so many attacks, a surprising number of people have no concept that pumas can be dangerous. Probably this can be explained by the way pumas look. Pumas seem very pretty to human beings and have the type of facial features often found on greeting cards — big eyes, round ears, and a small chin, all of which are guaranteed to reassure human beings. In this pumas are the opposite of wolves, whose facial features — long nose, pointed ears — frighten some of us. Some people react to the appearance of pumas very sensibly indeed, saying to themselves, Uh-oh — good thing the housecats aren't that big or we'd all be in serious trouble. Other people see what they take for cuteness and ignore the implications of the size. At the puma conference in Denver, a bizarre snapshot was presented. It showed a woman holding a baby while a puma peers around her, so that all three are looking at the camera, held by the baby's father. Evidently he thought it was safe to pose his wife and infant next to a large, wild, adult male puma who had been lurking in the bushes. In the photo, the wife is smiling and the puma looks puzzled. The puma's unsettling lack of fear should have raised a red flag in the minds of the little family but did not. All three escaped with their lives, as if by a miracle, but their misjudgment was on a par with that of another couple who, wanting a photo of their little boy being kissed by a bear, smeared jam on his cheek and shoved him out of the car. Going for the jam, the bear killed the child by accident, which of course resulted in the bear's death — she was shot by the park authorities.

(Animals who make such errors aren't always killed — the life of at least one Yellowstone grizzly was spared even though she had killed a photographer. She was saved by his photos, which showed how she had grown increasingly uncomfortable with his nearness and how she had warned him again and again to back off. Clicking away, he did not heed her warnings, and on that occasion, the authorities put the blame where it belonged.)

Meanwhile, an account describing similar naivety appeared in the August 21, 1991, *Wall Street Journal.* A committee was formed on Fire Island, in Long Island Sound, with the intention of introducing "thirty breeding pairs" of pumas to control the deer that overpopulate the island. Credit must be given to the committee for attempting an organic solution to a problem involving wildlife, but the plan would not have worked. Even if Fire Island were good puma habitat, which it is not, it might be big enough for one puma, but not for sixty, as the committee proposed, and certainly not for two hundred pumas eighteen months later if the original pumas bred as planned. Possibly no one had read the puma literature, which reveals that cats don't form breeding pairs; and surely no one had bothered with the math, which suggests that by the fifth year the swarming pumas would have required no fewer than fifty thousand deer, and, without a practical way to leave the island, would be looking around for another source of food. The mauled and sorrowing citizens might then hold the committee responsible for the misfortunes that would result, but that possibility didn't seem to have been visualized either, perhaps because the committee was under the grave misimpression that pumas "present ABSO-LUTELY NO DANGER to humans or their pets," as a poster proclaimed.

One result of the conference in Denver was that a sort of protocol was endorsed to encourage people to make their property less hospitable to pumas. Homeowners were advised to eliminate hiding places by cutting back their shrubbery, and to eliminate sources of food by bringing pets inside at night and not feeding the deer. Hikers were told of a canned pepper spray to be aimed at the face of an attacking puma but were warned against spraying into the wind, which could leave the hikers thrashing helplessly on the ground, unable to see or hear, right in front of the advancing puma. (When I tested a can, the product malfunctioned, letting fall a drop or two of peppery juice on my feet. What a disappointment that would have been if I had been trying to deter a puma!) More reliable methods for repelling puma attacks make use of the fact that pumas are sometimes susceptible to a display of force. If attacked, one might shout in a deep voice or make threatening gestures or brandish a stick. The key word here is *sometimes*, and the point is illustrated by the experience of a hiker who, against park regulations, had unleashed her miniature terrier at the head of a trail that led down a narrow canyon with steep walls. As the two entered the canyon — the dog first, the woman second — a puma, who evidently had been watching them from a ledge on the canyon wall, suddenly plopped down in front of them. The brave dog flew at the puma, who seemed aghast and fled along the trail with the terrier at his heels, demonstrating that even a tiny creature can rout a puma by showing some convincing aggression.

On the other hand, one shouldn't count on it. Rethinking the situation even as he fled, the puma suddenly spun around, seized the terrier, and leaped up the canyon wall with the dog in his mouth. Neither was ever seen again.

Of course, the more people present, the better the chance of spotting the attacking cat in the first place. Like Ruby in her mock attacks on Lissa, like most man-eating leopards and tigers who attempt to prey upon human beings, man-hunting pumas tend to attack from behind, with a bite to the back of the neck. According to Dr. Beier's survey, most people who were attacked by a puma and lived to tell the story reported that they never knew what was happening until they felt the terrible thump of its body, and then the teeth and claws.

Even so, some people were able to fight off the puma. According to Dr. Beier's survey, of the thirty-five children who were attacked, nine were alone and were killed, but the others were saved because someone else saw what was happening and came to the rescue. Also according to the survey, once the puma had launched its attack, fighting back turned out to be an effective form of defense. Playing dead, which seems to help people when attacked by bears, was strongly counterindicated in a puma attack, as the deception could result in the victim's being dragged to a more private location with fatal consequences. After all, the bear's aggression often results from his fear of the human being, who allays that fear by assuming a nonthreatening posture. The cat, in contrast, may be looking for a meal, and would find a nonthreatening posture inviting. When attacked by a cat, it would be much better to do what bears themselves do in tiger country — stand up tall and face the attacker. One might stare at the cat's eyes and shout "Bad puma!" or "Back off!" in a deep, menacing voice while brandishing something — one's jacket, say, or one's camera. The cat is only trying to eat, after all, and doesn't want trouble. But don't stoop down to get a stick or a rock — children and crouching people are the most frequent victims of puma attacks. Why so? Because most hunting, or hunting in the old way, is pragmatic food-gathering behavior and is best done carefully, wisely. Hunting for food (a different activity than hunting for sport) lacks the aggression that drives reckless, warlike behavior. One of the primary rules of hunting for food, at least for the animals and people who live in the old way, is simply this: be careful, tackle only what you think you can handle, and above all don't get hurt.

One of Dr. Beier's accounts of escape from pumas brought much laughter and even derision from the audience, as if he had intended the story as humor, which as far as I could tell he had not. I repeat the story here because of its implications and because, to me, it is the most intriguing of all the accounts. A woman who was backpacking alone on a remote trail was attacked by a puma. In the usual way, the puma leaped on the woman from behind, grabbing her by the pack and knocking her down. But she twisted herself around in her pack straps and kept the pack between herself and him. Face to face with her attacker, she spoke smoothly and encouragingly. Although he had her in his power and could have killed her at any time, he instead was willing to listen to her. Eventually, other hikers came along the trail and drove him away.

Why did this amuse some members of Dr. Beier's audience? Perhaps because the concept of making an emotional or intellectual connection with a puma at such a moment was remote from their experience, and they were unable to see themselves in a similar situation, to make the leap. "Nice kitty," some people joked, as if they thought that the puma had attacked because he was angry and that the woman had managed to placate him.

In fact, something very different was probably the case. Probably, the woman's voice and demeanor had taken the puma by surprise, so that his hunt metamorphosed into a different kind of encounter, requiring different behavior. He must have been wondering what that behavior should be, and in hopes of getting more information kept watching and listening.

After all, any intelligent, empathetic social being must often make decisions about his or her relationship to another being. Is the other being a friend or a foe or a meal? Because cats are creatures of the edge, dependent entirely upon animal protein, they usually select the third option, even to the point of occasional, opportunistic cannibalism. But they don't always select the third option. The puma had been sensitive enough to see that the woman didn't act like meat.

The men and women of Dr. Beier's audience, mocking suburbanites who typically interact with the natural world only by occasionally going hiking or hunting or camping, were very far removed from this kind of dilemma. But the puma was not. Nor, evidently, was the woman. And at one time, when our kind lived in the old way, as wild animals still live today, neither were we.

The episode, I believe, shows something common to all hunting species, of which we are one. Wherever people hunt, similar episodes appear in stories. A hunter spares the life of a bird or a roe deer or a fallow doe, only to find that she is an enchanted princess. Usually he marries her, thus acquiring a beautiful woman and a kingdom too; not bad for a lowly woodsman. The only disadvantage of his kindness is that he loses the food value of her body, but in fiction that consideration would be crass indeed and of course is never mentioned.

In the real world, though, they who hunt for a living really need the food, and if for any reason they spare the victim's life, they go hungry. So they must squelch the tendency to empathize.

Long ago, the /Gwi Bushmen told the true hunter's version of the story, but that version has a cautionary twist to it. In the /Gwi story, a man takes the role of the hunting puma and a female elephant takes the role of the backpacking woman. The man has married the elephant, which worries her parents very much. They suspect his intentions and those of his relatives too. The parents are right to worry — the husband's younger brother is plotting to kill their daughter. One day she has a premonition of disaster and tells her parents that they may never see her again. Her husbands people are on the move, and after taking leave of her parents she follows. The younger brother looks back and, noticing that she is trailing them, waits for her to catch up. Then he tricks her into letting him kill her. Finished, he builds a fire to cook one of her breasts, which he eats, sitting on her body. When the husband looks back and sees his brother sitting high above the bushes, he fears the worst, and when he returns to find his brother sitting on his wife's enormous corpse, he is furious. But the younger brother hands him some of the roasted breast, which presently he eats. "You fool," jeers the brother. "You were married to meat and you thought it was a wife."

If cats could speak, they, too, might tell the /Gwi's cautionary version of the tale. Meanwhile, though, when they're not hunting they think and feel like the rest of us. We, too, must suppress the wish to empathize when we are hunting. At other times, though, cats and people are much the same. I saw this during my first visit to Lissa Gilmour and her puma, Ruby, when chance provided me with an interesting tape recording. Ruby was sitting with us in Lissa's living room, where, in a confined space, the puma seemed much larger and more daunting than she had seemed outdoors. Worse yet, she seemed restless. While trying to keep track of her whereabouts and her changing moods, I found that I was missing much of the fascinating information that Lissa was sharing, so I got out my little recording device. Intended as a dictation aid, it records at an unnatural speed to save tape, making the words hard to understand and unpleasant to listen to. Tones, however, come through clearly, and, stripped of their purely logical sense, they sing of our thoughts and feelings, revealing far more than our words do.

At the beginning of the tape, Lissa and I are seated on her rug, with Ruby stretched out full length between us. Lissa and I are getting to know one another. I am excited to be with Lissa in her houseful of wonderful animals, and, as the tone of my voice attests, I am eager to please her. She, in turn, with her flawless western hospitality, seems happy to discuss her beloved animals with me. Our voices are soft and high, our speech is quick and often punctuated with brief stops — we are communicating enthusiastically but at the same time we are anxious not to interrupt each other. We do, though, and as women will, we keep laughing politely and saying, "I'm sorry!" Together we are singing a duet, the female version of the human species song.

Ruby, meanwhile, has found an odor on the rug. It is a drop of amniotic fluid from Lissa's pregnant Himalayan cat, Yehti, who, it turns out, has been in labor all this time. However, at the moment in question no one knows this, as Yehti is holding back her kittens, possibly because she is afraid of Ruby. Ruby does nothing to reassure her. Rather, she begins to rumble, then to spit. On and on she goes, sometimes so loudly that she drowns out other voices. She is singing the murderous song of a cat's dark feelings, a contralto solo of envy and displeasure, which fills Lissa's house and finds its audience of one, little Yehti, crouched in hiding

318

under a chair, quietly considering the seriousness of her situation.

Suddenly, Lissa's canaries begin to sing. They are males and rivals, whose burst into song, within a nanosecond of each other, seems miraculously coordinated, as if both had been on edge and on the mark, waiting tensely for a signal. Surely they are the most accomplished of finches — their song soars high above our heads, filling the air with an unquenchable cascade of music. Once started, each bird with head thrown back pours forth song as if to extinguish the other.

The rest of us don't seem to hear the canaries. Lissa and I keep right on talking, so involved are we with the relationship of guest and hostess that is developing between us. Prowling Ruby keeps up her disconcerting spits and growls. Thus the tape brings out the voices of five creatures — two people, one cat (just Ruby, because Yehti keeps quiet), and two canaries — each with its important, earnest message to the other of its kind.

As the afternoon passes, however, the canaries subside, and the rest of us — all but Yehti — seem to turn outward, we toward Ruby and she toward us. At first, I may have been somewhat frightened by Ruby. Well, maybe not exactly frightened — Lissa's confidence was reassuring — but Ruby was bigger than me, vastly stronger, a stranger, and a cat. For my part, I had never before been so close to a puma. Nor did I know very much about pumas. So I was cautious. On Side B of my tape, I hear my uncertain voice telling

Lissa that I respect Ruby.

Meanwhile, I am also very curious about her. Pumas are considered to be small cats, but how close to housecats are they really? I hear myself asking if Ruby eats crouched above her food in small-cat fashion, or if she stretches out beside it, the way the big cats do. Here Ruby, who had been prowling the room, turned and walked toward us, eyes front, as if she had every intention of passing between us, when plunk — as if her rump, not her head, had made the decision — her hip hit the ground beside us, gracefully followed by the rest of her. She then twisted onto her back and showed us her furry white belly. On the tape I am asking how many breasts she has. Has she six, like a housecat? Or four, like a leopard or a lion? Actually pumas have eight, but I don't know that at the time, and as Ruby remains on her back I ask if I can search for her nipples. In attentive silence, Lissa and I then do just that, with Ruby lying flat on her back very stiffly, her head raised, her paws bent at the wrists, her thighs spread, looking down at herself uneasily while our hands roam like spiders through her fur. However, as Lissa quietly predicts on the tape, we find nothing. Maiden pumas have absolutely no sign of nipples or breasts. This in itself is fascinating. I keep searching, but when Ruby's body tenses, I stop fast. A housecat at that point might have seized my hand, clapped it to her mouth, and bitten it, and I don't want that treatment from Ruby, whose eyeteeth seem as long as my fingers and whose triangular cheek teeth are as massive as my folded thumb.

In the late afternoon, Ruby grew more restless. Soon she was jumping on and off the furniture, which she dwarfed. Next, she nervously paced to and from the window, growling and switching her tail. Judging from my voice on the tape, her agitation must have been making me nervous. I keep asking what Ruby is doing. Lissa's voice is very gentle and soothing and her words can't be deciphered. Soon a silence falls. Lissa has offered Ruby her arm, and Ruby, stretched at full length, has started to suck it. Her massive paws knead alternately, slowly, making bread. Ruby is like a kitten and has even aligned herself to Lissa by heading in to Lissa's side as a kitten aligns itself to the body of its mother.

In a low voice, Lissa asks me if I'd like to let Ruby suck my arm. I whisper yes, I would. Lissa shows me how to take her place in front of Ruby, and I do. My arm slips under Ruby's mouth. Feeling the change, Ruby slowly opens her great, yellow eyes and looks up, but by now I am deeply moved by her tenderness and vulnerability, and I just wait, not speaking. In peaceful silence, we all wait. There is no tension in the moment. Ruby again begins to suck. Then she purrs. The room fills with her purring. Little Yehti creeps out from under the chair and leaves the room. She will later deliver two kittens on a rug behind the bathroom door. Ruby doesn't care and lets her velvet eyelids shut. On the skin of my arm I feel the slow gentle rasping of her rough tongue, which gradually turns as smooth and slick as a piece of raw liver. Has she turned her tongue over so that I am feeling the underside? Has she collapsed her papillae? I quietly mention this to Lissa, who nods. She knows what has happened, but not why. It doesn't matter. Ruby drowses, her black lips and smooth tongue gently pressed against my arm. And that is all. We stay a long time in the peace of Lissa's quiet room, not talking or whispering, just relaxing, purring, dreaming, gently breathing, mildly aware of cloud shadows, of the afternoon sun, of a light breeze from an open door, of being alive there together.

The next tape records the events of the evening, when we are in Ruby's pen, and Ruby is about to eat a pullet who has been accidentally suffocated by some other chickens. Crouching above the carcass in small-cat style, with her paws neatly together below her chest like a housecat eating from a dish, Ruby is preparing her food. Little bones snap as she severs the wingtips, then feathers rip as she plucks the breast with short, neat tosses of her head. Feathers float around us on the evening air. Soon Lissa shows me something strange. Ruby is not spitting out all the feathers. In the sides of her mouth, damp feathers are clinging, positioned to go down her throat if she swallows. Why is this? If she eats the feathers anyway, why does she pluck them first? Doesn't she know about them? Can't she get rid of them? In search of further information I lie down beside the chicken to look up into Ruby's mouth.

Thinking back, I occasionally wonder at myself for that. I wouldn't have put my face so near the eyeteeth of a feeding dog, let alone a dog I had met so recently. But, unlike dogs, cats don't snap, and anyway, by then I trusted Ruby. And Ruby trusted me. No longer did we view each other as unpredictable strangers, or care how closely we approached each other's faces and mouths. Not for a moment did I think she'd bite me. Nor was she afraid that I might snatch her chicken. Thanks to the soothing, the bliss, that we had experienced earlier, we seemed to understand each other. We had crossed our species' boundaries and had found the common center in each other, where all creatures rest.

Acknowledgments

Many people have helped me to gather the material for this book. I thank them all. Going cat by cat and beginning with the pumas, I'd like to thank Lissa Gilmour, the wildlife rehabilitator, and her puma, Ruby. My debt to these two friends is deep and very obvious. I wouldn't have attempted to write this book without first visiting them. I'd also like to thank Sue Morse, the forest ecologist, for her insights into tracks and tracking. For an unparalleled insight into puma behavior and habitat, and for the opportunity to see wild pumas, I'd like to thank Ken Jafek of War Eagle Outfitters in Malta, Idaho, and his colleague, Kevin Allred, as well as their extraordinary dogs. As Kevin once wrote for *Coonhound Bloodlines*: "Without [these dogs] there would be no [puma] study. They are always ready to go, even if it's two o'clock in the morning and 15 degrees below zero. Their devotion, courage, and desire is something to be respected." To that I have but one word to add: Amen.

For information on puma populations and puma attacks, I'd like to thank James C. Halfpenny. For supervising a fascinating puma study, I'd like to thank John Laundre. For invaluable help in understanding the pumas of the Denver-Boulder area, I'd like to thank Kathy Green, Betsy Spettigue, and Mike Sanders. For further information on puma populations in the Rockies, and also for information on deer populations without which there would be no pumas, I would like to thank Allen E. Anderson. Let me hasten to add, however, that any mistakes herein on the subject of animal populations are certainly my own.

For generous hospitality, and for much insight into circus tigers, I'd like to thank John Cuneo, Elke and Roelof de Vries, Trudy and Bill Strong, and the tiger grooms and tigers of the Hawthorn Corporation. In this context I'd also like to warmly thank Harry and Rowena Thomas and their tigers; and to offer special thanks to Ada Smieya-Blaszak and her husband and son, Klaus and Brunon Blaszak, and their tigers, especially Rajah and Rowena; and finally, I'd like to express my gratitude to Rodney Huey of the Ringling Brothers Barnum and Bailey Circus for his help and his courtesy. For much insight into zoo tigers and for generously explaining the captive breeding program I'd like to thank Dr. Ronald L. Tilson, director of biological programs at the Minnesota zoo.

For information about domestic cats I'd like to thank certain cats, namely the hefty, part-Siamese barn cat Manas; the wise, marmalade tomcat Rollo; the elegant tricolor Baby Cat, and her marmalade colleague Thomas; also the blind white cat Aasa (now Chushi); the white hunter Orion; the black huntress Wicca; the elegant Rose and her sister, Iris; the stealthy Goniff; the cheerful Max; the devoted Natasha; the loyal Fang, a neosaber-tooth, and also his associates and rivals, the cats who roam the short-grass plains of Marshall Lane in Austin, Texas; the vanished Fritz, whose owners are still searching; the shy Cleo; the valiant Eddie; the gray Christmas with her pure white stockings; the mauve, mottled Lilac; and the black wondercat Rajah, all for the insights they have afforded to anyone who would take the trouble to watch them over time.

For information about training housecats as circus performers I'd like to thank Dominique La Font and his very accomplished cats, Piggie, Sharkey, Spot, and Mars, whose wonderful work can be seen in Key West on Mallory Pier every evening at sunset; for his observations of housecats hunting deer I'd like to thank Dave Blanchette; for the story of a cat protecting a person, I'd like to thank Lisa Rappaport; for the story of Bubastis and the tomcat who climbed high buildings to find her, I'd like to thank Mab Gray of the publicity department at Houghton Mifflin; for the story of Wazo, I'd like to thank Margie Bourne; and for the story of the cat who soothed a person, I'd like to thank Lori-Ann Tessier.

For insight into Ju/wa hunting and for observations about the Bushmanland lions I'd like to thank my brother, John Marshall. As has been seen in the text, many of the most interesting observations included herein were made by him. I'd also like to thank Tsamko Toma and his late brother, /Gashe Martin, as well as their late father, /Toma — all three of /Gautscha in Bushmanland, Namibia — for many important insights and much information about lions over the years. I'd also like to thank the wildlife biologist Richard D. Estes, who constantly and generously shared his vast store of knowledge on the behavior of African and other mammals. For insight and advice about the Ju/wasi in general and about their relationship to lions in particular, I'd like to thank the *grande dame* of hunter-gatherer anthropology, Lorna Marshall. For insight into circus lions, I'd like to thank Trudy Strong and also Timba, a lion.

For including me in their research project on elephant vocalizations during two seasons in Namibia, I'd like to thank my dear friends Katy Payne and Bill Langbauer. If not for the time in the field spent with them I would never have been able to observe the cultural change exhibited by the local lions. Furthermore, Katy is as attuned to animals as it is possible to be — in this she's more like some of their kind than like some of our kind. To spend time with Katy in the presence of animals is an unforgettable experience, of which I've had many, and I also thank her for those.

In a slightly different form, much of the information herein about lions first appeared in *The New Yorker*. For this I'd like to thank Bob Gottlieb, and also Nancy Frankin and Hal Espen, whose skilled and careful work so greatly enhanced mine. For his help and friendship, as always, I'd like to thank Ike Williams, my agent. For the beautiful line drawings that so sensitively link this present work on cats to my past work on dogs, I'd like to thank the artist, Jared Williams. For her friendship and for being so pleasant to work with as well as for her wonderful editing skills, I'd like to thank my editor, Becky Saletan. For her generous help and her ability, I'd like to thank my assistant, Anita Marie Mann. Finally, I'd like to thank Irene Williams and Mab Gray of the publicity department at Houghton Mifflin for the wonderful work they did in publicizing an earlier book of mine called *The Hidden Life of Dogs*. Their excellent skills on behalf of that book have paved the way for this book, even though the two books were published by different houses.

Bibliography

The following is a partial bibliography of the publications I found most helpful:

Clutton-Brock, Juliet. *Cats: Ancient and Modern.* Cambridge: Harvard University Press, 1993.

Cole, D. D., and J. N. Shafer. "A study of social dominance in cats." *Behaviour* 27 (1966): 39–52.

Corbett, Jim. *More Man-Eaters of Kumaon.* London: Oxford University Press, 1954.

—. *The Man-Eating Leopard of Rudraprayag.* Suffolk: Richard Clay and Company, 1947.

—. *Man-Eaters of Kumaon.* New York: Oxford University Press, 1946.

Dunstone, N., and M. L. Gorman, eds. *Mammals as Predators.* Oxford: Oxford Science Publications, 1993.

Estes, Richard D. *The Safari Companion: A Guide*

to Watching African Mammals. Post Mills, Vermont: Chelsea Green, 1993.

—. *The Behavior Guide to African Mammals.* Berkeley: University of California Press, 1991.

Guggisberg, C. A. W. *Wild Cats of the World.* New York: Taplinger, 1975.

Hornocker, Maurice G. "Stalking the Mountain Lion — to Save Him." *National Geographic* 136, no. 5 (1969).

Kitchener, Andrew. *The Natural History of the Wild Cats.* Ithaca: Comstock, 1991.

Leyhausen, P. *Cat Behavior, the Predatory and Social Behavior of Domestic and Wild Cats.* New York: Garland STPM Press, 1979.

Macdonald, David. *The Velvet Claw.* London: BBC Books, 1992.

—,et al. "Social Dynamics, Nursing Coalitions and Infanticide Among Farm Cats, *Felis catus.*" In *Advances in Ethology.* Berlin: Paul Parey, 1987.

—,ed. *The Encyclopedia of Mammals.* Oxford: Equinox, 1984.

Marshall, Lorna. The *!Kung of Nyae Nyae.* Cambridge: Harvard University Press, 1976.

Mongtomery, Sy. *Spell of the Tiger.* Boston: Houghton Mifflin, in preparation.

Packer, C., and A. E. Pusey. "Cooperation and competition within coalitions of male lions (*Panthera leo*)." *Animal Behavior* 31 (1982): 334–40.

Schaller, G. B. *The Serengetti Lion: A Study of Predator-Prey Relations.* Chicago: University of Chicago Press, 1972.

—. *The Deer and the Tiger.* Chicago: University of Chicago Press, 1967.

Seidensticker, J., et al. "Mountain lion social organization in the Idaho Primitive Area." *Wildlife Monographs* 35 (1973): 1–60.

Sunquist, M. E. "The social organization of tigers *(Panthera tigris)* in Royal Chitawan National Park, Nepal." *Smithsonian Contributions to Zoology* 12 (1981): 239–41.

Thomas, Elizabeth Marshall. "The Old Way." *The New Yorker*, Oct. 15, 1990.

—. *The Harmless People.* New York: Knopf, 1989.

—. *Warrior Herdsmen.* New York: Knopf, 1966.

Tilson, Ronald L., and Ulysses S. Seal, eds. *Tigers of the World.* Park Ridge, N.J.: Noyes Publications, 1987.

Young, S. P., and E. A. Goldman. *The Puma: Mysterious American Cat.* New York: Dover, 1946.

We hope you have enjoyed this Large Print book. Other G.K. Hall & Co. and ISIS Publishing Limited Large Print books are available at your library or directly from the publishers. For more information about current and upcoming titles, please call or write, without obligation, to:

G.K. Hall & Co.
P.O. Box 159
Thorndike, Maine 04986
USA
Tel. (800) 223-6121 (U.S. & Canada)
In Maine call collect: (207) 948-2962

OR

ISIS Publishing Limited
7 Centremead
Osney Mead
Oxford OX2 0ES
England
Tel. (01865) 250333

All our Large Print titles are designed for easy reading, and all our books are made to last.